DEVIANT PEER INFLUENCES IN PROGRAMS FOR YOUTH

Deviant Peer Influences in Programs for Youth

Problems and Solutions

Edited by

KENNETH A. DODGE
THOMAS J. DISHION
JENNIFER E. LANSFORD

THE GUILFORD PRESS

NEW YORK   LONDON

© 2006 The Guilford Press
A Division of Guilford Publications, Inc.
72 Spring Street, New York, NY 10012
www.guilford.com

Printed in the United States of America

This book is printed on acid-free paper.

Last digit is print number: 9   8   7   6   5   4   3   2   1

Library of Congress Cataloging-in-Publication Data

Deviant peer influences in programs for youth : problems and solutions / edited by
Kenneth A. Dodge, Thomas J. Dishion, Jennifer E. Lansford.
    p. cm. — (Duke series in child development and public policy)
  Includes bibliographical references and index.
  ISBN-10: 1-59385-279-7   ISBN-13: 978-1-59385-279-5 (hardcover)
  1. Teenagers—Services for—United States.   2. Juvenile delinquency—United States—
Prevention.   3. Peer pressure—United States.   I. Dodge, Kenneth A. II. Dishion,
Thomas J., 1954–   III. Lansford, Jennifer E.   IV. Series.
  HV1431.D485 2006
  362.74—dc22
                                    2006002011

About the Editors

Kenneth A. Dodge, PhD, is the William McDougall Professor of Public Policy and Professor of Psychology at Duke University. He also directs the Duke Center for Child and Family Policy, which is devoted to finding solutions to problems facing youth in contemporary society through research, policy engagement, service, and education. Dr. Dodge has teamed up with colleagues to create, implement, and evaluate the Fast Track Program to prevent chronic violence in high-risk children, and he is now leading the Durham Family Initiative to prevent child abuse in Durham, North Carolina. He has been honored with the Distinguished Scientific Contribution Award from the American Psychological Association, the Boyd McCandless Award, and the Senior Scientist Award from the National Institutes of Health. Dr. Dodge is a fellow of the American Association for the Advancement of Science, the Academy of Experimental Criminology, the American Psychological Society, and the American Psychological Association.

Thomas J. Dishion, PhD, is Professor of Clinical Psychology and Director of Research at the Child and Family Center at the University of Oregon. His interests include understanding the development of antisocial behavior and substance abuse in children and adolescents, as well as designing effective interventions and prevention programs. Dr. Dishion's intervention research focuses on the effectiveness of family-centered interventions, and the negative effects of aggregating high-risk youth into intervention groups. He has published over 90 scientific reports on these topics, a book for parents on family management, and two books for professionals working with troubled children and their families.

Jennifer E. Lansford, PhD, is a Research Scientist for the Duke Center for Child and Family Policy at Duke University. Her research focuses on the development of aggression and other behavior problems in children and adolescents, with an emphasis on how family and peer contexts contribute to or protect against these outcomes. In particular, Dr. Lansford examines how experiences with parents (e.g., physical abuse, divorce) and peers (e.g., rejection, friendships) affect the development of children's behavior problems; explores how influence operates in adolescent peer groups and how peer influence can be harnessed to prevent adolescent substance use; and investigates how cultural contexts moderate links between parents' discipline strategies and children's behavior problems.

Contributors

James C. Anthony, MSc, PhD, Department of Epidemiology, Michigan State University, East Lansing, Michigan

Anthony Biglan, PhD, Department of Psychology, University of Oregon, Eugene, Oregon

Laine O'Neill Briddell, MA, Crime, Law, and Justice Program, Department of Sociology, Pennsylvania State University, University Park, Pennsylvania

Philip J. Cook, PhD, Department of Public Policy Studies, Duke University, Durham, North Carolina

Thomas J. Dishion, PhD, Department of Psychology and Child and Family Center, University of Oregon, Eugene, Oregon

Kenneth A. Dodge, PhD, Center for Child and Family Policy, Duke University, Durham, North Carolina

Jean E. Dumas, PhD, Department of Psychological Sciences, Purdue University, West Lafayette, Indiana

Greg Duncan, PhD, Institute for Policy Research Education and Social Policy, Northwestern University, Evanston, Illinois

J. Mark Eddy, PhD, Oregon Social Learning Center, Eugene, Oregon

Peter Greenwood, PhD, private practice, Malibu Lake, California

Malcolm W. Klein, PhD, Social Science Research Institute, University of Southern California, Los Angeles, California

Jennifer E. Lansford, PhD, Center for Child and Family Policy, Duke University, Durham, North Carolina

Cindy Lederman, JD, Juvenile Court Division, 11th Judicial Circuit Court, Miami, Florida

Mark W. Lipsey, PhD, Center for Evaluation Research and Methodology, Vanderbilt Institute for Public Policy Studies, Vanderbilt University, Nashville, Tennessee

Jens Ludwig, PhD, Georgetown Public Policy Institute, Georgetown University, Washington, DC

Kevin J. Moore, PhD, Oregon Social Learning Center, Eugene, Oregon

D. Wayne Osgood, PhD, Crime, Law, and Justice Program, Department of Sociology, Pennsylvania State University, University Park, Pennsylvania

Ron Prinz, PhD, Department of Psychology, University of South Carolina, Columbia, South Carolina

Wendy M. Reinke, PhD, Department of Mental Health, Bloomberg School of Public Health, Johns Hopkins University, Baltimore, Maryland

Joel Rosch, PhD, Center for Child and Family Policy, Duke University, Durham, North Carolina

Michelle R. Sherrill, MS, Department of Psychology, Duke University, Durham, North Carolina

Rebecca B. Silver, MS, Department of Psychology, University of Oregon, Eugene, Oregon

Emilie Phillips Smith, PhD, Human Development and Family Studies Program, Pennsylvania State University, University Park, Pennsylvania

Jeffrey Sprague, PhD, Institute on Violence and Destructive Behavior, College of Education, University of Oregon, Eugene, Oregon

Jacob Vigdor, PhD, Sanford Institute of Public Policy, Duke University, Durham, North Carolina

Hill M. Walker, PhD, Institute on Violence and Destructive Behavior, College of Education, University of Oregon, Eugene, Oregon

Melvin N. Wilson, PhD, Department of Psychology, University of Virginia, Charlottesville, Virginia

LaKeesha N. Woods, PhD, Department of Psychiatry, Yale University, New Haven, Connecticut

Series Editors' Note

This volume is the fourth in the Duke Series in Child Development and Public Policy, an ongoing collection of edited volumes that address the translation of research in child development to contemporary issues in public policy. The goal of the series is to bring cutting-edge research and theory in the vibrant field of child development to bear on problems facing children and families in contemporary society. The success of the series depends on identifying important problems in public policy toward children and families at the time that researchers in child development have accumulated sufficient knowledge to contribute to a solution.

The first volume addressed the growing problem of aggressive and delinquent behavior in girls. Although violent behavior rates have remained stable over the past decade, violence by girls has increased, to the dismay of public officials who are at a loss to how to prevent these problems or respond through placement and treatment. The volume reviewed the literature, identified points for intervention and policy engagement, and targeted areas for future research. The second volume examined emerging interventions and policies to promote secure attachment relationships between parents and infants. Developmental neuroscience, clinical therapies, and ecological analysis of family life all point toward the first several years of life as a crucial time for intervention to promote secure relationships between infant and parents. The third volume addressed the state of African American families in the 21st century. A portrait of these families finds many strengths to celebrate but also challenges, ranging from the wealth gap to cultural uniqueness in parenting styles. All three volumes highlight important problems facing children and families and the role of research in child development to solve those problems.

The current volume addresses a costly paradox in public policy toward youth. Recent research in child development has identified unfettered association with deviant peers as a major factor in the growth of deviant behavior among high-risk early-adolescent youth. Oddly, the most common public policy response to the problem of deviant youth is to segregate them from mainstream peers and aggregate them with each other. Aggregation occurs in education (e.g., special education classes, in-school suspension, alternative schools), mental health (e.g., group therapies, residential milieu therapy, group homes), and juvenile justice (e.g., training schools, boot camps, incarceration). Are these policies harmful to these youth? Does any benefit that accrues from removing these youth from the regular peer group get outweighed by damage to the segregated youth?

This volume represents the final report of a diverse working group that met numerous times over a 3-year period to address the problem of deviant peer influences in intervention programs and placements. The group, called the Duke Executive Sessions in Deviant Peer Influences, included over two dozen scholars from a wide range of disciplines, public policy officials, and community leaders. They reviewed the literature, visited programs, conducted a new meta-analysis, and deliberated over the problem and various solutions.

The product of their work is this volume, which concludes that aggregation of deviant youth is indeed a major and expensive practice in public policy, that the practice detracts from positive outcomes for these youth (compared with similar treatment in individualized settings) and has led to documented iatrogenic (i.e., harmful) outcomes under some circumstances, that individual treatments should be preferred whenever possible, and that program officials can alter their group settings and interventions in specific ways that are likely to minimize adverse effects.

The report goes beyond these recommendations to ponder whether the systemwide impact of these placements is positive or negative. That is, deviant youth are segregated from the mainstream because the citizenry believes that the mainstream peer group will benefit from their removal. Many citizens and professionals believe that classrooms are more orderly and neighborhoods are safer without these youth. Is there a societal benefit to removal of these youth, and does it outweigh any adverse impact of segregation on those deviant youth? The report articulates a way to contemplate systemic impact of a policy and calls upon scholars and policy officials to collect more systematic information about peer settings in government programs so that future analyses can examine these questions.

The current volume is being published simultaneously with a shorter, 20-page Executive Summary that is being disseminated by the

Society for Research in Child Development as a *Social Policy Report*. The shorter summary will reach numerous policy officials, practitioners, and scholars to alert them to the various issues at hand, but only the current full report can provide the in-depth analysis that is necessary to make crucial policy decisions.

This volume was inspired by a good friend and giant in the field, Joan McCord, who sadly passed away during the volume's preparation. It was her evaluation of the Cambridge–Somerville Youth Study that generated momentum about the potential dangers of group interventions and led others to scrutinize interventions and policies more closely. She was contagious in her enthusiasm for the topic, visionary in her recognition of its importance, and heroic in her dogged pursuit of the truth. We miss her, and we readily join the volume editors in dedicating this volume to her memory.

Like previous volumes, this report has benefited from financial support provided by the Duke Provost's Initiative in the Social Sciences. We are grateful to Duke Provost Peter Lange. We are also grateful for the support provided by a grant from the William T. Grant Foundation.

Upcoming volumes will address the prevention of depression in youth, the problems faced by immigrant families in the United States in the early 21st century, and the processes through which deviant peer influences operate. Each volume will follow the model of a partnership between scholars at Duke University and scholars at another university, and each volume will bring together leading scholars with practitioners and policymakers to address timely issues. More later . . .

KENNETH A. DODGE, PHD
MARTHA PUTALLAZ, PHD

Contents

Part III. Promising Solutions
and Recommendations

PART I

INTRODUCTION

CHAPTER I

The Problem of Deviant Peer Influences in Intervention Programs

Kenneth A. Dodge, Jennifer E. Lansford,
and Thomas J. Dishion

THE PROBLEM OF DEVIANT PEER INFLUENCES

Every parent understands the basic thesis of this volume: placing a high-risk youth in an unstructured group setting with deviant peers has the potential to worsen his or her problems. Deviant adolescents become more deviant by associating freely with deviant peers. Worse, when well-meaning government agencies act to place deviant youth together, they may contribute to the problem. Ironically, much of what we do as public policy is to remove deviant youth from the mainstream and segregate them, together, in groups. It happens in education, juvenile justice, mental health, and community programming. Recently, sociologists, developmental epidemiologists, psychologists, and economists have caught on and have begun to assemble a broad array of research studies that point toward the same conclusion. This volume summarizes the evidence and makes recommendations for public policy, practice, and research.

Sociological studies have long shown that deviant behavior is concentrated in certain adolescent groups. Gangs, cliques, and peer groups vary in their overall rates of deviance, but if one member of a group is deviant there is a high probability that other members are, or will be, deviant as well (Cairns, Cairns, Neckerman, Gest, & Gariepy, 1988; Dishion, Andrews, & Crosby, 1995). A high proportion of violence, drug use, and other deviant behaviors is committed in groups rather

3

than in isolation, especially among adolescents, who are reputed to be obsessed with peer culture (Warr, 1996). In fact, the finding that affiliation with deviant peers is associated with delinquent behavior is one of the most robust findings in the literature on juvenile delinquency (Thornberry & Krohn, 1997). Exposure to deviant peers has been linked to increases in a wide range of delinquent behaviors including drug use (Dishion & Skaggs, 2000; Thornberry & Krohn, 1997), covert antisocial behavior (Keenan, Loeber, Zhang, Stouthamer-Loeber, & Van Kammen, 1995), violent offenses (Elliott & Menard, 1996), and early and high-risk sexual behavior (Dishion, 2000). Additionally, deviant peer affiliation is a stronger predictor of delinquent behavior than such variables as family, school, and community characteristics (Elliott & Menard, 1996).

THE PROBLEM OF TREATING DEVIANT YOUTH IN GROUPS

Although the bulk of research examining peer group influences on delinquent behavior has been conducted in naturally occurring peer groups (e.g., informal peer networks, dyadic friendships, street gangs), it has recently been hypothesized that deviant peer influences may at times operate in groups or programs designed to reduce problem behavior. A common method (in fact, the *most* common method) of dealing with delinquent adolescents in this country is to segregate them from the mainstream of peers and to place them together, to aggregate them in settings such as alternative schools, therapy groups, and juvenile justice facilities. Such practices make meeting the needs of deviant youth more financially and logistically feasible and serve the potential function of protecting nondelinquent youth from harm or negative influence. However, when the reason that deviant youth are placed with each other is because they are deviant, their identity and common ground become deviance. The processes of deviant peer influence might well operate in educational, treatment, and correctional settings in a manner similar to that in natural settings. Thus a potential consequence of bringing adolescents with problem behavior together is that such strategies may serve to exacerbate rather than diminish their problem behavior.

Aggregation of deviant peers is common public policy in education, mental health, juvenile justice, and community programs. The purpose of this volume is to address the extent to which aggregation of deviant youth occurs in these settings, what the outcomes of such aggregation are, and under which conditions the outcomes of deviant peer aggregation may be negative. We start with the extent of the policy of aggregating deviant youth.

Educational Programs

How Pervasive Is the Policy and Practice?

Within the educational setting, instructional and disciplinary policie ten lead both directly and indirectly to the aggregation of deviant you Tracking on the basis of academic aptitude, for example, has the indirect effect of bringing together children with problem behavior due, in part, to the high comorbidity of behavioral and educational difficulties. A common response to children who display conduct problems is to refer them to special education for diagnosis as "seriously emotionally disturbed" (SED) or "behaviorally or emotionally handicapped" (BEH). Children in the special education system are often treated in groups. Sometimes these groups are treated in self-contained classrooms for the whole day, and sometimes they are treated in "pull-out resource classrooms" for some part of the day. The effects of this aggregation include both the possibility of deviant peer influence and the loss of opportunities for positive influence from well-adjusted peers. Education officials who understand these effects have lobbied for mainstreaming of special education children into regular classrooms as much as possible, but the malignant effects of children with conduct problems on the atmosphere of the regular classroom often prohibit mainstreaming for these children.

During the 2000–2001 school year, 39% of public school districts had at least one alternative school or program for at-risk students; this percentage translates into 10,900 public alternative schools and programs for at-risk students (Kleiner, Porch, & Farris, 2002). Of approximately 47.1 million public school K–12 students in the United States in 2000, an estimated 612,900 students (1.3% of all public school students) were enrolled in public alternative schools or programs for at-risk students (Kleiner et al., 2002); this number does not include aggregation of deviant students that may occur as a result of academic tracking into "low" groups in regular classrooms. During the 1999–2000 school year, 33% of districts with alternative schools and programs for at-risk students had at least one such school or program that had reached or exceeded full capacity (Kleiner et al., 2002). Demand for enrollment exceeded capacity within the last 3 years in 54% of districts with alternative schools and programs for at-risk students (Kleiner et al., 2002), suggesting that the practice of aggregating deviant youth would be even more prevalent if space limitations did not prevent some students from being placed in such programs.

In 2003–2004, 501.3 billion tax dollars were allocated for K–12 education in the United States (U.S. Department of Education, 2004). Although the precise amount spent on programs that aggregate deviant youth is difficult to determine because portions of the funds come from federal, state, and local sources that are not reported uniformly across districts, the costs of such programs are substantial. For example, in North Carolina in the 2001–2002 school year, 3% of state tax dollars spent on education were used to fund alternative schools and programs for at-risk students (Public Schools of North Carolina, 2003).

Effects of Deviant Peer Aggregation on Outcomes

Although limited research exists concerning the impact of tracking on behavioral outcomes, some evidence suggests that vocational education programs that bring together students at risk of dropout, particularly in the context of schools serving predominantly low-income students, have not produced positive effects on reducing later criminality (Ahlstrom & Havighurst, 1971, cited in Arum & Beattie, 1999). As an exception to these findings, Arum and Beattie (1999) found that participation in vocational programs reduced risk of later incarceration in schools if adequate financial resources were provided to structure the programs in ways that minimized deviant peer interaction and influence.

Although carefully conducted behavioral research is needed to assess the impact of aggregating children with behavior disorders in special education classrooms, initial evidence suggests that such policies may have adverse effects. Several studies indicate that students receiving special education services are more likely to be recommended for suspension and expulsion than non-special education students (Morrison & D'Incau, 1997). This relation holds despite federal legislation that prohibits suspension of special education students for offenses that may be a manifestation of their disability (Kingery, 2000). Additional evidence regarding the effectiveness of special education for children with conduct problems suggests that it acts not to reduce conduct problems but rather to increase problem behavior.

The disciplinary use of suspension and expulsion provides another example of educational policies that may indirectly lead to the aggregation of deviant youth and exacerbation of problem outcomes through deviant peer influence. For an increasing variety of offenses, especially in response to recent, federally mandated zero tolerance policies, students are being recommended for long-term suspension and expulsion in unprecedented numbers (Kingery, 2000; Morrison & D'Incau, 1997). According to Kingery (2000), this trend has continued to increase since the advent of zero tolerance policies, leading education researchers to question the premise that "hard-line" discipline serves to deter future offenses. More relevant to the current review, the increase in suspension and expulsion rates may have three potentially detrimental effects. First, suspended and expelled students not offered alternative placements are likely to wind up in the community, increasing the probability of their unmonitored exposure to other delinquent peers. Second, suspended and expelled students lose the opportunity of regular exposure to the positive influence of their conforming classmates. Although these two hypotheses have not been directly tested, evidence suggests that suspended students fall behind academically, are at increased risk of engaging in criminal activity in the community, and are more likely to drop out (Kingery, 2000). Similarly, Arum and Beattie (1999) reported that students who report being suspended in high school were 2.2 times more likely to be incarcerated as adults than students with no history of suspension. Importantly, this relation held even after controlling for related risk factors such as family characteristics, socioeconomic status (SES), prior delinquency, and years of education.

The third consequence of increased suspensions has been a rapid increase in the use of alternative schools with special educational programs, particularly for chronically disruptive and suspended students (Kingery, 2000). These schools involve the aggregation of deviant youth by official policy. Although early alternative schools were designed to serve students not optimally served in the traditional academic environment, alternative programs are increasingly used simply for disciplinary purposes (Raywid, 1994). In her review of the efficacy of alternative educational programs, Raywid (1994) identified alternative programs that focus on behavior management in group settings. There is little to no evidence to suggest that these programs are effective, and there is evidence indicating that they may cause harm. An analysis of state-wide use of in-school suspension in Florida during the 1979–1980 school year revealed that the roughly 58,000 assignments to in-school suspension had no impact on dropout or referral rates or on the rates of more serious disciplinary measures (Raywid, 1994). Officials in Oklahoma recently reviewed the state's use of alternative programs and concluded that although alternative educational programs appear to have some positive effects, programs with a disciplinary emphasis adversely affected student outcomes, including delinquency (Raywid, 1994). Although these studies do not directly examine the impact of aggregating deviant adolescents on delinquent behavior, the growing evidence suggests that it is worth asking the question of whether alternative programs designed to house chronically disruptive students have harmful effects and, if so, under which circumstances.

Mental Health Programs

How Pervasive Is the Policy and Practice?

In mental health settings, children with conduct disorders and children at high risk for these problems are often treated in groups. Outpatient treatment includes parent and child groups, where deviant children (and their parents) share stories with each other. Residential treatment in short-term hospital settings or long-term psychiatric facilities often involves placement with other youth with conduct disorders. Group homes, halfway houses, and day treatment programs typically involve treatment of youth with conduct disorders in "batch processing."

Based on data collected between 1994 and 1996, an estimated 4.1 million (8.2%) children in the civilian, noninstitutionalized population of the United States have a reported mental/emotional problem and/or functional limitation; 19.2% of children with such problems are currently seeing a mental health provider on a regular basis (Colpe, 2001). Extrapolating from Medicaid expenditure reports for North Carolina in state fiscal year 2002–2003, at least 15% of youth in the mental health system are treated by aggregation with other youth in the system (A. Holtzman, personal communication, February 8, 2005). This estimate includes children served for substance abuse and/or mental health problems in facility-based crisis centers, outpatient group therapy, partial hospitalization/day treatment, residential programs, and other inpatient settings; because the estimate is based only on Medicaid data in North Carolina, it is unclear how well the estimate generalizes to children with private insurance and with no insurance, or to other states.

In 1998, the direct costs for the treatment of child mental health problems (emotional and behavioral) in the United States were approximately $11.75 billion (National Institute of Mental Health, 2004). Although a relatively small proportion of children in the mental health system are treated by aggregating them with other deviant youth, 52% of the costs in the mental health system are generated by treatments that aggregate deviant youth (again extrapolating from Medicaid expenditure reports for North Carolina in state fiscal year 2002–2003; A. Holtzman, personal communication, February 8, 2005). The 52% figure seems to be a disproportionate amount of the funds if only 15% of children are served in group rather than in individual settings, but it is a function of the much greater cost of residential and inpatient than other services. For example, on average, $21,659 is spent per client served in a residential setting versus $669 per client for outpatient individual services (A. Holtzman, personal communication, February 8, 2005).

Effects of Deviant Peer Aggregation on Outcomes

Some researchers have begun to explore the possibility that mental health interventions that aggregate deviant youth may have harmful, or iatrogenic, effects on outcomes (Dishion, McCord, & Poulin, 1999). For example, in the Adolescent Transitions Program study assessing the relative efficacy of parent- and peer-based interventions, Dishion and Andrews (1995) randomly assigned 119 high-risk boys and girls to one of four treatment conditions: (1) parent focus only, (2) peer focus only, (3) combined parent and peer focus, and (4) minimal intervention control. Although short-term evaluations indicated that both parent-focused and peer-focused interventions had intended positive effects on reducing negative family interactions and increasing mastery of curriculum material, long-term analyses revealed adverse effects for peer-focused interventions at both the 1-year and 3-year follow-up. Specifically, participants who had been randomly assigned to the peer-focus intervention showed increases in tobacco use and teacher reports of delinquent behavior beyond the levels reported for youth who had received only minimal intervention.

Similar results have been reported with Group-Guided Intervention by Gottfredson (1987c), who found iatrogenic effects on smoking and aggressive behavior for high school students randomly assigned to nondirective peer- (vs. family-) based interventions.

Perhaps the most compelling evidence for the iatrogenic effects of placing high-risk youth with deviant peers for intervention purposes comes from the St. Louis Experiment by Feldman (1992). In this study, youth were randomly assigned to one of three treatment groups: one composed exclusively of referred youth, one composed entirely of nonreferred youth, and one composed of a mix of referred and nonreferred youth. This study was a direct test of the effects of placing high-risk youth with other high-risk youth versus with well-adjusted peers. Although overall effects for treatment were not large, evidence indicated that high-risk children who had been randomly assigned to all-deviant peer groups had more negative outcomes than did those high-risk youth who had been assigned to groups with well-adjusted peers.

It is very important to note that in all of these studies, the adverse effects of aggregating deviant youth could be muted under certain conditions or for certain groups. For Dishion's Adolescent Transition Program, younger children were less susceptible to these iatrogenic effects than were adolescent youth (Dishion et al., 1999). For Gottfredson's experiment with Group-Guided Intervention, the adverse effects were not evident for elementary school-age children, but only with high school youth. In the St. Louis Experiment, boys who had been randomly assigned to mixed groups with experienced leaders faired best, whereas youth assigned to unmixed groups with inexperienced leaders demonstrated the most significant behavioral regressions. Furthermore, boys who had been randomly assigned to a behaviorally oriented treatment were not adversely affected by being placed with other deviant peers (vs.

well-adjusted peers), whereas boys who had been randomly assigned to traditional nondirective therapy suffered ill effects when placed with deviant peers (vs. well-adjusted peers).

Meta-analyses of mental health interventions suggest that multiple effects may operate in therapy. First, most therapies have a generally positive effect on children; however, similar therapies when administered in a group setting have less positive effects (see Lipsey, Chapter 9, this volume; Weisz, Weiss, Han, Granger, & Morton, 1995). Groups that assemble youth in all-deviant groups have even less positive effects than groups that include a high proportion of well-adjusted children (Ang & Hughes, 2002). It is as if the positive effect of the therapy is partially (sometimes wholly) offset in the deviant peer group setting by another, opposing effect.

Taken together, studies in mental health provide compelling evidence for the potentially harmful effects of aggregating deviant youth in mental health treatment and suggest the need for additional examination of the consistency of these harmful effects across contexts and settings.

Juvenile Justice Interventions

How Pervasive Is the Policy and Practice?

A common juvenile justice system response to delinquent behavior is placement in a residential setting that is populated exclusively by other offending youth. These settings include detention centers, training schools, reform schools, prisons, boot camps, and wilderness camps. In all of these settings, youth interact primarily with other deviant youth under circumstances of limited adult supervision. Adults guard the boundaries, but most of the time youth are in rooms with peers and no adults present.

More than 1.6 million delinquency cases were handled by the courts in 2000 (Office of Juvenile Justice and Delinquency Prevention [OJJDP], 2003). In 20% of these cases, juveniles were held in secure detention facilities at some point between their referral to court and the disposition of their case (OJJDP, 2003). Thus at least 20% of youth in the juvenile justice system are aggregated with other offending youth in the system; this figure does not include juveniles who were never in a detention facility but who may be grouped with other delinquents in group-oriented parole or other activities. On a given day, approximately 109,000 juveniles are held in residential placements (OJJDP, 2003).

The 43 states that provided data for a Council of Juvenile Correctional Administrators survey spent a combined total of $4.25 billion on juvenile corrections (Loughran, Godfrey, Holyoke, Conroy, & Dugan, 2004). The average cost per state was $111 million, so a reasonable national estimate would be $5 billion. About 93% of these funds were spent on programs that aggregate deviant youth (e.g., in training schools, detention centers, other residential facilities, day treatment centers); the remaining 7% was spent on parole, probation, and home-based services that may or may not have aggregated deviant youth.

Effects of Deviant Peer Aggregation on Outcomes

Although evaluations of prevention and intervention programs for juvenile offending have not systematically isolated the effects of aggregating delinquents, considerable evidence suggests that the detention of juveniles in programs characterized by high exposure to deviant peers and minimal adult interaction fails to reduce and, in some cases, may exacerbate rates of recidivism. Seven studies of the heralded "Scared Straight" program for juvenile offenders, a program that intentionally brought together first-time offending adolescents in groups for the purposes of exposing them to incarcerated offenders, have yielded uniform conclusions that this program is not effective and may actually exacerbate criminal offending (Sherman & Strang, 2004).

In a meta-analytic review of more than 500 crime prevention programs, Sherman and colleagues (1998) identified effective, ineffective, and promising intervention programs across developmental periods. With respect to delinquent and at-risk youth, the only prevention programs with clearly positive results were those that treated youth individually and were aimed at family interactions (e.g., parent training and family therapy). Several peer group programs aimed at adolescents found no effects or potentially negative effects. Ineffective programs included school-based leisure-time enrichment programs, correctional boot camps using traditional military training, and wilderness camps. Counseling, and peer group counseling in particular, failed to reduce substance abuse or delinquency, and in some cases increased delinquency. A common element across all programs identified as ineffective is the aggregation of deviant youths.

In a similar meta-analytic review of interventions for serious juvenile offenders, Lipsey, Wilson, and Cothern (2000) found that outcomes differed somewhat for incarcerated and nonincarcerated offenders. For incarcerated offenders, the most effective programs include interpersonal skill development programs (e.g., social skills training, anger management) and teaching family homes (e.g., community-based, family-style group homes). Noneffective programs include milieu therapy, drug abstinence programs, wilderness/challenge programs, and vocational programs. For nonincarcerated offenders, programs involving individual counseling, interpersonal skill building, and behavioral interventions have the most beneficial effects. Once again, programs with minimum opportunities for deviant peer interaction may be the ones most likely to reduce delinquent behavior. Interestingly, an important factor in determining program efficacy for incarcerated youth is treatment delivery through mental health versus correctional officers. This finding is consistent with results reviewed in the previous section suggesting that experienced leaders may mute the adverse effects of deviant peer aggregation.

Community Programs

Although education, mental health, and juvenile justice are the systems in which practices that aggregate deviant youth are most common, other community programs and policies also aggregate deviant youth. A variety of programs that are designed to keep at-risk youth off the streets, and which are sponsored by public and private agencies in the United States, often offer little structure or adult supervision and simply provide a place for youth to "hang out." These programs may have the unintended effect of increasing behavior problems by increasing the aggregation of at-risk youth. In other domains, such as foster care and public housing, although policies do not explicitly aggregate deviant youth, these policies lead to the aggregation of deviant youth in practice. For instance, sometimes vulnerable children and adolescents who are removed from the homes of their biological parents risk increased exposure to negative peer influences through experiences in group foster care. Furthermore, in low-income neighborhoods, at-risk youth often come together in ways that may increase their risk for deviant behavior (e.g., in the case of street gangs). It is difficult to estimate how prevalent deviant peer aggregation is in such community contexts, both because the aggregation often takes place outside of formal contexts and because the contexts in which aggregation might occur differ considerably across communities.

In sum, all these reviews suggest that programs emphasizing individualized or highly structured skill-building interventions are more effective at preventing or reducing delinquent behavior than those programs that place deviant young adolescents in loosely structured group interactions with other deviant adolescents. However, few evaluations have tested this premise directly, and many evaluations have been flawed by nonrandomized designs or other threats to their validity. Also, published reviews of programs have not emphasized the aggregation of deviant peers as a moderating variable. Therefore, rigorous reviews are needed to test fully the hypothesis that the aggregation of deviant peers within interventions may increase rather than decrease deviant behavior.

Furthermore, because abandoning group interventions for deviant youth may not be logistically feasible, studies that examine factors that moderate the effects of deviant peer aggregation are also needed.

THE CHALLENGE OF INNOVATIVE ALTERNATIVES

The policy solution to the problem of deviant peer influence in group settings is not obvious. It may be implausible to require that deviant youth be kept apart from other deviant youth. "Batch processing" is the most common policy because it is financially feasible. Furthermore, the rest of society may intuitively believe that deviant youth pose a danger to nondeviant youth, suggesting that even if aggregating deviant youth exacerbates their problems, a large segment of well-adjusted society is being spared. The system-wide "net" effect of deviant peer aggregation policies has yet to be tested. Although the perception that segregating deviant youth from mainstream society has a net positive effect may, in fact, prove inaccurate (additional research is necessary to resolve this question fully), the political motivation to segregate deviant youth from mainstream society is strong, and financial constraints appear to make group treatment the setting of choice. Finally, there is little consensus within or across the domains of education, mental health, and juvenile justice regarding the components of an effective alternative response to the problem of delinquent behavior.

The challenge for scholars, practitioners, and policymakers—and the defined aim of this book—is to understand the problem of deviant peer aggregation more thoroughly and to generate innovative and cost-effective alternatives. A related challenge is to understand how group treatments and interventions might be structured so that deviant peer influence is minimized. It is possible that group treatment per se is not iatrogenic and that novel ways of structuring this experience or delivering treatment in group settings can be found. Serious scholars disagree about the conclusions that can be discerned from the available evidence (e.g., Weiss, Tapp, Caron, & Johnson, 2005), but all scholars agree that the question has not been addressed exhaustively.

Recent experimental studies suggest that the U.S. public is willing to pay large sums in taxes for programs that "work" and are truly effective in reducing crime (Cohen, 2004). Are we as willing to stop payment for programs that are truly ineffective or that might even bring about adverse effects?

CHAPTER 2

Deviant Peer Contagion in Interventions and Programs

An Ecological Framework for Understanding Influence Mechanisms

Thomas J. Dishion
and Kenneth A. Dodge

In this chapter, *deviant peer contagion* refers to inadvertent negative effects associated with intervention programs that aggregate peers in the delivery of a therapeutic protocol, educational service, or community program. The chapters in this volume suggest that under some conditions educational, juvenile justice, and mental health interventions are potentially undermined by deviant peer contagion. The evidence is clear that deviant peer contagion effects are conditional on the characteristics of the individual and the circumstances of the program (see Dishion & Dodge, 2005). It is therefore necessary that future research focus on isolating the individual, group, and contextual mechanisms that contribute to deviant peer contagion and the potentially negative effects of educational, rehabilitative, and intervention services. Research that advances our understanding of the dynamics of deviant peer contagion will certainly provide insights useful for the design of interventions and programs that minimize these effects and optimize benefits to participating youth.

In this chapter we offer an ecological framework for isolating and studying levels of influence and developmental factors that account for variations across studies, as well as for documenting negative intervention effects. An ecological framework was originally proposed by Bronfenbrenner (1979, 1989) during his efforts to organize the vast literature on individual differences in child and adolescent social development. An ecological perspective is not a theory of behavior but rather a conceptual heuristic for disentangling levels of influence. It is often true that various theories can be integrated as simply different levels of analysis (see Figure 2.1). For example, control theory (Hirschi, 1969) can be differentiated from social learning theory (Patterson, 1982) in that the former emphasizes the social-cognitive consequences of relationships with parents, while the latter emphasizes the specific social interactions that lead to effective parent–child relationships and socialization outcomes. From an ecological perspective, these two "mechanisms" may be integral to a general childrearing process, studied at different levels with unique measurement preferences.

In the service of identifying the mechanisms of deviant peer contagion, the framework provided in Figure 2.1 conceptualizes the "ecology" with respect to social contexts contrived by an intervention, program, or educational service. This volume is concerned with programs that aggregate clients, students, and/or individuals to deliver a service in a cost-effective and safe manner. There are many dimensions to programs with respect to the implied and explicit curricula guiding therapeutic efforts. Some of the contextual features of interventions that aggregate are intended (e.g., a targeted risk group), while others seem to be driven by convenience (e.g., after-school program).

Inspection of Figure 2.1 reveals three levels of analysis pertinent to deviant peer contagion. The first level, the *individual level*, refers to the characteristics of an intervention recipient that may influence his or her response to an intervention service. For example, individuals may understand or react to an intervention in such a way that they may deteriorate on the very dimension that the program is intended to improve. Characteristics such as age of the youth, gender, behavioral history, and temperament moderate the relation between intervention characteristics and outcomes. As is discussed below, it is likely that such individual characteristics are often social-cognitive in nature and depend heavily on information processing and individual interpretations of an intervention and subsequent reactions.

The second level of analysis, the *program or intervention service level*, describes the microsocial interactions (i.e., relationship processes) that are incidental to an intervention (i.e., informal interactions among group members) as well as those that are engineered into the intervention specifically to reduce problem behavior and develop positive behavior and skill among the participants. At a minimal level, these interactions consist of those with peers who are mutual recipients and participants in

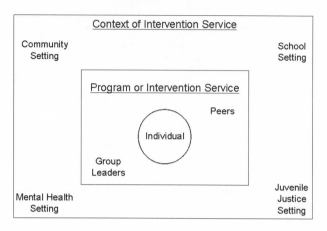

FIGURE 2.1. An ecological framework for understanding deviant peer contagion.

the program curricula and those with group leaders who are charged with delivering, monitoring, and problem solving the objectives of the intervention agenda. Such dynamics may be affected by the ratio of deviant to nondeviant peers, number of leaders per group, skill of group leader, and the like. Much of our thinking about deviant peer contagion implies that program interactions may account for iatrogenic, peer contagion effects.

The third level of analysis considered in this volume is the *context level* within which the intervention is embedded. As noted in Figure 2.1, there are four primary contexts considered with respect to deviant peer contagion. The first is interventions that are delivered within a community setting, which may include welfare services or other community programs such as after-school programs, gang prevention programs, recreational centers, or summer camps (Klein, Chapter 13; Wilson & Woods, Chapter 11; Lansford & Rosch, Chapter 5; Vigdor, Chapter 10; and Ludwig & Duncan, Chapter 17, this volume). The second context involves programs that are delivered within the public school setting. These may include "pull-out" programs that contrive a special context in mainstream public school or alternative school environments (Reinke & Walker, Chapter 7; Silver & Eddy, Chapter 14, this volume). The third context is the mental health setting where outpatient or inpatient mental health services, including those for substance use, are provided. Although there are relatively few studies regarding positive and/or negative effects associated with inpatient mental health and substance use settings, features of such programs likely contribute to or detract from intervention goals (Dodge & Sherrill, Chapter 6; Smith, Dumas, & Prinz, Chapter 16; Lipsey, Chapter 9, this volume). Thus mental health settings provide yet another systemic level of analysis for potential study of iatrogenic effects arising from aggregation. The fourth context is the juvenile justice setting, typically delivered within a community, that may include a variety of aggregation strategies ranging from weekly groups to residential containments that last for weeks, months, or even years within state institutions (Osgood & Briddell, Chapter 8; and Greenwood, Chapter 15, this volume).

An important feature of an ecological perspective is the ability to conceptualize and test *interaction effects among levels of analysis*. That is, it is very possible that problem behavior may escalate in some vulnerable individuals (e.g., young adolescents with marginal peer relationships) by means of informal interactions among peers that are facilitated by the service being offered at night in a community setting (e.g., they walk home together and smoke cigarettes). The point is that if this hypothesis were found to be true, then the iatrogenic effect would be explained by a two- to three-way interaction among three levels of interaction. Given the literature on deviant peer contagion contained in this volume, it is probably true that negative effects are a joint function of the developmental status of the individual, the informal and formal interactions of the participants, and the context of the program or service. Therefore, an ecological framework would seem to be a useful heuristic for considering a further study of iatrogenic effects.

QUANTIFYING LEVELS

Before proceeding to an exploration of potential mechanisms, it is useful to advance a formula that could be considered with respect to the parameters needed to quantify and test hypotheses regarding factors that may contribute to deviant peer contagion. Thus, in Figure 2.2, we provide a hierarchical linear model that includes three levels of analysis of the framework previously described, including individual characteristics of the intervention participants, the peer group dynamics of the intervention, and the social contexts of the interventions. This quantitative framework allows the specification of variation within each level of analysis, as well as a description of interactions among the three levels. The framework is derived from the influential work of Bryk and Raudenbush (1988) toward the development of a quantitative framework for considering levels of analysis. Currently, the ability to quantify multiple levels within a quantitative modeling framework is available in several multivariate statistical platforms (Muthén & Muthén, 2000). Anthony (Chapter 3, this volume) provides a thorough analysis of the quantitative strategies needed to identify a variety of potential deviant peer contagion mechanisms.

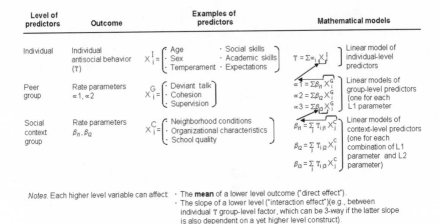

Level of predictors	Outcome	Examples of predictors	Mathematical models

FIGURE 2.2. Antisocial behavior in group and metagroup content.

Although program effects can be conceptually reviewed at the three levels described in Figure 2.1, it is rare that any study would provide the empirical data needed to evaluate the contribution of each level and their constituent interaction effects on deviant peer contagion. Most of the intervention and program outcome literature does not report variation in the social contexts within which the intervention or program is embedded. For example, a meta-analysis of many studies (at least 40) of a cognitive-behavioral intervention to reduce adolescent problem behavior would be needed, assuming a very large effect size of social contexts on intervention outcomes. Thus the framework is conceptually useful, but it is doubtful whether there currently exists a database to explore the contribution of the social context of the intervention (level three) as a main effect or in interaction with individual (level one) or peer group (level two) interactions of the intervention in a systematic way.

DESIGN LIMITATIONS

Today, it is noteworthy that the existing literature on intervention effects serves as a *barrier* for understanding such mechanisms. The primary empirical strategy for studying intervention effects is often randomized group intervention trials. Although these serve as state-of-the-art empirical strategies, there is an enormous loss of information in these group comparison studies. Jacobson and Truax (1991) provided a more useful framework for studying intervention effects at both the group and the individual level. Within that framework, four nominal outcomes were specified:

1. *Clinically significant change*, describing individuals who required an intervention service and who improved.
2. *Unchanged nondistressed*, describing individuals who probably did not require an intervention service but who participated nonetheless and subsequently did not change.
3. *Unchanged distressed*, describing individuals who clearly required or would have benefited from an intervention service, participated, but did not change.
4. *Deteriorated*, describing individuals either in the nondistressed or the distressed range who participated, but who clearly worsened as a function of the intervention service.

The advantage of the Jacobsen and Truax (1991) approach to studying change is the a priori statistical formulation of normative and distressed functioning, and the quantitative parameters for determining movement across those ranges, incorporating reliability of measurement in this determination. When considering deviant peer contagion, most investigators would be interested in two types of change: distressed individuals who remain distressed or get worse, and individuals who are functioning within the normal range who become distressed following their involvement with an intervention. Note that the majority of the literature on deviant peer contagion often does not separate these two potentially distinct outcomes, nor the underlying mechanisms.

Unfortunately, intervention science is often summarized by central tendencies for groups. Thus, it is frequently impossible to look at individual variations in response to interventions; however, to do so is critical for identifying mechanisms that could explain individuals' negative responses despite the majority's positive responses to an intervention service. This point will be taken up in the discussion section of this chapter.

In the sections that follow, we offer systematic hypotheses from the developmental, criminological, clinical, and epidemiological literature regarding mechanisms that could potentially account for iatrogenic effects resulting from peer aggregation.

INDIVIDUAL CHARACTERISTICS: VULNERABILITY AND RESILIENCE

The literature on the development of problem behavior in general and deviant peer contagion in particular describes a variety of individual characteristics that define vulnerabilities to deviant peer influence, as well as resilience against such influence. For example, the age and gender of the youth may attenuate or amplify the peer contagion effects. The available evidence also suggests that peer contagion effects may vary with respect to the kinds of behaviors that are influenced at diverse ages. For example, peer effects in terms of aggression have been noted at the preschool level (Hannish, Martin, Fabes, Leonard, & Herzog, 2005) and also in terms of both aggression and covert antisocial behaviors during the transition into elementary school (e.g., Snyder et al., 2005; Warren, Schoppelrey, Moberg, & McDonald, 2005). In early adolescence, peer effects appear to be most pronounced on early forms of substance use such as smoking (e.g., Chassin, Presson, Sherman, Montello, & McGrew, 1986; Dishion, Capaldi, Spracklen, & Li, 1995; Ennett & Bauman, 1994) and peer-oriented forms of delinquent behavior (Patterson, 1993; Warr, 1993).

Some youth may be more vulnerable to peer contagion effects than others. Youth with a history of peer rejection may be more vulnerable to deviant peer influences and even gang involvement (Dishion, Nelson, Winter, & Bullock, 2004). College-age males with a history of binge drinking are more vulnerable after random assignment to a roommate with a similar history with respect to observed increases in problem drinking in the young adult years (Duncan, Boisjoly, Kremer, Levy, & Eccles, 2005), whereas female college students appear unaffected by the characteristics of their same-gendered roommate.

It is also true that some individuals may be less susceptible to peer influences by virtue of their level of maturity, relationships with significant adults, temperamental characteristics such as level of self-control or self-regulation, or level of severity of deviance (Dishion & Patterson, in press; Goodnight, Bates, Newman, Dodge, & Petit, in press; Rothbart & Bates, 1998). For example, a group format is considered state of the art for delivering parenting information, and has the most compelling empirical evidence of effectiveness (e.g., Webster-Stratton & Hammond, 1990). Assuming that parents of children with behavior problems are themselves vulnerable to deviance or mental health problems, it nonetheless appears that their age and maturational status render them invulnerable to deviant peer contagion. Also, recent evidence by Waldron and Kaminer (2004) suggests that group interventions with adolescents with a documented substance abuse disorder are effective, and do not result in peer contagion. It is likely that deviant peer influence operates most strongly on those adolescents who are only marginally deviant (Caprara & Zimbardo, 1996; Vitaro, Tremblay, Kerr, Pagani, & Bukowski, 1997). Youth who are firmly well adjusted may be able to resist deviant peer influences, and youth with very severe levels of deviance may be beyond influence by others.

The study of individual characteristics associated with attenuation or amplification of deviant peer contagion is complex with respect to the scientific goal of identifying the mechanism that accounts for these effects. As shown in Figure 2.2, we presume that the individual characteristics that moderate deviant peer contagion effects are social-cognitive in nature. The general idea is that such individual characteristics are correlated with social-cognitive attributes, which in turn affect how a young person might respond to the interactive dynamics (i.e., peer group dynamics) of the intervention service. In this sense, the mechanism is likely interactive—for example, a high-risk young adolescent may be especially vulnerable to some specific contexts, but not all, depending on his or her own demographic or physical features (e.g., Magnussen, Stattin, & Allen, 1985). For this reason, we focus primarily on the individual's social perceptions as the most viable strategy for identifying the mechanism that may underlie demographic covariates such as age, gender, and social and emotional history.

Mechanisms that emphasize the individual level of analysis can be generally classified as social-cognitive and motivational. It is important to note that recent advances in developmental psychology and neuroscience support a perspective on human behavior as a joint function of individuals reading contextual cues and then responding to environmental events accordingly. For example, work by Dodge and colleagues (e.g., Dodge & Coie, 1987; Dodge, Murphy, & Buchsbaum, 1984) describes an information-processing paradigm for considering the contribution of individual social-cognitive to environmental cues in behaving aggressively. In general, it is clear that a key aspect of reading social and interpersonal environments is making inferences regarding the mental states, thoughts, and judgments of others (Malle, 1999). Developmental research reveals that a tendency to read and interpret the actions of significant others begins during infancy (Baird & Baldwin, 1999; Baldwin, 2000; Baldwin & Moses, 1994). An overview of the brain mechanisms that are associated with the active reading of others' behavior and responding accordingly is summarized by Frith and Frith (2001). In this work, "mentalizing" is located in the anterior cingulate cortex, which is also highly linked to the area of the brain concerned with self-regulation (Tucker & Luu, in press; Posner & Rothbart, 2000). Given the substantial evidence that is emerging regarding the importance of active reading and interpretation of environmental events and the regulation of behavior and motivation, it seems clear that the analysis of the individual's responses to interventions is an alluring focus for research in understanding deviant peer contagion.

The following mechanisms have been suggested as explanatory for such individual effects.

Labeling Theory

Inherent to human social living is the formation of cognitive categories into which we place other people (Allport, 1937; Rothbart, Ellis, Rueda, & Posner, 2003). Such social judgment may determine with whom one interacts and the nature of those interactions. High-risk youth may identify and label peers and group leaders in such a way as to enhance or to undermine the intervention's effects, and, conversely, group leaders and peer participants may perceive a child positively or negatively on the basis of his or her surface characteristics. Later in this chapter, we link the formation of social categories that underlie prejudice and that structure subsequent interactions under the general rubric of *rule-governed behavior* (Hayes, 1989). Social judgments related to interventions and programs that undermine intended outcomes have been referred to as *labeling*.

Since the 1970s, there has been an increasing awareness that juvenile justice interventions (Schur, 1973) and mental health interventions (Rosenthal, 1994, 2003) have potential negative effects if they involve labeling individuals as problematic. Labels such as *juvenile delinquent*, *seriously emotionally disturbed*, and *mentally ill* elicit a reaction from both the client and the service providers that is potentially iatrogenic. The very involvement in a program that aggregates individuals that fit such labels, therefore, would increase the negative effects of the intervention, a result of being assigned membership in a group of individuals with shared characteristics in addition to the pejorative label (e.g., *delinquent, high risk*). Analyses by Johnson, Simons, and Conger (2004) revealed that official processing in juvenile courts systems seemed to have negative effects on subsequent criminal offending (after controlling for prior offending). Although it is often thought that labeling is a potential mechanism, to date, the social-cognitive mechanism remains unmeasured and untested. Nor has the labeling hypothesis been systematically studied by random assignment studies. One promising exception was conducted by Rabiner and Coie (1989), who experimentally manipulated a rejected child's perception of his social standing among peers by telling him that he was a liked child (or by not telling him anything at all). They found that this labeling manipulation led the rejected child to achieve more favorable peer outcomes. They concluded that the self-label of *rejected* apparently interferes with the child's ability to achieve positive outcomes.

Ample evidence suggests the viability of self-fulfilling prophecies that fit within the labeling theory (e.g., Harris, 1994). Literature reviewed by Harris (1994) suggests that self-fulfilling prophecies are systematically derived from subtle nonverbal communications. For example, implanting expectations regarding the nature of a client's problems could, indeed, affect subtle interaction sequences that clearly communicated to the client the therapist's expectations regarding the client's adjustment and skill level. These communications were unconsciously read and interpreted by the client, and the expected effects in the client's behavior ensued.

It is also plausible that the participant's perception of the peers in the group and/or the group leader can have deleterious effects on deviant peer contagion. Prinstein and Wang (2005) presented data showing that high-risk youth tend to "overestimate" the problem behavior of their peers. Assignment to a group of high-risk children may create the impression in the minds of some participants that other members of the intervention group support and engage in deviant behavior. This perception leads to bragging about, boasting about, or exaggerating one's own deviant exploits in a group context. In groups involving a group leader, such interactions may inadvertently reinforce the participant who exaggerates his or her own problem behavior by virtue of mobilizing group attention. Thus, a self-fulfilling prophecy is enacted and provides an impetus for future, similar interactions.

To date, the labeling hypothesis has not been systematically tested with respect to negative effects associated with deviant peer contagion. However, if such effects did occur, one would expect that the characteristics and communications of the group leader and peers regarding the individual client would reinforce an expectation for more deviant behavior. This expectation would then lead to prophecy-fulfilling behavior in settings outside the group. Thus iatrogenic effects would occur, and group-level effects would be expected (see Figure 2.2). It is noted that with self-labeling effects, only "virtual" deviant peer aggregation, rather than actual peer aggregation, is necessary to lead to iatrogenic outcomes.

Construct Theory

McCord (1997) proposed a deceptively simple motivational perspective on the performance of delinquent behavior. She referred to this motivational theory as *construct theory*. The theoretical perspective is derived from the criminological theories of Shaw and McKay (1972) and Cohen (1955). This theory is decidedly cognitive with respect to the mechanism. McCord proposed that individuals derive meaning from their interactions with significant others, including both peers and adults. They listen, watch, and observe others interacting with their world. The end

result of this process is that they learn, through observation and thinking, a motivational framework for their own future behavior. The motivational framework is not dependent on reinforcement with respect to
observable contingencies. However, there is an expectation that the motivational stance will lead to rewarding circumstances as perceived by
the individual. For instance, a self-destructive pattern of behavior that is
voluntarily adopted may not be reinforced within the context of an individual's network of relationships, but the expectations themselves may
be rewarding to the individual. For example, a youth may expect that
significant others will be angry or upset and blame themselves for his or
her self-destructive behavior. Alternatively, a youth may expect that others will hold him or her in high esteem on the basis of delinquent or
problematic behavior or detection by the police. These are not reinforced circumstances; instead, they are cognitive expectations that may
or may not have bearing in reality.

Given the cognitive nature of construct theory, one would expect an
interaction between an individual's premorbid characteristics and the
group experience in predicting potential negative effects. That is, given
the emphasis on idiosyncratic interpretations of environmental events,
individual effects would dominate group effects in explaining negative
responses to interventions.

Very little research specifically tests the construct theory approach
to understanding iatrogenic effects that result from peer aggregation.
However, there is support in the social-psychological literature for individual interpretations of situations or tasks being embedded within a
larger cognitive framework and having influences on future behavior.
For example, Steele, Spencer, and Aronson (2002) discuss the role of stereotype and social identity threat in performance on academic achievement tests. These investigators were interested in providing a mechanism
for explaining ethnic differences in performance on standardized academic tests. Through a series of structured manipulations on the demand
characteristics of test performance, they gathered data in support of
their hypotheses. Under conditions in which the experimenters proposed
that test performance was indicative of innate ability, individuals responded in concordance with the social stereotype regarding their own
group. For example, minority participants performed more poorly under
conditions imputing innate ability when compared with white participants. Although these data are far removed from the real world of service and intervention dynamics, they do provide support for an essential
cognitive perspective regarding the formation of expectations that link
one's identity with social stereotypes that have a real-world impact on
behavior. From this perspective, it would be proposed that youth renego-
tiate their identities cognitively in the context of group interventions and

subsequently change their motivational stance with respect to delinquent and/or other problem behaviors.

Kaplan's formulation of self-derogation theory in explaining adolescent deviance might also be seen as a cognitive theory of deviant peer contagion (H. B. Kaplan, 1975, 1976, 1994; R. M. Kaplan, 1984). Self-derogation theory proposes that adolescent deviance is a motivational reaction to failure and rejection experiences in childhood and adolescence. High-risk children respond to such experiences with tobacco use and other deviant behaviors, especially those that are salient among the peer group at that age. Indeed, Kaplan found that in early adolescence smoking was associated with decreases in self-derogation. In the context of interventions that aggregate youth, the self-derogation hypothesis would predict that higher risk youth participating in interventions that aggregate would increase their level of deviance to enhance their sense of self-worth. These effects would be mostly individual in that self-enhancement through deviance would be a joint function of the individual's premorbid history (i.e., rejection and failure experiences) and the dynamics of a group with respect to providing a social context in which the youth would interpret deviance as a venue for improving his or her sense of self.

Control Theory

One very influential perspective on the performance of aggressive, delinquent, and other problem behaviors is the theoretical view originally proposed by Hirschi (1969). The essential notion of control theory is that most individuals would readily commit crimes if there were not a "stake in conformity." A commitment to conform to rules is based by and large on positive relationships with socializing agents. Although the foundation of a stake in conformity is a positive relationship with socializing agents, the mechanism is clearly cognitive. Individuals with a high stake in conformity interpret deviant behavior and deviant individuals in a negative light. They avoid social contexts and behaviors that are disruptive to their conformance values.

Therefore, in an updated version of the control perspective, Hawkins and colleagues (1992a) propose that bonding to parents and schools jointly reduces the likelihood of engaging in problem behaviors and substance use. From this perspective, deviant peer influences are not causal but merely an epiphenomenon or facilitative factor for increasing deviance. Bonding is seen as a social-cognitive mechanism that would explain why some youth are unaffected by peer aggregation and exposure to deviant norms and behaviors.

Control theory perspectives would assume that random assignment to interventions that aggregate peers would not have a deleterious effect on problem behavior unless interactions among those peers attenuated bonds to parents and schools. Therefore, again, we see that this perspective would predict that individual reactions to interventions would dominate with respect to negative effects. It would be hypothesized that groups that inadvertently attenuated relationships with parents and/or schools would be those that increased problem behavior in participating youth.

Very few studies support this hypothesis to date. In fact, in our analysis of the Adolescent Transitions Program, Dishion and Andrews (1995) found that group interventions that aggregate youth increased the positive interactions between the youth and parents as determined by direct observations. Therefore, the pattern of findings is inconsistent with control theory in which one would expect that an intervention that improved the parent–child interaction would also decrease the level of adolescent deviance. This was not found, and therefore control theory has as yet to provide a viable explanation for negative effects associated with peer aggregation.

Summary

Clearly, future research is required to understand the individual-level mechanisms that may account for negative responses to interventions that aggregate. In the hierarchically linear model presented in Figure 2.2, the expectation is that the individual and/or the individual by group interaction would account for the majority of the variance and negative effects associated with deviant peer contagion. Simply put, an emphasis on individual-level variables suggests that the group-level variable is less important than the individual-level variable in accounting for variation.

MICROSOCIAL DYNAMICS OF AN INTERVENTION SERVICE

Reinforcement Theory

Research on interpersonal influence breaks down social interactions into molecular units that often take place in a matter of seconds, then studies contingent reaction patterns by experimentally controlling consequences or using statistical procedures such as sequential analysis (Bakeman & Quera, 1995; Patterson, 1982). This research tradition is often based on a reinforcement theory of social behavior, which emphasizes the role of consequences and function in understanding individual differences in behavior patterns. A reinforcement perspective on deviant peer contagion proposes that the individual's deviant behavior in the group is functional with respect to some outcome of value to that individual. The functional dynamic of the group, therefore, strengthens the tendency for the individual to respond accordingly in other situations and settings. For this process to occur, it is not necessary for the individual to track and/or to monitor positive responses that have reinforcing value for him or her. Several investigators have identified the viability of unconscious shaping of behavior. For example, Byrne, Young, and Griffitt (1966) provide evidence suggesting that in conversations within an experimental laboratory, similar and dissimilar attitude statements could be defined, a priori, as reinforcing or not. The preponderance of similar attitude statements over dissimilar attitude statements accounted for neutral attraction within the context of an experimental conversation study. The participants were not aware of the reasons for their level of attraction. Others have argued, however, that conscious awareness of the reinforcing stimulus properties amplifies the conditioning effects (Fuhrer & Baer, 1965; Spielberger, 1965). Regardless, a reinforcement perspective on deviant peer contagion would propose that some arrangement of either negative reinforcement and/or positive reinforcement within the context of the group meetings would account for most of the variation in negative outcomes associated with deviant peer aggregation.

During the past 15 years, the reinforcement perspective has been expanded to include verbal learning in humans (Hayes, 1989; Hayes, Barnes-Holmes, & Roche, 2001). Reinforcement theory has often rather ambiguously combined the properties of classical conditioning with those of operant conditioning (Rescorla, 1987). In the analysis of social interactions in the natural environment, considerable utility is found in simply examining antecedent events as prompts for strong response tendencies such as aggression (Patterson, 1973; Patterson & Cobb, 1973). However, a case can be made that the combination of classical and operant conditioning results in a uniquely human sensitivity to verbal learning referred to as *rule-governed behavior*. This work is important because it provides a potentially integrative framework for linking social-cognitive mechanisms with the microsocial interactions that are known to influence behavior. From a rule-governed perspective, the central point in regard to contagion from deviant peers is that being reinforced for talking deviantly is equivalent to behaving deviantly. Therefore, group interactions that provide attention or reinforcement to individuals for their deviant talk are equivalent to group interactions that would reinforce deviant acts. More important, getting group attention for deviant talk would be associated with positive reinforcement, and would therefore lead to similar behaviors in other group contexts involving same-age peers.

Figure 2.3 provides a summary of reinforcement mechanisms. The critical point here is that the different learning mechanisms are potentially complementary in explaining responses to group interaction. Classical conditioning accounts for youths' perception that a particular class of peer interactions will be reinforcing. Operant conditioning can strengthen the response and later goal-directed behavior. Imitation and modeling can explain the influence of observing peer reinforcement in action within an intervention.

The relevance of integrating rule-governed mechanisms into a reinforcement perspective is that it provides a mechanism that can explain the generalizability of negative effects to some behaviors and not to others. For example, Dishion, McCord, and Poulin (1999) found that random assignment to peer interventions had a negative impact on delinquent behavior but not on aggressive behavior. Moreover, it had a negative impact on smoking but not on alcohol or marijuana use. The selective effect on specific behaviors within a problem behavior syndrome is difficult to explain. However, from a simple operant point of view, it is nearly impossible to explain, because it is clear that there were very few, if any, delinquent and/or smoking events in the peer groups. Therefore, the account must incorporate how the youth derived a rule from the group that is potentially salient for the future collection of peer reinforcement. Thus using an integrated perspective of reinforcement mechanisms is optimal in understanding deviant peer contagion.

Deviancy Training

Startling findings have been reported recently by Bayer, Pintoff, and Pozen (2003) on the learning of delinquent behavior within juvenile correction facilities. In a careful examination of 15,000 adolescents placed in juvenile corrections facilities in Florida, Bayer found a statistically reliable tendency for youth to acquire the delinquent behavior of their peers within their placement facility, and to demonstrate those behaviors following release from institutionalization. Bayer found that after release, an adolescent became more likely to be arrested for the type of crimes that had previously been committed by his or her cellmates. Somehow, these youth "learned" to commit the types of crimes that their cellmates had committed. Although reinforcement mechanisms within the correctional facilities were not observed, this study provides solid evidence that interactive dynamics within juvenile corrections facilities have an iatrogenic effect on delinquent behavior.

Theories of criminal behavior have often emphasized the role of peers in the commitment of delinquent acts. Differential association theory proposed that delinquent behavior was an outcome of selecting and

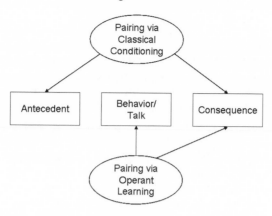

FIGURE 2.3. An integrated perspective of reinforcement mechanisms.

identifying with a deviant subculture (Short & Strodbeck, 1965). The emphasis on peer influence in differential association was soon translated into reinforcement theory by Burgess and Akers (1966). Their concept was relatively simple: youth prone to delinquency received relatively high rates of positive reinforcement from peers for committing delinquent acts. Measurement and testing of the differential association hypothesis was difficult. Buehler, Patterson, and Furniss (1966) examined the social interactions of delinquents within an institutional setting. Direct observations of incarcerated youth revealed that the reinforcement ratio of peers to parents was approximately 9 to 1, that is, for every one time an adult in the residential facility rewarded or praised the youth for a prosocial action, peers praised the youth nine times for his or her deviant acts.

The concept of differential reinforcement for delinquent behavior was more directly tested in research involving the Oregon Youth Study boys. In this study, 206 13-year-old boys brought their best friends into the research center for a 30-minute videotaped observation task. In this task, the youth were asked to discuss activities and to solve problems together. The videotapes were subsequently coded for deviant talk, normative talk, laughter, and pauses. The deviancy-training process was defined as contingent, positive responses (i.e., laughter) to deviant talk. This dynamic between two male friends was found to be predictive of growth in substance use, delinquency, and violent behavior in adolescence, after controlling for past behavior (Dishion, Capaldi, Spracklen, & Li, 1995; Dishion, Eddy, Haas, Li, & Spracklen, 1997; Dishion, Spracklen, & Patterson, 1996). Moreover, youths' tendency to select and engage in deviancy training with friends mediated the link between early antisocial behavior and young adult problem behavior and adjustment problems (Patterson, Dishion, & Yoerger, 2000).

Central to the notion of deviancy training is the concept of the *matching law* (Herrnstein, 1970; McDowell, 1988). The concept of the matching law depends on the notion of relative rate of reinforcement: it is not so much that peers provide reinforcement for delinquent behavior but rather that individuals prone to delinquent behavior receive relatively higher rates of reinforcement for deviance than for normative behavior. The matching law has been applied to studying choice behavior across species and fits rather well with the reinforcement dynamics of adolescents and their friends (Dishion et al., 1996; McDowell, 1988). Consistent with the matching law perspective on deviancy training, it was found that youth whose friendships were indeed organized around deviance were those most likely to continue antisocial and delinquent behavior 10 years later (Dishion, Nelson, Winter, & Bullock, 2004). From a dynamic systems perspective, youth who organize their relationships around deviance get "stuck" in deviant talk, much as one would expect from a dynamic attractor (Granic & Dishion, 2002). It is presumed that antisocial dyads provide high relative rates of reinforcement for deviant talk, compared to normative talk, in an effort to merge psychologically in the context of friendship. We have referred to this as the *confluence model* (Dishion, Patterson, & Griesler, 1994), but the formal testing of this process is yet to be conducted.

The identification of deviancy training within the natural environment has also been studied relative to iatrogenic effects associated with randomized peer intervention groups. In an analysis of the dynamics that were associated with negative effects for tobacco use and delinquency at school, peer intervention groups were videotaped and coded. Before the group began, during the breaks, and at the end of the group the incidental interactions among the youth in the intervention groups were coded across 12 2-hour weekly sessions. Several indices were derived from these codings, including deviancy training (i.e., the tendency to join with other group members around deviance), connection to older normative peer counselors, peer rejection, and other behaviors.

To examine the contribution of group dynamics to iatrogenic growth, a latent growth modeling procedure was used (Muthén & Curran, 1997). In the analysis of iatrogenic growth in tobacco use, there was a marginally reliable effect for deviancy training in the group. Individuals who engaged in deviancy training in the group were more likely to use tobacco during the 3 years following the intervention. Unexpectedly, a positive relationship with the older peer counselors was found to be correlated with reduced likelihood of tobacco use during the ensuing 3 years (Dishion, Poulin, & Burraston, 2001). Peer counselors were used in the delivery of the cognitive-behavioral groups to facilitate the youths' acceptance of the curricula, to model appropriate behavior in groups, and to facilitate role plays of prosocial skills. The peer counselors were typically high school students with a history of problem behavior who had turned their behavior around with respect to becoming abstinent, achieving satisfactory grades (above a C), and participating in prosocial activities such as sports.

In the analysis of growth in delinquent behavior in the 3 years following the intervention, again deviancy training significantly predicted growth in problem behavior. However, it was also noted that positive relationships with peer counselors seemed to reduce growth in problem behavior at school. Together, these findings suggest that group dynamics were indeed relevant to the positive and negative effects of the intervention aside from the stated curriculum. It is worth noting that the tendency to respond to the groups by increased tobacco use and delinquent behavior at school was not a group phenomenon. Individuals across groups seemed to be more or less at risk for iatrogenic reactions.

Poulin, Dishion, and Burraston (2001) found that the youths' initial level of deviance was predictive of iatrogenic growth in the groups. On the basis of our two sets of analyses and our perusal of the videotapes, we speculate that higher risk youth who enter into groups command attention from the group members and the group leader. Group attention, an explicit support for deviance among group members, reinforces delinquent lifestyle behaviors. In this respect, rule-governed behavior is an important principle. Borrowing from construct theory, we propose that what is rewarded is not the behavior per se but the overall set of values and attitudes that accompany a delinquent lifestyle. From group interactions youth derive support for a trajectory they have already established in their natural environment. Thus the effects are individual, and low-risk youth are apparently unaffected. The general conclusion can be made that some youth may be more susceptible to deviancy training than other youth. It seems that moderately deviant youth are most susceptible.

Modeling and Imitation

It is difficult to explain, however, from a reinforcement perspective, the strong moderating effects of relationships with the older peer counselors on iatrogenic growth. Bandura (1969) proposed that observations of reinforced models would elicit the same behavior patterns among observers. This effect is referred to as *modeling*. It is conceivable that for some youth, the older peer counselors served a function in that they modeled nondeviance and prosocial behavior. Therefore, youth in the group who established positive relationships with the older peer counselors were less likely to engage in problem behavior following participation in the groups. Alternatively, it may well be that individual youth who were unlikely to engage in deviant behavior following involvement with the group were those most likely to connect with the older peer counselors.

This issue demonstrates the methodological weakness of post hoc analyses of group dynamics associated with negative effects. Although these analyses are useful at a preliminary stage of research, it is difficult to disentangle individual characteristics from causal group dynamics. Both the deviancy training findings and the older peer counselor findings could be attributable to premorbid characteristics of the youth (Dishion et al., 2001; Poulin et al., 2001).

Adult Behavior Management

It is clear that interventions that mobilize adults, whether they be group leaders or parents, to supervise youth closely, to manage peer group dynamics, and to structure contact and interactions with peers are effective in reducing problem behavior. In classic intervention research with very high-risk adolescents, treatment foster care has been shown to be effective in reducing court-documented delinquent activity (Chamberlain & Reid, 1998). Importantly, the intervention effects on delinquent behavior were found to be mediated by reductions in deviant peer involvement (Eddy & Chamberlain, 2000).

In general, interventions that mobilize parents and support behavior management practices result in reduced problem behavior in children and adolescents (e.g., Dishion & Stormshak, in press; Henggeler, Mihalic, Rone, Thomas, & Timmons-Mitchel, 1998). However, research is rare that shows specific effects of these interventions on the nature and extent of deviant peer clustering. In a school-based intervention, Dishion, Kavanagh, Schneiger, Nelson, and Kaufman (2002) found that random assignment to a family-centered intervention in a school context resulted in reductions in deviant peer involvement. These effects were presumed to have been achieved through improvements in parental monitoring and behavior management practices.

In the Fast Track prevention program for high-risk elementary school students, Lavallee, Bierman, Nix, and the Conduct Problems Prevention Research Group (2005) studied the potential for deviancy training among first- and second-grade students. Although deviancy training in the intervention groups was rare, it did contribute to growth in problem behavior when it occurred. Likewise, Boxer, Guerra, Huesmann, and Morales (2005) found that in their intervention groups, initially moderately aggressive youth became more aggressive as a function of the presence of more highly aggressive youth.

In research attempting to replicate the Reconnecting Youth Program, Cho, Hallfors, and Sanchez (2005) found unintended negative effects as the result of aggregating high school students in special classrooms for "disaffected" youth. A post hoc disaggregation of the effects by school revealed significant site effects, whereas some schools did not show negative effects and others did. All used the same curriculum and participated in the same training. One might hypothesize that school staff behavior management skills were associated with the differences in negative effects observed for this intervention. Several studies that document negative effects from peer aggregation report that these effects vary by individual group or classroom, suggesting that adults' ability to manage and structure peer interactions may be a critical factor in deviant peer contagion. However, it is likely that certain peer contexts (e.g., a dense population of deviant peers) overwhelm even the most talented and skilled adults in their attempts to reduce or eliminate deviant peer contagion. In general, these findings suggest that carefully managed and supervised groups can avoid iatrogenic effects (Dishion & Dodge, 2005).

Increased Exposure and Opportunity

Yet another possible mechanism for iatrogenic effects in deviant peer groups is the increased exposure to opportunities for deviance that these peers offer. Some of these opportunities may occur directly within the peer group—for example, if deviant peers provoke fights among group members. Other opportunities occur through peers' behavior outside the group. For example, deviant peers might offer a youth an opportunity to purchase or sell illicit drugs. Beyond imitation of this behavior, the youth might adopt it merely because it is available (Thornberry, Krohn, Lizotte, Smith, & Tobin, 2003). Deviant peers might bring a youth to new neighborhoods and expose him or her to new stimuli for acting deviantly. These peers might provoke reactions from authorities that lead to deviant behavior by the youth merely because the youth was nearby at the time. These effects are more readily explained by an "opportunity" hypothesis than by learning, reinforcement, or imitation.

Summary

Given the relatively recent focus on understanding negative effects associated with interventions that aggregate deviant youth, the reinforcement perspective seems to have the most empirical support. Recent research reported by Lavallee and colleagues (2005) suggests that within elementary school social skills training groups with very high-risk youth, a process of deviancy training may account for individual differences in the growth of aggressive behavior, despite the intervention's overall positive effect. Note, however, that the studies to date primarily use global ratings and do not systematically disentangle individual effects from group dynamics. Therefore, the hypothesis proposed by McCord (1997) and the reinforcement perspective are difficult to differentiate empirically. It seems plausible that observation, modeling, and reinforcement collectively contribute to changes in behavior and social-cognitive motivations to commit problem behavior.

ECOLOGICAL AND SYSTEMIC DYNAMICS

An ecological-level analysis considers the broad context of the intervention, and a system-level analysis combines the perspective of the individual, his or her interactions with group members, and the ecological context of the intervention. An advantage of the ecological framework is the organization of levels of analysis to facilitate multilevel interactions to consider systemic effects. Systemic effects can involve a significant main effect for a contextual term such as *neighborhood effects* or an interaction term that combines neighborhood with individual effects, such as high-risk youth in a high-crime neighborhood. Three empirically supported systemic mechanisms may account for negative effects associated with aggregating peers into interventions.

Contagion Process

Phenomena such as crowd contagion, fads in deviance, and school-wide problem behavior such as weapon violence would be seen as potential contagion effects at the system level (Cook & Ludwig, Chapter 4, this volume). A contagion process implies a nonlinear increase in a "disease" or "problem behavior" that occurs among individuals defined by a geographic or media boundary. For example, an immediate increase in suicide as a function of a highly publicized suicide is a contagion process at the systems level.

   The mechanism explaining group-level contagion is decidedly cognitive, and most consistent with a control theory of crime and delinquency. Observing deviant behavior can have the effect of attenuating the inhibiting factors for one's own deviance. Novel, interesting, reinforcing behaviors and attention-getting behaviors (e.g., drug use, drinking, sexual behavior, vandalism) that are inhibited through voluntary control are most likely to be affected by this contagion process. It appears that the more individuals endorse a behavior, the less inhibition there is regarding that behavior. This effect can undermine preventive interventions for young people. For example, Moberg and Piper (1998) found that prevention programs aimed at reducing high-risk sexual behaviors linked to HIV infection actually increased these behaviors. It appears that providing a public context for discussing sexual behavior among adolescents weakens the cognitive factors inhibiting sexual experimentation among participating middle school students. Of interest is whether or not the microsocial interactions among participating students changed as a function of preventive intervention. That is, after the intervention, it is plausible that young adolescent friends spend more time talking about sex favorably.

Contagion effects, although nonlinear, would constitute a main effect for context in the equation presented in Figure 2.2. Contagion effects do not *require* direct interactions among the participants, other than knowing the behavior of another. Cook and Goss (1996) define many examples of contagion phenomena. The most compelling evidence for contagion processes at the system level are those that involve attenuated inhibitions. Examples include the clustering of bulimic behavior in sororities (Crandall, 1988), male delinquency and dropout in impoverished neighborhoods (Crane, 1989), and the clustering of suicide and hysteria (see Cook & Goss, 1996). The contagion metaphor is derived from considering the spread of infectious diseases. For example, nonlinear infectious rates can be predicted when there is extensive contact with infected agents. The communicability of the disease (e.g., airborne vs. fluid exchange) and the density of the contacts would give rise to nonlinear increases in the disease. If one conceptualizes deviance as a disease, then contact with deviant individuals would be seen as disinhibiting similar behavior among the members. Again, contextual conditions can moderate the spread of deviance within a group. For example, groups that provided reinforcement for deviance would be those that resulted in a high rate of change. This effect would be most pronounced in groups where there is a higher density of deviant individuals.

Empirically, the contagion model would predict that group-level effects would predominate. When examining outcomes of group interventions, some groups would be singled out as resulting in high levels of iatrogenic effects. This has indeed been found in the area of eating disorders. Post hoc examination of purging and binge eating in sororities revealed that such behavior is clustered by sorority house (Crandall, 1988). An interesting feature of the Crandall study (1988) is that sororities are not designed to address eating disorders in girls. However, there has been a recent surge in such problems. The contagion model may fit very well such behaviors in sororities because these behaviors are by nature subterranean and not monitored by supervising adults. In contrast, behaviors in intervention groups are monitored by adults, and an active effort to intervene in problem behaviors is clearly present. Therefore, a contagion model may fit the spread of some deviant behaviors more than others. This is very consistent with a systemic view of deviant peer contagion in that the context of the aggregation, the dynamics of the behavior, and the overall cultural characteristics combine to account for the rapid spread of unhealthy behavior.

Lost Exposure to Some Contexts

Peer Contexts

When interventions and programs are delivered in groups, we often focus on the microsocial interactions of youth with others in the same intervention. However, an alternative consideration is that high-risk youth are removed from normative contexts that reinforce the inhibition of deviance. Removing a youth from a public school environment to an alternative school serves several functions. First, it presumably improves the learning environment of the nondeviant youth left behind in the public school (Cook & Ludwig, Chapter 4, this volume), but it also changes the interactive world of the deviant student. The focus of this chapter has been on the increased contact with others that may reinforce antisocial attitudes and norms. However, iatrogenic effects may also result from reduced exposure to the positive socializing influences of nondeviant peers and other supervising adults. From the matching law framework for understanding the effects of reinforcement of individual differences in problem behavior, it follows that increases in problem behavior would result from the joint increase in reinforcement of deviance and decreased reinforcement of nondeviance (Dishion, Spracklen, & Patterson, 1996; McDowell, 1988). Thus, from a systemic view, it is important to consider the effects of an intervention on the youth's overall sampling of the social ecology. Strategies such as those reported by Osgood, Wilson, O'Malley, Bachman, and Johnston (1996) of sampling the ecology of high-risk youth may be necessary to understand the impact of interventions on changes in behavior.

Adult Contexts

Adults' monitoring and supervision of adolescents are absolutely essential protective factors for high-risk adolescents, both in reducing access to deviant peers and in minimizing their influence after exposure. Interventions that aggregate deviant peers may inadvertently attenuate natural, adult-led controls for deviant behaviors. Systemic family therapists (Minuchin & Fishman, 1981; Szapoznik & Kurtines, 1989) emphasize the importance of an executive system for behavioral control. By extension, it is plausible to suppose that some interventions reduce or attenuate the executive control of parents and other supervising adults. For example, high-risk youth who enter a treatment program may find themselves with more unsupervised opportunities to engage in deviance. The mechanism is that the supervising adults assume that the problem behavior was being addressed during the treatment and relinquished control over and monitoring of the adolescent's behavior. If this were true, then observations of parenting practices would reveal reductions in monitoring and other parental management practices as a function of peer aggregation.

In the analysis of iatrogenic effects in the Adolescence Transitions Program, this conclusion was not found to be true. There were no negative changes in parenting practices as a function of youth being randomly assigned to the peer interventions. However, the parent-only intervention resulted in the best outcomes with respect to reduced substance use, antisocial behavior, and delinquent behavior (Dishion et al., 1996). In addition, examination of youth in the natural environment reveals that association with deviant peers predicts decreases in parental monitoring over time (Dishion, Nelson, & Bullock, 2004). Bronfrenbrenner (1989) referred to the joint consideration of mutual changes in the peer and family settings as a *mesosystem model*. Indeed, high-risk youth have been found to increase their engagement in deviant peer group activity at the same time they were actively undermining and disengaging from adult control mechanisms such as parental monitoring (Dishion et al., 2004; Stoolmiller, 1992). This joint process of movement into the peer group while attenuating adult socialization influences is referred to as *premature autonomy*, and is highly related to the emergence of new forms of deviance from middle adolescence to early adulthood (Dishion et al., 2004). The extent to which some interventions exacerbate a youth's premature autonomy is worthy of further study.

New Opportunities

Exposure to situations, events, and behaviors that suggests deviance is reinforcing, valuable, and attractive may increase these behaviors among vulnerable youth. This perspective builds on a cognitive model for understanding iatrogenic effects (McCord, 1997). In general, the actor reads the situation in light of the cultural context, the intervention setting, and the interpersonal dynamics in deciding on future courses of action. For example, a high-risk youth who is sent to a summer camp on repeated occasions and who learns that his delinquent lifestyle has a certain attraction for organizing his social world may indeed adopt that lifestyle well into the future. Moreover, a marginally deviant youth who is impressed by such behavior in the summer camp context may decide to adopt a similar lifestyle and engage in deviant behaviors well into the future. The key operating variable in this circumstance is individual interpretations, not direct reinforcement. These idiosyncratic perspectives are potentiated by the systemic characteristics of the environment. For example, media depictions of gang violence can provide a glorified perspective on gang membership, dress, and correlated behavior. Thus, given exposure, those behaviors can "spread" rapidly as a collective function of the dynamics of the intervention program, school setting, and the community at large. Klein (Chapter 13, this volume) discusses the complexity of interventions designed to reduce gangs in Los Angeles and the systemic influences on gang proclivities and activities. Public school environments, for example, can create a readiness for gang activity by virtue of the systemic dynamics among youth of diverse socioeconomic backgrounds, peer relations, and relations among ethnic groups. Coupled with media portrayals of gangs, interventions designed to prevent gang involvement in some settings could have the disturbing effect of actually increasing and solidifying such behavior (Klein, Chapter 13, this volume).

Similarly, juvenile correction facilities may or may not provide contextual cues that are supportive of delinquent lifestyles. Moreover, juvenile correction facilities may consist of reactions to deviance that are punishing and/or punitive. In this sense, McCord's (1999) construct theory proposes that motivation to engage in deviance is a complex interaction between the individual's social and emotional history and the potentiating effects of the program and the context of the program.

Again, it is unclear to what extent this is a competing model from the reinforcement perspective as presented by Hayes (1989). That is, rules of behavior are derived from reinforcing circumstances that are complex and linguistically embedded. Rule-governed behavior, for example, has been used to explain rather complex problems such as suicide in which ostensible reinforcement is absent. However, the course of action leading to suicide can be derived from behavioral events that are linguistically linked. To date, the construct approach to understanding motivation to deviance has yet to be systematically tested. Below, suggestions regarding conceptualization and measurement are provided to encourage future research on the social-cognitive and motivational changes that can occur from potentiating effects that result from interventions that aggregate.

Summary

The ecological systemic dynamics that facilitate negative effects associated with peer aggregation suggest interactions in the equation summarized in Figure 2.2. It is proposed that, in essence, individual effects interact with program characteristics and the context of the intervention service to potentiate negative effects of intervention. These three-way interactions are testable in theory. Realistically, the vast majority of randomized intervention trials do not directly measure these multiple levels. However, it is possible that meta-analyses of intervention effects can estimate the characteristics of multiple levels and test systemic hypotheses accordingly.

CONCEPTUAL AND METHODOLOGICAL ISSUES AND CONCLUSIONS

It is clear from the findings presented in this volume that peer aggregation can potentially undermine the benefits of educational and intervention programs to youth in adolescence. The science of interventions, however, lags in identifying the critical mechanisms and conditions underlying iatrogenic effects. It is critical, at this juncture, that we specify and facilitate the advancement of the behavioral sciences with respect to providing the scientific basis for understanding the full range of outcomes associated with efforts to intervene with and benefit youth and adolescents. With this in mind, the following conceptual and methodological suggestions are made (also summarized in Table 2.1).

Conceptual Issues

The vast majority of the science on program effectiveness, evaluations, treatments, and prevention focuses exclusively on benefits. To date, the current standard is a randomized trial with pre–post assessments with data-analytic efforts comparing the control with the intervention condition with respect to a preestablished set of dependent variables that are presumed to be the outcomes of interest. This valuable methodological approach is but one strategy that is relevant to understanding the process and dynamics of behavior change as a function of a contrived inter-

TABLE 2.1. Summary of Methodological and Conceptual Issues in the Identification of Iatrogenic Mechanisms

Conceptual issues

- Study interventions and programs from a cost–benefits perspective, demarcating positive effects along with iatrogenic effects.
- Increase funding and support for identifying conditions under which regular effects are likely to increase.

Measurement issues

- Assess side effects, in addition to variables (Kelly, 1988).
- Observe attributes and interactions of an intervention.
- Identify nomological network of constructs that can be assessed in all interaction studies.

Design issues

- Analyze existing programs for iatrogenic effects (nonrandomized).
- Conduct longitudinal follow-up with repeated assessments.
- Conduct experimental studies to test hypothesis regarding mechanisms.
- Test single intervention strategies before combining.

vention. In general, it is suggested that the field should approach intervention research much like pharmacological research, in that an effort must be made to document more carefully the range of effects, both positive and negative, that can be expected or that are relevant to an intervention at any given developmental stage.

In this vein, it is clear that one response to the possibility of a negative effect from an intervention condition is to cease and desist funding. Unfortunately, this strategy may undermine our collective ability to develop a general framework for understanding the range of intervention effects that can be expected under various conditions. In this respect, it seems important that investigators be encouraged to report the full range of effects associated with any intervention trial. However, to progress in this area, we need to expand our measurement-and-design repertoire to enable progress with such research.

Measurement Issues

In applying the ecological framework to understanding deviant peer contagion underlying iatrogenic effects, a nexus is defined between community and conventional treatment research. Early pioneers of community psychology have often been sensitive to potential systemic effects of interventions that may be unanticipated. Kelly (1988) summarized an ecological approach to community intervention. This approach included a call for studying and assessing side effects to intervention conditions. Clearly, the work on iatrogenic effects associated with peer aggregation underscores this important point. Intervention research, in general, should incorporate a strategy for assessing potential side effects that may be both positive and negative in addition to main effects.

An advantage of the ecological perspective on development and intervention science is that it provides a framework for preestablishing a *nomological* network of constructs that are likely to be relevant at any stage of development. It would be helpful if intervention studies were guided by an ecological perspective and routinely assessed a range of constructs from the individual child to the context of the intervention to understand a range of effects. For example, intervention studies that focus on a cognitive-behavioral intervention for aggressive behavior should also assess delinquent behaviors such as smoking and/or covert antisocial behaviors. The developmental literature is clear, for example, that acts of proactive and reactive aggression are highly correlated but distinguishable behaviors. Proactive aggression includes delinquency, coercion, and bullying, whereas reactive aggression includes anger and passionate retaliation. Research by Poulin and Boivin (2000) reveals that the conditions of proactive aggression are different from the conditions of reactive aggression despite their high intercorrelation. Indeed, proactive aggression seems to be facilitated by peer coalitions, whereas reactive aggression seems to be facilitated by individual characteristics of the child or the stimulus. In this vein, proactive and reactive aggression, though highly correlated, may respond differently to the same intervention. Without measurement of the full range of the relevant constructs, it is impossible to detect negative effects on attributes or behavior. A critical point in measurement is the use of focused observational measures to capture intervention dynamics associated with positive and negative effects. The use of videotape and other methodologies facilitates the ability to analyze post hoc characteristics of interventions that benefited or harmed participants. Progress in understanding intervention effects is likely to come from the careful formulation of constructs that translate well into real-world behavior and subjective experiences of participants (Fiske, 1986, 1987).

Design Issues

There are considerable advantages to randomized studies with pre–post assessments. However, it is clear that repeated measurements over the course of time are critical for disentangling the dynamics of change. Thus the analysis of mediation requires more sophisticated measurement-

and-design strategies to assess the process of change within a program or intervention service.

It is proposed that examining existing programs, intervention services, and/or institutional rehabilitative efforts outside the context of a randomized trial can lead to considerable progress. Thus, the work by Bayer, Pintoff, and Pozen (2003) is exemplary. Studying youth who are being processed through the juvenile justice system and considering the characteristics of their dispositions (e.g., group treatment, group homes, and institutional placement) provides a basis for modeling program characteristics associated with growth or reductions in problem behavior. Similarly, Andrews (1980) also examined characteristics of juvenile justice programs with respect to negative effects on criminal offending. The focus on pre–post outcomes and anticipated benefits is complementary to the analysis of existing programs with respect to positive and negative effects. Even generally effective programs might have negative effects for some individuals. The dynamics of these negative effects, if understood, could inform the design of even more effective intervention strategies and/or the training of more effective interventionists.

Finally, the mechanisms that account for iatrogenic effects can be studied using a variety of social-psychological strategies under experimental conditions. Collaborations with basic scientists, especially those in the field of social psychology, will benefit from our collective understanding of how individuals (youth or adults) are likely to respond to social programs and interventions.

Analytic Issues

Intervention science has progressed to consider mediation as a centerpiece to progress in intervention research (Kazdin & Weisz, 2003). The real issue considered in this volume is the influence that deviant peers exert over a youth, but rarely, if ever, does an intervention isolate this single factor in a child's development. Instead, interventions simultaneously manipulate multiple aspects of a child's life. Also, single interventions indirectly affect a distal outcome by exerting multiple proximal effects. Testing of mediation thus becomes a crucial aspect of data analysis to understand how an intervention operates.

Progress in mediation analysis has enhanced the field tremendously. Several outcome studies have not only documented significant intervention effects, but also the processes that accounted for those effects (e.g., Martinez & Forgatch, 2002). Nonetheless, mediation analysis in the context of a randomized trial should never be considered to have the methodological rigor of an experiment. By their nature, mediation analyses test relations among correlated variables, without the benefit of randomized assignment.

Conclusion

The evidence specifying the mechanisms that are associated with adverse effects of peer aggregation is somewhat limited as of this writing. It is clear that the majority of the negative effects are an interaction between the premorbid characteristics of the individual and the dynamics of the group. However, it is also apparent that the developmental status of the individual is relevant. For example, research by Kellam, Ling, Merisca, Brown, and Ialongo (1998) reveals that highly aggressive children placed in highly aggressive classrooms tended to increase their aggressive behavior and were at heightened risk for long-term adjustment problems. In our work with young adolescents, overt aggressive behaviors were not affected by aggregation, but covert delinquent behaviors were affected. Recent research by Duncan and colleagues (2005) indicates that random assignment of male drinkers to the same dormitory room resulted in nonlinear increases in drinking for both participants. Other salient problem behaviors were unaffected by random assignment. Future research may reveal that specific behaviors may be critical for defining adaptation during developmental transitions. Such behaviors may be novel, socially salient, and sensitive to peer aggregation. This evidence suggests that a transactional perspective (Sameroff, 1981) is needed to fully understand the mechanisms of deviant peer contagion. It is likely that such research efforts will feed back to form basic theories of development and behavior change. To quote an overused adage, "If you wish to understand behavior, try to change it" (Lewin, 1936).

CHAPTER 3

Deviant Peer Effects

Perspectives of an Epidemiologist

James C. Anthony

For the purposes of this chapter, "contagion" is conceptualized as a process during which an aftereffect on one or more individuals is caused by a prior effect on some other individual, where both the aftereffect and the prior effect are members of the same general set or domain of life experience. To be clear about set membership, consider that most epidemiological studies of chicken pox contagion would seek focus on both clinically apparent cases of chicken pox and clinically inapparent infections with the varicella zoster virus (VZV), without which chicken pox cases won't be seen. Here, the general set or domain of life experience would encompass both clinical chicken pox and antibody response to VZV, if not recovery of active VZV. Alternately, consider an epidemiological study of the potentially contagious spread of vandalism in the form of intentional fire setting. The idea would be that the intentional fire setting by one individual has been causally determined, at least in part, by the prior intentional fire setting of some other individual. Of course, intentional fire setting by one individual might exert a causal influence on later substantially different fire behaviors of others (e.g., the firefighters who put out the fire), but, in general, fire-extinguishing behavior would not be considered as a member of the same general set or domain of life experience that encompasses intentional fire setting if the goal is to study the potential contagious spread of intentional fire setting.

For reasons that will become more clear in this chapter, it is my judgment that studies of peer contagion processes can shed more light on

44

these processes when they focus on quite fine-grained, distinctive, and specific facets of youthful misbehavior, conduct problems, or violations of norms that tend to be valued by society at large ("antisocial behavior"). A fine-grained example would be intentional fire setting, or even a more specific form of intentional fire setting (e.g., by using a magnifying glass and sunlight). Of course, the individual distinctive and specific elements are members of a more general set of "problem behaviors." The study of the individual distinctive and specific elements might be conducted in complement with research on more diffuse and generic ideas such as "levels of antisocial behavior" or a "problem behavior syndrome." However, in this context, the evidence of a contagious process will tend to be more definitive to the degree that the responses of interest are fine-grained, distinctive, and specific elements of behavior.

In epidemiology, when the aftereffect and the prior effect are both infections or diseases, we try to trace the contagion within a predefined group back to a specific time point or interval of life of the first affected individual within that group (our so-called index case) and forward to aftereffects in the lives of the later affected individuals in the group (our so-called secondary cases). To the extent that the infection (or disease) is spread by a contagious process with multiple waves, we have tertiary cases, quaternary cases, and so on.

There are some clear advantages to this formulation of contagion in terms of transitions from one state to another (e.g., not infected to infected, not diseased to diseased). Because each individual starts out without the characteristic (e.g., not diseased) and shifts to having the characteristic (e.g., becoming diseased), the characteristic can be represented as a time-varying binary value, and while this value for an individual is constantly zero, it can have no direct influence (e.g., no influence on other individuals).

In many instances, the evidence of a contagious process seems obvious, but is it really? Suppose two individuals are standing together in a line on the sidewalk outside the theater, waiting to buy a ticket to a show. It's been a long day and a long wait. One person yawns; a microsecond later, the other person yawns, and then complains, "You made me yawn!" The first person who yawned is the index case; the second person who yawned is the secondary case. Yawning by the index case causes the aftereffect of yawning by the secondary case (Platek, Mohamed, & Gallup, 2005; Schurmann et al., 2005). Really and truly? A sharp observer standing off to the side might have been able to see a process not apprehended by the two individuals in question. Namely, a stranger to the front of both of them in the line yawned just before they yawned, and though they didn't "see" this yawn, the stranger actually was the index case in the "group," and they were secondary cases, as essentially simultaneous aftereffects of the index case-stranger's yawn. Plus, as the sharp observer later reveals, in the seconds before the index case's yawn, he observed a large smoke-spewing truck drive past, blasting everyone with exhaust fumes, including carbon dioxide. Busy as they are within the microexchange of communication about the first individual causing the second individual to yawn, the two of them just hadn't paid much attention to the truck. Of course, unbeknownst to the observer, it seems likely that CO_2 concentration does not precipitate yawning, as discussed by Provine, Tate, and Geldmacher (1987). Because the sharp observer didn't know this, the attribution to an exogenous cause is made (i.e., via an appeal to a causal influence other than the aftereffects of a contagion process).

In recent years, epidemiologists have added the theories and tools of molecular biology and phylogenetics to enrich their data and to help strengthen causal inference about aftereffects, secondary cases, and index cases in relation to the contagious spread of some infectious diseases. Advances in theory and methods have produced an increased specificity in relation to the identity of what is being spread by a contagious process from individual to individual. In some instances the spread of a specific virus strain from index case to secondary cases can be documented with fine-grained detail—no longer solely via antibody response to the virus as virus, but also via analysis of what amounts to a crude genetic "fingerprint" of a specific virus strain. A newsworthy instance in the early 1990s involved an HIV-infected dentist whose alleged suboptimal infection control practices had aftereffects in the form of subsequent HIV infections among his patients. A series of increasingly refined phylogenetic analyses produced evidence in favor of the hypothesized contagion, with the dentist as an index case for at least some of the secondary cases among his patients, based upon nucleotide sequences of virus sampled from the patients being compared to nucleotide sequences of virus sampled from the dentist, and where few of the patients had other known or documentable exposures that might have accounted for their infections (e.g., history of prior unprotected sexual contact between dentist and patient either directly or indirectly via sexual partners shared in common). In this instance, the specificity of the virus strain with respect to quite rare nucleotide sequences was an aid in the epidemiological analysis of HIV's spread through that group. Even so, there were arguments that the patients might have acquired the virus by some means other than a contagious process involving the dentist (Ciesielski et al., 1992; Crandall, 1995).

Whether the argument of alternative causes seems compelling or not, consider the loss of strength of evidence if there had been no genetic fingerprint for the rare specific virus strain infecting the dentist. In this circumstance, there would be nothing more than evidence that both the dentist and the patients were generically HIV-infected without reference to strain. It is in this sense that the evidence of a contagious process becomes stronger when we can state, with a high degree of certainty, what it was that was spread from the index case to secondary cases. The strength of evidence is increased not only by the existence of genetic material that can be used to distinguish *this* HIV strain from *that* HIV strain, but also by two implications of the evidence. First, there is the issue of chance co-occurrences. Second, there is the issue of ruling out alternative causes.

With respect to chance co-occurrence as an explanation for an apparent contagious process, consider that a cluster of HIV-infected cases within a dental practice might arise by chance alone, but the chance of seeing a cluster of a rare specific HIV strain within a dental practice is smaller. (Think of drawing a card at random from a standard deck of playing cards, 52 to a deck, four suits of 13 cards each, two red suits and two black suits. With one random draw, the chance of drawing a black suit card is $\frac{1}{2}$, while the chance of drawing a black ace is $\frac{2}{52} = \frac{1}{26}$. Once the first drawn card is replaced in the deck, the chance of drawing a black suit card again is $\frac{1}{2}$ and, again, after replacement of that first card, the chance of drawing a black ace is $\frac{1}{26}$. So, under these conditions of drawing first one card, replacing it in the deck, and then drawing another card, the chance of drawing a pair of black suit cards in succession is $\frac{1}{4}$ [$= \frac{1}{2} * \frac{1}{2}$] while the chance of drawing a pair of black aces in succession is $\frac{1}{676}$ [$= \frac{1}{26} * \frac{1}{26}$].) Within a group of individuals, a cluster of conditions arises by chance co-occurrence more often when the condition is common and generic, less often when the condition has specificity and is rare.

With respect to ruling out alternative causes of an apparent contagious process within a group, the specificity (and rare occurrence) of a condition also can be valuable. Consider two groups of 15 preadolescent boys. In one group, 100% of the boys are wearing baseball caps, with the front of each cap depicting a commercially embroidered logo of a different Major League Baseball team (i.e., a different team for each boy). In addition, within this group, all boys are wearing the cap with the cap's bill facing forward. In the other group, five of the boys are hatless, but the other 10 are wearing baseball caps with the hand-embroidered logo "FCUK" on the back of the cap, and all 10 of these boys are wearing the cap with the bill facing backward. Given these observations about the two groups, and with all else being equal, which peer group is more likely to have experienced a process of contagion that involves an index case and secondary spread to other individuals? To date, most observers have nominated the second

(FCUK) group as more likely to have experienced a contagion process; the explanation given for this choice is the specificity of the FCUK cap worn backward relative to the more generic nature of the commercial Major League Baseball caps. Of course, it is possible that, unbeknownst to us, a sales representative of FCUK Inc. handed out those caps to the 10 boys all at one time and gave them a dollar if they promised to wear the caps backward so that people would see the advertisement better. As in the HIV example, neither the specificity of the condition nor the final-state frequency distribution permits a firm inference that a contagion process is at play.

PRIMARY AND SECONDARY ATTACK RATES

When the event or condition under scrutiny for contagion is discrete and binary in character, it can be studied in a quantitative comparison of primary attack rates and secondary attack rates. A few technical details about primary attack rate analysis and some elementary examples may help to motivate secondary attack rate analysis (and multivariate attack rate analysis), as well as the other developments to be mentioned in cursory detail within this chapter. One elementary example is represented in Figure 3.1. This figure depicts three nested structures, which may be regarded as households, classrooms, or predefined peer groups (A, B, C), as observed during four successive time intervals of equal length ($t = 1$, 2, 3, 4). To reduce complexity, this is a closed population (no in-migration, no out-migration), and each nest (A, B, C) contains eight individuals, with capital M and F denoting adults, male and female, and lowercase m and f denoting minors within each nested structure. Furthermore, within each nest, the position of each individual within the nest remains the same. That is, within each nest, if we let X_{hijty} denote nest h, row i, column j, time t, and a response variable named y, which is a binary case status indicator ($y = 0$ for at-risk noncase, $y = 1$ for case), then the MA1110 adult male in row 1, column 1 of nest A at $t = 1$ is the same person as the MA1120 adult male in row 1, column 1 of nest A at $t = 2$. Similarly, mB3110 is a male minor (child) noncase in nest B at time $t = 1$ who becomes a case as mB3121 in nest B at time $t = 2$, whereas mC4110 is a male minor noncase in nest B at time $t = 1$ who remains a noncase in nest C from time $t = 1$ through $t = 4$.

In primary attack rate analysis, we are not attempting to scrutinize for a contagion process and we can disregard the sequencing of affected cases. The attack rate for a group is estimated at a specific time point (e.g., the end of a time interval). For example, by the end of $t = 1$, summarizing the experience across all nests, we observe that two individuals

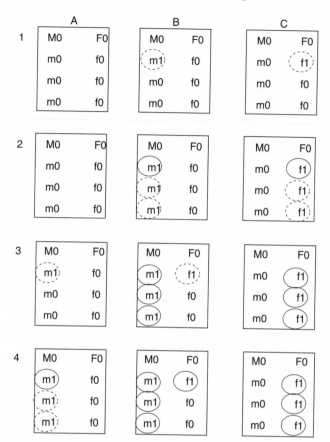

FIGURE 3.1. This figure is intended to help convey concepts of "primary attack rate" and "secondary attack rate," as explained in the text. Uncircled individuals within each nest (A, B, C) are unaffected "at-risk" members of the nest. When encircled with a dashed line, the individual has just become a case in the time interval under observation. When encircled with a solid line, the individual is a past case, but is not a newly incident case.

have just become cases, out of the total of 24 individuals who were at risk for becoming a case at the start of the interval. Hence, the attack rate is $\frac{2}{24}$, or roughly 8%. Between the end of $t = 1$ and the end of $t = 2$, four newly incident cases are observed, out of a total of 22 at-risk individuals (24 minus the two prior cases observed at $t = 1$), for an attack rate of $\frac{4}{22}$, or roughly 18%. By the end of $t = 3$, two newly incident cases are observed, out of a total of 18 at-risk individuals, for an attack rate of $\frac{2}{18}$, or roughly 11%. Finally, by the end of $t = 4$, two more newly incident cases are observed, out of a total of 16 at-risk individuals, for an attack rate of $\frac{2}{16}$, or 12.5%.

Figure 3.2a plots the number of cases across the time intervals without respect to the underlying size of the at-risk population, showing two newly incident cases in the first interval, four new cases in the second interval, two new cases in the third interval, and two new cases in the fourth interval. This plot, by itself, is not terribly informative about any underlying process of contagion. This observed count of cases across time might be consistent with a single point source exposure to an infective agent or a toxin, with a peak and a median incubation (or induction) period some two units of time after exposure, and with variance of the incubation/induction period allowing for some rapid-onset cases as well as some late-onset cases. In general, a single point source epidemic gives rise to a sharply leptokurtic (or sometimes normal or truncated normal) distribution of cases plotted across units of time, particularly when the point source can be identified and removed promptly. When there is a single point source followed by contagious spread, the right-hand side of the curve has what epidemiologists call a "prosodemic" elaboration. For example, consider the labor force within a factory where there is a change in a manufacturing material from one nontoxic ingredient to a new ingredient that tends to produce a contact dermatitis within a median of 8 hours of epidermal contact (i.e., one work shift), and suppose that in the context of a gender-role-stratified society the factory workers all are male while the homemakers and laundresses all are female. The factory work is arduous and dusty, such that workers are required to wear a newly laundered uniform every day. Once the new ingredient is used, the male workers experience the contact dermatitis within the 8-hour induction interval (plus or minus some function of its variance), but there continue to be new cases of contact dermatitis beyond that induction period when the homemakers and laundresses come into contact with the ingredient as they launder the prior day's uniforms. This type of process, originating in a point source, can yield an originally leptokurtic distribution of onsets, followed by a prosodemic elaboration as secondary cases come into contact with the intermediaries of the process (i.e., contaminated uniforms).

Based upon data shown in Figure 3.1, Figure 3.2b shows the primary attack rates plotted across the time intervals, showing attack rates of 8% for the first interval, 18% for the second interval, 11% for the third interval, and 12.5% by the end of the fourth interval. This plot represents a minor challenge to the idea that the outbreak is due entirely to a single point source exposure, in that the risk of becoming a newly incident case among at-risk individuals has not declined much across the span from the second to the third time intervals to the fourth time interval.

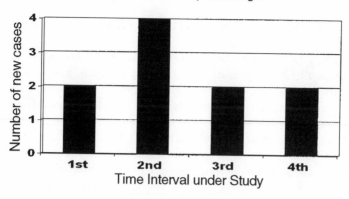

FIGURE 3.2a. The number of new cases observed in each time interval under study.

In the factory example, an occupational epidemiologist faced with a mounting number of workers coming to the factory clinic with contact dermatitis might restrict the denominator of theoretically "at-risk" population to the male workers, in which case the observed attack rates might drop off sharply. Only by extending epidemiological surveillance and case ascertainment to the workers' households and more specifically to the laundresses would the epidemiologist become aware of the prosodemic elaboration in the form of newly incident cases in that segment of the labor force.

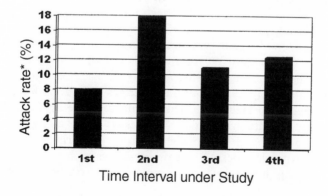

FIGURE 3.2b. Primary attack rate for each time interval under study. (A primary attack rate is the number of newly incident cases observed during the interval, divided by the number at risk of becoming a new case as observed at the start of that interval.)

ANALYSIS OF SECONDARY ATTACK RATES

The analysis of secondary attack rates provides a way to probe more deeply into the underlying dynamics of the outbreak and to provide a quantitative assessment of whether a contagion process might be at play. A secondary attack rate is "secondary" by virtue of drawing a distinction between primary affected cases within each nest of nested structure (e.g., household) versus the secondary and later cases. Turning back to Figure 3.1, there is no way to estimate a secondary attack rate at time = 1 because there is no distinction between primary and secondary cases. However, at time = 2, the secondary attack rate is formed by removing each primary case from the denominator of the attack rate. For example, the denominator of the primary attack rate for each of the nests A, B, C is the same value at time = 1, when it is equal to eight (8) per nest.

In contrast, the denominator of the secondary attack rate at the start of $t = 2$ is undefined for nest A (because there still are no primary cases within that nest and we do not calculate a secondary attack rate until there is a primary case in the nest). The denominator is 7 for nest B, and it is 7 for nest C, the prior incident case having been removed from the denominator for each of these two nests. Carrying forward in time, we see in nest A at $t = 3$ we have one newly incident case but no other cases; hence, the denominator of the secondary attack rate for nest A will be 7 at the start of the next interval. At the start of $t = 3$, the denominator is 5 for nest B and also is 5 for nest C. Any decrement in the number of vulnerable (yet unaffected) individuals within each nest tends to elevate the value of the secondary attack rate until all vulnerable individuals have become affected or the outbreak ends.

Calculation of the secondary attack rate (SAR) for time $t = 2$ yields a value of $2/7$ for both nests B and C, or roughly 29%; an SAR of $1/5$, or 20%, for time $t = 3$ (again, with nests B and C contributing values); and an SAR of $2/7$, or roughly 29%, for nest A during time $t = 4$, but an SAR of 0% for nests B and C during time $t = 4$. The non-zero values are shown in Table 3.1, along with primary attack rate values for each time interval depicted in Figure 3.1. The sustained nature of the underlying dynamic and potentially contagious process is conveyed by the secondary attack rates of each nest in the structure. The primary attack rates convey the dynamic process of the outbreak for the community at large, but do not help us to rule in or to rule out a contagion process within households.

Of course, this analysis of secondary attack rates, by itself, does not constitute definitive evidence of an underlying process of contagion, but if this type of analysis fails to disclose elevated secondary attack rates, it

TABLE 3.1. Analysis of Primary and Secondary Attack Rates

Time interval	Numerator and denominator for primary attack rate	Primary attack rate	Numerator and denominator for nonzero nest-specific secondary attack rates	Secondary attack rate
1	2/24	8%	Not defined[a]	Not defined[a]
2	4/22	18%	2/7 (based on B&C)	29%
3	2/18	11%	1/5 (based on B&C)	20%
4	2/16	12.5%	2/7 (based on A only)	29%

[a] The secondary attack rate remains undefined for a nest within the nested structure until after a primary case has been observed.

can be difficult to argue that the underlying process is one of contagion. To be more definitive, we must be able to rule out other potential sources of the within-nest concentration of newly incident cases (the analogy to the truck exhaust fumes and CO_2 in the initial yawning example).

The analysis of secondary attack rates was developed some 100–120 years ago, was made popular by Charles V. Chapin, one of Rhode Island's most famous public health leaders of the 19th century, and was refined by Professor Wade Hampton Frost, first professor of epidemiology at the Johns Hopkins School of Hygiene and Public Health. The early foundation of this tradition of attack rate analyses began with the work of Peter Panum, one of the earliest quantitative epidemiologists, who is mainly known for his investigation of measles outbreaks on the Faroe Islands of Denmark during the early 1800s. What was noteworthy about the Faroe Islands was that the history of measles on the islands was known, on the basis of historical records showing no recent outbreaks, and it was possible for Panum to investigate a measles outbreak under conditions of almost 100% vulnerability. All but a few elderly residents of the islands had previously never been exposed to measles, and as a result it was possible to trace the progress of the epidemic through this "virgin" population (i.e., a population completely unaffected by prior measles exposure).

Later epidemiologists were able to show that an analysis of secondary attack rates within nested structures of a community (e.g., households, school classrooms) can help to approximate investigations of these rare "virgin" populations. Of course, distortions can arise unless it is possible to assume relative homogeneity of vulnerability among members of the nest or among members of a specified stratum within the nest (e.g., minors vs. adults). For example, the pattern of affected cases shown in Figure 3.1 suggests some degree of invulnerability of the adult members within each nest. Across $t = 1$ through $t = 4$, there is no accumulation of adult cases. Unless these adult cases have some characteristic that has shielded them from exposure (i.e., near-zero opportunity to be exposed) or a characteristic that has increased their resistance nonspecifically (e.g., a general, or "autarceologic," defense associated with having matured to adulthood), one might suspect that the adults had been affected at some prior interval of time, and thereby are effectively nonvulnerable at $t = 1$. Of course, we can see this at the end of the final interval, but midcourse through an outbreak this type of pattern of vulnerability can be difficult to apprehend.

In summary, when there is no contagion within the nested structure, the secondary attack rate will be roughly equal to the total community's primary attack rate. A contagion process within the nested structure tends to give rise to an elevated secondary attack rate relative to the primary attack rate for the community at large, but the evidence of an elevated secondary attack rate is not sufficient to declare that a contagion process is occurring. More detailed and formal expositions of secondary attack rates within the context of a generalized "susceptibles, infections, removals" (SIR) model are provided by Daley and Gani (1999) and by Rhodes, Halloran, and Longini (1996). Baker and Stevens (1995) have extended the SIR model in two interesting directions: (1) to allow for random effects heterogeneity in an individual's susceptibility to becoming a case, and (2) to estimate heterogeneity in the SAR for different types of contacts. That is, the estimated likelihood of transmission from person to person is allowed to vary; in the example provided by the authors, an estimated within-household secondary attack rate value of 9% was derived for adult–adult transmission during a community outbreak of *Shigella sonnei*, the bacteria causing shigellosis, for which the main clinical features are diarrhea, fever, and stomach cramps starting 1–2 days after exposure. In contrast, when the authors applied a scaling factor within the SIR model, the investigators found that the SAR estimate was consistently 9% if the infecting household member had been a child and there had been subsequent contact with a male adult, while the SAR estimate was 54% if the infecting household member had been a child and there had been subsequent contact with a male child. This type of analysis approach, with a scaling factor applied to transmission coefficients, may be especially useful in microanalysis of peer contagion because this approach allows for underlying individual-level heterogeneity in susceptibility to peer influence, and also permits study of variation in the contagious process when the members of a peer group have different social status, roles, or other individual-level characteristics (e.g., age, sex, prestige within the peer group).

ANALYSIS OF MULTIVARIATE ATTACK RATES

Analysis of secondary attack rates remained at a fairly rudimentary level during the early 20th century. Nevertheless, conceptual, methodological, and computational advances in the last decades of the century opened a door to an approach we can call "multivariate attack rate analyses," in the sense that these analyses involve multiple response variables. The nature of the multiple response variables can be understood by returning to Figure 3.1 and letting each individual be denoted by the types of subscripts described in the introduction to that figure. For example, the unaffected status of the adult male in the first row and first column of nest A at $t = 1$ can be indicated by a subscripted response variable, YA111; at $t = 1$, YA111 = 0 because that individual is unaffected at that time point. The affected status of the male minor in the second row and first column of nest B at $t = 1$ can be indicated by a subscripted response variable, YB211; at $t = 1$, YB211 = 1 because that individual is affected at that time point. As a final illustration, the unaffected status of the male minor in the second row and first column of nest A at $t = 2$ can be indicated by a subscripted response variable, YA311, and in between $t = 2$ and $t = 3$, the YA311 value changes from a 0 (unaffected) to a 1 (affected). Of course, when there is a possibility of a contagious process that helps account for some individuals becoming affected while others are spared, or when there are other sources of variation in the probability of becoming affected (e.g., shared genes within the nest; shared drinking water supply; shared meals), these multiple response variables within the nest are not statistically independent of one another; they are interdependent response variables in the multivariate matrix.

A conceptual advance in relation to the analysis of this type of interdependent binary response variables within nested structures was made by McNemar, who appreciated that the strength of association between a binary response variable and some other binary variable (e.g., an exposure) might be estimated by taking the odds ratio (i.e., the odds of disease among exposed individuals divided by the odds of disease among nonexposed individuals, where the concept of "odds" is simply the ratio of the probability of disease to the complement of that same probability; odds = {Pr / [1 − Pr]}). McNemar noted, however, that in the case of nested structures of size two ($n = 2$), within which the response of one individual nest member is interdependent with the response of the other individual nest member, the multivariate character of the binary responses can be ignored at peril. This line of thinking led to the development of McNemar's test to estimate the odds ratio for matched-pair data (i.e., with interdependent binary responses of two individuals within a matched set, such as a pair of monozygotic twins). This form of the odds ratio, as a gauge of strength of association for matched pairs, involves a focus upon the matched pairs in which there is discordance. Let's take as an example the idea that early serious head trauma increases risk of Alzheimer's-type dementia (AD), a condition that also is known to be determined in part by genetic vulnerability traits (e.g., as measured by the number of alleles for apolipoprotein epsilon-4), and let's consider a study of monozygotic (MZ) twins (i.e., twins whose individual genomes at conception are 100% concordant). By studying MZ twins, it is possible to impose tight constraints on that genome (near 100% matching of genes at that point in development) in order to shed light on variation in the risk of AD that might be induced by experience or environmental exposures such as head trauma. Under these constraints, given interdependent binary responses within each matched twin pair, the odds ratio linking history of serious head trauma (HT) to risk of developing AD by a given age is expressed as the ratio of two specific numbers: (1) the number of twin pairs in which the AD-affected twin has experienced prior HT but the nonaffected cotwin has not, divided by (2) the number of twin pairs in which the nonaffected twin has experienced prior HT but the affected cotwin has not.

The resulting odds ratio estimate for the strength of association between AD and HT also can be derived under a "conditional" or "fixed effects" form of the logistic regression model (also called "McFadden's choice model"), which includes a subscripted intercept term for each "nest" (cotwin pair) within the nested structure of the MZ twin study, as well as a common slope that gauges the increase in log odds of AD as we look across the HT-exposed and HT-nonexposed discordant twin pairs. An advantage of this logistic regression formulation is an extension to multiple logistic regression models, under which multiple covariates can be held constant in order to probe the statistical independence of each observed association. For example, the history of prior HT might be confounded by a history of tobacco smoking—if both are manifestations of an underlying sensation-seeking trait, and if history of tobacco smoking has its own independent association with risk of AD. If so, the slope for the AD–HT association can be estimated under a model that controls for history of tobacco smoking, and the slope for the AD–tobacco association can be estimated under a model that controls for history of HT.

The McNemar formulation for a basic multivariate attack rate analysis is most tractable when the nested structure consists of pairs of individuals, matched on one or more characteristics (e.g., genetically matched, sex-matched, age-matched). The conditional form of multiple logistic regression can accommodate matched risk sets of individuals, with the risk sets allowed to include a varying number of affected cases and still-vulnerable noncases. Originally, epidemiologists often constrained their matched risk set studies to include just matched pairs or just fixed ratios of affected cases to noncases for risk sets of a fixed size, due to the tedious hand computations for estimation of the matched pairs odds ratio. They also might start a matched pair or risk set analysis with the conditional form of logistic regression to estimate the "crude" form of the odds ratio (i.e., without ancillary covariates), and then proceed to an unconditional form of multiple logistic regression in order to hold constant the ancillary covariates—again, because computation by hand was tedious, or due to extreme cost of access to the computational power of a mainframe computer's central processing unit (CPU). Advances in computational sciences, reduced cost of CPU access (e.g., via personal computers), and new software programming put the conditional form of multiple logistic regression within reach (e.g., via PECAN and MLR software of the early to mid-1980s).

Regrettably, these original methods for multivariate binary responses had two features that were not optimal. First, the conditional form of multiple logistic regression does not always yield the smallest possible variances for the resulting regression slopes—because the analyses are focused upon the discordant members of the matched pairs (as in the McNemar test) or the risk sets. Second, this regression approach does not yield an estimate of the degree to which the outcome or response of interest might be appearing with greater than expected clustering within the risk sets.

The desire for small variances is most pronounced when one conducts a matched pair study, but the number of discordant pairs is too small to yield statistically robust results; many concordant matched pairs are discarded when the estimate is focused solely upon the discordant pairs. However, in 1988, Liang and Zeger showed that it was possible to derive the correct odds ratio estimates and smaller variances by taking into account the information value of the nondiscordant pairs. They demonstrated how to accomplish this task in an application of estimating equations. The essence of this solution involves use of the generalized linear model and a logistic link, with the estimating equations used to take into account the interdependencies of the responses (e.g., within matched pairs).

In our research group's work on clustering of drug involvement within regions, communities, schools, and neighborhoods, we have used an advanced multivariate statistical method known as the "alternating logistic regressions" (ALR), which also takes advantage of an estimating equations approach (GEE) in order to quantify the magnitude of local area clustering of drug involvement, while concurrently probing into the suspected causal determinants of a binary response variable of interest. In this work, applying an extension of a GEE developed by Vincent

Carey, with Scott Zeger (Carey, Zeger, & Diggle, 1993), we mainly have been interested in whether drug involvement might be clustering in patterns that might stimulate additional research on the possibility of contagion processes. The ALR approach yields a readily interpretable pairwise odds ratio estimate of the magnitude of clustering within groups, concurrent with derivation of covariate-adjusted estimates of causal (or noncausal) associations. Unlike so-called subject-specific or individual-level random effects models, the ALR approach treats the interdependence of responses of individuals as an important object of study to be estimated; the interdependence is not "absorbed" within the distribution of the individual's "random intercept" or "random slope" where it cannot be inspected or estimated directly. In this work with the ALR, as in the analysis of secondary attack rates, when the ALR model estimates disclose no evidence of clustering within groups, it is difficult to claim that a contagion process is at work. Nonetheless, observed clustering is not sufficient to infer presence of a contagion process, and we have been careful to note that the patterns of observed clustering of drug involvement cannot, by themselves, be interpreted as evidence of contagion processes (e.g., see Bobashev & Anthony, 1998; Petronis & Anthony, 2003).

An appreciation that observed clustering of health conditions is ambiguous with respect to contagion is not new, and can be found in early biometrics work by Karl Pearson (1912), as well as Greenwood and Yule (1920). Greenwood and Yule characterize three possible processes that might give rise to these "dependent happenings"—namely, (1) uncomplicated chance (of the type that operates in card games), (2) mechanisms arising or operating in relation to mixtures of heterogeneous populations (e.g., self-selection or other selection processes that combine higher risk and lower risk segments of the population), and (3) contagion or contagion-like processes. Taibleson (1974) characterized the contagion-like processes as those "where the occurrence of an event has an after effect that increases the probability that the next event will occur" (p. 877). He went on to assert that there is a mythical quality to the belief that longitudinal or "over-time data" can be used to draw the distinction between a contagion process and the "heterogeneous population" mechanism mentioned by Greenwood and Yule. About 20 years later, Manski (1993) illuminated this conclusion in a clear but technically demanding exposition of three different hypotheses "often advanced to explain the common observation that individuals belonging to the same group tend to behave similarly":

(a) *endogenous effects*, wherein the propensity of an individual to behave in some way varies with the behavior of the group;

(b) *exogenous (contextual) effects*, wherein the propensity of an individual to behave in some way varies with the exogenous characteristics of the group, and

(c) *correlated effects*, wherein individuals in the same group tend to behave similarly because they have similar individual characteristics or face similar institutional environments. (p. 532)

Manski also provided this useful example of these three distinctive effects, and explained certain policy implications of these effects:

> Consider the high school achievement of a teenage youth. There is an endogenous effect if, all else equal, individual achievement tends to vary with the average achievement of the students in the youth's school, ethnic group, or other reference group. There is an exogenous effect if achievement tends to vary with, say, the socioeconomic composition of the reference group. There are correlated effects if youths in the same school tend to achieve similarly because they have similar family backgrounds or because they are taught by the same teachers.
>
> . . . Consider, for example, an educational intervention providing tutoring to some of the students in a school but not to the others. If individual achievement increases with the average achievement of the students in the school, then an effective tutoring program not only directly helps the tutored students but, as their achievement rises, indirectly helps all students in the school, with a feedback to further achievement gains by the tutored students. Exogenous effects and correlated effects do not generate this "social multiplier." (pp. 532–533)

In an echo of Taibleson's pessimistic remarks about longitudinal observational data, Manski (1993) concluded his essay with an assertion that "richer" data from "experimental" studies are needed in efforts to learn about endogenous social effects in the form of contagion processes (p. 541). Extending this theme in the domain of social policy analysis, Moffitt (2001) identified three classes of interventions that might hold promise for experimental research on endogenous social effects:

(a) interventions that change group membership, either by forcibly reassigning individuals to schools, neighborhoods, or other groups, or that offer taxes or subsidies for voluntarily changing group membership;

(b) interventions that alter the fundamentals for only a subset of a group with the intention of affecting the entire group [where "fundamentals" for a subset of a group are defined as private incentives: incomes, prices, and public goods for the subset]; and

(c) interventions that seek to operate directly on social norms. (2001, p. 49)

Manski advocated greater reliance upon "subjective data, the statements people make about why they behave as they do," in parallel with his recommendation for experimentation, but this topic is beyond the scope of a chapter intended to have a focus upon quantitative methods.

Manski's characterization of contagion processes and other endogenous social effects in relation to an individual's high school achievement relative to the average achievement of students in the youth's school is of interest. It represents a shift from the traditional focus of epidemiological analysis of contagion, which from the time of Fracastoro (16th-century Verona, Italy) to the present has been a discrete binary health event: alive versus dead, infected versus not infected, diseased versus not diseased.

This shift in the direction of a nonbinary characteristic, such as achievement test scores with a possibly normal (bell-shaped) distribution, takes us out of the realm of attack rate analyses, McNemar's approach to estimation of the odds ratio in matched pair data, the conditional form of logistic regression, and the multilevel ALR models into the realm of alternatives such as ordinary linear regression models, as well as subject-specific hierarchical linear models with multiple levels. Under these circumstances, it would appear that the problem of contagion has been reworked in a direction that might make its detection more difficult rather than less difficult—to the extent that a contagion process is disclosed more readily as we increase the specificity and unique or distinctive character of the event or behavior, and to the extent that we no longer have the nonvarying zero value advantage mentioned at the end of the fourth paragraph of this chapter. Rather, when the response variable is allowed to vary prior to the start of an observation interval for a contagion process, we have a situation in which the variation of the response variable for an individual can exert an influence upon the variation of the reference group's averaged value of that response variable, and vice versa. In these situations, we have more than 30 years of pessimism that strictly observational studies can yield definitive evidence about these causal influences. As argued by Manski (1993) and Moffitt (2001), formal experimental trials become crucial in this context.

What follows is not a comprehensive review of experiments intended to study contagious processes, which is a theme that recurs throughout this volume. Instead, what follows is a description of two formal experiments in which there has been an effort to probe into peer-to-peer contagion. The following remarks are mainly focused upon the quantitative methods used to study peer contagion in these experiments, and some sources of remaining uncertainty about peer contagion processes in these studies.

FORMAL EXPERIMENTS FOCUSED UPON POSSIBLE PEER INFLUENCE

Duncan, Boisjoly, Kremer, Levy, and Eccles (2005) have described a remarkable experiment in which incoming college freshmen were invited to be assigned at random to same-sex dormitory roommates, with follow-up assessments of multiple responses, including discrete problem behaviors such as heavy episodic drinking (termed by the authors as *binge* drinking but measured as consuming four to five drinks within a single drinking occasion). An array of precollege assessments also was taken prior to roommate assignment (e.g., history of any *binge* drinking during the high school years). There have been prior (and subsequent) experiments of this type, with random assignment of students to dormitory rooms (or to school classrooms). However, in these other experiments the focus of inquiry generally has been on topics such as school achievement, grade point average, or decisions about joining fraternities (see, e.g., Kang, 2005; Sacerdote, 2001), or attitudes on social topics such as marijuana (see, e.g., Nickerson, 2005). The experiment by Duncan and colleagues is special because of its focus on discrete aspects of peer-influenced behavior such as *binge* drinking (hereinafter noted without italics).

In their paper, Duncan and colleagues (2005) offer a very clear explanation of the value of random assignment of the roommates in experiments of this type, including the research design's control over threats to validity in the form of self-selection and other processes that fall under the Greenwood–Yule category of "mechanisms arising or operating in relation to mixtures of heterogeneous populations." For example, without random assignment, one binge-drinking roommate might select another binge-drinking roommate; with random assignment, the pairs of binge-drinking roommates occur at random, as do pairs of binge-drinking and light-drinking or nondrinking roommates. Random assignment of roommates within dormitories also helped to bring into balance what Manski has characterized as "exogenous [contextual] effects" and "correlated effects" (e.g., to the extent that roommates within dormitories share much of their living and learning environments in common).

Among the options for statistical approaches for analysis of their experimental data, Duncan and colleagues (2005) organized their data set with one row for each respondent and chose a "fixed effects" multiple regression model, with current (recent) frequency of binge drinking as the response. They included multiple dummy-coded covariate terms, one for each dormitory or college housing unit (less one), and one or more covariate terms for "control" or background variables for statistical adjustment (e.g., white vs. nonwhite, father's and mother's level of education). Under the multiple regression model with covariates for statistical adjustment, they then estimated the peer effects by regressing the response value for recent frequency of binge drinking in college upon terms coded to reflect (1) whether both the respondent and the roommate had been binge drinkers in high school, (2) whether the roommate but not the respondent had been a binge drinker in high school, and (3) whether the respondent but not the roommate had been a binge drinker in high school; the reference category consisted of respondents who had been binge drinkers in high school but the roommate was not. As for results, among males but not females, the derived estimates are consistent with the hypothesized excess frequency of college binge drinking when random assignment paired up two roommates with a prior history of binge drinking during high school, relative to the incoming freshmen who had been binge drinkers before college but who were paired up with a roommate who had not been a binge drinker. (Note: An estimate consistent with a peer effect among females might emerge if these data were reanalyzed using Liang's GEE adaptation of logistic regression analysis for matched pair data, with the response recast as *any* binge drinking during college. In that approach to analysis, the estimates gain strength because information is contributed by both types of discordant roommates [i.e., all high school binge + nonbinge pairs]. In addition, this model holds constant socially shared aspects of roommate pairs' environments [e.g., each dorm advisor's level of tolerance for binge drinking], even when there has been no explicit measurement of these socially shared environmental conditions or processes.)

The evidence from this study suggests that pairing up two male binge drinkers represents a particularly noxious combination, but this evidence may not be sufficient to demonstrate the presence of peer contagion because the contrast actually might be showing us the "protective" influence when a nonbinging male roommate is paired up with a binging roommate (also a male). A group of incoming binge drinkers assigned at random to singleton rooms might be needed to help us split the difference between these two types of potential peer influence: (1) a hypothesized contagious process that involves pairing up two male roommates who arrive at college with a history of binge drinking, and (2) A hypothesized protective process that involves pairing up one male who brings to college this type of history of binge drinking with a male roommate who brings no such history.

But perhaps more to the point is that contagion is a process, not a result. It might be helpful to superimpose a more fine-grained assessment process on an experiment of this type, with microlevel assessment of what each respondent is experiencing during a short interval just before the "hazard" episode of binge drinking versus what that same respondent experienced during a short interval (of the same length) that is *not* followed by a binge-drinking episode. This approach has been termed the "epidemiological case-crossover design" or more recently the "self-controlled case method" (Whitaker, Farrington, Spiessens, & Musonda, 2005). It requires a type of microlevel assessment that may be required if we are to understand peer influence as a process of "contagion" and to distinguish between a possibly noxious combination that involves the group aggregation of "similarly behaving" peers versus a possibly protective combination with group aggregation of "dissimilarly behaving" peers. One form of contagion process that might be occurring as a result of putting together two male binge-drinking roommates is that an escalating number of drinks in one roommate prompts an escalating number of drinks in the other roommate. If so, under the self-controlled case (case-crossover) method, during a short interval just before one roommate's binge-drinking episode, there should be an excess occurrence of escalating drinks in the other roommate's life, relative to an appropriately chosen "control" interval not followed by a binge-drinking episode. Here also, because it is a "subject-as-own-control" design, this approach imposes constraints on both genetic and environmental conditions and processes, as we have discussed elsewhere (see, e.g., Wu & Anthony, 2000).

An experiment conducted by Dishion, McCord, and Poulin (1999) and Poulin, Dishion, and Burraston (2001) also is remarkable because of its random assignment of youths with identified antisocial behaviors or conduct problems to either an individualized intervention or a group intervention, and because of its finding that the aggregation of this type of youths within the groups might have produced iatrogenic (cure-caused) adversity. In particular, under a subject-specific random-effects growth trajectory model, the youths assigned to the group intervention showed more growth of conduct problems during postassignment follow-up assessments, as compared to the growth trajectory for youths assigned to the individualized (nongroup) intervention.

Here also there is some ambiguity in the evidence with respect to peer contagion, mainly because the experiment included no youths randomly assigned to a "no intervention" condition. This "complaint" is not a challenge to the inference that the group-assigned youths are "doing worse" relative to the individualized intervention youths; the research group was able to make a creative use of videotaping in order to document "deviant talk" processes that might be conducive to a contagion process. Nonetheless, as in the experiment conducted by Duncan and colleagues, the experimental results are subject to a possibility that the contrast group (here, the individualized intervention youths) might have benefited from a nongroup intervention. Hence, the individualized intervention youth growth trajectory is not completely counterfactual in nature; it does not cleanly estimate the conduct problems growth trajectory that might have been observed if the group-assigned youths had not been gathered together. A solution exists for future experiments in the form of an additional experimental arm of the study, with randomized assignment of one group of youths to an individualized intervention known to be completely inert with respect to growth of conduct problems.

In addition, within this experiment, there is no study of contagion as a process, and the inference of contagion depends upon the contrast of averaged trajectories for the group-intervention-assigned youths relative to the individual-intervention-assigned youths. Leaving aside the possibility that, by chance, youths with greater liability toward conduct problem growth ended up in the intervention group, one additional difficulty in the interpretation of the evidence with respect to a possible underlying contagion process is that the analysis has no response variables of the discrete, specific variety (i.e., nothing analogous to a specific HIV virus strain, or FCUK baseball caps worn bill-backward).

In future experiments, it should be possible to blend the strengths of the longitudinal latent growth trajectory modeling with strengths of contagion process measurements, and it might be possible to conduct new analyses of the existing experimental data that would shed light on these processes. For example, the evidence in favor of contagion would be strengthened if the research team were to be able to show that fire setting or graffiti vandalism of a specific variety were rare (but not absent) at the start of the study, but then that specific variety of fire setting or graffiti vandalism became more widespread throughout the growth of deviance among the group-aggregated peers (but not among the individualized youths) during the study interval. The case for a contagious process with respect to this type of conduct problem would become even more compelling if the videotape evidence documented "deviant talk" about these specific varieties of conduct problem (i.e., fire setting, graffiti vandalism). Evidence of a discrete and specific character also might be found in relation to specific forms of drug involvement—for example, not only actual use of possibly unusual drugs such as methylenedioxymethamphetamine or ketamine, but also special slang terms or code names used to convey information about these drugs (e.g., "XTC," "Special K").

Under some circumstances, a committee for protection of human subjects in research might allow the investigator to attempt to kindle a mildly deviant contagious process within the context of the experiment under study. For example, youths can be taught to play and win an online video game at the end of the first session, via individualized tutoring, and at random (or systematically, as described below), youths can be taught a specific way or ways to cheat in order to increase the score or likelihood of winning (or they might be taught to find an "Easter Egg" deposited within the game by the software developer). The contagion process with respect to this specific form of cheating (or Easter Egg discovery) then can be inspected automatically by having the computer game record when and by whom the cheating (or discovery) step is invoked. Systematic assignment of one unique cheat/discovery method to youths with higher social prestige (within the group) versus assignment of a different unique cheat/discovery method to youths of lower social prestige would permit study of the contagion process using models such as the Baker–Stevens random effects SIR differentiation of secondary attack rates for *Shigella* transmission from a child to a male adult versus from a child to another child (Baker & Stevens, 1995).

CONCLUSIONS

There are many different traditions for research on contagion. In epidemiology, the tradition is one of studying contagion as a process, and the research approaches tend to focus upon highly specific and discrete events or characteristics (e.g., infections) and the transmission of these events or characteristics from person to person via direct contact or via indirect contact. Some of the research approaches developed in epidemiology may have utility in social and behavioral sciences research on peer influences. By applying an epidemiological perspective to the study of peer contagion, we come to an evaluation of the evidence that may differ somewhat from the evaluations made from other perspectives, as well as suggestions for novel analysis approaches (e.g., Liang's adaptation of logistic regression analyses of matched pair data), research designs (e.g., the case-crossover or "self-controlled case method"), and elements of peer influence research (e.g., random effects SIR model estimation that can shed light on peer contagion processes through which specific antisocial behaviors spread from peer to peer). Moreover, it is possible that for the most probing research into peer contagion processes, the response variables must be specific, discrete, and perhaps of a unique character (e.g., the special mode of cheating to win or Easter Egg discovery that otherwise remains hidden unless there is a peer-to-peer contagious process for spreading that novel information). As was learned many years ago in research on epidemiology of infectious diseases (see, e.g., Taibleson, 1974), an inspection of the end distribution of a supposed contagious process may often yield uncertain conclusions about the generating mechanisms of primary interest.

ACKNOWLEDGMENTS

I wish to thank the editors and Dr. Greg Duncan for helpful comments on prior drafts of this chapter, as well as Ms. Sara Vasilenko for expert bibliographic assistance. In addition to foundation funds provided for support of the Duke Executive Session meetings and completion of this chapter, the writing was supported in part by a K05 Senior Scientist award from the National Institute on Drug Abuse (U.S. National Institutes of Health award number 5K05DA015799) and by research funds made available by Michigan State University.

CHAPTER 4

Assigning Youths to Minimize Total Harm

Philip J. Cook
and Jens Ludwig

A common practice in the fields of education, mental health, and juvenile justice is to segregate problem youths in groups with deviant peers. In education, disruptive or delinquent youths may be assigned to self-contained classrooms for in-school detention or even to alternative schools. In mental health interventions, youths with conduct disorders and drug abusers may be assigned to group therapy or placed with similar youths in group homes and day treatment programs. In the juvenile justice system, youths are placed with other offenders in camps, training schools, and detention centers. It is entirely possible that assignments of this sort, which concentrate deviant youths, may lead to perverse outcomes. Instead of helping their transition to a healthier, more productive trajectory, these assignments may actually facilitate a greater commitment to deviant behavior. The result may be an increase in the rate or seriousness of problem behaviors, either during the course of the placement or in subsequent years (Dishion, McCord, & Poulin, 1999; McCord, 2003).

This possibility of an iatrogenic effect from interventions with troubled and troublesome youths is relevant in designing policy, and adds to the list of arguments in support of "mainstreaming" or diffusing them among other youths whenever possible. But there are other concerns that help justify segregated group assignments. Delivery of treatment through specialized resources may be accomplished more efficiently in settings dedicated to that purpose, and that may also be true for monitoring and controlling the behavior of youths with conduct disorders. In any event, segregating such youths has the desirable effect of insulating other youths and adults from them. And the *threat* of assignment to in-school detention or a training school may itself have some deterrent effect on bad behavior. In considering alternative assignment policies, the validity and strength of these rationales should be weighed against the possible perverse results from concentrating deviant youths.

Our analysis is intended to help organize the discussion about these trade-offs. First, we show that the number of deviant youths (relative to the size of the relevant population or to the number of assignment options) may well determine whether the harm-minimizing assignment calls for diffusion, segregation, or some of both. Second, the way in which individual behavior cumulates to collective harm can be of considerable relevance in characterizing the harm-minimizing assignment; in cases where bad behavior has a direct detrimental effect on others who share the assignment (including youths who are not deviant), then there is a stronger case for segregation than when harm occurs outside of the assignment location. Third, the capacity for behavior control matters, and may make the difference in a choice between segregation and integration; an innovation that enhances control over disruptive youths may make integration more attractive.

We briefly discuss the empirical literature, which with some exceptions is inadequate to the task of providing clear guidance about optimal assignment strategies. Empirical investigations often focus solely on the behavior of deviant youths under different kinds of assignments without considering the effects on others or the overall social costs of the assignments. There are some exceptional cases where the evidence, while limited, may nonetheless be sufficient. It should be noted that the conceptual and methodological matters discussed here are also relevant to almost any policy dilemma involving sorting and mixing of different sorts of people across locations. Our review of the literature includes examples involving race, residential location of families in poverty, and students of differing abilities, as well as deviant youths.

Given the inherent complexity of the assignment problem and the limited evidence, decisions will have to be made under uncertainty about costs and consequences. Furthermore, alternative assignment possibilities are likely to bring into conflict the interests of the deviant youths, other youths, and the taxpayers. Under these circumstances, is there an ethical obligation to give priority to the interests of the group that is to be directly acted on, the deviants? We reflect briefly on the medical practice principle "First do no harm," and contrast it with the claims of potential victims of deviants.

CONCEPTUAL ISSUES

Much of the relevant literature has been concerned with establishing whether the decision of how to distribute deviant youths across locations (assignments) has an effect on their behavior. That inference has proven quite challenging in practice, as we discuss in a subsequent section. But even when this empirical effort produces reliable results, it may leave us far short of having the information necessary to make a normative judgment. To make that judgment, it is also necessary to make inferences about how the assignment affects the quantity and distribution of total harm to anyone affected by the assignment, including bystanders.

One important distinction is whether the harm is limited to the individuals judged to be at risk or whether their behavior victimizes others as well. If there are victims, then it is important to distinguish between cases where the victims are in the same assigned location or are outsiders. These distinctions suggest three logical cases: no other victims, victims elsewhere, victims in the assigned location. In what follows we combine the first two cases and contrast it with the third. The distinction, then, is whether the behavior harms those who share the assigned location or not. The two types are labeled "D" and "S."

- Type D behaviors are those that have an effect on others who share the assigned location, such as classroom disruption (hence the "D") and bullying.
- Type S behaviors are those that do not have a direct impact on others who share the assignment. Included here are a variety of harms to the deviant youths themselves both during and after the particular assignment in question. Examples include smoking (the "S"), alcohol and drug abuse, and inattention to schoolwork. But this category is not limited to "victimless" behaviors. Also included are gang involvement and other criminal activity, as long as their impact is outside of the assigned location.

Of course it is quite possible that Type D and Type S behaviors are both affected by the assignment.

To gain leverage on the assignment problem, we stipulate several simplifying assumptions and refer specifically to the school official's task of assigning students to classrooms. The students are of two sorts, "nondeviants" (the As) and "deviants" (the Bs); their identities are predetermined and known to the official. There are a fixed number of classrooms and teachers. The considerations relevant to the official's decision will depend on the nature of the problem behavior.

The consequences within the classroom of Type D behavior are obviously relevant in assigning students. Other considerations may also come to bear for both types of students. Most interesting is the possibility of social influence among deviant peers. The actual behavior of a deviant youth (either Type D or Type S) may well depend on whether there are other deviant youths in the same classroom to serve as models, guides, accomplices, or an appreciative audience.

Also relevant is the capacity of teachers and other resources to influence bad behavior in the classroom or outside it. If such influence is possible, whether exercised through discipline or some sort of constructive (therapeutic) programming, then the actual behavior of deviant youths will depend on the level of resources relative to the "load" in the classroom. Resource considerations may lend weight to a prescription for either diffusion or segregation of deviant youths, depending on what might be deemed the "technology of control."

This conceptual setup provides the basis for developing some guidance for the assignment problem. Of the various assumptions, the one that may seem most artificial is that there are only two types of youths (A and B). One generalization is to assume that youths form a continuum with respect to their propensity to engage in deviant behavior, ranging from those who will initiate it under almost any circumstance to those who require a powerful stimulus, such as a complete breakdown of order. While this generalization is more flexible and realistic, we stick with the more tractable assumption of a dichotomy for now. Whether dichotomy or continuum, the mix of propensities can be understood as producing aggregate behavior that is conditioned on peer influence and external social control.

Another note on the basic setup: While our discussion is for the most part presented with reference to the problem of distributing students among classrooms or among schools, the logic is applicable to a variety of other assignment problems. For example, the state of North Carolina is in the process of demolishing its large juvenile corrections institutions and is building a series of smaller units. Among the relevant questions are how large these new units should be and whether the protocol for assigning juveniles among them call for concentrating the most serious delinquents or mixing them in with the rest of the population. Other examples from the school context include those facing a district school system: whether to start an alternative school for deviant students, whether to locate ninth graders in middle school or high school, and whether to retain large numbers of failing students for a repeat in grade.[1] More broadly, it is relevant to any scheme that sorts youths across neighborhoods or schools, including housing relocation programs and school voucher programs. We return to these examples in the empirical section.

Case 1: Assignment When There Is No Social Influence and No Control

If deviant peers do not influence others' behavior, and the issue of concern is limiting Type S behavior (smoking, crime outside the classroom, etc.), then the assignment problem appears trivial: the amount of Type S behavior would not be affected by how students are sorted among classrooms. Two exceptions should be noted: First, in some cases the assignment to a segregated classroom is justified as punishment, as in the case of in-school detention. One rationale is that the threat of such an assignment will deter bad behavior. Second, it is possible that deviant behavior is influenced by the capacity of the teacher and other resources to influence such behavior. A discussion of that possibility is left for the next section.

For disruptive (Type D) behavior, the assignment matters even if there is no social influence. In a recent theoretical article that analyzes this circumstance, Edward Lazear (2001) provides a rationale for segregation. He postulates that any one student can disrupt the productive teaching and learning activity in the classroom for a spell, and that some students are more prone to being disruptive than others. Lazear sets up the analysis by assuming two types of students, A and B, where the A students are less disruptive. A students are disruptive a fraction of the time given by $(1 - p_A)$, while the B students are disruptive a larger fraction $(1 - p_B)$ of the time. Under the assumption that episodes of disruption are uncorrelated random events, the total amount of productive, nondisrupted time is given by the product $p_A{}^a p_B{}^b$, where the exponents a and b signify the number of A and B students, respectively.

The cumulative harm (assumed to be proportional to unproductive time) due to Type D behavior in any one classroom is then

$$1 - p_A{}^a p_B{}^b$$

and the total harm associated with any given assignment of students to classrooms is the sum over all classrooms.

Under this setup, consider the marginal cost to the students in a classroom (in terms of additional time lost to disruption) of replacing an A student with a B student in that classroom. That marginal cost will be

$$p_A{}^a p_B{}^b - p_A{}^{a-1} p_B{}^{b+1} = p_A{}^a p_B{}^b [1 - p_A^{-1} p_B],$$

which is a positive number because by assumption $p_A > p_B$. This marginal cost declines as the number of B students, b, grows. The intuition here is simply that the marginal cost of an extra B student is in the form of a proportional reduction in nondisrupted time. As B increases, that proportion is applied to a shrinking base of productive teaching time, $p_A{}^a\, p_B{}^b$. One more disruptive student added to a classroom that is already mostly out of control makes little difference to the amount of teaching and learning that takes place there.

The mathematical result under Lazear's assumptions is that an assignment that separates all the A students from the Bs, placing them in different classrooms, maximizes the total amount of nondisrupted time, and hence minimizes total harm.[2] If that is the goal, then segregation is the answer. Of course, that segregated assignment may raise an equity concern, since the B students will end up with a more meager educational opportunity than the A students. That concern may be more compelling if the "disruption" in question takes the form of epileptic seizures or failure to follow directions due to attention-deficit/hyperactivity disorder, rather than to clowning or getting in fights; if the latter behaviors are viewed (rightly or wrongly) as volitional and the former as not volitional, then we might be more hesitant to assign the former group to an inferior placement. The question of whose interests should have priority is a deep one, to which we return at the end of this chapter.

Other assumptions may lead to still different conclusions. The robust lesson from this analysis is that social influence is not the only mechanism that should be considered in making assignments—for example, the influence that youths' behavior has on the productivity of the classroom or (more generally) the well-being of other students may also be relevant. That set of concerns raises issues of both fairness and overall harm to the affected population.

Case 2: Assignment When Resources Matter

In Case 1, we assumed that the youths' behavior is exogenous, that is, not influenced by the classroom context. A more realistic assumption is that the amount and quality of behavior depends on the circumstances. A "deviant youth" can then be identified as one that has a relatively high potential for exhibiting deviant behavior, in the sense that it doesn't take much of a stimulus to set him or her off. In particular, the presence of other deviant youths may facilitate this potential. Here we consider one mechanism by which that may happen: the dilution of authority. The next section addresses another mechanism of this sort: direct social influence.

Assume that each classroom has a teacher who exerts some control over the behavior of the students. The focus here is again on disruptive (Type D) behavior. A teacher may be able to "handle" one or two disruptive kids in his or her classroom, constraining their tendency to disrupt the proceedings, but at some point the "load" on the teacher will become too great. Discipline will begin to break down, and the deviant (B) students' disruptive tendencies will be given greater scope.

When authority is subject to dilution, then the best assignment of students to classrooms will depend on the capacity of teachers—what "load" they can "handle"—and the number of B youths relative to the total number of classrooms. For example, if each teacher is capable of fully constraining one B student at most, and there are fewer B students than classrooms, then the harm-minimizing assignment is to disperse the B students so there is no more than one anywhere. Note that that assignment is not random, but rather requires an explicit policy of identifying and assigning the Bs with an eye to the load per teacher.[3]

If there are more B students than classrooms, then the nature of the harm-minimizing assignment may still be dispersion or it may become segregation. In general, the answer will depend on how behavior and control capacity interact.

The addition of another B student into a classroom has both a direct and an indirect effect on total disruption in that classroom. The direct effect is whatever that new youth adds to the total, given the circumstances. The indirect effect stems from the fact that the addition of that youth changes the circumstances by diluting control capacity, with the result that the behavior of all Bs in that classroom may deteriorate.

This is a familiar dynamic in community youth programs, mental health placements, and, most obviously, the criminal justice area. If, for example, a new criminal gang forms, its crimes will add to the load on the local police department and court system. Unless there is excess capacity, the result is likely to be a reduction in the probability and severity of punishment for any given crime. With the sanction threat reduced, criminal activity will become more profitable, with the result of further increases in the crime rate and further dilution of criminal justice resources. The new "equilibrium" may be characterized by a much higher crime rate than could be explained in a direct sense by the formation of that new gang. This type of vicious cycle has been used, for example, to explain the extraordinarily high rates of homicide in Columbia (Gaviria, 2000).[4]

While it is certainly possible to adapt the Lazear model (discussed under Case 1) to this new circumstance, there is not much to be learned, since the implications for the harm-minimizing assignment will be sensitive to the specific assumptions about how behavior responds to dilution of control. Some qualitative statements can be made if we stipulate a sharp threshold phenomenon with respect to "load." First, if there are too many Bs to keep every classroom inside this threshold, then some segregated classrooms may be part of the harm-minimizing solution so that the other classrooms can remain relatively calm. That is to say, the harm-minimizing solution will entail a combination of diffusion and segregation. Second, if teachers differ in their capacity to handle Bs, then the assignment should be adjusted accordingly. Similarly, if there are extra control resources that can be allocated, then they should be assigned together with the students with an eye to staying within threshold in as many classrooms as possible.

If there is no threshold, but rather a pattern of steadily increasing disruption per B as the number of Bs increases, then it might appear that equalizing the load across classrooms would minimize harm. But the Lazear model makes clear that that is not necessarily the case. The question becomes just how the behavior in question contributes to total harm. If the concern (as in that model) is classroom time available for productive activities, then there is a limit to just how bad things can be— namely, zero productive time. So even an explosive growth in disruptiveness (resulting from the addition of Bs to the classroom) will result in a muted growth in harm, asymptotic to the limit.

In sum, if actual behavior depends on the relationship of load to control capacity, then the total harm resulting from a given number of Bs may be quite sensitive to their assignment among classrooms. The harm-minimizing assignment will depend on the number of Bs relative to the number of classrooms and the capacity of ordinary (unspecialized) teachers to assert control.[5]

The capacity of a teacher to maintain control may be expanded through training and adoption of effective innovations, which in turn could affect the harm-minimizing assignment. One important example is the Good Behavior Game, developed in the 1960s by Montrose Wolf, one of the founders of behavior analysis, with two graduate students (Barrish, Saunders, & Wolf, 1969; Embry, 2002). This game adopts a simple behavioral strategy to help maintain order in a classroom. The teacher divides the class into teams and for preset intervals keeps a visible scorecard of "fouls" committed by each team. Teams that behave well (i.e., that commit fewer fouls than some preset limit) receive a prize. This method has been subjected to extensive testing, including a large randomized trial with first graders, the Baltimore Prevention Project, in 1985–1986. The game was demonstrated to be effective at reducing classroom disruption and increasing pedagogic productivity; what's more, and more surprising, it appears to have caused long-term improvements in behavior, so that even in sixth grade the experimental students were better behaved, less likely to smoke, and so forth (Kellam, Ling, Merisca, Brown, & Ialongo, 1998). Embry (2002) has nominated the Good Behavior Game as a "behavioral vaccine" for its power to reduce impulsive, disruptive behaviors and set deviant youths on a healthier course.

Thus the Good Behavior Game provides teachers with the capacity to reduce both Type D and Type S behaviors. The harm associated with having deviant youths in the classroom is thereby reduced. If the game were difficult to implement (as suggested by the fact that it is not currently used much in ordinary classrooms), it would provide an impetus to segregate deviant youths into classrooms with teachers that do use the method. On the other hand, if it were widely adopted, as suggested by its advocates, then it would reduce the costs of mainstreaming deviant youths.

Case 3: Assignment When Deviant Peer Influence Is Important

As in Case 2 we assume that the behavior of deviant youths depends on the circumstances, but now consider a different mechanism: youths may influence each other directly, in addition to whatever indirect influence may occur via the dilution of authority. Deviant peer influence of this sort is akin to the spread of a contagious disease, and is often referred to as "social contagion" (Cook & Goss, 1996).

We initially assume that contagious transmission for deviant behavior is limited to those with a propensity for that behavior. Three recent studies from widely differing contexts are among those that offer general support for this assumption. First, in the Baltimore Prevention Project cited above, Kellam and colleagues (1998) found that first graders with aggressive tendencies were the ones whose behavior were most affected by the presence of other aggressive children in the classroom. Second, an analysis of the influence of randomly assigned roommates for first-year students at a university found that males who had been drinkers in high school had a positive effect on the quantity of drinking by their college roommates, but only if that roommate had also been a drinker in high school (Boisjoly, Duncan, Kremer, Levy, & Eccles, 2003). Third, an analysis of the postrelease behavior of delinquents in Florida training schools found that the likelihood of postrelease recidivism was positively related to the concentration of youths who happened to be in that reformatory with similar criminal histories—for example, auto thieves were more likely to steal cars again following release if they had been locked up with a relatively high number of other auto thieves (Bayer, Pintoff, & Posen, 2003).

In evaluating alternative assignment strategies, contagion is analytically similar to the problem of authority dilution. The addition of a badly behaved individual to a classroom adds to the total harm directly (by his or her own behavior), and also indirectly through his or her influence on other deviants in the room. This process may exhibit a threshold phenomenon. In the analysis of disease epidemics, a critical point occurs where there is enough contact between infected contagious individuals and "susceptible" individuals so that each case of infection results in more than one additional case, initiating explosive growth. The concentration of deviants required to produce this result is akin to the capacity of a teacher to handle a load of disruption. And the two mechanisms may be related substantively, as well as by analogy: the teacher's ability to respond effectively to disruption may be instrumental in stopping the spread of a contagious process.

The possibility of social influence is not limited to Type D (disruption) behavior, but also includes Type S behavior. As with auto thieves in the training school study mentioned above, the behavior of a deviant youth outside of the immediate assignment may be influenced by who was in the same location with him or her. But there is an important difference between S and D behavior in evaluating alternative assignments. Much of the harm from D behavior may fall on nondeviant classmates, but, by assumption, the harm from S behavior occurs outside of that setting. Thus one of the main justifications for segregation is absent in the case of S behavior.

If S behavior is the issue and social contagion a real possibility, then the best assignment depends (as usual) on the number of deviants relative to classrooms, and the shape of what might be called the "social influence function." If there are fewer deviants than classrooms, then no more than one per classroom is the harm-minimizing solution. If there is more than one per classroom, it is important to know something about how the behavior of Bs responds to the concentration of other deviants. Here are two possibilities:

1. If social influence is characterized by a threshold phenomenon, such that social amplification of S behavior does not begin until there are at least $n + 1$ deviants in the classroom, then the key issue is how the ratio of deviants to classrooms relates to that threshold. If there are 10 classrooms and fewer than $10n$ deviants, then systematic diffusion is the harm-minimizing solution. If social influence is characterized by a threshold phenomenon, but there are more than $10n$ deviants to be divided among the 10 classrooms, then a mixed approach may be best, with some Ss assigned to "dilute" classrooms (n deviants) and others to classrooms that are more concentrated. In some cases the best assignment may include a few segregated classrooms with all Bs, and the rest integrated. But it may also work out that equal division is the harm-minimizing solution. Finding the best answer depends on knowing the shape of the relationship between harm and deviant concentration.

2. Second is the possibility that there is contagion without a threshold, so that deviant influence grows stronger as the concentration of Bs

in the classroom increases. In other words, suppose that the addition of another B to the classroom tends to make each of the others in that classroom more committed to deviant behavior, and that effect increases monotonically with the number of Bs. In this case, the harm-minimizing solution is (once again) equal division of Bs among available classrooms.

At the beginning of this chapter, we noted that our analysis of sorting and mixing is relevant to other domains besides deviant behavior. Consider a quite different domain, taken from the influential Coleman Report of 1966 (Coleman, 1966). That report analyzed the effect of racial segregation in schools. The empirical analysis was based on a national sample of U.S. schoolchildren. James S. Coleman and collaborators estimated the effect of the racial makeup of the student's school (percentage black) on his or her achievement test score. His estimation procedure assumed that the effect was linear, and possibly different for black than for nonblack students.

To preserve as much of the previous notation as possible, we define the following variables and analyze a representative school:

a = number of nonblack students in the school (type A)
b = number of black students in the school (type B)
k = total number of students in the school, $k = a + b$
Y_i = achievement test score of student of type i (i = A or B)
p_i = constant associated with student of type i
β_i = parameter indicating the effect of racial concentration

We follow Coleman in assuming a linear relationship that may differ between groups, as follows:

$$Y_i = p_i + \beta_i b/k$$

If the goal is to maximize the sum of achievement test scores for the classroom, then the maximand is

$$ap_a + a\beta_a b/k + bp_b + b\beta_b b/k$$

or

$$ap_a + \beta_a b(k - b)/k + bp_b + \beta_b b^2/k$$

A couple of interesting cases come out of this setup. If the effect of the race mix is the same on blacks and nonblacks, so that $\beta_a = \beta_b = \beta$, then the expression simplifies to

$$ap_a + bp_b + \beta b$$

In this case, the number of black students in the school has a linear effect on total achievement. If we then sum across all schools, all that is relevant is the total number of black and nonblack students—their distribution across schools has no effect. So in this case the decision of how to mix different types of students matters in the small (at the level of the individual school) but not at the systems level. This point has been noted as well by other analysts of peer and neighborhood effects (Galster, Quercia, & Cortes, 2000; Jencks & Mayer, 1990).

Another possibility, made interesting by the fact that Coleman concluded that it best fit the data, is that the black concentration in a school affects black scores but not white scores. In that case, we have the total score in the school equal to

$$ap_a + bp_b + \beta_b b^2/k$$

If we sum over all schools in the system, it turns out, assuming $\beta_b < 0$ (as found by Coleman), that uniform integration is the policy that maximizes total scores.

Summary

One lesson is that an evaluation of the effects of an assignment policy for deviant youths should not be limited to the behavior of the youths in question. Also required is an assessment of the harm to all who are affected by the assignment, including the bystanders.

A slight generalization of our analysis serves as a useful summary. The harm in any one classroom is a function of the number of deviant youths in that classroom. Total harm in the system is the sum over the classrooms. Thus:

$$\text{Harm in classroom } c = H_c = H(b_c, a_c)$$

$$\text{Total harm} = \Sigma_c H_c$$

If H_c is a linear function of b_c, then total harm is determined only by the total number of Bs in the system. But under a variety of circumstances harm is decidedly not linear in b_c and the assignment does matter. We reviewed cases in which there was a limited capacity to maintain order, existence of deviant peer influence, or harm that is not proportional to bad behavior (as in the case of classroom disruption).

A full analysis would also take account of the budget impact on the relevant agencies and other mechanisms that may be relevant—especially the deterrent effect of the threat of assignment to a segregated classroom (or training school).

EMPIRICAL ISSUES

In choosing an assignment policy, it would be useful to know the outcomes for all youths in the system for each of the options under consideration. To keep things simple, suppose that only two schemes are under consideration, one that segregates deviant youth ($T = 1$) and the other that "mainstreams" such youth into classrooms with nondeviant youth ($T = 0$). In a randomized experiment in which entire school systems are randomly assigned to the segregated or integrated conditions, the net effect of the difference in assignment schemes can be estimated by regressing outcomes for each youth on an indicator for the system's treatment assignment. In the equation below, a limited number of parameters are to be estimated, allowing for different intercepts and response coefficients for nondeviant (A) and deviant (B) youths. The residual terms ε_c and ε_i represent other characteristics of classrooms and individuals, respectively, that affect the outcome; because of random assignment, the distribution of these characteristics will be balanced across treatment conditions (i.e., orthogonal to the assignment indicator T). In this equation, the variable I_i is an indicator for whether the individual is type A ($I_i = 1$) or type B ($I_i = 0$).

$$Y_i = \alpha + \beta I_i + \beta_A I_i{}^*T + \beta_B (1 - I_i)^*T + \varepsilon_c + \varepsilon_i$$

In this setup, β_A provides an estimate of the average effect on As of segregated classrooms, while β_B provides the same information for the Bs. A weighted average of these two coefficients would provide an overall estimate. The relationship between these estimates and "harm" depends on the nature of the outcome measure. Positive βs indicate segregation is harmful if the outcome measure is crime, injury, absenteeism, or smoking. If the outcome is an achievement test score, then a positive β indicates that segregation is beneficial.

In practice there may be a number of outcome measures that are deemed relevant. A complete analysis would require combining them in some fashion to produce a comprehensive measure of welfare (Nagin, 2001).

This group assignment experiment highlights conditions under which analysts could reliably compare two (or more) assignment practices. This ideal is rarely achieved in practice. Among the limitations of available research literature are inadequate measurement and uncertain interpretation.

Measurement

Often, the outcome measures are limited to one or several measures of the behavior of the target youth (usually the deviant youths). That approach is inadequate if the behavior of other youths may also be affected by the assignment. Furthermore, data on the behavior measures, even if collected for all youths, may not adequately capture the effects on welfare, as in the case of classroom disruption, bullying, and so forth.

Adding Up

A comprehensive assessment should consider the system-wide effects, although that is not standard practice. For example, a finding that the behavior of Bs tends to deteriorate in the presence of a high concentration of Bs may be presented as evidence that Bs should be integrated. But that conclusion does not necessarily follow, since it only looks at the costs of concentration and not at the possible benefits to those classrooms and students that avoid contact with Bs in a concentrated assignment.

Self-Selection

The Coleman Report discussed above provides one well-known example of estimating peer effects on youth outcomes. Coleman's estimates, like most estimates of peer effects in the literature, were based on natural variation rather than experimentally induced variation. In "nature," students in integrated classrooms are likely to differ in relevant ways from students in segregated classrooms. Coleman's analysis attempts to adjust for this problem by controlling for measures of family background and other student characteristics available to him in his data set. But those measures are far from comprehensive. Inevitably there remains a question: Why do two observationally equivalent minority students wind up in very different types of schools?

Suppose, for example, that parents who choose an integrated school for their children tend to have different attitudes toward race and education on average than those who choose a more segregated school. ("Choice" in this case may be exercised by choosing where to live or choosing between private and public schools.) If African American parents who are most committed to education are the ones who manage to navigate their child's way into an integrated setting, and parent competence and attitudes cannot be "controlled for" (because they are not measured adequately), then Coleman's analysis and similar nonexperimental estimates will confound the effects of unmeasured parent attributes with the effects of school racial composition. Put differently, the self-selection of families and youth into different educational or other social settings may compromise the internal validity of estimates for peer effects on youth outcomes, causing biased estimates.

Self-selection could also affect the external validity (generalizability) of estimates of peer effects if peer influences differ among settings. For example, suppose that in the mid-1960s, when the EEOS was collected, minority families who sent their children to integrated school settings only did so in areas where the local white population was relatively progressive and open to the idea of school desegregation. In this case the effect of racial desegregation on whites in desegregated schools may be quite different from the hypothetical effect on whites of integrating all-white schools. Introducing minority students to all-white schools may have more negative effects on the whites in those schools (and the newly introduced black students as well) than the estimates in the Coleman Report would suggest. (For more on the issue of "local average treatment effects," see Angrist, Imbens, & Rubin, 1996; Imbens & Angrist, 1994.)

Classrooms: Control or Contagion?

Even if, despite the self-selection problem, the parameter estimates are valid, there remains the question of just what can be learned from them. The parameters measuring peer context in a standard observational study do not identify the causal mechanism that is responsible for the estimated effect. Possible mechanisms include social contagion, the effects of "load" on control, and unmeasured or poorly measured aspects of the classroom environment itself (Manski, 1993). Understanding the mechanism is usually important in designing an appropriate assignment and related policies.

This discussion suggests that standard practice within the empirical literature on peer effects is unlikely to be informative about the net impact of different assignment processes within our public school or juvenile justice systems. But there is a growing experimental literature that eliminates most of the self-selection problem and is helpful in other respects as well. Here we review a small sample of such experiments.

First-Year Dormitory Assignments

Many residential colleges and universities assign some first-year students to dormitory rooms more or less at random. That assignment scheme provides a natural experiment for studying peer effects. Usually membership in social groupings is influenced in part by individual choice, which makes it difficult to distinguish the effects of the group from the characteristics of the people who tend to join that group. Random assignment eliminates that problem. In one study, randomly assigned roommates at a large midwestern university were found to influence each others drinking under some circumstances (Boisjoly et al., 2003). The effect was only found for males, and only when both roommates had been drinkers in high school—drinking in college by those who had been abstainers in high school was not affected by first-year roommate assignment. But when two drinkers were assigned to the same room, the effect (in the male dorms) was to amplify their drinking.

If the university's goal were to reduce drinking by undergraduates, then these results are sufficient to point the way. It would be advisable in making dormitory assignments to match high school abstainers with drinkers. That conclusion is strongest if drinking is primarily a Type S behavior rather than a Type D behavior. If, on the other hand, a roommate's drinking tends to negatively affect the quality of life in the dorm room (i.e., it is a Type D behavior), then the normative circumstance is more complicated. It could be argued that the abstainers should be spared the disruptive influence of a drinking roommate, even if the total prevalence of alcohol problems would be reduced by forced integration.

Baltimore Prevention Project

In the Baltimore Prevention Project, introduced above, first graders were assigned to classrooms on a random basis. Kellum and colleagues (1998) evaluated the effects on behavior of this assignment (and the application of the Good Behavior Game) years later, when the children were in sixth grade. One finding was that the initial assignment had a long-term effect on the behavior of the most aggressive boys. Those who were identified as aggressive in first grade behaved worse 5 years later if they happened (by chance) to end up in a first-grade classroom with a relatively high concentration of other aggressive boys.

Because the initial assignment was made randomly, it can be concluded with some confidence that Kellam's finding reflects a causal process involving peer effects. Perhaps the first-grade exposure to other aggressive boys exacerbated their tendencies, or perhaps the first grade provided an opportunity for the aggressive boys to find each other and become troublemaking companions thereafter.

What does this finding imply about assigning aggressive children to first-grade classrooms? Assuming we only care about their subsequent behavior, and that behavior translates into social harm in a straightforward (additive) manner, then the answer could potentially be derived from the analysis of these data. Given an estimated relationship between first-grade class composition and subsequent behavior, simulations could be run to determine the total amount of trouble associated with different hypothetical assignments. The best assignment may well be an even distribution of these boys among classes, but not necessarily—if they are sufficiently prevalent, it may be best to concentrate some of them and diffuse the rest. In any event, the "right" answer would require that the objectives be identified explicitly.

Moving to Opportunity

The best available evidence to date on the existence of "neighborhood effects" on youth outcomes derives from the U.S. Department of Housing and Urban Development's Moving to Opportunity (MTO) housing voucher experiment. MTO overcame the self-selection problem that plagued previous studies of neighborhood effects by randomly assigning families who lived in public housing who volunteered for the demonstration into different mobility treatment groups, two of which were offered housing vouchers to move to lower poverty areas and one of which—the control group—received no additional services under the program.

Short-term findings from MTO suggested that moving from high- to low-poverty neighborhoods reduces youth involvement in problem behavior and may increase achievement test scores (Goering & Feins, 2003; Katz, Kling, & Liebman, 2001; Ludwig, Duncan, & Hirschfield, 2001; Ludwig, Ladd, & Duncan, 2001). Additional years' worth of postrandomization data suggest that moving to a neighborhood with less poverty produces lasting behavioral benefits among adolescent girls but not boys (Kling, Liebman, Katz, & Sanbonmatsu, 2004; Kling, Ludwig, & Katz, 2005).

Most relevant for our purposes, MTO tells us nothing about the effects of moving youth across neighborhoods on those who reside in either the origin or destination neighborhoods of MTO participants. The harms to neighbors of Type D behavior are ignored. For that reason it is not possible to assess the net social benefit of the mobility induced by the experimental intervention. Even more problematic is projecting what would happen if housing vouchers were offered to *all* public housing families under the same terms as the MTO experimental group.

School Vouchers

As another example, consider the case of school vouchers, which, like housing vouchers, help move youths to new social settings. Much of the recent evidence comes from local randomized school voucher experiments. The first and perhaps best-known program comes from Milwaukee. While students in Milwaukee were not actually randomly assigned to "voucher" or "no voucher" groups, as in a classical randomized experiment, private schools in the program that had more applicants than slots were required to admit students on the basis of a random lottery. In this sense the Milwaukee voucher program provides a particularly credible natural experiment. The best available study of Milwaukee suggests that attending private rather than public school produces gains in math but not in reading (Rouse, 1998).

More recent voucher programs in New York City, Washington, DC, and Dayton, Ohio, use formal randomized experimental designs and yield suggestive evidence of positive private school effects, at least on some students in some grades, although the experimental designs behind these programs is undermined somewhat by low response rates to the follow-up surveys used to measure student outcomes (Howell & Peterson, 2002; Howell, Wolf, Campbell, & Peterson, 2002).[6]

In all of these school voucher experiments, the causal mechanism is not well identified. It could be that the private schools offer better instruction on average, or that the peer environment is more conducive to academic achievement. If the latter mechanism is part of the mix, then the system-wide effects of a voucher program may be quite different than the effects on those who take up the vouchers. For example, suppose that those who volunteer for these voucher experiments are among the best students in their old public schools but now are among the weakest students in their new private schools. In this case their take-up of the voucher offer leads to a reduction in average student quality in both the origin and destination schools. If individual achievement is positively influenced by the average quality of peers, then the result would be that the voucher students would benefit (by association with better students) while all others—both public and private—would lose. So once again we need a more comprehensive measure.

System-Level Studies

The case of school vouchers provides a useful example of the distinction between "mover" and "systems-level" studies. What would happen to the average achievement of all U.S. youth if our country adopted a large-scale school voucher program? Because no such system has ever been implemented in the United States, we cannot answer this question directly. But intriguing evidence on this point comes from Chile, which has offered students private school vouchers for the past two decades.

The number of new private schools that operate in Chile has increased substantially over this time, with the growth in the size of the new private sector varying considerably across metropolitan areas within Chile over time. Hsieh and Urquiola (2002) estimate the effects of this resorting program by comparing trends in average student outcomes across metropolitan areas within Chile that experienced differential growth in the local private school market.

Their "difference-in-difference" analysis suggests that Chile's school voucher program has redistributed students from public to private schools. As a result, average test scores have declined in the public schools and increased in the private schools. That pattern may in principle be the result of the concurrent effects of several mechanisms: the direct effects and peer effects of changes in the quality of the public and private student enrollees, as well as productivity changes in public and private schools. It is telling in this respect that the aggregate effect of the growth in the private school market appears to be nil—when public and private students are considered together, students in areas that had more voucher-induced movement into private schools did no better than students in areas with less movement. These results suggest that whatever gains the "switchers" enjoyed were compensated by losses to those left behind in the public schools.

The Chilean experience highlights the trade-off between mover experiments and systems-level studies. The former provide highly credible evidence on the effects of assignment policies on a subset of youth within the social system of interest, but provide limited information about systems-level effects. Studies conducted at the systems level, on the other hand, capture the overall effects of changing assignment procedures within a system. However, these systems-level studies come at the cost of losing the experimental variation that drives differences in peer settings in mover studies. In the case of Chile, the private school sector developed more rapidly in large, urban, wealthy metropolitan areas. Whether changes over time in student outcomes within smaller, rural areas of Chile provides a good control group for large wealthy areas is not clear.

Recommendations for Research

The main lesson from the analysis above is that when deviants' behavior is either influenced by social context or victimizes bystanders, a complete evaluation may require going well beyond observations on the deviants themselves. The study of first-year dormitory assignments was especially illuminating because it included information on the college drinking behavior of roommates who were "nondeviant" in that they did not drink in high school; the study may be considered deficient in that it did not include measures of disruption within the dormitory setting. An important limitation of the MTO study was that it lacked measures of the effects of those who relocated under the program on either their new neighborhoods or their old neighborhoods.

The problem, of course, is that a more comprehensive study tends to be more costly to implement. Judging whether it is worthwhile to measure contextual effects in any given evaluation project requires knowledge of when they are likely to be important. The accumulation of such knowledge should be a goal of any long-term research strategy.

NORMATIVE CONSIDERATIONS

Empirical evidence, even when reliable, is inevitably an incomplete guide to formulating assignment policies for deviant youths. Also needed is a clear statement of values. Here we offer several observations, focusing on how to take account of the possibility of deviant peer influence.

If the welfare of the deviant youths is the benchmark for judging policy, then negative effects from clustering such youths for the delivery of services are of great concern. The possibility that an intervention would actually do harm to the group that it was intended to help is not just ironic but downright scandalous. That's the power of McCord's findings concerning the summer camps for the Cambridge–Somerville Study's delinquent youths; she concludes that by concentrating such youths for an extended period, the camp experience not only did not set them straight, but actually served to reinforce their deviant propensities (McCord, 2003).

The Hippocratic stricture "First do no harm" applies in this case: physicians are to be especially sensitive to the possibility that their prescriptions will hurt rather than help their patients. While the operational significance of this stricture is not clear, it may be a useful check on the tendency to demonstrate professional know-how by offering some active remedy rather than allowing nature to take its course. Of course, even well-advised remedies may be harmful for some patients, but "evidence-based medicine" is supposed to be guided by the empirical probabilities, insisting on an expectation of benefit and the informed consent of the patient or his or her guardians.

While this standard is not irrelevant to assignment policies for deviant youths, it should be noted that the choice between mainstreaming and some form of segregation brings into play the welfare of other youths—those who would have more or less contact with the deviant youths depending on the assignment—and, of course, cost. If mainstreaming is good (on average) for the deviant youths, but harmful (on average) to the others, then the welfare of the deviants alone may be deemed an inadequate standard for making the judgment. But there is no consensus on this matter.

Indeed, since the 1970s those who favor mainstreaming children with mental and physical disabilities have had the dominant voice in school assignment policies. Public Law 94-192 guaranteed children with disabilities the right to an education in a mainstreamed setting with their peers, rather than in separate classrooms (Dodge, Kupersmidt, & Fontaine, 2000, p. 42). In the Willie M case beginning in 1979, this right was extended by a federal court to violent delinquents with mental health problems. Among the advocates' arguments are that, first, mainstreaming is in the disabled youths' interest, and, second, that their interest should be given priority over other considerations, including financial cost and classroom management problems.

Suppose that we accept the principle of a rebuttable presumption that deviant youths should be mainstreamed. The rebuttal then might take one of several forms: first, an argument that with available resources and technology, deviant youths would make better progress in a segregated setting; second, that other youths would benefit from removing certain deviant peers to segregated settings; or third, that a particular class of deviant youths did not deserve the "mainstreaming" presumption because they should be held culpable for their actions (rather than deemed "disabled"). The first two of these arguments would be based on empirical evidence.

Several observations about such arguments follow from the analysis in this chapter: Since the evidence on the consequences of alternative assignment policies for deviant youths and other youths is typically incomplete or weak, rejecting the null hypothesis (rebuttable presumption) is going to be difficult in practice. Where mainstreaming is the norm, as in public schools, the presumption will be difficult to overcome, given the difficulties of inferring causal effects from available evidence. In those cases where there is experimental evidence, it is typically incomplete. So even when the preponderance of the evidence suggests that mainstreaming would cause more harm overall than segregation, that conclusion will not be beyond reasonable doubt.

On the other hand, if there is no presumption of mainstreaming (as in public housing policy, for example, or with respect to youthful offenders who are not deemed disabled), then the preponderance of the evidence should rule, and the interests of all who are affected be taken into account. In that case the more complete analysis of harm suggested in our analysis above is relevant in principle, although still difficult in practice. A finding that concentrating deviant youths tends to facilitate negative peer influence makes a difference, but only as one of several relevant mechanisms.

The complexities introduced by uncertainty about the effects of alternative policies, and concerns about how those effects are distributed, can be illustrated by the example of a school system assignment policy that is to be guided by projected effects on an end-of-grade achievement test. The hypothetical choice is between mainstreaming a group of deviant students and concentrating them in special classrooms or in a separate school. Evidence is available on how the choice of assignment will affect achievement test scores for each group; the evidence yields probability distributions of results for deviant students, other students, and overall. Here are several of the possible decision rules, in order of increasing sensitivity to the welfare of the deviant group:

1. Choose segregation unless mainstreaming causes a higher expected achievement score for the nondeviant group. This standard might be considered if the deviant group in question were deemed to be criminals or otherwise blameworthy, and deserving of assignment to a segregated setting.
2. Choose the assignment that has the higher overall expected average achievement score (averaging deviants with others).
3. Choose mainstreaming unless reliable evidence indicates that there is at least a 95% chance that the deviant students will have higher average scores if separated. This standard is the implementation of the "rebuttable presumption" in favor of mainstreaming.
4. Choose the assignment that has the higher expected average achievement score for the deviant students, regardless of the effect on the other students.

The interplay of values and statistical reasoning presents an interesting challenge for policymakers in this case and similar cases in other domains.

ACKNOWLEDGMENTS

We thank Al Blumstein, Ken Dodge, and other members of the Executive Session for their very helpful comments. We also benefited from discussions with Allen Buchanan and Charles Clotfelter.

NOTES

1. Thanks to Al Blumstein for suggesting these examples.
2. If there are not enough B students to fill a classroom, then they should still be assigned to the same room, filling in with As.

3. While systematic dispersion of Bs is ideal, it may not be feasible. In that case it is of interest to ask whether random assignment would be better than segregation. The answer will depend on the shape of the function relating concentration to disruption.

4. A related dynamic is in reference to the informal social control exerted by a community over its miscreants. That capacity is also limited. One mechanism that may be relevant is the attenuation of norms condemning bad behavior. As such behavior becomes more common, the result may be an implicit downward shift in the cultural definition of "deviance." Daniel Patrick Moynihan popularized this idea as "defining deviance down."

5. This summary suggests that another policy margin relevant to the segregation–integration choice is classroom size. Smaller, more numerous classrooms provide an opportunity to separate deviant youths and expand control capacity. General evidence that smaller classroom size is helpful to student learning is provided, for example, by Alan Krueger in his analysis of Tennessee's experiment with reduced classroom size for students in kindergarten through third grade (Krueger, 1999).

6. If we were certain that the characteristics of nonrespondents in the voucher treatment and control groups were on average identical, then relatively low response rates would reduce the statistical bias of the analysis but not introduce bias. However, as an incentive to participate in follow-up surveys, control group families who responded to these surveys were entered into a new voucher lottery (Howell, Wolf, Campbell, & Peterson, 2002, p. 196). This raises the possibility that the voucher treatment group respondents may have been the families who were most satisfied with their voucher experiences, while the control responders consisted disproportionately of those families who were least satisfied with their public school experience. This response pattern would lead the analysis to overstate the effects of voucher receipt on achievement.

CHAPTER 5

Is Deviant Peer Influence a Problem, and What Can Be Done?

Qualitative Perspectives from Four Focus Groups

Jennifer E. Lansford
and Joel Rosch

This chapter describes a qualitative study of beliefs about deviant peer influence among practitioners, educators, and adolescents. The data come from four focus group sessions that were conducted to gain insight into the issue of deviant peer influence from the perspectives of practitioners, educators, adolescents who had been expelled from school, and adolescents in regular schools. The purpose of the discussions was to gain qualitative descriptive information from individuals who were selected because they possessed certain attributes that made them expert informants about the issue of peer influence. Because the number of participants was small and their representativeness may be questioned, the goal was not to reach definitive conclusions; rather, the goals were to check tentative conclusions that had been reached in previous quantitative studies with the real stakeholders in these processes and to generate hypotheses that could be tested in future studies.

Separate focus group discussions were conducted with four targeted groups: (1) practitioners ($n = 12$; two males; one African American, 11 European American; backgrounds in social work, social service management, and mental health); (2) educators ($n = 8$; one male; six African Americans, two European Americans; one principal, two assistant principals, five teachers; three at alternative schools); (3) adolescents expelled from public schools and attending a voluntary program for expelled youth in an alternative school ($n = 9$; six males; all African American; ages 15–18); and (4) adolescents in regular schools ($n = 10$; six males; nine African Americans, one European American; ages 13–17; eight students at public schools, two students at private schools). Each group met once for a 60- to 90-minute discussion. Discussions were guided by open-ended questions about peer influence. In particular, moderators asked whether group members perceived peer influence (both positive and negative) to be an important issue and what solutions they would recommend if they perceived negative peer influence to be a problem. The following sections describe issues that each group identified as being particularly salient to them.

PRACTITIONERS

Practitioners were well aware of the potential problem of deviant peer influence. This was no surprise to anyone, and at least one professional spoke about deviant peer influence as a well-established phenomenon among savvy professionals in his field. This group described how deviant youth can identify other deviant youth and quickly connect with each other. It was reported that at-risk students who are new to a school quickly find friends and are readily admitted to deviant groups. In contrast, they believed that it took prosocial youth longer to form connections with other prosocial youth. In their view, some youth struggle with social isolation, such that social isolation may be a greater problem for them than the potential harm from deviant peer influence. To fulfill their need for peers, deviant youth may seek any peers they can find, putting them at risk for gravitating toward other deviant youth.

Not only were the practitioners aware of the potential problem of deviant peer influence, some described specific strategies to minimize such effects in their own work with deviant youth. One strategy involved mentoring programs that pair a deviant and a nondeviant student. However, the practitioners believed that such programs benefited the nondeviant students more than they did the deviant students. Mentoring programs or buddy systems might open the eyes of the nondeviant youth to those who are less fortunate, but the practitioners generally had not witnessed positive effects on the deviant youth, perhaps in part because the deviant youth may not trust the nondeviant youth.

One practitioner who treated juvenile sex offenders said that his agency used to run more adolescent treatment groups but since becoming aware of research on the problem of negative peer effects, the agency has moved away from that approach and now uses family counseling instead. The practitioners' view was that negative peer effects are associated primarily with conduct disorder. Therefore they continue to use group therapies for some (non-conduct-disordered) youth, but they are more vigilant about avoiding aggregating youth with conduct disorders.

In a situation where aggregating deviant youth is necessary, one practitioner described staggering the timing of entry of new youth into a program so that they could establish positive group norms with some youth before others entered the program. These "experienced" youth could then "scaffold" in new members by modeling the group's established prosocial norms. The practitioner was consciously trying to minimize the risk of deviant influences. This process is similar to that used by preschool teachers in multiage Montessori programs, where establishment and maintenance of a prosocial peer group norm is crucial to the program's success.

A number of practitioners described strategies to help youth develop their own rules so that they would be more invested in them. They also guided youth to establish consequences for infractions of rules. Adult leaders could then encourage youth within a group to intervene when a peer acts out.

Most of the practitioners spoke about ways to structure groups' activities in ways to minimize deviant peer influence, such as having youth work on a specific project with a defined goal. The key to minimizing deviant peer influence seemed to be to avoid unstructured "hanging out" time when youth could engage in deviant activity or conversation and instead to take up all of their time with highly structured, productive activities. Many of the practitioners believed that the right kinds of adult leadership could counterbalance negative peer pressures, but they all were aware of those pressures.

EDUCATORS

The educators spent much of their time discussing the problem of gangs within the schools. Interestingly, the educators perceived "copycat" or "wanna be" gangs as being more problematic than real gangs because the former groups have less structure and are invested in emulating deviance. The educators' perception was that in real gangs many of the activities are run by adults who provide structure and some stability. The educators described the real gangs as having rules and leaders who can get followers to behave appropriately with just a hand signal. In their view, the challenge is to target this leadership potential in a prosocial way. The teachers were more disturbed by the unpredictability of youth in copycat or wanna-be gangs acting like they thought gang members were supposed to act.

The educators believed that peer influence works by filling a void left by parents, teachers, and other adults. They used the metaphor of nature abhorring a vacuum and believed that if prosocial influences are not in place, deviant peer influence will be more likely to occur.

The educators debated among themselves whether more support should be given to deviant youth in regular classrooms or whether deviant youth should be pulled out of regular classrooms for alternative programs using some of the same concepts discussed elsewhere in this volume (see Cook & Ludwig, Chapter 4, this volume). On the one hand, the educators found it nearly impossible to teach if some disruptive youth were not removed from the classroom. If the most deviant youth are not pulled out, all children in the classroom suffer, with the most vulnerable children at the greatest danger of becoming more deviant because of the disruptive classroom culture. For example, one teacher estimated that because of deviant students, she spent 60% of her time on discipline, leaving little time for teaching. On the other hand, the group recognized the potential for the deviant youth removed from the class to be negatively influenced if they were pulled out of regular classrooms and grouped with other deviant youth. Overall, the educators were pessimistic about the prospects of helping deviant youth no matter the setting in which they are placed and did not have clear solutions for how to remedy the problems created by deviant youth in the education system.

ADOLESCENTS

Like the educators, the adolescents who had been expelled from school and were attending an alternative program perceived peer influence as filling a void left by adults and community institutions that were not meeting their needs. However, they also emphasized that they were influenced not just by their peers but also by their parents and the media. For example, several of the youth said that their parents are in gangs and use drugs; if parents are modeling deviant behaviors, the void of positive influences leaves especially fertile ground for potential negative influences of peers. In addition, the youth mentioned specific examples of antisocial acts that they had viewed in movies and on television that they then imitated with their friends. The youth also claimed that antisocial behavior often stemmed from trying to get money.

The youth in this group described school as a place for them to relax and get away from home, attesting to the difficult circumstances they faced with their families. However, they often found school to be dangerous and unpredictable as well. This group liked being aggregated in an alternative school where they felt safe and received more individual attention. This self-selected group said all the right things about individual responsibility and wanting to do well. They also described a desire for adults to talk to them about everyday topics, not just their deviance.

In the context of the focus group discussion, the adolescents attending a regular school appeared to be acting more deviant than they really were, even though they were in a group of presumably average youth. The youth appeared to be trying to impress one another with how much experience and knowledge they had with regard to deviant behaviors. Indeed, some deviancy training appeared to be occurring (see Dishion & Dodge, Chapter 2, this volume, for an elaboration of this issue).

The experience of running this group highlighted for the group facilitators the need to be cautious even in seemingly innocuous discussions because of the potential for such discussions to alter the group members' beliefs about how common deviant behaviors actually are.

CONCLUDING THOUGHTS

The idea of deviant peer influence was not new to the practitioners, educators, and youth who participated in the focus group discussions. The practitioners, in particular, were already taking steps to try to minimize negative effects of peers within groups.

Several themes emerged across groups. All groups emphasized the desire youth have for rules and structure, the influence that gangs and lack of parental involvement can have on youth problems, and the importance of adult leadership. Overall, the focus group discussions posed the dilemmas faced by those working with deviant youth. That is, there are good reasons that deviant peers are aggregated, such as removing them from regular classrooms to enable teachers to focus more on teaching and less on discipline. Goals regarding which harms to reduce will be important considerations in shaping practices with deviant youth.

PART II

REVIEWS OF PEER EFFECTS

CHAPTER 6

Deviant Peer Group Effects in Youth Mental Health Interventions

Kenneth A. Dodge
and Michelle R. Sherrill

In spite of the fact that for over 30 years evaluators have cautioned mental health care providers about the dangers of treatments that group deviant youth (Dishion, McCord, & Poulin, 1998; Fo & O'Donnell, 1975; Gottfredson, 1987c; McCord, 1978; Slaikeu, 1973), group therapies to treat or prevent mental disorders in youth often remain the treatment of choice (or default). Group therapies have been found to be, on average, less effective than individual therapies (Weisz, Weiss, Alicke, & Koltz, 1987; Weisz, Weiss, Han, Granger, & Morton, 1995), and about one-third of all published controlled studies of interventions for delinquency, including group therapies that aggregate deviant youth, yield an adverse effect on behavioral outcomes (Lipsey, 1992; updated by Lipsey, Chapter 9, this volume). The scientific conundrum is that most studies of the effects of aggregating deviant youth in therapeutic groups, even randomized experiments, confound deviant peer aggregation with other factors such as group versus individual treatment or therapeutic philosophy, rendering a test of the specific effect of deviant peer aggregation difficult. The clinical conundrum is that, because both therapeutic and practical rationales often compel treatment in groups, any offsetting adverse effect of interacting with deviant peers in those groups may be missed, ignored, or discounted.

The purpose of this chapter is to review various group approaches in child mental health in order to understand whether (1) group treatment per se is iatrogenic (we conclude that it is not) or (2) the aggregation of disordered youth with each other in groups for treatment decreases the beneficial effects and increases the likelihood of adverse effects (we conclude that it probably does, under some circumstances). The domain of "child mental health" includes psychiatric diagnoses and behavioral outcomes of psychosocial adjustment that are altered by preventive interventions and postdiagnosis treatments that are implemented by clinical psychologists, psychiatrists, social workers, and counselors. It is noteworthy that the most common psychiatric diagnosis among children involves antisocial behaviors commonly called "externalizing problems," and the most common interventions in child mental health address antisocial behavior disorders (Coie & Dodge, 2006). Increasingly, these interventions are being implemented in diverse settings that include schools and juvenile justice placements, and so overlap occurs with other domains considered in this volume.

This review complements the systematic meta-analytic approach by Lipsey (Chapter 9, this volume) by analyzing features of deviant peer group treatments that may exacerbate problem behavior and other features that may protect against problem outcomes. We conclude that enough well-designed studies have been conducted to lead us to warn the field about the potential adverse effects of bringing together deviant youth in group therapies, under some circumstances. Furthermore, the variations in outcomes that have been identified by Lipsey seem to be systematic. These variations are affected by the characteristics of the peers with whom a child is placed, the child in treatment, the size and structure of the group, the type of therapy, and the qualifications of the therapist. We are able to make recommendations about group treatments and mental health policy from this analysis.

We begin with a brief background on group therapies and the rationale for treating youth in groups. We next review in detail four major "exemplary" studies of the effects of deviant peer group treatment. Then we synthesize the literature according to features that might moderate outcomes. Finally, we conclude with recommendations for practice and research.

THE HISTORY, RATIONALE, AND EFFECTIVENESS OF GROUP THERAPY

McCorkle (1953) was among the first to advocate group psychotherapies for young criminal offenders. His rationale was that because delinquents undoubtedly commit most of their deviant behavior with, and learn deviant attitudes and norms from, deviant peers, the deviant peer group provides a necessary context for "undoing" deviant attitudes and behaviors and "relearning" more acceptable attitudes and behaviors. His Guided Group Interaction (GGI) therapy uses free discussion in an open atmosphere guided by a leader who asks questions non-directively to help participants recognize their own problems and change their behavior. This therapy was initially hailed as a successful innovation for delinquent youth (Empey & Rabow, 1961), has been extended to school contexts for the treatment of high-risk youth by social workers (Gottfredson, 1987a), and continues to be used in schools today. Residential group homes and halfway houses were created as milieu therapy treatment contexts for delinquents either for similar therapeutic reasons (Almond, 1974) or for contexts to implement behavioral token economies (Phillips, Wolf, Fixsen, & Bailey, 1975); these models continue to function in most communities today (Leve & Chamberlain, 2005). Summer camps for behaviorally disturbed youth were once popular (Rickard & Dinoff, 1974), and now nondirective after-school programs targeted toward high-risk youth are growing (Gottfredson, Gerstenblith, Soule, Womer, & Lu, 2004).

Quite a different rationale for placing deviant youth with deviant peers in deviant contexts is to force them to realize the horrible consequences of their own behavior. In the "Scared Straight" program, which grew in popularity in the 1980s, deviant adolescent offenders are grouped together and brought to prisons, where they are exposed to inmates who tell them about the "horrors" of imprisonment. A random assignment study of California's version of this approach, called the "Squires Program at San Quentin," revealed that 12 months after the intervention 81% of the youth in the group intervention had been arrested, in contrast to just 67% of the youth in the control group (Lewis, 1983). Six other randomized trials of this program have yielded similarly dismal outcomes. Nonetheless, the governor of Illinois recently signed legislation that requires Chicago schools to use this harmful program with all high-risk youth (Sherman & Strang, 2004).

Other psychiatric disorders are often treated in groups as well. Alcoholics Anonymous has long utilized a peer group approach with addicts, and group psychotherapy is often used for girls with eating disorders (Polivy & Federoff, 1997). Social skills training groups have proliferated for children with social problems (Bierman, 2004).

The rationales for group treatment range from theoretical and strategic to practical and cost containment. The conceptual basis for group work has been explained by psychodynamic theory, behavior modification, social skills theory, and ecological theory, and groups have been implemented by all of the helping professions from psychiatrists and psychologists to counselors and social workers.

Meta-Analyses

One of the challenges in evaluating the impact of peer group interventions is to identify the appropriate counterfactual control group. Should the intervention be compared to no intervention at all, to a similar intervention administered in an individual context, or to a similar intervention administered in a group context that does not aggregate deviant youth? Meta-analyses indicate that psychotherapies administered in groups generally yield significantly less positive effects than similar therapies administered individually. Weisz and colleagues (1987) found that, relative to individually administered therapy, group-administered therapy reduced the average effect size (Cohen's δ) by 40%, from 1.04 to .62. Weisz and colleagues (1995) updated their meta-analysis a decade later and found that the reduction in effect size was 26%, from .63 to .50.

Lipsey's (Chapter 9, this volume) meta-analysis of treatments for delinquency yielded a relative (to individual treatment) decrement in effect size for group-administered prevention programs of 30% (from .10 to .07). Peer group counseling approaches to prevention were found to be 33% less effective (decrement from .12 to .08) than individual counseling approaches. Thus about one-third of the positive effects of therapy are offset by the adverse effects of therapy administered in a group context. What is not clear is whether this relative offset of positive effect is due to the aggregation of deviant youth with each other in a way that allows deviancy training or to some other factor that distinguishes individual from group treatments (e.g., different amount of therapist attention).

Ang and Hughes (2002) conducted a meta-analysis of social skills training interventions for children with conduct problems specifically contrasting all-deviant peer groups with mixed groups (including both deviant and nondeviant children) and with individual interventions. For overall outcomes immediately after treatment, they found that individual context yielded the largest average effect size (.78), followed by mixed groups (.60), and then all-deviant groups (.55). On measures of social adjustment, the all-deviant groups yielded an effect size (.41) that was about one-third less than the other contexts (.64). At follow-up (about 1 year later), the all-deviant peer group context yielded an average effect size of .30, which was one-third less than that of other contexts (.46). Thus social skills training as a therapy has been found to produce favorable effects on children, but about one-third of the possible positive effect is offset when the intervention is administered in a context consisting solely of deviant peers.

We speculate that (at least) four effects are operating: one positive effect of therapy, one dilution of this positive effect by administration in a group context, one adverse effect of interaction with deviant peers, and the sum of an array of moderating factors that could exacerbate or minimize the adverse effects of interaction with deviant peers. Each of these four effects independently contributes to the outcome:

$$\text{Total intervention outcome effect} = (T - \Gamma - I) + \Sigma\,(\mu i \,{}^{*}I)$$

where T is the therapeutic effect; Γ is the group context effect; I is the deviant peer-group effect; and μi are moderator factors.

It is plausible that, in the absence of a very strong positive effect of the intended therapy, adverse effects of deviant peer aggregation could lead to overall iatrogenic outcomes, as illustrated in Figure 6.1. This figure illustrates the hypothetical findings that the positive effects of a psychotherapy are diminished when administered in a group context and become adverse when that group consists of deviant peers. Indeed, 42% of group-administered prevention interventions and 22% of group-administered probation interventions yield adverse effects (Lipsey, Chapter 9, this volume), although individually administered interventions also sometimes yield adverse outcomes. Ang and Hughes (2002) found that seven of the 29 all-deviant group interventions (24%) yielded an adverse effect size, in contrast with none of the individual or mixed-group interventions.

A growing number of controlled experiments leads to the conclusion that therapies that aggregate deviant peers can, under some circumstances, lead to worsening of problem behavior. Four "exemplary" stud-

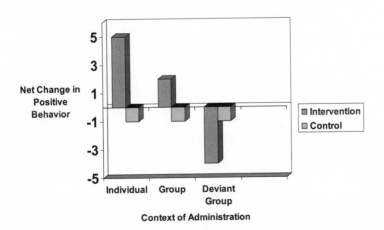

FIGURE 6.1. Model of hypothesized prototypic effects of mental health interventions.

ies are reviewed next. These studies reveal that adverse effects of deviant peer group aggregation can occur, but that their magnitude depends on circumstances (called "moderators"). We then synthesize the literature on moderators and conclude with recommendations for practice and science.

FOUR MAJOR EXPERIMENTS IN DEVIANT PEER GROUP TREATMENT

Cambridge–Somerville Youth Study

In 1939, Judge Richard Clarke Cabot began the largest and longest randomized experiment ever conducted of preventive intervention for boys at high risk for delinquency. He identified 10-year-old boys through community referrals (mostly "troublemakers," although a minority were average in behavioral adjustment but had a background risk factor), placed them into matched pairs so that each of the two boys were equivalent on a variety of characteristics, and then randomly assigned one to receive the Cambridge–Somerville intervention and one to act as a nontreated control. The intervention included a variety of friendly guidance and supportive actions, some of which aggregated the boys (e.g., after-school activities) and some of which did not (e.g., tutoring). The intervention lasted an average of 5.5 years, through World War II. Disappointingly, evaluations conducted at the end of treatment indicated that the groups did not differ in adjustment (Powers & Witmer, 1951). Court record searches soon after the intervention ended revealed that the boys assigned to treatment were slightly more likely to have had a court appearance and had been brought there for a larger number of offenses (McCord, 1978, 2003). Thirty-year follow-up reviews of archival records revealed that in adulthood, treatment boys were *more*, likely than control boys to have experienced a "bad" outcome, defined as having been convicted of serious street crimes, to have died, or to have received a diagnosis of alcoholism or a psychiatric disorder (McCord, 1978). What went wrong?

McCord (1992) has completed admirable post hoc analyses of a variety of dose–response relations to determine which aspect of the program might be responsible for the preponderance of bad outcomes in the treatment group. Her strategy was to identify treatment condition boys who had a particular kind of dose (e.g., tutoring, longer involvement) and compare them to their matched pair. Ultimately, she found that the group of 66 boys who had been sent to summer camp for two consecutive years was the only group that was much more likely to experience a bad outcome as adults than its matched controls.

This study has been cited as proof that assignment to summer camp for two consecutive years yields adverse outcomes for high-risk youth. Although it certainly warrants closer scrutiny of other similar intervention programs, this conclusion cannot be made definitively because the analyses are post hoc and have a methodological limit. Treatment group families self-selected or were selectively encouraged by staff members to attend summer camps, but their matched controls did not self-select into the subgroup of controls for this analysis. They were included simply by virtue of being paired with an intervention child. This asymmetry destroys the randomized nature of assignment to the two conditions because for this subanalysis the intervention self-selected and the control did not. Because the matched controls had no part in self-selecting summer camp, it is possible that an unmeasured pretreatment characteristic that was present in the treatment group member of these pairs (but not the matched control) caused both summer camp placement and the long-term poor outcomes.

Whether biased self-selection in this circumstance is likely or not is debatable, but the methodological limit tempers the conclusions that can be made about the effects of peer group experiences on outcomes for deviant youth in this study. The self-selection problem in subgroup analysis is similar to the methodological problem inherent in propensity score analysis and instrumental variables analysis (Imbens, 2003) and in any analysis that relies on a self-selected subgroup. The virtues of randomized assignment get lost. These method problems do not detract from the importance of scientific data; rather, they increase the importance of truly randomized experiments.

School Action Effectiveness Study of Guided Group Interaction Therapy

Although the Cambridge–Somerville Youth Study raised alarms about the danger of placing high-risk youth in groups where they might become even more deviant, a definitive conclusion was eluded. During the mid-1980s, around the time that U.S. Secretary of Education Bill Bennett called them the worst and most dangerous schools in the nation, the Chicago public schools participated in a randomized experiment of a modification of the highly acclaimed GGI therapy, called Peer Culture Development (PCD; Gottfredson, 1987a). This delinquency prevention peer group intervention assembled 360 school children into groups on a daily basis for 15 or 30 weeks, during which they confronted problem behaviors and discussed them in a nondirective manner. Each group was composed of a majority of youths experiencing behavior problems as well as a minority of those not experiencing such problems. The focus was delinquency prevention. This study offered an opportunity to test impact on the high-risk youth as well as the non-high-risk youth. At the end of the year, outcomes were measured by self-report and archival school records.

Among high schoolers, significant adverse effects of assignment to the peer group intervention were found for self-reported delinquency, drug use, and attachment to parents, and school records for tardiness. Police contacts were more frequent for intervention youth than for control youth, but not significantly so. These effects were found for both the high-risk and the non-high-risk youth. No adverse effects (and no positive effects) were found for the elementary school groups.

Although proponents of nondirective peer group interventions for deviant youth responded by suggesting that the intervention still had worthy components but simply needed "tweaking," Gottfredson (1987a) concluded that "in contemplating future field trials . . . it may be useful to seek ways to avoid delinquent peer interaction entirely rather than to attempt to modify its nature" (p. 710).

This peer group intervention was rigorously evaluated and found to cause adverse effects on its high school participants, relative to not administering the intervention at all. Whether the deviant peer group aggregation aspect of the intervention was responsible for the adverse effects was not clear. Perhaps any intervention that focused on peer interaction, even without actual contact with deviant peers, could be harmful.

Adolescent Transitions Program Study

Dishion came a step closer to a rigorous test of the deviant peer group hypothesis. He created a peer group intervention to prevent substance use that employed cognitive-behavioral techniques to regulate behavior. The intervention targeted skills development in self-monitoring, goal setting, problem solving, and limit setting, and it aggregated high-risk youth with six or seven deviant peers. Dishion randomly assigned 158 11- to 14-year-old high-risk boys and girls to receive his peer group intervention, a parent group intervention, both, or neither. The design included two contrast groups for the peer group intervention: one was a self-directed change condition, in which participants received all curricular materials but were directed to view and learn them on their own. The other was a condition in which the child's parents received training in monitoring and management but the children were never seen. His method included true randomization, high fidelity, and low attrition.

Dishion and Andrews (1995) reported that the immediate goals of the peer group intervention were met: youth in these two conditions acquired the skills that were being taught and lowered their family conflict. However, within 1 year, teacher report of conduct problems and self-report of tobacco use were significantly higher for youth who had been assigned to one of the two peer group intervention conditions than to either of the other two conditions. Benefits of learning the prescribed curriculum in the peer group intervention condition and even the benefits of the parent training in the combined condition were undermined by some process occurring when deviant peers were brought together. These findings were not a fluke. The effects persisted in the 2-year follow-up and again in the 3-year follow-up, using reports by teachers who had no knowledge of the original intervention (Dishion, McCord, & Poulin, 1999; Poulin, Dishion, & Burraston, 2001). Furthermore, the iatrogenic effects were most severe for youth who began the intervention with modest levels of delinquency. That is, the iatrogenic process did not add to negative outcomes for the already highly deviant youth but catalyzed antisocial development among the initially moderately deviant youth.

This study sharpened the concern about interventions that bring together deviant peers to discuss social behavior. Such an intervention produced strikingly adverse outcomes compared to a self-directed change intervention that delivered similar content but without any peer group interaction. Furthermore, the adverse effects undermined the otherwise positive effects of parent training. But what is still unclear is whether it was the placement with other *deviant*, peers that was iatrogenic or merely placement with any peers.

St. Louis Experiment

We now go back in time to an extremely important study. In 1970, Feldman (1992), a social work professor at Washington University, wanted to test whether any peer group intervention, or more narrowly one that aggregates deviant youth only, alters youth development. He randomly assigned 263 early adolescent high-risk boys and 438 low-risk boys to a 24-session peer group intervention administered through local community centers. The high-risk boys were referred by social service agencies, juvenile courts, and mental health centers and met criteria for high deviance. Low-risk boys were volunteers. The boys were assigned to one of three kinds of 10- to 15-person groups, populated by high-risk-only boys, low-risk-only boys, or mixed groups (which included one or two high-risk boys, with the rest being low-risk boys). The last of these three conditions is critical because the high-risk boys here were exposed to all of the therapeutic content but in a context where they interacted only or predominantly with well-functioning peers. Another asset of this design was the opportunity to study effects on well-functioning peers:

one worry of policymakers is that interventions to maximize help for high-risk youth might bring a cost to low-risk youth.

Feldman's experimental design cleverly included two other randomized factors: (1) group leaders were either experienced or inexperienced at leading groups; and (2) the theory guiding the therapeutic intervention varied as traditional, behavioral, or minimal. The "traditional social work" intervention group was based on the practices developed by Vintner (1967) and the GGI movement of nondirective insight and group dynamics focused on problem behaviors. The behavioral groups were highly structured attempts to apply group contingencies and systematic reinforcement for group, rather than individual, behavior. The minimal treatment condition brought the youth together but without any structure, goals, or therapeutic tasks. Outcomes were assessed by direct observation, self-report, and therapist ratings.

Direct observations of behavior during each boy's first and last group sessions revealed a striking set of findings. High-risk boys assigned to all-deviant peer groups nonsignificantly increased their rate of directly observed antisocial behavior from 5.4% to 5.7% of all behaviors, whereas high-risk boys assigned to groups with nondeviant peers significantly decreased their antisocial behavior rate from 5.4% to 3.2% of all behaviors ($p < .01$). Youth self-reports before and after treatment revealed that high-risk boys assigned to all-deviant peer groups reported a highly significant *exacerbation*, of antisocial acts, from 57.5 acts per week to 126.6 acts per week ($p < .001$). In contrast, high-risk boys assigned to groups with nondeviant peers reported a slight improvement from 57.5 antisocial acts per week before treatment to 46.6 antisocial acts per week after treatment, an overall pattern that was significantly better than that for high-risk boys in deviant peer groups ($p < .01$). Therapist reports of changes in behavior also support a main effect of peer group composition. This study provides rigorous support that intervention peer group membership can affect a high-risk boy's outcomes.

Several significant interaction effects suggest ways to minimize the iatrogenic impact on high-risk boys if they must be assembled in all-deviant peer groups. The first was an interaction between peer group composition and therapist experience. During group sessions, in mixed-peer groups, both experienced and inexperienced therapists were able to achieve favorable outcomes. However, in all-deviant peer groups, high-risk boys who had been placed with inexperienced therapists became increasingly antisocial over time and fared the most poorly, whereas experienced therapists were able to keep high-risk boys from becoming more antisocial. This beneficial dampening effect of an experienced therapist extended to observers' coding of disruptive behavior and therapists' reports of outcomes but not to youth self-reports.

Second, the theoretical basis for the treatment had a large impact in tempering the adverse effect of all-deviant peer groups. In both traditional and minimal interventions, high-risk youth in all-deviant peer groups displayed worse behavior problems than did high-risk youth in mixed groups. In contrast, high-risk youth in the behavioral intervention condition showed a reduction in antisocial behavior and fared as well in all-deviant peer groups as they did in mixed groups, based on most measures. The authors concluded that the high degree of structure in the behavioral groups dampened any deviant peer contagion effect.

Finally, Feldman addressed the impact on the low-risk youth. The low-risk youth were not adversely affected by association with one high-risk youth in a group of eight (vs. interaction with only other low-risk youth). Generally, these low-risk youth changed little across time. Thus a mixed group of one high-risk boy and seven low-risk boys appears to retain a cultural norm of prosocial behavior and to yield a positive effect on the high-risk boy without any negative impact on the other boys.

These findings point to the conclusion that high-risk early adolescent boys can be adversely affected by being placed in a therapy group with other high-risk boys, but that these iatrogenic outcomes can be averted by placing the high-risk boy in a group with all nondeviant peers and can be minimized by increasing the experience of the therapist and by using highly structured behavioral methods.

Additional Findings in the Disruptive Behavior Disorders

Numerous other studies (listed in Table 6.1) have yielded less positive or adverse effects of deviant peer group aggregation, albeit with ambiguity about the precise potent factor. Shelton and colleagues (2000) tested a classroom intervention for children identified to be highly at risk for oppositional defiance disorder (ODD) and attention-deficit/hyperactivity disorder (ADHD). They designed special kindergarten classrooms where treatment group participants received training in social skills and self-control. Compared to the control group participants, who attended kindergarten in regular classes, treatment participants were 17.3% more likely to develop ADHD and 12.5% more likely to develop ODD (Shelton et al., 2000).

Two randomized trials have examined the efficacy of multidimensional treatment foster care (MTFC) for high-risk youth, which is also reviewed in other chapters. MTFC is an individual foster family alternative to group home care for delinquent youth. A focus of MTFC is on close monitoring and supervision by trained foster parents so that the adolescent is not allowed to interact with deviant peers. In the first trial, MTFC boys had significantly lower rates of official and self-reported delinquency at the 12-month follow-up and lower rates of violent offend-

TABLE 6.1. Randomized Control Trial Studies Yielding Adverse Effects of Deviant Peer Group Aggregation on Youth Mental Health

Source	Outcome	Age	Nature of intervention	Who is in it?	Leader-to-student ratio	Negative effect of treatment
Prevention programs						
Berger et al. (1975)	Court records	Adolescents	Control: Ordinary court services Treatment: Group counseling, tutoring	Delinquents	Main effect	
Boxer et al. (2005)	Behavior problems	Grade 3 Grade 6	Control: Classroom only Treatment: Added small groups	At risk	1:5	Process effect More negative effect for those in groups with more aggressive peers
Catterall (1987)	High school dropout	Grades 10–12	Control: Wait-list Treatment: Residential camp	High risk	6:100	Main effect
Feldman et al. (1983)	Behavior problems	Grades 7–9	Mixed-risk, high-risk or low-risk groups	Mixed risk	1:10–15	Main effect
Fo & O'Donnell (1975)	Behavior problems	10–17 years	Control: No intervention Treatment: Buddy system intervention	High risk	1:1	Mixed

Study	Outcome	Age/Grade	Condition	Risk	Ratio	Effect
Gottfredson (1987a)	Delinquent behavior	Grades 9–12	Control: No intervention Treatment: Peer culture development	Mixed risk		Main effect
Gottfredson et al. (2004)	Behavior problems Substance use	Grades 4–5 Grades 6–8 Grades 4–5 Grades 6–8	Afterschool programs	Any	22–45 students	Partial effect More positive effect for older children when addressing substance use
Lavallee et al. (2005)	Aggressive behavior	Grade 1	Control: Standard classroom Treatment: Social skills group	High risk	2:3–7	Process effect Less positive effect for those with less engagement in group sessions
Mann et al. (1997)	Eating disorders	College freshmen	Control: No intervention Treatment: Discussion groups	Any	2:10–20	Main effect
McCord (1978)	Alcoholism Mental illness		Control: No intervention Treatment: Youth study intervention	At risk		Main effect
McCord (1992)	Behavior disorders	Mean age of 10.5	Control: No intervention Treatment: Summer camp	At risk		Main effect
Palinkas et al. (1996)	Substance use	14–19 years	Control: Educational curriculum	High risk	1:8–12	Main effect

(continued)

Treatment: Added skills training

TABLE 6.1. (continued)

Source	Outcome	Age	Nature of intervention	Who is in it?	Leader-to-student ratio	Negative effect of treatment
Petrosino et al. (2000)	Delinquency	Teenagers	Nine Scared Straight programs	Very high risk		Main effect
Poulin et al. (2001); Dishion & Andrews (1995)	Behavior disorders	Grades 7–8	Control: No intervention Treatment: Teen focus groups	At risk	1:7–8	Main effect Moderated effect More negative results for higher risk children
Trembley et al. (1995); Vitaro et al. (1999a)	Behavior disorders	Kindergarten	Design: Mixed groups	At risk	1:4–7	Moderated effect Negative effect of friends' aggressiveness for higher risk participants
Classroom-based programs						
Cavell & Hughes (2000)	Aggressive beliefs	Grade 3–4	Control: Standard classroom Treatment: Social skill groups	High risk	1:2–5	Main effect

110

Study	Target	Grade	Control/Treatment	Risk		Effect
Cho et al. (2005)	Substance	Grades 9–11	Control: No intervention Treatment: Reconnecting youth	High risk		Moderated effect More negative effect for less at-risk site; Positive effect at higher risk site
Donaldson et al. (1995)	Substance use	Grades 5 and 7	Control: Information only Treatment: Refusal skills training	Mixed risk	Moderated effect	Moderated effect Less positive results for lower risk participants
Ellickson et al. (1993)	Smoking	Grades 7–8	Control: No intervention Treatment: Project ALERT	Mixed risk		Moderated effect Negative effect only for higher risk participants
Gottfredson (1987c)	Delinquent behavior	High school	Control: Standard classrooms Treatment: Peer culture development groups	High risk		Main effect
Hanish et al. (2005)	Behavior disorders	Pre-K–K		Low risk	1:3–5	Main effect
Hawthorne (2001)	Substance use	Grade 6	Control: No life education Treatment: Life education curriculum	Mixed risk		Main effect

(continued)

111

TABLE 6.1. (*continued*)

Source	Outcome	Age	Nature of intervention	Who is in it?	Leader-to-student ratio	Negative effect of treatment
Shelton et al. (2000)	Behavior disorders	Kindergarten	Control: Standard classrooms Treatment: Special classrooms	High risk	2:14–16	Main effect
Warren et al. (2005)	Behavior disorders	Grades 1–4				Negative
Inpatient and residential programs						
Duncan et al. (2005)	Alcohol overuse	College freshmen	Random roommate assignment	Any		Moderated effect Negative effect only for at-risk males
Leve & Chamberlain (2005)	Behavior disorders	Middle and high schoolers	Control: Group home Treatment: Foster home	At risk		Negative

ing at the 24-month follow-up than did group care youth (Chamberlain & Reid, 1998; Eddy, Whaley, & Chamberlain, 2004). A second randomized trial with girls generally paralleled the boys' trial, with MTFC girls spending fewer days in locked settings, having fewer adult-reported delinquent behaviors, and showing a trend toward fewer arrests at the 12-month follow-up (Leve & Chamberlain, 2004).

Catterall (1987) reported a school dropout prevention study that yielded nonsignificant adverse effects. One hundred high schoolers at risk for dropping out were sent to a 4-day residential program designed to target their low academic performance and negative social relationships. Although the difference was not statistically significant, the later school dropout rate for treatment participants was 17% compared to 13.5% in the control group (Catterall, 1987).

Findings in Substance Use

In addition to Poulin and colleagues' (2001) findings about increased tobacco use among deviant peers grouped together, reported above, Palinkas, Atkins, Miller, and Ferreira (1996) reported iatrogenic effects that occurred after a substance use prevention intervention. In their study, control participants received a routine educational curriculum. Treatment participants both received the curriculum and attended social skills training discussion groups. All participants were females considered to be at high risk for substance use. After 3 months, those girls randomly assigned to the treatment group were more likely to use alcohol, marijuana, and tobacco (Palinkas et al., 1996).

A quasi-experimental study of a non-mental health intervention with college roommate assignment also suggests that iatrogenic effects on alcohol use may occur when deviant peers are grouped together. Duncan, Boisjoly, Kremer, Levy, and Eccles (2005) found that increases in binge drinking occurred for freshman males who had been randomly assigned a roommate who had been a drinker in high school, but only if the male had also been a high school drinker. This finding demonstrates the synergy of deviant peer aggregation: only when a high-risk male was grouped with another high-risk male did the negative behavior increase.

Eating Disorders

Mann, Nolen-Hoeksema, Burgard, Wright, and Hanson (1997) used random assignment to test an intervention to prevent disordered eating among college females. The intervention consisted of attending a special discussion group where guest speakers talked about the symptoms of eating disorders, explained how to get help, and told their own personal recovery stories. After 3 months, females assigned to the no-intervention control group reported a slight decrease in eating disorder symptoms ($M = -.08$), whereas females assigned to the group intervention reported an increase in these symptoms ($M = .24$), a significant iatrogenic effect. Intervention participants were more likely than controls to report bingeing, vomiting, laxative use, and both bulimic and anorexic symptoms. Although the participants in this study were not initially deviant or disordered, the assembly of college females in a group to hear a new female who had an eating disorder apparently led to the increase in eating disorder symptoms.

STUDIES OF THE PROCESS OF CHANGE

Supporting the hypothesis that aggregation with deviant peers is a component of intervention that can exacerbate a deviant youth's behavior problems are analyses of the mediation of intervention effects. Although such analyses rely on correlational data within experiments, they provide theoretically plausible explanations for how exposure to deviant peer groups might lead to negative effects. Leve and Chamberlain (2005) used structural equation modeling to conclude that their effect of treatment foster care on reduction of antisocial outcomes could be statistically accounted for by intervening effects on foster parents' success in reducing the youth's time spent with delinquent peer groups.

Cavell and Hughes (2000) found that their social skill training intervention, delivered in a deviant peer group context, had negative effects on antisocial behavior outcomes, and that these effects were mediated by the children's development of more favorable attitudes toward aggressive behavior, attitudes that grew in the deviant peer group intervention context. In their study, children who had been randomly assigned to a peer group intervention displayed more favorable attitudes toward displaying aggressive behavior, as measured by private survey responses, following intervention than did control group children. In turn, this effect of intervention on these attitudes statistically accounted for the intervention effect on exacerbating children's antisocial behavior. Thus the findings are consistent with the hypothesis that aggregating deviant youth leads them to develop more favorable attitudes about aggression, which leads to enhanced antisocial outcomes.

FACTORS THAT ALTER THE IATROGENIC EFFECT

Some programs that group deviant youth together have been effective at reducing the targeted problem behavior (e.g., Mager, Milich, Harris, &

Howard, 2005), whereas other programs actually report increases in problem behavior compared to control groups (e.g., Mann et al., 1997; Poulin et al., 2001), and still others report no effects of the treatment (e.g., Gottfredson et al., 2004). Some of this apparent inconsistency may be attributed to the fact that youth who are assigned to the "control" group experience a variety of treatments that are not thoroughly reported in published articles. Understanding the characteristics of interventions that moderate their impact is the challenge of this review. In the following sections, we synthesize this literature.

Ratio of Deviant to Nondeviant Youth

One important characteristic appears to be the ratio of deviant to nondeviant youth in the intervention group. *Our review of the literature suggests that there is a nonlinear effect of group membership.*

Interventions with deviant youth that have been found to be effective usually include one or very few deviant members. Trembley, Pagani-Kurtz, Masse, Vitaro, and Pihl (1995) and Vitaro, Brendgen, Pagani, Tremblay, and McDuff (1999) tested an intervention that aimed to prevent behavior problems in high-risk male kindergarteners. Participants were screened for risk and participated in social skills training groups. A trained professional led these groups, consisting of three or four prosocial and one or two target members. A positive long-term effect of the treatment was found such that treatment participants reported engaging in fewer delinquent acts and their teachers reported that they engaged in less disruptive behavior (Trembley et al., 1995).

Lavallee, Bierman, Nix, and the Conduct Problems Prevention Research Group (2005) randomly assigned high-risk first graders to intervention or not, and then randomly grouped high-risk children with each other for social skills training groups. They found that, even though the overall effect of assignment to the intervention was positive relative to assignment to the control condition, random assignment to a group with a high ratio of highly aggressive peers was associated with greater group disruption than assignment to a group with less aggressive peers; the deviant peer influence effect operated, but within a context of an overall net positive effect.

Boxer, Guerra, Huesmann, and Morales (2005) also randomly assigned high-risk youth to intervention groups and found that children were influenced by the relative level of aggression of the peers in their groups. Children who had been randomly assigned to a group with more highly aggressive peers became more highly aggressive themselves, whereas children who had been randomly assigned to a group with less aggressive peers became less aggressive themselves, a phenomenon that the authors called the "discrepancy-proportional peer-influence" effect.

On the other hand, Mager and colleagues (2005) used a group intervention to prevent behavior problems with early adolescents in mixed versus all-deviant groups. The positive effects of intervention were stronger for participants who were in all-deviant groups consisting of all target children than for those in mixed groups (Mager et al., 2005). Their report provides evidence that personal involvement in the intervention predicted the effectiveness of the intervention. Deviant group members participated more often in group activities when they were in all-deviant groups than when they were combined with lower risk peers (Mager et al., 2005).

An additional concern of researchers is the potential deleterious effect on the lower risk participants who may be aggregated with higher risk peers during mental health interventions. Feldman, Caplinger, and Wodarski (1983) randomly assigned low-risk youth to groups with one or no deviant peers and found no adverse effects on the low-risk youth of being assigned to a group with one deviant peer. However, it is plausible that a nonlinear effect (a tipping point) also operates with low-risk youth, such that once the ratio of deviant to nondeviant youth exceeds a controllable level the low-risk youth become adversely affected. Some evidence suggests that this may be a valid concern.

Severity of Deviance of the Youth

A second important characteristic is the initial severity of deviance of the affected youth. Arnold and Hughes (1999) suggested that youth who are at risk but without a history of serious antisocial behavior may be more likely to be influenced by placement with more deviant peers. Indeed, both Lavallee and colleagues (2005) and Boxer and colleagues (2005), as described in the previous section, found that initially moderately aggressive children are likely to become more aggressive when placed in a group with highly aggressive peers; in contrast, highly aggressive children are not adversely affected when placed with moderately aggressive peers. At the deviant extreme, some youth may be so far along a trajectory of deviant development that peer group exposure is not a significant additional risk process in their development. At the low extreme of severity of deviance, findings by Feldman and colleagues (1983) indicate that well-adjusted, nonaggressive youth are relatively immune to the adverse effects of being placed with a deviant peer, with the caveat that the number of deviant peers and the length and amount of deviant peer exposure remain modest.

In a follow-up analysis of the intervention reported by Tremblay and colleagues (1995), Vitaro, Brendgan, and Trembley (2000) divided the high-risk participant boys according to teacher ratings of their disruptiveness at ages 11–12. When the impact of associating with aggressive-disruptive friends was analyzed in terms of the boys' prior history of conduct problems, Vitaro and colleagues found that it was the moderately disruptive boys whose delinquent activity at age 13 showed the negative consequences of deviant friends' influence, in contrast to highly disruptive or lower risk socially conforming boys.

Following Caprara and Zimbardo (1996), we hypothesize that it is the marginally deviant youth who are most susceptible to the influence of deviant peers and are damaged most by placement in highly deviant peer settings. By definition, these youth have begun to try out a behavior pattern of deviance, but their intermittent displays and wavering indicate that they are not yet committed to a life of deviance, nor to a life of social conformity. According to the theory of marginal deviation (Caprara et al., 2005), the path from marginal deviance to permanent deviance follows the self-fulfilling prophecy, with social-perceptual processes operating in the youth, their peers, and outside observers.

Age

Although some research has investigated the effects of aggregation of peers at two age levels (e.g., Boxer et al., 2005; Gottfredson et al., 2004), it is difficult to make conclusions about how age may moderate iatrogenic effects in group interventions. One hypothesis is that the moderating effect of age is curvilinear, such that children are particularly susceptible to deviant peer group influences during their early adolescent years and less sensitive to those influences at younger and older ages. The rationale for this hypothesis grows from knowledge in social development that early adolescence is an era of life when peers are highly salient and the notion of "deviance" is particularly attractive (Cillessen & Mayeaux, 2004). Evidence by Poulin and Dishion (2002) indicates that the relation between deviance and peer social status changes in early adolescence, when aggression and deviant behavior become less negatively associated with social preference than in earlier age groups. In a longitudinal study of the same boys across time, Pope, Bierman, and Mumma (1989) found that aggressive behavior predicted negative sociometric nominations when the boys were in elementary school but not in middle school. Several studies have found that in adolescence, aggressive behavior is actually positively correlated with high peer status (Mayeux, Bellmore, & Kaplan, 2002; Rodkin, Farmer, Pearl, & Van Acker, 2000; Rose, Lockerd, & Swenson, 2001).

Unfortunately, the evidence that iatrogenic effects are moderated according to this curvilinear hypothesis is inconclusive. Negative effects of participation in a deviant peer group have been found at every age level from prekindergarten (e.g., Lavallee et al., 2005; Shelton et al., 2000) to college (Duncan et al., 2005; Mann et al., 1997).

Additionally, research examining interventions with children at different age levels does not provide evidence of age-related differences in susceptibility to peer influence. Gottfredson and colleagues (2004) reviewed after-school programs for their success in preventing substance use and delinquency. Although they found that the after-school programs did not prevent delinquency in either grades four and five or grades six through eight, they did find that the programs prevented substance use for participants who were in grades six through eight. Additionally, Boxer and colleagues (2005) found similar results of peer aggregation for children in grade six as for children in grade three. Children in each grade were equally and adversely affected by aggressive peers.

It is difficult to make a conclusive statement about the effect of age given that age is confounded with the type of behavior addressed in interventions. Interventions with younger children tend to focus on problem behaviors. As children age, the relevant interventions become more focused on delinquency and substance use. Older children, such as those in high school and college, are more likely to experience interventions on substance use, alcohol overuse, or eating disorders.

Type of Behavior

Not all deviant behaviors are equally susceptible to deviant peer influence effects. Effects appear to be more likely for behaviors that are normally acquired through peer influence processes and less likely for behaviors that are acquired through other processes, such as biological risk or early trauma. Delinquent behaviors more frequently yield a deviant peer contagion effect than does reactive anger. Substance use more frequently yields the effect than does major depression. A surprising effect has been demonstrated with eating disorder symptoms (e.g., bingeing following by purging, anorexic eating habits), which had not been described in the literature as being acquired directly through peer influences. Perhaps the influence of peers on eating disorders is more direct than previously considered, operating through an adolescent's perception about the frequency of such behaviors among peers and the value of those behaviors and their outcomes.

Individual Susceptibility

Botvin (1985) introduced the concept of resistance efficacy to describe individual differences in susceptibility to peer influence that may explain moderation effects in intervention studies. The problems that he addressed were the intervention goal to increase such efficacy and the variation in impact of preventive intervention across different adolescents, but it can be applied here as well. It is possible that a personality characteristic of "susceptibility to peer influence" renders one adolescent more likely to be affected by placement with a group of deviant peers than another adolescent. No studies have tested this notion, so it remains just a hypothesis at this time.

Sometimes so-called personality characteristics that are introduced to explain individual variation in behavior merely describe the variation rather than produce any additional understanding. More helpful in this context than a description of individual variation in susceptibility would be empirically supported factors in a child's background or current context that moderate his or her likelihood of resisting deviant peer contagion. Although no direct tests have been completed, several candidate factors should be examined in future studies. For example, friendships and social acceptance in the mainstream group provide security to a peer-oriented youth (Bierman, 2004) that may protect that child from the temptations of deviant peer groups.

Structure of the Group

Feldman and colleagues (1983) found that when deviant adolescents participated in unstructured groups that were devoted to free-flowing discussion without judgment or in groups that had little therapeutic mission other than "free time," the effects on the youth were more adverse than when the group had a behavioral orientation with clear rules for reinforcement of appropriate behavior. Given theories of how deviancy training occurs during unfettered peer conversation, it is reasonable to assert that a high degree of structure can mitigate the adverse effects of aggregating deviant youth.

Expertise of the Leader

Just as effective in the Feldman and colleagues (1983) study was the expertise of the group leader in maintaining control of the group. That is, youth who had been randomly assigned a group leader with relatively more experience were buffered from the adverse effects of being aggregated with deviant peers.

Fidelity of Intervention Implementation

Many intervention program developers are aware of the potential for deviancy training in peer groups and therefore integrate components that are designed to minimize opportunities for deviant peer contagion, such as a high degree of structure and behavioral contingencies for misbehavior. Because these components are usually not the primary focus of the intervention, which, instead, is designed to address a specific psychopathology, they receive lower priority and may get lost when the intervention program is disseminated. Reviews of the literature (Weisz, 2004; Weisz & Jensen, 2001) indicate that interventions that are administered in the community as part of "usual care" often are not very effective at all. Cho, Hallfors, and Sanchez (2005) suggest that one contributing factor in the decline of effectiveness when programs are disseminated into the community may be the lack of adherence to intervention features that are specifically designed to minimize deviancy training. Thus lack of fidelity to the prescribed intervention plan may contribute to iatrogenic effects.

CONCLUSIONS AND RECOMMENDATIONS

The findings reviewed here lead to the conclusion that mental health interventions for deviant youth are more likely to be effective when administered individually rather than when the youth is aggregated with other deviant youth. Individual interventions could include family members, and, indeed, family-based interventions administered to individual families have proven highly effective (Dishion & Stormshak, in press). When cost or practical constraints force the intervention to be administered in a group context, the effect is likely to be diluted by about one-third. If the other members of the group are all deviant, the effects are likely to be diluted even further and, under some circumstances, can even become adverse; this latter is called an "iatrogenic deviant peer contagion effect."

Characteristics of the child, the peer group, the broader peer culture, and the leader can alter the impact of group interventions. Children who are most susceptible to deviant peer contagion effects are likely to be those who have begun deviant behavior but are not yet fully committed to a deviant way of life. Peer groups that foster adverse effects are those populated by a preponderance of youth who are slightly more deviant than a particular youth in question. Deviant peer influence effects are most likely in cultural contexts in which deviance is seen as exciting, novel-but-possible, and valued for its sensational impact. Deviant peer influence effects can be mitigated by leaders who have the expertise to know how to impose a high degree of structure and control and who administer the intervention with high fidelity.

These findings lead to the conclusion that mental health interventions that can be administered in individual contexts should be so administered. School counselors should avoid all-deviant groups for nondirective counseling. Therapists should attempt to find ways to intervene with individual youth and their families. If a group context is necessary, it should be constituted so that the within-group culture remains one of endorsement of prosocial values. Ways to increase the probability that a prosocial culture can be fostered include populating the group with a majority of well-adjusted youth, imposing a high degree of structure that does not allow deviancy training to occur, employing a high ratio of leaders to youth, and employing leaders who have sufficient expertise to maintain control over group behavior. Given the possibility that adverse effects can occur merely through "virtual" aggregation by labeling a youth as a member of a deviant group even without actual contact with deviant peers, these methods might not guarantee that adverse effects are avoided. However, they improve the probability.

Public policies should be shaped to attend to the possibility of iatrogenic effects. Programs should be required to report how groups are constituted, the characteristics of all members and leaders, and the outcomes of each member across time. Outcomes should be reported not only by average effects but also by the distribution of effects, including the proportion of youth who display adverse outcomes. Because the only way to be confident that these outcomes accrue through the intervention, appropriate control groups are essential features of good intervention programming, even in contexts for which research is not a primary motive.

CHAPTER 7

Deviant Peer Effects
in Education

Wendy M. Reinke
and Hill M. Walker

School reform, student safety, and achievement accountability pressures have transformed the nature of schooling. Strong incentives exist in today's schools to improve schooling outcomes by raising academic expectations, using high-stakes testing tied to rewards and punishments for schools, and dealing with marginalized students through control, containment, and exclusion strategies. Zero tolerance policies to enhance school safety, combined with grade retention practices to cope with pervasive academic failure, are resulting in large numbers of marginalized students who are assigned to socially restrictive settings and who often leave school early. When they do, their risk status for such outcomes as delinquency, gang membership, and drug use escalates substantially. Additional incentives that drive these school-based practices are (1) the creation of more homogeneous classroom and school cultures in order to make them easier to manage, (2) the protection and support of students who adhere to the normative school culture, and (3) the management of school resources and costs.

Within this schooling context, students are subjected to aggregation practices that can include academic-tracking/ability-grouping systems, use of resource and self-contained classrooms for special education students, and assignment of disruptive, aggressive students who are chronic disciplinary problems to alternative school settings. These practices serve the school's need for convenience and efficiency by reducing the accommodation demands on teachers associated with individualizing instruction; as a means of neutralizing the impact of disruptive, challenging students on the classroom's ecology; and through facilitating group instructional processes. However, the benefits that accrue to the students, particularly those grouped with peers exhibiting deviant behaviors, have not been clearly documented. Furthermore, other than discussions of the potential stigmata and exclusion issues associated with these common aggregation practices, there has been little treatment in the educational literature of the possible harmful effects on students of schools' broad-based investment in these procedures. The deleterious effects of aggregating peers are discussed throughout this volume. Association with deviant peers is a strong predictor of multiple youth problem behaviors, including academic failure, delinquency, substance use, and antisocial behavior. Thus the routine use of aggregation practices that congregate deviant and at-risk students may carry substantial levels of risk for destructive outcomes of the type that have been empirically demonstrated in the psychological literature on deviant peer influence (Dishion, McCord, & Poulin, 1999).

The school setting, by its very nature, provides many opportunities for naturally occurring aggregation of deviant at-risk peers. This is particularly true of disorderly classroom settings and low-traffic, poorly supervised areas of the school such as the playground, the lunchroom, restrooms, and locker rooms where peer-based abuse, intimidation, and physical victimization are most likely to occur. Bullying, mean-spirited teasing, and peer harassment are salient examples of destructive social outcomes resulting from this kind of natural peer aggregation that school staffs and parents have great difficulty in controlling (Espalage & Swearer, 2003). Schools also serve as a staging area for recruitment into deviant peer networks and cliques, such as gangs, youth drug cultures, and formal deviant peer groups whose members commit delinquent acts during nonschool hours (Reid, Patterson, & Snyder, 2002).

This chapter reviews the phenomenon of deviant peer influence (DPI) within school settings and addresses current educational policies and practices that contribute to the aggregation of deviant peers. It also provides a guide to principles that may minimize deviant peer influence effects. To date, few research studies have directly addressed this problem within school settings in terms of organizational and operational features that possibly allow DPI to occur and none have investigated it experimentally. However, school environs appear to provide a supportive context for DPI and are an excellent setting for studying it. A research agenda for the study of DPI within the school setting is proposed at the end of this chapter.

DOCUMENTING DEVIANT PEER
INFLUENCE EFFECTS IN CLASSROOMS

Classroom ecologies have particular salience for school-age children. The collective competencies and problems of students comprising today's classrooms contribute to the overall quality and nature of peer interactions, which in turn affect children's social development (Hoglund & Leadbeater, 2004; Kellam, Ling, Merisca, Brown, & Ialongo, 1998; Ladd, 1990). While there has been a paucity of research in documenting DPI effects resulting from school institutional policies that knowingly aggregate at-risk and deviant students (e.g., through the use of self-contained behavior disorder classrooms, academic tracking), an empirical literature is now beginning to emerge on the negative long-term impact of the *naturally* occurring aggregation of aggressive students in the classroom setting.

Research indicates that classrooms containing high numbers of students with poor academic skills and/or behavior problems are more likely to promote these attributes among individual students. Barth, Dunlap, Dane, Lochman, and Wells (2004) examined how variations in academic and social classroom compositions affected student behavior over a 2-year period. Their results indicated that classrooms having larger numbers of students with academic and behavioral problems were associated with higher levels of student aggression, lower quality peer relations, and a decreased academic focus. Another study, evaluating classroom context with regard to aggression, found similar results. Aber, Jones, Brown, Chaudry, and Samples (1998) investigated the interaction effects of classroom contextual factors for over 5,000 elementary students. Their results indicated that students placed within classrooms in which the prevailing norm was that the use of aggression was "perfectly OK" reported higher rates of aggression, used more aggressive strategies, and had lower levels of social competence than students placed in classrooms in which aggression was not the norm. Furthermore, Stormshak and colleagues (1999) investigated the determinants of peer preference for first-grade students participating in the Fast Track program. They found that as classroom levels of aggression increased, the negative effects of child aggression on peer preference decreased, particularly for boys. In fact, for boys, aggression and peer preference were positively related in highly aggressive classroom environments.

The distal impact of naturally occurring aggregation of aggressive students in the classroom setting has also been investigated. Kellam and colleagues (1998) investigated the influence of classroom context on the course and malleability of aggressive behavior for children upon entrance into first grade through their transition into middle school.

Results of this longitudinal study indicated that aggressive males who were in highly chaotic, poorly managed first-grade classrooms were at substantially increased risk for being aggressive in middle school. In contrast, aggressive males assigned to well-managed first-grade classrooms had a reduced risk for becoming highly aggressive in middle school.

Recently a group of researchers replicated and extended the findings of Kellam and colleagues (1998). Warren, Schoppelrey, Moberg, and McDonald (2005) investigated the relationship between group aggression in the classroom context and individual aggression outside the classroom. Their results indicated that parents' ratings of their children's aggressiveness were predicted by group levels of aggression recorded in their school classrooms. Children exposed to higher levels of aggression in the classroom were significantly more likely to exhibit high levels of aggressive behavior outside the school setting 2 years later.

In summary, according to the most recent literature on DPI in the classroom setting, the influence of higher than normal levels of aggression within the classroom exerts a substantial negative influence on the current and future behavior of individual students. Thus a case can be made that the aggregation of high-risk and/or deviant youth within the school setting, through either naturally occurring or deliberate organizational means, is associated with risk for experiencing later destructive outcomes. Given this risk, policies and practices that affect the aggregation of deviant students should be evaluated and monitored for deleterious effects prior to being mandated or becoming universal practice by the field of education.

RECENT POLICIES THAT AFFECT THE AGGREGATION OF DEVIANT STUDENTS

Educational policies and their resulting effects on students' schooling are a key consideration in any discussion of school-based DPI. A number of school policies have been instituted that may mediate DPI processes and outcomes within the school setting. The following policies are reviewed with a view toward their possible facilitation of deviancy training among aggregated, at-risk students: (1) No Child Left Behind, (2) The Gun-Free Schools Act, and (3) Individuals with Disabilities Amendment of 1997 for disciplining special education students.

No Child Left Behind

No Child Left Behind (NCLB) was signed into law on January 8, 2002. It is the latest revision of the 1965 Elementary and Secondary Education

Act and imposes significant changes to educational policy. The intent of this law is to ensure that all students meet the highest learning standards of the state in which they live. To ensure that schools and districts meet the goals of NCLB, the law provides a blend of requirements, incentives, and resources. NCLB requirements include the following: (1) annual testing; (2) verification of each state's assessment system; (3) analysis and reporting of student achievement results; (4) state definitions and timelines for determining whether a school, district, and state are making "adequate yearly progress" toward the goal of 100% of students meeting state standards by the 2013–2014 school year; and (5) sanctions for schools, districts, and states that fail to make adequate yearly progress. Furthermore, NCLB allows students enrolled in schools that are not making adequate progress to transfer to another public school.

While NCLB is well intentioned, several components of its implementation may actually contribute to DPI within the school setting. First, in an effort to achieve the goal of all students meeting state standards, today's students are being retained when they do not meet state criteria. In some instances, students who have earned passing grades throughout the year are held back from being promoted to the next grade when they fail the annual state-wide assessment. The practice of academic retention has long been documented as ineffective (see Holmes, 1989). In fact, students who are academically retained are more likely to drop out of school than similar low-achieving students who are socially promoted, leaving at-risk peers the opportunity to naturally aggregate unsupervised in the community, elevating the risk of DPI (Jimerson, Anderson, & Whipple, 2002).

Second, when parents and caregivers have the option of transferring children from schools deemed not meeting state standards, students of families with the most resources and education are likely to transfer, leaving behind a host of children in a school that is at higher risk for academic and behavioral difficulties. This movement is consistent with sociological research regarding the emergence of the underclass, specifically in urban settings (Wilson, 1987). Those schools not meeting the state standards do not receive monetary incentives, thereby creating a gap between the funding of these schools when compared to other schools within the state. Thus schools that have the lowest standards will receive the least funding, and likely the most difficult students. Consequently, DPI is increased by aggregating at-risk students within school settings that are not adequately funded and have undertrained staffs.

Gun-Free Schools Act

In 1994, the Clinton administration passed the Gun-Free Schools Act into law. This law mandates that students in possession of a firearm at school be expelled for one calendar year. The intent of this mandate was to send the message to offenders that certain types of behavior at school would not be tolerated in any form (i.e., zero tolerance). While the act only covers firearms, the language of the bill has since been expanded to include any instrument that can be used as a weapon (e.g., pencils). Furthermore, state and local school districts have broadened zero tolerance practices beyond the federal mandate of weapons to include drugs and alcohol, fighting, unauthorized used of pagers or laser pointers, and sexual harassment (Skiba & Peterson, 1999).

This mandate has led to the overuse of expulsion and suspension practices. Despite the significant increase in the use of suspension and expulsions when disciplining students, there appears to be little evidence that supports expulsion or suspension practices to improve student behavior. Rather than teach appropriate behavior that could improve outcomes for students it is likely that zero tolerance procedures lead to the aggregation of unsupervised at-risk youth in the community, increasing the risk for DPI among these youth.

Individuals with Disabilities Education Act

The reauthorization of the Individuals with Disabilities Education Act (IDEA) Amendments of 1997 instituted some key changes in the regulations regarding discipline of students with disabilities. The new rules have allowed public schools to discipline special education students as they would their classmates who do not have disabling conditions. The final regulations reflect concerns expressed by school administrators and teachers regarding maintaining school safety without dealing with unduly burdensome requirements. Therefore, school personnel became able to order a change in the placement of a special education child to an interim placement or suspension, but for not more than 10 school days without a formal review. A disciplinary change of placement occurs when the child is removed for more than 10 consecutive school days or when the child is subjected to a series of removals that constitute a recurring pattern because they are for more than 10 school days in a school.

The changes in how schools discipline special education students are relevant to DPI within schools because, along with the reauthorization of the IDEA Amendments of 1997, came increasing pressures to develop and rely upon alternative education practices for students failing to adjust to the demands of general education settings. If a special education student is removed from a current placement for more than 10 school days in the same school year, subsequent removals require that the school provide services to the extent necessary to enable the student to progress academically. The need to service special education students who require a change in placement by IDEA has stimulated interest in the design of interim alternative education programs that can be more effective than the commonly used homebound tutoring placement option (Tobin & Sprague, 2002). Thus alternative education placements become an option for schools to both discipline students and to serve those with specialized educational needs. These alternative educational settings have the potential for producing iatrogenic effects, particularly when the setting is poorly managed by staff and students have regular contact with deviant peers.

To date, as we have noted earlier, relatively little research attention by educators has focused on institutional policies and practices that aggregate peers. Given what is currently known about deviancy training and its iatrogenic effects (Dishion et al., 1999), it is likely that some policies and practices meant to increase academic outcomes and reduce negative behavioral outcomes for children and adolescents may in fact have the opposite effect. Yet school policies and organizational practices have been relatively ignored with regard to the potential negative outcomes due to DPI. In fact, researchers Wilson and Herrnstein (1985, p. 280) noted that "it is remarkable and a bit dismaying . . . that so little effort has been made to find out if different kinds of schools lead to different behavioral outcomes." Some 20 years later, the same statement can be made with considerable accuracy.

CURRENT PRACTICES THAT AFFECT THE AGGREGATION OF DEVIANT STUDENTS

Organizational practices within the school context can lead to formal as well as informal aggregation of deviant peers. In this section we review the effects of school instructional practices such as (1) retention, (2) academic tracking, (3) special education resource rooms and self-contained classrooms, and (4) disciplinary practices including alternative school placements, suspension, and expulsion practices that lead to the aggregation of deviant peer populations. The processes and the outcomes associated with each practice are briefly described.

Retention

Schools are under severe pressures to produce high achievement levels among students with an emphasis on educational standards and accountability. Accountability procedures, such as high-stakes testing, have rekindled debates about the accelerated use of grade retention as an intervention to remedy academic deficits. Census data indicate that the percentage of students retained has risen steadily during the past few decades. Whereas in the mid-1960s about 24% of boys and 16% of girls were at least a year behind grade level by sixth grade, in 1990 those percentages ranged from a low of 24% for white females to a high of 47% for Hispanic males (U.S. Department of Commerce, Bureau of Census, 1966, 1990, cited in Dawson, 1998).

The steady increase in the practice of academic retention is of concern for several reasons. First, results from research during the past century examining the effectiveness of academic retention fail to demonstrate any consistent achievement, socioemotional, or behavioral advantages of retaining students (Jimerson, 2001; Jimerson & Kaufman, 2003). In fact, retention is often viewed as punishment and children who are retained feel anxious about the reactions of their peers and others to their status as a "school failure" (Brynes & Yamamoto, 2001). Although the practice of retention may not lead to higher concentrations of low-achieving students in classrooms, assuming that similar proportions of students are retained across grades, students who are retained suddenly share a common experience that could lead to bonding between peers who otherwise may not have associated. Thus, consistent with social identity theory (Tajfel & Turner, 2004), students identifying as school failures may seek to enhance their self-esteem by identifying positively with shared characteristics of others who lack school bonding and display disengagement with school (e.g., poor grades, disruptive classroom behavior, and school dropout).

Second, the long-term outcomes for retained students are often damaging, leading to dropout and increased risk for potential DPI in community settings. Jimerson and colleagues (2002) reported that retention was the best predictor of school dropout. They found that retained students were 11 times more likely to drop out than nonretained students and 25% more likely to drop out of high school than low-achieving, socially promoted peers.

The use of grade retention as an academic intervention is an ineffective practice that has risen to new heights of usage and acceptance stemming from political pressures to increase academic gains for public schools. Educational policies that are linked to student failure and that contribute to early school leaving may inadvertently lead to affiliations with troubled youth in the community where there is little or no adult supervision. Youth who fail to complete school commit a significant majority of crimes in the larger society (Office of Juvenile Justice and Delinquency Prevention, 1995). The connection between retention and DPI has not been directly examined but cannot be dismissed as a possible contributing factor in the negative outcomes associated with the retained student population, particularly in comparison to the more positive outcomes associated with peers who struggle academically but are socially promoted.

Academic Tracking

One of the most well-researched and critically examined instructional practices by schools is the use of academic tracking. Tracking is nearly universal in U.S. secondary education, although its nature varies across schools. The main goal of tracking is to segregate students according to ability in order to maximize their academic potential. The tracking process assigns students to a prescribed curriculum based on the perceived academic aptitude of the student. In general, academic tracking systems are hierarchical, with the sequences of classes preparing students for 4-year college requirements at the top of the hierarchy. Moreover, while student movement across tracks is possible, tracking assignments tend to be stable (Dornbusch, Glasgow, & Lin, 1996) and students rarely exercise choice in their track assignments (Kubitschek & Hallinan, 1998).

Several additional problems are associated with academic tracking. First, tracking systems tend to mirror racial and economic inequalities within the larger society (Hochschild, 2003). Second, lower track students tend to lag behind other students in school achievement and school engagement, even when controlling for initial ability levels (Bennett & LeCompte, 1990). Third, and most important for this review, tracking placement can have negative behavioral consequences. Because of the high comorbidity of behavioral and academic difficulties, tracking may inadvertently aggregate students with behavioral problems in the lower academic tracks. Thus classrooms with high numbers of students having poor academic skills and deviant social behavior may actually perpetuate these destructive outcomes through DPI.

Kubitschek and Hallinan (1998) investigated the mechanism by which academic tracking influences students' friendship choices. They used a subsample of the first (1980) wave of the High School and Beyond data, a national sample of approximately 58,000 sophomores and seniors from 1,000 public and private schools in the United States. Results indicated that track placement affected friendship choice independent of other factors. Academic track placement explained more variance in friendship choice than the preexisting factors of gender, race, socioeconomic status (SES), and grades, indicating that track placement had a direct effect on friendship choice. Furthermore, the researchers examined whether background similarities, which cause students to be placed in the same track, are similar to those that cause students to become friends. There was no evidence that the effects of track placement on friendship were due to the background similarities of students, suggesting that any organizational grouping would have similar effects on friendship choice. These findings imply that organizational structures, even when designed for other purposes, act independently to exacerbate or ameliorate patterns of friendship choice.

Crosnoe (2002) conducted a similar investigation of high school curricula tracking and friendship development. Using structural equation analyses of data from 2,899 students, Crosnoe investigated curriculum track as a moderator of friendship relations and additionally investigated the potential for curriculum track as an organizer of delinquent friendship groups. Students in the sample reported their own involvement in delinquent behavior as well as the delinquent activities of their friends. Crosnoe's results were consistent with prior findings that tracking generally organized friendship groups, but tracking was not a strong predictor of delinquent friendship groups. Academic achievement was a better predictor of association with delinquent peers. Students with high academic achievement, despite academic track placement, were less likely to associate with deviant peers.

Nevertheless, non–college preparatory track students had lower levels of academic achievement and reported higher rates of self-reported delinquency and higher levels of delinquency among their friends. Additionally, findings indicated that the non-college preparatory track students became more similar to their delinquent friends over time. Furthermore, the study found that the relation between friends' delinquency and later respondent delinquency was strong and significant for non-college preparatory track students, yet it was not significant for college preparatory track students. Thus having delinquent friends is a risk factor, but this risk is more likely to translate into problem behavior within the lower tracks. The increased vulnerability to delinquent friends for lower track students appeared to arise from lower bonding to conventional institutions and pathways of achievement.

The institutional aggregation of peers through academic tracking leads to a greater similarity or homogeneity of students in the group and increasing affiliation among those students. However, it appears that low-achieving, low-track students are most vulnerable to DPI, particularly when they identify with disengagement from school and lack bonding to the conventional pathways to success. Academic tracking was never intended to increase or decrease the likelihood of particular students to become friends or to expose students to DPI. Thus it is important to note and consider the indirect effects that institutional aggregation practices and policies may have on the long-term development of students.

Special Education

Special education services operate within the school setting to increase academic and behavioral outcomes for students identified as needing additional supports outside the general education classroom. Students identified for such services are typically aggregated in resource rooms or self-contained classrooms where they receive specialized instruction for all or part of the school day. Within the school setting, youth displaying serious and disruptive behavior, including antisocial behavior, may be eligible for special education services under the label of emotionally disturbed (ED) depending on their specific behavioral characteristics.

Self-Contained ED Classrooms

In many states, students served under the disability category of ED who exhibit disruptive behaviors felt to be inappropriate for the regular education classroom setting are placed in self-contained classrooms. These placements typically include smaller number of students, have higher staff-to-student ratios, and provide support for achieving individualized behavior goals. Although IDEA requires placement in the least restrictive educational setting possible, most students assigned to self-contained ED classrooms spend their entire school day within them interacting with the same classroom peers.

Because the majority of students eligible for ED exhibit primarily externalizing behavioral characteristics, students aggregated in these classrooms are exposed to chiefly deviant peers. Although a portion of these ED students can succeed in regular classrooms, many of them and their teachers do not currently receive the supports they need to succeed in regular class environments. According to the National Longitudinal Transition Study (NLTS), of students with ED who were served in regular education environments, only 11% had behavior management plans (Wagner, 1995). Often, special education teachers of self-contained classrooms are left with few good inclusion opportunities for students with ED who can be defiant, disruptive, and difficult management problems within the regular education setting.

Outcomes

The majority of ED students experience poor academic and behavioral outcomes (Wagner et al., 2003). Compared to other disability groups, students with ED fail more courses, earn lower grade point averages, have lower reading and math scores, miss more days of school, are retained on average a grade more often than other students, and have lower graduation rates (Kauffman, 2005; Wagner, Blackorby, & Hebbeler, 1993). In fact, the majority of students with ED leave school before graduating with a graduation rate of only 42% (Wagner, 1991). Wagner and her associates have found that within 3 years of leaving school, a majority of ED students have been arrested one or more times. As a result of academic failure, ED students often experience a lifetime of problems in personal, educational, and employment domains and are likely to become involved with the criminal justice system at an early age (National Research Council, 2002).

The extent and magnitude that DPI contributes to the array of negative outcomes for students with ED is unclear at this time. However, the persistent finding in the naturally occurring peer influence literature that the aggregation of peers who display aggressive and delinquent behavior is particularly problematic for children who are themselves at risk for aggressive and delinquent behavior points toward DPI as a contributing factor (Dishion et al., 1999; Kellam et al., 1998; Warren et al., 2005). Students aggregated in self-contained ED classrooms are consistently exposed to peers exhibiting deviant behaviors. Thus these students have ongoing association with aggressive and delinquent peers. In poorly managed self-contained ED classrooms, students have ample opportunity to practice observed deviant behaviors, and have sufficient motivation to exhibit the behaviors in order to gain peer acceptance and/or to prevent themselves from being victimized by fellow classmates. Therefore, DPI is in full effect when self-contained classrooms of at-risk students associate, practice deviant behavior, and have their deviant behaviors maintained by cycles of positive reinforcement (i.e., peer acceptance and respect for aggressive and delinquent acts) and negative reinforcement (i.e., avoidance of victimization by aggressive peers). It seems evident that school personnel must take significant steps to deter the negative affects associated with intentionally aggregating deviant peers in the classroom setting.

Alternative Education Programs for Disruptive Students

The Office of Juvenile Justice and Delinquency Prevention first promoted alternative education programs and schools for delinquency prevention in the 1980s. Alternative schools were designed to remove disruptive students from traditional public schools and provide them with a smaller, more supportive environment. In general, alternative school programs have been designed to create a more successful learning environment with lower student-to-teacher ratios, individualized and self-paced instruction, noncompetitive performance assessments, and a less structured classroom regimen (Raywid, 1983). The premise underlying alternative education programs was that at-risk youth would be more motivated to attend this type of school, thus creating bonding and attachment to the schooling experience that would help curb future delinquent behavior (Gottfredson, 1987b). Unfortunately, alternative schools are often used as a form of punishment for troublesome students with little regard for providing specialized programming and supports (Arnove & Strout, 1980).

According to a nation-wide survey of alternative educational programs conducted by the U.S. Department of Education (National Center for Education Statistics, 2001), 1.3% of all public school students attended alternative schools and programs for at-risk students during the 2000–2001 school year. Twelve percent of the students attending public alternative schools and programs were special education students. The survey indicated that students entered public alternative schools and programs for a variety of reasons. Behaviors recognized as disruptive to others, such as possession of firearms or other weapons, possession of alcohol or drugs, physical attacks, and disruptive verbal behavior, were sufficient for transfer of a student to an alternative school or program. Districts with a high minority enrollment and those with a high poverty concentration were more likely than their counterpart districts to report assigning teachers involuntarily to teach at alternative schools or programs.

Cox (1999) addressed the methodological shortcomings plaguing the alternative school literature by employing a true experimental design with a follow-up component by randomly assigning 83 middle school students (sixth–eighth grade), referred for alternative educational placement by school officials, to attend an alternative school for one school semester or to remain in their traditional school. Information was collected from student interviews and official school records and included attitudes toward school, self-esteem, self-reported delinquency, academic achievement, and school attendance. Results showed there were no differences between the program participation group and the control group on self-reported delinquency, attitudes toward school, or academic achievement. The alternative school students had higher self-esteem, better grade point averages, and improved attendance while attending the alternative school, but these gains dissipated when the students returned to their traditional school.

Interestingly, while not significant, the mean score of self-reported delinquency reported by students who attended the alternative school gradually increased at 1-year follow-up (mean score of 2.90 delinquent acts at preprogram, 3.07 postprogram, and 3.20 at 1-year follow-up). Students who remained at the traditional school had no change in their reported delinquent acts (mean score of 2.83 delinquent acts at preprogram, 2.71 postprogram, and 2.83 at 1-year follow-up), ending with the same mean rate as baseline. While not significantly different, these trends may point to potentially negative effects on delinquent behavior over time for students placed within alternative educational settings. Further research utilizing experimental designs with a focus toward DPI is necessary to fully understand peer effects in alterative school placements.

Suspension and Expulsion

The prevalence of zero tolerance policies that predetermine consequences for specified offenses is broadly in evidence, with the majority of schools reporting policies that range beyond weapons and firearms. Suspension and expulsion are the cornerstones of schools' zero tolerance policies. A recent study by Harvard University's Advancement Project and The Civil Rights Project (2000) reported that over 3 million students were suspended and 87,000 expelled in 1998. In the Chicago public schools alone, the number of expulsions increased from 14 in 1992–1993 to 737 in 1998–1999. Relative to the general population, a disproportionately large number of these students were minorities. Furthermore, other studies have shown that children with disabilities constitute a disproportionately large percentage of expulsions and suspensions (see Morrison & D'Incau, 1997).

The increase in use of suspension and expulsion, particularly with children having disabilities, has led to increased aggregation of deviant peers. Disruptive, aggressive, and delinquent students are placed together in in-school suspension settings as punishment, placed in alternative school settings as interim placements, or expelled from school altogether and left unsupervised to conspire with other at-risk or delinquent peers in the community. Yet, despite these substantial increases in the use of suspension and expulsions in disciplining students, there appears to be little evidence that expulsion or suspension improve student behavior or contribute to overall school safety. This is likely due to the fact that schools characterized by high levels of antisocial behaviors and low academic expectation tend to reactively rely on suspensions and expulsion as the preferred response to disruptive behavior (Le Blanc, Vallieres, & McDuff, 1992; McEvoy & Welker, 2000). Therefore, school safety will not be impacted by the removal of one or more deviant students because the overall climate of the school contributes to underachievement and disruptive behavior. These school climates with high levels of antisocial behavior and low school attachment are primed for DPI.

Additionally, studies of school suspension have shown that up to 40% of suspensions are due to repeat offenders (Bowditch, 1993). This suggests that students targeted by school suspension are not getting the message or learning from their punishment(s). In fact, Tobin, Sugai, and Colvin (1996) found that past suspension was the best predictor of a future suspension. Furthermore, analyses of the data from the national High School and Beyond survey revealed that 31% of sophomores who dropped out of school had been suspended, as compared to a suspension rate of 10% of same-age peers who stayed in school (Ekstrom, Goertz, Pollack, & Rock, 1986). Some argue that suspension causes low-achieving students and those viewed as troublesome to leave school before graduation (Skiba, 2000). For a student at risk for antisocial or delinquent behavior, being expelled or suspended simply accelerates the course of delinquency.

PRINCIPLES TO MINIMIZE DEVIANT
PEER INFLUENCE EFFECTS

The aggregation of high-risk and/or deviant youth within the school setting, through either naturally occurring or deliberate organizational means, is associated with risk for experiencing later destructive outcomes. The impacts of these processes have been largely unexamined by educational researchers to date. Yet numerous reviews of scientific literature have concluded that a variety of proactive preventive school-based programs and practices can be effective in preventing, or reducing, disruptive problem behaviors in youth, and have the potential to reduce the need to aggregate deviant peers and the risk for DPI. The following section briefly summarizes promising principals to minimize DPI.

School-wide Principles to Minimize Deviant
Peer Influence Effects

Prevention research indicates that the school ecology should be a central focus of intervention (Greenberg, Domitrovich, & Bumbarger, 2001). An alternative to the student-by-student approach of intervention is the development of a school-wide behavioral support system. School-wide systems of behavioral support define, teach, and reward expected behaviors; develop peer support systems; and implement clear and consistent consequences for inappropriate behavior (see Sprick, Sprick, & Garrison, 1992; Sugai, Horner, & Gresham, 2002). A school-wide system also emphasizes the development of a positive school climate, practical policies, well-defined physical spaces, and monitoring systems that will reduce conditions that will trigger problem behaviors among students (Taylor-Green et al., 1997). Such a system allows school administrators, teachers, and other school personnel to tailor a behavioral support program to the specific needs of the school.

Recently, the Office of Special Education Programs and the Safe and Drug Free Schools Office collaboratively supported a program of research to identify effective schools and programs and to synthesize information that could help others to replicate effective programs. Results of this study were included in a special report titled *Safe, Drug-Free Schools, and Effective Schools for ALL Students: What Works!* (Quinn,

Osher, Hoffman, & Hanley, 1998). The report indicates that successful schools have high behavioral and academic expectations and provide students and staff with the needed support to achieve them. Furthermore, these schools combine school-wide prevention efforts with early intervention for those students who are at risk of developing ED, and provide individualized services for those already identified with ED. Additionally, successful schools provide students with positive behavioral supports, offer ongoing training to staff, collaborate effectively with families, and coordinate services across agencies (Mayer, 1995; Nelson, Crabtree, Marchand-Martella, & Martella, 1998; Sugai et al., 2002).

The effectiveness attributes of schools and programs listed can serve as offsetting protective factors for at-risk students in many cases. An effective school-wide system would likely reduce the risk of DPI by reducing student disruptive behaviors by actively teaching and reinforcing students for appropriate behaviors, thus reducing the need to aggregate deviant peers through reactive suspension and expulsion practices.

Classroom Management Practices to Minimize Deviant Peer Influence Effects

Given that the collective competencies and problems of students comprising the classroom setting contribute to the overall quality and nature of peer interactions, increasing the use of effective classroom management strategies will likely minimize DPI. In fact, well-managed classrooms can buffer children from adverse emotional and behavioral effects of particular school and family risk factors (Hoglund & Leadbeater, 2004; Kellam et al., 1998; Ladd, 1990). Therefore, providing training and support to teachers with a focus on critical classroom management variables, such as use of proactive classroom management practices, improving the teacher–child relationship, and increased monitoring, would likely lead to more orderly classrooms and reduce opportunities for DPI.

Individual Behavior Support Practices to Minimize Deviant Peer Influence Effects

A small percentage of students within a school will continue to display behavioral difficulties despite the implementation of school-wide and classroom management systems (Sugai et al., 2002). There are school practices that can help to minimize or prevent the behavior problems displayed by these students, and reduce the need for more restrictive environments. For instance, conducting a functional behavior assessment and developing a behavior support plan specific to the needs of the indi-

vidual student can decrease the frequency and intensity of problem behaviors displayed by students (see O'Neil et al., 1997). With an effective
behavior support plan in place, larger numbers of students exhibiting
disruptive behavior ranging from mild to severe levels can remain within
the regular education setting. A few students will not respond to behavior support plans implemented within the regular education setting and
will require more restrictive placements and intensive supports. However, this does not become clear until functional behavioral assessments
and behavior support plans have been implemented. Without an effective individual behavior support plan in place, many students are unnec-
essarily placed in more restrictive educational settings (e.g., resource
rooms, self-contained ED classrooms, alternative settings). This is a
practice that aggregates severely disruptive youth with malleable youth
who simply need more structure and behavioral support within the regular classroom setting, placing these students at great risk for DPI through
the expanding use of restrictive alternative placements.

CONCLUSIONS

The available evidence and reviews of current school practices indicate
that (1) school settings provide ample opportunities for the naturally
occurring aggregation of behaviorally at-risk youth that are largely un-
controlled or mediated by adults and (2) a majority of U.S. schools
have institutionalized practices that involve and inadvertently promote
DPI through long-standing organizational and operational procedures.
Yet psychological researchers interested in school-based prevention,
bullying and harassment, and peer group dynamics have conducted the
vast majority of school research that has focused on naturally occurring DPI within school settings (see Juvonen & Graham, 2001). It is
urgent that the potentially deleterious effects of school aggregation
practices become known through descriptive and experimental research.

The relative absence of research on school practices that cause or
carry a risk of facilitating DPI makes reaching firm conclusions about
the current educational landscape difficult. However, as we've noted,
schools provide rich environments for research on this topic. The main
points of this chapter along with suggestions for future research are provided below.

1. Evidence exists that the natural aggregation of aggressive and
low-achieving peers within classroom settings leads to DPI among students. Researchers should continue to examine and carefully document

the developmental outcomes associated with naturally occurring peer aggregation utilizing longitudinal methods.

2. It is likely that some policies and practices meant to increase academic outcomes and reduce negative behavioral outcomes for students may in fact have the opposite effect. Therefore, it is imperative that politicians and school administrators are fully informed of the potential deleterious effects of DPI prior to developing and implementing overarching broad decisions to aggregate at-risk youth in the school setting. Researchers can contribute to informing decision makers by conducting research specifically targeting policies and practices institutionalized in school settings that lead to the aggregation of at-risk peers (i.e., alternative education, self-contained classrooms).

3. Pervasive school challenges such as the poor classroom management skills of staff and the absence of school-wide behavioral systems continue to plague schools. Adopting a system of school-wide behavioral supports should be in place in all schools to maximize the school's ability to accommodate a broader range of students with diverse social, behavioral, and academic attributes. Increasing the accommodation capacities of schools in this manner would likely reduce school dropout rates, help create a positive school climate, and indirectly lead to reductions in DPI. The promotion of positive school values and establishing peer cultures that discourage peer harassment would also do a great deal to facilitate achievement of this important goal. Studying the impact of school-wide systems of behavioral support on student outcomes, such as reported association with delinquent peers and reported instances of delinquent acts, would contribute to the literature on DPI.

4. As practitioners, we have witnessed kindergarten students with ED placed into self-contained behavior classrooms who display mature acts of deviance such as attacking their teachers and assaulting peers. The classroom settings in which they function are often chaotic, out of control, and unpredictable. Self-contained behavior classrooms appear to be a training ground for deviance *if they are not carefully structured and well managed.* Studies that focus on the behavior management training of teachers and support staff who supervise classroom and playground settings could potentially be effective and provide long-lasting intervention supports for children who are likely to develop later delinquent behavior. A study focusing on behavioral consultation within self-contained classrooms as well as general education classrooms geared toward reducing DPI effects is urgently needed.

5. Research should focus not only on the outcomes of current school practices but also include scientific intervention studies that allow experimental evaluations of efforts to reduce DPI by adopting effective schooling practices that avoid and/or buffer and offset DPI effects. Im-

plementation of large-scale, randomized control trials and single case studies can begin to shed light on the potential for preventing and reducing DPI in the school setting. Controlled studies that randomly assign students, classrooms, or schools to intervention and control conditions are particularly difficult within the public school setting. However, in order to fully understand the potential mechanisms leading to the school failure of so many disruptive and delinquent youth, we must find ways to research DPI within the schooling context.

6. It cannot be argued with certainty that peer aggregation is always detrimental due to the institutionalized peer aggregation practices of schools. However, DPI is an established and well-documented risk that has been observed to operate across a broad range of settings and contexts as described within this volume. In our view, schools have an obligation to address this issue and to evaluate its impact.

As we have noted herein, research focused on the potential effects of DPI must be initiated before broad policy changes to control and manage them are adopted by schools. It is possible, but not as yet fully established, that a number of current school practices may be causing long-term harm to selected at-risk students. Until researchers discover creative and meaningful ways to investigate the existence and extent of school-based DPI, and to change potentially harmful environments and practices, these controversial but important questions will remain unanswered.

ACKNOWLEDGMENT

Thanks are due Steve Forness for his review and comments on an earlier draft of this chapter.

CHAPTER 8

Peer Effects in Juvenile Justice

D. Wayne Osgood
and Laine O'Neill Briddell

Recent studies of deviant peer influence (Dishion, McCord, & Poulin, 1999) raise the troubling possibility that programs intended to reduce delinquency will do more harm than good if they bring together groups of delinquent or high-risk youth. Because it is standard procedure for many programs of the juvenile justice system to aggregate deviant youth in this way, it is critically important to determine the strength of deviant peer influence as well as the conditions under which it arises. This chapter takes on part of that job. We leave to Lipsey's chapter (Chapter 9, this volume) the key task of comparing the effectiveness of programs that aggregate delinquent youth with the effectiveness of programs that do not. We will try to set the context for that chapter, as well as for Greenwood's chapter (Chapter 15, this volume) on juvenile justice policy, by noting the long history of concern with negative peer effects in the juvenile justice system, by discussing the role of aggregation in various types of juvenile justice programs, and by reviewing the limited set of studies that specifically address peer influence processes in juvenile justice programs.

Deviant peer contagion is a distinctive form of peer influence in program settings that may arise when deviant youth are brought together (Dishion et al., 1999). Deviant peer contagion entails a positive feedback loop in which youths influence one another to become more delinquent or deviant than they would have been in the absence of the program. Thus deviant peer contagion exacerbates rather than reduces the problems the program was meant to solve. For instance, Poulin, Dishion, and

Burraston (2001) studied high-risk youth assigned to a program designed to use peer group reinforcement to promote positive change. They found that 3 years after completing the program the youth who had participated in it had higher rates of tobacco use and delinquency than youth in a control group. Dishion and colleagues (1999) argued that this result was a reflection of negative peer influence among the youth who participated in the program, a finding that is consistent with the large body of research indicating that peers can influence one another's delinquency (reviewed by Dishion & Dodge, Chapter 2, this volume). As we discuss below, there appears to be considerable potential for deviant peer contagion in the many juvenile justice programs that bring together deviant youth.

THE JUVENILE JUSTICE SYSTEM

For the purposes of this chapter we define the *juvenile justice system* rather broadly to encompass the full range of agencies and programs that address the problem of juvenile delinquency and that are targeted to youth identified either as delinquent or as at high risk for delinquency. Much of the juvenile justice system is devoted to apprehending juveniles who have broken the law and to deciding the consequences that will follow. Our interest is not in these activities of the police and juvenile court, however, but rather in those programs that constitute our society's organized efforts to prevent further lawbreaking.

It will be useful to distinguish between residential programs, serving juveniles removed from their homes, and nonresidential programs, serving juveniles who continue to live with their families. Residential programs range from large state training schools and reformatories to small group homes operated by private groups. Typically, youth are committed to residential settings by the juvenile court, but they are sometimes sent by their families. Juveniles can reach nonresidential programs through probation following adjudication as delinquent, informal probation prior to adjudication, or referral from sources outside the juvenile court. Probation is itself also a specific nonresidential program in which probation officers supervise and provide services to youth. The content of nonresidential programs addressing delinquency varies enormously, from all types of group and individual counseling to mentoring (e.g., Big Brothers and Big Sisters) to recreation (e.g., Boys and Girls Clubs, YMCA) and to almost any other sort of social service program.

Though only youth adjudicated by the juvenile court are legally designated as delinquent, juvenile justice programs (in the sense we are using the term) serve many other youth as well. Some of their clientele have been apprehended for illegal acts, but were diverted from the formal justice system or received informal dispositions short of adjudication. Other parties such as parents, school officials, and mental health workers send youth to these programs as well, and such cases may not entail any legal processing at all. Because all of these programs are part of our society's organized attempts to ameliorate the problem of juvenile delinquency, we include them in the scope of this chapter. This chapter does not consider primary prevention programs delivered to the general population. Though it would be reasonable to view these programs as part of the juvenile justice system in its broadest sense, issues of deviant peer contagion are not pertinent to their nondelinquent target populations.

THE OUTCOMES OF INTEREST

The principal concern of this chapter is the impact of peer processes in juvenile justice programs upon subsequent delinquency. The term "delinquency" is generally used to refer to violations of the criminal law by persons who have not reached the age of jurisdiction for the criminal court (Jensen & Rojek, 1998), which is 18 in most states, but 17 or even 16 in some. The criminal law proscribes a wide variety of behavior, ranging from grave but rare offenses such as murder, rape, and armed robbery, to relatively minor and very common acts such as disorderly conduct, fistfights (misdemeanor assault), and shoplifting.

The two primary sources of data for measuring individual delinquency are official records and self-reports. Official records of delinquency include police records of arrests and juvenile court records of petitions filed and cases adjudicated delinquent. Self-report measures ask respondents questions about their own behavior, relying on assurances of confidentiality and proper rapport with interviewers to obtain accurate responses. Each source has distinct strengths and weaknesses. Official records emphasize more serious offenses that may be of greater interest, while self-reports have the potential to capture the large proportion of illegal acts that are not detected by law enforcement. Official records are subject to any biases in justice system case processing while self-reports are subject to respondent biases. The standard wisdom of the field of criminology is that both sources are valid and useful, and that findings are most convincing when they are consistent across both (Hindelang, Hirschi, & Weis, 1979; Huizinga & Elliott, 1986). In addition to these two primary sources of data, some studies have been able to measure delinquency through reports of other parties such as parents or teachers (e.g., Poulin et al., 2001).

In addition to delinquency itself, two other types of factors are also relevant to our interests. First, for a more comprehensive understanding of the processes by which peer processes impact youth in juvenile justice programs, it is useful to consider effects on risk and protective factors for delinquency. For instance, association with deviant peers or lack of parental supervision (Eddy & Chamberlain, 2000) are possible mediators that would be likely to foretell increases in delinquency. Also of interest are measures pertaining to the programs, such as acceptance of program goals and attitudes toward the staff (Gold & Osgood, 1992). Such measures are potentially useful for identifying the circumstances that either promote or prevent deviant peer influence. They may also serve as mediators of negative peer processes—for instance, if peer influence interferes with program effectiveness by engendering an inmate culture of resistance to program goals (Sykes, 1958).

SCOPE OF THIS CHAPTER

Though the term "deviant peer contagion" may be recent, concern with negative peer effects in programs for delinquent youth is not. The next section of the chapter reviews this history of concern. We then discuss the variety of programs that serve delinquent or high-risk youth, giving special attention to the ways that those programs do or do not bring youth together to set the conditions for potential deviant peer influence. After that, we review in more detail the small set of studies of juvenile justice programs that examine peer processes and their effects. This material should provide a useful background to Lipsey's discussion (Chapter 9, this volume), which reviews the broader set of results from program evaluations to establish the relative effectiveness of programs that do and do not group deviant adolescents.

A HISTORY OF CONCERN ABOUT NEGATIVE PEER EFFECTS IN JUVENILE JUSTICE

The present volume is inspired by recent findings that aggregating delinquent youth may lead treatment programs to have harmful rather than beneficial effects (Dishion et al., 1999). Yet concern that grouping antisocial youth would result in negative social influence among participants is anything but new. Indeed, it goes back at least as far as the history of the juvenile justice system itself, which is usually traced to the founding of Houses of Refuge, the first institutions specifically intended to keep troubled youth from lives of crime (Bernard, 1992).

The first House of Refuge was founded in New York in 1825. It was widely viewed as an innovation that made the United States a world leader in addressing the problems of children and youth (Schlossman, 1977). A primary rationale for the House of Refuge was to create an alternative to placing children in prisons with adults, and one of the reasons for this apprehension was the assumption that adult criminals would influence children toward a life of crime (Schlossman, 1977, p. 23). Foreshadowing the now common notion that correctional institutions can be "schools of crime," an 1819 report of the group that created the first House of Refuge stated that the penitentiary serves as "a college for the perfection of adepts in guilt" (Bernard, 1992, p. 61).

Houses of Refuge temporarily established a legal basis for a separate institutional placement for juveniles, but that legal precedent was lost in an Illinois state supreme court decision of 1870 (Bernard, 1992). Housing children in adult jails and prisons therefore remained a major social concern. In 1890 the Chicago Board of Public Charities issued a report that deplored the practice and illustrated the belief that adult prisoners would have a negative influence on children, stating "what a shame, to place these little boys in such a school of vice" (Platt, 1977, p. 122). The creation of the juvenile court, first in Chicago in 1899 and soon after throughout not only the entire United States but also much of the industrialized world, finally provided a legal framework for keeping juveniles out of adult jails and prisons. The existence of the juvenile court was not always sufficient to effect this change, however, for as late as 1994 the Office of Juvenile Justice and Delinquency Prevention (OJJDP) was still working to compel states to separate juveniles and adults in detention and correctional facilities (OJJDP, 1994). The issue of separating juveniles from adult prisoners became more prominent once again in the 1990s as virtually every state of the union increased provisions for the transfer of juveniles to the adult criminal justice system (Snyder, Sickmund, & Poe-Yamagata, 2000).

The concern that adult facilities exposed innocent juveniles to hardened criminals soon extended to institutions created specifically for juveniles. Though the Houses of Refuge were built on high-minded ideals about protecting innocent children from the depredations of the street (Bernard, 1992), by 1850 there was widespread criticism that conditions in them were little better than in prisons. Among the many negative features of the environment cited by critics was again the idea that "incarceration provided a perfect setting for mutual instruction and reinforcement of the norms and techniques of criminal behavior" (Schlossman, 1977, p. 36). One of the responses to criticisms of Houses of Refuge was support for a cottage system, developed in Europe, in which groups of about 12–30 juveniles would live in a home-like setting with an adult couple serving as surrogate mother and father. Part of this plan was also to group youth with similar levels of past delinquency in order to minimize the negative peer influence of the more seriously delinquent on the more innocent (Schlossman, 1977, p. 38). The cottage system was widely implemented, and variants of the approach are still popular today (such as the teaching family model; see Fixsen, Phillips, & Wolf, 1978). Even so, this idea of small living units with a personal and supportive atmosphere was soon overshadowed by the dominance of large new state reformatories and training schools (Schlossman, 1977), which did little to address concerns about negative peer influence. According to Schlossman, by the 1890s there was a "critical consensus" about the many ills of these institutions, including that "the great majority of reformatories still mixed criminal and relatively innocent youth, thereby facilitating 'the contaminating influence of association' and turning reformatories into schools for crime" (1977, p. 64, quoting Homer Folks's 1891 speech to the National Conference of Charities and Correction).

The theme of peer influence toward deviance is also central to the classic social science works on the culture of correctional institutions. Though these authors emphasized institutions for adults rather than juveniles, their writings set the agenda for research in juvenile corrections as well (see, e.g., Gold & Osgood's review, 1992, pp. 6–18). Clemmer's (1940) influential study *The Prison Community* described an institutional culture in which inmates collaborated to oppose institutional authority and to support crime. Clemmer theorized that this culture stemmed from the values inmates brought with them to prison; this position came to be known as *importation theory*. Clemmer also believed that the oppositional culture of inmates had negative consequences that correspond to deviant peer contagion, in that the concentration of criminals engenders a synergistic peer influence likely to increase future crime among this already criminal group. In *Society of Captives* Sykes (1958) put forth *deprivation theory*, which portrayed inmate culture as a collective response to the deprivations inherent in institutional life, such as the loss of liberty, goods and services, and autonomy. In his well-known book *Asylums*, Goffman (1961) applied his close analysis of interpersonal interaction to these same themes for inmates of all total institutions, including settings such as mental institutions as well as prisons and juvenile reformatories. Sykes and Goffman agreed with Clemmer that aggregating criminals produced peer influence that would support values opposing reform, but they differed in attributing much of that opposition to the conditions of confinement.

Responding to the late-nineteenth-century criticisms of correctional institutions for juveniles, the juvenile court instituted the innovation of relying on probation as the standard disposition for juveniles adjudicated delinquent, rather than on incarceration. In addition to keeping youth away from the negative peer influence of institutions, probation had important advantages such as allowing the court to serve many more youth for the same cost and enabling court employees to enter the homes of the poor and attempt to alter their standards of childrearing (Schlossman, 1977). The same logic underlay calls for deinstitutionalizing status offenders that began in the 1970s (Empey, 1982) and more recent efforts to promote intermediate sanctions and community alternatives to corrections (Byrne, Lurigio, & Petersilia, 1992).

A reform movement beginning in the 1970s sought to remove as many youth as possible from all involvement in the juvenile justice system, including probation and any other nonresidential programs operated by juvenile justice agencies (Empey, 1982). The primary inspiration for the movement was *labeling theory*, which holds that involvement in the justice system increases rather than decreases the likelihood of future offending. According to labeling theory, both being legally designated "delinquent" and being sent to a program for delinquent youth carries a harmful stigma in the eyes of conventional youth and adults, and that stigma generates social forces that produce further delinquency. It is not clear whether aggregating delinquent youth played a major role in these concerns. Labeling theorists endorsed the common view that correctional institutions serve as schools for crime (e.g., Schur, 1973), but the reforms they proposed did not clearly distinguish between nonresidential programs that aggregated delinquent youth and those that did not. Interestingly, Tannenbaum's (1938) original version of labeling theory gave an important role to peer influence as a source of delinquency that arises once stigma cuts off opportunities to associate with conventional peers.

This brief historical review illustrates that concern about the potential for negative peer influence in juvenile justice programs is long-standing and widely shared and that it has been important in shaping the evolution of the juvenile justice system. The new research on deviant peer influence builds on past thinking in two important ways. First, in the past the dominant theme was negative effects that exposure to serious offenders would have on more innocent youth. The current work in this area raises the possibility that delinquent youth may have a negative social influence upon one another even if they were equally delinquent. Processes such as deviancy training or altering social networks to include proportionally fewer conventional or prosocial friends could produce a synergistic peer influence that leads all program participants to become more delinquent. Second, attention to negative peer influence in juvenile justice historically has focused almost exclusively on correctional institutions, while the current concerns place equal emphasis on nonresidential programs that aggregate deviant youth. Indeed, the prime example discussed by Dishion and his colleagues (1999) is a program for high-risk youth who are living with their parents.

PEER AGGREGATION IN
JUVENILE JUSTICE PROGRAMS

The potential for deviant peer influence is largely dependent on whether a program brings together groups of delinquent youth. This section of our chapter surveys the widely varying amounts and types of peer grouping that take place in juvenile justice programs. We also discuss some of the ways in which programs attempt to reduce the chances of negative peer influence, or even to convert it to prosocial influence. We hope that this discussion will provide some information that is useful background for Peter Greenwood's discussion of policy issues for juvenile justice (Chapter 15, this volume).

Residential Programs

Correctional institutions for juvenile offenders appear to offer conditions that are exceptionally conducive to deviant peer influence. They gather delinquent youth, keep them together 24 hours a day, and cut them off from their nondelinquent friends. Though this is necessarily true of all residential placements, there are many variations in residential programs that could affect the potential for negative peer influence.

An overarching dimension that differentiates juvenile correctional institutions is the extent to which they take a treatment versus custodial orientation (Berk, 1966; Street, Vinter, & Perrow, 1966). Custodial institutions focus on maintaining order and ensuring that residents follow rules, while institutions emphasizing treatment place a higher priority on bringing about positive change toward reform. Institutions with a treatment orientation typically have a less punitive atmosphere and more positive relations between residents and staff. Scholars such as Street and colleagues (1966) and Berk (1966) hypothesized that a treatment orientation would reduce the deprivations of institutional life, with the result of reducing support for an inmate counterculture. A number of studies have presented evidence supporting this position, but their research designs cannot rule out the possibility that results might be due to institutions with a custodial orientation serving different sorts of youth than institutions with a treatment orientation (Gold & Osgood, 1992). For instance, it would not be surprising if youth sent to custodial institutions had more serious offense histories.

Programs with a treatment orientation also often have features that may decrease the potential for deviant peer influence (Gold & Osgood, 1992). First, the activities of the treatment program are likely to increase the interactions of residents with staff in forums such as counseling sessions, meetings (Vorrath & Brendtro, 1985), and teaching interactions (Fixsen et al., 1978). These interactions increase the staff's opportunities for monitoring peer interactions, and they might also improve residents' attitudes about the staff, enhancing staff members' potential as a source of positive influence to counter negative influence from other residents. Second, treatment programs tend to impose greater structure on residents' time and interactions with one another, thus reducing chances for deviancy training and other forms of social influence. Where custodial programs typically allow residents to interact freely for long periods while watching television or milling in an exercise yard, treatment programs tend to engage them in group discussions, homework, and chores. Third, institutions with a treatment orientation are likely to divide residents into smaller units such as cottages or wings, and to organize much of institutional life around those groupings. For instance, in the original design of the cottage system, groups lived, worked, and went to school together, and they had minimal contact with residents in other groups (Schlossman, 1977, p. 38). This organization separates the social organization among residents into small divisions that may be more readily managed by staff.

Some programs with the strongest treatment orientation combine all of these elements into a milieu approach, which also includes involving all staff members in treatment delivery, whether they are counselors, teachers, or late-night hall staff. This increased communication across the staff could allow the staff to more closely monitor and alter the patterns of influence among residents, perhaps giving them leverage to reduce deviant peer influence.

The program models of guided group interaction (GGI; Empey & Rabow, 1961) and its offshoot positive peer culture (PPC; Vorrath & Brendtro, 1985) are especially interesting in relation to deviant peer influence. These programs are founded on the assumption that peer influence is an exceptionally powerful force, especially in the isolated social world of a correctional institution. These programs seek to convert the power of peer influence toward reform in a setting where it would normally oppose reform. GGI applied these principles to a group home setting, and PPC extended them to a more pervasive milieu program in an institutional setting. The PPC program design includes detailed guidance for ways that staff should make residents hold one another accountable for working to improve their current and future behavior and monitor one another for any antisocial influence. This program gives residents considerable power over one another in these regards. The centerpiece of the PPC program is a therapeutic meeting each day at which the group addresses an important personal problem of one resident. Residents take the active roles in these meetings, and the staff member in charge of the meeting is expected to intervene only when necessary to ensure that the group process remains on task. The design of the PPC program can be interpreted as an attempt to reverse the deviancy training process so that these delinquent youth reinforce both prosocial behavior and accepting responsibility for one's actions. Nevertheless, it is also possible that, if not properly managed, the same interactions could inadvertently reinforce respondents' talk about their prior misdeeds. Greenwood (Chapter 15, this volume) suggests that PPC may not have the desired effect of reducing delinquency.

Group Homes

As in correctional institutions, residents of group homes have been removed from their families' residences to live with other delinquent youth, but in contrast they also attend community schools and have at least some contact with nondelinquent youth. Thus opportunities for deviant peer influence remain high, though less so than in a correctional institution. Group homes typically are much smaller than correctional institutions, so they should present simpler social systems that might be more easily managed by staff. Yet the time residents spend in the open community also means that staff have less complete control over residents' interactions with their peers.

The teaching family model (Fixsen et al., 1978) is an interesting example of a sophisticated program developed for a group home setting. This program is built on a large base of behaviorally oriented research, and it entails extensive staff training in careful management of residents' interactions with staff and with one another. The program eschews counseling in favor of teaching interactions in which staff members work directly with residents to teach them prosocial skills. As a behavioral program, the teaching family model requires residents to earn points through prosocial behavior in order to receive extra privileges. The emphasis is on positive reinforcement rather than punishment. Lipsey and Wilson's (1998) meta-analysis of treatment programs indicated that the teaching family model is one of the more effective programs for reducing delinquency, which suggests either that these measures are effective for minimizing deviant peer influence or that deviant peer influence is not as problematic as some suspect.

Nonresidential Programs

A large proportion of the youth processed through the juvenile justice system are sent to nonresidential programs, some operated by justice agencies and some operated by community groups. The process may be designated probation, informal probation, diversion, or simply referral. Many other delinquent or high-risk youth arrive at similar programs, or even the same programs, by other routes.

Unlike residential programs, nonresidential programs need not aggregate deviant youth. Yet many do. For instance, the standard juvenile justice disposition of probation entails supervision and services by a probation officer for a specified period of time. Youths on probation are required to follow a set of rules, such as meeting with their probation officer once a month, attending school regularly, not being out late at night, and not associating with known offenders. Probation officers are also responsible for delivering services to their charges, though in recent decades this aspect of their work has receded in favor of greater emphasis on supervision and on contracting services from community agencies (Mays & Winfree, 2000). In the past, however, it was common for probation officers to hold group counseling sessions, meeting with perhaps a dozen probationers at a time to discuss their problems and offer guidance. If deviant peer contagion is indeed a powerful force that increases future delinquency, then group counseling of this sort would be exactly the wrong approach.

In relation to the issue of peer aggregation, there would appear to be three basic program strategies. The first is to bring together groups of delinquent or high-risk youth in order to provide a program addressing the issues that they share in common. Among the potential benefits of doing so would be efficiency, the likely mutual acceptance among youth with similar experiences, and the use of program activities that capitalize on shared experience and understanding. Yet Dishion and colleagues (1999) concluded that activities of this sort were the forum for deviancy training that led to deviant peer contagion.

A second strategy would be to place delinquent or high-risk youth in programs that also serve nondelinquent youth. For instance, these youth could be sent to programs that serve the general population of youth in their neighborhoods such as Boys Clubs or summer camps for inner-city children. There are many such programs, and this strategy has long been the stock-in-trade of programs that divert youth from the juvenile justice system. This strategy brings little risk of deviant peer contagion unless a pattern of concentrated interaction develops among the subset of deviant youth. A limitation of this approach is that it is an unlikely means of delivering intensive services that target the specific needs of highly delinquent youth. One study that did involve nondelinquent adolescents in counseling sessions with delinquent adolescents concluded that this pattern of interaction reduced future delinquency for the delinquent youth, without increasing it for the originally nondelinquent youth (Feldman, Caplinger, & Wodarski, 1983). We return to this study in the next section.

Finally, programs can serve youth, and perhaps their families, individually rather than in groups, thereby totally avoiding any possibility of contagion. Consider, for instance, the successful programs of multisystemic therapy (Henggeler, 1998) and multidimensional treatment foster care (Chamberlain & Reid, 1998). Both are intensive programs that work with key adults involved in the lives of delinquent youth to provide the youth with strong supervision and support, and there is no aspect of the programs that require the youth to interact with other delinquent youth. Instead, the adults are trained to be sure that the youth are not allowed to spend unsupervised time with other youth, especially youth who have reputations for misbehavior. As we discuss in more detail below, Eddy and Chamberlain (2000) found evidence that the success of multidimensional treatment foster care was at least partially due to reducing deviant peer association.

STUDIES OF PEER EFFECTS
IN JUVENILE JUSTICE PROGRAMS

Based on theory and research on peer influence and delinquency, the history of concern about negative peer influence in justice program settings, and the aggregation of deviant peers in so many programs, there would seem to be considerable potential for deviant peer influence in juvenile justice. Yet research directly examining peer effects in programs is rare. Consider, for instance, that neither Empey and colleagues' well-known studies of GGI (Empey & Erickson, 1972; Empey & Lubeck, 1971), nor Andrews's (1980) prison studies testing differential association theory gathered any data about peer relations. In this section of our chapter we review those studies we have identified as directly investigating peer effects in juvenile justice programs.[1]

Reinforcement of Behavior in Institutional Settings

Buehler, Patterson, and Furniss (1966) presented a set of three relatively simple pilot studies that provide information very relevant to the peer processes that could produce deviant peer contagion in residential programs. In these studies of groups of girls who resided together in a correctional institution, trained observers coded sequences of behaviors and responses. They identified behaviors classified as deviant or rule break-ing and those classified as normative or encouraged by the program. Buehler and colleagues then analyzed the proportion of times that each type of behavior was followed by positive reinforcement versus punish-ment. They determined that peers were considerably more likely to observe and to respond to youths' behavior than were staff, which would give peers greater power to shape behavior. Furthermore, the overwhelming majority of peers' responses to deviant acts were reinforc-ing (ranging from 70% to 88%), while normative behaviors were usu-ally punished. When staff did respond, they showed no consistent pat-tern of punishing or reinforcing either type of behavior. Thus, according to standard behavioral principles, interactions among these deviant peers should exert a strong influence toward deviance, which the actions of staff would do little to counter.

There are obvious limitations to this set of small studies. They in-clude no measures of the effects of these processes on later delinquent behavior, and they are based on small samples of individuals studied for brief periods at a single institution. Yet this research provides a useful model of the sort of data that would be helpful for determining the na-ture of deviant peer influence and the conditions under which it does and does not occur.

Multidimensional Treatment Foster Care Evaluation

Eddy and Chamberlain (2000) present a unique analysis that combines a sound evaluation of a juvenile justice program's effectiveness with a test of the influence of deviant peers. Previous analyses of this sample of 53 chronic and severe offenders had shown that multidimensional treat-ment foster care reduced both official and self-reported delinquency rela-tive to a randomly assigned control group (Chamberlain & Reid, 1998). The control group members were placed in group homes, which was the standard justice system disposition for this sample. Eddy and Chamber-lain examined several potential mediators of program impact, all of which were variables targeted by multidimensional treatment foster care. Their analysis is of special interest here because one of those medi-ators was associating with deviant peers. They found that assignment to the treatment program greatly reduced deviant peer association ($r = -.78$), which in turn was associated with both official delinquency ($r = .35$) and self-reported delinquency ($r = .25$). The mediation analyses they report are not informative about the specific mediating role of deviant peer as-sociation because they combine this variable with the other mediators. Fortunately, the correlations they report allow us to calculate the relevant indirect effects (McClendon, 1995). Doing so reveals that the reduction in deviant peer association produced by the program could account for almost all of the program's impact on official delinquency (94%) and roughly two-thirds of its impact on self-reported delinquency (63%). This pattern is quite consistent with the themes of deviant peer contagion.

It would be overinterpreting the findings, however, to view this result as a definitive demonstration of the causal impact of aggregating deviant adolescents in juvenile justice programs. Reducing deviant peer association was only one of several goals of multidimensional treatment foster care; the program also succeeded in improving the youth–adult relationship, increasing discipline, and enhancing supervision. All of these variables were associated with delinquency and highly correlated with one another. Given the small sample size of the study, it is impossible to disentangle the mediating effects of these variables from those of deviant peer association. Doing so would require a much larger sample size, or, even better, a comparison of programs that differ in fewer respects, such as a study contrasting multidimensional treatment foster care with a group home version of the same treatment strategy.

St. Louis Experiment

In their intriguing book *The St. Louis Conundrum*, Feldman and his colleagues (1983) posed a question that directly addresses the idea of deviant peer contagion: Will delinquent youth fair better in treatment groups whose members are mostly conventional youth than they do in groups all of whose members are delinquent youth? Feldman and colleagues addressed this issue through an intensive study of 60 groups of boys at Jewish community centers in St. Louis. In one-third of the groups all members were delinquent youth who had been referred from a variety of sources, one-third of the groups consisted of one or two such delinquent youth mixed with the usual clientele of the community centers, and one-third of the groups consisted of only the usual clientele. The delinquent youth were allocated to the two types of groups by random assignment. The researchers gathered observational data on the group sessions, and youth and group leaders completed questionnaires four times during the treatment process. Parents and referral sources also completed interviews before the start of the program and at its end.

Feldman and his colleagues concluded that the antisocial behavior of delinquent youth was lower when they were in the mixed groups than in the all-delinquent groups, while there was no increase in antisocial behavior for nondelinquent youth assigned to the mixed groups rather than to entirely nondelinquent groups. This finding would appear to be one of the strongest pieces of evidence of deviant peer influence in juvenile justice programs. Nevertheless, a careful reading of their book reveals reasons for caution in accepting that conclusion. The design of the study included an equal number of groups in the three conditions, which resulted in assigning 237 delinquent youth to the all-delinquent groups and only 26 delinquent youth to the mixed groups (Feldman et al., 1983, p. 68). Thus statistical power for detecting differences between these two conditions was limited. Indeed, though comparisons of outcomes for delinquent youth tended to favor the mixed groups, the differences did not approach statistical significance for the observational measures ($p = .37$; p. 142), group leaders' reports ($p = .53$; p. 165), referral agents' ratings ($p = .61$; p. 209), or parents' reports ($p = .19$; p. 210). The one statistically significant finding favoring the mixed groups was for lower self-reported delinquency by the delinquent youth ($p < .01$; p. 163), but that result was also accompanied by a finding of higher self-reported manifest aggression for the same group ($p = .02$; p. 163). Interpretation of these findings is also complicated by quite a few significant interactions of the effect of group composition with the other factors manipulated in the experiment, which were group leaders' experience (experienced vs. inexperienced) and type of treatment program (a behavioral method vs. a traditional social work group therapy vs. a minimal intervention placebo condition). Furthermore, the findings are limited to the period of the treatment program. An attempted follow-up 1 year later yielded too little data to analyze. Though the findings do favor mixed rather than entirely delinquent groups, the evidence must be regarded as only suggestive.

Another interesting aspect of the St. Louis Experiment is the researchers' analyses of peer influence of the groups on individuals. These analyses were not very sophisticated as far as separating influence from the contributions of selection factors or other influences in the shared environment (Jussim & Osgood, 1989). Rather, they simply tracked individuals' own scores in relation to the mean of the other group members. In doing so, Feldman and his colleagues were able to demonstrate a strong association between individuals' adjustment and that of their groups. This suggests a substantial potential role for peer influence in group programs.

The St. Louis Experiment was an ambitious study directed toward issues central to the concerns of this volume. Its long-term contribution to the field is limited by its unbalanced research design and a lack of resources that precluded meaningful follow-up data. In many ways, however, this study points the way to the type of study that would be most useful for furthering our understanding of deviant peer influence in juvenile justice.

Building Criminal Capital Behind Bars

Bayer, Pintoff, and Pozen (2003) took a unique approach to examining peer effects in juvenile justice. These economists hypothesized that individuals specialize in areas of crime where their returns are greatest and that they will acquire criminal capital primarily in those areas. Bayer and colleagues used the phrase "criminal capital" to refer to skills, knowledge, and networks that enhance the capability of committing illegal acts. They hypothesized that exposure to peers with similar criminal histories will result in increased acquisition of criminal capital and therefore an increase in subsequent illegal behavior. Reasoning from their strong assumption of specialization, they argued that exposure to peers with dissimilar criminal histories will not result in an increase of capital and thus will have no effect on recidivism.

To test these hypotheses, Bayer and colleagues (2003) analyzed Department of Juvenile Justice records in Florida for all individuals under the age of 18 who were released from juvenile facilities in Florida over a 2-year period. Their data included records for almost 15,000 individuals released from 169 facilities, including community and institutional settings ranging from group homes to boot camps to residential treatment programs. These records provided information on past offenses, facility assignment, and offenses for a year following release.

Bayer and colleagues' (2003) primary focus was on the effects of serving time with peers who had similar and dissimilar criminal records. They addressed this issue in terms of the set of peers who resided in a facility at the same time as each target individual. They formulated a strong quasi-experimental design for this purpose by controlling for differences between facilities (which are likely to serve clienteles with very different risks of recidivism) in order to limit their analysis to within-facility variation. Preliminary analyses demonstrated that within-facility variation in the overlap of interest was effectively random.

Analyses provided considerable support for Bayer and colleagues' (2003) hypotheses. For about half of the offenses they studied, being placed with more peers who had committed that offense had a significantly greater effect on recidivism for those youth who previously committed the same offense. They found the strongest evidence of this peer influence for felony drug crimes, and significant evidence for burglary, petty larceny, and felony weapon offenses. In contrast, analyses revealed no consistent evidence of any effect of being placed with peers who had committed an offense with which the individual had no experience. Analyses also showed that peer effects decline as age increases and that older peers have greater influence than younger peers.

Bayer and colleagues (2003) acknowledged that overlapping stays within a facility do not guarantee actual interaction between any pair of residents, so that may be too broad of a definition of peer influence. They therefore repeated their analyses for small facilities, in which there is likely to be more interaction between all individuals. They found stronger evidence of influence in this case, which supported their interpretation of the results.

Though Bayer and colleagues (2003) conducted a strong study of peer influence on illegal behavior, it does not directly address deviant peer contagion. Deviant peer contagion refers to a general increase in offending that results when programs bring together groups of offenders. Bayer and colleagues' research focuses on a narrower pattern of influence that applies when a target individual's offense specialization matches that of the peers with which he or she is placed. Indeed, their analyses have limited potential to address the effects of overall levels of peer deviance because there is little systematic variation in those levels within facilities over time. In other words, their approach gains its methodological strength from a feature that precludes an effective analysis of the general phenomenon of deviant peer contagion. Nevertheless, their findings should be of interest to program designers because it suggests that negative peer effects will be most problematic when programs group offenders who share an offense specialization. Finally, research generally indicates that juveniles are more often versatile offenders, committing many different types of offenses, than they are specialists (e.g., Farrington, Snyder & Finnegan, 1988). Thus the potential for differentiating offenders by their offense specialties is likely more limited than Bayer and colleagues suggest.

Peer Influence Project

The Peer Influence Project (Gold & Osgood, 1992) was a study of 336 boys placed in 45 living units at Michigan's four largest juvenile correctional institutions. Two of these institutions were the state's training schools and the other two were long-standing private facilities. The purpose of the project was to study peer influence processes in a setting where peer interaction was intensive and where participants were assigned to rather than chose their peer groups.[2]

Unlike most other studies we have reviewed, the Peer Influence Project did not focus on differences between types of treatment, but rather analyzed variation within a single treatment approach. All four institutions used PPC, which largely restricts social interactions to the youth who share a living unit. Gold and Osgood reasoned that this division into relatively isolated peer groups made an excellent laboratory for the study of peer influence.

Though the researchers were not able to control the assignment of youth to living units, they limited the study to sets of groups among which assignment was effectively random. At all four institutions, the basic policy was to assign newly placed youth to the first available living unit. Observation of the assignment process revealed that this policy was followed in the vast majority of cases, and that exceptions to that policy were in the direction of heightening similarity across groups rather than differentiating them (e.g., avoiding putting too many youth with drug problems in the same group). Preliminary data analyses supported the comparability of groups within institutions, and analyses of peer effects controlled for differences between institutions.

To study peer influence, the Peer Influence Project first gathered data from all residents in the 45 groups, doing so on three occasions over the year in which the target sample entered the institutions. The target sample members were interviewed upon entering the institutions, 4 months later, at the time of their release, and 6 months after departing. Analyses of peer influence related measures of target youths' adjustment to group norms measured between 4 months before and 2 months after their arrival. This timing assured that the norms reflected a preexisting property of the group, established before the target individual could play a substantial role in shaping them. Measures of group norms were the mean of residents' responses to questions about "most members of your group" with regard to delinquent values, support for an inmate counterculture of resistance to institutional authority, and accepting the goals of the program.

The findings of the Peer Influence Project gave clear evidence that peer influence occurs in these correctional settings, but they also indicated that peer influence may not be the potent force that many have thought. Four months after arrival, members of groups with norms supportive of an inmate counterculture engaged in more behavior violating institutional rules, were more supportive of the counterculture themselves, and showed poorer overall adjustment. This pattern held for delinquent behavior and general adjustment at the time of release as well (when support for the counterculture was not measured). Yet these relationships were not strong; standardized regression coefficients were no greater than .2. Furthermore, group norms were not significantly associated with behavior and adjustment 6 months after leaving the institution, a striking result given the intensive experience of having spent a year interacting only with fellow members of that small group.

Jussim and Osgood's (1989) conceptual model helps us to understand these findings by distinguishing two stages of the influence process. The first is perception or communication of the group norm, as reflected in the correspondence between the group norm and the individual's perceptions about the group. The second is subjective influence, which is the influence of that perception on the individual's own behavior or adjustment. The findings of the Peer Influence Project showed that the weak link in the influence process was perception of the group norm. Correlations between norms and perceptions were in the range of .25–.34, values insufficient to produce strong peer influence. In other words, there was not sufficient agreement among members about a group's norms for those norms to provide a clear social reality that could dramatically shape members' attitudes and behavior.

We see two principal questions about the breadth of the implications of these findings. The first is whether the contribution of peer influence is dampened by the study's focus on a single treatment approach. Perhaps more substantial differences in group norms will only emerge when contrasting different treatment models. We did not think this was the case because we observed wide and stable variation across living units for the staff's morale and their orientation toward their work (e.g., support for group decision making, emphasis on treatment vs. custody). Of course, whatever differences existed among these living units, all of these youth did spend a year in the full-time company of other delinquent youth, and the study is not informative about the contrast to residing in the open community. The second possibility is that group norms and the accompanying subjective processes are not the key to peer influence. For instance, it is possible that the deviancy training processes portrayed by Dishion and his colleagues (1999) operate without the awareness of the participants, and if so, our methods would be unable to detect them.

CONCLUSIONS

Deviant peer influence is an issue of enormous consequence for juvenile justice. If this increase in delinquency that stems from bringing together troubled youth is a powerful and widespread phenomenon, then juvenile justice programs must be carefully designed to avoid it or they will have considerably less success at their mission to reduce delinquency. Concern about the possible negative effects of peers in juvenile justice reaches back as far as 1825 when Houses of Refuge were founded as an alternative to placing children in adult prisons, where it was assumed that adults would lead the juveniles toward a life of crime. Further innovations in juvenile justice, such as the cottage system and probation, attempted to address potential negative peer influence from other juveniles. Today, attention to iatrogenic effects of peer influence has expanded to include any setting in which juveniles are brought together, from correctional institutions to nonresidential programs.

Deviant peer influence might occur in several different ways. Juvenile justice programs that bring together delinquent youth necessarily expose each to new delinquent peers, thereby increasing the potential for influence. In addition, grouping deviant adolescents may also increase the frequency of interaction among delinquent peers, both during program sessions and potentially during time away from the program. Programs can seek to minimize deviant peer influence by not bringing juveniles together at all, or they can choose strategies that reduce unstructured or unsupervised interactions of juveniles (Osgood, Wilson, O'Malley, Bachman, & Johnston, 1996).

The research we have reviewed in this chapter provides consistent evidence that associating with deviant peers influences youth toward greater delinquency, a pattern that holds both for adolescents' friendships in general and for peer contacts arising in juvenile justice programs. Yet it is also clear from these studies that deviant peer influence is not as potent a force as some have argued. The few studies in the general population that address the methodological problems of selection and same-source bias find that peer influence is genuine, but modest (see Haynie & Osgood, 2005). Similar conclusions result from studies of peer processes in juvenile justice programs.

It is still not clear exactly how deviant peer influence operates, especially under the conditions of various juvenile justice programs and among groups of different types of juveniles. Our review of specific studies makes clear that research about peer processes in juvenile justice programs remains quite limited. There is also little if any available evidence about whether deviant peer contagion is equally applicable across lines of gender, race/ethnicity, and social class. Furthermore, though troubled youth are often involved in multiple programs, we know little about the combined effects, especially when some of these programs may group deviant youth while others do not. Most importantly, we know very little about the effectiveness of different strategies for overcoming deviant peer influence.

Many important topics concerning peer influence in juvenile justice merit further research. The studies that have directly addressed peer processes in these settings are interesting and valuable, but there are so few of them that they raise as many questions as they answer. Further research on this topic is critically important both for designing effective programs and for furthering our understanding of delinquency in general. Juvenile justice programs provide unique research opportunities that rarely arise in the more typical settings of adolescent life, such as bringing together previously unacquainted adolescents for periods of intensive interaction, often in constrained settings potentially subject to observation by researchers.

To enable us to improve programs and to advance our knowledge, future research should have several attributes. First, strong research designs are essential. Only true experiments and strong quasi-experimental studies can give confidence that findings are more likely due to the peer processes of interest than to preexisting differences between the youth in different conditions. Second, our greatest need is for studies that measure and analyze peer relationships such as friendship and interaction patterns. Without such data there is little hope of clarifying the mechanisms of deviant peer contagion and the conditions under which it does and does not occur. Finally, the studies must be large enough to have sufficient statistical power for detecting effects of modest size and for determining variation in the strength of effects, and they must be of sufficient duration to differentiate immediate consequences of peer processes from longer term effects.

NOTES

1. We omit Dishion and colleagues' (1999) Adolescent Transitions Program Study from our discussion because it is thoroughly considered in other chapters of this volume. It would fit well here, however, because it shows higher rates of delinquency and problem behaviors resulting from a group treatment program, and the authors did gather data about peer interactions.

2. Ted Newcomb, a founding father of social psychology and of the study of peer relations, was one of the original designers and principal investigators of the Peer Influence Project. The design of the project was in many ways analogous to that of Newcomb's famous study of social influence among the women of Bennington College (Newcomb, 1943). Unfortunately, Ted passed away during the early phases of the Peer Influence Project, but he and his work had great influence on the study.

CHAPTER 9

The Effects of Community-Based Group Treatment for Delinquency

A Meta-Analytic Search for Cross-Study Generalizations

Mark W. Lipsey

Research reviewed in other chapters in this volume has found negative effects for treatments that work with juvenile offenders or juveniles at risk for delinquency in groups (Dodge, Lansford, & Dishion, Chapter 1; Osgood & Briddell, Chapter 8, this volume). Moreover, as those reviews demonstrate, there is substantial evidence indicating that affiliation with antisocial peers can lead to increased delinquency among such youth (also see Dishion & Dodge, Chapter 2, and Klein, Chapter 13, this volume). These findings make it plausible that exposure to antisocial peers in treatment conditions may produce increases in delinquency that outweigh whatever therapeutic influence the treatment has for reducing delinquency. The treatment circumstances under which such negative effects may occur could be circumscribed and relatively rare or they could be more general and pervasive. The latter case would be especially problematic for juvenile justice programs, which routinely collect delinquent and predelinquent youth into groups for reasons of practical necessity and efficiency in delivering treatment.

The greatest concentration of juvenile offenders in groups within the juvenile justice system occurs in training schools, camps, and other residential facilities to which juveniles are sentenced for sufficiently serious offenses. Although rehabilitation programs are usually provided within those facilities, whatever distinct grouping of juveniles they involve is embedded within the broader, continuous aggregation of delinquent youth within the facility itself. Under these circumstances, the residential arrangements themselves, not treatment sessions within that context, are the most likely source of potential negative peer effects on delinquency. There is some evidence that confinement in such facilities is associated with increased delinquency (Osgood & Briddell, Chapter 8, this volume), but it is a difficult matter to study. Juvenile justice processes and legitimate concerns about public safety do not readily permit experimental comparisons of the subsequent delinquency of juveniles sentenced to residential facilities and comparable juveniles with alternative dispositions that do not entail high levels of contact with delinquent peers.

The juvenile justice programs that affect the largest number of juveniles, however, do not involve institutional confinement. The most frequent disposition for juvenile court cases is probation, that is, court supervision within the community. Also, in many systems, significant numbers of offenders are diverted to social service programs before they get to court. In addition, prevention programs are often provided for minor and first-time offenders and other youth identified by various social agents as being at risk for delinquency. These community-based programs use a wide range of treatment approaches in formats that involve individual juveniles, juveniles in groups, or juveniles with family members. Programs using a group format often bring youth together who are not previously acquainted and who would not likely be in such close contact in the absence of the program. If peer influences have negative effects on the potential for subsequent delinquency, these programs are especially vulnerable. Moreover, if such negative effects occur under relatively common program circumstances rather than being limited to unusual conditions, we would expect the whole category of programs using group formats on average to produce negative or at least diminished effects relative to comparable programs that do not use a group format.

This chapter describes an exploration of a large body of delinquency prevention and intervention studies aimed at finding across-study generalizations about the effects of treatment in peer groups relative to treatments that do not work with juveniles in groups. Admittedly, this is a challenging task. There is no significant body of research that attempts to directly compare outcomes for youth treated in peer groups versus those treated in other formats. Even if such studies existed in useful numbers, it would be difficult to determine if different outcomes were a result of negative group influences or a difference in the actual treatments delivered, some of which would be inherent in the nature of the respective treatment formats (e.g., differential amounts of individual attention).

Similarly, when we compare studies of group and nongroup treatment, any differences in outcomes could stem from differences in the juvenile samples involved, other aspects of the treatments provided, or even the methods employed in the studies. The best we can do under these circumstances is to select groups of studies for comparison that are as similar as possible except for group versus nongroup treatment format and/or use statistical controls to adjust for differences other than the treatment format. This chapter attempts to make such comparisons using data developed in a large meta-analysis of research on delinquency interventions. It focuses on community-based programs for preventing or reducing delinquent offenses among juveniles 12–18 years old that are divided into two categories: (1) prevention programs that treat (usually minor) offenders and juveniles at risk for offending who are not adjudicated or under court supervision, and (2) probation programs that treat adjudicated offenders who are on probation or under an analogous form of court supervision, but not institutionalized.

The analysis first identifies studies that found negative effects, that is, less subsequent delinquency among juveniles in the control group than juveniles in the intervention group, whether or not those differences were statistically significant. Next, within the sets of prevention and probation studies, those reporting negative and positive effects are compared to determine if treatments using group formats are disproportionately represented among the negative ones. The analysis then examines interventions for which different programs provide services in individual, group, or mixed formats. In these cases, the effects on delinquency are compared across individual and group formats with other characteristics of the studies statistically controlled. A separate analysis compares individual and group counseling with other study differences controlled. Counseling is the most common type of intervention provided in both individual and group formats and thus allows comparison under circumstances where the nature of the treatment itself is relatively similar across formats.

The final analysis considers only interventions provided in a group format to investigate moderator variables potentially associated with the delinquent outcomes. The first moderator variables of interest in this analysis are those relating to the characteristics of the juveniles and the groups into which they are aggregated for treatment (e.g., risk level, heterogeneity of risk, gender mix, age). The second group of moderators examined relate to the nature of the treatment and the leadership and supervision of the groups. These analyses attempt to identify circumstances in which the effects of group treatments are negative or especially weak.

META-ANALYSIS DATA

This review draws upon an extensive meta-analysis of the effects of intervention on delinquency (Lipsey, 1992, 1995; Lipsey & Wilson, 1998) that employed a thorough bibliographical search to identify published and unpublished studies that met specified criteria, summarized as follows:

- Juveniles ages 12–18 received an intervention that could potentially have some positive effect on their subsequent delinquency.
- Quantitative results were reported for a comparison between a treatment and a control condition for at least one delinquency outcome measure. In addition, the assignment of juveniles to conditions was random or, if not, pretreatment group differences were reported that allowed an assessment of initial group equivalence—for example, a pretest on the dependent variable, demographic comparisons, matching, or the like.
- The study was conducted between 1950 and 2002 in an English-speaking country and reported in English.

Studies meeting these criteria were retrieved and coded by trained personnel on more than 150 items describing study methods and procedures, subject characteristics, treatment and program characteristics, outcome effect sizes, and other related matters (the bibliography of studies included is available at www.vanderbilt.edu/cerm). Two subsets of this larger database were used for the analyses reported here.

1. The *"prevention" database* included 174 experimental and quasi-experimental studies of the effects of community-based prevention programs on the subsequent delinquency of the participants. These studies met the criteria for the overall meta-analysis but were selected to include only those in which the treated juveniles were not adjudicated or under court supervision at the time of treatment.
2. The *"probation" database* included 197 experimental and quasi-experimental studies of the effects of community-based programs on the recidivism of juvenile probationers. These studies also met the criteria for the overall meta-analysis and were selected to include only those in which the treated juveniles were identified as being under court supervision as probationers or in some comparable status, but not in a custodial institution or residential placement.

The delinquency outcome variables selected for analysis from the studies in these databases (one per study) were those representing subsequent arrests or, if that was not available, whatever delinquency outcome was most similar to arrests. For the probation database, 55% of the outcomes were expressed in terms of arrests, 6% as probation violations, 29% as court contact, 3% as incarceration, and the remainder as school disciplinary actions or self-report. For the prevention database, 50% were reported as arrests, 2% as probation actions, 10% as court contact, 1% as incarceration, 16% as school disciplinary actions, and 20% as reports from the juveniles, parents, teachers, or other observers. The intervention effects in these outcomes were represented as standardized mean difference effect sizes, that is, the difference between the mean treatment and mean control group outcomes divided by the pooled standard deviation. Statistical controls were used in all analyses to adjust for differences in effect sizes associated with the form in which the outcome variables were expressed. Hedges's (1981) small sample correction was applied to the effect sizes, and outlier effect sizes and sample sizes were Winsorized (i.e., recoded to less extreme values) prior to analysis. In all analyses, the effect sizes were weighted by the inverse of the sampling error variance (Hedges & Olkin, 1985) and fixed effects statistical models were used throughout (representing these particular sets of studies only but accounting for subject-level sampling error within the studies).

ANALYSIS AND RESULTS

Group Treatment and Negative Effects

A straightforward examination of whether group treatment of juveniles is associated with negative effects (i.e., more delinquency in the treatment group than in the control group) can be made by determining if studies that yield negative effect sizes show a disproportionate representation of group treatments. It must be kept in mind, however, that negative effect sizes do not necessarily mean that the corresponding interventions have harmful effects. Sampling error is associated with every effect estimate. Especially with small samples, therefore, a certain proportion of effect sizes in any set of studies will be negative on a chance basis. Nonetheless, if group treatment tends to produce negative effects, the proportion of such effects should be higher for group treatments than for those provided in other formats.

For each study represented in the meta-analysis, the primary treatment format was coded as individual (including juvenile alone, juvenile and provider, and juvenile with parents), mixed (more than one format, none primary), and group.[1] The 174 studies in the prevention database include 84 involving treatments provided in youth groups, 58 that do not involve groups, and 32 that are mixed. The overall mean effect size is 0.10, which is statistically significant but small enough that the distribution around it includes negative effect size values. Within that distribution, 58 effect sizes were negative, 104 were positive, and 12 were exactly zero. Table 9.1 shows the relationship between group versus nongroup treatment and positive versus negative effect sizes. It reveals no significant tendency for treatments provided in group format to produce more negative effects than treatments that do not involve groups. Table 9.1 also shows the results when this analysis was repeated using only studies with high internal validity (i.e., those with random assignment and no attrition). In addition, it presents the results when the analysis was repeated using only studies reported in dissertations and technical reports, which should be less influenced by any publication bias against negative effects. Both these versions also showed no significant relationships between group treatment and negative effect size values.

A similar analysis was done with the studies in the probation database. Of the 197 studies, 58 involved treatments in youth groups, 94 did not, and 45 involved a mix of group and nongroup treatment formats. The overall mean effect size for these studies is 0.13, which, like the prevention studies, is statistically significant but small enough for the distribution around it to include a number of negative effect size values. Those effect sizes divided into 48 with negative values, 140 with positive values, and nine in which the value was exactly zero. Table 9.2 presents the breakdown of positive and negative effect sizes for the group and nongroup treatments. As with the studies of prevention treatments, this

TABLE 9.1. Positive and Negative Effect Sizes for Group versus Nongroup Prevention Studies

	All studies[a]		Randomized No-attrition studies[b]		Studies reported in dissertations and technical reports[c]	
	Negative effect size % (n)	Positive effect size % (n)	Negative effect size % (n)	Positive effect size % (n)	Negative effect size % (n)	Positive effect size % (n)
Group	42.1 (32)	57.9 (44)	46.2 (12)	53.8 (14)	46.3 (25)	53.7 (29)
Nongroup	41.8 (23)	58.2 (32)	36.0 (9)	64.0 (16)	48.4 (15)	51.6 (16)

[a] Chi-square = .001; df = 1; p = .97.
[b] Chi-square = .54; df = 1; p = .46.
[c] Chi-square = .04; df = 1; p = .85.

TABLE 9.2. Positive and Negative Effect Sizes for Group versus Nongroup Probation Studies

	All studies[a]		Randomized No-attrition studies[b]		Studies reported in dissertations and technical reports[c]	
	Negative effect size % (n)	Positive effect size % (n)	Negative effect size % (n)	Positive effect size % (n)	Negative effect size % (n)	Positive effect size % (n)
Group	21.8 (12)	78.2 (43)	26.7 (4)	73.3 (11)	26.5 (9)	73.5 (25)
Nongroup	26.4 (24)	73.6 (67)	26.3 (5)	73.7 (14)	30.2 (16)	69.8 (37)

[a] Chi-square = .38; $df = 1$; $p = .54$.
[b] Chi-square = .001; $df = 1$; $p = .98$.
[c] Chi-square = .14; $df = 1$; $p = .71$.

comparison shows no significant tendency for treatment in groups to produce more negative effects. The analogous breakdowns for the random assignment, no attrition studies and those reported in dissertations and technical reports also showed no significant relationships between group treatment and negative effect size values (Table 9.2).

These analyses reveal no indication of a general tendency for treatment provided in youth groups to more frequently produce negative effects than treatment not provided in groups. The studies in both the prevention and the probation databases do include a number with negative effect size values, but this mainly reflects sampling error in estimating effect sizes around overall means that are modest. Of the 58 negative effect size values in the prevention database, for instance, only six are reliably different from zero at $p < .05$. Similarly, of the 48 negative values appearing in the probation studies, only eight were significantly lower than zero. With no evidence that group treatments generally produce disproportionate negative effects, we next take up the question of whether treatment provided in youth groups tends to produce smaller average effects than comparable treatments not provided in groups.

GROUP TREATMENT COMPARED WITH INDIVIDUAL TREATMENT

Treatment Provided in Peer Group Format versus Individual Format

The nature of the treatment provided in the individual, group, and mixed formats described above was coded from study reports with a checklist that identified a wide range of treatment components that might be present—for example, individual counseling, tutoring, and recreation. This procedure was adopted because most treatments involved multiple components rather than a single treatment modality. However, when there was a dominant component, as there often was, it was coded as such and other components were coded as secondary treatment elements.

If we select studies of treatments that involve a given treatment component, for example, interpersonal skills training, and break out the format in which treatment was provided, we find many components that are present in treatments provided in all three formats: individual, group, and mixed. This applies in some cases even though the treatment component itself involves only one format. For instance, individual counseling is, of course, provided in an individual format. However, individual counseling is part of many multicomponent treatment packages for which the primary format across all the components is group or mixed.

If treatments provided mainly in individual versus group formats involve rather different types of treatment, represented in our coding as different combinations of treatment components, any differences in their outcomes might well represent differential treatment effectiveness, not the influence of the format. To maintain some overall comparability in the nature of the treatments, therefore, we first identified treatment components that appeared in combinations provided in all three formats. Table 9.3 lists those components. We then selected studies involving these treatment components from each database and divided them according to the primary treatment format. This procedure resulted in 96 prevention studies (32 individual format, 16 mixed format, 48 group format) and 105 probation studies (38 individual format, 33 mixed for-

TABLE 9.3. Treatment Components Represented in the Sets of Individual-Format, Mixed-Format, and Group-Format Studies Selected for Analysis

Individual counseling	Employment related
Group counseling	Sports/recreation
Interpersonal skills	Multimodal
Life skills	Mentoring [a]
Tutoring/remedial education	Drug/alcohol [b]
Cognitive-behavioral	Health education [b]
Behavior management	

[a] Prevention studies only.
[b] Probation studies only.

mat, and 34 group format). In each case, therefore, the individual, mixed, and group format treatments to be compared involve the same mix of treatment components, though not necessarily in the same proportions.

Table 9.4 shows the mean effect sizes by treatment format for these sets of studies. For neither the prevention nor the probation studies was the mean effect size for treatments provided in group format notably smaller than those provided in individual format. For the prevention studies, however, it was smaller than treatment provided in mixed format. Because the mixed format also involves some treatment in groups, the significantly larger effect size for that format among the prevention studies is unlikely to represent solely the influence of the treatment format. Table 9.4 also shows the standard deviations, which might be expected to be larger for treatments in group format if some were more likely to produce negative effects that were offset in the mean by others producing larger positive effects. No such differences are evident, however.

The studies in each of the categories shown in Table 9.4 differ in other ways, so the mean effect sizes are not as fully comparable as desired for purposes of assessing the relative magnitude of treatment in group versus treatment in nongroup formats. We thus repeated this comparative analysis using only the individual and group treatments and with control variables included to adjust for some of the other study characteristics that might distort the comparison.

One set of appropriate control variables relates to variation in the methods and procedures used in the studies, many of which are partially confounded with treatment characteristics. In previous analyses using the prevention and probation databases we defined factors that combine variables from our coding into conceptually related clusters predictive of effect sizes. These were developed separately for each database and thus are somewhat different for each. In both cases, however, they represent variables related to study design and initial group equivalence, attrition after initial assignment to conditions, and characteristics of the delin-

TABLE 9.4. Mean Effect Sizes (and n) for Prevention and Probation Studies with Similar Treatment Components by Treatment Format

Study type	Overall mean ES (SD; n)	By treatment format		
		Individual	Mixed	Group
Prevention	.10 (.29; 96)	.07 (.27; 32)	.25 (.28; 16)	.06 (.29; 48)
Probation	.11 (.26; 105)	.09 (.24; 38)	.12 (.27; 33)	.14 (.27; 34)

Note. Each of these mean effect sizes is significantly greater than zero. The differences between the formats are significant for the prevention studies but not for the probation studies.

quency outcome measure. Specifically, the method control variables are as follows:

1. *Attrition*. A composite of the treatment group attrition rate and the control group attrition rate, with attrition represented as the proportion of the original treatment or control sample not included in the outcome measurement.

2. *Design*. The research design ranked by the expected internal validity of the procedure for assigning the treatment and control groups (random, matched, neither). This was not correlated with effect sizes in the prevention database, so it was used only in the analysis of the probation database.

3. *Initial equivalence*. A factor score combining 3-point ratings for whether the initial treatment–control comparisons on gender, age, ethnicity (minority/majority), and delinquency history favor the treatment group, neither/cannot tell, or the control group.

4. *Measurement 1*. A factor score combining a binary variable indicating whether the delinquency outcome was measured using official juvenile justice records or other sources (e.g., self-report, others' report) and a few other variables correlated with it in each database—for example, rating of potential for social desirability bias, whether the outcome was based on a dichotomous (e.g., arrested, not arrested) or continuous (e.g., number of delinquent acts) measure.

5. *Measurement 2*. A factor score combining a variable for the number of weeks covered by the delinquency outcome measure (e.g., a 26-week period after treatment) and a few other variables correlated with it in each database—for example, whether general or only specialized offenses were reported.

Other control variables were available that represent critical sample characteristics: mean age, gender mix, and risk level (prior delinquency/antisocial behavior history). Most samples were entirely or predominately male, so there was too little variation on gender mix to be useful, but the other two variables are relevant for controlling characteristics that may vary between treatments in group and individual formats. Another set of control variables represents the amount of treatment provided, summarized in terms of the duration of the treatment period and the estimated total hours of service provided during that period. For the final set of control variables, we included binary codes for the presence or absence of each of the pertinent treatment components shown earlier in Table 9.3 that were independently related to effect sizes at $p < .15$. These variables allowed the analysis to at least approximately equate the mix of treatment components represented in each of the treatment formats under consideration. These control variables were all included in a multiple regression model[2] as predictors of the effect sizes for delinquency outcomes. The test variable in these analyses was a binary code for group (coded 1) versus individual (coded −1) treatment formats; studies of treatment using mixed formats were not included in these analyses. Summaries of the results are presented in Tables 9.5 and 9.6.

The multiple correlation for the regression model applied to the prevention studies was $R = .65$ and that for the probation studies was $R = .64$. In both cases the overall model accounted for a significant portion of variance but there was still a significant residual variance unaccounted for. On the key test variable comparing group versus individual treatment formats with the other variables in the model controlled, a significant difference favoring group formats was found for the probation studies and no significant difference appeared for the prevention studies. To better describe the nature of these differences, we computed the adjusted mean for each treatment format, that is, the mean effect size adjusted for the covariates controlled in the regression model. These means are presented in Table 9.7; comparison with Table 9.4 shows the effects of including the control variables in the analysis.

Group Counseling versus Individual Counseling

Of all the treatment variations represented in the two databases, counseling is one of the most frequent and also one for which both group and

TABLE 9.5. The Effect of Group Treatment Format in Prevention Studies with Method, Sample, and Treatment Characteristics Controlled

Variables in regression	β	p
Method factors		
Attrition	−.03	.76
Initial equivalence	−.21	.01
Measurement 1	.09	.28
Measurement 2	−.46	.00
Sample characteristics		
Risk	.39	.00
Age	.24	.01
Treatment characteristics		
Duration	.14	.22
Total hours	−.26	.06
Individual components	−.57 to .39	.00 to .02
Individual–group format	−.19	.07

Note. $n = 80$.

TABLE 9.6. The Effect of Group Treatment Format in Probation Studies with Method, Sample, and Treatment Characteristics Controlled

Variables in regression	β	p
Method factors		
Attrition	−.03	.62
Design	−.13	.18
Initial equivalence	.27	.00
Measurement 1	.10	.15
Measurement 2	.36	.00
Sample characteristics		
Risk	.05	.45
Age	.18	.05
Treatment characteristics		
Duration	.02	.84
Total hours	−.84	.00
Individual components	−.23 to .17	.02 to .13
Individual–group format	.23	.02

Note. n = 72.

individual treatment formats are common. This makes it an especially good case for comparing the two formats—the nature and content of the treatments can be expected to be relatively similar in that both are forms of counseling, but they differ on the extent to which peer groups are involved. To examine whether youth group counseling and individual counseling show differential effectiveness, we first selected studies from each database in which either was identified as the primary treatment component. Among the prevention studies, 21 were found with individual counseling as the main treatment component and 26 were found with group counseling as the main treatment component. Among the probation studies, there were 19 studies of individual counseling and 22 of group counseling. Table 9.8 shows that, for the prevention studies,

TABLE 9.7. Mean Effect Sizes for the Different Treatment Formats Adjusted for the Covariates in the Regression Models

	Treatment format	
Study type	Individual	Group
Prevention	.08 (32)	.05 (48)
Probation	.09 (38)	.14 (34)

Note. The number of effect sizes in each mean is shown in parentheses. The individual–group mean effect size difference is significant at $p < .02$ for the probation studies.

TABLE 9.8. Mean Effect Sizes for Outcomes When Individual or Group Counseling Is the Main Treatment Component

	Type of counseling		
Study type	Individual mean (SD; n)	Group mean (SD; n)	Q-between
Prevention	.08 (.29; 21)	.14 (.28; 26)	1.97 (1), p = .16
Probation	.21 (.20; 19)	.13 (.27; 22)	3.40 (1), p = .07

Note. The number of studies in each category is shown in parentheses.

the mean effect size was larger for group than individual counseling; the reverse pattern appeared for probation studies. In neither case, however, was the difference statistically significant. The standard deviations were similar for the prevention studies but, for the probation studies, the standard deviation was larger for group counseling.

As in the analogous comparison earlier of group and individual treatment formats, this comparison takes no account of other variables that may be confounded with the type of counseling. We therefore conducted regression analyses controlling for the same variables as shown earlier in Tables 9.5 and 9.6 but applied it only to the studies in which group or individual counseling was the main treatment component. The test variable for these analyses was a binary variable contrasting group counseling (coded 1) with individual counseling (coded −1). The results are shown in Tables 9.9 and 9.10.

TABLE 9.9. The Effect of Group Counseling versus Individual Counseling in Prevention Studies with Method, Sample, and Treatment Characteristics Controlled

Variables in regression	β	p
Method factors		
Attrition	.004	.98
Initial equivalence	.11	.42
Measurement 1	−.004	.98
Measurement 2	−.67	.00
Sample characteristics		
Risk	.11	.31
Age	−.02	.91
Treatment characteristics		
Duration	.21	.10
Total hours	−.14	.37
Individual components	−.49 to .43	.00 to .10
Individual–group counseling	−.28	.04

Note. n = 47.

TABLE 9.10. The Effect of Group Counseling versus Individual Counseling in Probation Studies with Method, Sample, and Treatment Characteristics Controlled

Variables in regression	β	p
Method factors		
Attrition	−.11	.30
Design	−.40	.00
Initial equivalence	−.05	.76
Measurement 1	−.33	.01
Measurement 2	.41	.00
Sample characteristics		
Risk	.09	.55
Age	−.14	.36
Treatment characteristics		
Duration	.18	.30
Total hours	−.42	.01
Individual components	−.36 to .58	.00 to .09
Individual–group counseling	.18	.22

Note. n = 41.

The multiple correlation for the analysis of prevention studies was R = .60 (Table 9.9); that for the probations studies was R = .67 (Table 9.10). In both cases this value was statistically significant, as was the residual variance the model did not account for. The group counseling versus individual counseling comparison was statistically significant in the prevention studies but not in the probation studies. The covariate-adjusted mean effect sizes for group and individual counseling derived from these analyses are shown in Table 9.11. The pattern of means is much the same as in Table 9.7 for the individual versus group treatment format, though it was the probation difference that was significant in that comparison. Group formats and group counseling show smaller effect sizes among the prevention studies and larger ones among the pro-

TABLE 9.11. Mean Effect Sizes for Group and Individual Counseling Adjusted for the Covariates in the Regression Models

Study type	Type of counseling	
	Individual	Group
Prevention	.12 (21)	.08 (26)
Probation	.15 (19)	.19 (22)

Note. The number of effect sizes in each mean is shown in parentheses. The individual–group mean effect size difference is significant at $p < .04$ for the prevention studies.

bation studies, but not all of those differences were statistically significant.

Age and Risk Interactions with Group versus Individual Treatment

Among the ways in which the prevention and probation studies differ, age and risk are especially discriminating. The youth represented in the prevention studies are younger on average than those in the probation sample and, again on average, are less at risk for antisocial behavior as indicated by prior offense histories. The differential effectiveness of individual and group counseling between the prevention and probation studies seen in Table 9.11, and the somewhat similar differences for individual versus group treatment formats seen in Table 9.7, suggest the possibility of interactions between sample age or risk and group/individual treatment. The regressions reported in Tables 9.5, 9.6, 9.9, and 9.10, therefore, were each extended to add interaction terms representing differential group and individual effect sizes for mean sample age and risk, each dichotomized at their respective medians. Table 9.12 reports the results for the risk interactions and Table 9.13 reports them for the age interactions, showing the covariate adjusted mean effect sizes in each instance. The three-way interactions between age, risk, and group versus individual treatment were not examined because the number of studies in some of the cells was very small.

Table 9.12 shows that there was no significant interaction between risk and treatment format for either the prevention or the probation studies. The interactions between risk and group versus individual counseling, on the other hand, were significant for both sets of studies but in opposite directions. For the prevention studies, group counseling was less effective than individual counseling for lower risk juveniles and

TABLE 9.12. Mean Effect Sizes for Risk Interactions with Group and Individual Treatment Adjusted for the Covariates in the Regression Models

	Lower risk		Higher risk		p-value for interaction
Study type and contrast	Individual	Group	Individual	Group	
Prevention					
Treatment format	.09 (11)	.05 (32)	.08 (21)	.03 (16)	.89
Type of counseling	.18 (9)	.06 (19)	.09 (12)	.20 (7)	.001
Probation					
Treatment format	.10 (17)	.13 (15)	.08 (21)	.14 (19)	.82
Type of counseling	.13 (7)	.67 (5)	.20 (12)	.16 (17)	.001

Note. The number of studies in each category is shown in parentheses.

TABLE 9.13. Mean Effect Sizes for Age Interactions with Group and Individual Treatment Adjusted for the Covariates in the Regression Models

Study type and contrast	Lower risk		Higher risk		p-value for interaction
	Individual	Group	Individual	Group	
Prevention					
Treatment format	.12 (18)	.02 (23)	.06 (14)	.07 (25)	.04
Type of counseling	.15 (16)	.01 (12)	.09 (5)	.11 (14)	.001
Probation					
Treatment format	.09 (20)	.17 (13)	.10 (18)	.12 (21)	.20
Type of counseling	.15 (10)	.32 (10)	.16 (9)	.19 (12)	.21

Note. The number of studies in each category is shown in parentheses.

more effective for higher risk ones. For the probation studies, group counseling was more effective for the lower risk juveniles and somewhat less effective for the higher risk ones. Table 9.13 shows a somewhat different pattern for age. The two significant interactions showed group treatment to be less effective than individual treatment with the younger juveniles in the prevention studies. Neither of the interactions with age was significant for the probation studies.

Amount of Treatment Interactions with Group versus Individual Treatment

As group treatments continue for longer periods of time and/or involve more hours of contact, they will provide more opportunity for peer interaction, and therefore more opportunity for negative peer influences. More treatment contact, of course, may represent a larger dose that could make the treatment more effective. The dose effect, however, should also apply in somewhat similar form to individual treatment but without the accompanying increase in peer contact. The two variables in the analysis used to capture amount of treatment were duration, the total time in weeks from the beginning to the end of treatment, and the mean number of hours of treatment contact per person over whatever period the treatment lasted. To explore the relationship between amount of treatment and peer group effects, each of these variables was dichotomized at its approximate median and the interaction with group versus individual treatment was examined, much as for the interactions with age and risk described above.

For the probation studies, none of these interactions were significant. Specifically, the interactions between treatment duration and individual versus group treatment format and individual versus group counseling were not significant, nor were the interactions between total hours of treatment and either of these individual versus group treatment contrasts. For the prevention studies, neither of the interactions involving individual versus group treatment format were significant. However, both the interactions involving individual versus group counseling were significant. And, in both cases, the effects of group counseling tended to be smaller than those of individual counseling for greater amounts of treatment. The covariate adjusted means for these interactions are shown in Table 9.14.

VARIABLES THAT MODERATE GROUP TREATMENT EFFECTS

Across the combined prevention and probation databases, we selected all the studies of nonresidential programs that provided their primary treatment in juvenile peer groups for closer scrutiny. There were 138 studies in this set, which included studies with treatment components that eliminated them from the analyses described above, that is, they did not match studies of similar treatments provided in individual formats. For these 138 studies, we revisited the original study reports and completed additional coding on the characteristics of the group treatment and the juvenile samples to which they were applied. The additional variables coded, in summary form, are identified in Table 9.15.

These variables represent varying characteristics of group treatments that may differentiate more and less effective versions, and which were reported widely enough to provide sufficient information for analysis. Because these moderator variables may themselves be correlated with other characteristics of the study or treatment that might influence their relationship with effect sizes, the moderator analysis was con-

TABLE 9.14. Mean Effect Sizes among Prevention Studies for Amount of Treatment Interactions with Individual and Group Counseling Adjusted for the Covariates in the Regression Models

Study type and contrast	Type of counseling		p-value for interaction
	Individual	Group	
Duration of treatment			.001
12 weeks or less	.11 (16)	.18 (12)	
More than 12 weeks	.13 (5)	.03 (14)	
Mean contact time			.01
12 hours or less	.06 (9)	.17 (19)	
More than 12 hours	.15 (12)	.04 (7)	

Note. The number of studies in each category is shown in parentheses.

TABLE 9.15. Regression Results for the Relationships between Selected Moderator Variables and Effect Sizes Controlling for Methodological Characteristics, Amount of Service, and Type of Primary Treatment

Variables in regression	β	p
Control variables		
Initial equivalence	.17	.002
Measurement	.15	.004
Treatment dose	.18	.001
Treatment type	.25	.001
Sample characteristics		
Mean age	−.03	.63
Age range (low–high)	−.04	.49
Gender mix (male–mixed)	.06	.29
Risk (low–high)	−.17	.01
Risk heterogeneity (low–high)	−.14	.01
Group and leader characteristics		
Group sessions primary (yes–no)	−.00	.94
Mean group size (small–large)	−.00	.98
Number of adults (one–more)	−.01	.92
Peer leaders present (yes–no)	.02	.68
Police leaders	.08	.19
Psychologist/psychiatrist leaders	−.02	.72
Counselor/youth worker leaders	.04	.50
Teacher leaders	−.20	.003
Researcher leaders	−.13	.01

ducted as a multiple regression that included control variables for some of those other characteristics. The control variables created for this set of studies were identified as predictors of effect size through preliminary regression analyses. They included a factor representing the initial equivalence between the experimental and control subjects (e.g., design type, sex and race differences, attrition), characteristics of the outcome variable (e.g., arrest vs. other forms of recidivism, whether from official records), amount of treatment provided (e.g., duration, frequency, hours per week), and the primary treatment type (e.g., counseling, academic training). The treatment type variable summarized information about a number of distinct treatment categories and was coded as a rank-order variable for the worst to best treatment type in terms of mean effect sizes.

The overall mean effect size for the 138 studies used in the moderator analysis was 0.12. Table 9.15 shows the standardized regression coefficients (beta weights) for the control variables and each moderator variable along with the p value assessing the statistical significance of the relationship with effect size. The results showed surprisingly little differentiation in the effect sizes as a function of the moderator variables tested. In particular, there were no significant relationships associated with the mean age, age range, and gender mix of the juvenile participants. The two sample characteristics that were significantly related to effect size were risk level, with higher risk juveniles associated with smaller effect sizes, and the heterogeneity of the risk mix, with more heterogeneity being associated with smaller effect sizes.

Among the group and leader characteristics, there were also relatively few significant moderators of effect size. Whether group sessions were primary to the treatment activities, mean group size, number of adults participating, and presence of peer leaders were unrelated to effect size. Dummy codes for the professional backgrounds of the leaders were significant only for teachers and researchers, both of which were associated with smaller treatment effects.

SUMMARY AND DISCUSSION

The research studies included in the meta-analysis reported here all investigated the effects of community-based treatment programs. Those programs therefore did not involve juvenile offenders in residential facilities where frequent interactions with delinquent peers would be an inherent part of the program context. On the other hand, it is unlikely that the juveniles in these community-based programs had no affiliation with antisocial peers prior to participation in the programs. Juvenile offenders often commit their offenses in peer groups rather than individually, and they are also likely to have contact with delinquent youth as a function of natural peer affiliations and the nature of their home neighborhoods and schools. The juvenile probationers represented in the probation studies are especially likely to have antisocial peer affiliations prior to program participation. We would expect fewer of the at-risk juveniles who participated in the prevention programs to have significant prior affiliations with delinquent peers, but cannot assume that there were no such relationships.

The group treatment programs examined in this meta-analysis therefore were unlikely to provide the participating juveniles with their first opportunity to interact with antisocial peers. At most, we would expect group treatment to add an increment of interaction with deviant peers to whatever ongoing antisocial peer affiliations the participating juveniles already maintained. That added increment is likely to be larger relative to prior experience for the prevention cases than for the probation ones, which is part of what makes the comparison of the two interesting for purposes of analysis.

The interaction with antisocial peers that results from participation in group treatment may come in more than one form. First, of course, the youth interact during the group program itself. In addition, however, group programs may provide incidental opportunities for informal peer interaction before and after program sessions. For instance, juveniles may gather in a waiting area or on the streets outside a program facility and perhaps elect to do other things together during these periods. The studies of program effects available for meta-analysis take no account of such incidental peer interaction. What appears as group treatment effects in those studies encompasses all aspects of group treatment that contrast with the respective control conditions. The latter typically involve probation as usual or no treatment at all for juveniles in prevention programs. Neither of these typically involves much deliberate or incidental aggregation of youth.

The intent of group treatment programs, of course, is to reduce delinquent behavior, not to increase it. To the extent that a program is effective in achieving that purpose, it may counteract any negative influence of interaction between antisocial peers. It would not be correct to assume that treatment programs for delinquent and at-risk youth are generally ineffective. The overall picture from meta-analysis shows modest positive mean effects on recidivism across all interventions with some program configurations demonstrating relatively large effects (Andrews, Zinger, Hoge, Bonta, Gendreau, & Cullen, 1990; Lipsey, 1992).

The community-based group treatment studies in the meta-analysis here thus involved a rather complex situation with regard to potential influences on subsequent delinquency. The group treatment format provides both direct and incidental opportunities for antisocial peer influence with its potential to exacerbate delinquent behavior. On the other hand, many or most of the participating juveniles likely already had affiliations with antisocial peers prior to their encounter with the program. In addition, the treatment is intended to exercise a countervailing influence which, if effective, should reduce subsequent delinquency. Under these circumstances, quite different effects might result depending on the peer influences in place when juveniles enter treatment, those they are exposed to during treatment, and the effectiveness of the group treatment for decreasing the potential for antisocial behavior.

The body of research on the effects of community-based treatment does not differentiate these various aspects so that their relative influence on delinquency outcomes can be assessed. Without such studies, we can only examine the net effects that result from the particular mixes of countervailing peer and therapeutic influences captured in the currently available studies. The meta-analysis reported here examines those net effects for different subsets of studies in an attempt to identify any generalized patterns of diminished effects associated with group treatment.

The worst-case scenario is one of such strong deviant peer influences and weak positive treatment influences that the net effects of group intervention are negative, with more delinquency resulting from group treatment than would have occurred without treatment. The meta-analysis found no evidence supporting this scenario for any subset of studies examined. Many studies produced negative effect sizes, but most of these were within a range easily produced by sampling error and, in any event, they were not disproportionately associated with interventions that used a group format. Moreover, these findings held for the most methodologically sound studies (i.e., those randomized with low attrition), as well as for the full set of experimental and quasi-experimental studies. Further analysis of selected subsets of probation and prevention studies involving treatment components used in group and individual formats, group and individual counseling, lower risk and higher risk juveniles, older and younger juveniles, and greater and lesser amounts of treatment revealed no instances where the mean effect size was negative.

The extensive collection of studies covered in this meta-analysis therefore showed no indication of negative effects on subsequent delinquency for group treatment of juvenile probationers or at-risk youth in prevention programs. Any adverse peer influences community-based group programs add to preexisting peer relationships are apparently not sufficiently strong to produce net negative effects with any generality. Such adverse influences, nonetheless, could still diminish the effectiveness of group treatment by offsetting whatever therapeutic value it has.

For studies of interventions with juvenile probationers, the meta-analysis showed no decrement in the recidivism effects of group treatment relative to those of comparable individual treatment. This was true for the general comparison of similar treatments provided in group and individual formats, as well as for the more specific comparison of group versus individual counseling. Nor did group programs in this category show any pattern of diminished effectiveness relative to individual programs for older or younger juveniles or for higher or lower risk cases. The one significant interaction involving these variables (Table 9.12) mainly represented enhanced effects of group counseling on lower risk juvenile probationers.

For prevention programs for at-risk youth, however, the meta-analysis did show somewhat smaller effects on subsequent delinquency for group treatment than for individual treatment. This difference reached statistical significance only for group versus individual counseling, but was in the same direction for the more general comparison of group versus individual program formats (Tables 9.7 and 9.11). The group programs in both cases showed mean effect sizes about one-third smaller than those for comparable individual programs. It should be noted, though, that the overall mean effect sizes were modest in these instances and the magnitude of this difference was on the order of an even more modest .03–.04 standard deviation units. Further analysis of the statistical interactions involving group versus individual treatment for prevention cases and other variables revealed few consistent results. Group counseling and programs using group formats more generally showed smaller effects for younger juveniles (age 14 and under) than did individual programs. Group counseling, relative to individual counseling, showed smaller effects for lower risk prevention cases and larger effects for higher risk cases, but this pattern was not replicated for programs using group versus individual formats generally. Group counseling also showed smaller effects than individual counseling for programs of longer duration and those providing more hours of treatment, but this pattern also was confined to the counseling programs and did not appear in the more general case of group versus individual program formats.

In a final analysis, all the studies of treatment in a group format irrespective of the type of treatment were examined in relation to the potential moderator variables we were able to code from the study reports. This analysis was aimed at identifying any characteristics of group treatment independently associated with delinquency outcomes, especially circumstances yielding very small effect sizes that might indicate adverse peer influences. No significant relationships with effect size were found for most of these variables. This analysis did show smaller effects for group treatment with higher risk juveniles (those with more prior offenses), which is at least somewhat inconsistent with the generally larger effects of group treatment found for probation cases than for prevention cases (Tables 9.7 and 9.11). It also showed smaller effects when there was more heterogeneity in the risk levels of the juveniles participating in the group programs, a situation that might be conducive to negative influences on less delinquent peers by those more delinquent. The only other significant differences showed smaller effects when the group leaders were teachers or researchers, which could reflect less experience than the other categories of leaders (police, psychologists, counselors) in dealing with antisocial youth.

Overall, the results of this meta-analysis provide no evidence that working with antisocial youth in groups in community-based programs has negative effects on their subsequent delinquency. Nor does it show much indication that the net effects of group treatment are diminished by whatever mix of peer influences and therapeutic efficacy occurs in such situations. It appears likely, as others have argued (e.g., Weiss,

Tapp, Caron, & Johnson, 2005), that for community-based programs the deviant peer influences in group treatment of antisocial youth are generally negligible relative to such influences outside of the treatment setting and the countervailing influence of the treatment. The one possible exception that emerged from the analysis presented here warrants additional investigation, however. Smaller effects were found for group treatment of at-risk youth with limited involved in delinquent behavior at the time of treatment (prevention cases), particularly for group counseling programs of longer duration or more total hours of contact and for younger juveniles (age 14 and under). Smaller effects were also associated with treatment groups that were heterogeneous in the risk levels of the participating juveniles and groups with teachers or researchers as leaders. The pattern that emerges from these findings is one of relatively unstructured and/or ineffectively supervised groups comprised of a mixture of more and less antisocial youth, but mainly young and at-risk youth not yet heavily involved in delinquent behavior. Group treatment appears from the meta-analysis to be especially ineffective under such circumstances, though not necessarily negative. Further investigation of this possibility would require studies designed specifically for that purpose, unlike those currently available for meta-analysis.

NOTES

1. For purposes of this analysis, we omitted several miscellaneous categories (e.g., parents only, teachers or probation officers only).
2. The regression analyses reported here used a fixed effects model in which each effect size was weighted by its inverse variance (Hedges & Olkin, 1985).

CHAPTER 10

Peer Effects in Neighborhoods and Housing

Jacob Vigdor

Over the past two decades, researchers in the United States have documented increasing disparities in poverty rates across neighborhood areas and an increase in the fraction of persons who live in extreme poverty neighborhoods (Jargowsky, 1997; Madden, 1996; Wilson, 1987). Recent data suggest that the processes of urban gentrification and widespread suburbanization have ameliorated these trends (Cutler, Glaeser, & Vigdor, 1999; Vigdor, 2002a). Moreover, data from the most recent U.S. Census suggest that the number of extreme poverty neighborhoods declined during the 1990s (Jargowsky, 2003). Nonetheless, both social scientists and policymakers continue to pay significant attention to highly disadvantaged neighborhoods.

Why are disadvantaged neighborhoods more than a simple demographic curiosity? For several decades, economists and sociologists have posited and tested numerous hypothetical links between neighborhood characteristics and individual outcomes. While some of these links concern the impact of neighborhood on adult outcomes (see, e.g., Kain, 1968), most focus on the potential role of neighborhood factors—community institutions, adult role models, and peers—on the behavior and development of youth. Identifying any such causal links is of substantial policy importance, as the residential locations of both the poor and the affluent are influenced by government actions related to subsidized housing, tax subsidies for home ownership, and school districting, among other things.

Epidemic models of deviant peer influence are one of many theorized causal mechanisms hypothesizing a link between neighborhood characteristics and child outcomes (Gephart, 1997). As discussed below, few if any careful studies of neighborhood influences on individual outcomes utilize a methodology that permits distinctions between hypothesized causal mechanisms. Indeed, the majority of studies in the neighborhood effects literature have focused on outcomes related to educational attainment and labor market success rather than on deviant youth or adolescent behavior. Thus, even though empirical social scientists have studied this question for decades, the voluminous literature on neighborhood influences on development has yet to provide convincing evidence documenting the existence or magnitude of contagion effects operating between high-risk youth within neighborhoods.

CONCEPTUAL ISSUES

From a theoretical perspective, not every hypothesized link between neighborhood factors and individual outcomes points toward a common definition of the term "neighborhood." One researcher looking at the impact of community institutions might consider a neighborhood to be the geographic area served by a single school or recreation center. A second researcher examining peer interactions might define a neighborhood as a single city block where youth spend the greater part of their unstructured social time. In most of the studies reviewed in this chapter, convenience dictates the definition of neighborhood more than any other factor. This reflects the widespread use of census publications as a source of data on neighborhood characteristics.

The widespread use of census data reflects two essential benefits: the data are essentially free and are collected in a uniform process for the entire nation. With these benefits comes a countervailing cost: neighborhoods as defined by the census are not necessarily the most relevant units from a scientific perspective. Using a census tract to define a neighborhood when a unit of some other size is more appropriate introduces statistical error into the measurement of truly relevant neighborhood characteristics. Measurement error can in turn lead to biased estimates of the impact of neighborhood factors on individual outcomes. The researcher's primary alternative is to collect more detailed and accurate neighborhood information using a costlier process, such as the effort undertaken by the Project on Human Development in Chicago Neighborhoods (see, e.g., Sampson, Raudenbush, & Earls, 1997). This alternative gains more accurate and detailed measurement at the expense of smaller sample sizes and lower statistical power. In the absence of strong prior beliefs regarding the size of the truly relevant neighborhood, neither strategy is foolproof.

Having identified a neighborhood, a study of peer contagion within neighborhoods must identify the set of peer characteristics most relevant to individual behavioral outcomes. Most studies of neighborhood effects use very basic measures such as poverty rates to capture average peer characteristics. While relationships between these basic measures and child outcomes or behavior could conceivably be driven by peer influence, it is difficult to rule out any of several alternative causal mechanisms.[1]

MEASUREMENT ISSUES

There are three daunting obstacles to the measurement of peer contagion effects in neighborhood contexts, each with analogues to difficulties faced by scholars studying peer influence in other settings. To facilitate discussion, the following equation represents a stylized social scientific model of an individual child's behavior:

child's behavior = f (child's background,
peers' behavior, peers' background, contextual factors)

A *contagion effect*, as commonly defined, is a direct link operating between peers' behavior and child's behavior, independent of any other individual, peer, or contextual factors. Economists, following Manski (1993), often refer to this type of contagion effect as an *endogenous social effect*. A simple example of a contagion effect would be a child's decision to initiate drug use because her next-door neighbor decided to initiate drug use.

The first obstacle to empirically identifying contagion effects is what Manski (1993) termed the *reflection problem*: absent further assumptions on the nature of peer influence, it is impossible to distinguish the causal impact of peers' behavior on an individual's behavior from the causal impact of peers' background characteristics on an individual's behavior. Manski refers to this second type of causal influence as an *exogenous social effect*. In the simple example of the substance-abusing dyad mentioned in the preceding paragraph, we cannot distinguish the hypothesis that the peer's behavior caused the individual's behavior from the hypothesis that some peer background characteristic, such as a substance-abusing parent, caused both children to adopt the same behavior. The distinction between these explanations is important for policy purposes. When true contagion effects operate, intervening to alter one child's behavior may have the net effect of changing several children's behavior. In other cases, such as when children initiate substance use because adults in their neighborhood provide opportunities to do so, these *multiplier effects* do not exist (Brock & Durlauf, 2001). Correctly distinguishing endogenous from exogenous social effects is necessary for any effort to gauge the true net impact or social benefits of any behavioral intervention. Most existing studies remain silent on the issue of whether neighborhood effects represent endogenous social effects.

The second obstacle relates to the nonexperimental process of assigning families to neighborhoods. Correlations in behavior between neighboring youth may result from similarity of underlying background characteristics rather than from any true contagion effect of one on the other. Residential sorting of similar individuals into neighborhoods is both a prediction of standard political economy theory (Tiebout, 1956) and an empirical regularity.[2] In theory, it would be possible to surmount this obstacle by statistically controlling for all background characteristics determining households' location choice decisions. Indeed, the modal methodological strategy pursued in the studies reviewed below is to control for as many background characteristics as possible. In practice, the more promising strategies for surmounting this obstacle involve programs that randomly assign individuals to neighborhoods. Some authors have also pursued an instrumental variable strategy, identifying factors that partly determine a household's neighborhood choice but otherwise have no impact on behavioral outcomes. Other studies have acknowledged the difficulty of separating "treatment" effects from "selection" effects and simply referred to their estimates as upper bounds on the true impact of neighborhoods on outcomes.

The final obstacle, related in many ways to the first two, is the presence of multiple potential causal mechanisms linking neighborhood to youth behavioral outcomes. Neighbors may mimic one another's behavior, but there are numerous shared contextual factors that might also generate such correlations, even after perfectly controlling for each child's own background characteristics. Neighbors regularly attend the same schools, where they are exposed to potentially common sets of peers, and to similar curricula, teachers, and other educational inputs. Other local institutions, including community recreation facilities, churches, and social service agencies, may also exert common effects. Neighboring children are also exposed to a similar set of adult role models. Finally, neighborhood characteristics may influence other intermediate factors, such as parenting practices, that directly impact youth outcomes (Klebanov, Brook-Gunn, Chase-Lansdale, & Gordon, 1997; Pinderhughes, Nix, Foster, Jones, & TCPPRC, 2001). Existing studies often look for correlations in outcome measures across neighboring children as potential evidence of "neighborhood effects." These studies, by and large, treat neighborhoods as a black box, exerting influence through unspecified causal mechanisms. Thus even literature that identifies a significant role for neighborhood influence generally fails to identify peer influence as the root cause of that influence.

Beyond these obstacles inherent in identifying neighborhood effects, translating research findings into efficient and effective policy interventions entails two additional difficulties. First, evaluating any such intervention from a cost–benefit perspective requires the fundamentally subjective attachment of monetary values to intangible outcomes. Second, the reduction of population rates of deviant behavior hinges on the existence of nonlinearities in peer influence effects. If peer-related neighborhood effects are purely linear in nature, redistributing individuals across neighborhoods will have no impact on population rates (see Cook & Ludwig, Chapter 4, this volume, for further discussion).

In this context, nonlinear contagion effects could take several forms. The probability of an individual adopting a particular behavior could be a nonlinear function of the proportion of neighbors engaged in that behavior. Using a more continuous behavior measure, an individual's expected behavioral outcome could be a nonlinear function of neighbors' mean behavior, or could be a function (either linear or nonlinear) of moments in the distribution of behavior other than the mean. For example, an individual's predicted behavior might worsen when the dispersion of neighbors' behavior increases, holding the mean constant. Nonlinear effects also encompass "tipping"-type phenomena and other threshold effects. Generally speaking, nonlinear effects imply that there is a distribution of individuals across neighborhoods that minimizes total deviant behavior. The nature of this distribution—for example, whether it involves segregating or dispersing high-risk youth—depends on the nature of the nonlinearity.

SCOPE OF THIS CHAPTER

Building on the thorough literature reviews by Jencks and Mayer (1990), Ellen and Turner (1997), Gephardt (1997), and in the two-volume study of neighborhood poverty edited by Brooks-Gunn, Duncan, and Aber (1997a, 1997b), this chapter focuses particularly on efforts to identify neighborhood effects on the outcomes of children and adolescents within the past decade.[3] While studies will be distinguished in part by the nature of their findings, they are also classified by the strategy they pursue to separate causal impacts from correlations arising from familial selection into neighborhoods. These strategies range from standard efforts to statistically control for any confounding factors to experimental or quasi-experimental studies of situations where youth have been assigned to neighborhoods randomly.

BODY OF EVIDENCE

Nonexperimental Evidence

The set of studies examining neighborhood influences on youth outcomes in nonexperimental settings spans a wide range of methodological approaches. These include standard ordinary least squares (OLS) or logistic regression analyses that attempt to control for a wide array of family background characteristics, studies of siblings raised in the same family but different neighborhoods, propensity score matching methods, and nonparametric efforts to bound the correlation in outcomes among neighboring children. This section considers each of the four types of study in turn.

Five noteworthy recent studies employ traditional regression techniques incorporating extensive family background controls. These studies use either nationally representative or smaller site-specific data sets to study the relationship between neighborhood characteristics and child outcomes. The set of analyzed outcomes includes standardized test score measures of cognitive ability, educational attainment, indicators of behavioral problems, and teen childbearing. In general, the studies point toward the conclusion that the magnitude of estimated neighborhood effects depends critically on efforts to control for family background characteristics. The largest effects are derived from models with the weakest claims to have isolated causal relationships. Family background controls often attenuate estimated neighborhood effects; in other cases the relationship between neighborhoods and individual outcomes is moderated by family characteristics.

Chase-Lansdale, Gordon, Brooks-Gunn, and Aber (1997) use nationally representative data on children born to mothers who were themselves born between 1958 and 1965 from the National Longitudinal Survey of Youth (NLSY) and the Infant Health and Development Program (IHDP), which follows a set of low-birth-weight infants as they mature in eight different sites. They examine the effects of five different census tract-level neighborhood characteristics on both behavioral and cognitive outcomes. While they find some evidence of a relationship between neighborhood factors and child outcomes, particularly for early school-age children, the magnitude of these relationships pales in comparison to the importance of family background factors. Once family background characteristics have been controlled for, adding a set of five neighborhood characteristic variables explains no more than 2% of the variation in outcomes in any reported specifications.

Halpern-Felsher and colleagues (1997) report some similar patterns in their study of somewhat older children in the Panel Study on Income Dynamics (PSID) and in smaller samples collected from a set of U.S. metropolitan areas. In the Halpern-Felsher and colleagues study, neighborhood characteristics appear to have the strongest impact for adolescents, with additional variation in impact by race and gender. Spencer and colleagues (1997), who use the same data sets as Halpern-Felsher and colleagues to study mental health outcomes; Ginther, Haveman, and Wolfe (2000), who examine educational attainment and teen childbearing outcomes in the PSID; and McCulloch and Joshi (2001), who use data from the British National Child Development Study to examine the impact of neighborhood poverty on children's vocabulary test scores, echo the common finding that controls for family background characteristics diminish the estimated relationship between neighborhood inputs and individual outcomes.

While the inclusion of family background controls generally diminishes the impact of estimated correlations between neighborhood characteristics and outcomes, it should be noted that the residual effects are often of considerable magnitude. For example, Halpern-Felsher and colleagues (1997) report that a 1-standard deviation increase in the concentration of high-SES (socioeconomic status) neighbors predicts as much as a 0.93-year increase in educational attainment in their PSID sample, with effects differing significantly across racial and gender groups. The effects are largest for white males, significant for white and African American females, and insignificant for African American males. While it is difficult to prove that any causal association drives these residual effects, or to identify a mechanism that would predict this particular array of effects across race and gender groups, they are consistent with the existence of such relationships.

Of additional interest are studies that find interactive, or moderating, relationships between family and neighborhood characteristics. Ginther and colleagues (2000) report that educational attainment tends to be higher among those whose family income is high relative to the neighborhood average. Gordon and colleagues (2003), who study the vocabulary test scores of white children in three suburban communities, find the opposite result: children from low-income families exhibit the strongest positive returns to neighborhood income levels. Lopez Turley (2003) finds that the relationship between neighborhood income and standardized test score or behavioral outcomes in the PSID varies by race: there is a positive effect of neighborhood median income on outcomes for white children and among black children who live in predominantly black neighborhoods. Lopez Turley also notes a number of patterns that point toward true causal effects of neighborhoods rather than selection effects. Correlations between neighborhood median income and outcomes are weakest among those who have lived in their neighborhood a short time and among those who know fewer than 15 neighborhood peers. The predicted impact of a $10,000 increase in neighborhood median income on test scores is a statistically significant 0.22 standard deviations among children living in their neighborhood at least 3 years, and statistically insignificant among other children. Within the group that knows 15 or more peers, a $10,000 increase in median income predicts a 0.1 standard deviation increase in test scores, and a 0.4 standard deviation increase in self-esteem. Effect magnitudes in the less-connected group are one-tenth to one-half the size and statistically insignificant. These results are not consistent with the hypothesis that families predisposed to poor outcomes select into poor neighborhoods; however, they are consistent with causal mechanisms other than neighborhood peer influence, such as peer influence in schools or other locally shared contexts.

Three studies estimate neighborhood influences on child outcomes by comparing siblings raised in the same household but in different neighborhoods. These so-called family fixed effect models operate under the presumption that family background measures are identical for both siblings, eliminating any correlation between unobserved factors and neighborhood characteristics. Restricting analysis to sibling comparisons assuages concerns regarding *time-invariant* family background characteristics. Many important family background characteristics may change over time, however. For example, families may move into less desirable neighborhoods when one parent loses a job or when parents divorce. These events might easily have an independent impact on individual outcomes.

Setting these concerns aside, results from these studies are mixed. Aaronson (1997, 1998) uses the PSID to study the relationship between neighborhood educational attainment levels and individuals' propensity to complete high school. In both studies, Aaronson finds a significant positive relationship, suggesting that a 10% increase in the density of high school dropouts in the neighborhood predicts a 0.6% decrease in the probability of high school graduation. Plotnick and Hoffman (1999), by contrast, use the same data set to examine neighborhood effects on the outcomes of females, including teen childbearing, high school graduation, and family earnings in adulthood. They find no significant neighborhood effects in their cross-sibling comparisons.

Perhaps the most extensive effort to control for family background characteristics is Harding's (2003) study of neighborhood influences on high school graduation and teen pregnancy in the PSID. Harding employs propensity score matching methods to pair individuals residing in high-poverty neighborhoods with nearly identical individuals residing in moderate- or low-poverty neighborhoods.[4] Harding reports significant relationships between neighborhood poverty levels and the outcomes under consideration. Individuals residing in neighborhoods with poverty rates above 20% have high school dropout rates 12 percentage points higher, and teenage pregnancy rates 11–16 percentage points higher, than otherwise identical individuals living in neighborhoods with poverty rates under 10%.

By matching individuals with nearly identical background characteristics, the propensity score methodology avoids some pitfalls associated with simpler linear regression techniques. However, the possibility remains that unobserved background characteristics vary even for those individuals with nearly identical observed characteristics. Harding conducts a sensitivity analysis to estimate the magnitude of impact such unobserved characteristics would have to exert in order to significantly bias the results. An unobserved variable with the same impact on outcomes as a dichotomous variable measuring whether a parent graduated from high school would be sufficient. Harding concludes that it is unreasonable to expect unobserved variables to exert this much impact; however, it is impossible to reach any definitive conclusion on this subject.

Given the extreme difficulty of accounting for unobserved background characteristics in the identification of neighborhood effects, one reasonable strategy followed by several recent researchers is to place an upper bound on the impact that neighborhoods could conceivably have on individual outcomes. This strategy is most interesting in the event that the identified upper bound is small; a finding that neighborhoods explain no more than 99% of the variance in outcome measures, for example, would be completely uninformative.

The first in this series of papers, Solon, Page, and Duncan (2000), used PSID data to estimate the correlation in educational attainment between children who grew up in the same neighborhood but in different families. This correlation, which serves as an upper-bound estimate to the true impact of neighborhood-specific factors, is estimated to be on the order of 0.1. The true impact will be lower than this to the extent that families residing in the same neighborhood share important unobserved background characteristics. Thus the net impact of neighborhood characteristics is likely to be small relative to family background measures, a conclusion shared by much of the research profiled above. Duncan, Boisjoly, and Harris (2001) use a similar methodology, examining a set of outcome measures—measures of school achievement and delinquency—more directly relevant to the study of peer influence. Comparing the relative magnitude of correlations between siblings, neighbors, self-identified peers, and grademates, the authors conclude that neighborhood-level correlations are small, especially in comparison with sibling-level correlations. Page and Solon (2003) extend the methodology to examine adult earnings, and do find a stronger neighborhood-level correlation, but they attribute this pattern to the widely documented tendency for wages to be higher in urban areas, and for adults to choose residential locations that match their childhood home in terms of urbanicity.

Instrumental Variable Techniques

Instrumental variable (IV) methodology resembles the propensity score strategy in one essential respect: both involve multistage statistical estimation where the first equation models the process by which individuals sort into neighborhoods and the second stage analyzes the relationship between neighborhoods and outcomes. At the heart of the IV strategy lies one or more instruments, or factors that have no impact on the ultimate dependent variable except through the factor analyzed in the first stage. In this case, an instrument must influence a household's choice of neighborhood but have no other conceivable relationship with the outcome measure under consideration.[5] Evans, Oates, and Schwab (1992) receive credit for first applying IV methodology to studies of peer effects in their study linking schoolmate characteristics to teen childbearing and high school dropout decisions in the NLSY.

Two noteworthy recent papers have used IV techniques to relate neighborhood characteristics to the outcomes of children, adolescents, or young adults. A third paper utilizing IV methodology, Liebman, Katz, and Kling (2004), uses assignment to an experimental group as an instrument for neighborhood poverty and will be covered in more detail in the discussion of experimental evidence below.

Cutler and Glaeser (1997) study the relationship between residential segregation and differentials between white and black outcomes using 1990 U.S. Census Public Use Microdata Samples (PUMS) on a cross-section of metropolitan areas. Outcomes considered include indicators for single motherhood, high school graduation, and labor market measures. Both OLS and IV estimates indicate that segregation is associated with wider gaps between black and white outcomes, an indication that blacks fare worse when congregated in racially distinct neighborhoods. As instruments for segregation, Cutler and Glaeser employ measures of local government fragmentation in each metropolitan area and a count of rivers and streams flowing through each metropolitan area.[6]

Currie and Yelowitz (2000) study the impact of residing in public housing projects on children's probability of being held back in school. The IV strategy makes use of the fact that families with two opposite-sex children are entitled to a larger housing unit than families with two same-sex children under federal policy. Since no additional rent is charged to families for the larger unit, the value of the implicit public housing subsidy is larger for families with opposite-sex children. As economic theory would predict, otherwise identical families with opposite-sex children are more likely to take up residence in a public housing project than families with same-sex children.

The estimated effect of residing in a housing project is positive: children predicted to reside in projects are 11 percentage points less likely to have been retained relative to otherwise identical children in private-sector housing. The authors conclude that housing projects provide families with superior environments relative to the private-sector alternatives that would otherwise be available to poor households. Families residing in projects are less likely to be overcrowded and less likely to live in large (50+ units) buildings. Public housing projects thus do not appear to be focal points of poor child outcomes relative to private-sector developments.

An alternative interpretation of the results focuses on the possibility that families may differentially understand the incentives embedded in the public housing entitlement policy. Families responding to incentives may differ from those that do not in ways that also carry implications for the performance of their children in school. Similar concerns regarding instrument validity plague many studies employing IV methodology.

Experimental and Quasi-Experimental Evidence

In the study of neighborhood effects, experimental methodology implies randomly assigning families to neighborhoods with different characteristics and observing the differences in outcomes that emerge. This random assignment ensures the absence of any correlation between neighborhood characteristics and family background characteristics, observed or unobserved. There is at least one example of a true mobility experiment designed to estimate neighborhood effects. There are also several quasi-experimental analyses of individuals subjected to policies where their residential locations were chosen for them in an effectively random manner.

The most widely known and most widely studied residential mobility experiment is the federal Moving to Opportunity (MTO) program, implemented in five different metropolitan areas.[7] Most of these analyses are focused on the estimation of treatment effects, or the mean differences in outcomes between individuals assigned to experimental and control groups (e.g., Duncan, Clark-Kauffman, & Snell, 2004; Kling & Liebman, 2004a, 2004b; Kling et al., 2004; Sanbonmatsu, Kling, Duncan, & Brooks-Gunn, 2004). In this case, the treatment group was offered a voucher redeemable for housing in a low-poverty neighborhood and the control group was not. As Ludwig and Duncan note, results suggest differential patterns of outcomes for male and female children of program participants. Deviant behaviors such as criminal behavior and substance use increased among males assigned to the treatment group; such behaviors decreased among females. Ludwig and Duncan address this somewhat puzzling pattern in Chapter 17 (this volume).

While treatment effects represent valuable information for those interested in evaluating the impact of the policy intervention, they do not address the more fundamental question of how neighborhood characteristics relate to individual outcomes. As noted above, Liebman and colleagues (2004) exploit the fact that assignment to the treatment or the control group is an ideal instrument for neighborhood characteristics, as assignment is by design uncorrelated with any family characteristic. The instrumental variable is a set of indicators for treatment status interacted with metropolitan areas. The neighborhood characteristic of interest is the average tract-level poverty rate families experience over a 4- to 7-year span. Their IV analysis thus relates MTO experimental results to much existing literature that directly measures the relationship between neighborhood poverty rates or similar measures and individual outcomes. Consistent with other MTO research, this study concludes that neighborhood poverty has a positive effect on indices of female risky behavior but a negative effect on the same index for males. The magnitude of estimated effects is fairly large: a 10% reduction in neighborhood poverty levels is associated with a 0.1 standard deviation reduction in female risky behavior, and a 16% increase in male risky behavior.

Two other recent studies employ quasi-random methodology to examine the impact of neighborhood characteristics on youth. Oreopoulos (2003) analyzes the experiences of adults born between 1963 and 1970 who were assigned as children to reside in a housing project in the Toronto metropolitan area. In Toronto, families queue for limited available slots in public housing units, and are assigned the first available unit when they reach the top of the queue.[8] Toronto's public housing offerings vary widely in terms of neighborhood location and project environment.

Oreopoulos compares indicators of adult SES, including earned income and welfare receipt, for individuals assigned to projects of differing size and construction style (high-rise buildings vs. low-rise buildings), and to neighborhoods with different underlying poverty rates. He consistently finds no significant evidence of differences in adult outcomes. The estimated correlation in outcomes for children who resided in the same housing project but different families never exceeds 0.005.

Jacob (2004) analyzes the experiences of youth forced to relocate as a result of the Chicago Housing Authority's decision to demolish certain public housing projects. Households forced to relocate were given vouchers redeemable for rent subsidies in private-market housing. The Chicago Housing Authority typically did not demolish all buildings within a project at the same time, which enables Jacob to compare the outcomes of individuals forced to move with those of individuals who were permitted to stay. Outcomes considered include standardized test scores and whether a child over 16 continued to be enrolled in school. Consistent with the work of Currie and Yelowitz (2000) described above, Jacob finds no significant evidence of any adverse effect of residing in public housing.

An important limitation of Jacob's study is that those families forced to relocate generally took up private-market housing in neighborhoods very similar to the ones they had previously inhabited. So, rather than estimating the impact of residing in a high-poverty neighborhood, the results are best interpreted as the impact of residing in a public housing project.

Can the apparently conflicting MTO and quasi-experimental results be reconciled? The outcome measures considered vary across study; one explanation is that the behavioral outcomes considered in MTO research are not significant predictors of educational attainment or adult SES. Indeed, MTO research has found only limited evidence of a link between neighborhood and educational attainment. It can easily be argued that Jacob's study addresses a different question than the MTO research. MTO research subjects differed from subjects in Oreopoulos's study not only in terms of nationality, but also in terms of race (MTO subjects were almost entirely nonwhite; Toronto public housing occupants are majority white), female headship (MTO families had mostly female heads; less than 50% of the Toronto public housing families had female heads), and nature of selection into the sample (MTO subjects volunteered for the study; Toronto subjects did not). It is certainly possible that some of these additional characteristics moderate the relationship between neighborhood characteristics and outcomes.

SUMMARY AND CONCLUDING COMMENTS

The studies described in this chapter vary widely in methodology, particularly in their choice of outcome variables; strategy for addressing endogenous residential choice; and neighborhood measures. In such a case, it would be very intellectually appealing to report that the literature has reached a broad consensus on the existence and magnitude of neighborhood effects. Unfortunately, this is not the case. Studies with methodological approaches that appear suitably sound a priori reach qualitatively different conclusions. In spite of these differences, it is possible to glean four general conclusions from the literature on neighborhood effects:

1. Overall, evidence suggests that neighborhood-level factors play at most a modest role in individual outcomes, relative to family-level influences. The strongest relationships are found in studies that examine youth behavior or the consequences of that behavior. The weakest relationships tend to be found in studies that consider the relationship between an individual's childhood neighborhood and adult outcomes such as earnings or educational attainment, possibly indicating that neighborhood effects are of low persistence and do not influence long-run trajectories. Few if any studies report a positive effect of adverse neighborhood conditions on outcomes.

2. Neighborhood effects are heterogeneous; however, this heterogeneity is underexplored and poorly understood. Many studies ignore the issues of effect heterogeneity, including the important question of whether neighborhood effects are nonlinear. The exceptional studies have found intriguing patterns: neighborhood effects often appear stronger among females, for whites, and for children of early school age. Studies have found conflicting results regarding the moderating effect of family income. The understanding of these disparate moderating effects is hampered by a shortage of clear conceptual models identifying potential causal mechanisms.

Perhaps the greatest obstacle to pursuing the estimation of moderating effects is the sheer number of potentially interesting interactions that exist. Similarly, an obstacle to estimating nonlinear effects is the great variety of plausible nonlinear models. A sensible placement of the highest priority would be on explaining patterns that have already appeared in the literature. Detailed meta-analyses of reported neighborhood effect results could draw inferences from the ways in which these results vary across study populations, institutional settings, and range of neighborhood characteristics observed in the analysis. These meta-analyses could then inspire a new round of research identifying the specific environments where neighborhood characteristics are likely to exert the strongest influence on individual outcomes.

3. No studies have addressed the issue of whether neighborhood effects reflect peer influence. From an intuitive standpoint, some result

patterns do point to the importance of deviant peer influence operating in neighborhoods. Nonetheless, existing literature can be seen as exposing a vast thicket, the disentangling of which will require significant additional research effort. While much of this required research is empirical in nature, further efforts to conceptually model possible mechanisms linking neighbors and individual outcomes are also essential.

4. The existing literature does not point to any specific policy recommendations. As discussed above, the policy implications of neighborhood effects depend critically on their nonlinearity. Given the paucity of evidence on this topic, and on the more general subject of effect heterogeneity, any attempts to advise current policy efforts would be little more than shots in the dark. The identification and isolation of specific causal mechanisms would also greatly further the goal of minimizing neighborhood peer contagion through sound policy.

How might future research on neighborhood effects isolate the impact of deviant peer influence from other hypothesized causal pathways? As discussed above, it is difficult to separate an endogenous social effect such as that in a contagion model from exogenous social effects that lead to similar correlation patterns but do not imply the existence of social multiplier effects. An ideal methodology would randomly assign groups of peers that vary in the proportion of deviant youth. In theory, the random assignment procedures of the Toronto housing project experiment offer an opportunity to follow such a strategy, if it were possible to measure youth deviancy prior to experimental assignment. There may be other, more promising, assignment policies currently practiced by individual housing authorities that would offer more feasible opportunities to execute such a study.

A somewhat less ideal but still promising strategy would be to combine a rigorous methodology, such as experimental, instrumental variable, or propensity score matching, with a population data set with information on residential location. Such a study would take advantage of the fact that the age cohort distribution of high-poverty neighborhoods, especially if defined at a suitably fine level, is likely to vary. Suppose that the study found equal relationships between neighborhood characteristics and individual outcomes, even among individuals who have no same-age peers residing in the immediate neighborhood area. In such a scenario, causal mechanisms other than neighborhood peer influence are likely to be responsible. Such a research design would build on Lopez Turley's (2003) findings that the link between neighborhood and behavioral outcomes is moderated by peer network density.

High-frequency population data sets might also prove useful in the study of deviant peer contagion in neighborhoods. For example, databases of disciplinary infractions that identify the date of infraction could be used to trace out patterns of behavior diffusion over time and space. The fundamental objective of such a study would be to estimate the change in likelihood of a particular infraction occurring when a same-neighborhood peer is recorded as committing a similar infraction. A study of this sort would face the standard difficulties in distinguishing true social effects, but reasonable extensions such as observing how patterns vary with the nature of the initial infraction could provide some insight.

Where might one look for the data necessary to conduct these more intensive analyses? Researchers are now studying administrative data sets covering public school students in several states, and some of these databases incorporate disciplinary records (see, e.g., Figlio, 2005). There is at least one data set that combines these disciplinary records with information on student home addresses, which can be geocoded into neighborhoods of unlimited specificity. This data set, pertaining to North Carolina public schools, is described in Clotfelter, Ladd, and Vigdor (2005).

Existing result patterns in the literature suggest that neighborhood effects are quite small for the mean individual and that interventions targeted at the entire population will have little if any effect. Moreover, the failure to isolate specific causal mechanisms implies that there is little support for any intervention strategy save physically moving youth from one environment to another. Extending the literature in the two directions suggested here—by focusing more attention on specific causal mechanisms, and by more precisely identifying the subset of individuals for whom neighborhood contagion matters the most—would provide vital information to those interested in improving life outcomes of youth raised in impoverished neighborhoods.

NOTES

1. A more minor conceptual issue relates to the duration of exposure to neighborhood characteristics. Most cross-sectional studies allow observation of neighborhood-level variables at only a single point in time. More advanced studies using longitudinal data occasionally average neighborhood-level variables for individuals who move between observations, or who reside in neighborhoods undergoing demographic change. As with the use of census tracts as neighborhood constructs, the use of point-in-time indicators to measure long-term neighborhood characteristics may introduce measurement error and lead in turn to biased estimates of causal effects. Kunz, Page, and Solon (2003) argue, however, that this potential errors-in-variables bias associated with using point-in-time neighborhood indicators is likely to be small because the serial correlation

in neighborhood characteristics experienced by individuals tends to be high. Lopez Turley (2003), discussed below, also addresses the issue of duration of exposure as a moderator of neighborhood influence.

2. While the most common presumption is that individuals predisposed toward more negative outcomes sort into lower quality neighborhoods, it is also conceivable that individuals in higher quality neighborhoods have lower quality unobserved background characteristics. For example, children of a given socioeconomic background residing in better neighborhoods may interact with their parents less frequently, if those parents must work extra hours to offset higher housing costs (Duncan, Connell, & Klebanov, 1997). Some parents may be motivated to choose better neighborhoods because they perceive that their children are at high risk for deviant behavior (Kling, Ludwig, & Katz, 2004).

3. Explicitly excluded from this review are studies such as Sampson et al. (1997) where the unit of observation is a neighborhood rather than an individual. In these studies, the problem of identifying a causal mechanism linking neighborhood characteristics to behavior is especially acute, since by definition no individual-level covariates can be incorporated in such a study.

4. This method involves a multistage estimation procedure. The first stage is a logit model where the dependent variable measures discrete neighborhood characteristics individuals experience while 11–20 years old and independent variables capture individual characteristics from the first 10 years of life. Predicted values from this equation thus offer an estimate of the likelihood that an individual resided in a high-poverty neighborhood while 11–20 years old. These predicted likelihoods are referred to as "propensity scores." Individuals with near-identical propensity scores but differences in the neighborhoods actually lived in are then compared on the two outcome measures. If the relationship between background characteristics and outcomes is nonlinear, and the background characteristics of individuals residing in different neighborhoods tend to differ substantially, propensity score matching is a clear improvement over OLS regression.

5. In practice, the identification of a suitable instrument is a formidable barrier to this research strategy. In the social sciences, it is almost always possible to link two observable phenomena together by more than one causal channel, involving more than one possible set of mediating factors. Many studies attempt to prove the validity of their instruments by the use of statistical tests, such as an "overidentifying restrictions" test (Hausman, 1978). The Hausman test checks whether instrumental variable estimates derived with two or more instruments are statistically different from each other. These statistical tests are relatively weak, though, since instrument validity is usually set up as the null hypothesis rather than as the alternative that must be proven correct. These caveats must be borne in mind when considering the IV-based literature.

6. Interestingly, Cutler and Glaeser's findings cannot be replicated with earlier editions of PUMS data (Collins & Margo, 2000). Vigdor (2002b) hypothesizes that the emergence of harmful effects associated with segregation reflects changes in black migration patterns over time. Before World War II, highly educated migrants were more likely to move to cities with higher degrees of segregation. After the war, this pattern reversed. Such a selection story would argue against a causal interpretation linking segregation to black outcomes. This illustrates a serious caveat with IV studies: even if one can credibly argue that only one mediating factor—the variable of interest—causally links instruments to outcomes, any mere correlation between the instruments and unobserved factors can lead to biased estimates of true effects. In this case, government fragmentation and rivers make metropolitan areas more segregated without otherwise affecting blacks. The fact that highly skilled blacks display an increasing aversion to segregated

cities, regardless of the root cause of that segregation, threatens the validity of the IV estimation strategy.

7. The design of the MTO program and a detailed survey of results obtained from analyzing differences between treatment and control groups can be found in Ludwig and Duncan (Chapter 17, this volume).

8. Families have the right to refuse one assignment but if they refuse two they are dropped from the queue. Oreopoulos reports that families only rarely rejected their first offer.

CHAPTER 11

Iatrogenic Outcomes of the Child Welfare System

Vulnerable Adolescents, Peer Influences, and Instability in Foster Care Arrangements

Melvin N. Wilson
and LaKeesha N. Woods

Unlike the other settings discussed in this volume, the child welfare system does not automatically place children in peer settings where negative influence could occur. However, an interesting anomaly about the child welfare system makes it worthy of consideration. Although intended to protect the well-being of children and adolescents, sometimes vulnerable children and adolescents are at an increased risk of exposure to negative peer influences through selection into and experiences in group foster care placements that are initiated by the child welfare system. Two facts warrant an examination of the peer influences in child welfare services. First, approximately 20% of all youth in foster care reside in group homes or institutions, and 50% are ages 11–18 (Administration for Children and Families, 2003; Jonson-Reid & Barth, 2000a, 2000b). Second, child welfare studies consistently have found positive correlations among child maltreatment, foster care, and juvenile justice system involvement. Thus this chapter examines the associations among unstable families of origin, inadequate supervision in traditional group foster care placements, and vulnerability to negative peer influences and antisocial outcomes. Efforts to increase stability and decrease negative peer and other social influences on vulnerable children are also reviewed.

THE CHILD WELFARE SYSTEM
AND VULNERABLE CHILDREN AND FAMILIES

In the United States, the child welfare system has been designed to ensure that the family environment is healthy for its members. Child welfare specifically is interested in the well-being of families who are unable
to care for and defend their children fully. Beginning in the 19th century,
childhood began to be viewed as a particularly innocent and vulnerable
time that required special consideration and protection (Barnett, Manly,
& Cicchetti, 1993). Orphanages were established to house children
whose parents were deceased or whose families could not provide for
them. Foster homes began as a form of indenture, as foster parents were
not compensated and the children had to work for their shelter and care
(Chipungu, 1991).

Today, child maltreatment represents a common reason that children are placed in foster care, and maltreatment has replaced parental
death as the main reason that children are "orphaned." *Child maltreatment* is defined as injury, abuse, exploitation, or neglect of a child by a
guardian, under circumstances that harm or threaten the child's health
or welfare (Tatara, 1991). *Violence* is any act carried out with the intention of causing physical pain or injury to another, and *abuse* is an act of
violence with a high probability of causing injury (Straus, Gelles, &
Steinmetz, 1980). Physical injury (e.g., major, minor, or unspecified);
neglect (i.e., deprivation of necessities and failure to provide shelter,
nourishment, health care, education, supervision, and clothing); sexual
abuse, which is the fastest growing category; and emotional maltreatment (i.e., failure to provide emotional and psychological support or
commission of abusive acts that are emotionally detrimental) are the categories of child maltreatment.

Child maltreatment represents a primary source of child vulnerability. Family instability increases the risk of child maltreatment and foster
care placements. Single parenthood, divorce, poverty, substance abuse,
living in a shelter, and institutionalization have been implicated as conditions that can increase a child's vulnerability to maltreatment and other
negative developmental outcomes (Sternberg, 1993). High rates of child
maltreatment are also associated with neighborhood characteristics
(Garbarino, Kostelny, & Grady, 1993). Children who subsequently are
placed in foster care are staying longer, and a significant number reenter
foster care (Wells & Guo, 1999).

African American families experience more changes, disruptions,
and separations than do other families (Hampton, 1991; Kapp, McDonald, & Diamond, 2001; Wilson & Saft, 1993). Children of color constitute 40–50% of the foster care population, although they comprise only

20% of the national population (Garland, Ellis-MacLeod, Landsverk, Ganger, & Johnson, 1998; McRoy, Oglesby, & Grape, 1997). Youth of color, especially African American youth, are more likely to remain in foster care longer, make multiple foster care moves among familial situations, receive fewer services and contacts with caseworkers, and have faster rates of reentry into the child welfare system than do Caucasian youth (Avery, 2000; Garland et al., 1998; McRoy et al., 1997; Wells & Guo, 1999).

Prolonged family separation is associated with a variety of child and family characteristics. Children who are in poor health, from single-parent and low-income homes, enter foster care because of dependency or neglect, do not receive preplacement services, or are placed in kinship care often have slower and lower family reunification rates (Courtney, 1994; Davis, Landsverk, & Newton, 1997; Wells & Guo, 1999). Children experiencing long delays in placement also are more likely to have substantial disabilities, and be male, older when they enter care, part of a sibling group, and involuntarily removed from the birth parents' home (Avery, 2000). In addition to children with health and family difficulties, children who had a high number of placements during their first period in foster care had the fastest rates of reentry into the child welfare system (Courtney, 1994; Wells & Guo, 1999). The rising numbers of children entering the system are met with declining numbers of available foster homes (Wilhelmus, 1998).

Juvenile Delinquency Outcomes

Research has found a relationship between early child maltreatment and later delinquency, particularly for children who have experienced instability in foster care placement. However, the literature on foster care placements and juvenile delinquency does not adequately address the question of group foster home placement and subsequent juvenile delinquency. A critical limitation in the child welfare research is that group and individual family care placements are often combined simply as "foster care." Disentangling the type of placement is critical in understanding possible negative outcomes of placing children in foster care.

Several researchers (Jonson-Reid, 2002a; Jonson-Reid & Barth, 2000a, 2000b; Ryan & Testa, 2005) have reported an increasing number of incidents of dependent children who are placed in multiple foster home situations during a single period of separation from their family of origin. Jonson-Reid and Barth (2000a, 2000b) explored foster care placement and subsequent juvenile adjudication. They found that multiple placements and race/ethnicity were predictive of subsequent placement in juvenile detention facilities. In addition, they found that minority adolescents who received child welfare services had a lower risk for subsequent juvenile delinquency than did nonminority adolescents who received services and all adolescents who received no services.

Likewise, Ryan and Testa (2005) reported that children who were substantiated victims of maltreatment average 47% higher delinquency rates relative to children who were not maltreated. Approximately 16% of maltreated children placed into substitute care experienced at least one delinquency petition compared to 7% of all maltreatment victims who were not removed from their families. Adolescents in foster care have also been found to display decreased social and academic competency compared to the general population (Khan, 2001). Of course, selection biases among maltreated children might contribute to the higher later delinquency rate in the family-removal group, and so the direct impact of family removal, and group foster care placement, is difficult to estimate.

Important gender correlates with delinquency also have been found (Jonson-Reid, 1998; Ryan & Testa, 2005; Testa, 2004). Ryan and Testa (2005) indicated that girls who were placed into a foster home, even if stable, showed a 6% rate of delinquency versus a 3% rate for those who remained in their family homes. The rate of delinquency for all girls placed into multiple foster homes was 8%. In contrast to girls, for males, placement instability, rather than simply placement into foster care, was associated with increased risk of delinquency for victims of maltreatment (Ryan & Testa, 2005). The rate of delinquency among boys with one or two placements in a foster home and boys who remained in their family homes was nearly identical (12% and 11%, respectively). Boys with three placements had a delinquency rate of 16%, while the rate of delinquency for boys with four or more placements was 21%. Overall, 23% of the boys in substitute care had at least one delinquency petition. Regarding child welfare practice, the study's results may indicate a need to improve efforts to match children with foster parents, cutting down on multiple placements. In addition to sorting out selection biases from effects of placement, research is needed that disentangles the type of foster care services provided to adolescent victims of maltreatment.

SECURE ATTACHMENT, DEVIANT PEER ASSOCIATIONS, AND CHILD OUTCOMES

How does child maltreatment push a child toward a trajectory of deviant development, and how does the placement of that child affect the trajectory? Secure attachment to adult caregivers is compromised in cases of parental maltreatment of children, and insecure attachments are associated with negative outcomes throughout the lifespan. Bowlby (1969, 1982) hypothesized that attachment behavior is activated during a period of stress in which the child seeks comfort from his or her attachment figure. The attachment paradigm has distinguished attachment types, including secure, anxious, ambivalent, and disorganized attachment strategies. Moreover, Bowlby (1980) contended that although attachment behavior is activated less readily in older individuals, a propensity to monitor the accessibility of attachment figures and to seek them out as "stronger and wiser" in times of stress exists throughout the lifespan.

The majority of parentally maltreated children have been found to have disorganized attachments (see Cicchetti, Toth, & Lynch, 1995). Disorganized attachment is considered a risk factor for mental disorders (Carlson & Sroufe, 1995). Disruptive and aggressive school behaviors have also been associated with disorganized attachments in 4- to 6-year-olds (Greenberg, Speltz, DeKlyen, & Endriga, 1991; Lyons-Ruth, 1996; Solomon, George, & DeJong, 1995).

Leathers (2002) explored correlates of attachment in older children. The relation among specific experiences, the quality of attachment to parents, involvement in community institutions, and behavioral disturbance were tested. Children with secure attachments to caregivers and a high level of involvement in the community had fewer behavioral problems than did their counterparts. Weak interpersonal attachments and little involvement in community institutions accounted for child and adolescent experiences in care and behavioral disturbances.

Allen and colleagues (2002) examined adolescent attachment organization and autonomy in interactions, revealing that adolescent attachment organization was associated with the development of social skills and delinquent behavior for moderately at-risk adolescents at ages 16 and 18. A disorganized attachment organization predicted increasing delinquency during this period. Moreover, Allen and his colleagues found long-term sequelae of early attachment difficulties in severe adolescent psychopathology that could be explained from the perspective of adult attachment theory. Unresolved trauma with attachment figures accounted for much of the insecure attachment rating. The results suggest a substantial and enduring connection between disorganized attachment organization and severe adolescent psychopathology.

Children who grow up with insecure attachment relationships with adult caregivers often appeal to peers for their interpersonal needs. Peer groups are social networks for adolescents. Affiliation with delinquent peers is considered a risk factor for delinquency and recidivism, and family support is a means of mitigating this risk (Lipsey & Derzon, 1998; Peeples & Loeber, 1994; Shepherd & Farrington, 1995). Garnier and Stein (2002) completed an 18-year longitudinal study of conventional and nonconventional families and their children. The interrelation of family and peer influences predicted adolescent behavior problems. Although adolescent behaviors were associated with both family and peer relationships, peer behaviors were correlated more strongly with adolescent problems.

Of course, youth who engage in delinquent activity can select themselves into delinquent peer groups, as well as be further influenced by these deviant peers. Woods (2004) found that, after controlling for peer group association, the relation between communal and individualistic cultural factors and delinquency severity tended to attenuate in a sample of African American adolescents in settings such as a group home and a detention facility. A positive relation, however, occurred between delinquency frequency and report of being highly communal, or other-centered. Some of the most frequent delinquent behaviors were skipping class, using illicit substances, and disorderly conduct (Woods, 2004), behaviors that often are committed in groups, suggesting that the youth were engaging in antisocial behavior with their peers. Lack of affiliation with social networks and environments that are protective against delinquency can contribute to a vulnerability to affiliation with maladaptive networks. Delinquent peer affiliation can influence vulnerable youth and exacerbate the frequency and severity of antisocial activity in youth with a history of delinquent behavior.

MALADAPTIVE OUTCOMES RELATED TO THE CHILD WELFARE SYSTEM AND FAMILY INSTABILITY

Beyond the trauma of maltreatment, subsequent placement into foster care can be an additional extremely unsettling experience for some children, contributing to increased vulnerability to negative peer influence and maladaptive outcomes. Many children who are insecurely attached to adult caretakers and who move from their maltreating families into group foster care facilities are exposed to deviant peer influences in those facilities or through inadequate adult supervision of their free time. Maltreated children often display externalizing and deviant behaviors, further making them vulnerable through selection into deviant peer groups. Children with conduct disorder, hyperactivity, emotional difficulties, and social adjustment problems are more likely to experience placement instability than are children who are victims of neglect (Jonson-Reid, 2002a; Khan, 2001).

Moreover, Leve and Chamberlain (2005) found that youth who

have been placed in group homes reported more delinquent peer associations than did youth placed in individual foster care homes. Likewise, Jonson-Reid (2002b; Jonson-Reid & Barth, 2000a, 2000b) found that children who were placed in group foster homes had a higher risk of juvenile detention than did those children who received in-home or individual foster care services. These findings suggest that conventional group home care is not the most appropriate alternative for adolescents with conduct disorder (Jonson-Reid, 2002a, 2002b).

Several researchers suggest that family foster care generally means that there may be other foster care children living with the foster family (Jonson-Reed, 2002a, 2002b; Ryan & Testa, 2005). For instance, Moore, Osgood, Larzelere, and Chamberlain (1994) suggested that the average number of children in foster care was three. They found a positive direct relationship between the number of foster children in a family and disruptive and deviant behaviors. Such literature points to the serious iatrogenic effects that might occur as a function of placing vulnerable youth in group care. Maltreated children who are placed in group care with inadequate adult supervision may be especially vulnerable to deviant peer influences as a result of their poor decision making in attempting to repair their attachment systems.

INTERVENTION STUDIES OF FOSTER CARE AND GROUP PLACEMENT

Foster care programs that provide adequate adult supervision, care, and consistency could be a successful intervention for delinquent youth (Chamberlain, 2003a, 2003b). Poor parental supervision, lack of consistent discipline, low parental involvement, friendships with delinquent peers, and school failure have been considered risk factors for antisocial behavior and delinquency during adolescence (Chamberlain, 2003). Antisocial behaviors also depleted and deteriorated the adult resources that potentially could guide the youth to acceptable behavior. Once the adolescent became involved in delinquent activity, either by compromising community safety or by participating with groups of youth who are delinquent, the court intervened.

Research over the last decade has noted that individualized, stable, and treatment-oriented foster care placements may help decrease negative outcomes related to selection into out-of-home placements and exposure to negative peer influences. Barber (2001) noted evidence that children placed into individualized foster care have more positive outcomes than do children placed into institutional or group care settings. Browne (2002) found that similar positive outcomes of foster care were dependent upon the maltreatment experiences and sociodemographic characteristics of the child.

Random-Assignment Studies of Peer Group Placement

Chamberlain and colleagues have conducted the most compelling work on the effect of group care placement on adequate supervision by adults, deviant peer involvement, and subsequent delinquency, through random-assignment experiments with youth in the child welfare system. Chamberlain, Ray, and Moore (1996) compared staff assumptions and program practices in two models of residential care for adolescents. Group care (GC) settings had from six to 15 youths in residence and used peer-mediated treatments. Treatment foster care (TFC) settings had one youth placed in each home and treatments were adult-mediated. The findings revealed several critical distinctions between the GC and TFC program models. First, comparisons were computed for staff opinions about the source of influence on boys' success, degree and type of supervision rules and restrictions provided by the programs, discipline strategies used, and the role of peers and adults in the treatment process. Although the staff of both programs reported similar levels of peer influence, TFC staff reported significantly more influence of adults than was reported by the GC staff. Boys in the TFC program spent significantly less time with peers and more time with adults than did the boys in the GC programs. Both programs reported about the same level of overall monitoring (i.e., knowing where the boys spent time). Reports from the participating boys concurred with staff impressions. That is, boys in the TFC program spent less time without supervision than did the boys in GC. In terms of problem behaviors, the adult caretakers reported about the same level of problem behavior occurrence. However, the boys in TFC reported fewer occurrences of problem behaviors than did the boys in GC. In the adult-mediated TFC model, both the boys and the caretakers reported that consequences occurred more frequently than did their counterparts in the GC program. Both approaches were consistent between their program assumptions and practices in terms of overall reduction of problem behaviors.

Overall, the TFC program demonstrated several improvements over the GC program. TFC offered a consistent adult-focused program that provided necessary supervision, monitoring, and an adult presence in the lives of vulnerable youth. The critical mechanism of change was reflected in the importance of adults as the source of positive mature influence on the youth. In addition, other specific mechanisms of the TFC approach known to reduce conflict in the therapeutic milieu and to contribute to successful outcomes for youth include a proactive approach to reducing problem behavior, the creation and maintenance of a consistent and reinforcing environment for the participating youth, and the separation and stratification of staff roles (Eddy, Whaler, & Chamberlain, 2004).

Differences in other types of foster care treatment programs have also been examined. Chamberlain (2003a, 2003b) compared multidimensional treatment foster care (MTFC) to group care interventions. Youth in the intervention condition participated in MTFC, in which each youth individually was placed in a treatment foster family recruited from the local community. Youth in the control condition participated in group care interventions, the standard service for this population. Chamberlain hypothesized that providing the child welfare system adolescent with the powerful socialization force of functional family life could intercede in his or her continual decline. MTFC programs provide youth with families who have positive experiences with adolescents, are willing to act as treatment agents, and can offer a nurturing environment. Families were selected based on a telephone screen, an application form, a home visit, and 20 hours of preservice training. The training emphasized parent management skills such as monitoring and setting clear rules. Foster parents were taught to track positive and negative behaviors and to respond appropriately and consistently. Adolescents were supervised closely, all free time was prearranged, and contact with delinquent peers was prohibited. Foster parents learned how to implement an individual plan for each adolescent.

MTFC was a more effective treatment for severe antisocial behavior in comparison to the traditional group care home services and was the best choice for foster care in terms of significantly fewer crime referral outcomes. Youth in MTFC placements demonstrated lower rates of later delinquency than did youth who had been assigned to control conditions. MTFC also was found to produce large positive effects on increasing placement permanency and the social skills of the children as well as moderate positive effects in reducing serious behavior problems and improving psychological adjustment (Eddy & Chamberlain, 2000).

Eddy and Chamberlain (2000) examined mediational factors in MTFC in a sample of boys. Several factors mediated the relationship between the randomly assigned group condition and boys' later criminal referral and self-reported delinquency rates. The variables included close and consistent supervision by adults, effective discipline, adult mentoring, and separation from delinquent peers. Thus, the findings suggest that placing children in group foster care settings may lead to exposure to deviant peer influence and subsequent criminal behavior, which can be mitigated by individual foster care placement with foster parents who have been trained in MTFC.

Early intervention foster care (EIFC) is an age-appropriate, early entry program designed for preschoolers who were placed in a new foster home (Fisher, Ellis, & Chamberlain, 1999). Similarly to MTFC, EIFC provides foster parents with positive parenting strategies that they maintain over time (Fisher, Gunnar, Chamberlain, & Reid, 2000). A quasi-experimental evaluation study indicated that EIFC children's behavioral adjustment improved. On the other hand, regular foster care children exhibited decrements in functioning in several areas over the same time period. Overall, a parent training approach that emphasizes close supervision and monitoring of the youth's interactions with deviant peers (along with building the foster child bond with his or her family) appears to provide a more effective alternative to warehousing children in group settings.

In addition to type of care, children's history, ethnicity, and gender are important considerations in MTFC. Changes in arrest rate decreased significantly over time for both male and female adolescents for property crimes, with boys showing faster improvement. In addition, 15-year-old girls had a decrease in the rate of status offenses. Participants who had suffered sexual abuse tended to have more total risk factors and more status offense outcomes than did those youth who had not been abused. Although the MTFC has demonstrated positive long-term outcomes for those foster youth and children, one caveat of the MTFC approach is the relatively low minority participation, in which the range is about 6–8% (Chamberlain & Reid, 1998; Eddy & Chamberlain, 2000; Leve & Chamberlain, 2005). It is important to determine whether MTFC is effective with the minority population because nearly half of the population of foster children is minority. Indeed Jonson-Reid and Barth (2002b) have noted that differences between the African American and Caucasian youth participants in the type of out-of-home placements they received after controlling for sociodemographic variables. African American youth were more likely to be placed in correctional facilities and foster care, whereas Caucasian youth were more likely to be hospitalized.

Separate male and female intervention trials have yielded similar mediational findings. Leve and Chamberlain (2005) examined data from two randomized intervention trials with delinquent adolescents who had been placed either in MTFC or in group care. Path analyses indicated that the MTFC youth had fewer associations with delinquent peers at 12 months postplacement than did the group care youth. Further, associating with delinquent peers during the course of the intervention mediated the relation between group condition and 12-month delinquent peer association.

In sum, Chamberlain has suggested that three specific mechanisms of the MTFC approach contribute to successful outcomes for youth and their families. According to Chamberlain, a proactive approach to reducing problem behavior, the creation and maintenance of a consistent and reinforcing environment for the participating youth, and a mature consistent adult caretaker can help mitigate the risks associated with negative peer affiliations. Put another way, the MTFC approach centers on family management skills that include supervision, discipline, and positive adult–youth relationships.

CONCLUSION

Children (and adults) have a need for affiliation and attachment, and a child's parents are his or her first social support network. Child maltreatment, however, threatens secure attachment to parents and is a primary reason that children enter the child welfare system. Although the child welfare system was designed to protect and provide a stable environment for maltreated and orphaned children, the system is not adaptive for all children. The anomaly occurs for insecurely attached children. Cumulative effects of unstable environments, particularly multiple foster care placements, can have a negative impact on vulnerable children. African American children are particularly vulnerable, as disproportionate numbers of youth of color are in foster care. Youth of color are more likely to remain in care longer and receive fewer services than their Caucasian counterparts. Interestingly, research indicates that minority youths are more responsive to child welfare interventions than are nonminority youths (Jonson-Reid & Barth, 2000a, 2000b).

Maladaptive correlates of family instability include social and academic difficulties, externalizing and delinquent behavior, and negative peer affiliation. Peers are a primary social system for adolescents and can be influential to youth in a variety of ways. Children seeking alternative strong attachments are particularly susceptible to peer influence. Given the correlation between child maltreatment and delinquency, peer influence is a risk for adolescents with a history of maltreatment and unstable environments. Youth in group foster care placements can be particularly vulnerable. Youth who have experienced instability in their families and the child welfare system can be affected through introduction to deviant behavior or exacerbation of delinquency through selection into delinquent peer groups. Research has supported the hypothesis that youth with histories of maltreatment and family and placement instability are vulnerable to peer influence through selection into and association with negative peer groups.

Clinically oriented, individualized foster care placements have been found to be successful ways to provide protective, meaningful relationships and to manage, maintain, and monitor dependent children and adolescents. Random-assignment experiments have demonstrated their superior efficacy over placement into group care settings. An important limitation in the literature, however, is that both group and individual family care placements are often referred to simply as "foster care." Disentangling the type of placement is critical in understanding possible negative outcomes of placing children in foster care.

Child welfare services afford an assurance of safety to children who are living with maltreating families. However, there has been limited research on the influence of grouping dependent children in foster care. To address the anomaly of the child welfare system, outcome research should continue to distinguish between group and individual foster care placements and demographic differences such as gender, ethnicity, and children's specific maltreatment and behavior history. Increasing the stability of foster care environments further can help child welfare aid in the healthy adjustment of youth, particularly those who are vulnerable to negative peer influences.

CHAPTER 12

Peer Effects in Community Programs

Jennifer E. Lansford

The Midnight Basketball League was founded in 1986 with the goal of providing 17- to 25-year-old males with a safe and structured activity between the hours of 10:00 P.M. and 2:00 A.M., when they presumably were most vulnerable to risks associated with drugs and crime. Along with games and practice, participants were obligated to attend educational workshops on topics such as safer sex, substance use, and job skills. Leagues quickly formed across the country. Communities often rallied around the players, with crowds of up to 200 coming to watch the late-night games (Midnight Basketball: How . . . , n.d.). Initial claims about the benefits of Midnight Basketball looked promising (see Midnight Basketball, n.d.). For example, the founder of Midnight Basketball asserted that the crime rate in Glenarden, Maryland, had dropped by 30% during the first 3 years of the program (see Hartmann, 2001). Farrell, Johnson, Sapp, Pumphrey, and Freeman (1995) reported a similar reduction in crime in Milwaukee.

Despite the initial heralding of this program, in 2001, the U.S. surgeon general issued a report warning that programs such as Midnight Basketball that attempt to turn deviant gangs into benign clubs either have no effect or even increase gang-related delinquency (Youth Violence, n.d.). How could such a well-intentioned community program with an auspicious start result in these unintended consequences? Why did the surgeon general issue such a warning?

The main problem with the early claims regarding the reduction of crime in areas with Midnight Basketball programs is that there were no scientific controls and no assurance that the programs were not simply

215

operating during a period when the crime rates in particular cities were decreasing overall. Evaluations to date have been either qualitative interviews with participants and staff to assess their perceptions of how the program has affected their lives (Derezotes, 1995) or surveys conducted after participation in the program with no preparticipation surveys or control groups (Farrell et al., 1995). Although no rigorous evaluations of Midnight Basketball have been conducted, there are reasons to doubt that the program has been as successful as proponents would like to believe. First, Midnight Basketball serves only a small proportion of high-risk youth in disadvantaged communities. For example, the Chicago Housing Authority League included a mere 160 participants from two of the highest risk public housing projects in the city; the two projects together housed 6,600 at-risk youth, and the entire Chicago Housing Authority housed 85,000 at-risk youth (Hartmann, 2001). Second, Midnight Basketball shares several features with other community programs that have been found to increase levels of problem behaviors among participants, perhaps in part because they aggregate deviant, high-risk peers and promote their group identity and solidarity.

The aim of this chapter is to evaluate whether the aggregation of deviant peers that occurs in some community programs may be associated with increases or decreases in adolescent antisocial behavior. Evidence for positive and negative peer effects is examined in the following youth programs and community settings: (1) incidental/informal peer aggregation (e.g., unsupervised and unstructured time with peers in popular youth "hangouts"); (2) programs sponsored by public agencies such as libraries and parks and recreation departments; (3) broad-based private organizations (e.g., religious organizations); (4) programs sponsored by national youth-serving organizations (e.g., Boys Clubs/Girls Clubs, Boy Scouts/Girl Scouts, YMCA/YWCA, Girls, Inc., 4-H); and (5) school-based extracurricular programs (although these are not community programs per se, they share the key function of serving the recreational and social needs of adolescents). Several conceptual and measurement points deserve comment before turning to the body of evidence regarding peer effects in community programs.

CONCEPTUAL ISSUES

Conceptually, for the purposes of this chapter, community programs are included if they were designed primarily to meet the recreational, social, or spiritual needs of deviant or high-risk adolescents. A key feature of such community programs is that they aim to increase adolescents' competencies and build their skills, not just prevent negative behaviors; the philosophy is that youth are "resources to be developed rather than problems to be managed" (Roth & Brooks-Gunn, 2003, p. 172). In focusing on promoting the healthy development and normal socialization of youth, these programs' goals are distinct from the goals of programs explicitly designed for the prevention or treatment of mental health- or behavior-related difficulties (Quinn, 1999). Programs that provide only academic instruction and those that do not involve aggregation of deviant or high-risk youth (such as mentoring programs) are also outside the scope of this chapter.

MEASUREMENT ISSUES

The report of one task force concluded that "in the United States, it is easier to obtain a million dollars to study juvenile purse-snatching than a thousand dollars to study youth theater or dance groups" (quoted in Quinn, 1999, p. 109). Overall, there is a paucity of research on community programs for adolescents, particularly regarding programs designed to enhance positive development (vs. targeted prevention or intervention programs) and particularly regarding effects of peer aggregation in community programs. The studies of effects of community programs on adolescents' adjustment that have been conducted often lack experimental rigor and are limited in several ways. Limitations include using local nonrepresentative samples, not controlling for potential confounds (e.g., family socioeconomic status [SES], behavior problems present before program participation), and employing cross-sectional designs (making it impossible to make inferences about causality or to know whether effects of programs endure over time; Catalano, Berglund, Ryan, Lonczak, & Hawkins, 2002). Other evidence is largely in the form of testimonials— for example, Moss (1996) found that 87% of the clergy in San Antonio believed that the church was successful in combating juvenile delinquency, but there are likely to be subjective biases in such reports.

Perhaps the most troublesome barrier to understanding the efficacy of these programs is that adolescents choose whether to participate in particular community and extracurricular activities. It is likely that better adjusted adolescents will choose to participate in extracurricular activities. Moreover, factors such as costs and parental and peer influence shape adolescents' decisions (Bartko & Eccles, 2003). Without random assignment to a control group versus a community program participation group, the possibility that better adjusted adolescents select themselves into the programs cannot be eliminated. There is evidence suggesting that there are indeed large selection biases (e.g., Fejgin, 1994). Despite these limitations, the existing evidence can help inform understanding of peer effects in community programs. It is to this evidence that we turn next.

BODY OF EVIDENCE FOR POSITIVE AND NEGATIVE PEER EFFECTS

Incidental and Informal Peer Aggregation at Popular "Hangouts"

Juvenile offending is related to adolescents' time spent socializing with one another in unstructured settings that are unsupervised by authority figures (e.g., Agnew & Petersen, 1989; Wallace & Bachman, 1991). Hundleby (1987) found that the strongest correlate of adolescents' deviance (including sexual behavior, substance use, and delinquency) was an index reflecting informal socializing with peers. At a societal level, adolescent antisocial behavior is more common in cultures in which adolescents spend more time with peers and less time with adults (Schlegel & Barry, 1991).

Osgood, Wilson, O'Malley, Bachman, and Johnston (1996) argue that individuals will be more likely to succumb to deviant behavior if they spend a great deal of time in situations that are conducive to deviance (e.g., if no authority figure is present, if the time is unstructured) and if they perceive the rewards of deviance to be important. Using five waves of longitudinal data from the Monitoring the Future study, they examined within-individual changes over time and found that higher levels of criminal behavior, alcohol use, marijuana use, use of other illicit drugs, and dangerous driving were associated with riding in a car for fun, visiting with friends, going to parties, and spending evenings out— all of which are forms of unstructured activities. However, going on dates, going to movies, being involved in community affairs, participating in sports, and going shopping were unrelated to deviant behavior, perhaps because each of these activities had a more structured agenda than simply "hanging out."

Young adolescent respondents to a large survey in the United Kingdom indicated that informal recreational hangouts (e.g., mall, arcade, bowling alley) were the second most common place to witness teen tobacco use (Alesci, Forster, & Blaine, 2003). In addition, frequent visitors to arcades and amusement centers reported more frequent tobacco use, drug use, and minor delinquent behavior than did nonregular visitors (Fisher, 1995). A large proportion of adolescents reported going to arcades to "hang around" their friends, and 7% and 6%, respectively, went specifically to smoke cigarettes and to drink alcohol with their friends. Frequent visitors (i.e., once a week or more) were more likely than less frequent visitors to engage in problematic behaviors such as selling possessions, spending money designated for other purposes, and stealing money to be able to keep playing arcade machines (Fisher, 1995).

To what extent are negative outcomes for adolescents who informally aggregate with peers in community settings the result of aggregating versus selection to aggregate? And to what extent do these effects depend on the characteristics of the peer group and the individual youth? Pettit, Bates, Dodge, and Meece (1999) found that unsupervised contact with peers in grade six was related to increased externalizing behavior problems by grade seven, but only among adolescents who already had high levels of behavior problems in grade six. Thus they found a real effect of interacting with peers in unsupervised settings, but the effect held only among youth who were predisposed to deviance. Because adolescents choose to associate with peers who are similar to themselves with respect to interests and behavioral characteristics (called "homophily"; see, e.g., Hamm, 2000) and because adolescents influence the behavior of others in their peer groups (see, e.g., Dishion & Owen, 2002), one might infer that adolescents who spend time with deviant peers in informal community settings are likely to be susceptible to deviant behavior and to influence and be influenced by their peers to engage in such behaviors.

How can informal aggregation among deviant peers be avoided? Parental monitoring may play an important role in this regard. The adolescents at highest risk for externalizing behavior problems in the Pettit and colleagues (1999) longitudinal study were those who associated with peers in unsupervised settings, whose parents engaged in little monitoring, and who lived in unsafe neighborhoods. In a descriptive longitudinal study, Oxford, Harachi, Catalano, and Abbott (2001) found that parental rules, monitoring, and attachment when their children were in fourth or fifth grade reduced their children's association with antisocial peers as well as their initiation of substance use 1 year later. Similarly, in a longitudinal study following boys from the age of 11 to 18 years, Dishion, Capaldi, Spracklen, and Li (1995) found that ineffective parental monitoring predicted adolescents' subsequent association with deviant peers. Thus it appears that adolescents whose parents monitor their activities are less likely both to associate with deviant peers and to experience the behavior problems that such informal peer aggregation can instigate.

The literature reviewed here suggests five conclusions.

1. Interacting with a deviant peer as a friend or with a group of deviant peers appears to increase an adolescent's risk for increasing his or her own deviance, and should be avoided.
2. Interacting with well-adjusted peer friends and groups appears to

protect a youth from deviant development, and thus should be encouraged.

3. The adverse effects of deviant peer group interaction can be minimized through close supervision and monitoring by adults. Adult supervision can prevent a child's gravitation toward deviant peers in the first place and can minimize adverse effects while interacting with that peer group.

4. Adverse effects of group interaction among deviant youth can be minimized through a high degree of structure and organization within the group, such as being task-oriented, skill-development-focused, or tightly scheduled. "Hanging out" informally is the most problematic kind of deviant peer group interaction because it fosters deviancy training.

5. It appears that the youth who are most susceptible to being influenced by deviant peers are those who are marginally deviant or who are just becoming deviant. Children who are very well adjusted may be able to resist the effects of deviant peers, and children who are already very deviant may not be influenced any further.

Programs Sponsored by Public Agencies

Youth development programs provided by public agencies such as libraries and parks and recreation departments constitute a somewhat more structured community context in which youth congregate than do the informal "hangouts" described above. For example, the American Library Association has encouraged the nation's 15,000 local libraries to develop youth development programs, and youth are the main constituents of parks and recreation services such as pools, athletic fields, tennis courts, arts and crafts programs, drama, and special events (Quinn, 1999). Furthermore, in response to the concerns that 8 million children are left alone and unsupervised after school each day and that children are most likely to commit crimes or to be the victim of crime in the hours immediately after school, the U.S. Department of Education has provided grants to more than 7,500 schools in over 1,400 communities to fund 21st Century Community Learning Centers housed at public schools to keep children safe after school (U.S. Department of Education, Office of the Undersecretary, 2003). A typical center serves 156 children; centers primarily serve students in rural and inner-city areas, minority students, and students living in poverty (U.S. Department of Education, 2000). Thus, although many centers do not explicitly target deviant high-risk youth, they may do so merely because of where they are located or who enrolls.

Mathematica Policy Research, Inc. has released findings from their ongoing evaluation of the effectiveness of the centers (James-Burdumy et al., 2005; U.S. Department of Education, Office of the Undersecretary, 2003). In the evaluation of the elementary school centers, it was possible to assign children randomly to participate or not because there were more applicants than spaces available in 18 centers. In the evaluation conducted 2 years after children were randomized to the treatment or to the control group, the treatment and the control students did not differ on several outcomes (e.g., academic grades, parent involvement in school). The treatment group reported feeling safer after school than did the control group. However, the other outcomes assessed favored children in the control group rather than those who participated in the centers. In particular, children in the treatment group were found to have schools contact their parents more frequently about behavior problems during the school day, to have their privileges removed during the school day because of misbehavior more often, and to be suspended from school more often than children in the control group. Furthermore, teachers were less likely to report that students in the treatment group got along well with others, and students themselves were less likely to rate themselves as working well in a team than were control students.

In the evaluation of the middle school centers, random assignment was not possible, but analyses included statistical controls when comparing the participants and nonparticipating children who attended schools where the centers were located. Middle school participants were more likely than nonparticipants to indicate that they had sold drugs, had smoked marijuana, and had experienced the destruction of their property (U.S. Department of Education, Office of the Undersecretary, 2003). Although statistical controls were applied, because middle school participants were more at risk than nonparticipants prior to attending the centers, it is unclear to what extent the differences between the two groups are attributable to participation. Because the centers were housed in relatively disadvantaged communities (e.g., 71% of elementary school centers were located in schools with over 75% eligibility for free and reduced-price lunch) and designed to provide after-school care for children who would otherwise be unsupervised, one might surmise that the centers aggregated youth who were at moderate risk for behavior problems. The possibility that these at-risk youth influenced one another's propensity to use and sell drugs remains strong.

A comparison of children involved in four different types of after-school care highlights the importance of considering both the context of the after-school care and the available alternatives (Mahoney, Lord, & Carryl, 2005). In a sample of first- through third-grade children from an urban, disadvantaged area of the United States, Mahoney and colleagues (2005) found that children who participated in an after-school program at their school had higher academic achievement and motivational attributes than did children who were cared for after school predominantly by their parents, by parents and nonadults, or by other adults and nonadults. Children were not randomly assigned to these after-school care groups. Children in after-school programs at their school had parents who were more likely to be employed, and their families were less likely to be in poverty; these demographic variables were statistically controlled in analyses. The comparison groups are also noteworthy. The nonadult care in two of the four categories generally involved either self-care or care provided by siblings. After-school programs at schools in this study may have proved superior given the alternatives and because they were structured, adult-supervised contexts that emphasized promoting academic skills. The other contexts considered in this investigation likely provided fewer resources (see Mahoney et al., 2005).

A substantial body of research on programs sponsored by public agencies has been conducted by Mahoney and colleagues (e.g., Mahoney & Stattin, 2000; Mahoney, Stattin, & Lord, 2004; Mahoney, Stattin, & Magnusson, 2001), who have conducted several studies on the effects of participating in youth recreation centers in Sweden. These recreation centers were designed to prevent youth from wandering the streets at night and are targeted at 13- to 19-year-olds (Mahoney et al., 2001). Activities available at the centers include pool, table tennis, video games, darts, TV, and music. Adults are present, but they do not structure the youths' activities.

Mahoney and colleagues (2001) report the results of a prospective longitudinal investigation that followed 498 boys from age 10 to age 30. The sample was drawn from a single medium-sized Swedish city. Teachers and peers rated boys' social and behavioral adjustment at the age of 10. At the age of 13, boys reported how often they attended any of the 18–20 recreation centers that were operating throughout the city at the time. Official records that documented all criminal offenses were available both for juvenile offenses (that occurred between the ages of 13 and 17) and adult offenses (that occurred between the ages of 18 and 30).

Boys who had both social and academic problems at age 10 participated in the recreation centers more frequently at the age of 13, as did boys from economically disadvantaged homes (Mahoney et al., 2001). In addition, participation at recreation centers was related to boys' subsequent juvenile offending and persistent offending up to age 30, even after controlling for individual, economic, and family factors that preceded involvement at the recreation centers. In regression models that included aggression, hyperactivity, school achievement, peer preference, SES, marital status, and parent concerns about child behavior, participation in the youth center was the best predictor of criminal offending (Mahoney et al., 2001).

In a separate 2-year longitudinal investigation of 1,163 eighth-grade boys and girls, Mahoney and colleagues (2004) found that after controlling for initial selection factors that predicted participation in youth recreation centers (i.e., problems with parents and at school), participating in the recreation centers increased antisocial behavior over time. Recreation centers that aggregated many antisocial youth were especially likely to promote the development of antisocial behavior among new participants. Youth who began participating in the recreation centers during the course of the study showed a marked increase in their antisocial behavior that corresponded to the time they began attending the centers.

In a cross-sectional sample of 703 14-year-old Swedish boys and girls, Mahoney and Stattin (2000) found that youth who reported participating in structured leisure activities (e.g., sports, music, church, Scouts, or other groups with peers that had an adult leader and met at least once a week at a regular time) had lower rates of antisocial behavior, whereas youth who participated in unstructured leisure activities at a recreation center had higher rates of self-reported antisocial behavior (e.g., stealing, vandalizing, fighting, skipping school). Boys' antisocial behavior was particularly strongly linked to the combination of low participation in structured activities and high participation in unstructured activities (Mahoney & Stattin, 2000).

One of the main problems with the Swedish recreation centers is that they are not age-graded, so young adolescents associate with older adolescents, who are likely to be engaging in more problem behaviors. For girls, the route to delinquency might be through the romantic relationships they form with older delinquent boys. Indeed, Persson, Kerr, and Stattin (2002) found that center participation was a risk factor for girls' subsequent norm breaking (e.g., shoplifting, getting drunk, vandalizing property, forging a signature) only if heterosexual relationships were involved. Overall, girls engaged in more norm breaking with boys than with other girls, but they engaged in more norm breaking with girls who participated in centers than with girls who did not participate in centers (Persson et al., 2002).

Mahoney and colleagues (2001) emphasized that their findings did not suggest that the Swedish recreation centers should be closed because no evidence was available to indicate how the adolescents would have fared if the centers had not existed or it they had chosen not to participate in them. The findings do suggest the need for experimental investigations in which adolescents are randomly assigned to center participation or not to investigate these links further. Mahoney and colleagues also suggested quasi-experimental alternatives such as comparing criminal offending in communities that do and do not have recreation centers or comparing criminal offending in a particular community before and after the introduction of a recreation center.

An Internet search for teen recreation centers suggests that hundreds of such programs are currently operating in the United States. Programs appear to vary substantially in the number of structured activities and the level of supervision provided, but many bill themselves as a place for middle school- and high school-age children simply to "hang out." Despite the substantial number of such centers currently in operation, very little research appears to exist (Mahoney et al. notwithstanding) evaluating the impact of these programs on developmental outcomes.

The degree of deviant peer aggregation that occurs in community programs sponsored by public agencies is likely to depend on the intended clientele and whether the programs are located in high-risk communities. The 21st Century Community Learning Centers and Swedish recreation centers described above were intended to serve relatively high-risk children who would not have had another productive place to spend time after school or in the evening. Thus these programs may have inadvertently increased some behavior problems by aggregating at-risk children in unsupervised settings. However, future research will be needed to determine whether programs sponsored by public agencies in advantaged communities targeting low-risk children would produce similar results (note, however, that public programs under these circumstances enroll fewer youth because the perceived need is less).

Broad-Based Private Organizations

One-third to one-half of U.S. youth participate in religious programs such as confirmation classes, special youth-led worship services, and retreats (Quinn, 1999). Adult service clubs such as Rotary and Kiwanis have chapters of the adult groups that are tailored for youth (e.g., Interact Clubs of Rotary and Key Clubs of Kiwanis). Museums often provide opportunities for youth to learn about art, science, diverse cultures, and history through hands-on experiences. Grassroots organizations have taken shape for youth in many communities; although these certainly have the potential to affect adolescents' adjustment, they have rarely been studied (Quinn, 1999).

It is difficult to find research on private or quasi-private community organizations; most program "evaluations" are little more than testimonials from participants. Evidence does not suggest that participation in such groups leads to increases in delinquent or deviant behavior, but some researchers have found no effects of participation on adolescents' adjustment. Overall, deviant youth are unlikely to be aggregated in such programs because the programs are not targeted for at-risk youth. In fact, in one study, the effect of church attendance on delinquency was indirect, through effects of church attendance on the likelihood of having nondelinquent peers (Mitchell, Dodder, & Norris, 1990). Zimmerman and Maton (1992) found that participating in a voluntary organization can compensate for otherwise risky life choices. For instance, youth who dropped out of high school and were not involved in meaningful activities were at higher risk for alcohol and substance use than were youth who dropped out but were involved in a church (Zimmerman & Maton, 1992). Although the mechanisms are unclear, one possibility is that church involvement provides a social venue in which youth do *not* aggregate with deviant peers as they might in the community at large.

National Youth-Serving Organizations

Community-based youth programs are offered by over 17,000 state and local organizations and 500 national organizations such as Boys and Girls Clubs, Boy Scouts/Girl Scouts, YMCA/YWCA, and 4-H (Task Force on Youth Development and Community Programs, 1992). The 25 major youth-serving organizations operating in the United States annually serve over 30 million youth, which is second only to public schools in the number of youth served each year (National Collaboration for Youth, 1990); approximately 50% of eighth graders participate in a program sponsored by one of these organizations (U.S. Department of Education, 1990).

The most typical structure of youth programs sponsored by these organizations is a small group of adolescents led by an adult who is meant to serve as a mentor and positive role model, but the programs are diverse in their structure and logistical details of operation (Quinn, 1999). For example, some programs are facility-based (e.g., YMCA/YWCA, Boys and Girls Clubs) and tend to be staffed by paid employees, whereas other programs are operated through groups that meet in a variety of locations (e.g., Boy Scout troops that meet in schools, churches, or homes) and tend to rely on adult volunteers (Quinn, 1999). The length of time that programs operate also varies widely from 1–2 hours per week for troop-based programs up to 40 hours per week for some facility-based programs (although few youth would participate in that extent of programming; Quinn, 1999). Some national organizations provide guidelines for programs across the country (e.g., handbooks and badges for Girl Scouts), whereas others give local branches autonomy to shape their own programs (Quinn, 1999). Programs also differ along a continuum of providing for the needs of the "whole child" versus focusing on a specific area of skills and knowledge (Quinn, 1999).

Children tend to be engaged more by youth development programs than by prevention programs that target behavior problems such as substance use or sexual activity (Roth, Brooks-Gunn, Murray, & Foster, 1998). Unlike prevention or intervention programs that identify children who are at risk, youth development programs are typically not stigmatizing and can enhance youths' strengths in a variety of domains rather than focusing on a set of more narrowly defined problems (Roth et al., 1998). For youth who feel disconnected from schools, youth-serving organizations may play an especially important role by offering fun and challenging experiences that are not solely academic (St. Pierre, Mark, Kaltreider, & Campbell, 2001). Such organizations may also be successful in connecting with high-risk parents, who may also have had negative experiences in school (St. Pierre et al., 2001). The degree of aggregation of deviant or at-risk youth is likely to differ by program. For example, Boys and Girls Clubs typically serve at-risk communities whereas Boy Scouts/Girl Scouts typically do not. Thus one might expect effects of these programs to differ according to features of the program as well as characteristics of peers who attend.

Youth development programs have rarely been evaluated rigorously. Self-report testimonials by youth, parents, and program leaders have been more common, but there are clear limitations on this type of anecdotal evidence. Some recent evaluations have been more rigorous, particularly in relation to Boys and Girls Clubs; however, even these evaluations have not addressed whether aggregation of deviant peers occurs in these programs and, if so, how that aggregation affects children's developmental outcomes. The Boys and Girls Clubs of America serve almost 3 million youth in over 2,850 clubs across the country; 71% of the youth live in low-income urban areas (Anderson-Butcher, Newsome, & Ferrari, 2003; Roffman, Pagano, & Hirsch, 2001). These clubs offer five core program domains: character and leadership development; education and career development; health and life skills; the arts; and sports, fitness, and recreation (Anderson-Butcher et al., 2003). In their study of youth in one urban club, Anderson-Butcher and colleagues (2003) found that 59% of youth reported playing in the games room, 33% did arts and crafts, 29% played sports, 28% were involved in life skills/prevention activities, 20% conducted service projects, and 17% engaged in educational activities.

One of the more rigorous program evaluations compared a group of high-risk elementary school students who participated in a 2-year substance use prevention program at their Boys and Girls Club with a control group that did not receive this program (St. Pierre et al., 2001). At each of five elementary schools, children were rated by their first-grade teachers on math and language skills; these ratings were used to create blocks of students within each school. Within each academic block, children were randomly assigned either to the program or to the control group. Each group completed a pretest and several posttests. Compared to the control children, the children who participated in the prevention program showed higher levels of competency skills in refusing wrongdoing, solving problems, being courteous, and behaving ethically (St. Pierre et al., 2001).

In an assessment of a substance use prevention program offered in Boys and Girls Clubs in public housing communities, five clubs were assigned to receive the intervention, one club was assigned not to receive the intervention, and one locale did not have a club at all. The substance use prevention per se was less important than the mere presence of the club in the community. That is, youth in clubs that offered the substance use prevention program did not differ from youth who were not offered the program; however, youth with access to a club were less involved in deviant and dangerous activities and were more involved in school activities (Boys Clubs of America, 1991). This might suggest that the Boys and Girls Club itself, rather than the specific targeted intervention, effected positive change, and the benefits of participation outweighed the potential detriments of grouping youth from at-risk communities. However, an alternate possibility is that this was a neighborhood effect rather than an intervention effect. That is, it is possible that neighborhoods that had a Boys and Girls Club also had other characteristics (e.g., better schools, more involved adults) that made them less likely to house youth involved in deviant activities.

Participation in other organized clubs sponsored by national youth-serving organizations (Girl or Boy Scouts, 4-H, etc.) has been linked to higher academic competence (Fletcher, Nickerson, & Wright, 2003). Among African American and European American fourth graders attending a suburban school, more participation in club activities (primarily scouting organizations) was related to higher grades and higher teacher ratings of academic competence but not to higher standardized test scores (Fletcher et al., 2003). This suggests that instead of improving actual academic performance, club participation may affect teachers' perceptions that students are meeting goals and expectations (Fletcher et al., 2003). Deviant peer aggregation is probably unlikely to occur in many of those club activities.

School-Based Extracurricular Activities

This category of programs has been studied more extensively than have other types of community programs. Most studies show that participation in extracurricular activities positively affects youth development, with some variations in effects depending on the type of extracurricular activity and the outcome assessed. For example, Eccles and Barber (1999) found that participating in sports, school-based leadership activities (e.g., student council), school spirit activities (e.g., pep club), academic clubs (e.g., math club), and prosocial activities (e.g., religious or volunteer groups) predicted better high school grade point averages. Larson's (1994) longitudinal analyses showed that participating in extracurricular activities other than sports decreased adolescents' involvement in delinquent behaviors. Mahoney, Schweder, and Stattin (2002) found that participating in after-school activities was associated with lower levels of depressed mood, especially for adolescents who were detached from their parents but received support from the leader of the activity. Broh (2002) found that participating in music groups enhanced students' educational outcomes, but that participating in student council, drama, and the yearbook club had limited academic benefits. Using data from the National Education Longitudinal Study of 1988, Zaff, Moore, Papillo, and Williams (2003) found that participating in extracurricular activities from eighth through twelfth grade predicts prosocial behavior in early adulthood, even after controlling for potentially confounding variables. Rates of cigarette, alcohol, and marijuana use were lower for adolescents who participated in extracurricular activities than for adolescents who did not participate (Elder, Leaver-Dunn, Wang, Nagy, & Green, 2000).

Overall, extracurricular activities are relatively unlikely to aggregate deviant peers because they are open to all students and not targeted at particular risk groups. Extracurricular activities might provide opportunities for at-risk adolescents to interact positively with conventional adolescents who support the values of the school and to do so in a setting that is tailored to the interests of the participating adolescents (Mahoney & Cairns, 1997). However, studies investigating effects of participation in extracurricular activities have not been designed to test hypotheses about the effects of peer aggregation in the activities.

Of the activities investigated by Eccles and Barber (1999), participating in sports is the type of extracurricular involvement that has been studied most frequently. The majority of studies demonstrate that participating in school sports increases prosocial behavior or decreases involvement in delinquent activities. Using data from the National Educational Longitudinal Study of 1988, Fejgin (1994) found that participation in sports improves students' grades and decreases discipline problems, even controlling for prior grades and discipline problems. Athletes have been found to have higher grade point averages during their athletic season than out of that season (Silliker & Quirk, 1997), and nonathletes have been found to drop out of high school at four times the rate of athletes (Schafer & Armer, 1968).

Mahoney and Cairns (1997) found in a longitudinal investigation of youth followed from seventh to twelfth grade that the students at highest risk of dropping out of school benefited more from participation in extracurricular activities than did more competent students. These researchers hypothesized that because socially and academically competent students are connected to the school in positive ways already, they have less to gain by participating in extracurricular activities (at least in terms of reducing the risk of dropping out, because they are already unlikely to do so). However, at-risk students who are less connected academically to the school might be induced to stay in school if they are engaged by extracurricular activities in that setting (Mahoney & Cairns, 1997). Mahoney (2000) found that participating in extracurricular activities at school was related to lower rates of dropping out of high school and lower rates of criminal arrest during young adulthood, particularly for high-risk adolescents. However, the benefits for these high-risk adolescents were found only if adolescents' social networks also participated in extracurricular activities, suggesting that peer influence within extracurricular contexts is a critical factor.

As described above, participating in extracurricular activities generally has been found to promote adolescents' academic achievement, self-concept, and mental health, and to reduce delinquency (e.g., Eccles & Barber, 1999). The main area that has led to mixed findings is the relation between participation in certain extracurricular activities and alcohol use. It appears that although participating in athletics is related to academic achievement in high school and enhances the likelihood of college attendance, it is also related to more alcohol use in high school and college (Barber, Eccles, & Stone, 2001). However, Eccles and Barber (1999) highlight the importance of considering individual risky behaviors within the broader contexts in which they occur. In the case of athletes who are more likely to drink alcohol but who also have higher academic achievement and are involved with high-achieving peer groups, they argue that drinking alcohol in high school may not have long-term negative outcomes. However, if drinking alcohol is part of a broader constellation of problem behaviors engaged in by a group of peers who are disconnected from school, then it may be a sign of long-term problems to follow (Eccles & Barber, 1999).

SUMMARY AND CONCLUDING COMMENTS

Community Program Characteristics Associated with Deviant Peer Influence

Mahoney and Stattin (2000) argued that "the issue is not whether an individual is engaged in an activity—the issue appears to be what the individual is engaged in and with whom. In terms of antisocial behavior, it may be better to be uninvolved than to participate in an unstructured activity, particularly if it features a high number of deviant youth" (p. 123). Along with the level of structure, the composition of the group is a key feature associated with how community programs are related to deviant peer contagion. Although assessing effects of peer aggregation per se has generally not been a feature of research investigating participation in community programs, results are consistent with the hypothesis that the more unstructured time youth spend in the company of deviant peers, the worse the associated outcomes will be. Table 12.1 summarizes key features of different types of community programs.

Level of Structure

Mahoney and Stattin (2000) emphasize the importance of the demands of an activity increasing in complexity and level of challenge as the participants become more skilled, which is characteristic of many structured activities (e.g., band, athletics), but not of unstructured activities (e.g., hanging out with peers). In theory, organized activities benefit adolescents because they provide opportunities to learn specific skills and prosocial values, foster socialization with peers and adults in positive settings, and take time that otherwise may be spent on risky activities (Eccles & Barber, 1999). An additional benefit of youths' participation in structured activities is that such participation facilitates parents' attempts to monitor their adolescents' activities, companions, and whereabouts, which may, in turn, foster trust between the parent and the adolescent (Mahoney & Stattin, 2000). Structured activities also offer less time for adolescents to spend socializing without adults' supervision. On the basis of this research, *to minimize the potential for deviant peer influence, programs should avoid giving youth unstructured time to "hang out."*

Composition of Group

Youth development programs that are open to all children appear to have better outcomes than prevention programs, which are ostensibly targeted to at-risk youth only. Some of the positive effects associated with activity involvement may arise because adolescents who participate in extracurricular activities have more structured leisure time with peers who are likely to be academically oriented and less likely to skip school and use drugs (Barber et al., 2001). Barber and colleagues (2001) argue that the types of peers who participate in the activities in which an adolescent is involved have the potential to shape the adolescent's emerging social identity, and voluntarily participating in an activity provides the adolescent with the opportunity to declare publicly that he or she is a

TABLE 12.1. Characteristics of Community Programs

Type	Level of structure	Adult involvement	Evidence of negative peer influence	Positive outcomes	Negative outcomes
Informal groups	Low	No	Yes	Fun, perceived benefits of peer group affiliation	Risky sexual behavior, substance use, delinquency, other risk taking (e.g., dangerous driving)
Public agency programs[a]	Variable, often low	Maybe	Yes	Parent involvement in school	Using and selling drugs, delinquency, victimization
Private agency programs	Moderate	Usually	No	Less substance use, less delinquency	None consistently documented
National youth-serving organizations	Generally high	Yes	No	Skills and knowledge, less delinquency, higher grades	None consistently documented
School-based extracurricular activities	High	Yes	Only in relation to athletes' alcohol use	Higher grades, more prosocial behavior, less delinquency, less depressed affect	More alcohol use for athletes

[a] Restricted to programs that concentrate high-risk youth with little structure or supervision.

particular type of person with values and interests congruent with those of the group. Activity involvement may exert its influence on adolescents' adjustment by contributing to the consolidation of adolescents' identity, as well as by enhancing the development of particular skills and increasing social capital (e.g., by bringing the adolescent in contact with adult leaders; Barber et al., 2001). *To minimize the potential for deviant peer influence, programs should avoid targeting only at-risk youth and should avoid aggregating youth who might define their collective identity in terms of deviance.*

Adult Involvement

Not only is the youth composition of the group important, adult involvement is important as well. Caring relationships with adults are important but these do not necessarily need to be one on one. Programs with active adult involvement and oversight are more successful than programs with less adult involvement. *To minimize the potential for deviant peer influence, programs should actively involve adults in the group activities to provide supervision, act as role models, and deter youth from encouraging one another to behave deviantly.*

Future Directions

As described above, much of the research on effects of community programs on adolescents' adjustment is limited in several ways. Because adolescents choose whether to participate in these programs, it is difficult to rule out the possibility that putative positive program effects are actually the result of better adjusted adolescents choosing to participate in the first place. Most importantly, in terms of determining whether deviant peer aggregation contributes to increases in problem behavior, evaluations of community programs have not been conducted in a manner that would allow separate testing of effects of peer aggregation versus other program aspects.

One direction for future research would be to conduct random assignment experiments whenever doing so is feasible and ethically acceptable. By randomly assigning youth to participate in a community program or not, one could help elucidate program effects by eliminating selection biases as an explanation for differences between groups. The peer aggregation component would be more difficult to randomize; because the vast majority of community programs are designed for groups of adolescents (e.g., team sports, recreation centers as a place for adolescents to "hang out"), there would be no comparable way of delivering the program to an individual adolescent in isolation from others. Clearly, in many circumstances, it will not be possible to conduct experiments such as these. However, some of the hypotheses generated in this chapter could be subjected to experimental tests (e.g., the hypotheses that high degree of structure, adult supervision, and presence of some well-adjusted peers could mitigate any adverse effects of deviant peer aggregation). Experiments might alter the structure and composition of peer group activities. Furthermore, it may be possible to conduct natural experiments that could provide useful information. For example, using archival data from school records, it might be possible to chart school suspensions, expulsions, and other disciplinary actions for youth before and after the introduction of a particular extracurricular activity to the school.

On the basis of the research to date, a guiding hypothesis for more rigorous future research is that community programs will have positive effects on youth adjustment to the extent that they provide adult-supervised, structured activities that build adolescents' skills and competencies and do not aggregate only high-risk youth. On the other hand, community programs will have negative effects on youth adjustment if they provide little structure and focus instead on adolescents "hanging out" and if they aggregate groups of high-risk youth.

CHAPTER 13

Peer Effects in Naturally Occurring Groups

The Case of Street Gangs

Malcolm W. Klein

Never underestimate peer effects, especially peer contagion, among young people. Such effects can overwhelm even the most well-designed and sustained efforts at interventions in peer group processes. I was sorely reminded of this many years ago at the end of a highly successful 18-month project in reducing street gang activity. I wrote then that "I've had it with gangs," a declaration often since thrown in my face by facetious colleagues aware that the statement was followed by an additional 30-year career in gang research.

What occasioned my outburst was a simple example of peer contagion, but one that upset my professional complacency. Based strictly on group-related data gathered in prior gang research, my research team had mounted an intervention project with one of Los Angeles's most notorious traditional gangs. The group had existed for about 30 years, constantly regenerating itself in a gang-spawning community that featured not only the Latins (a pseudonym), our gang, but four surrounding rival gangs.

Our object was to manipulate individual, group, and neighborhood factors in such a way as to reduce the cohesiveness of the Latins, in the belief that a reduction in this group process would in turn lead to a reduction in the delinquent and criminal activity of the 100-plus active male and female members of the gang. And that is what happened. Daily

observational data collection and final arrest data showed a cohesiveness reduction of about 40% and, as a result, a similar reduction in recorded crime. Recruitment into the gang had ceased after the initial 6
months of intervention. Such a direct gang intervention result had never
before been empirically demonstrated. So we were pretty pleased with
ourselves. We had successfully reduced peer contagion effects in a naturally occurring youth group. The Latins has been quiet for a year after
some very intensive, data-based, and conceptually designed efforts.

But on my last night in the field, the group reminded me that it was
still a group. A fairly large number of leftover Latin core members was
hanging out with several members of our project team in a church basement. Someone was playing the piano, a group was tossing around a
basketball, and the room was filled with the sound of normal youth
chatter. This almost idyllic scene was suddenly interrupted by the sound
of heavy boots bounding down the basement steps, bringing in the ex-
cited Madman and Narco, aptly named gang "veteranos." They an-
nounced that the rival Gaylords and High Riders were challenging each
other down the street from the church. The trigger was pulled: my quiet,
relaxed Latins leapt up the stairs, out the door, and on to the melee. I
didn't follow to observe the mayhem; I was too upset at seeing this insult
to my "success." Instead I drove rapidly home, poured myself a scotch,
and retreated to my study to pen "I've had it with gangs."

Since this incident was merely one aberration within an overall success in reducing the Latins' cohesiveness and criminal behavior, it might
seem appropriate to describe the project. However, that has been done
elsewhere (Klein, 1971), and to be honest, the interventions carried out
then would be very hard to replicate today. The gang project was conceptualized and organized by a dedicated researcher whose purpose was
less to solve the gang problem than to demonstrate in an action setting
that a carefully planned intervention could reduce gang cohesiveness,
and thereby (rather than directly) reduce gang crime. It included a full-
time staff of three researchers and three field staff working 5–7 days a
week for 18 months, with extreme control over every field decision
made daily, sometimes hourly, by the research director. The point was
demonstrated, but a replicable experiment probably did not result.[1]

NATURALLY OCCURRING GROUPS
AND STREET GANGS

I offer the incident above to remind the reader that natural group processes exist whether groups form themselves or are brought together by
others. Groups are more than aggregations of individuals; they are units

having their own special *group* properties to be analyzed at the *group* level. Communication and interaction imply more than individual-level activities. Norms and cohesiveness are group-level phenomenon. Esprit de corps, or group pride, requires more than individuals. A sense of identity can be derived from group affiliations. Anthropologist James Diego Vigil reminds us that in street gangs, weak self-esteem can be traded for strong group esteem.[2]

The other chapters in Part II of this book are concerned with deviant individuals brought together in groups to facilitate their treatment. This chapter on naturally occurring groups such as street gangs reminds us that individuals already bring learned group processes with them to group treatment settings. They have been "natural" group members prior to treatment, and will be again after treatment. I emphasize street gangs specifically in this chapter because they are groups already involved in deviant behavior *as groups*, and because they have become so prevalent.

The change in street gang prevalence in this country (I will note changes in Europe later) is worth some comment. In the early 1960s, when much of the now classic gang literature was written, there were about 50 cities with street gang problems. In the next two decades that number more than tripled but was still in the low hundreds. Then, in the early 1980s, there was a veritable explosion of gang prevalence (Klein, 1995), to the point that the law enforcement surveys conducted by the National Youth Gang Center (NYGC) reveal over 4,000 gang-involved jurisdictions, peaking in the late 1990s but still very high in our new century (NYGC, 1998). No longer is gang prevalence a "big city" problem; street gangs are found in large, medium, and small cities, many with less than 10,000 in population. Rural areas and Native American reservations are included in the list of gang sites. For one seeking to study peer contagion in naturally occurring groups, it can be done within a short distance of home regardless of one's location.

Of course, most boys and girls affiliate with both formal and informal groups. Clubs, teams, classes, and cliques take up much of youth time in modern society. Most of these, however, are not deviant groups. My contention is that the normal group-level processes in such groups become exaggerated in street gangs, with a product—illegal behavior—that harms both them and us. With the advent of a number of longitudinal youth studies that included questions on gang membership and offending patterns, we learned that joining gangs leads to a marked increase in delinquent behavior, above and beyond that to be expected from gang-prone youth and above and beyond that to be expected from having delinquent peers (Battin, Hill, Abbott, Catalano, & Hawkins, 1998; Bradshaw, 2005; Esbensen & Huizinga, 1999; Gatti, Tremblay,

Vitaro, & McDuff, 2003; Gordon et al., 2004; Thornberry, Krohn, Lizotte, Smith, & Tobin, 2003). Gang joiners are more delinquent than nonjoiners from their own neighborhoods, but the process of membership greatly amplifies crime levels (which drop again after members leave the gang). This is a very robust finding: the authors listed in the citations above report data from such disparate locations as Rochester (New York), Edinburgh, Montreal, Denver, Pittsburgh, and Seattle. One must wonder how likely it is that correctional settings alone could diffuse such an effect.

This chapter concentrates on issues of street gangs because, as I note throughout this chapter, these groups have proven to be *qualitatively* different from other youth groups, even deviant youth groups such as tagger and party crews.[3] In accord with recent work in the Eurogang Program (to which reference is made later), I define street gangs for purposes of this discussion as follows: a *street gang* is any durable, street-oriented youth group whose involvement in illegal activity is part of their group identity.

By this definition, there are four "necessary and sufficient" defining factors: durability, a street orientation, youthfulness, and self-identity as a criminally involved group. Other characteristics are descriptors rather than definers: special clothing, tattoos, or argot; territoriality; special *patterns* of criminality; group names; subgroup patterns; gender and ethnic components; and the like. Gangs may vary widely on these various characteristics, yet share the four defining components that establish their generic character. The definition further allows us to distinguish between street gangs and the multitude of other naturally occurring youth groups. Finally, it allows us to distinguish between street gangs, on the one hand, and other criminal groups such as prison gangs, motorcycle gangs, adult criminal groups and cartels, and terrorist groups, on the other hand.

A final advantage of the four-component nominal definition provided above is that it lends itself readily to operational measures. In materials developed by the Eurogang Program (Weerman & Decker, 2005) operational measures for each component have been pretested and applied in the United States and a number of European countries. These can be used in youth surveys (questionnaire or interview), adult surveys (questionnaire or interview), and as explicit guidelines in ethnographic descriptions. This allows for both nominal and operational comparisons across sites and across methods. Work is now underway in several countries, including the United States, to compare the results of these operational procedures with those of the more common, robust self-report operationalization of street gang membership ("Are you now . . . have you ever been a member of a gang?" and variations on this question).

GANG STRUCTURES

Another approach to determining whether or not a naturally occurring youth group is a street gang derives from recent typological research on the structures of street gangs. Reported elsewhere and most fully elaborated in Klein and Maxson (in press), this research describes five street gang structures that apply to 75–90% of all street gangs to which they have been applied. Any naturally occurring youth group that fits one of the five patterns can be called a street gang.

Although partially sharing certain characteristics, the five structured types are sufficiently different that they provide meaningful depictions and some implications about both useful and counterproductive interventions. The briefest descriptions are these (paraphrased from Klein, 2004):

• *Traditional gangs* are large, territorial, and long enduring, with a wide age range, subgroups or sets based on age or residence, and a versatile crime pattern.

• *Neotraditional gangs* are similar to the traditional form but newer (usually in existence for 10 years or less), smaller, with a narrower age range of members.

• *Compressed gangs* are so labeled because of their smaller size (usually fewer than 50 members) and the restricted age range of their members. Typically, these are adolescent or very early adult groups without well-defined subgroups. They generally endure for less than 10 years as members mature but are not easily replaced by new generations of recruits.

• *Collective gangs* are more loosely structured than the other types. They have some amorphous community ties but are not strongly territorial. They manifest low cohesiveness yet a large membership. They seem transitional, likely to be forced into a more traditional form by outside pressures (rival gangs or law enforcement) or to retract into a smaller form or to dissolve on their own.

• *Specialty gangs* do not show the crime versatility of the other forms. As the name suggests, they specialize in a few patterns such as drug distribution or burglary or auto theft or extremist pursuits (e.g., skinheads). They tend to be the smallest in membership and also the most organizationally structured in order to carry out their criminal activities.

It is notable that these depictions tell us nothing about gender or ethnicity. Research on females in gangs is not yet so definitive that the typologies clearly relate to female membership. Within traditional gang structures, female subgroups have often been described (Klein, 1971; Miller, 1973; Moore, 1991), but beyond this only Jody Miller (2001) has commented on the gender and structure connections of more modern gangs. The lines of distinction between structures and ethnicity are also unclear, but mostly because group process trumps ethnicity. That is, the structures serve group goals, not ethnic goals, and each structure can be found among Hispanic, black, Asian, and white gangs (although not in identical proportions).

Attempted interventions are probably better based on the structural characteristics of gangs than on their gender or ethnic makeups. Critical in this is the notion of gang cohesiveness. Contrary to many media and law enforcement characterizations, most gangs are not highly cohesive nor hierarchically structured. The problem in intervening with their structures is that almost any intervention serves to increase gang cohesiveness (Klein, 1995). By drawing attention to the special nature of the group, both social service and law enforcement attention reinforce the identity, sense of belonging, status, and reputation that attracted youth to the gang originally. Increased cohesiveness, unfortunately, yields increased involvement in delinquent activities (Klein, 1971), just as increased cohesiveness yields positive outcomes for many prosocial groups (sports teams, work groups, study groups, etc.). Peer contagion can be healthy in prosocial groups, but quite the opposite when it results from interventions with deviant groups.

A single exception to this pattern may have been produced by Operation Cease Fire in Boston (Kennedy, Braga, Piehl, & Waring, 2001). Here an intervention into firearm use based on an intense deterrence format resulted in street gang intervention because so many of the city's gun problems proved to be gang-based. After-the-fact evaluations of the project and several replications showed promising results, but it is remarkable that none of the reports were based on experimental designs and all are subject to alternative (regression) interpretations.

With this possible exception, negative results from interventions have been demonstrated among traditional gangs (Klein, 1971) and probably exist for neotraditional and compressed gangs as well. The case is less clear among collective gangs where neighborhood affiliations may be as strong as gang affiliations (Fleisher, 1998) and normal membership dissolution may be expected.

By way of contrast, one might expect specialty gangs to be subject to dissolution under law enforcement pressure as applied by selective enforcement (harassment), civil injunctions, and antigang legislation. Highly structured criminal enterprises often wither when attacked by equally well-structured enforcement agencies simply because their "business" is interrupted. Increased cohesiveness is not a problem for gangs already tightly cohering around their well-structured business roles.

GANG PROCESSES

As is the case with cohesiveness, the usual processes in "normal" groups are to be found within gangs. However, they often take on a gang-specific tone that requires recognition prior to any planned intervention. The "oppositional culture" (Moore & Vigil, 1989) that develops in a street gang stands ready to resist and turn to its own advantage any intrusion from outside, no matter how well intentioned that intrusion may be. Tenuous levels of group cohesiveness can be raised by inadvertently triggering this oppositional culture, but also can be lowered by promoting individuation of the members and by avoiding actions that legitimize the gang.

Beyond this, some of the more important of a gang's group processes include:

- *Rivalries with other gangs*, which sometimes inadvertently and sometimes by design cement in-group identity. This happens both in the community and within correctional institutions.
- *Group norms of loyalty and commitment*, which are often stronger in rhetoric than in fact. Group norms are broad, variable, and dependent on place and time. Stereotyping these norms, which both the media and law enforcement agencies have a tendency to do, overstates their strength and immutability, which in turn discourages useful attempts to counteract them among individual gang members.
- *Gang cohesiveness and group identity*, which serve to isolate members from prosocial peers, almost demanding disdain for nongang associations. Especially among the youngest and oldest gang members whose emotional bonds to the group are more tenuous, prosocial associations are engageable—girls, jobs, family roles, military service, mentors, and other external time commitments can all be encouraged at the expense of gang group identity.
- *Variations in kind and degree of gang commitment.* Some gang members become committed to the group principally because their own personal deficiencies and penchant for aggression make group identity a salient option. Others become committed because of an already established social propensity for peer and group associations (see Klein, 1971, Ch. 3). In either case, the strength of commitment to gangs is highly varied across members, and also variable across time for each individual member. A most instructive exercise is to observe gang members at times

of high stress—for example, when they are under attack by a rival gang—and note how some members disappear from the street, while others gather closely together in temporarily highly cohesive cliques. Gang intervention without recognition of variability in commitment to the group will miss many marks.

• Elsewhere in the volume, and especially in Chapter 2 (Dishion & Dodge), authors have stressed many *mechanisms that trigger and reinforce peer contagion.* Many of these are easily observable, and are implicit in the materials presented above, in the open street gang setting[4]: "deviance-training" identity reinforced by the treatment setting (i.e., iatrogenesis), exposure to antisocial norms, personal vulnerabilities to group processes, sensitivity to like-minded peers, and direct recruitment of like-minded peers. What the gang setting adds to all this is perhaps greater appreciation of group-qua-group processes above and beyond those that might seem to be "merely" interpersonal. There is, in other words, a legitimate analysis at the group-as-unit level, such that concerns for the iatrogenic processes for youth peers in treatment settings are more than accumulated individual and interpersonal processes. If peer aggregation triggers new gang identities and commitments, then the street gang analogue becomes even more relevant.

This is a generic phenomenon, not just a U.S. gang phenomenon. Pinnock's (1997) description of group processes in South African gangs has a familiar ring. He describes these processes as contributing to the "separation" of the gang member from other peer connections: "It can begin from the moment a youth flashes his first gang sign . . . a gradual process of assimilation of gang disposition: conforming to certain gang criteria, posturing on the street corner, adopting a style of talking, mobilizing around certain territories and around certain real and imaginary symbols" (pp. 31–32). Pinnock refers to "the particular argot specifically used by gang youths to differentiate between those who are a part of the normal or gang community" (p. 33). Finally, Pinnock describes the process in a gang named, ironically, "The Americans": "Within the house little defined them as a gang: they simply appeared to be a group of friends laughing, joking and spending time together. Outside, the performance began the moment they became aware of being in the public eye" (p. 37).

This leads us to the final point in this listing, described by Pinnock as "a greased pole of deviance":

• *Crime amplification* can be the most destructive of all group processes in street gangs. As noted at the beginning of this chapter, earlier ethnographic observations have been amply confirmed by recent longitudinal survey studies of gangs that joining gangs leads to a very marked increase in delinquent and criminal activity by individual members. Anything that increases gang cohesiveness and size—including well-intentioned interventions—will likely increase members' involvement in criminal activity, further removing them from prosocial alternatives.

DIFFERENTIATING FACTORS

To this point, I have stressed the point that street gangs are qualitatively different from most other naturally occurring groups. The four-component nominal definition serves to highlight this difference. The five gang structures described earlier are not descriptive of most other youth group forms. The group processes just discussed similarly paint a somewhat unique portrait of street gangs. Yet, in addition to these concerns, there are other factors that help us to understand street gangs as qualitatively different groups, probably requiring special understanding if we are to develop useful interventions and controls.

For instance, it is generally understood that street gangs are either Hispanic or black, although occasionally the notion of Asian gangs— Chinese, Japanese, and Vietnamese gangs are the most common—is accepted. And for the most part, this image is correct. Yet there are white gangs in the United States (of various ethnicities and mixes), and Native American gangs, and gangs of mixed origins. Upon study, what becomes clear is that street gang membership tends to derive from socially marginalized populations. Even white gangs seem to be composed of marginalized youth, those not "making it" in their own settings. Thus it is not the race, nor the national origin, nor the color, nor the religion that provides the fodder for gang development, but the process of marginalization from the social mainstream. The old Italian, Jewish, Irish, and other white gangs of the 1930s and 1940s largely disappeared as these nationally and religiously marginalized groups found acceptance in the U.S. social structure. Deviance in social background led to an outsiders' stature, and this in turn to the outsiders' behavioral deviance. The same is true today—only the names of the national and racial groups have changed (granted, a slight exaggeration, but useful to stress the point).

Thus in earlier times, the first half of the 20th century, gangs flourished principally in the major eastern and midwestern cities where white immigrants set their new American roots. Blacks and Hispanics were there too, but not as remarkably distinctive minorities. As noted earlier, today's gangs, reflecting the presence of marginalized populations in cities and towns of all sizes, can be found in over 4,000 jurisdictions, ranging from rural entities and small towns to the largest cities, wherever a sufficient segregated or marginalized youth population is located. Poverty—*relative* poverty—helps to reinforce the process as it is manifested in poor resources, inadequate educational and welfare responses, deeply rooted unemployment, and a discriminatory criminal justice system that can't accept minority status and poverty as mitigating circumstances.

This leads one to a second differentiating factor: it is not so much the gangs that are the problem, but the neighborhoods that spawn them. Communities are not tabulae rasae, innocent contexts that somehow become "gang territories." Larger communities and smaller neighborhoods create the setting for gang emergence and inadvertently reinforce the process once it starts. It's not like starting up a basketball team, a boys and girls club, or a student council. Gangs are spawned where marginalized youth are located (not by random assignment), where their needs are not adequately recognized or supported, and where informal (adult) social controls are no longer adequate. These are neighborhoods of low "social efficacy" (Sampson, Morenoff, & Earls, 1999). If direct interventions with gangs are ineffective or counterproductive because of their effects on group cohesiveness, then we had better turn our attention to the nature of the communities that spawn and reinforce gang existence. And if someone suggests that the answer lies in taking the gang members out of the neighborhood for a while via detention and incarceration, let us remember that the gang member will return to that neighborhood, or one very much like it. What was the old saying about rural America? "You can take the boy out of the farm, but you can't take the farm out of the boy."

There is a third gang-differentiating factor of another sort, equally important to the notion of gangs being qualitatively different. It is often incorrectly assumed that street gangs are composed of delinquents who are merely more delinquent than other deviant youths. Thus, the implication is, the variables that predict to delinquency will also—and even more clearly—predict to gang membership. But the implication is not supported by most recent research: gang membership (with its attendant greater delinquency) is actually less predictable by reference to the usual variables associated with delinquent behavior.

These variables, the ones that are predictive of delinquent behavior, may number well over a hundred (depending on how narrowly they are defined). There are delinquency predictors at the level of individual characteristics—for example, intelligence, self-esteem, various attitudes and perceptions, gender, and ethnicity. There are predictors in the family domain—for example, family size, family structure, supervision, family criminality, consistency of discipline, and family resources. There are predictors in the peer domain—some of which are our strongest predictors—such as numbers of delinquent peers, numbers of prosocial friends, and amount of time spent with both. There are predictors in the school domain, such as commitment to education, grade point average, respect for teachers, being liked by teachers, involvement in school activities, and absenteeism. And there are predictors in the neighborhood domain, including local social resources, deviance gathering spots, police presence, exposure to violence, and community efficacy.

Predicting to delinquency is easy, although accounting for a lot of its variance is not. What differentiates the predictors of gang membership is that only a subset of the individual delinquency predictors are useful in distinguishing gang members from nongang delinquents. Perhaps this should not surprise us, given the well-demonstrated fact that most delinquents do not become gang members, even in high-gang-incidence neighborhoods. There is something quite special about joining gangs, something above and beyond being delinquently oriented (see, in particular, Thornberry, Krohn, Lizotte, & Chard-Wierschem, 2003). For example, in the family domain, a special attempt was made to find the risk factors for gang joining among a broad array of family predictors of delinquency. Of 21 family variables known to predict delinquency, only 10 yielded bivariate predictions to gang involvement. Of these, only six survived a multivariate analysis (Whitlock, 2004).

In an attempt to provide intervention guidelines for a large gang prevention project a few years ago, I compared the findings of two California-based cross-sectional studies of gang joining (Long Beach and San Diego) with the results of the extensive longitudinal comparisons of gang and nongang youth in Rochester, New York (Thornberry et al., 2003), and Denver, Colorado (Esbensen & Huizinga, 1999). All four projects used similar and identical measures of many delinquency predictors, as well as basically the same self-report measures of delinquent behavior. In addition, the same basic self-report measures of gang membership were used and applied to youth samples expected to include both gang and nongang respondents. Only the following constructs (Klein, 1997) were commonly found to predict to gang as compared to nongang youth:

1. Earlier involvement in delinquent activities.
2. Earlier self-concept as a delinquent.
3. Absence of helpful adults outside the family.
4. Exposure to a set of stressful critical events, such as parental breakup, death in the family, broken love matches, etc.
5. Family members in a gang or in serious legal trouble.
6. Lower family supervision or monitoring.

7. Delinquently oriented friends.
8. Friends who accept or endorse violent forms of conflict resolution.
9. Enjoyment from "hanging around" the neighborhood with friends.
10. Lower commitment to school, lower expectations for higher education.
11. Higher levels of exposure to violence in the neighborhood.
12. Higher levels of disrespect for officials, especially police.

The point of this listing is less the specifics of the variables listed than the restricted number of such variables. This small number confirms the assertion that gang membership is in no way merely the extreme of delinquency, but something above and beyond it. While research has not yet adequately documented this "above and beyond" complex of variables, it seems clear that it must have to do with the additional matters associated with group membership, which includes the attraction of the group to potential members, the settings in which such groups manage to emerge, and the reaction of local youth and adults to the presence of such groups. Thus when we take gang members out of their neighborhoods to treat and punish them in correctional settings, we renew much of what spawns and reinforces their group membership. This expectably leads to inappropriate, perhaps even counterproductive, intervention because gang members will return to their original habitat. Naturally occurring groups may best be handled—and *very* carefully— in their natural settings.

GENERALIZING TO OTHER SETTINGS

How natural are our naturally occurring youth groups? One way to test this question about street gangs is to seek them out elsewhere, as my colleagues and I have done in the Eurogang Program. Are the characteristics, structures, and processes described in the previous pages to be found as well in counterpart groups in Europe? If not, then the particular U.S. context for street gangs may have to be highlighted in our concerns for assessing peer contagion problems. But if the similarities are strong, then we can be more secure about the generalizability of our understanding about peer contagion in naturally occurring groups.

Until the very recent past, European research on gangs has been scattered and episodic. In large part, this is probably due to the sparse appearance of gangs until the 1980s. Much of the following discussion is based on reports emanating from the Eurogang Program, a joint enterprise among U.S. and European gang researchers initiated in 1997 and first catalogued in *The Eurogang Paradox* (Klein, Kerner, Maxson, & Weitekamp, 2001). Eight workshops to date have been held in the United States, Germany, Holland, Spain, Belgium, and Norway. Since 2001, more research reports have emerged, a second compilation has been produced (Weerman & Decker, 2005), and significant gang patterns are emerging in 50 or more locations ranging from the British Isles to Russia's Volga region, from Scandinavia to Italy, and most countries in between. These patterns, and some open questions, can be summarized as follows:

1. There is every reason to believe that similar group processes occur in U.S. and European street gangs. European gang reports contain descriptions similar to those in U.S. reports, regardless of whether or not the European writers show familiarity with U.S. gang research. Limited group cohesiveness, oppositional culture, exaggerated norms of loyalty and commitment, and crime amplification can be gleaned from many of the European reports, most of which are ethnographic in nature.

2. Perhaps surprisingly, these general similarities appear despite some notable differences from the U.S. street gang. The ethnic or national origins are different; access to and reliance on firearms is far lower than in U.S. gangs; female participation appears to be lower than in the United States; and the accumulated gang traditions in Europe seem less shared than in the United States.

3. The similarities and differences have led to extended discussions about how best to define street gangs. Significantly, scholars on both sides of the Atlantic have been able to come to a consensus on the nominal definition cited earlier in this chapter, with its four necessary and sufficient components. A common nominal definition would not be possible if the U.S. gang picture were not reflected in its European counterparts. Empirical attempts to test common operational definitions are currently under way and will be published in subsequent reports.

4. Differences requiring further research include the impression that the European gang scene includes a higher proportion of non-minority groups (including skinheads) than is the case in the United States, and more groups with a political focus.

5. Still under investigation is the question of whether the five-structure typology described earlier adequately encompasses the bulk of European street gangs. Indications to date suggest the answer is yes, but with different proportions (e.g., fewer traditional gangs). This tentative conclusion derives from secondary analyses, however, rather than from research deliberately designed to test the typology's suitability.

6. As with U.S. street gangs, the importance of antisocial and crimi-

nal behavior to the self-identity of European street gangs does not seem to be in doubt among the European gang scholars. Just as serious violence was not a major factor in the earlier stages of gang formation in the United States, so it is not in Europe. However, there is great variety on both sides of the Atlantic, with some very violent gangs among the larger number of gangs where violence is a lesser proportion of overall criminal involvement. The most extreme case in Europe was reported in Glascow in the 1970s (Patrick, 1973).

7. I will discuss below some of the principal attempts at gang intervention in the United States. The European situation, being far newer, provides very few descriptions of gang prevention, intervention, or suppression (the three foci of U.S. efforts). Police prevention programs have been described in Denmark, and a detached worker street program is ongoing in Berlin. By and large, however, little is known of gang intervention in Europe. The most common public or official response to street gangs has been to deny their existence (most clearly in England) or to deny the seriousness of the problem (see comments throughout Klein et al., 2001).

GANG CONTROL PROGRAMS

The primary difficulty in describing the effects of street gang control programs in a chapter about peer effects—especially "peer contagion"—is that there has been such a disjuncture between the two. In most instances of gang control programs, peer effects have been all but ignored, or at best poorly conceived and therefore not subject to planned and conceptualized intervention. One might conclude that practitioners and policymakers have forgotten that street gangs are groups and have complex group properties.

Similarly, the majority of scholars doing research on gangs have failed to appreciate group processes, or have adopted research methods that are unlikely to uncover these processes. The exception to the generalization lies in selected observational and ethnographic studies (as opposed to youth surveys, archival studies of news reports and police records, and interviews with gang service agencies).

The final difficulty lies at the intersections of the above: What research methods have been used to assess gang intervention programs in which peer effects or contagion or group processes have been adequately recognized and conceptualized? I would submit that only three major exercises in assessing such effects have been undertaken in such a way as to influence our appreciation of peer effects in street gang behavior. All three predate 1970.

1. Short and Strodtbeck (1965), in a nonevaluative study of Chicago gangs, paid special attention to peer processes and group leadership, finding them so pivotal that they titled their book *Group Process and Gang Delinquency.*

2. Mattick and his associates, also in Chicago, looked closely at peer influence processes among gang members and how interventions can be perverted by these processes (Caplan, 1968). They found that gang members receiving the most intensive services manifest the greatest increases in delinquent behavior (Carney, Mattick, & Callaway, 1969).

3. Klein, working in Los Angeles during this same period, concentrated some effort on measuring changes in gang cohesiveness during street work programs. In the first project, he documented that greater program intensity led to increased cohesiveness and thereby to increased delinquency. In a second project, he demonstrated that deliberately reducing the sources of cohesiveness led to a reduction of gang recruitment and to group-level (but not individual-level) decreases in delinquency.

Each of these three programs looked deliberately at peer contagion and associated group process. Yet they are exceptions in the general gang literature, and especially in that limited literature that reports on program interventions with gangs. Ethnographic studies have tended to accumulate incidents rather than tie them to group processes (but note the concern for honor stressed by Horowitz [1983]). Archival studies, deriving their data from news reports and analyses of police and court data, almost never find peer process data in the materials available to them. Survey studies generally report aggregated *individual* responses to questions and seldom ask individuals to report on peer relations or group structures and processes. Although it is an exaggeration to say so, I must conclude that gang research has largely omitted the fact that gangs are groups.

The most recent, large-scale efforts at gang control have shown two trends that make them, at best, tangential to our own concerns in this chapter and volume. First, several of them have failed to build in independent evaluations that specifically draw forth data on gang members (the "L.A. Plan," "L.A. Bridges," and the Illinois Attorney General's Gang Prevention Program, all of which are reviewed by Klein and Maxson [in press]). Three others built in major research evaluation procedures. The Gang Resistance Education and Training Program (G.R.E.A.T.), built on the D.A.R.E. (Drug Abuse Resistance Education) model, failed to show any effects at the gang level. The national Comprehensive Gang Intervention program (the "Spergel Model") has as yet failed to demonstrate a generalizable result over five sites. The Safe Futures program, as studied in St. Louis, showed such low program implementation that results in gang change cannot be assessed (these three projects are also reviewed by Klein and Maxson [in press]).

In sum, our concern with peer contagion in the gang setting had been addressed sporadically since the 1960s, and almost not at all in the context of attempts to intervene in the processes connected with peer contagion. Further, the desire to study these processes experimentally, as expressed in various chapters of this volume, has never been addressed in the context of street gang research (nor is it clear how it might be addressed). Our best understandings, hopefully summarized in the preceding pages, come primarily from uncoordinated ethnographic and observational studies. Systematic, comparative studies of this sort, designed a priori, remain our best single methodological hope. Their value would be increased by combining them in time and space with survey research on gang and nongang youth. A proposal to do just this is a part of the Eurogang Program, in which ethnographic guidelines, youth surveys, and community surveys have been developed with an identical common core of variables to be collected across cities and across countries. The rationale for such comparative studies is elucidated by Klein (2005). Until then, numerable incidents such as that described at the beginning of this chapter remind us of the strength of peer contagion effects. Thus I close with another such incident.

THE F—— ROSE GARDEN (JUNE 2003)

On a warm day, with a slight breeze wafting in from the west where the ocean determines the day's weather, the odors of thousands of roses lie in waves above the colored bushes. Reds, yellows, flame oranges, and striped hybrid flowers cover the sunken grounds of the Exposition Park rose garden. Hispanic families, sheltered from the roars of nearby boulevards, wander along the pathways, grandparents taking toddlers to the edges of the plants to poke their noses in the blooms. A flock of green parrots circles overhead, then passes on in its daily path above the many communities that call themselves Los Angeles.

I am in this idyllic setting to escape from writing page 10 of this chapter, to clear my head before plunging back into the issues of treating gang members in group rehabilitation settings. Strolling through the gardens is a balm, watching the kids at play, the birds in flight, considering the decades of dedicated horticulture that has led to the beauteous variety in one of the region's finest flower displays.

In each corner of the garden there is a white and green cabana, often the sites of colorful weddings and family celebrations, with Mexican music punctuating the air. But today the sounds from two of the cabanas are strikingly different. A dozen young men, black and Hispanic, form groups in each spot, yelling and laughing and then suddenly quiet as if a bubble had burst. As I pass by each group, studiously attending to the roses but with ears pointed like Mr. Spock toward the cabana, I hear more f-words in a half hour than I did in some 40 years of street gang research. The f——ing counselors and m—— f——ing police, and the f——ing just-about-everyone-else in this f——ing world, including each f——ing member of both f——ing groups were the targets of intense discussion.

The local correctional halfway house had come to the rose garden: rehabilitation among the blooms, another setting for peer contagion in group treatment. I had not escaped page 10 after all. Some of us, it seems, are fated to find our professional lives displayed even in the most unlikely places. And as I walked up and out of the garden, I noticed what I had overlooked on the way in—gang graffiti along the walls. No roses there.

NOTES

1. The project is described by Klein (1971) and the incident is offered in the "Introduction and Epilogue" section of the book. Various procedures were used to reduce cohesiveness. At the individual level, gang members targeted for intervention were chosen only on the basis of their relationship to the group: leaving it, becoming more active in it, stirring up group feeling, and so on. At the group level, all sponsored group activities were stopped or discouraged: outings, meetings, joint activities, and the like. At the neighborhood level, alternative opportunities were enhanced—for example, the Boys Club and a teen center reopened their doors to the Latins. Tutors and members were engaged. Most importantly, employment opportunities were aggressively sought out, resulting in over 100 jobs engaging 45 Latin members over an 18-month period.
2. Vigil (1988) draws this conclusion from his extended experience with Chicano gangs, but I have found it to be apt far more broadly.
3. A somewhat inconsistent depiction of these three types of groups can be found in Valdez (2000). His very loose definition of street gangs would incorporate a wide variety of youth groups, losing the special nature of street gangs.
4. Pinnock (1997, p. 30) observes, "In the desperation of the streets, peer admiration is the only admiration around."

PART III

PROMISING SOLUTIONS AND RECOMMENDATIONS

Research-Based Prevention Programs and Practices for Delivery in Schools That Decrease the Risk of Deviant Peer Influence

Rebecca B. Silver
and J. Mark Eddy

Addressing student misconduct has long been a part of the daily routine for teachers and administrators in elementary and secondary schools. Responses are typically reactive, after the misconduct has occurred, rather than proactive, or *preventive*, in nature. Depending on the type, severity, and pattern of misconduct, common responses to student misbehavior include disciplinary meetings, detention and suspension, referral to group counseling, assignment to a special education classroom or an alternative school, and expulsion from school. The major theme in this set of responses is the exclusion of chronically and seriously misbehaving youth from the general population of students. Exclusion appears to accomplish two important goals: (1) it ensures a safe and nondisrupted educational environment for the majority of students, and (2) it provides highly disruptive students with specially trained teachers who may have more success than regular classroom teachers in managing and even improving their behavior and academic performance. Unfortunately, very little is known about how well these goals are met through the use of reactive strategies. There is some evidence that such strategies simply don't work, at least in terms of reducing the occurrence of problem behaviors (Bear, 1998; Larson, 1998). Furthermore, over the long run, there is evidence that these strategies may actually lead to increases in disruptive behaviors through an increase in the frequency of association between the "problem" youth and similarly "deviant" peers. As discussed throughout this volume, association with deviant peers is a significant predictor of a variety of interrelated youth problem behaviors, including student misconduct, academic failure, delinquency, substance use and abuse, and early sexual behavior.

In the case of responses that cluster deviant youth within a school setting (e.g., group counseling, special education classroom assignment), exacerbation may occur because youth are given both the means and the opportunity to make new friends with whom they may subsequently misbehave, whether at school or in the community. In the case of responses that remove a youth altogether from the school setting (e.g., suspension, expulsion), exacerbation may occur because the amount of time youth spend unsupervised by adults is likely to increase. If a youth in this situation "wanders" about the community in the company of other deviant youth and/or criminal adults, the probability is high that the quantity and diversity of problem behaviors exhibited by the youth will increase. Subsequently, if the youth returns to school—and he or she well may not—his or her behavior problems may be more problematic than before the sanction was applied.

While reactive responses remain a mainstay of school policy (Gottfredson & Gottfredson, 2001), schools within the United States traditionally have been given some version of a mandate to contribute to the prosocial development of youth, most typically through the shaping of student "morals," "beliefs," or "citizenship," and more recently through the encouragement of responsible youth decisions and behaviors in areas such as driving, sexual behavior, and substance use. To date, numerous reviews of the scientific literature have concluded that a variety of these school-based programs and practices are effective in terms of preventing, or at least reducing, a variety of youth problem behaviors both inside and outside of the school setting (e.g., Bear, Webster-Stratton, Furlong, & Rhee, 2000; Gottfredson & Wilson, 2003; Hawkins, Farrington, & Catalano, 1998; Larson, 1994; Samples & Aber, 1998; Tobler & Stratton, 1997; Wilson, Gottfredson, & Najaka, 2001). Prevention programs that emphasize proactive strategies can serve as *complements* to schools' reactive strategies, and, if effective within a particular school, have the potential to reduce the need for strategies that lead to the clustering of deviant peers and the consequences that may result.

In this chapter, we attempt to provide some clarity for policymakers and school personnel on the issue of prevention by beginning with an overview of the school-based programs that have received the greatest research support. Of note is that the majority of these programs *do not* group children with behavior problems together for intervention. If grouping does occur, it is often within the context of a variety of other ongoing interventions. Because failing to remove or segregate problematic children from the regular education classroom may increase risk for a variety of undesirable events, we follow our overview with a close consideration of what is known about how these programs influence not only the behavior of the most troublesome students (i.e., the primary targets of reactive practices), but also the behavior of students with few or no behavior problems (i.e., the students who might suffer if deviant students are not segregated). We conclude by outlining principles that school staff can use to guide the selection of preventive strategies.

DEFINITION OF A RESEARCH-BASED PREVENTION PROGRAM OR PRACTICE

A commonly accepted definition of a *prevention program* is a program that attempts to delay or eliminate the onset of serious problem behaviors by enhancing protective factors and decreasing risk factors present in the life of targeted youth (Mrazek & Haggerty, 1994). A wide variety of prevention programs have been developed over the past 40 years, but rigorous research on prevention programs is still relatively rare. Perhaps because of this, deciding whether or not a program has been studied sufficiently enough to be called "research based" is difficult and little consensus exists. In the absence of consensus, we included programs in this chapter using the following three-step search process. Programs that targeted elementary, middle, or high school students were included in our search.

Step 1. We first applied the functional definition used by Metzler, Eddy, Taylor, and Lichtenstein (2005) that a program or practice is "research based" if deemed as such by at least three independent, scientifically rigorous reviews of the research literature on youth problem behaviors. To apply this definition to the literature, we searched the 11 reviews examined by Metzler and colleagues. Expert panels conducted many of these reviews, and most programs that make even one of these lists could legitimately be labeled "research based" by most researchers. Making three lists was chosen as the standard to be absolutely certain that a program was widely viewed as supported by research. Step 1 yielded 26 school-based programs. Almost all of these programs have been studied within the context of a "randomized controlled comparison group" research design, which is generally considered the most unequivocal way to determine whether a program is, or is not, efficacious.

Step 2. The risk with our initial search strategy is that we may have failed to identify a class of programs or strategies (rather than a specific program) that is efficacious. For example, there might be 10 differently named parent education programs that share similar content and instructional practices. While no particular program may have enough evidence to be considered "research based," when the evidence from all the programs is pooled together this class of programs might actually be quite strongly supported by research. Thus we searched recent meta-analyses of school-based prevention and intervention programs (Durlak & Wells, 1997; Stage & Quiroz, 1997; Tobler & Stratton, 1997; Wilson et al., 2001) to find out if we missed any strategies. This search did not identify any particular class of programs or strategies that were not represented in the 26 programs found in Step 1.

Step 3. The first two steps were sufficient to create an adequate "research-based" set of school-based programs. However, because of the relatively slow timeline in which studies are conducted and published, it was likely the list was incomplete. To ensure that we did not leave out programs, we searched a variety of recent narrative reviews of school-based prevention programs and practices. This strategy yielded eight additional "promising" programs. As would be expected, the quality of research designs and the strength of research findings for these programs tended to be inferior to those for the programs found in Step 1. Nevertheless, the available evidence indicates that these programs may be useful tools in the prevention of youth problems. We note whether a particular program was identified as "research based" or as "promising" throughout this chapter. All programs that we reviewed are listed in Table 14.1.

RESEARCH-BASED AND PROMISING PREVENTION PROGRAMS

The programs identified through our search strategy can be classified in two primary ways: based on the characteristics of the targeted population or based on the characteristics of the intervention. In terms of characteristics of the population, programs can be sorted into three major types, "universal," "selective," and "indicated," based on how broad a population the program targets and the risk status of that population (Mrazek & Haggerty, 1994). *Universal* prevention programs are those that target an entire population of children (e.g., an entire classroom or school) who are not identified based on their risk status. Each member of the population receives the program. Aggregation of deviant peers does not explicitly occur in these programs. *Selective* prevention programs target a subgroup of individuals who are considered "at risk" for

TABLE 14.1. Preventive Interventions Reviewed

Program[a]	Evidence[b]	Target age	Universal versus selective	Person versus environment	Strategies for change[c]
Adolescent Transitions Project/Project Alliance (Dishion & Kavanaugh, 2002)	Research based	Middle school	Universal and selective (tiered)	Environment	Parent competencies
All Stars Program (Harrington, Giles, Hoyle, Feeney, & Yungbluth, 2001)	Research based	Middle school	Universal	Person	Child competencies (SU)
Athletes Training and Leading to Avoid Steroids (Goldberg et al., 1996)	Research based	High school	Selective (football teams)	Person	Child competencies (SU)
BASIS (Gottfredson, Gottfredson, & Hybl, 1993)	Promising	Middle schools	Universal	Environment	School-wide reform
Brain Power (Hudley et al., 1998)	Promising	3rd–6th grade	Selective (highly aggressive)	Person	Child competencies (SS in mixed groups)
Bullying Prevention Program (Olweus, 1997)	Research based	4th–7th grade	Universal	Environment	School-wide reform
CASASTART (Harrell, Cavanaugh, & Sridharan, 1998)	Research based	Elementary and middle schools	Selective (high risk in low-income areas)	Person and environment	Partnership of social services, school, law enforcement
Child Development Project (Battistich & Hom, 1997)	Research based	Elementary school	Universal	Environment	School-wide reform

(*continued*)

TABLE 14.1. (*continued*)

Program[a]	Evidence[b]	Target age	Universal versus selective	Person versus environment	Strategies for change[c]
Fast Track Program (Conduct Problems Prevention Research Group [CPPRG], 2002a, 2002b, 2002c)	Research based	Children identified in kindergarten, continuous services for 10 years	Universal and selective (aggressive in kindergarten)	Person and environment	• Child competencies (e.g., universal SS, selective SS in mixed groups) • Parent competencies
First Step to Success (Walker et al., 1998)	Research based	Early elementary school	Selective (aggressive in kindergarten)	Person and environment	• Parent competencies • Teacher competencies
Good Behavior Game (Ialongo, Poduska, Werthamer, & Kellam, 2001)	Research based	Early elementary school	Universal	Environment	Teacher competencies
I Can Problem Solve (Shure, 2001a, 2001b)	Research based	Elementary school	Universal	Person	Child competencies (SS)
Incredible Years, Dina's Dinosaur School (Webster-Stratton & Hammond, 1997)	Research based	Elementary school	Selective (children with oppositional defiant disorder or conduct disorder)	Person	Child competencies (SS)

Program	Status	Ages	Level	Environment	Competencies
Incredible Years, Teacher Training Component (Webster-Stratton, Reid, & Hammond, 2004)	Promising	Ages 4–8	Selective (children with oppositional defiant disorder or conduct disorder)	Person and environment	• Parent competencies • Child competencies (SU) • Family functioning
Iowa Strengthening Families Program (Spoth, Redmon, Shin, & Azevedo, 2004)	Research based	6th-grade students and families	Universal	Person and environment	• Child competencies (SU, SS)
Life Skills Training (Griffin, Botvin, Nichols, & Doyle, 2003)	Research based	Middle school	Universal	Person	• Child competencies (SU, SS)
Linking the Interests of Families and Teachers (Eddy, Reid, Stoolmiller, & Fetrow, 2003)	Research based	1st and 5th grade	Universal	Person and environment	• Parent competencies • Teacher competencies • Child competencies (SS)
Metropolitan Area Child Study (Metropolitan Area Child Study Research Group & Gorman Smith, 2003)	Promising	2nd, 3rd, and 5th grade	Universal and selective (high-risk for aggression)	Person and environment	• Teacher competencies • Parent competencies • Child competencies (SS)

(continued)

TABLE 14.1. (continued)

Program[a]	Evidence[b]	Target age	Universal versus selective	Person versus environment	Strategies for change[c]
Midwestern Prevention Project (MacKinnon et al., 1991)	Research based	Middle school	Universal	Person	Child competencies (SU)
Montreal Longitudinal Study (Vitaro, Brendgen, & Tremblay, 1999)	Research based	Children identified in kindergarten, continuous services	Selective (disruptive in kindergarten)	Person and environment	• Parent competencies • Child competencies (SS in mixed groups)
Positive Behavior Supports (Sugai & Horner, 2002)	Promising	Elementary, middle, and high schools	Both universal and selective (tiered)	Environment	• School-wide reform • Teacher competencies
Peacebuilders (Flannery et al., 2003)	Promising	Elementary school	Universal	Environment	• School-wide reform • Teacher competencies
Peer Coping Skills Training (Prinz, Blechman, & Dumas, 1994)	Promising	1st–3rd grade	Selective (highly aggressive)	Person	Child competencies (SS in mixed groups)
Preparing for the Drug Free Years (Spoth et al., 2004)	Research based	6th grade	Universal	Environment	Parent competencies

Program					
Project Achieve (Knoff & Batsche, 1995)	Promising	Elementary school	Universal	Person and environment	• School-wide reform • Teacher competencies • Child competencies (SS)
Project Alert (Bell, Ellickson, & Harrison, 1993)	Research based	Middle school	Universal	Person	Child competencies (SU)
Promoting Alternative Thinking Strategies (Greenberg, Kusche, Cook, & Quamma, 1995)	Research based	1st–3rd grade	Universal	Person	Child competencies (SS)
Project Northland (Perry et al., 2002)	Research based	Middle and high school	Universal	Person and environment	• Child competencies (SU) • Parent competencies
Responding in Peaceful and Positive Ways (Farrell, Meyer, Sullivan, & Kung, 2003)	Research based	Middle school	Universal	Person and Environment	• Child competencies (SS) • Peer mediation
School Transitional Environment Project (Felner et al., 1993)	Research based	9th grade	Universal	Environment	School-wide reform

(continued)

261

TABLE 14.1. (*continued*)

Program[a]	Evidence[b]	Target age	Universal versus selective	Person versus environment	Strategies for change[c]
Seattle Social Development Project (Hawkins, Catalano, Kosterman, Abbott, & Hill, 1999)	Research based	Initiated with 1st-grade children, services through 6th grade	Universal	Person and environment	• Parent competencies • Teacher competencies • Child competencies (SS)
Second Step (Grossman et al., 1997)	Research based	2nd and 3rd grade	Universal	Person	Child competencies (SS)
Social Decision Making and Problem Solving Program (Bruene-Butler, Hampson, Elias, Clabby, & Schuyler, 1997)	Research based	Kindergarten–8th grade	Universal	Person	Child competencies (SS)
Towards No Tobacco (Dent et al., 1995)	Research based	5th–8th grade	Universal	Person	Child competencies (SU)

[a] When more than one article was reviewed for a given program, only the most recent is cited. See references for additional citations.
[b] Research based, identified in three or more rigorous reviews; promising, identified in narrative reviews.
[c] SS, social skills training; SU, substance use prevention programming.

developing a certain behavior problem or disorder based on specified risk factors. *Indicated* preventive interventions target a subgroup of individuals who exhibit "subclinical" levels of a specific behavior problem or disorder but who do not yet meet diagnostic criteria (i.e., students who are clearly having troubles, but do not yet qualify to be labeled). In the school-based literature, it can be difficult to differentiate between selective and indicated interventions; therefore, in this chapter, any program that targets a subgroup for intervention will be labeled "selective." High-risk peers are often explicitly aggregated in this type of program.

In terms of intervention characteristics, school-based programs can be classified into those that take an environment-centered approach or those that take a person-centered approach (Durlak, 1995). Programs that take an environment-centered approach generally do not include direct work with children, but instead attempt to change child behavior indirectly by modifying aspects of the environment(s) in which they spend time. In contrast, person-centered approaches focus on working directly with children and aim to teach specific skills or behaviors to decrease child risk and enhance child competencies. We now overview the programs identified in our search, grouping programs by their population and intervention classifications.

Universal, Environment-Centered Programs That Focus on School-Wide Reform

A variety of environment-centered prevention programs have been developed and tested that initiate school-wide changes in an effort to address behavior problems. These types of programs generally target for change the policies and procedures that schools employ to control and suppress student misbehavior. Among the strategies commonly used in these school-wide reform efforts are (1) clearly explicated expectations for student and staff behavior, (2) consistent utilization of proactive school discipline strategies, (3) active monitoring of "hot spots" for behavior problems (e.g., hallways, restrooms, playgrounds, parking lots, and cafeterias; Welsh, Stokes, & Greene, 2000), and (4) improved systems to monitor student achievement and behavior.

One promising example of a program is Positive Behavior Support (PBS; Sugai & Horner, 2002). One of the defining elements of PBS is its emphasis on all members of the school community (i.e., students, parents, teachers, and support staff) learning and adhering to clearly defined behavioral expectations. PBS is implemented in such a way that members learn a common language about key school rules. In addition, although clearly stated consequences are put in place, the focus of PBS is on positive reinforcement for adherence to behavioral expectations. PBS takes a multisetting approach to reinforcement and monitoring, such that positive student behavior is supported throughout all spaces in the school, and particularly in typical hot spots. Vital to PBS is the monitoring of progress through the continual assessment and evaluation of outcomes (e.g., office discipline referrals, academic achievement, student behavior). In a number of evaluations, PBS has been shown to decrease office discipline referrals (e.g., Colvin & Fernandez, 2000; Lohrmann-O'Rourke et al., 2000; Taylor-Greene & Kartub, 2000).

Universal and Selective, Environment-Centered Programs That Improve Teacher Competencies

A promising type of prevention programming that is often a part of school-wide change efforts is the use of effective classroom management strategies by teachers throughout a school. Although a plethora of classroom management strategies have been examined, a recent meta-analysis (Stage & Quiroz, 1997) found that the three most effective management strategies were group contingencies (i.e., token economies in which the behavior of a group of students is evaluated to receive reinforcement), self-management techniques (i.e., self-monitoring, self-evaluation, self-reinforcement), and differential reinforcement (i.e., positive reinforcement for a specified amount of prosocial behavior or the absence of a disruptive behavior in a given time limit). Consistent with these findings, it has been suggested by numerous reviewers that teachers who (1) clearly state expectations for student behavior, (2) utilize high and consistent rates of praise and positive reinforcement for student prosocial behaviors, and (3) consistently apply developmentally appropriate consequences for student misbehaviors will not only help promote academic, social, and emotional development within their classes, but also will decrease levels of disruptive behavior (Bear et al., 2000; Brophy, 1996; Reinke & Herman, 2002; Walker, Colvin, & Ramsey, 1995). It is important to note that even if these programs are selective (i.e., target the behavior of teachers of children identified as at risk), not universal, these programs do not aggregate deviant youth and may provide benefit for the larger classroom population.

One example of a program that has focused on training teachers in effective classroom management is the Incredible Years Teacher Training Component (Reid, Webster-Stratton, & Hammond, 2003; Webster-Stratton, 2001; Webster-Stratton, Reid, & Hammond, 2004). This program was developed to promote and generalize the reduction of early-onset behavior problems to the classroom and focuses on training teachers in proactive classroom management practices, strategies to improve the teacher–child relationship, increased monitoring in hot spots, strengthening teachers' ability to teach social skills and problem solving, and methods for increasing communication with parents. A randomized trial that examined the relative effectiveness of parent training, child training, and combinations of these programs with teacher training found that adding the teacher training component to either the parent or child training programs decreased negative behaviors and increased positive behaviors at home and at school for children who showed pervasive behavior problems. Furthermore, and importantly, children with pervasive problems at home and at school whose teachers did not receive training did not show consistent improvement within the school setting (Reid et al., 2003).

Several randomized trials have illustrated that a simple, team-based incentive program, the Good Behavior Game (GBG), can be effective in reducing aggression (Dolan et al., 1993; Ialongo, Poduska, Werthamer, & Kellam, 2001; Ialongo et al., 1999; Kellam, Regok, Ialongo, & Meyer, 1994). During the GBG, teachers create heterogeneous teams of students comprising deviant and prosocial peers. Teams are rewarded for adhering to prescribed levels of behavioral standards. Initially, the "game" is played at set and clearly stated times. To increase generalization, the game is soon expanded to different times of days and different activities and is often started without warning. The effects of this program have been found to have long-term effects (e.g., sustained through the sixth grade when administered in first grade), especially for boys and those children with the highest levels of baseline aggression (Ialongo et al., 2001; Kellam et al., 1994).

Although it is likely that many teachers do utilize effective classroom management strategies, it is probable that a significant number do not. Many teachers receive little or no training during college in behavior management techniques (Larson, 1998). Not surprisingly, many new teachers state that they feel underprepared in classroom management strategies, especially in strategies designed for students with the most challenging and disruptive behaviors. If teachers are unequipped to handle student misbehavior, it is likely that they will overutilize punitive techniques (Cook, Landrum, Tankersley, & Kauffman, 2003; Skiba & Peterson, 2000). It has been suggested that training in effective teaching strategies should be a mandatory part of all teachers' professional training, similar to training in curriculum development (Sawka, McCurdy, & Mannella, 2002). While this idea has not yet caught on around the country, schools can utilize ongoing in-service trainings to ensure that all teachers are well versed with the techniques.

Further, regardless of the training a teacher has received, applying techniques effectively on a day-to-day and year-to-year basis can be quite challenging, particularly in the face of high numbers of students and heavy academic demands. Given this reality, some researchers have posited that the ongoing availability of teacher consultation services focused on effective classroom management strategies may be a vital part of a proactive approach (Sawka et al., 2002). Teacher consultation has been successfully employed within several programs reviewed here (Peacebuilders, Metropolitan Area Child Study, Project Achieve, First Step to Success). Although each of these programs used outside consultants, in-house school personnel trained to consult and to be readily available on an as-needed basis would be most ideal. Additionally, other trained teachers within a school can serve as mentors and provide ongoing support.

Universal and Selective, Environment-Centered Programs that Improve Parent Competencies

A large body of research supports the effectiveness of family-centered interventions for reducing problem behaviors (Reid, Patterson, & Snyder, 2002). In the past, much of this work has focused within a clinical setting, but in recent years there has been a strong movement to create family-centered interventions appropriate for a wide variety of settings, most notably for the school setting (Spoth, Kavanaugh, & Dishion, 2002). Similar to programs focusing on improving teacher competencies, even when these programs target high- or at-risk youth, deviant peers are not aggregated.

For example, the research-based Adolescent Transitions Program (ATP; Dishion & Kavanaugh, 2000, 2002; Dishion, Kavanaugh, Schneiger, Nelson, & Kaufman, 2002) is a family-centered preventive intervention program designed for public middle schools. ATP includes several levels of programming, with each level providing additional services for children with higher levels of need. The "universal" level includes a family resource center, located in the school and staffed by a parent consultant. The parent consultant works to foster collaboration between parents and the school, delivers universal prevention programming (e.g., a classroom-based health curriculum), writes a monthly newsletter emphasizing family management skills, and provides resources and materials to parents in the family resource center. At the second level, for children identified with behavior problems, the Family Check-Up (a family-based assessment followed by a motivational feedback session) is offered. During the feedback session, parents are given a sense of how their child compares to others the same age, and are assisted in the creation of a menu of options about what actions might be taken to resolve various problems. At the third level, for children with severe behavior problems, family-based therapy and parent skills training groups are offered. While an evaluation of ATP (known as "Project Alliance") is ongoing, there is initial evidence that the approach is successful in preventing substance use and decreasing rates of antisocial behavior.

Universal and Selective, Person-Centered Programs That Improve Student Competencies

Programs that take a person-centered approach aim to teach youth specific skills that reduce their risk for more extreme behavior problems. These programs can be universal or selective, and are typically developed to address specific student problems, most notably antisocial and delinquent behavior and/or substance use. Given our emphasis on deviant peer influence, we first provide a brief overview of these programs, in general, and then review the programs that aggregate deviant peers in more detail.

Most of the programs that focus on decreasing aggression and conduct problems are based on some combination of (1) social problem-solving strategies (e.g., Shure & Spivack, 1982), (2) social information-processing strategies (e.g., Crick & Dodge, 1994; Dodge & Crick, 1990), and/or (3) emotional/social competence development strategies (e.g., Elias et al., 1997). These programs have been evaluated both as stand-alones and as part of a variety of multimodal programs. Programs usually utilize a variety of teaching strategies and often target the development of more than one type of cognitive or emotional skill. Instructors vary from classroom teachers to trained specialists to clinicians.

These programs consistently show at least some positive effects, although many of the effects have been small and relatively short term. When programs are effective, it appears that they result in increases in competence-enhancing skills and behaviors as well as decreases in risk factors and problem behaviors (Durlak & Wells, 1997). Meta-analytic results (Durlak & Wells, 1997; Wilson et al., 2001) indicate that person-centered programs are most effective when cognitive and cognitive-behavioral strategies (e.g., modeling, role playing) are incorporated and when provided to young children (age 2–7 years). While peer mediation is another common component of several programs (e.g., Resolving Conflict Creatively, Responding in Peaceful and Positive Ways), the effectiveness of peer mediation programs per se is unclear (Johnson & Johnson, 1996).

The most common program targeting substance use in the schools is D.A.R.E. (Drug Abuse Resistance Education), with over 34% of schools in one survey reportedly delivering the program (Gottfredson & Gottfredson, 2001). Unfortunately, as typically implemented, D.A.R.E. is not effective for reducing drug use in either the short or the long term (Lynam et al., 1999; Ringwalt et al., 1994). It is important that schools utilize alternative strategies. Reviews of school-based substance use preventive interventions generally conclude that effective programs do more than simply provide information. Effective programs teach students specific skills (Botvin, 2000; Gottfredson & Wilson, 2003) through the use of interactive teaching strategies (Tobler & Stratton, 1997). In particular, effective programs utilize interactive teaching strategies that allow for interactiveness between peers. The two types of programs that have utilized these techniques and proven most effective (Botvin, 2000) are social influence training (e.g., education on norms and training in resistance skills) and competence enhancement training (i.e., social influence combined with more general social skills training). Both types of programs are usually taught within the regular classroom, although some programs, such as ATLAS (Athletes Training and Leading to Avoid Steroids), are designed to target only one group of students (in this case, athletes).

Selective Programs

Within schools, social skills interventions are often directed toward children thought to be at risk for the development of behavior problems or to children who are already exhibiting symptoms of behavior problems. The content of these programs is generally consistent with that discussed above. Here we distinguish between programs that integrate the selected children with prosocial peers (i.e., peers thought not to be at risk for future behavior problems) and those that create homogeneous groups of deviant youth. Selective social skills programs are often incorporated into multimodal programs such that universal components may also be included (e.g., revised school rules).

In three programs designed for such children (i.e., Brain Power, Peer Coping Skills Training, the Montreal Longitudinal Study), the children identified to be at risk for the development of future problem behaviors were exposed to the social skills training component while participating in groups of prosocial peers. Not only do these programs appear to be successful at improving the behavior and skills of the high-risk children, there is no evidence to date of detrimental effects for the prosocial peers. Other research-based strategies aimed at high-risk children include bringing the person-centered component into the regular classroom via an individualized, consultant-based behavioral modification plan (e.g., First Step to Success) and using a peer-pairing program in which each target child is paired with a classroom peer for a weekly guided play session (e.g., Fast Track). These strategies are an effective way to provide services to high-risk children while decreasing the degree of deviant peer aggregation.

Several programs (e.g., Fast Track, Dina's Dinosaur School) explicitly aggregated high-risk children together for social skills training groups. However, these research-based programs were found to be effective at promoting child competencies and reducing negative behaviors. What factors might contribute to the success of the programs that aggregated deviant peers? Such information may guide decisions made by schools when they are faced with the "necessity" of aggregating deviant peers.

First, groups were highly structured yet allowed for high levels of student involvement (vs. didactic teaching strategies). Second, group leaders had high levels of training in behavior management strategies and utilized specific behavioral (e.g., reinforcement) strategies for maintaining order in the groups. Third, the groups included a small number of children and had a low student-to-leader ratio. Fourth, the programs reviewed in this chapter that included homogenous groups of deviant peers targeted younger students; it is possible that the impact of deviant peer influence increases as children age. In fact, the Fast Track program discontinued the use of social skills training groups that aggregated deviant peers after elementary school due to the risk associated with aggregating deviant peers in older children.

These variables may contribute to the presence of group process variables that have been found to lead to improved outcomes among deviant youth aggregated in preventive intervention programming (Lavallee, Bierman, Nix, & the Conduct Problems Prevention Research Group, 2005). In a set of follow-up analyses of social skills training groups in the Fast Track program, Lavallee and her colleagues (2005) found positive outcomes were more likely among at-risk children aggregated in groups when children were highly engaged in the group activities, had a high number of positive interactions, and experienced a low amount of negative peer interaction and deviancy training. Utilizing strategies such as highly structured, interactive teaching methods and highly trained group leaders may increase positive outcomes in social skills groups that aggregate deviant peers.

Multimodal Efforts That Combine Several Types of Programs over Time

Many of the programs highlighted above combine several types of programs, but most have been applied over short periods of time rather than on a continuous basis. Programs that target multiple risk and protective factors across multiple domains over time (i.e., those that are multimodal) are widely believed to be most effective, although evidence on this conclusion remains slim (e.g., Greenberg, Domotrovich, &

Bumbarger, 2001). The utilization of multimodal programs that are co-ordinated within or across schools has added benefits, including the decreased tendency for schools to utilize fragmented and uncoordinated short-term programming efforts and increased collaboration between families and schools.

Even though the targeted content of the interventions may differ, they share several commonalities in program structure. First, each program uses a developmental approach to prevention by targeting developmental periods that are critical for the initiation of problem behaviors (usually early elementary school for conduct problems and middle school for substance use). Second, several programs incorporate prevention efforts across several years in an attempt to increase the impact of programming efforts. Third, all programs use some combination of child-focused, classroom-focused, and parent-focused prevention components, although the specifics vary. Most use a universal, classroom-based approach (primarily a social skills or drug prevention curriculum), although some utilize "selective" components as well. Many programs that incorporate services for both parents and teachers also emphasize increased home–school collaboration or communication.

One example of a research-based multimodel program is the Linking the Interests of Families and Teachers (LIFT) preventive intervention for conduct problems. LIFT was implemented in first- or fifth-grade classrooms and participants are still being followed today. LIFT combines parent training, a classroom-based social skills program, a recess incentive program (a modified version of the GBG), and systematic communication between teachers and parents. In the short run, LIFT has been found to reduce child physical aggression, decrease aversive maternal behavior, and increase child positive behavior with peers, all of which are precursors and correlates of conduct problems (Eddy, Reid, & Fetrow, 2000; Reid, Eddy, Fetrow, & Stoolmiller, 1999; Stoolmiller, Eddy, & Reid, 2000). Over the middle school period, LIFT has been shown to decrease the likelihood of first contact with police as well as initiation of patterned alcohol use (Eddy et al., 2000). Across adolescence, LIFT has been shown to decrease substance use, and this effect was mediated by changes in child aggression on the playground and parental monitoring (DeGarmo, Patterson, & Forgatch, 2004).

THE IMPACT OF RESEARCH-BASED AND PROMISING PROGRAMS ON DEVIANT PEER INFLUENCE

There are many promising and research-based strategies that schools can utilize to prevent youth problem behavior. Of interest in the context of this book are what impact these programs have on the phenomenon of deviant peer influence. For example, does a universal social skills program that prevents or reduces aggression in the student population as a whole have negative effects on a subgroup of students (e.g., low-risk students who gain increased exposure to the aggressive behavior of high-risk students who are not removed from the classroom)? Are these universal programs successful at reducing the negative behaviors of the most deviant youth? Furthermore, do prosocial children who participate in mixed-group social skills programs with highly aggressive peers become more aggressive due to increased contact with deviant peers? To examine these types of questions, each program reviewed in this chapter was categorized based on the level of deviant peer aggregation in the program and by the subpopulations actually examined during statistical analyses (e.g., all students were analyzed as one group vs. high-risk youth were evaluated separately; please see Table 14.2).

As illustrated in Table 14.2, very little research has directly answered the types of questions posed above. The majority of the programs reviewed are universal programs that do not aggregate peers. In the rare case in which selective programming is provided to high-risk children within the context of the general education classroom (e.g., First Step to Success), only the impact of the program on the targeted students has been examined. Furthermore, among the universal programs, the effectiveness of the program is usually evaluated for the entire student population instead of subgroups within this population. Exceptions to this have found that the program is equally effective among children of various levels of deviancy (e.g., Project Alert). Importantly, several of these programs have had the most impact on a subgroup of children who enter the program with the highest baseline level of deviancy (e.g., Peacebuilders, Responding in Peaceful and Positive Ways, Good Behavior Game, LIFT), indicating that these universal programs are indeed an effective strategy for impacting the misbehavior of the most deviant students. While examined rarely, there is no evidence that low-risk peers who continue to gain exposure to the high-risk youth due to universal or other classroom-based programming are negatively impacted.

When peer aggregation does occur, there are two ways in which deviant peers are grouped: (1) in a homogenous group of deviant peers (e.g., Dina's Dinosaur School) or (2) nested within groups of prosocial peers (e.g., Brain Power, Montreal Longitudinal Study). Positive effects of the programs for high-risk targeted youth have been found in both of these types of programs. Importantly, in programs with the second type of aggregation, no negative impact has been found on the low-risk youth (e.g., nonaggressive, prosocial) who are grouped with the deviant youth. Also of interest is whether targeted interventions for deviant students have an impact on the rest of the general student population. Little to no

TABLE 14.2. Preventive Intervention Programs by Level of Deviant Peer Aggregation and Analysis

Analysis by child deviancy level	Level of deviant peer aggregation in intervention		
	Peers not aggregated	Mixed	Peers aggregated
General population[a]	All Stars Program (BG)		Athletes Training and Leading to Avoid Steroids (B)[g]
	BASIS (BG)		
	Bullying Prevention Program (BG)		
	Child Development Project (BG)		
	I Can Problem Solve (BG)		
	Iowa Strengthening Families Project (BG)		
	Life Skills Training (BG)		
	Midwestern Prevention Project (BG)		
	Preparing for the Drug Free Years (BG)		
	Positive Behavior Support (BG)		
	Project Achieve (BG)		
	Promoting Alternative Thinking Strategies (BG)		
	School Transitional Environment Project (BG)		
	Seattle Social Development Project (BG)		
	Second Step (BG)		
	Social Decision Making and Problem Solving Program (BG)		
	Towards No Tobacco (BG)		
	Project Northland (BG)[e]		
Low[b]	Project Alert (BG)	Brain Power (B)	
	Project Northland (BG)[e]	Peer Coping Skills Program (BG)	

272

Medium/at risk[c]	Adolescent Transitions Project/Project Alliance (BG) Life Skills Training (BG) Linking the Interest of Families and Teachers (BG)[f] Project Alert (BG)		
High[d]	First Step to Success (BG) Good Behavior Game (BG)[f] Peacebuilders (BG)[f] Project Alert (BG) Project Northland (BG)[e] Promoting Alternative Thinking Strategies (BG)[f] Responding in Peaceful and Positive Ways (BG)[f]	Brain Power (B) Montreal Longitudinal Study (B) Peer Coping Skills Program (BG)	Fast Track (BG) Incredible Years, Dina's Dinosaur School (BG) Incredible Years, Parent, Teacher, and Child Training Program (BG) Metropolitan AreaChild Study (BG)

Notes. For multicomponent programs, programs were included in the table at their highest level of aggregation. B, only boys were included in the study; BG, both boys and girls were included in the study.

[a] All participants were analyzed together, reporting main effects of the intervention condition.

[b] Children identified as low risk for problem behavior were analyzed as a subgroup.

[c] Children were identified as at risk (e.g., have friends who use alcohol, are in the middle group of a continuous distribution) for problem behavior, but were not yet exhibiting high levels of deviant behavior. These children were analyzed as a subgroup.

[d] Children were identified as high risk or already exhibiting clinically significant levels of problem behaviors. These children were analyzed separately as a subgroup or were the only children included in the study.

[e] Project Northland is a multicomponent program that includes some aggregation of peers; however, the composition of these groups was not determined by the intervention and was not reported.

[f] A continuous interaction between baseline levels of problem behavior and intervention was examined; general population effects also reported.

[g] ATLAS targets the general population of athletes who are assumed to be "at risk" for steroid use, and is delivered only to groups of athletes.

work has been done to systematically investigate the impact of removing deviant youth and segregating them in pull-out programs on the rest of the student population. It is thus unclear if and how removing or segregating deviant youth has benefits for the rest of the school community.

Finally, although many positive effects of these prevention programs and strategies have been reported, it is rare that these studies directly examine (or report) the impact of the program on the level of deviant peer association among students. Only two programs reviewed here (CASASTART, Seattle Social Development Project) reported a positive effect of the program on a measure of deviant peer involvement or association (Harrell, Cavanaugh, & Sridharan, 1998; O'Donnell, Hawkins, Catalano, Abbott, & Day, 1995). In addition, evaluations of the Adolescent Transitions Program (Dishion & Kavanaugh, 2000, 2002; Dishion et al., 2002) have incorporated deviant peer association into a general deviancy construct and found that the program reduced growth in deviancy across middle school.

RECOMMENDATIONS FOR SCHOOL-BASED PREVENTION PROGRAMMING

Based on the current evidence on the efficacy of school-based prevention programs, there are several principles that schools can utilize in designing and implementing effective prevention intervention programming for problem behaviors. These principles, and brief comments on the degree of empirical support available for each, are listed below.

1. *Take a preventive approach that engages students and families early in elementary school and continues through middle and high school.* Although this is commonly stated in the field of preventive intervention and has very strong theoretical support, the degree of empirical support remains small. One source of confirmation comes from the Seattle Social Development Project, in which children exposed to the intervention from first through sixth grade reported fewer negative outcomes at age 18 than the students who did not receive the intervention or youth who received programming only in grades five or six (Hawkins, Catalano, Kosterman, Abbott, & Hill, 1999).

2. *Create school-wide discipline policies that include both behavioral norms and expectations for all community members and proactive discipline approaches, including a heavy emphasis on positive reinforcement.* Unfortunately, the experimental rigor of the evaluation studies for most programs that utilized these strategies (e.g., Positive Behavior Support) has not been as high as other preventive interventions, but the re-

search is quite promising. In addition, there is evidence that reactive and punitive discipline techniques are less effective for managing student behavior over the long term than are proactive and positive approaches (Bear, 1998; Brophy, 1996; Larson, 1998).

3. *Increase use of effective and proactive classroom management techniques by (a) incorporating these skills into teacher degree programs, (b) providing in-service training in these skills, and/or (c) providing ongoing consultation services and support to teachers.* The efficacy of utilizing specific classroom management techniques has been supported by numerous empirical studies (see Stage & Quiroz, 1997, for a meta-analysis) and several rigorously designed prevention studies (e.g., Good Behavior Game, Incredible Years Teacher Training Component, First Step to Success). Providing teachers with the training and support they need to work effectively with difficult students has the added benefit of improving the relationship between these demanding students and teachers, which has been found to have important implications for the development of classroom behavior problems (e.g., Pianta, Steinberg, & Rollins, 1995; Silver, Measelle, Essex, & Armstrong, 2005).

4. *Use universal child-centered preventive interventions (e.g., social skills training) whenever possible.* There is empirical evidence that supports the use of child-focused universal prevention programs (e.g., PATHS, Second Step). The universal approach has several benefits above and beyond a selective approach to child-centered interventions including (a) teaching skills to high-risk youth without aggregation, (b) teaching skills to the entire student population, and (c) decreasing stigma for high-risk youth often associated with being pulled out of the regular education setting.

5. *When using selective prevention programs (which target at-risk or deviant youth), utilize strategies that minimize the risk of deviant peer influence. Such strategies include (a) creating a highly structured program with a low teacher–student ratio and extensive training for group leaders, (b) integrating prosocial and deviant youth in mixed intervention groups or peer-pairing programs, and/or (c) bringing selective interventions to the regular education classroom (e.g., behavioral modification strategies supported by consultation services).* There is a noticeable lack of research that investigates the most effective ways in which programs that target at-risk youth can reduce the likelihood of deviancy training. However, the selective programs (e.g., Brain Power, Peer Coping Skills Training, Incredible Years) that utilized the techniques discussed above were effective in reducing problematic behaviors *and* found no evidence of iatrogenic effects (for either deviant or prosocial youth). There is also promising support for consultation-based services within the regular education classroom (e.g., First Step to Success, MACS).

6. *Actively monitor hot spots (e.g., hallways, restrooms, play-grounds, parking lots, cafeterias) to increase school order and decrease antisocial behavior during unstructured and unsupervised time.* This strategy has not been evaluated as a stand-alone program. However, programs that incorporated this strategy (e.g., Bullying Prevention Program) reported encouraging results. In addition, antisocial behavior is often highest in the least monitored areas of the school (Welsh et al., 2000).

7. *Make parenting resources (e.g., parent training classes) accessible through schools.* There is much empirical support for the effectiveness of family-centered interventions. In addition, there is promising evidence that family-based preventive intervention programming specifically embedded within schools can be effective at reducing problem behaviors and promoting parenting skills (e.g., ATP/Project Alliance, LIFT). An added benefit is that this approach increases exposure while avoiding the stigma associated with accessing such resources in mental health clinics.

8. *Foster home–school collaboration by increased communication between families, teachers, administrators, and other school personnel.* Although this is a stated target of many of the research-based preventive interventions reviewed in this chapter (e.g., LIFT), and the theoretical significance of communication between parents and teachers is commonly discussed (Christenson, Rounds, & Franklin, 1992), it is unclear whether there is empirical evidence for the direct effect of increased home–school collaboration on the prevention of problem behaviors.

9. *School-based preventive efforts are most likely to be effective when they target multiple risk factors in several contexts of children's lives. Child-, parent-, classroom-, whole-school-, and community-focused components should all be considered.* Similar to the first principle, this is an oft-stated claim consistent with an ecological approach to human development and preventive intervention strategies (Stormshak & Dishion, 2002). Empirical evidence suggests that for children with pervasive behavior problems, intervention programming must at least target both the classroom and the family in order to achieve positive results at both home and school (Reid et al., 2003).

CONCLUSIONS

There are still gaps in our knowledge of how school-based programs address the issue of peer aggregation and deviant peer influence. Although some strategies have been identified that address ways to minimize the risks associated with deviant peer aggregation, more research in this area is sorely needed. In addition, a broader research agenda is needed on the risks and benefits of deviant peer aggregation within the school context. Most notably, research needs to be directed toward understanding whether there are negative consequences for the school community to *not* removing disruptive or deviant children from the regular classroom setting. Examining whether preventive intervention strategies are more or less effective for different subgroups of students (e.g., more or less aggressive) needs to be included as part of all school-based prevention studies. Finally, it is important to highlight that little is known about the effectiveness of school-based preventive intervention programs when implemented outside of the relatively tight control of research teams.

Despite these limitations, scholars have made significant progress in designing and evaluating preventive interventions. Many empirically supported strategies have been developed that school policymakers and personnel can utilize to minimize and prevent youth problem behavior while reducing the risks associated with aggregating deviant peers. These strategies range from child-centered social skills curricula, to enhanced classroom management strategies, to parent resources provided in schools, to school-wide reform efforts aimed at discipline policies and procedures. With a careful assessment of individualized needs within the school community, schools have a variety of strategies from which to choose. These strategies hold great promise for making full use of the research base to guide schools' efforts to promote the development of healthy, safe, and well-adjusted children.

CHAPTER 15

Promising Solutions in Juvenile Justice

Peter Greenwood

Other contributors to this book have described the phenomenon of *deviant peer contagion* (DPC), the mechanisms through which it is thought to occur, susceptible populations, and the available evidence regarding its strength. In particular, Osgood and Briddell (Chapter 8) describe the juvenile justice system and how DPC is thought to affect specific populations at various points of contact within that system. Lipsey (Chapter 9) presents the results from a meta-analysis designed to measure the strength of DPC effects in several critical contexts.

From these chapters we have learned that:

- Peer influence is real, though perhaps not as strong as many have assumed.
- Several forms of DPC have been well documented by research.
- All things being equal, the risk of DPC is thought to increase with increased contacts with deviant peers, but to decrease with increasing program structure.
- There are opportunities for DPC throughout the juvenile justice system.
- The opportunities for DPC increase with the intensity of the sanctions and other interventions.
- Measurable effects of DPC are greatest for younger, less serious offenders.

- Many current programs appear to facilitate DPC.
- The most successful delinquency prevention programs specifically address DPC in multiple ways.
- We know little about the relative strength of DPC compared to other risk factors for specific populations.
- We know little about the marginal effects of alternative prevention strategies on DPC.

The goal of this chapter to use the available evidence on DPC and program effectiveness to first identify a set of programs and strategies that appear to be effective in reducing DPC, and then, from them, to articulate a set of principles that can be used to guide future program decisions in juvenile justice.

The chapter is divided into three sections. The first section reviews methods for identifying, describing, and categorizing evidence regarding the effectiveness of juvenile justice programs. The second section describes the body of evidence that those methods have produced, and the strategies and programs that show the most promise. The third section summarizes what that evidence has to say about the effectiveness of strategies designed to deal explicitly with DPC, and the overall impact of such strategies on delinquency prevention.

METHODS OF GENERATING AND SUMMARIZING EVIDENCE REGARDING EFFECTIVENESS

Methods of Generating Evidence

The primary evidence base that is now used to identify the most promising strategies and programs for delinquency prevention and treatment consists of the large body of evaluations that meet established methodological standards, and the growing number of reviews that attempt to sort out and synthesize them. Only a decade ago reviewers were using many different ways of evaluating programs and many different strategies to assess the effectiveness literature. In recent years there has been a good deal of convergence as to how these tasks should be done.

An evaluation using random assignment of subjects to treatment and comparison groups—a true experimental design—is in most situations the optimal way in which to establish the causal effect of a prevention program on youth crime outcomes. However, in some situations they are impractical, too time-consuming, or prohibitively expensive. In fact, in most situations in delinquency prevention, and all the other social sciences as well, a randomized experiment is not the evaluation design selected. Most evaluations of crime prevention efforts employ so-called quasi-experimental, nonexperimental, or more judgmental designs.

The random assignment of units to treatment and comparison groups assures that other factors that might influence the outcomes are also randomly assigned across these conditions, thus allowing the researcher to assume that the only systematic differences between the treatment and control groups are found in the treatments or interventions that are applied. Without random assignment, comparisons between treatment and nontreatment conditions must always be made with the assumption that the groups are nonequivalent and causal inferences about the effects of the programs are more difficult to make. Furthermore, a recent analysis by Weisburd, Lum, and Petrosino (2001) concluded that research design does have a systematic effect on outcomes in criminal justice studies. The weaker a design, the more likely it is to report a result in favor of treatment and the less likely it is to report a harmful effect of treatment. These considerations have led most professional review groups to be extremely skeptical of any reviews of interventions that are not supported by at least one randomized trial (Office of Management and Budget, 2004; Shadish & Meyers, 2002).

Methods of Summarizing and Synthesizing the Evidence

The four primary techniques that have been used to summarize and synthesize the evaluation literature are subjective reviews, meta-analysis, the development of certified lists, and cost-effectiveness analysis. Progress in identifying proven or promising program strategies and methods was hampered by an almost complete lack of effort and standards for program evaluation. It is still a rarity to find a juvenile intervention program that measures outcomes. The few evaluations that did take place were usually of inadequate quality to produce reliable results (Sherman et al., 1997).

A new chapter in the search for effective programs began with the use of meta-analysis, a more objective and reproducible method of summarizing the findings from many different studies. A meta-analysis of both juvenile and adult corrections programs by Andrews and colleagues (1990) identified a number of characteristics that were associated with the more effective programs. The first meta-analysis focused specifically on juvenile justice was produced by Lipsey (1992). Lipsey's analysis did not identify specific programs but did begin to identify specific approaches that were more likely to be effective than others. Lipsey has continued to expand and refine this work to include additional studies and many additional characteristics of each study (Lipsey & Wilson, 1998; Lipsey, Chapter 9, this volume).

The next major development in the identification of promising programs was the publication of the first set of Blueprints (Elliot, 1997) by the Center for the Study and Prevention of Violence at the University of Colorado. The original group of Blueprint Proven Programs included 10 programs that met rigorous criteria for proving their effectiveness and were prepared to help others to replicate their models. A program is not considered *proven* by Blueprints until it has demonstrated its impact on problem behaviors with a rigorous experimental design; the impacts have been shown to persist after youth leave the program; and the program has been successfully replicated in another site. The current Blueprints web site (www.colorado.edu/cspv/blueprints/) lists 10 *model* programs and 20 *promising* programs. The design, research evidence, and implementation requirements for each model are available on the site. A number of other professional groups and private agencies have developed similar processes for developing their own recommended list of promising programs (Mihalic, Fagan, Irwin, Ballard, & Elliot, 2002; U.S. Department of Health and Human Services, 2001). There is some variation in the programs identified on these lists due to differences in the outcomes on which they focus and the criteria they use for screening. But there is also a good deal of consistency.

The most recent development in efforts to identify promising programs is the use of cost-effectiveness and cost–benefit analysis to evaluate the relative efficiency of alternative approaches in addressing a particular problem. In 1996 a team at RAND published a cost-effectiveness study showing that parenting programs and the Ford Foundation–sponsored Quantum Opportunities Program to be much more cost-effective than long prison sentences mandated by Three Strikes (Greenwood, Model, Rydell, & Chiesa, 1996). A later RAND report (Karoly et al., 1998) demonstrated that even expensive early childhood programs such as David Olds's Nurse Home Visiting program and the Perry Preschool program could be cost-effective crime prevention strategies if savings in educational costs, welfare costs, and unemployment benefits were factored into the equation. In more recent years systematic cost–benefit studies of alternative delinquency prevention and intervention programs have been conducted by the Washington State Institute for Public Policy (Aos, Phipps, Barmoski, & Lieb, 2001).

In summary, different reviewers produce different lists of "proven" and "promising" programs because (1) they focus on different outcomes, and (2) they apply different criteria in screening programs. Some reviews simply organize and summarize the information contained in the literature, grouping studies together to arrive at conclusions about particular models or approaches (Greenberg et al., 1999; Mendel, 2001; Posey et al., 1996; Sherman et al., 1997). Some use statistical meta-analysis techniques to develop more rigorous estimates of outcomes for interventions for which there are many reported studies (Lipsey & Wilson, 1998). Finally, some "rating or certification systems" use expert panels or some other screening process to assess the integrity of individual evaluations and specific criteria to identify *proven*, *promising*, or *exemplary* programs (Elliot, 1997; Mihalic & Aultman-Bettridge, 2002; U.S. Department of Health and Human Services, 2001). These reviews also differ from each other in the particular outcomes they emphasize, such as delinquency, drug use, mental health, or school-related behaviors; their criteria for selection; and the rigor with which the evidence is screened and reviewed.

At the very top of the promising program pyramid, on everybody's list, are the very small number of rigorously evaluated programs that have consistently demonstrated significant positive effects and have developed effective strategies for helping others to replicate their model and achieve similar results. At the bottom are the vast number of programs that have never been evaluated. In the middle are those for which there is some evidence to support their claims of effectiveness in at least one site.

WHAT WORKS AND WHAT DOESN'T

The most recent reviews, meta-analyses, certified lists, and cost-effectiveness analyses provide a variety of perspectives and a wealth of knowledge regarding what works and what doesn't in preventing delinquency. The research is strongest and most promising for early interventions, that is, ones conducted prior to the need for residential placement. In this area a number of well-specified, proven cost-effective programs have emerged. For youth in custodial settings there is much less research to draw on and what there is suffers from serious methodological problems. Still, there are some findings that appear to hold up across various settings. In this section we review the evidence regarding "what works" in delinquency prevention and intervention. We begin our review by focusing on the most serious youth who are usually found in custodial settings and work our way back to those who pose less of a threat or require less intervention. All of the evidence cited in this chapter is summarized in Table 15.1 by source.

Delinquents in Residential or Custodial Settings

Juvenile courts, like criminal courts, function as a screening agent for the purpose of sanctions and services. Only a fraction of the cases reaching

TABLE 15.1. What Works for Delinquency Prevention and Intervention By Source

Andrews et al. (1990)

Meta-analysis of adult and juvenile corrections evaluations
  Focus on higher risk youth
  Focus on dynamic risk factors associated with crime
  Treatment method appropriate to individual
  Use of proven methods

MacKenzie (2002)

Review of sentencing and corrections literature
  Does work
    Boot camps instead of longer term custody
    Therapeutic communities
  Might work
    Intensive supervision with appropriate services
  Does not work
    Intensive supervision/surveillance
    Boot camps instead of probation

Lipsey and Wilson (1998)

Meta-analysis of more than 400 programs for juvenile delinquents
Effective programs produce larger effects in community versus custodial settings.
Different factors explain success in different settings
Effective for noninstitutional settings
  Duration of treatment
  Researcher involvement
  Interpersonal skills training
  Individual counseling (more effective for the more serious offenders)
  Behavioral programs
Not effective for noninstitutional settings
  Bringing younger delinquents together in groups
  Wilderness challenge, early release from probation or parole, deterrence
  Vocational training
Effective for institutional settings
  General program characteristics more important than treatment type
  Integrity of treatment implementation
  Duration of treatment
  Well-established programs
  Treatment administered by mental health professionals
  Interpersonal skills training(ART)
  Teaching family home (behavior modification, counseling, advocacy)
Not effective for institutional settings
  Wilderness challenge
  Employment related

Rating systems

Blueprints (Elliot, 1997)
  Functional family therapy (FFT; Alexander et al., 1998)
  Multisystemic therapy (MST; Henggeler et al., 1998)
  Multidimensional treatment foster care (MTFC; Chamberlain, 1998)

(continued)

TABLE 15.1. (*continued*)

Surgeon General (U.S. Department of Health and Human Services, 2001)
  Effective
    FFT, MST, MTFC
    Intensive protective supervision
  Not effective
    D.A.R.E.
    Scared Straight
  Cost effective
    WSIPP (Aos et al., 2001)
    FFT, MST, MTFC
    Aggression replacement training
    Adolescent Diversion Project
    Diversion with services
    Intensive probation as alternative to incarceration
    Boot camps as alternative to longer residential program
    Other family-based therapy approaches

any one stage of the process are passed on to the next stage. Out of all the juveniles arrested in 1999, only 26% were adjudicated delinquent and only 6.3% were placed out of their homes (Puzzanchera, Stahl, Finnegan, Tierney, & Snyder, 2003). Even in the cases of those arrested for one of the more serious Crime Index offenses, only 35% were adjudicated delinquent and only 9.2% were placed out of their homes. Those that are placed out of their homes are referred to a wide variety of group homes, camps, and other residential institutions.

The meta-analysis by Andrews and colleagues (1990) identified several factors that were associated with the more effective correctional programs:

- They focused their intervention efforts on the higher risk youth, where the opportunity for improvement and the consequences of failure are both the largest.
- They focused their interventions on dynamic or changeable risk factors behavior, such as drug use and relationships with negative peers, that have been shown to promote criminal behavior.
- They used evidence-based interventions that were appropriate for the issues and individuals they were working with.

These factors provide the basis for the Correctional Program Inventory (CPI), a program assessment instrument that is now being used by Latessa and colleagues to rate the quality of programming in individual correctional facilities (Latessa, Listwan, & Hubbard, 2005).

A more subjective review of correctional programs undertaken by

MacKenzie (1997) as part of the Sherman and colleagues review of prevention programs for the U.S. Congress reported the following findings:

- Boot camps for less serious youth offenders are more cost-effective than longer term custody, but not as effective as regular probation.
- Voluntary therapeutic communities, in which inmates take an active role in providing therapy, are effective in custodial settings.

Lipsey and Wilson's (1998) meta-analysis identified a number of characteristics associated with the more successful institutional programs:

- General program characteristics were more important than specific treatment type.
- The integrity with which a treatment program was implemented, as indicated by the specificity of its design and the fidelity of the operational program to the original design, was significant.
- Longer duration of treatment was more effective than shorter treatments.
- Well-established programs were more effective than newer programs.
- Treatment programs administered by mental health professionals were more effective than similar programs administered by regular correctional staff.

The most effective treatment methods in custodial settings were interpersonal skills training (12 1-hour social skills training sessions in groups of four, over a 6-week period) and teaching family home, a community-based, family-style, behavior modification group home for six to eight delinquents. Ineffective approaches identified by Lipsey and Wilson included wilderness challenge and employment-oriented programs.

Delinquents in Community Settings

Community settings for delinquency prevention programming can result from diversion, informal or formal probation, or parole. They can include the individual home, schools, teen centers, parks, or the special facilities of private providers. They can involve anything from a 1-hour monthly meeting to intensive daily supervision and services.

MacKenzie's (1997) review identified only intensive supervision with appropriate services as a community-based strategy that might be effective, and intensive supervision and surveillance alone as one that did not. Lipsey and Wilson's (1998) meta-analysis found that the character istics associated with effective programs in the community were somewhat different than those that distinguished effective programs in custodial settings. It also found that, all other things being equal, community-based interventions were more effective than similar interventions in custodial settings. Other factors identified by Lipsey and Wilson as associated with the more effective programs in community settings included:

- Longer duration of treatment was more effective than shorter treatments.
- Researcher/evaluator involvement in operating the program.
- The use of interpersonal skills training.
- The use of individual counseling, particularly with the more serious delinquents.
- The use of behavioral programs.

Program strategies that Lipsey and Wilson found did not work in community settings included wilderness challenge, early release from probation or parole, deterrence, and vocational training.

Unlike the case in custodial settings, where no proven program models have yet emerged, for community-based settings a number of proven program models have been identified. The three community-based programs for delinquents that meet the rigorous evaluation and replication standards established by the University of Colorado's Blueprints Program are functional family therapy, multisystemic therapy, and multidimensional treatment foster care (Elliot, 1997). These same programs along with intensive protective supervision have been identified as proven program models by the U.S. surgeon general (U.S. Department of Health and Human Services, 2001). Cost–benefit analyses by the Washington State Institute for Public Policy (WSIPP; Aos et al., 2004) have shown that each one of these programs can produce taxpayer savings in excess of $7.00 for every $1.00 invested in operating them.

Functional family therapy (FFT) is a clinical intervention that targets youth within the age range of 11–18 who have problems with delinquency, substance abuse, or violence. The program focuses on altering interactions between family members, and seeks to improve the functioning of the family unit by increasing family problem-solving skills, enhancing emotional connections between family members, and strengthening parental ability to provide appropriate structure, guidance, and limits to their children (Alexander et al., 1998). FFT is a relatively short-term program that is delivered by individual therapists, usually in the home setting. Each team of four to eight therapists works under the direct supervision and monitoring of several more experienced therapist/ trainers. The effectiveness of the program has been demonstrated for a wide range of problem youth in numerous trials over the past 25 years, using different types of therapists, ranging from paraprofessionals to trainees, in a variety of social work and counseling professions. The program is well documented and readily transportable (U.S. Department of Health and Human Services, 2001).

Multisystemic therapy (MST) is another clinical intervention whose overriding purpose is to help parents deal effectively with their youth's behavior problems, including disengagement from deviant peers and poor school performance. To accomplish family empowerment, MST also addresses barriers to effective parenting and helps family members build an indigenous social support network. To increase family collaboration and treatment generalization, MST is typically provided in the home, school, and other community locations. Master-level counselors provide 50 hours of face-to-face contact spread over 4 months.

MST takes about as long to work with an individual family as FFT, but it is more intensive and more expensive. In addition to working with parents, MST will locate and attempt to involve other family members in supervising the youth, as well as involving teachers, school administrators, and other adults who interact with the youth. MST therapists are also on call for emergency services, while FFT therapists are not. Evaluations of the program demonstrate that the therapy is effective in reducing rearrest rates and out-of-home placements for a wide variety of problem youth enmeshed in both the juvenile justice and social service systems (Henggler, Mihalic, Rone, Thomas, & Timmons-Mitchel, 1998).

The third *model* program in this group, multidimensional treatment foster care (MTFC), is a cost-effective alternative to group residential treatment for adolescents who have problems with chronic delinquency and antisocial behavior. MTFC is based on social learning concepts. Community families are recruited, trained, and closely supervised to provide MTFC treatment and supervision to participating adolescents. MTFC parent training emphasizes behavior management methods to provide youth with a structured and therapeutic living environment. After completing preservice training, MTFC parents attend a weekly group meeting run by a program case manager where ongoing supervision is provided. Supervision and support are also provided to MTFC parents during daily telephone calls. Family therapy is also provided for the youth's biological family.

Evaluations of MTFC have demonstrated that compared to control group youth (typically in group home placements), during a 12-month follow-up period, MTFC youth spent 60% fewer days incarcerated, had significantly fewer arrests, ran away from their programs on average three times less often, had significantly less hard drug use, and received quicker community placement from more restrictive settings (Chamberlain, 1998; Chamberlain & Reid, 1998). The large effect sizes achieved by MTFC, in comparison to traditional group homes, are in all probability partially due to the difference in DPC between the foster home and group home settings

In addition to the three Blueprint family interventions, the surgeon general's report (U.S. Department of Health and Human Services, 2001) identified a fourth model program, intensive protective supervision (IPS), which targets non-serious status offenders. Offenders assigned to IPS are closely monitored by counselors who carry reduced caseloads and interact more extensively with the youth and his or her family than traditional parole officers. The counselors make frequent home visitations, provide support for parents, develop individualized service plans, and arrange for professional or therapeutic services as needed. An evaluation of the program found that youth assigned to IPS were less likely to be referred to juvenile court during supervision or during a 1-year follow-up period, and were more likely to have successfully completed treatment than youth assigned to regular protective supervision (MacKenzie, 1997; Sontheimer & Goodstein, 1993). IPS is listed as *promising* by both Blueprints and the surgeon general.

PRINCIPLES THAT SHOULD GUIDE JUVENILE JUSTICE PROGRAMMING

The evidence described in the preceding sections regarding what works and what doesn't can be combined with the knowledge about DPC presented in previous chapters to suggest a number of principles that can inform delinquency prevention programming. The development of those principles is our task here.

DPC is only one of the many issues that juvenile justice policymakers and practitioners must deal with in working with delinquent youth. It is but one of the many factors that affect future delinquent behavior. However, it appears to be a significant factor in particular situations and with particular kinds of youth. In this section we attempt to identify these critical combinations and identify strategies for avoiding or reducing the negative consequences of DPC. The overriding principle in avoiding DPC is to avoid placement of delinquents in institutional settings whenever possible. This principle divides the rest of our discussion up into two distinct categories: those in which youth are placed in institutional settings, and those in which they are not.

Community versus Custodial Contexts

If peer contagion is a serious risk factor, then it does not makes sense to place delinquent youth together in group settings except when there are overriding concerns about immediate public safety and there is no other option. There have not yet been the kind of comparative studies that would allow us to estimate the specific effects of placing a youth in an institutional or group home setting as opposed to an appropriate community alternative. Tolerance for risk of further criminal activity and the availability of alternative options will depend on state laws, local politics, community attitudes, and local conditions.

There are many arguments that support this line of reasoning. From a DPC perspective, the argument is that the negative effects of peer contagion will tend to counteract whatever positive effects that programming in a group setting is able to produce. From a "labeling" perspective, the argument would be that the mere act of placing a youth out of his or her home is likely to have a negative impact on the way others will see that youth in the future, and on his or her own perception of him- or herself. Youth who are removed from their homes and placed in institutional or group programs will inevitably be seen as more at risk than those who are not removed: by their family and peers, by those who work with them in the system, and by themselves (Lemertt, 1951, 1972). Being placed in an institutional or group setting only adds to the cumulative negative labeling process that includes all previous attempts to intervene.

Another reason for avoiding group placements is that they provide an unnatural and unrealistic setting for youth in which to develop and practice the social and relationship skills they will require to survive back in their communities.

However, the most important reason for avoiding group placements is the clear evidence that all types of preventive programming produce better results in community settings rather than in institutions (Lipsey & Wilson, 1998). The effects of DPC may well account for some of this difference. During the past decade a number of intervention models have been developed and sufficiently tested in a variety of community settings that we can have a relatively high degree of confidence in the effects they appear to produce.

Given this evidence, it seems clear that the only reasons for removing a youth from his or her home and placing him or her in an institutional or group home setting would be (1) the inappropriateness of the current home setting and an inability to find a more suitable community placement, or (2) the public safety risk posed by the youth. In these two instances placement in a group setting is still likely to occur.

Programs for Institutionalized Youth

In the two situations described above, in which it is likely that youth will be placed in some type of institutional or group living arrangement, we have theories that tell us how DPC is likely to affect the group but very little evidence on how to reduce those effects. What we know about the mechanisms of DPC suggests that the following approaches might lessen its negative impacts.

Since DPC is a risk factor that all institutional and group living programs have to deal with, we might expect that one of the characteristics that distinguishes the more effective institutional programs is their ability to neutralize or at least diminish the consequences of DPC. Although the evaluation literature does not speak to this point directly, it does identify some factors that distinguish the more effective programs that may be related to DPC. These include the integrity and duration of treatment, how long the program has been in existence, and the use of the "teaching family home" approach. Surprisingly, a program's general characteristics appear to be more important than the specific methods it employs (Lipsey & Wilson, 1998). Of course, most residential programs have not been subjected to rigorous evaluation, and there have been few serious attempts to compare them.

Assuming that most program developers and providers are aware of the risks of DPC, we might also assume that they include some active measures within their programs to reduce the likelihood of it occurring. Looking back at the characteristics that distinguish the more effective programs, we can speculate on how they might be related to reducing DPC. If active countermeasures are required to reduce the negative effects of DPC, then the integrity with which the program is implemented is clearly related to the prevention of DPC. The program's designer is far more likely to be aware of the need to control DPC than the regular staff members who operate the program. A poorly implemented program is not likely to contain the kind of integrated structure and specific programming that may be required to counteract DPC. Likewise, a program that has only been in existence for a short while may not have developed effective mechanisms for suppressing DPC, or they may not yet be effectively implemented. Studies of the implementation of Blueprints model programs have shown that even with extensive staff training, these highly manualized programs require about 2 years to achieve a high degree of therapeutic integrity (Elliot, 2003).

Lipsey and Wilson's (1998) meta-analysis found empirical support for one custodial programming approach that is theoretically designed to reduce DPC effects in custodial settings: the teaching family model. The teaching family model involves assigning youth to small residential living units, where they live in a family atmosphere and are supervised by a resident parent couple using a variety of behavioral approaches. The model has been adopted to institutional as well as group home settings.

Development of the teaching family model has been supported by a long line of National Institute of Mental Health (NIMH) grants, beginning with the Achievement Place group home in 1967 (Phillips, Phillips, Fixsen, & Wolf, 1974). The teaching family model was selected as a model program by the American Psychological Association in 1993 and was identified in Lipsey and Wilson's (1998) meta-analysis as one of the most effective treatment methods for institutionalized juveniles.

Two characteristics of residential programs that DPC theory suggests might be critical are staffing ratio and the degree of structure in daily activities. DPC would seem to thrive best in situations where youth are only loosely supervised and free to interact with each other at will for extended periods of time. This would be the case where youth, in a residential facility, are turned out into a yard or dayroom for extended periods of recreation. Opportunities for this kind of unstructured interaction can be reduced by providing more structured and organized activities in the daily routine, and by increasing the level of direct staff supervision and interaction. As was the case with integrity of treatment, skill in developing and monitoring appropriately structured activities is probably something found in more mature programs rather than in brand-new ones.

In summary, the potential harm from DPC is one of several reasons for not placing youth in congregate custodial settings. However, when public safety concerns require such placements, there do appear to be a number of techniques that can reduce or mitigate the negative effects of DPC. These include organizing the youth into small family-like living units, minimizing the amount of unstructured time the residents have for interacting with each other in unstructured settings, maintaining a high level of direct staff supervision, and attempting to minimize contact with deviant peers upon release. Incentives for program directors to develop countermeasures for DPC can be provided by monitoring the use of evidence-based practices and increasing their accountability for outcomes. The evidence suggests that it will take a new program about 2 years to reach its full potential in reducing DPC and recidivism rates.

Programs for Noninstitutionalized Youth

As we indicated in the previous section, the negative effects of DPC and deviant labeling both argue for restricting the use of custodial placements only to those youth that pose a sufficiently high risk to the community. For all others, community-based interventions or no intervention at all are the preferred option from a crime control and youth protection perspective. Since we have just completed our review of appropriate strategies for dealing with the more serious institutionalized youth, we will begin this review of community-based programs by considering the programming requirements for the most serious youth in this category.

Here we will invoke the basic principle of avoiding the bringing together of delinquent youth, for either programming or supervision purposes, more sparingly. This admonition only holds for younger, less serious delinquents under the age of 15. According to the meta-analysis reported by Lipsey (Chapter 9, this volume), effects are larger for group treatment than individual treatment for youth above 15 years of age.

Some programs now bring such youth together to provide day treatment or run special schools for delinquents. Others assemble delinquent youth in groups to perform community service or for other special activities. For the younger, less serious offenders, all such activities run the risk of enhancing DPC and should be evaluated to determine if they do. Mainstreaming of less serious delinquent youth into regular school and program settings is the preferred alternative, where they will not be surrounded by delinquent peers. The value of this mainstreaming approach is illustrated by the positive outcomes produced by MST, another one of the Blueprint model programs (Henggler et al., 1998). MST combines clinical intervention with the families of delinquent youth with efforts to improve the youths' interactions and connections with the local school system and other community-based resources.

With older, more serious delinquents, group interventions are not only allowed, but they are the preferred modality, again according to Lipsey's meta-analysis. However, when delinquent youth are brought together in the community, then all of the principles that were articulated for dealing with youth in custodial settings should probably apply, but we can not be sure. The evidence is unclear. Small groups, a high level of substitute parental supervision, well-structured activities, and a minimum of unstructured time should be the rule. Bringing delinquent youth together in the community, without recognizing these principles, may run the risk of facilitating their continued participation in delinquent activities through the process of DPC.

Even in those instances where delinquent youth are not required to assemble in the community, there is still a risk of DPC through their own initiative. Delinquent youth in a neighborhood are likely to seek each other out or to already be acquainted. In order to guard against this natural form of DPC, it is necessary to prevent delinquent youth from associating with each other. The specific steps that are required to operationalize this concept include (1) identifying a youth's delinquent peers; (2) setting ground rules and consequences for inappropriate contacts with these peers; and (3) employing close supervision and monitoring to make sure that such contacts do not take place, and are detected if they do. Some of the protocols utilized by MST and MTFC train parents in how to carry out these tasks. The most difficult and time-consuming part is the monitoring. In order to have youth accountable at all times, it is necessary not only to check up on where they are going, but also to ensure that they are where they are supposed to be, and that none of their delinquent peers are present. This requires cooperation and communication between parents to ensure that adequate supervision and monitoring are provided at all times.

THE POLICY PERSPECTIVE

Previous chapters of this book have laid out the case for the existence of DPC and suggested the mechanisms by which it occurs. In this chapter we have identified a number of programs and principles that point toward successful strategies for reducing DPC in both institutional and community settings.

The number one rule is to avoid unnecessary institutional placements whenever possible. The number two rule is to avoid bringing younger, less serious delinquents together for *any* purposes even in community settings.

One example of the kind of unnecessary and harmful use of group placements that currently exists within the juvenile justice system involves juveniles with mental health problems. A *New York Times* story entitled "Many Youths Reported Held Awaiting Mental Help," dated July 8, 2004, summarizes the findings of a congressional study into the treatment of children with psychiatric disorders. The study found that 15,000 such children had been improperly incarcerated the previous year because no mental health services were available to serve them. The figures were compiled by the Democratic Party staff of the House Committee on Government Reform in the first such nationwide survey of juvenile detention centers. More than two-thirds of the 510 detention centers responding to the survey reported that youth with mental disorders were being locked up with delinquent youth because there was no other place for them to go while awaiting treatment. Seventy-one centers in 33 states said they were holding mentally ill youngsters with no charges.

For those youth who must be placed in institutional settings, there are still a number of strategies that can be used to reduce DPC. Utilization of the *teaching family* model and appropriate skills training are two approaches. Providing small living units, high levels of structure in daily activities, and a high staff-to-youth ratio are others. Finally, it is important to avoid unnecessary turnover among program providers so that programs can reach a mature level of competence.

These findings lend support to arguments for further restricting or reducing the number of unnecessary institutional placements, particularly the use of secure detention for less serious youth who have a high likelihood of being contaminated by the more serious youth they are likely to meet in detention. They suggest that programs that do serve youth in aggregate settings should be required to collect data on potential peer contagion effects in both naturalistic and experimental settings. They also lend support to the concept of restricting community-based placements solely to those programs based on proven models that also include rigorous quality control mechanisms.

Another apparent principle is that all of the most cost-effective strategies support parents and other significant adults in developing appropriate behavior management and monitoring skills for dealing with at-risk youth. Program developers that expand on this strategy are more likely to produce effective programs than those who fail to utilize it.

FUTURE RESEARCH

The most consistent finding of this whole inquiry has been the weakness of research efforts in identifying the conditions under which DPC takes place, the size of the effects, and the value of alternative strategies for reducing these effects. This lack of information about what works in preventing DPC is only part of a much larger void regarding the effectiveness of alternative methods of organizing and operating group residential programs. One of the most pressing needs identified in this field, particularly in regard to institutionalized youth, is the need to develop and test alternative strategies for reducing DPC in institutional settings.

Approximately 150,000 delinquent youth are placed out of their homes in any given year. These youth represent the most high-risk pool of individuals that can be identified with respect to future criminality. Any reduction in future criminality that can be produced by reducing the effects of DPC will have long-term payoffs in reduced crime and criminal justice expenditures. Yet few states or individual localities can afford the kind of rigorous experimental design and measurement that are required to determine the effectiveness of a new program in curbing recidivism and DPC. This issue should be an obvious choice for funding by the Office of Juvenile Justice and Delinquency Prevention, the National Institute of Justice, or any foundation that is interested in helping at-risk youth.

Other questions that need to be answered before juvenile justice authorities can make intelligent choices about program designs and placements of youth include:

- How does susceptibility to contagion vary with age, gender, and delinquency record?
- How does the effectiveness of the strategies discussed above vary with these same characteristics?
- Are there minimum exposure or dosage effects?
- Do some of the effects decline with continued exposure?
- Are all youth equally at risk?
- Does it matter whether an emergency residential placement facility is called a shelter, detention, or a hall?
- What are the real costs and availability of alternatives for youth currently in congregate care?

Efforts to deal with DPC must compete with the many other demands that are placed on programs that deal with delinquent youth. If this issue is going to receive the attention it deserves, there will need to be considerably more research regarding the conditions under which DPC will flourish or be suppressed.

CHAPTER 16

Prevention Approaches to Improve Child and Adolescent Behavior and Reduce Deviant Peer Influence

Emilie Phillips Smith, Jean E. Dumas,
and Ron Prinz

In the past decades, a number of advances have been made in prevention approaches to improve child and adolescent behavior, particularly in the areas of reducing violence, aggression, and substance abuse (Lochman & van den Steenhoven, 2002; Spoth, Kavanaugh, & Dishion, 2002). This is quite a notable departure from the early 1970s when policymakers questioned whether anything "worked" in reducing juvenile crime and problem behavior (Martinson, 1974). Since that time a generation of prevention science has delineated the individual youth, family, peer, and neighborhood risk and protective factors that are influential in youth behavior (Elliott, Huizinga, & Menard, 1989; Elliott et al., 1996; Loeber, Farrington, Stouthamer-Loeber, Moffitt, & Caspi, 1998; Patterson, Reid, & Dishion, 1992; Sampson, Raudenbush, & Earls, 1997; Thornberry, Krohn, Lizotte, & Chard-Wierschem, 1993; Tremblay, Masse, Vitaro, & Dobkin, 1995). With this type of information in hand, prevention science has developed, tested, and identified effective approaches in reducing violence, aggression, and substance abuse. Numerous guides have been published to help assist practitioners and policymakers in selecting programs that will be effective in promoting positive youth behavior (see, e.g., *Best Practices in Youth Violence Prevention* [Thornton, Craft, Dahlberg, Lynch, & Baer, 2000]; *Youth Violence: A Report of the Surgeon General* [U.S. Department of Heath and Human Services, 2001]; or the *Blueprints for Violence Prevention* series [Elliott & Mihalic, 1998]). This chapter does not attempt to duplicate the important work of these reviews, but does pay special attention to prevention approaches that improve child and adolescent behavior and reduce deviant peer influence, the focus of this volume.

Deviant peer influence is the potentially iatrogenic, or unintended, consequence of implementing programs that group children and youth together who are at high risk for exhibiting problem behavior (Dishion & Andrews, 1995; Dishion, McCord, & Poulin, 1999). In implementing programs intended to benefit youth, care should be taken to use approaches that actively limit or eliminate the possibility for peer modeling and reinforcement of antisocial behavior. Having meaningful adult involvement in the lives of youth, be they parents, teachers, or community mentors, is instrumental in accomplishing this goal.

This chapter explores prevention approaches that are effective in promoting positive child and youth behavior and limiting deviant peer influence. These include approaches designed to strengthen families, school-based programs focused on enhancing student and teacher skills, well-implemented community-based after-school and/or mentoring programs that expose children to positive role models and relationships, and multimodal programs that may include some or all of the aforementioned strategies. The collection of these prevention strategies vary in terms of the developmental point at which they intervene. Some are focused on preschoolers, others on elementary school-age children, and still others focus on adolescents. Some programs are designed to prevent problems from arising in youth and families at risk and others attempt to limit the scope and duration of early delinquency and/or substance abuse. The following sections explore prototypical examples found to be effective upon youth behavior and examine the extent to which the issue of peer influence has been addressed.

THE IMPORTANCE OF INVOLVING THE FAMILY

Etiological research on youth risky behavior has recognized the crucial role of parents. For children across different stages of development, parental disciplinary practices with clear standards, rewards, and consequences are found to be superior to inconsistent, coercive, and unresponsive discipline (Lutzker, Touchette, & Campbell, 1988; Maccoby & Martin, 1983; Snyder & Huntley, 1990). Inconsistent parenting fails to establish clear limits that are rewarded or sanctioned with regularity. On the one hand, in coercive parenting, the parent gives in to nagging misbehavior or child noncompliance, thereby unwittingly encouraging youth to continue this maladaptive behavioral pattern (Chamberlain & Patterson, 1995; Martinez & Forgatch, 2001; Patterson, Reid, & Dishion, 1992). On the other hand, harsh punishment involving intense physical punishment and caustic verbal abuse (Lochman & van den Steenhoven, 2002) is emotionally damaging for children and does not model nor teach them positive ways to behave.

Communication and responsiveness are important dimensions of family relationships. Parenting strategies that express care, concern, and warmth, in which parents communicate with their young by listening and helping them to think about the consequences of their actions, promote children's moral development and good decision making (Brody & Shaffer, 1982). Communication between parents and children helps to build closeness in the family relationship (Rodick, Henggeler, & Hanson, 1986). Furthermore, parents who communicate effectively with their children are more aware of *who* youth are with, *what* they are doing, and *where* they are, and are less likely to have children and youth involved in deviant peer groups or delinquent activities (Dishion, Patterson, Stoolmiller, & Skinner, 1991). Overall, youth who report good family relationships are less susceptible to the influence of delinquent peers. Clear behavioral expectancies, monitoring and supervision, parental warmth, and good communication are all important dimensions of families that promote behavioral and social competency and good decision making in youth.

Based upon the etiological research examining the critical role of family in children's lives, many studies of family-based programs have been conducted. Programs have been developed for pregnant and new mothers (Olds, 2002), and for parents of preschoolers (Webster-Stratton, 1998), young children (e.g., Conduct Problems Prevention Research Group, 2002a; Dumas, Prinz, Smith, & Laughlin, 1999; Eddy, Reid, & Fetrow, 2000), and adolescents (e.g., Alexander & Parsons, 1973; Dishion & Kavanaugh, 2000; Henggeler, Melton, Brondino, Scherer, & Hanley, 1997; Spoth & Redmond, 2002). At all ages, family-based programs employ a variety of universal, selected, and indicated approaches. The following sections will explore the degree to which various models of providing parenting support also address the issue of deviant peer influence.

Universal Family Approaches

Universal family-based programs are delivered to the entire population of youth, often for specified grade levels in a school (Mrazek &

Haggerty, 1994). Because it is desirable to extend programming to as many families as possible, universal family programs often use group-delivered modes instead of individual modes of delivery. Part of the rationale for family groups concerns the possibility to reduce costs using a group-delivery modality rather than an individual one (Cunningham, Bremner, & Boyle, 1995). Another rationale for group-based approaches is the opportunity to build networks among families coping with similar issues and problems (Pantin et al., 2003; Smith, Gorman-Smith, et al., 2004). This section considers universal family programming approaches, the degree to which peer influence is addressed in these programs, and effects upon youth behavioral outcomes.

Research on family-oriented programs has demonstrated their impact upon deviant peer affiliation among youth. The Adolescent Transitions Program (Dishion, Bullock, & Granic, 2002) is a "tiered strategy" that offers increasingly intense family services and support based upon family motivation and need. The universal program available in selected schools involves all sixth-grade students in a 6-week curriculum and accompanying home activities designed to promote positive behavior and achievement. All sixth-grade families (including a racially diverse sample of African Americans, European Americans, and other racial-ethnic groups combined) are invited to receive the Family Check-Up, a brief assessment of youth and parent attitudes, behaviors, and needs. On the basis of this checkup, families are then offered a "menu of options" including brief consultation from an onsite family therapist (parent consultant), parenting groups, family therapy, and community referral. Research revealed that deviant peer affiliation grew among all adolescents in grades six through nine who participated in the study, but those in the intervention group, even those initially highest in deviant peer involvement, showed the least growth across a 4-year period (Dishion, Bullock, & Granic, 2002).

Eddy, Reid, and Fetrow (2000) developed a universal program for the families of school-age children called Linking the Interests of Families and Teachers (LIFT), a multimodal school-based program that has been evaluated in 12 Oregon schools. Universal group-based parent training, classroom-based social and problem-solving skills, and playground-based behavioral modification were the components delivered to children and parents. The program included two age groups, one early in school entry (first grade) and the other in preadolescence (fifth grade), an appealing feature of this program that facilitates the examination of program effects developmentally. Universal parent training included weekly parenting training groups for 6 weeks. The format of the sessions included review, lecture, discussion, role plays, and home practice. Parents who were involved in the group-delivered parent training were more supportive and exhibited less aversive behavior during parent–child problem-solving sessions. The developmental trajectories for fifth-grade program youth revealed that they were slower in exhibiting problem behavior with peers as reported by teachers and slower in being arrested by police for alcohol use and marijuana use. The effects were most dramatic for youth exhibiting the highest rates of initial problem behaviors and were still evident 3 years after the program ended. Though there is concern that grouping high-risk children might have unintended negative effects, universal group-delivered parent training accompanied by universal classroom and playground components with program availability to a cross-section of parents and youth from the school demonstrated benefits for youth. Adverse effects were not apparent; parents and youth, and especially high-risk youth, seemed to benefit from parent group participation.

A program of research using universal family prevention for families of preadolescents has been examined by Spoth and Redmond (2002). They examined the Iowa Strengthening Families Program (ISFP), a program developed based on earlier work on family programs conducted by Kumpfer, Molgaard, and Spoth (1996). ISFP involves seven sessions delivered to groups of 10–12 parents recruited through rural schools. In the first part of each session, sixth-grade youth met as a group while their parents also met as a group. In the second part of the session, youth and parents met together to practice skills they had learned separately. Approximately 51–68% of youth and families solicited within these rural schools participated. One and a half years after initial participation, there were differences in alcohol initiation for youths whose families attended more than half of the family groups.

Spoth and Redmond (2002) carefully pointed out that this program addressed the issue of peer contagion by offering access universally to all sixth graders and not just to youth at high risk for substance abuse and aggression. Since the youth who participated represented varying levels of risk, some youth demonstrated prosocial behavior and less proclivity toward substance abuse. Furthermore, parents were actively involved with youth for a portion of the session and were at the same site even during the time youth met as a group. Involvement in the program had an important impact upon youth tobacco initiation, frequency of alcohol use, and self-report of aggressive behavior in eighth and tenth grade. Parental involvement in programming in addition to having a mixed group of youth meeting together are both likely important factors in addressing peer influence in universal family programs.

Few universal programs developed explicitly with the needs of ethnic minority families in mind have undergone rigorous evaluation. One exception is Familias Unidas, a group-based, universal program that specifically addresses the issues facing Latino parents of sixth and seventh graders in the Florida public schools. This randomized intervention study involved multiparent groups consisting of 10–12 individuals who met weekly for approximately 9 months. Parents attended an average of 24 sessions. The program demonstrated success in increasing parental investment among Latino parents, which in turn predicted reduced adolescent behavior problems. In Familias Unidas, families with lower levels of initial parental investment attended more group sessions on average and appeared to benefit most from the intervention (Pantin et al., 2003).

Among the programs discussed here, group-based family programs did not seem to result in the same unintended negative consequences possible for groups of high-risk youth alone. First, the programs were universally delivered, appealing to a cross-section of families and youth who demonstrated varying levels of competency and problem behaviors (Dishion, Bullock, & Granic, 2002; Eddy et al., 2000; Pantin et al., 2003). In some programs the youth were separate for a period and were rejoined by their parents later in the session so that both parents and youth could apply their learning (Spoth & Redmond, 2002). The presence of parents, in addition to the involvement of a broad cross-section of youth and families, begins to address the issue of peer influence among these universal parenting groups, some with individually oriented youth components.

Selected and Indicated Family Approaches

Selected prevention approaches are used when the focus population is evidencing risk factors associated with the development of a disorder or other adverse outcome. Indicated programs are used when the population is showing evidence of the disorder or adverse outcome itself (Mrazek & Haggerty, 1994). In this chapter, selected and indicated programs are considered together because both involve the identification of youth who are at risk of or are already showing evidence of conduct disorder and/or substance abuse.

One rationale for selected and/or indicated programs concerns the proportion of crime committed by a small proportion of youth. In terms of juvenile delinquency, juveniles account for approximately 19% of all arrests in the United States (Snyder, 1997). Longitudinal surveys indicate that 20% of the serious offenders account for 75–90% of self-reported violent crimes (Elliott et al., 1989; Loeber, Wei, Stouthamer, Huizanga, & Thornberry, 1999). Given that these serious offenders have a developmental trajectory in which various risk factors are apparent fairly early in their life, these youth can be identified using multiple screening procedures with some degree of accuracy (Patterson, Reid, & Dishion, 1992).

In terms of comorbidity, family problems have also been found to be an important issue for those who escalate in substance use in the adolescent years (Wills, McNamara, Vacarro, & Hirky, 1996). To prevent and reduce risk factors and negative child behavior, selected/indicated family programs have been developed for parents of preschool children (Webster-Stratton, Reid, & Hammond, 2001), as part of multimodal prevention in childhood (Conduct Problems Prevention Research Group, 2002a), and for adolescents (Henggeler et al., 1997; Sexton & Alexander, 2002). Description of selected/indicated family approaches and their attention to the containment of deviant peer influence are described in the next section.

Cunningham, Bremner, and Boyle (1995) examined the effectiveness of a clinic-based individual parent training program compared to a community-based parent training group. Children who scored high on the screening questionnaire were selected for participation, matched by family structure (one- or two-parent family) and gender of the child, and randomly assigned to the 12-week clinic-based individual training, the 12-week community-based group, or a waiting list control group. The researchers found that family group participants reported greater improvements in behavior problems, demonstrated better scores on behavior observations of the children, and showed higher maintenance of gains at 6-month follow-up than those in the individual therapy administered in clinics. They also found the groups to be one-sixth the cost of clinic-based individual programming. (It is important to note that the comparison here is to clinic-based individual therapy and not to home-based individual programs that exhibit both long-term effects and cost-effectiveness; see, e.g., Olds, 2002.) The benefit of participating in the clinic individual component was that families reported feeling more competent sooner, suggesting that the intensity of a family meeting with one leader attending to their issues resulted in quicker growth. Yet those who were involved in the community groups benefitted from reports of better child behavior not immediately after intervention but 6 months later when compared to families involved in the clinic intervention or no intervention. Additionally, families in the community groups seemed more aware of community resources than those in the clinic individual programming (Cunningham et al., 1995).

Parent groups have also been found to be effective in improving parenting strategies for divorcing mothers of elementary-age sons (Forgatch & DeGarmo, 1999). Divorce is a transition for parents. In spite of the enormous emotional drain they are experiencing, they must continue to parent effectively to promote the adjustment of their child or children (Forgatch & DeGarmo, 1999). In randomized studies, parent groups with divorcing mothers have been found to decrease coercive parenting (where mothers give in to antisocial behavior or display similar behavior themselves) and to reduce a loss of positive involvement with their children during this transition phase (Forgatch & DeGarmo, 1999). The groups were found to be supportive and to help mothers identify successful educational and career trajectories that were beneficial to them personally and to their families.

There are other prevention trials with selected and indicated youth and families that used family groups as a mode of addressing issues within the family in combination with other modes of intervention. The Fast Track intervention was developed to interrupt the early developmental trajectory of conduct disorder in children by attending to multiple spheres of influence upon children (Conduct Problems Prevention Research Group, 2002a). Among these components were weekly parent/child groups (22 sessions in first grade, 14 sessions in second grade, and nine sessions in third grade) in which parents met to focus upon parenting strategies to enhance child adjustment. At the same time, groups of five to six high-risk children met in "friendship groups" (Bierman, Greenberg, & Conduct Problems Prevention Research Group, 1996). These sessions focused upon developing social, communication, friendship-building, and problem-solving skills. The child groups convened concurrently with the parent groups. After each parent and child group session, pairs of children and parents spent 30 minutes practicing positive parenting skills via joint reading and arts and crafts cooperative activities. There were also sessions at school in which high-risk youth interacted in 30-minute play sessions with classroom peer partners who were rotated over the course of the year. These pairings included heterogeneous peers, while the friendship groups occurring during the parent groups focused on the high-risk children. Other program components included tutoring from paraprofessionals three times weekly for 30 minutes during school and the socioemotional PATHS curriculum (Greenberg, Kusche, Cook, & Quamma, 1995) delivered universally by classroom teachers during school. Adults and higher functioning peers were positively involved in several ways in this intervention approach. Several benefits emerged from this multicomponent prevention program. Intervention children made more socially competent responses and fewer hostile peer attributions, parents indicated less reliance on physical punishment and improved parenting behavior, and teacher ratings of behavior problems showed improvement.

This study is particularly salient given the interest in peer contagion. The Fast Track prevention trial involved highly structured and closely supervised small groups of young children coming together while their parents were meeting nearby and then interacting with their families immediately afterwards. In combination with the other program components, positive results were evident. Factors potentially important to the containment of peer contagion might include the small size of the friendship groups, close staff supervision, proximity and interaction with parents, and the comprehensive and longitudinal nature of the prevention trial. With the available data from this longitudinal trial, further investigation might examine the role of child age and whether peer influence is more of an issue with young children than with adolescents. Further study work could also provide more in-depth analyses of the high-risk groups and the nature of peer reinforcement and sanction. Such analyses could more emphatically ascertain whether contagion was nonexistent or if it was moderated by a structured, comprehensive, intensive, and longitudinal theory-based intervention. These are all important questions to address in implementing groups with high-risk children that also inhibit peer contagion.

Waldron, Slesnick, Brody, Turner, and Peterson (2001) compared the effects of individual youth cognitive-behavioral therapy (CBT), adolescent group therapy, family therapy, and combined individual youth and family therapy. The individual CBT program focused upon communication, problem solving, peer refusal, negative mood management, social support, and relapse prevention. The adolescent group program covered similar topics as the individual therapy (Botvin & Botvin, 1992). The family therapy was based on the Functional Family Therapy model (Alexander & Parsons, 1973) and focused on family communication, problem solving, contingency management, behavioral contracting, and effecting change in the family. Both the family therapy and the combined individual and family therapy conditions evidenced lower percentages of days using marijuana at 4-month follow-up, at which time positive effects of the individual and group programs for youth were not evident.

It is difficult to ascertain whether the lack of effects in the adolescent group condition was potentially due to peer influence whereby the program unwittingly fosters reinforcement of substance abuse behavior among peers. At any rate, neither the individually oriented cognitive-behavioral condition nor the adolescent group condition demonstrated significant effects on marijuana usage. For the adolescents in this study, involving families in the behavior change process proved to be an important element leading to effectiveness. When family therapy was provided alone or in combination with intervention aimed at increasing youth understanding and skills, substantial reductions in drug use behavior were obtained. This research again illustrates that adult involvement seems to be an important part of reducing youth susceptibility to risky behaviors and to negative peer influences.

A number of programs for adolescents in the area of indicated prevention for juvenile delinquency have taken great care to prevent deviant peer influence. These programs have typically included behaviorally based or family systems intervention in the homes of the participants, and have been careful not to gather the delinquent youth in groups (Davidson, Redner, Amdur, & Mitchell, 1990; Henggeler et al., 1997; Sexton & Alexander, 2002). These programs focused on building parental management, communication, and linkages to community support for youth and families. All have demonstrated effects upon family relationships and recidivism measured by both self-report and official delinquency. These home-based approaches eliminate the potential of adolescent peer contagion in the program among youthful offenders and also exhibit effectiveness as much as 3 years postintervention (Henggeler et al., 1997).

PEER SOCIAL SKILLS TRAINING

Research on the role of peer relations in childhood aggression has delineated the role of early child coercive behavior upon peer rejection (Asher & Coie, 1990). In the pathway to peer rejection, children's coercive and aggressive behaviors are reinforced by parents. Moving into school and other social settings, this aggressive and aversive behavior can result in rejection by more socially competent peers, leading to more affiliation with aggressive peers. The Peer Coping Skills (PCS) program developed by Prinz, Blechman, and Dumas (1994) seeks to interrupt this chain of events by pairing children showing aggressive behavior with children who are more socially competent and nonaggressive. The children are placed by pairs into groups that help to teach children to actively listen to each other, exchange information more effectively, use and attend to nonverbal cues, and learn to effectively communicate their feelings. Implementing PCS with heterogeneous groups of children was found to increase social skills among both the competent nonaggressive children and the aggressive children. Aggression was also reduced among the children displaying higher initial levels of problem behavior (Prinz et al., 1994). Peer interactional training like that in PCS addresses peer contagion by pairing mixed-ability children and by enhancing the social and communication skills of both groups. Peer interventions have also been included in multimodal programs like Fast Track (Conduct Problems Prevention Research Group, 2002a).

UNIVERSAL CLASSROOM- AND SCHOOL-BASED APPROACHES

School bonding and academic achievement are important factors related to reducing the likelihood that youth become involved in violence, delinquency, and substance abuse (Dishion, Patterson, Stoolmiller, & Miller, 1990; O'Donnell, Hawkins, Catalano, Abbott, & Day, 1995). Feeling valued and supported by teachers and school staff contributes to helping youth feel connected and perform well in school (Bowen, Richman, Brewster, & Bowen, 1998; Smith, Boutte, Zigler, & Finn-Stevenson, 2004). Attachment to school and adults in that setting is an important theme in research on prevention of youth problem behavior. Research on consistent teacher disciplinary strategies, like that on consistent parental disciplinary strategies, shows that teachers who attend to and reward the students who are on task and behaving well, and who set and enforce clear academic and behavioral standards, have classrooms with students who behave better and achieve more academically and are at reduced risk for conduct disorder, aggression, and substance abuse (Abbott, O'Donnell, Hawkins, Hill Kosterman, & Catalano, 1998; Ialongo, Werthamer, Brown, Kellam, & Wang, 1999).

Classroom management approaches have been tested in randomized prevention trials in which school classrooms are assigned to conditions in which behaviorally oriented classroom management is compared to treatment as usual (Abbott et al., 1998; Kellam, Rebok, Ialongo, & Mayer, 1994). The beneficial results of clear, rewarding school disciplinary practices are most pronounced among students with higher initial levels of aggression; follow-up studies have detected effects well into middle school (Kellam et al., 1994). Universal classroom management of this sort has also been incorporated into multimodal prevention programs (Conduct Problems Prevention Research Group, 2002a; Eddy et al., 2000). Prevention strategies that enhance classroom management do not seem to aggravate peer contagion. On the contrary, these approaches are implemented classroom-wide and results indicate that such programs improve classroom climate overall and impact the behavior of the most aggressive children in class as well (Kellam et al., 1994).

A number of classroom programs include regular communication between school and families, a pattern of interactions that *begins* with teachers sharing children's *successes* with families and keeping families informed about children's progress and attainment (Abbott et al., 1998; Kellam et al., 1994). In turn, families have the opportunity to reward and encourage what is being learned in school at home. A partnership is built between home and school that places communication and encouragement of the child's behavior at the core of efforts at home and school.

Universal approaches have been extended to include the entire school building. In these types of initiatives, school staff and students work together to establish clear, visibly posted guidelines for behavior and actively reinforce success in the school environment (Metzler, Biglan, Rusby, & Sprague, 2001). Such approaches include school-wide efforts to encourage teachers to reinforce student performance with incentives redeemable at the school store and to communicate important accomplishments with parents and the local media. These approaches have been found to reduce student aggression and increase student-perceived safety significantly more than in comparison nonintervention schools. Similarly, school-wide efforts in reducing bullying seeks to create an environment in which students feel comfortable reporting bullying to teachers and developing a peer culture that sanctions and discourages bullying behavior (Olweus, 1993). Bullying prevention strategies tested in Germany, England, and the United States have been found to reduce aggressive behavior, vandalism, and truancy, and to result in improvements in school climate (Olweus, 1993).

COMMUNITY-BASED APPROACHES

Neighborhood and community become increasingly important to youth as they grow and develop. In addition to the neighborhoods in which they live, there are various communities with which youth may affiliate that may or may not be located within their residential neighborhood (Burton & Jarrett, 2000). The community of the school that they attend where they may or may not be involved in extracurricular activities, their faith community, and the places or communities where they spend their leisure time are all potentially influential settings in the lives of youth (Brooks-Gunn, Duncan, Kato, & Sealand, 1993; Burton & Jarrett, 2000).

Preadolescents and adolescents are afforded more freedom and autonomy that allows them to explore their neighborhood and community more than younger school-age children. Some research underscores the need to consider the influence of unstructured time with peers in the neighborhood and community because it can lead to increased crime and delinquency when youth lack adult supervision (Osgood, Wilson, Bachman, O'Malley, & Johnston, 1996). Living in an impoverished and violent neighborhood setting is a factor related to increased youth crime and delinquency (Attar, Guerra, & Tolan, 1994; Elliott et al., 1996). However, positive attributes are also available even in the most impoverished neighborhoods that can be galvanized to benefit youth. For example, *collective efficacy*, the availability of adults in the community who are ready and willing to intervene on behalf of children, is a feature identified as beneficial even in impoverished neighborhoods (Sampson et al., 1997).

Community-based approaches to promote positive youth development encompass a wide range of program types. However, even though a number of empirically validated family approaches are available, there is a serious dearth of community approaches tested with rigorous research methods. After-school programs, mentoring initiatives, and involvement of youth and adults in civic-minded endeavors are examples of community-based approaches that are potentially quite appealing to practitioners. These strategies often involve bringing youth together in groups. Given the need to contain potentially harmful iatrogenic effects, it is important that community-based programmatic efforts be fully tested scientifically.

After-school programs are becoming an increasingly greater part of the fabric of U.S. society. The increase in dual-career working families and single-parent households (Bianchi, 1995) has helped to fuel the need for quality after-school care. The U.S. Department of Education has funded thousands of programs across the nation for after-school programs and for the creation of 21st Century Community Learning Centers (as cited in Gottfredson, Gerstenblith, Soule, Womer, & Lu, 2004). These programs vary substantially in structure and content. However, work on after-school programs in Maryland shows that after-school programs have an impact especially upon the behavior of middle school students but not substantially on elementary school children. Furthermore, programs that incorporate attention to social skills development have higher levels of efficacy. Analyses of program effects reveal that these programs seem to work by increasing positive peer associations of youth. After-school programs present an area of potential promise, if effectively delivered, reducing negative peer associations and encouraging competency among youth (Gottfredson et al., 2004).

Many mentoring programs are conducted by community-based agencies that do not evaluate them. However, Big Brothers/Big Sisters (BB/BS) developed a community-based mentoring program that has been found to have positive effects for youth in a rigorous scientific evaluation (Grossman & Tierney, 1998). The evaluation was conducted in the eight largest BB/BS agencies in Texas, Ohio, New York, Minnesota, Kansas, and Arizona. A total of 959 youth ages 11–13 were included in the study. Approximately half of them were minority and/or youth from families eligible for food stamps or cash assistance. Their mentors were mostly upwardly mobile professionals; 60% of them were white and 60% had a college degree. Mentors were carefully screened, trained, and supervised by BB/BS staff, who contacted them monthly. The youth and family were contacted at least four times per year. Forty percent of the children reported seeing their mentor every week and another 44% two or three times per month.

At 18-month follow-up, youth participating in the mentoring program were significantly less likely to have initiated drug or alcohol use. They reported less aggressive behavior, slightly higher grade point averages, fewer days of skipping school, higher scores on academic self-competency, and better family relationships, particularly trust.

Many other mentoring programs are conducted by community-based agencies that either do not evaluate the programs or do not publish them in the empirical research literature. Meta-analytical reviews of mentoring programs reveal that there are several factors that help to determine the success of mentoring programs (DuBois & Neville, 1997). More effective programs have a clear conceptual framework that specifies what outcomes the program should influence and the process of effects. Ongoing training and supervision of the mentors and mentoring relationship are important features of more successful mentoring programs (Grossman & Tieney, 1998).

Mentoring and/or tutoring programs are also often included as components in multimodal prevention trials. In our experiences in implementing the EARLY ALLIANCE prevention trial, the structure of an after-school mentoring and reading tutoring program is critically important (Dumas, Prinz, Smith, & Laughlin, 1999). Because of the intense effort required to recruit and train volunteer mentors, programs using mentors and tutors may not use a design in which lower risk children also receive the mentors. In the EARLY ALLIANCE program alone, 75 reading mentors who committed on average to 4 hours every week were engaged in a single year. Thus, when this type of program occurs in an after-school setting, an important strategy is to structure the program to make predominant use of one-on-one contact to help contain potential contagion among children who are at risk for problem behavior. Structured programming, staff supervision, and a focus on youth social and communication skills are components found in effective after-school programs (Gottfredson et al., 2004). Given the popularity of mentoring and after-school programs, there is an unfortunate lack of a conceptual and theoretical framework for how these programs should work, or empirical data supporting their effectiveness. This little-researched area deserves much more theoretical and empirical attention.

SUMMARY

In the past decade or so, numerous approaches to improving child and adolescent behavior have been developed. Many show substantial support for their effectiveness. In general these effective approaches include parents, teachers, and other important adults in children's lives in the prevention and intervention strategies. Parental monitoring and parenting practices are important in guiding youth toward more positive activities and settings where they are less likely to become involved with deviant youth. Furthermore, when youth feel supported by their parents and communicate well with them, they are less susceptible to the influence of deviant peers. Family-oriented approaches may sometimes facilitate supportive groups of parents, an approach that has been found to be effective. Often in these models the youth are close by and program sessions often include a period of reunification where youth and parents work together to learn and apply what they have learned. Home-based programs with more intensive attention have been found to contain peer contagion and be effective for youth presenting more serious problems and juvenile delinquency.

Similarly, in the school setting, when practices are enacted by teachers and school-wide staff that promote good behavior and achievement, students often not only behave better but they feel closer to school staff and are more positive toward schooling in general. Many school-based efforts are universally available to youth either at a specified grade level or throughout the school. In these instances, the children who are included represent varying levels of competence, behavior, and social skills. In these instances, models of positive child competence are available in the setting to counter models of deviancy and antisocial behavior. Positive peer diffusion is another topic that could inform us about the possibility of youth being good models for each other (Prinz et al., 1994).

Finally, the community setting is yet another one where supportive programming may be provided to youth. After-school programs that include a mix of children can be helpful in exposing youth to positive peers (Gottfredson et al., 2004). However, there are also after-school programs that seek to include mentoring or tutoring as part of the program. If the program is for children and youth who are exhibiting behavioral difficulties, one strategy is to focus on the use of more one-on-one time and highly structured group times. The involvement of adults, as well as older adolescents, who are highly trained and well-supervised mentors and volunteers could likely prove critical. More efficacy and effectiveness research, especially as it pertains to peer contagion, is needed on these types of programs.

In multimodal programs we have much that can be learned about peer contagion in the varying types of intervention components. Data pertinent to this issue are being collected with respect to family-oriented, classroom management, and peer skills training programs. Further work could examine whether some components are especially effective in containing and redirecting potential contagion. Additionally, more process information is needed on the behavior and conversation that occurs in family groups and accompanying groups of adolescents that reunify with parents.

There are practical issues that arise relevant to contagion in programming that deserve more scientific inquiry. For example, though many staff may want to involve families in celebrations at the conclusion of home-based programs with more serious offenders, one might want to err on the side of caution and use gifts and awards to individual families instead of group-based types of celebrations. This has been less of an issue with universally administered family groups where the youth are more heterogeneous in their behavior and abilities. Another practical issue concerns field trips and important enriching activities for children in community-based programs. Many practitioners and children enjoy excursions of these sort and they may play a role in the children's developing sense of identity and future orientation. However, for these types of activities, a small adult-to-child ratio is likely quite important for effective behavioral management of children along with guidelines, rewards, and sanctions that are made clear to youth well in advance.

The field has amassed information on effective models in promoting positive behavior and competence in youth that reduce contagion. These models include mixed groups of children that offer positive young behavioral models along with the involvement of adults, be they parents, teachers, or community mentors in very meaningful ways in programming. Adults help to structure children's learning environments and provide a source of support and communication that decreases the allure of deviant peers.

CHAPTER 17

Promising Solutions in Housing and the Community

Jens Ludwig
and Greg Duncan

Housing policy affects the level and trend in neighborhood economic segregation found in the United States, which in turn affects the concentration of disadvantaged, at-risk youth.[1] If peer interactions affect the propensity to engage in antisocial behavior, then concentrated neighborhood poverty may lead poor youth to engage in more crime than they would in a more economically integrated environment (Glaeser, Sacerdote, & Scheinkman, 1996; Sampson, Raudenbush, & Earls, 1997). There are two general approaches to the problem of concentrated disadvantage. The first involves moving low-income parents and children to different neighborhoods to change the peer environments of youth. The second involves place-based interventions designed to directly address the types of social interactions through which peer influences might operate, such as substituting time with mentors for time with peers, to improve the life chances of youth and their families (i.e., make youth less disadvantaged, which may change the character of their peer associations) or to improve the conditions of the communities themselves.

The first half of our chapter reviews a variety of place-based approaches to the problem of deviant peer associations and youth crime. If peer effects are empirically important, then peer associations may play an important role in understanding the impacts of even those placed-based interventions that focus on reducing youth crime directly rather than targeting peer associations per se. The reason is that interventions that change the benefit–cost calculus associated with crime within a community will reduce the propensity that youth engage in crime, which depresses the overall delinquency of neighborhood youths' peer associations, which in turn further reduces the propensity that youth engage in crime. Put differently, if peer influences affect behavior, then the impacts of place-based interventions on crime may be amplified through "social multipliers" (Glaeser, Sacerdote, & Scheinkman, 1996, 2003).

The second part of our chapter reviews the efficacy of residential mobility programs that move high-risk youth out of high-crime neighborhoods. We pay particular attention to the Moving to Opportunity (MTO) housing mobility program, which is also discussed (but in less detail) in the chapters in this volume by Vigdor (Chapter 10) and by Cook and Ludwig (Chapter 4).

As noted by Cook and Ludwig (Chapter 4, this volume), the conditions under which mobility-based approaches will succeed depend in part on (1) the nature of the "social contagion function" and (2) the efficiency gains in public expenditures on social control from the concentration of high-risk youth. Put differently, there remains some uncertainty about whether the most efficient way to reduce crime in high-crime neighborhoods is through the use of place- versus mobility-based interventions.

PLACE-BASED INTERVENTIONS

In what follows we consider two distinct types of place-based interventions: (1) social programs that seek to either replace potentially delinquent peer associations with prosocial adult interactions or increase the opportunity costs of criminal activity (i.e., the benefits of engaging in prosocial behavior); and (2) criminal justice programs that seek to minimize the degree to which delinquent peer associations translate into action (criminal behavior) or more generally increase the direct cost of criminal behavior.

Social Programs

Concern about the limited economic opportunities available to those in disadvantaged urban neighborhoods has led to a variety of public programs that seek either to increase the supply of jobs available to city residents, or to increase the demand for labor by increasing the human capital of those who live in such communities. The best available evidence suggests that skill development is a more promising approach than efforts to spur the number of jobs in impacted urban areas.

Efforts to increase the supply of jobs in highly disadvantaged urban communities typically involve the provision of tax incentives to private firms to locate in such areas, known as "urban enterprise zones." Unfortunately, this type of intervention is difficult to evaluate, in large part because of the reliance on tract-level census data. Most existing urban enterprise zone programs are operated by state governments. Because most taxes are levied at the federal rather than at the state level, changes in state tax incentives may produce employment effects that are too modest to discern from other trends in economic outcomes found in tract-level data over time. Census tracts that are targeted for economic development programs may be unusual in a number of ways, so that comparison census tracts that were not targeted may provide a misleading picture of trends that would have been observed in targeted areas had they not received economic development services. And, more generally, we cannot be sure whether any changes in the average socioeconomic characteristics of tract residents over time reflect desired improvements in the economic conditions of those who lived there when the program began or, as with gentrification, the higher socioeconomic status (SES) of families moving into the neighborhoods.

With these caveats in mind, prior evaluations of U. S. enterprise zones suggest that they are unlikely to be a cost-effective means of improving economic opportunities in disadvantaged urban areas (Ladd, 1994). Setting aside the difficulties of deriving causal estimates for the effects of such programs, the estimated cost per new job created often equals or exceeds the annual earnings of these jobs. The main effect of such programs appears to be to siphon economic activity away from other areas (Ladd, 1994; see also Bushway & Reuter, 2002).

More promising are programs that boost the skills—and thus the employment and earnings prospects—of those who live in distressed areas. The evidence for early childhood programs appears to be particularly encouraging (Karoly et al., 1998). Early childhood may be a particularly promising time to intervene in the lives of disadvantaged youth because of suggestive evidence that the rate of learning may decline as children age (Entwisle, Alexander, & Olsen, 1997). Learning is also a cumulative process, so correcting the early disadvantages of low-income and minority children that lead to achievement differentials at the start of their schooling careers could affect their lifetime achievement trajectories.

Experimental evaluations of model early childhood interventions such as the Perry Preschool program suggest that very intensive, small-scale efforts may be able to reduce involvement with crime during adolescence (Schweinhart et al., 2005). Moreover, the magnitude of the benefits from such interventions is quite large, perhaps large enough to justify program costs (Donohue & Siegelman, 1998). Interestingly, the

Perry Preschool setting was a poor urban area (Ypsilanti, Michigan) in which social contagion forces are likely to be present. Other intensive preschool programs (e.g., the Abecedarian Program) located in more rural settings failed to generate significant reductions in crime, in part because of the relatively small amount of crime committed by the children in the control group (Campbell, Ramey, Pungello, Sparling, & Miller-Johnson, 2002).

Less clear is whether the early childhood education programs that governments operate on a large scale can reduce crime. A recent evaluation of the Chicago Child–Parent Centers (CPC) program also finds evidence for beneficial effects on criminal activity (Reynolds, Temple, Robertson, & Mann, 2001), although the simple regression-adjustment for other characteristics between participants and nonparticipants leaves open the possibility that the difference is driven by self-selection. More credible evidence on the effects of a publicly provided early childhood program comes from Gormley and Gayer's (2005) evaluation of the Tulsa universal prekindergarten program, which exploits the regression discontinuity in program participation generated by the age cutoff for eligibility. While Tulsa's program seems to have improved achievement test scores for disadvantaged minority students (but not for more affluent students or whites), given that the program is relatively new nothing is known about effects on later criminal offending.

Of particular importance is understanding the effect on delinquency and crime from the largest preschool intervention in the country, the federal government's Head Start program. One previous evaluation has found that Head Start participation may reduce later criminal activity, at least among black youth (Garces, Thomas, & Currie, 2002). To control for unmeasured family characteristics that may be associated with both youth outcomes and selection into Head Start, Garces and colleagues compared outcomes for siblings within the same family who differed with respect to Head Start participation. While this approach will control for unmeasured family attributes that are associated with Head Start enrollment, such sibling difference estimates are still susceptible to either time-varying family characteristics or unmeasured child-level attributes. A more recent evaluation uses a discontinuity in Head Start funding across counties generated by the way that the federal government launched the program in 1965 to identify impacts (Ludwig & Miller, 2005). Head Start appears to reduce child mortality from disease and other causes addressed by the program, increases educational attainment, and, while the effects on self-reported arrests are not statistically significant, the impact estimates are large as a fraction of the control mean and point in the direction of fewer arrests in areas with higher levels of Head Start funding.

Evidence from randomized experiments suggests that intensive programs targeted at older youth can also help reduce crime. For example, Job Corps is a 1-year intensive skills training program for disadvantaged youth that appears to reduce arrests by 16%, increase educational attainment (at least high school or GED completion), and increase earnings (Schochet, Burghardt, & Glazerman, 2000). These benefits taken together appear to justify the program's cost of $15,000 per participant.

A less expensive means of altering youth behavior is through mentoring programs—that is, by creating intimate, positive peer or adult influences in a teen's life. Evidence for the effects on crime from the well-known and intensive Quantum Opportunity Program (QOP) is somewhat mixed, with encouraging initial findings that are not clearly replicated in a follow-up multicity random assignment study.[2] More encouraging is a randomized evaluation of Big Brothers/Big Sisters (BB/BS) programs, which finds that 18 months after matching high-risk teens to mentors, teens in the mentored group were less likely to use drugs or alcohol or to hit someone else, and were more likely to attend and succeed in school (Tierney & Grossman, 1995). No statistically significant differences were found for self-reported property offending or vandalism. One concern is that this evaluation relies on self-reported youth behavior, and so in principle cannot disentangle a mentoring effect on youth willingness to report rather than engage in antisocial activity. In any case, the BB/BS program costs far less per participant (around $1,000) than more intensive youth interventions such as QOP or the Job Corps. Whether the program benefits justify these costs remains unclear to date, since we are not familiar with any attempt to monetize the program benefits. But given the substantial costs of crime to society—perhaps as much as $1 trillion per year (Anderson, 1999)—even modest reductions in criminal offending can lead to substantial dollar-valued benefits to society.

Recent evaluations of after-school programs find little evidence for changes in achievement test scores, but do suggest some improvements in the degree to which participating children and their parents engage with the child's school (Kane, 2004). One reason for the lack of detectable effects on achievement scores is that attendance in many of the programs was sporadic, which serves to further reduce the statistical power of the attendant evaluations to detect program impacts that are likely to be modest in magnitude. Whether these programs reduce youth involvement with crime is not clear.

Note that each of these programs (perhaps with the exception of Big Brothers/Big Sisters) serve to aggregate high-risk youth together, given that eligibility is typically limited to those from families with very low incomes. Increasing the representation of nondisadvantaged children to change the peer composition of such programs would divert program resources away from serving poor children.[3] Whether disaggregation in this case is a sensible policy will depend on the magnitude of any positive peer effects compared to the costs, both in terms of any negative peer effects on nonpoor youth who participate and in terms of the budget costs of enrolling nonpoor participants.

Criminal Justice Programs

Over the past several decades the United States has substantially increased its commitment to an involuntary housing program that serves to aggregate together the highest risk youth and adults in the society: prison. From 1970 to 1999, the incarceration rate in the United States increased by more than a factor of 4 (Blumstein, 2002), with this new prison population drawn disproportionately from low-income residents of our nation's most disadvantaged urban communities.

The net effect of this expansion in the prison population on crime will depend on the relative magnitudes of any negative peer effects that make prisoners more criminally active on prison exit than they were on prison entry, versus whatever deterrence and incapacitation effects that prison may generate to reduce crime, as well as any reductions in criminal offending that naturally occur as people serve out their prison sentences (i.e., age). The best available evidence to date, by Levitt (1996), suggests that expanding the prison population on net reduces crime. Importantly, Levitt's estimate is identified by using plausibly exogenous variation across states over time in the rate at which prisoners are released early. Put differently, Levitt's estimate suggests that any criminogenic peer influences on this sample from the aggregation of high-risk people within prison are outweighed by the crime-reducing effects of incarceration. The control/contagion calculus outlined by Cook and Ludwig (Chapter 4, this volume) suggests that there are net benefits to concentration.

We hasten to add that even though the net effects of prison expansion are to reduce crime, at current levels of incarceration the marginal criminal justice dollar may be more efficiently spent on policing than on prisons (Levitt, 2004). Levitt (1997, 2002) suggests that given current police practices, crime reductions from increased police spending are larger than crime reductions from increased prison spending. Levitt's analysis overcomes the problem that police spending may be both cause and consequence of local crime conditions by exploiting the fact that police and other forms of government spending tend to increase before mayoral elections. This finding is consistent with the idea that increasing society's capacity for control (in Cook and Ludwig's [Chapter 4, this volume] framework) helps contain the influence of negative peer associations and other criminogenic factors on people's behavior.

More relevant for our present purposes is whether policing programs that target the high-crime neighborhoods where high-risk youth aggregate can increase the effectiveness of police spending on crime. Available evidence suggests that the answer may be yes. The Minneapolis Hot Spots Patrol experiment during the late 1980s randomly assigned half of the city's highest crime places—"hot spots"—to receive 2.5 times more police resources than the other half of the city's worst hot spots, which received standard policing. An evaluation of the program suggests that the stepped-up policing helped reduce crime by around 13% (Sherman & Weisburd, 1995), suggesting an elasticity of crime with respect to police of $-0.13/2.5 = -0.05$. A related program in Pittsburgh assigned additional police resources to combat illegal gun carrying in the highest risk parts of towns during the highest risk times, and appears to have reduced gun crime (Cohen & Ludwig, 2003).

These types of targeted or hot spot patrol programs relate directly to the issue of economies of scale in formal social control discussed by Cook and Ludwig (Chapter 4, this volume). The specific mechanisms through which such patrol operations reduce crime will depend in part on why targeted hot spots are hot spots. For example, a disproportionate share of all crime in the Georgetown neighborhood of Washington, D.C., occurs on Thursday, Friday, and Saturday nights within a short distance of the main commercial intersection of Wisconsin Avenue and M Street. Presumably this stretch experiences unusually high crime rates because of the tendency of youth to aggregate on these evenings at the substantial number of bars located in this area. One policy option to reduce the number of high-risk (i.e., drunk) youth who aggregate in one place at one time would be to reduce the number of bars that could receive zoning permits within a given commercial area. The effects on crime of reducing high-risk peer interactions in this case would need to be weighed against the efficiency gains to the Washington, D.C., Metropolitan Police Department from being able to target policing at areas saturated with establishments that serve alcohol.

Some policing programs are targeted at the concentration of high-risk youth rather than at high-risk places. For example, in recent years a number of cities have used civil injunctions for relief from the "public nuisances" created by gang members engaging in certain activities within certain geographic areas. A recent evaluation of Los Angeles's experiences suggests that such injunctions may reduce violent crime by 5–10% (Grogger, 2002).

Ridding the nation of its most crime-infested public housing has also become a popular approach to combating neighborhood violence.

Created in 1992, the HOPE VI program has demolished or slated for demolition 72,000 public housing units and promoted mixed-income housing and voucher subsidies. Since 1993, the U.S. Department of Housing and Urban Development (HUD) has awarded nearly $5 billion for redevelopment and client services. Hope VI has replaced demolished units with 41,500 new public housing units and 15,000 homeownership units, "affordable units" for the working poor, and market-rate units.

One way that Hope VI could affect crime is by altering the physical space in which low-income families live. For decades urban planners and criminologists have been concerned with the possibility that some building designs contribute to crime—for example, through the construction of enclosed stairwells that are difficult for local residents to monitor. Alternatively, some Hope VI programs may reduce the concentration of high-risk youth by either redistributing poor families across different neighborhoods or by constructing mixed-income housing developments to replace the old public housing sites.

Unfortunately, to date little reliable empirical work is available about the effects of the Hope VI program on criminal offending or other youth outcomes. Credible empirical evidence on the effects of building design and physical space is also in short supply. Better evidence is available on the effects of redistributing public housing families to different neighborhoods, an issue that is taken up in the next section of this chapter.

RESIDENTIAL MOBILITY INTERVENTIONS

A long-standing federal policy approach to solve the problem of crime-infested public housing developments is housing mobility programs, such as HUD's Section 8 tenant-based rental subsidy programs. These Section 8 programs (now called "housing choice vouchers") provide low-income families with a financial subsidy to move to a private-market apartment or house that meets certain program requirements.

Currently, around 2.1 million low-income families receive housing vouchers, up from 162,000 vouchers in 1977 (Center on Budget and Policy Priorities, 2003; Olsen, 2003). Housing vouchers hold some appeal for both conservatives and liberals: they rely on the private market rather than the government to provide housing services to the poor (a plus for conservatives) and at the same time improve housing quality for low-income families and provide them with greater choice over where they live (a plus for liberals). And yet the increased residential mobility that housing vouchers have allowed poor families is controversial, since residents of working- and middle-class neighborhoods fear that the arrival of low-income neighbors will lower their property values and increase their own children's social problems.

How might mobility programs affect youth criminal offending? Deviant peer influence is neither a necessary nor a sufficient condition for mobility programs to influence youth crime. While mobility programs change the peer group choice set of youth, it is possible that youth simply reselect into the same sort of peer group as in their old neighborhood (Jencks & Mayer, 1990). In this case mobility may have little net effect on youth crime even if deviant peer influence is quite important in practice. Alternatively, mobility programs could have very large effects on youth crime even if deviant peer influence is unimportant, because such programs also change a variety of other neighborhood characteristics that might influence youth crime, such as the quality of local public schools or policing and the availability of prosocial adult role models.

How successful in practice are mobility programs in reducing criminal offending by youth in households that receive vouchers? With over a quarter century of history, the Chicago-based Gautreaux residential mobility program has been the subject of a number of evaluation studies (Rubinowitz & Rosenbaum, 2001). Gautreaux resulted from a 1976 Supreme Court decree in a lawsuit against the Chicago Housing Authority (CHA) and HUD in which the Supreme Court found that CHA and HUD had engaged in "systematic and illegal segregation." It authorized an expansive remedy, allowing African American families to relocate within and beyond the city limits into the six-county Chicago metropolitan area. Between 1976 and 1998, over 7,000 families participated in the Gautreaux program.

Rubinowitz and Rosenbaum's analyses focused on the distinction between families whose program-induced moves were to a city-of-Chicago versus a suburban address. One key to the Gautreaux study is that public housing families were assigned to a wait list organized by the agency implementing the relocation effort. This local housing agency also identified apartments for families on the voucher wait list, and most families reportedly accepted the first apartment that was offered. The degree to which Gautreaux breaks the link between family preferences and mobility outcomes—the self-selection problem that plagues most previous studies of neighborhood effects more generally—remains unclear. Convincing documentation of the voucher offer and acceptance process remains difficult to reconstruct from available administrative records.

In any case, several studies of Gautreaux have found that the suburban moves have conferred advantages for both mothers (in terms of labor market outcomes) and children (in terms of school outcomes), although more recent studies of Gautreaux show smaller impacts (Keels, Duncan, & Rosenbaum, 2004; Mendenhall, Duncan, & DeLuca, 2003). Studies of impacts on youth crime outcomes have not been completed. Nor, given their design, could any of the Gautreaux-focused work compare outcomes for program movers relative to either nonmovers or to comparable families not offered the chance to participate in the program.

The Moving to Opportunity program was designed with a random assignment, experimental evaluation in order to provide exactly these kinds of comparisons. Given the unusually large scale to this program, and the high quality of its implementation and evaluation, we review its structure and results at some length, which are summarized in Orr and colleagues (2003).

In operation since 1994 in five cities (Baltimore, Boston, Chicago, Los Angeles, and New York), HUD's Moving to Opportunity (MTO) demonstration assigned low-income families living in public housing within high-poverty neighborhoods into one of three research groups. Families in the *control group* received no special assistance but were eligible for all programs other than Section 8. A *Section 8 group* received conventional Section 8 private-market housing subsidies with no constraints on relocation choices.

Most interesting was the *experimental group*, which consisted of families that received Section 8–type housing vouchers but could only redeem them with moves to low-poverty census tracts (those with poverty rates under 10%). Movers in both the experimental and the Section 8-only groups were required to sign leases for 1 year. Those who moved again before the initial lease expiration date lost their eligibility for their financial subsidy, while families who wished to relocate after the first year were free to do so without restriction and were allowed to keep their subsidy. The experimental group also received substantial counseling and search assistance from a local nonprofit agency. With such dramatic changes in neighborhood conditions, the MTO experimental group may provide an upper bound on estimates of what might be accomplished through neighborhood mobility programs.

To understand the nature of program impacts, it is important to realize that most control families moved at least once during the study period and most who moved improved their neighborhood conditions. This is hardly surprising since control families who volunteered for the MTO opportunity did so with the specific goal of gaining help with a move, and all controls were free to move at any point without either financial or counseling resources to facilitate their moves. In fact, all low-income families move at surprisingly high rates (Gramlich, Laren, & Sealand, 1992). Further adding to mobility rates among the control group is the operation over this period of HUD's Hope VI program (described above), which led to the demolition of many of the public housing buildings from which MTO program participants were drawn.

To focus attention on the moves to low-poverty areas, we ignore the Section 8 treatment group (results for which are detailed in the Orr et al., 2003, report) and focus exclusively on the "experimental" group, all of whom were offered the opportunity to move to neighborhoods with poverty rates under 10%. Taken as a whole, the neighborhood poverty rate of all families assigned to the experimental group was 31%, which was significantly lower than the 39% rate averaged across all controls. As might be expected, the mean neighborhood poverty rate (22%) was lower still for experimental families who moved under the terms of the program. And at the time of the follow-up, experimental families who continued to reside in their destination units enjoyed the lowest neighborhood poverty rates of all: 13%. The higher poverty rates for the larger set of experimental families moving under the terms of the program than for the subset of experimental families moving only once shows that the subsequent mobility of experimental families undid some of the likely advantages of their initial moves.

The fact that many experimental group families moved to neighborhoods with poverty rates above 10% once they were allowed to under MTO program rules suggests that there may be some optimal degree of neighborhood change from the perspective of the program participants themselves. To the extent to which families have some preference for living near their baseline neighborhoods or near similar "types" of families more generally, such preferences should factor into an accounting of the costs and benefits of mobility interventions.

Despite the partial convergence in neighborhood conditions between experimental and control families, experimental families nonetheless experience substantial and sustained improvements in neighborhood quality. When asked at follow-up, nearly half (45%) of MTO controls reported feeling either "unsafe" or "very unsafe" on the street near their homes at night, while a quarter had similar feelings during the day. Assignment to the experimental group cut these respective fractions to 31% and 16%. Similar improvements were found in other indicators of neighborhood safety (Orr et al., 2003, Ch. 3). Moreover, the neighborhoods of families in the experimental group were also richer in "collective efficacy" (Sampson et al., 1997), with 60% of adults moving under the terms of experimental group conditions saying that it was likely that neighbors would do something about misbehaving youth. This is almost twice as high as the corresponding fraction (37%) of control group adults reporting that their neighbors would get involved in a similar situation. All in all, the MTO intervention proved very successful at addressing the neighborhood crime problems that sparked most adult participants' interest in the program.

What about the criminal involvement of the children in MTO experimental families? The pattern of findings observed for MTO youth is more complicated than "better neighborhoods, less crime." We focus on MTO's "intent-to-treat" effect, defined as the difference in average outcomes between all youth assigned to the experimental group (regardless of whether they move through the MTO program or not) and all youth assigned to the control group. Note that this intent-to-treat effect is not susceptible to bias from the fact that only some (self-selected) members of the experimental group actually relocated through the MTO program, since the comparison is between all families assigned to the experimental group (movers and nonmovers together) with all families assigned to the control group. If assignment to the experimental group has no effect on youth in families that do not relocate through MTO, then the effect of moving on the movers—the "effect of treatment on the treated" in evaluation jargon—will simply equal the intent-to-treat effect divided by the fraction of families assigned to the experimental group who move as part of MTO (Bloom, 1984).

Initial findings from the Baltimore and Boston MTO sites found short-term reductions in violent and other problem behaviors among experimental boys compared to controls (Katz, Kling, & Liebman, 2001; Ludwig et al., 2001). These short-term reductions were quite consistent with what one might have expected given that the most important reason parents reported for signing up for MTO was to get away from crime and drugs—that is, to improve the safety and peer environment for themselves and their children.

More recent data provide evidence for similar short-term reductions in violent criminal offending across the full set of MTO cities, although this program impact appears to fade over time. More worrisome are positive treatment–control difference in property crime arrests. On net, 4–7 years after random assignment and compared to control boys, boys in families assigned to the experimental group had been arrested more, and exhibited significantly worse behavior according to both self-report and parents' reports. Affected items in the behavior problem index include being disobedient at home or school, being withdrawn, or bullying or being cruel to others (Kling, Ludwig, & Katz, 2005).

For female youth in MTO the pattern of program impacts is more encouraging: relative to controls, girls in the experimental group experience fewer arrests for violent, property, and other crimes, and exhibit improvements in behavior and well-being along a variety of other measures as well (Kling et al., 2005; Kling & Liebman, 2004a, 2004b). Interestingly, experimental group families with boys and girls appear to move into similar types of neighborhoods, so this difference in MTO impacts appears to reflect gender differences in how youth respond to similar types of moves. This conclusion is supported most clearly by a sibling analysis showing that brothers respond quite differently from their sisters to the same family moves (Kling et al., 2005). One implication is that the "fade out" of the beneficial effects of mobility on violent crime for male youth after the first few years after random assignment is not due to their moving back to their baseline neighborhoods.

All school-age children spend substantial portions of their day away from home, with adolescents having the greatest latitude to choose where and with whom they spend their time. Children in families assigned to the experimental group were significantly less likely to report gangs in their neighborhoods or schools, or hearing gunshots recently in their neighborhoods (Orr et al., 2003). But no statistically significant impacts emerged in reports of witnessing drug sales, shootings or stabbings, nor in the child him- or herself reporting being threatened or injured by a knife or gun. Apparent in these data is the failure of better neighborhoods, which might be expected to breed much less crime-related social contagion than the origin neighborhoods, to translate into uniformly safer neighborhoods for and less crime committed by youth. Why might this be the case?

As mentioned above, a first important fact is that experimental group families undertook steps that undid some of the possible advantages of moving to middle-class neighborhoods. Subsequent moves undertaken by experimental group families put them in neighborhoods that were considerably less affluent than their original placements, although still more affluent than the neighborhoods of control families. Although experimental families moved to more affluent areas, most did not move to racially or ethnically integrated neighborhoods. Discrimination may have limited the availability of high-quality public services in minority neighborhoods.

Second, the quality of the schools attended by experimental group children did not improve as much as might be expected. Orr and colleagues (2003, Ch. 6) show that the test-score ranking of schools attended by children in experimental group families who moved in conjunction with the program was only the 25th percentile. While significantly higher than the 17th percentile ranking of schools attended by control group children, it is certainly not the case that MTO led many experimental group children to attend high-quality schools.[4] When youth themselves were asked to characterize the climate and resources of their schools, virtually no experimental/control group differences were found (Orr et al., 2003, Ch. 6). Evidence from a qualitative study of MTO families (Popkin, Harris, & Cunningham, 2001) suggests that school choice now built into many urban school systems gave parents the choice of sending their children to schools close to their origin neighborhoods near where relatives lived, and parents took advantage of these opportunities. Perhaps they did so because they were more comfortable with their children's original schools or schools in neighborhoods with which they were familiar.

Third, and closest to the point of deviant peer influence, it appears that children's own choices of peers and activities may have maintained (for girls) or undone (for boys) some of the potential advantages of the safer and more affluent neighborhoods. Adolescent girls, but not boys, in the experimental group were significantly more likely than their control group counterparts to participate in sports teams, engage in structured after-school activities, and have good school attendance records (Orr et al., 2003, Appendix E). In contrast, experimental group adolescent boys but not girls were more likely than their control group counterparts to have friends who use drugs. Of course, given the nature of the MTO experimental design, it is not possible to determine whether these program effects on peer influences are cause or consequence of the program's effects on youth delinquency.

Fourth, it appears that neighborhood advantages failed to translate into the kinds of family advantages that might have promoted children's well-being. Adults moving in conjunction with the MTO program were similar to their control group counterparts in their employment status, welfare dependence, family income, parenting practices, and connections to their children's schools and the parents of their children's friends. A concern with much of the nonexperimental literature on neighborhood influences is that it may be difficult to distinguish neighborhood effects from family influences. Perhaps something similar is operating with MTO—truly effective policies may require both neighborhood and family changes.

CONCLUSIONS

We have considered both place-based and residential mobility strategies for addressing the problems of youth crime in areas of concentrated urban poverty. Intervention evaluations have done a much better job of indicating what doesn't work than in pointing to promising program models.

Briefly, local community development efforts are unlikely to be helpful in reducing youth deviant behavior. Evidence for programs that promote stepped-up policing and punishments for criminal behavior, and for social programs targeted at both preschool children and adolescents, is more hopeful.

While the beneficial programs appear to produce more benefits than costs, the costs themselves are far from trivial. On the criminal justice side, policing appears to be a more cost-effective way of reducing crime than increasing the severity of punishment, perhaps in part because the United States has already substantially increased the scale of imprisonment over the past several decades. In terms of social programs, evidence suggests that intensive early childhood programs can improve long-term behavior among high-risk children. Whether less-intensive, large-scale programs such as Head Start can accomplish similar ends is less clear. Moreover, from a political perspective, intensive early childhood education has the potential drawbacks of being expensive and only relevant for crime rates 10–15 years into the future, when participants reach their peak criminal offending ages. Teen mentoring programs have the advantage of targeting the highest risk offending population. Interestingly, unlike the case of early childhood education, the best available evidence to date is stronger in support of less intensive mentoring programs (such as Big Brothers/Big Sisters) than for more intensive programs such as the Quantum Opportunities Program.

Neighborhood violence and other ills may indeed contribute to the behavior problems of children growing up in impoverished, high-crime communities. But the MTO evidence suggests that dramatic changes in neighborhood quality may not produce corresponding reductions in the level of violence experienced by children and adolescents. Girls appear more responsive than boys to neighborhood-based opportunities and are more likely to enjoy the mental health benefits that these improved opportunities may provide. In contrast, deviant behavior for males may actually increase rather than decrease.

In thinking about these conclusions, it is useful to consider exactly what it is that we are seeking to minimize: the number of criminal events perpetrated by youth, or the social harm inflicted by youth deviant behavior? In the case of MTO, the intervention seems to reduce the social costs of crime committed by males, even if the number of offenses increases, because the intervention leads to fewer costly violent crimes but even more less-costly property offenses (Kling et al., 2005). A related advantage of an MTO-type program is that there are few costs that show up in the government budget explicitly, although nonbudget costs in the form of spillover peer effects on destination-area youth may be very important (but are currently not well understood).

From a policy perspective, it is also important to think about the effects of mobility programs on society as a whole. Despite the fact that subsequent mobility undid some of the initial advantages of MTO-induced moves, the MTO experimental design provides a powerful research platform for learning about the causal effects of neighborhood mobility on highly disadvantaged youth, even if we cannot convincingly disentangle the effects of changing peer options from the effects of changing adult role models, schools, police, or other neighborhood attributes. Yet MTO provides us with little power in detecting the effects of resorting disadvantaged youth across neighborhoods on the overall volume of youth crime in U.S. society. To answer this question we would need some understanding of how the influx of MTO youth into more affluent communities affects criminal behavior by youth already living in such areas.

The possibility of deviant peer influence means that even if MTO is good for program participants, it may be less beneficial for youth living in destination areas. Destination neighborhood impacts are impossible to detect, since MTO purposively avoided reconcentrating families in low-poverty areas, leaving too few MTO families in any given neighborhood to convincingly identify their impact on local youth. Some understanding of both the system-level effects of mobility programs and the role played by deviant peer influences in particular are likely to require nonexperimental analysis, which raises a number of important research challenges (see Vigdor, Chapter 10, this volume). Given their importance for public policy, these are challenges that are very much worth taking on.

NOTES

1. Despite a decline in the fraction of Americans living in high-poverty census tracts (with poverty rates > 40%) from 1990 to 2000, nearly twice as many Americans lived in such high-poverty areas in 2000 as in 1970 (Jargowsky, 2003). Housing policies that affect the concentration of poverty include decisions about how much housing assistance to provide to poor families, the form that such housing should take (people-based subsidies such as housing vouchers or place-based subsidies such as public housing), the locations in which place-based housing projects should be built, the ability of low-poverty townships to engage in exclusionary zoning that limits low-cost housing within the jurisdiction, and the degree to which the government enforces antidiscrimination laws.

2. Initial evaluations of the Quantum Opportunities Program (QOP) provided suggestive evidence that participants were less likely to be involved with crime than nonparticipants (Hahn, Leavitt, & Aaron, 1994). However, more recent evidence from Mathematica Policy Research's randomized QOP evaluation in seven cities finds short-term improvements in educational attainment but not for crime (www.mathematica-mpr.com/education/qop.asp, accessed May 9, 2004).

3. Only if nonpoor parents were asked to cover the full cost of the program for their children would this not be the case, although most early childhood proposals include some subsidy to even nonpoor families to encourage their participation (see, e.g., Wolfe & Scrivner, 2003).

4. In contrast, the percentile ranking of neighborhood poverty was 22 percentile points higher for experimental than for control families (Sanbonmatsu et al., 2004).

CHAPTER 18

Creating a Legal and Organizational Context for Reducing Peer Influence

Joel Rosch
and Cindy Lederman

The final decision about whether to place a deviant youth in a group set-ting where he or she is likely to experience peer influence is often made not by social scientists, but in the legal system by judges, prosecutors, magistrates, school officials, clerks, and other hearing officers. These de-cisions are often made while balancing a number of issues, including both the immediate and long-term safety of the child, concerns about public safety, the civil liberties of child and his or her family, and adher-ence to justice principles that require like cases to be treated alike.

Understanding how and why these decisions are made, the con-straints on these decisions, and how these decisions might be better in-formed by information about deviant peer influence is essential if the recommendations in this volume are going to have an impact on public policy. Many of the policies and interventions discussed in earlier chap-ters on juvenile mental health and education highlight programs that re-quire a level of coordination, client control, and surveillance that may not exist in many communities. This chapter describes the changing legal and organizational context within which decisions about whether to place youths in a group setting are made. Although it focuses primarily on juvenile justice, mental health, and, to a limited degree, child welfare, some of the lessons might also apply to educational settings.

The first part of this chapter describes the origins and purpose of the juvenile court and the intent of the juvenile court movement. The second part describes the development and workings of therapeutic courts, which developed out of the juvenile court movement. The third part describes legal innovations growing out of these movements that support the development and implementation of interventions that decrease the probability of aggregating deviant peers. The last part addresses some of the challenges that these kinds of programs face and how to bring new information about peer contagion into these decisions.

THE ORIGINS OF JUVENILE COURT

"Little Jim" Guild was 12 years old when he was convicted of murder and sentenced to death after a 2 day trial. As thousands of people arrived to witness the hanging of the boy, "Little Jim" was conducting a mock trial in his cell with the mice he had captured. (Shepard, 1999, p. 13)

Until the early 19th century in the United States, children as young as age 7 could be tried in criminal court and, if convicted, sentenced to death. The establishment of special courts and incarceration facilities for juveniles was part of the Progressive Era's reforms, along with kindergarten, child labor laws, mandatory education, school lunches, and vocational education (McCord, Widom, & Crowell, 2001). All these reforms recognized that children were not just small adults and that it was necessary to treat juveniles in a way quite different from adults. Thereafter, the specific reason why a juvenile was brought to court (whether suffering from abuse and neglect or charged with committing a crime) was less important than understanding the child's life situation and finding appropriate, individualized rehabilitative services (McCord et al., 2001).

Since the inception of the first juvenile court in the United States, authorized by the Illinois Juvenile Court Act in 1899, the emphasis has been on the child, not the offense. The children were accorded confidentiality, and the institution was less formal than other courts. The act gave courts jurisdiction over delinquent youth under age 16 and

any child who for any reason is destitute or homeless or abandoned or dependent on the public for support: or has not proper parental care or guardianship; or who habitually begs or receives alms; or who is living in any house of ill fame or with any vicious or disreputable person; or whose home, by reason of neglect, cruelty or depravity on the part of parents, guardian or other person in whose care it may be, is an unfit place for such child; and any child under age 8 who is found peddling or selling any article or singing or playing a musical instrument upon the street or giving any public entertainment. (Illinois Juvenile Court Act, 1899)

By 1925, a functioning juvenile court existed in every state except Maine and Wyoming (McCord et al., 2001).

The social reformers who created the juvenile court over 100 years ago believed that children's culpability for their actions was limited and that delinquency was closely related to poor parenting, neglect, poverty, and lack of moral values. They believed that children were malleable and that rehabilitation could occur under the jurisdiction of a benevolent juvenile court through which the state adopted the philosophy of *parens patriae* (Lederman, 1999). By their design, these courts were supposed to have the power to fashion solutions to meet the needs of the child, even if this meant being able to impose various kinds of controls on the child's behavior that would never be imposed on adults. These courts also had the ability to remove children from their parents if such removal was seen as being in the best interests of the child. In practice, however, decisions were based on the idea that it was usually better to remove children from unfit parents; it was assumed that an alternative placement would be better for the child. There was usually no way to weigh whether an institutional placement, which could exacerbate the child's maladjustment by warehousing youth or aggregating them in large, unsupervised groups, was actually better for the child in comparison to continued home placement (Kernan & Lansford, 2004).

The juvenile court was explicitly charged with the duty of protecting and rehabilitating children even when everyone else had failed them. It was supposed to be a place where the needs of children are paramount. Unfortunately, the juvenile court of the 1990s has shifted from an institution focused on social welfare and acting in a child's best interest to one focused on children's due process rights (see In re Gault, 387 U.S. 1[1967]), and more recently on accountability and punishment (Lederman, 1999). However, by their design, courts that serve children are still supposed to have the power to fashion solutions to meet the needs of the child, even if this means being able to impose various kinds of controls on the child, and often on the parent.

Because they were supposed to meet the needs of specific children, these courts regularly accepted testimony from "experts" about what kinds of interventions/sanctions would be most likely to lead to the rehabilitation of the child. These courts were supposed to act in the long-term interests of the child and were not supposed to impose sanctions that increased rather than decreased the likelihood of future deviant behavior. The sanctions imposed on children by the juvenile court have always been influenced by widely held understandings of the development of antisocial behavior among children. For the most part, the sanctions developed for children were variations on sanctions developed for adults. Most involved putting children in group settings with children like themselves. If a new consensus is developing that aggregating deviant peers leads to an increased likelihood of future deviance, the juvenile court is one institution that is uniquely suited to take this information into account to help fashion new ways to deal with juveniles (Berman, 2004).

THE RISE OF THERAPEUTIC JURISPRUDENCE

Therapeutic jurisprudence is a relatively recent movement that is based on many of the same ideas as the juvenile court (Corrigan & Becker, 2003). The term was first used in 1987. It usually describes courtrooms where judges retain jurisdiction over a case after fact finding and adjudication; administer case management functions under judicial order; and, within legislatively set boundaries, rely on social science as they exercise discretion over what to do with clients. As in the juvenile court, under therapeutic justice judges have a broad range of powers to act in the interests of clients who are deemed to be more in need of treatment and protection than of punishment. One of the goals of therapeutic justice is to allow judges to make better use of social science (Corrigan & Becker, 2003; Slobogin, 1996).

While these courts continue to decide what people *deserve* because of their past actions, they put much greater emphasis on what people *need* for future success. Therapeutic jurisprudence tries to use legal rules, legal procedures, and, most importantly, a more active role for judges and other legal actors to promote the psychological or physical well-being of the people it affects (Wexler, 1992). Therapeutic justice has extended this approach to substance abusers, the mentally ill, and parts of the child welfare system. The decisions of these courts can have an impact on educational institutions as well as on mental health, juvenile justice, and social welfare agencies (Wexler, 2005). Where successful treatment depends on coordinating services, the courts are often used to forge new collaborative relationships between agencies.

With therapeutic justice (sometimes also called "problem-solving courts"), judges usually retain jurisdiction over cases beyond fact finding and sentencing in order to monitor cases to see that orders are properly enforced and the clients' problems are addressed. Clients often come back into court for monitoring. In some settings, judges also monitor, and sometimes require, higher levels of interagency coordination (Berman, 2004; Wexler, 2005). This directive can include ordering agencies to work together and encouraging the creation of community-based treatment. In addition to keeping some jurisdiction over cases until the treatment is complete, and actively supervising the monitoring of clients in community programs, this process enables judges to make better use of social science in making decisions about how clients will be treated. Depending on the amount of information and resources available to the courts, these programs have been very successful in a number of communities and exist in various stages in a growing number of states (Gilbert, Grimm, & Parnham, 2001).

The focus on consequences and on empirically verifiable results based on various social sciences sets therapeutic jurisprudence apart from other jurisprudential philosophies. Not only does it suggest that rulings be examined for their *actual* effects as compared to their *desired* effects, it also encourages the use of the social sciences throughout the rule-making process. Increasingly, both legislative and administrative rules are requiring agencies to adopt and use evidence-based programming. Judges are often required to see that this programming occurs. This marriage of the law and science opens the door for research to affect decision making. Therapeutic jurisprudence also puts judges into different and (for some) sometimes uncomfortable roles, ones often associated more with executive rather than with judicial functions (Arrigo, 2004; Bentley, 2003; Berman, 2004; Carson, 2003). Under this model, a judge may retain a case for a number of years, while getting reports and issuing orders based on the advice of clinicians rather than legal precedent.

This is a different role for judges. A judge is traditionally understood as a public servant who must balance the law, the public's interest, the well-being of the parties before him, and his or her own conscience. The role of the judge and the law itself is quite limited. Edmund Burke, in the 18th century, claimed that the vocabulary and syntax of natural law were too impoverished to reflect adequately the reality of moral choices in a political society (Cover, 1975). Under therapeutic justice, judges must play a more active role in cases and use a wider range of information in making decisions (Casey, 2004; Nolan, 2003).

A major obstacle to the exercise of therapeutic jurisprudence is the lack of training in social science for the legal actors charged with implementation. One of the challenges of this volume is to develop a strategy to disseminate information about the iatrogenic effects of peer aggregation to legal practitioners and to offer judges new ways to use their authority to improve the placement of children. This information should include not only when and how the iatrogenic effects of peer aggregation occur, but also programmatic options available to mitigate these effects.

INNOVATIVE MODELS OF LEGAL INTERVENTION THAT DO NOT AGGREGATE DEVIANT YOUTH

Courts and communities adopting therapeutic jurisprudence are already using a growing number of approaches to facilitate the treatment or rehabilitation of deviant juveniles that do not aggregate deviant peers. Many of these programs, which are described in more detail elsewhere in this volume, require the ability to monitor and control juveniles in their home communities. Others include general approaches to early diversion from institutional settings; various forms of restorative justice, including victim–offender mediation and teen court; and new forms of civil orders that increase our ability to control the behavior of individuals in community settings. As documented throughout this volume, there is growing evidence to support these kinds of interventions as preferable to interventions that group children with other deviant youth (National Institutes of Health, 2004). However, public acceptance of these programs is likely to be dependant on our ability to ensure increased monitoring and control.

Although the growth of therapeutic jurisprudence is fraught with dangers and challenges, these trends increase the likelihood that the social context needed for the programs described in this volume can be created. These are emerging practices and are not without their critics. One of the challenges is to demonstrate how these changes can support the emergence of clinical and social practices that will give us more effective and efficient interventions. The best known of these programs are carried out in the juvenile justice system and in some educational settings. They include the following.

Early Diversion Programs

These programs are attractive because even the formal processing by juvenile justice agencies appears to aggregate deviant peers and may amplify criminal activity and future problem behavior (Smith & Paternoster, 1990). Diversion programs vary greatly in design, implementation, and eligibility. In a controlled group study of juvenile diversion programs, the most positive recidivism-reduction effects were among juveniles who were held individually accountable for their actions, but were diverted from the justice system and any attempt to aggregate them with other delinquent youth (Eccles & Goodman, 2002; Emshoff & Blakely, 1983; Patrick, Marsh, Bundy, Mimura, & Perkins, 2004).

Victim–Offender Mediation

Victim–offender mediation (VOM) is a restorative justice mechanism that has been studied over the past 20 years in the United States, Canada, New Zealand, and Scotland and is regarded as an effective means of holding offenders accountable for their actions without prolonged exposure to deviant peers (Umbreit, Coates, & Vos, 2001). Instead of spending time with groups of other offenders, youth in VOM programs interact with victims. One study found that VOM participants re-offended at a rate 32% lower than nonparticipants (Nugent, Umbreit, Winimaki, & Paddock, 2001). In addition to the reduction in their delinquent behavior, VOM participants are more likely to complete restitution (Umbreit, 1993). Addressing community safety, victims have a positive response to VOM, including less fear and anxiety (Braithwaite, 2002; Umbreit, 1994).

Teen Court Programs

These programs bring juvenile offenders who admit their guilt into a courtroom setting where other teens play the role of defense attorney, prosecution, and jury to determine the offender's sentence. These programs are usually restricted to nonviolent offenders. Although most teen courts are administered by juvenile justice agencies, some are led by school systems. The majority of the jurors are supposed to be normative teen volunteers. As part of their sentence, teens are sentenced to participate in future teen court sessions and help sentence other delinquent teens. These programs bring together both deviant and nondeviant peers and ask them to make judgments about other deviant youth. Many of these programs also require a parent to be present to watch his or her child be judged by other children. In controlled experiments, successful teen court programs reduced recidivism rates by an average of 8–12% compared to 20% for similar cases handled in juvenile court. These programs are usually set in courtroom or school settings (Butts, Buck, & Coggeshall, 2002).

In the mental health and child welfare arenas, new options are also being developed to give judges more control over placements in community settings, reassuring clients and the community that agencies will do what they are supposed to be doing. Increasingly, judges are being asked to play a greater role in ensuring that juveniles receive appropriate mental health services (Giffin & Jenuwine, 2002; Petrucci & Hartley, 2004).

Community Commitment Orders

These and other civil remedies are designed to control behavior in community settings. The failure of many community-based treatments is often attributed to a lack of funding. However, studies of these programs show that more often failure comes from organizational failures and the lack of an effective mechanism to ensure that treatment protocols were being followed (Monahan, Swartz, & Bonnie, 2003).

One advantage of group settings is supposed to be increased control of both clients and treatments. These controls include monitoring and enforcement of medication plans and adherence to therapies. Community commitment orders allow judges to re-create this control and to enforce adherence in community and foster care settings. People can be ordered to allow home visits from staff, to appear at a certain time to take medication, to be at a particular place, to stay away from other places, or to adhere to treatment regimens. These orders can be combined with a variety of technological aids, including electronic monitoring, web cams, GPS tracking devices, and the like to increase compliance as well as community and patient safety. There is a growing body of evidence that community-based therapeutic plans have the greatest likelihood of long-term success and usually cost much less than institutional care (Swartz et al., 2001). As long as these tools are used *instead of*, rather than as *additions to* institutional placement, there is usually little objection from clients and their advocates (Monahan, 2003).

Civil orders have also been used with varying degrees of success to control gang and other criminal enterprises. Nuisance abatement orders, building condemnations, orders about with whom people can associate, changing traffic patterns and zoning, and a host of civil and regulatory tools have been used as part of community policing efforts across the United States. Survey research shows that citizens' satisfaction with community policing programs and perceptions of improvement to public safety is often affected by these kinds of civil changes as much or more than by the number of arrests police make or the density of police patrols (Sherman, 2002; Trojanowitz & Bucqueroux, 1994).

Psychiatric Advance Directives

Psychiatric advance directives (PADs) are another kind of civil order that has been developed to deal with risk management and adherence to treatment issues outside of institutional settings (Duke University Program on Psychiatric Advance Directives, 2005). These directives were originally designed for use with individuals who lapse in and out of mental illness. Whereas community commitment orders are usually imposed by the court on an individual or family and are not voluntary, PADs are voluntarily drawn up by individuals and brought to the court. Like a living will, with a PAD, an individual signs an order allowing a custodian, usually a parent or close relative, to use the legal system to enforce compliance with treatment if that person is judged by the custodian not to be competent to make decisions any longer. The individual signing the PAD sets the limits on what the custodian can and cannot do. Recent studies are exploring whether PADs can be an effective way to increase compliance with community-based mental health treatment (Duke University Program on Psychiatric Advance Directives, 2005). Parents can sign PADs to allow treatment for their children. Some school districts ask parents to sign advanced directives allowing them greater freedom, including drug testing, when dealing with disruptive students (C. Duber, personal communication, May 15, 2003).

Given that compliance is a major obstacle to the success of community-based treatment programs, therapeutic jurisprudence, community commitment orders, PADs, Early Diversion, VOMs, and teen courts, although far from foolproof, hold the potential to increase the acceptance of treatment programs that use community and family settings because they are a mechanism to ensure compliance. Increasingly, states are exploring the use of these tools (Monahan, 2003).

OBSTACLES TO OVERCOME

Although the research in this volume may demonstrate that placing deviant youth in settings with other deviant youth leads to bad outcomes for many children in the education, mental health, child welfare, and juvenile justice systems, officials place youth into group settings for a variety of reasons. Group placement serves a number of functions. Understanding these reasons and the functions that they serve are essential in order to gauge the feasibility of strategies designed to replace existing policies and to begin looking for ways to mitigate the negative effects of deviant peer contagion that occurs in group settings.

In mental health, and often in juvenile justice, antisocial peers are grouped in institutions for reasons that go beyond safety and treatment. Although the thrust of research into grouping antisocial peers focuses on treatment impact, antisocial peers are also placed in group settings for stabilization, assessment, and respit. Grouping children for mental health treatment purposes may not make therapeutic sense, but hospital settings may be the only place for stabilization, adjustment of medication, and assessment. Many evidence-based programs (e.g., multisystemic therapy and therapeutic foster care) offer respit services to children and families. Respit often requires a group setting. The key to any successful therapeutic intervention is often accurate assessment, and complex assessment may often require temporarily placing a youth into a group setting (Monahan, 2003).

In education settings, alternative schools are commonly thought of as a place for children with conduct problems, but they are also used as a last-resort voluntary placement for children who cannot learn in a regular classroom. Sometimes alternative schools are used to transition those youth who are returning to the community from group settings. Some districts also use alternative schools for children with physical disabilities who require expensive specialized services, where economies of scale make grouping children a financial necessity. Ironically, as some school districts strive to prevent grouping too many high-risk youth in a single school or a single class, they are often forced to remove the most disruptive students in order to placate well-adjusted students so that they remain in the system, even though their parents have the ability to move them elsewhere. As Cook and Ludwig note elsewhere in this volume (see Chapter 4), removing children from regular classrooms may not lead to positive outcomes for an individual child or a small group of children, but it is plausible that it leads to better outcomes for the entire population of children.

In the juvenile justice system there is tremendous pressure from both neighborhood and victims' groups to segregate children who are perceived to be dangerous from other children. As in the mental health system, these children often need expert diagnostic and therapeutic services that many professionals believe will be available only in large institutions.

Practical and ethical issues are also important. Whereas the research cited in this volume is based on studies across a variety of populations, public officials often have to make immediate decisions about individual children. In the long run, being placed with antisocial peers may lead to adverse outcomes for that child, but being allowed to remain in his or her current setting might also lead to adverse outcomes if, for example, the youth is shot by a member of a rival gang, lives in an abusive home, or lives without structure or proper supervision. One horrific case also has the potential to undermine public support for the best evidence-based practice model that may be providing benefits to many children. Even if a great deal of money is saved and 100, or even 1,000, children benefit from being placed in a nongrouped setting, newspapers write their stories about, law suits are files against, and elections often hang on the one child who gets hurt because someone was not placed in a secure setting with other troubled youth. The long-term negative consequences for a population exposed to deviant peer contagion is often far removed from the immediate context within which therapists, principals, social workers, teachers, judges, and prosecutors have to make decisions about what to do with the individual children who stand before them every day.

MEETING FUTURE CHALLENGES

None of these obstacles is insurmountable. Therapeutic justice programs are growing, and courts are developing a number of ways to monitor and enforce orders that avoid grouping deviant peers. This increased capability for monitoring and program compliance should improve program implementation and promote public safety. Nonetheless, non-aggregating interventions will find greater acceptance only when public concerns about the safety of those placements are addressed. One task for program evaluators is to provide detailed evidence regarding the effects of a program on the safety of the overall community. As documented in earlier chapters, there is increasing evidence for the success of programs that avoid group placement or try to mitigate the impact of inevitable group placements. This evidence is building in education, juvenile justice, housing, child welfare, and mental health. A recent National Institutes of Health (2004) consensus conference report recognized that group placements contributed to the development of youth violence through deviant peer contagion processes. We should not be surprised if, over time, avoiding the aggregation of deviant peers slowly becomes part of widely accepted best practice in juvenile justice, mental health, education, and child welfare. However, inertia is a powerful force in public policy, and agencies are not going to stop existing policies that aggregate deviant peers overnight.

Three kinds of activities could increase the likelihood that the programs and recommendations that are the focus of this volume will have an impact on public policy. The first activity is continued research, especially studies using stronger research designs that demonstrate the effectiveness of interventions that avoid aggregating deviant peers. The second activity is research that demonstrates the cost-effectiveness of these kinds of interventions. The last activity is the development of a dissemination and advocacy strategy to build support for these kinds of programs.

More Reliable Information

The most reliable information, which is likely to have the greatest impact, comes from evaluations that use an experimental design. Research using experimental designs is increasingly recognized as the best way to test the efficacy of programs, both those that aggregate deviant youth and those that provide an alternative to deviant peer group aggregation. Such designs are likely to bolster the case for changing current public policies that encourage aggregating deviant peers. However, studies using true experimental designs are rare in criminal justice, mental health, social welfare, and education settings. There is great difficulty in engaging public institutions in an empirical random assignment experiment when society believes that justice demands equal (or even identical) treatment for everyone. Experimental designs require different programming for equivalent clients. There is an even greater fear when courts are part of this process because courts can use the force of the law in an effort to alter behavior, force people into programs, and diminish the rights of clients (Bersoff, 2002). There are also concerns, however unsubstantiated they may be, of unethically denying treatment, net widening, and loss of due process. The justice system is an institution that has historically been reactive, not proactive. However, the more that courts and other public institutions can be convinced to use experimental designs when allocating scarce treatment resources, the greater the likelihood that a case will be built for mitigating the effects of deviant peer contagion.

We can also learn from past attempts to implement random assignment experiments. In 1997, a random assignment experiment, funded by the National Institute of Justice, began in the Broward County Domestic Violence Court. The goal of the study was to test the efficacy of court-mandated counseling for men convicted of misdemeanor domestic violence. As a component of the sentence, the men were placed in either an experimental condition, involving 1 year of probation and 6 months of counseling, or a control condition that involved probation alone. The process became a nightmare for the researchers, who were greeted with hostility, newspaper reports that drew parallels between the research and experiments in Nazi Germany, and a lawsuit filed by the prosecutor's office attempting to end the experiment and order the trial court to resentence the men in the control group (Feder, Jolin, & Feyerherm, 2000). This experience may not bode well for future random assignment experiments in our courts until the parties in the justice system are better educated about the value of experiments as the best method to learn whether court processes are effective in changing human behavior. This case is instructive for those persons who are looking for ways to perform experiments with this kind of population. Researchers wanting to use random assignment in courtroom settings have to choose their strategies carefully and must be able to make their case not only with court officials, but also with the media and the defense bar. A prosecutor who initiated an experiment for adolescent delinquents in Orange County, California, largely escaped this kind of criticism because of his successful use of upfront communication strategies (Orange County Probation Department, 2005).

Costs and Benefits

Although we know that children's conformity to their peers and susceptibility to negative peer influences peaks during early adolescence, it is often argued that a lack of resources in the juvenile justice system precludes individual treatments for youth that would avoid aggregating deviant peers. But suppose it were shown that individual treatment is actually more cost-beneficial than group treatment? Although few states have the capacity to make these calculations, some states have made the investment to develop this activity (Aos, Phipps, Barnoski, & Lieb, 2001). Both the State of Washington and Orange County, California, have been able to measure the outcomes of programs that serve delinquent youth. Using the results of these analyses, they were able to implement policies that placed adolescents in what proved to be more effective community-based individual programs rather than more expensive and less effective institutional group programs. The case for moving from group to individual programs is much stronger when the individualized programs are shown to be more cost-beneficial than existing group-based programs. The Washington state legislature, which now regularly receives cost–benefit information on programs, has funded a number of the programs that are recommended in this volume, including multisystemic therapy, functional family therapy, and treatment foster care (Aos, Lieb, Mayfield, Miller, & Pennucci, 2004). The more that researchers rigorously gather reliable information about the outcomes of programs, including costs and benefits, the greater is the likelihood that the effectiveness of programs can be translated into dollars and get the attention of policymakers.

Building an Advocacy Agenda

It is one thing to design programs that are economical, meet society's needs, and avoid deviant peer influence, it is another to get them put into place. Advocacy outreach and marketing can help create a demand for effective programs among both potential clients and the street-level professionals who will have to implement those programs. It is not enough to publish research that will be read only by other researchers and hope that these findings will create a demand among the public for new and better services. Nor can we assume that they will eventually reach the next generation of professionals through graduate programs or in-service training. A more proactive strategy is to target advocacy groups, professional associations, widely read newsletters, and practitioner journals with easy-to-read articles based on peer-reviewed research.

Frontline professionals usually value the authority of rigorous science, but they get information about best practices from a variety of sources that rarely include academic journals. Professionals are most likely to accept this information if it comes through what they see as their own professional channels. Likewise, parents usually want the best services for their children, but they often have a healthy skepticism of advice from researchers. They are more likely to accept information from organizations that they know and trust.

This premise suggests that researchers need to disseminate their findings to the professional and advocacy organizations that have more direct contact with the necessary recipients of that information. Researchers need to find out what those organizations are and how to get good information to them. This task is especially important because many of the programs highlighted in this volume rely on parent and/or family participation. Pursuing effective public policy involves more than following the paths laid out by the best clinical research. It also involves understanding how to ensure that programs generated by that research are implemented properly; creates ways to manage risk reasonably; keeps good records that enable evaluators to weigh long-term successes against short-term failures reasonably; and, perhaps most important of all, proactively create reasonable expectations among policymaking elites, street-level professionals, the media, and the general public about what public programs can and cannot do.

CHAPTER 19

A Functional Contextualist Framework for Affecting Peer Influence Practices

Anthony Biglan, Jeffrey Sprague,
and Kevin J. Moore

This chapter presents a framework for research on influencing practices relevant to deviant peer contagion. The present volume documents practices that increase the likelihood of antisocial behavior and drug abuse due to the clustering of adolescents. Presumably, if we reduce the prevalence of these practices, we will reduce the prevalence of deviant adolescent behavior. Yet we currently have no effective analysis of how to change these practices. We thus present a theoretical framework for analyzing organizations that work with adolescents in order to contribute to a pragmatic scientific understanding of how to shape and maintain effective practices. We focus on schools and—to a lesser extent—juvenile justice organizations because we have more thoroughly analyzed those organizations.

PRACTICES TO TARGET

The conclusion of this volume (Chapter 20) summarizes practices of schools, juvenile justice organizations, mental health providers, and child welfare agencies that seem to increase peer contagion. In it, the authors present a set of alternative practices that could make peer contagion less likely. These are the practices we need to influence if peer contagion is to be reduced.

Schools

Reinke and Walker (Chapter 7, this volume) identify two practices that seem to foster peer contagion. They are the tendency to track students according to academic skills or emotional difficulties and the absence of school-wide systems for supporting positive behavior that could prevent peer harassment (Metzler, Biglan, Rusby, & Sprague, 2001) and aggressive behavior, thereby reducing the likelihood of deviant peer group formation (Rusby, Forrester, Biglan, & Metzler, 2005). We focus especially on how we might increase the prevalence of positive behavior support (PBS) systems, since, besides reducing the tendency of adolescents to form distinct and often mutually hostile peer groups, they have many other benefits in preventing aggressive behavior (e.g., Embry, Flannery, Vazsonyi, Powell, & Atha, 1996; Mayer, 1995).

Space prohibits a thorough review of the evidence for PBS, but there is considerable evidence about the efficacy of each of its component practices, such as use of a small number of clear rules and high levels of positive reinforcement. Two types of evidence helped to develop PBS. There is substantial empirical evidence about school conditions that contribute to development of antisocial behavior (Sprague, Sugai, & Walker, 1998a, 1998b; Walker, Stieber, & Bullis, 1997). A wealth of evidence exists on the teaching practices that reduce such behavior and support development of appropriate behavior (Acker & O'Leary, 1987; Becker, 1986; Colvin, Sugai, & Patching, 1993; Embry et al., 1996; Gottfredson, Gottfredson, & Hybl, 1993; Hawkins, Von Cleve, & Catalano, 1991; Hops, 1978; Lewis, Sugai, & Colvin, 1998; Mayer, 1995; Mayer, Butterworth, Nafpaktitis, & Sulzer-Azaroff, 1983; Nafpaktitis, Mayer, & Butterworth, 1985; Olweus, 1992; Pfiffner & O'Leary, 1987; Pfiffner, Rosen, & O'Leary, 1985; Walker, Colvin, & Ramsey, 1995).

Besides its school-wide components, PBS employs applied behavior analysis to address the behaviors of the 10–15% "at-risk" and 3–5% "high-risk" (Sugai, Sprague, Horner, & Walker, 2000) students whose behavior is not sufficiently affected by the universal elements. School-wide PBS was developed when it became clear how difficult it is to maintain optimal behavior management for individual students in the absence of a system implemented and supported by all teachers and staff (Colvin, Kame'enui, & Sugai, 1993; Mayer, 1995).

Juvenile Justice System

Greenwood (Chapter 15, this volume) concludes that deviant peer contagion effects are greatest for younger, less serious offenders; that many current programs facilitate deviant peer contagion; and that most successful delinquency prevention programs specifically address deviant peer contagion in multiple ways. Specifically, programs such as multidimensional treatment foster care (MTFC; Chamberlain & Mihalic, 1998) and multisystemic therapy (MST; Henggeler, Pickrel, & Brondino, 1999) directly prevent adjudicated youth from associating with deviant peers. Greenwood's analysis suggests that two appropriate goals for changing the juvenile justice system would be not aggregating young, less serious offenders and implementing an empirically supported delinquency intervention such as MTFC or MST.

Mental Health Agencies

Smith, Dumas, and Prinz (Chapter 16, this volume) delineated a variety of mental health interventions likely to reduce peer contagion effects. In addition to those mentioned above, they describe school-based programs that include family interventions shown to reduce child problem behavior. In the concluding chapter of this volume, Dishion, Dodge, and Lansford argue that family-centered treatment programs directed to individual children are likely to avoid peer contagion and that, if aggregation is necessary for treatment, the process requires careful monitoring in order to prevent practices that foster peer contagion.

Child Welfare Agencies

Wilson and Woods (Chapter 11, this volume) and Dishion and colleagues (Chapter 20, this volume) argue that organizations should avoid foster care practices that aggregate at-risk youth. They recommend instead a program such as multidimensional foster family care, which provides intense supervision and training to foster parents and focuses on reducing youths' association with deviant peers.

   In sum, there are a variety of practices that empirical evidence indicates are likely to be beneficial for preventing deviant peer contagion and fostering positive youth development. Developing a science that can guide the adoption, implementation, and maintenance (Glasgow, Vogt, & Boles, 1999) of these practices should be a high priority.

A FUNCTIONAL CONTEXTUALIST ANALYSIS

Efforts to influence the practices of publicly funded organizations such as schools, mental health clinics, and youth correction facilities have mostly been unsystematic, haphazard, and ineffectual. For example, empirically supported school practices to teach children and adolescents effectively or to minimize disruptive behavior have been known for at least 30 years (e.g., Abelson, Zigler, & DeBlasi, 1974; Becker & Gersten, 1982; Engelmann, Becker, Carnine, & Gersten, 1988; Madsen, Becker, & Thomas, 1968). But progress in disseminating these practices has been depressingly slow (Carnine, 2000; National Council on Disability, 2003).

One reason for the lack of progress is that effective analyses of organizational practices necessarily lag behind advances in the understanding of individual behavior; understanding how to bring about organizational change depends, to some extent, on our understanding of the factors that influence individual behavior. Another reason for the lack of progress is that scientific analyses of organizations often fail to focus on identifying manipulable variables that influence organizational practice.

A functional contextualist framework (Biglan & Hayes, 1996; Hayes, Hayes, Reese, & Sarbin, 1993) guides the present analysis. The goal of this philosophical framework for research is to identify variables that enable the prediction *and* influence of the phenomena of interest with precision, scope, and depth. *Precision* refers to the degree to which the concepts in the analysis can be unambiguously applied to a given problem. For example, the analysis of reinforcement effects is precise in the sense that the events that constitute discriminative stimuli or reinforcers in any given analysis are unambiguous (e.g., a reinforcer must follow the behavior it is said to reinforce and must increase the subsequent likelihood of the behavior due to the contacted response–consequence contingency). *Scope* means that the analysis is effective for a broad range of phenomena. *Depth* means that analysis at any given level coheres with analyses at other levels. Here, depth is particularly important, since changing organizational practices requires us to influence the behavior of individual members, their relationships and coordinated actions, and the practices of the organization as a whole.

Prediction *and* influence comprise one goal: the strategy seeks variables that not only allow prediction, but also, when manipulated, can affect the behavior or practice of interest. The strategy is characteristic of behavior analysis (Hayes, Hayes, & Reese, 1988) and of the cultural materialist approach of Marvin Harris in anthropology (Biglan, 1995; Harris, 1979).

Prediction and influence necessarily lead to a focus on the context for the behavior or practice under study. Only events in their context can influence behavior and group practices. Arguably, one behavior (such as someone's attitude) can influence another behavior, but, practically speaking, even when attitudes affect behavior, one must still determine how to influence the attitudes. Similarly, although a given form of leadership may influence the adoption of a practice, we must still establish how to influence that form of leadership. Thus, to be effective, we must identify manipulable variables in the context of the behavior or practice that, if manipulated, would affect the behavior or practice. Accordingly, we analyze the behavior of individuals in organizations, the relationships among organization members, and the context for organizational practices in an effort to identify manipulable influences that can help develop an empirically testable strategy for changing organizational practices that affect peer contagion.

ANALYSIS OF THE PRACTICES OF ORGANIZATIONS

We divide this analysis into three levels. First, we consider the behavior of individual organization members. Second, we examine the relations among organization members that seem to influence implementation of human services practices. Examples include the organization's "social climate" and its governance and management practices, including group norms, goals, values, and leadership practices. Third, we examine the influence of the context external to the organization that affects the practices we seek to modify.

Figure 19.1 presents a schematic of the analysis. The *practices* of an organization consist of the interlocking behavior of individual members of the organization (Glenn, 2004). For example, the implementation of positive behavior support requires the faculty and staff of a school to define school-wide rules and set up a system for reinforcing behavior that is consistent with those rules. The behaviors are said to be "interlocking" because each person's behavior depends on the behavior of others in the group. For example, one person may propose a rule, but others must agree to it. We also must be concerned with the factors that influence individual members' willingness to engage in the necessary behaviors. For example, members' psychological functioning, such as whether or not they are depressed or "burned out" may affect whether they cooperate with others or are willing to try innovations. Whether group members adopt a particular set of interlocking behaviors may also be a function of other aspects of the organization's functioning, such as the degree to which there is a climate of social support and collegiality and the amount of administrative support for innovations. Finally, whether a given organizational practice continues depends, in part, on the effect that the practice has on the context for the organization's practices. For example, a practice that contributes to increased funding of the organi-

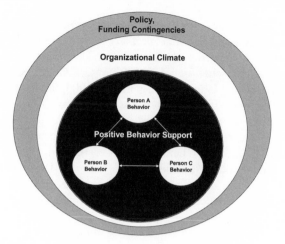

FIGURE 19.1. Contextual analysis of the practices involved in positive behavior support.

zation is more likely to survive. Laws and other policies may also affect what organizations do.

Influences on the Behavior of Individual Members of the Organization

Ultimately, the success of any strategy for fostering the adoption of a practice depends on getting individual organization members to adopt, implement effectively, and maintain it (Glasgow et al., 1999). Recent evidence suggests several variables as important correlates of whether organization members will adopt an innovation. Although most evidence comes from research in schools, it is relevant to other human service organizations.

Depression and Burnout

These states negatively affect teachers' self-efficacy and willingness to implement innovative practices (Evers, Brouwers, & Tomic, 2002), and predict teacher turnover (Hughes, 2001; Maslach, 1999) and absenteeism (Bartoli, 2002); inconsistent staffing then leads to poor implementation of evidence-based programs (Mihalic & Irwin, 2003).

Depression is one of the most prevalent adult mental conditions. The National Comorbidity Survey Replication study puts its prevalence at 16.2% for lifetime and 6.6% for a 1-year period (Kessler et al., 2003). Women are approximately twice as likely as men are to develop major depression. It is associated with impaired social, occupational, and other role functioning (Hirschfeld et al., 2000; Spitzer, Cupp, & Parke, 1995; Stewart, Ricci, Chee, Hahn, & Morganstein, 2003; Wells & Sherbourne, 1999). Since the majority of teachers are women, we would expect many studies of depression among teachers. Yet we found only one study of its prevalence among teachers. Jurado, Gurpegui, Moreno, and de Dios (1998) found 27% of teachers currently depressed, according to the Center for Epidemiologic Studies Rating Scale for Depression (CES-D; Radloff, 1977). Since depression typically involves reduced motivation, its prevalence among teachers could significantly impede the adoption of new practices.

Teacher depression and burnout are more likely in schools with high levels of student disruptive behavior (Beer & Beer, 1992; Dorman, 2003; Hastings & Bham, 2003; Schonfeld, 1992). Depressed teachers will likely manage student behavior less effectively, contributing to an escalating cycle of student misbehavior and teacher depression. Given evidence that parental depression can increase parents' notice of children's negative behavior (e.g., Johnson & Jacob, 1997) and that attention to children's negative behavior increases such behavior (e.g., Mayer, Sulzer, & Cody, 1968; Walker et al., 1995), it is likely that depressed teachers are less effective at behavior management.

Stigmatization

In the present context, *stigmatization* refers to negative attitudes toward an organization's clients. Stigmatization often accompanies depression and burnout. Certainly, negative attitudes toward people at work contribute to burnout (Maslach & Jackson, 1984). Teachers and others serving human development want to like and think well of the people they serve. Yet the social demand for consistently positive attitudes leaves no room for feelings of dislike or frustration when students or clients prove difficult. For example, students with disruptive behavior may cause teachers to be frustrated and angry. These feelings are unwanted and incompatible with their beliefs. It is quite common to try to suppress unwanted thoughts and feelings (Hayes, Strosahl, & Wilson, 1999). Unfortunately, suppression only makes unwanted thoughts and feelings more likely (Wegner, 1992). Moreover, there is growing evidence that efforts to avoid unwanted thoughts and feelings lead to many psychological problems, including job burnout, depression, and anxiety (Hayes et al., in press; Teasdale, 2004).

Psychological Inflexibility

Recent research identifies an aspect of the performance of organization members that is closely related to depression, burnout, and an unwillingness to adopt new practices. *Psychological inflexibility* involves a tendency to avoid unpleasant thoughts and feelings and to be unable to move in valued directions. Hayes (2004) reported a meta-analysis of the relationship between a measure of psychological inflexibility and various measures of psychological well-being, including psychopathology (e.g., depression, anxiety, posttraumatic stress, trichotillomania), stress, pain, and job performance. The studies included 5,616 participants and 67 correlations between the inflexibility measure and these outcomes. The weighted effect size of these relations was .42 (95% CI: .40, .44). Below we describe a strategy for helping organization members accept unwanted thoughts and feelings, while simultaneously committing to valued actions.

Organizational-Level Factors

Several aspects of the relationships among organization members influence whether those organizations will adopt and effectively implement a given practice. All have to do with creating a working environment that is supportive of individual autonomy, fosters positive social relationships, and generates group consensus about relevant practices.

Climate

Bryk and Driscoll (1988) identified five features of school organizations associated with their effectiveness: (1) shared values and purpose, (2) clearly defined behavioral expectations, (3) high learning expectations, (4) activities designed to foster meaningful social interactions in the school, and (5) social relations marked by caring. The authors studied relationships between an index of these features and staff and student behavior in several secondary schools. After controlling for average academic achievement, school social class, minority concentration, school size, and ethnic and social diversity, they found the index of community accounted for variance in teacher satisfaction, staff morale, teacher and student absenteeism, classroom disorder, student dropouts, and academic achievement. Unfortunately, the study did not analyze the degree to which the separate components of this index accounted for different parts of the variance in dependent variables.

Some studies have examined these features separately. In a study of

52 high schools, Yasumoto, Uekawa, and Bidwell (2001) found growth in achievement in math and science to be greater when faculty in these areas communicated regularly, shared norms about appropriate instruction, and consistently employed that instruction. Cook, Murphy, and Hunt (2000) reported greater academic achievement after implementation of the Comer School model, emphasizing faculty, student, and parent participation in choosing goals and practices. Others concluded that norms of collegiality benefit academic effectiveness (Little, 1982; Rosenholtz, 1985).

Teacher autonomy also seems to benefit school effectiveness. Rowan, Chiang, and Miller (1997) found teacher control of decisions associated with higher student achievement when controlling for other correlates of achievement. Ingersoll (1996), in a study of 2,975 schools, found teacher autonomy in instruction associated with less staff–student, faculty–faculty, and teacher–principal conflicts. Faculty influence on policy regarding instruction, student tracking, and socialization were associated with lower levels of each type of conflict. Models stressing broad-based participation in shaping goals and practices (Cook et al., 2000) and choices in governance structure (Bryk & Driscoll, 1988; Mihalic & Irwin, 2003) show better academic achievement.

Not all studies show the value of a communitarian school climate, however. Phillips (1997) analyzed longitudinal data from 5,600 students in 23 middle schools and found communal organization unrelated to attendance or math achievement, but found academic press (i.e., demanding curricula and high academic expectations) related to both variables. The study controlled for school ethnicity and student socioeconomic status (SES). Although we should interpret cautiously a study with only 23 schools, the findings suggest that good school climate does not directly translate into effectiveness. A democratic and collegial climate may benefit students only when teachers agree on and support each other in adopting effective practices; collegiality might also support implementation of bad practices. Ringwalt and colleagues (2003) found high teacher discretion about covering substance abuse lessons to be associated with lower fidelity of implementation of those lessons. Presumably, fidelity of implementation was not a goal for these teachers.

Administrative Support

Hallinger and Heck (1998) reviewed evidence on a principal's contribution to school effectiveness, concluding that principals "exercise a measurable though indirect effect on school effectiveness and student achievement" (p. 186). Kam, Greenberg, and Walls (2003) report that principals' ability to initiate and sustain innovation is related to successful program implementation, although some studies show effective program implementation without this feature (Fagan & Mihalic, 2003). The presence of highly committed project directors with time for program implementation and with good meeting facilitation skills also appears to ensure successful program implementation (Ellickson & Petersilia, 1983; Kramer, Laumann, & Brunson, 2000).

Gottfredson and colleagues (2000) examined relationships between school organization and the degree to which schools implemented effective prevention activities. They found that central support (training, supervision, and principal support), strong leaders, and high organizational morale were associated with implementing effective prevention programs. High levels of administrative support also accompany a sense of community, high student expectations, teachers' sense of self-efficacy (Newmann, Rutter, & Smith, 1989), and less staff turnover (Ingersoll, 2001).

A Limitation of Existing Research

A shortcoming of this research is that all of it is correlational. Schools with shared goals, values, collegiality, good communication, and considerable teacher autonomy have fewer behavior problems and more effective instruction, but this may be due to the fact that having better behaved and more academically advanced students contributes to positive social climate. We need research that shows, through experimental evaluations, that an intervention can improve social climate and foster the adoption of empirically based practices.

The Impact of Organization-Level Factors on Individuals

The individual factors discussed above (depression, burnout, and stigmatization) likely mediate the effects of negative school climate and inadequate administrative support on teacher turnover and poor implementation. Ingersoll (2001) found high teacher turnover among elementary and secondary teachers to be associated with low levels of administrative support, faculty decision making, and autonomy, and with greater levels of student conflict. These factors may increase burnout, depression, and stigmatization, contributing to teacher turnover and poor implementation of effective teaching practices.

Based on this review, we conclude that organizations with a positive social climate are more likely to adopt, implement, and maintain new practices—provided that they have explicit goals for doing so. Given such goals, the organizations most likely to succeed in utilizing new programs are those with low levels of conflict, high levels of cooperation among teachers and administrators, considerable employee participation in decision making (e.g., Bryk & Driscoll, 1988), and supportive administrators and adequate resources (Ennett et al., 2003; Gottfredson et al., 2000). Previous research has identified other potentially manipulable organizational factors associated with successful implementation of school innovation. These include a history of successful program adoption and implementation and organizational procedures enabling management of multiple concurrent programs (Gottfredson et al., 2000), a broad base of community support (Gendreau, Goggin, & Smith, 1999), and low staff turnover and consistent staffing (Ennett et al., 2003; Mihalic & Irwin, 2003).

The Context for Organization Practices

There is little scientific understanding of how the context of organizational practices influences those practices. Yet there are numerous factors that obviously influence them. In the case of the organizations we are discussing, state and federal policies are examples. However, these influences seldom undergo empirical evaluation. Indeed, we seldom even conceptualize them as something to study empirically.

Funding Contingencies

Recently, analyses have emerged on the way consequences lead to selection of group and organizational practices. Much of these analyses focus on the evolution of human societies, including agriculture, war making, capitalism, and democracy (Diamond, 2004; Harris, 1979; Ponting, 1991). However, the same analytic techniques have been applied to the evolution of the practices of organizations (Biglan, 1995; Glenn, 1986, 2004; Harris, 1981).

Oddly, although it is clear that organizations cannot exist without sustaining funds, there is little scientific analysis of the influence of this basic contingency on organizational practices or on factors that might influence creation of such contingencies. There may be two reasons for this: (1) organizational research seldom focuses on contextual influences on organizational practices, and (2) it is difficult to manipulate such a contingency for the purpose of studying its impact.

Glenn (1988, 2004) developed the concept of a metacontingency to account for the evolution of group and organizational practices. This involves a relationship between the interlocking behavior of two or more people and an outcome affecting whether the interlocking behavior continues. Without sustaining outcomes, the practice diminishes, ends, or alters. Or the practice may produce an outcome enabling the interlocking behavior or practice to survive or even expand. Experimental evaluation of this construct is difficult, but the evolution of for-profit organizations provides numerous examples. Halberstam (1986) described the evolution of quality control (QC) procedures in the auto industry as Japanese automakers implemented QC, contributing to the growth in their market share. U.S. companies adopted these practices only when Japanese penetration of the U.S. auto market resulted in deep cuts in U.S. profits. As QC began to foster the profits of the companies, the practice spread.

In schools, juvenile justice organizations, and human service agencies, it may seem that selection by consequence does not occur. Certainly, schools are not subject to contingencies of the marketplace in the way for-profit organizations are (Chubb & Moe, 1990). Indeed, this observation motivated economists such as Milton Friedman (Friedman & Friedman, 1980) to argue that schools and other government-run agencies might be more efficient if exposed to market forces. The movement advocating vouchers or charter schools arises from a belief that giving money to parents to choose their children's schools, or allowing charter schools, would create a market requiring schools to satisfy their customers. Opponents contend that such contingencies might induce schools to satisfy parents, but would not ensure that schools were any more effective in providing education (Brown, 1999; Hirsch, 1998). Recent evidence on the performance of charter schools, although quite limited, does not indicate better academic outcomes (Nelson, Rosenberg, & Van Meter, 2004).

Whether or not the privatization of schools and juvenile justice practices will grow is unclear. But it is doubtful that simply unleashing market forces on these problems will shape the selection of practices that are more effective. Nonetheless, advocacy for a move to a market system stems from a basic and important insight, namely, that practices are shaped and maintained by their consequences. The problem with the current arrangement (i.e., government support) is that funding is not contingent on using the practices found to be most effective. Rather, governments disperse funds based on existing precedent, modified slightly in light of fiscal considerations, such as whether tax revenues are growing or contracting. The ability of organizations to obtain funding depends on the bureaucratic skill of the organization's leaders. Additionally, political leaders who support drastic cuts in these budgets risk the wrath of unions, parents, crime victims, and others. Thus, government-funded practices tend to be insulated from the influence of funding contingencies due to entrenched bureaucracies skilled in maintaining the status quo (Chubb & Moe, 1990).

Nonetheless, incremental changes in institutional practices may be achievable. What can help is systematic research on the effects of making funds contingent on such practices and on how to engineer support for creating such contingencies. This research could develop a science-based strategy for shaping the practices of publicly funded organizations so they adopt and maintain empirically supported practices, and further evaluate whether such practice adoption does achieve the outcomes that existing research indicates are likely to occur (Biglan, Mrazek, Carnine, & Flay, 2003).

A POPULATION-BASED STRATEGY FOR INCREASING PRACTICES TO PREVENT PEER CONTAGION

Here, we present an admittedly speculative discussion of a strategy to influence organizations to adopt practices preventing peer contagion. We base each component on existing empirical evidence—either the evidence just reviewed or that from the social and organizational change literature. For the purpose of this *gedanken* (i.e., thought) experiment, we assume we are trying to increase the prevalence of relevant practices in the youth-serving agencies of an entire state.

One thing to consider in this context is the degree to which the relevant systems—the schools, the juvenile justice system, and the mental health agencies—coordinate their efforts. In general, they do not. For example, in most communities, it is entirely possible for one system to engage in practices designed to prevent peer contagion while another implements practices that foster peer contagion. An effective strategy to prevent peer contagion or, more generally, to foster successful youth development, would more likely succeed if all organizations affecting youth in a community coordinate efforts so they are aware of what each organization is doing and they employ compatible strategies.

Organizing for Change

As noted above, members of organizations are more likely to embrace a practice if they have substantial autonomy and a choice in doing so (Chen, Subramanian, Acevedo-Garcia, & Kawachi, 2005; French & Raven, 1960; Kanfer & Grimm, 1978). However, the typical method of attempting reform in schools and other human services agencies is through policies requiring staff simply to adopt and implement practices. This can increase resistance to the mandated practice, since people tend to resist influence when their autonomy is threatened (Cialdini, 1993).

A Task Force

It is challenging to honor the principles of autonomy and participation in a service system, especially since providing choice does not necessarily guarantee effective practices. A way to address this would be to create a state-level "blue ribbon" task force on problems of promoting positive social behavior and minimizing aggressive, disruptive behavior. The task force would include directors and staff of juvenile justice and mental health agencies and schools. Ideal members would have experience in roles of this sort and be credible leaders to those they represent. Other members of the task force would include school board members, legislators, state officials, and behavioral scientists. We hope these members would be able to represent the views and concerns of their constituencies and could facilitate obtaining support from those constituencies for any initiatives the task force begins. The behavioral science representation would be there to brief the task force on the empirical evidence on the strengths and weaknesses of specific school governance and behavior management practices.

A Survey

Despite its structure, a task force would not speak simply for its constituencies. Rather, its role would be to formulate a survey of teachers, human service workers, and administrators from a population-based or representative sample of schools, correctional agencies, and mental health agencies in the state. The survey would obtain a more accurate understanding of the current state of practices in relevant agencies. It would obtain data on these organizations' current work in preventing peer contagion. It would examine core values regarding youth development, since, as we will describe, people are more likely to adopt innovations that advance their own core values. The survey would assess levels of burnout, depression, psychological flexibility, autonomy, and participation. It would ask for opinions regarding the types of research-based practices the task force is most likely to advocate and will assess perceived obstacles to adopting specific practices. The results would form an accurate picture of relevant practices in the state and of the individual and organization conditions that might need attention in order to foster adoption of research-based practices.

Feedback to Staff, Educational Leaders, and Policymakers

The survey would lay the foundation for fostering organizational change. If it documents relatively high rates of depression and burnout and the roles they each play in staff turnover, it could generate greater consideration for teachers and other staff and for the unique challenges of their jobs. Providing feedback to teachers and agency personnel about the survey and about efforts to publicize its findings could build trust in the task force, which could speak on behalf of those workers.

Setting Priorities

Based on the survey, the task force would set priorities to reduce peer contagion and to improve influences on youth development. Scientists would brief the task force on empirical evidence regarding interventions. Assuming improvement of behavior management and reduction of burnout and depression as common and related problems, the scientists would present evidence addressing those problems. Ideally, this would result in specification of policies regarding the practices to be adopted.

Policies

Those accustomed to doing research on individuals and families do not always consider the influence of policies on practice. State and federal laws or regulations can greatly influence organizational practices. A first step in changing state practices that have an effect on peer contagion would be devising policies that specify practices to adopt and consequences to the organizations that adopt them. Policies should specify which practices to increase or decrease and the contingencies for funding the adoption and implementation of specific practices.

Examples of policies specifying research-based practices do exist. In 2004, Oregon Senate Bill 267 took effect. It requires juvenile corrections (and four other agencies) to utilize evidence-based practices. The agencies will phase in the funding requirements (contingencies) through 2011 to allow time for changes needed to meet the requirements of the legislation. In this unique approach, the law does not require specific programs or services, but does require evidence-based practices, including those involving assessment of client risk, assigning program services based on risk and need, and culturally or gender-specific services.

Another contextual policy example helping Oregon juvenile corrections to meet this legislative mandate began in 1995 when the U.S. Department of Justice Office of Juvenile Justice and Delinquency Prevention (OJJDP) initiated development of Performance-based Standards for Youth Correction and Detention (PbS). OJJDP developed these standards in response to a report of the dismal conditions of juvenile confinement in approximately 1,000 facilities (U.S. Department of Justice, 1994). This performance-based program provides tools for agencies and facilities to identify, monitor, and improve conditions and treatment services provided to incarcerated youths using national standards and outcome measures. Each cycle of tool use consists of data collections, site report analyses, and development and implementation of facility improvement plans. As of April 2005, over 140 facilities in 27 states and the District of Columbia are at various stages of participation in the system. Of those participating, 17 states have implemented performance-based standards state-wide. The Council of Juvenile Correctional Administrators (CJCA, 2005) currently directs the program. Oregon is able to use these PbS standards and assessment tools to provide ongoing data for the evidence-based quality improvement required by Senate Bill 267.

Within juvenile justice, a recent complementary contextual strategy that operates at the organizational level (actually in policy in Oregon) is the Correctional Program Assessment Inventory (CPAI; Gendreau & Andrews, 1994; Latessa, 2004). This is an assessment system for evaluating and monitoring the development and use of evidence-based juvenile justice practices. The CPAI advances the typical audit and assessment procedures that assess only whether a program or facility is doing what it says it is by also ascertaining whether the practices have their basis in principles and practices shown to be effective. The CPAI assess six contextual areas: (1) program implementation and leadership, (2) offender assessment, (3) program characteristics, (4) staff characteristics, (5) evaluation, and (6) other (including ethical guidelines for intervention, stakeholder involvement, and funding support). Using data gained from this assessment, the CPAI identifies strengths and weaknesses of programs, provides recommendations for program improvement, and is useful for benchmarking—it also has a rapid feedback cycle. Moreover, the inventory allows comparison of results for any given program with those obtained across all programs assessed.

What is important about these examples from Oregon juvenile corrections is the emphasis on the shaping of practices at state and organizational levels by using empirically based contextual assessment and feedback strategies with fiscal contingencies attached to their development and use. Moreover, the potential problem of peer contagion is not lost on legislative emphasis of good stewardship of scarce fiscal dollars, the development of these assessment and monitoring strategies, and on Oregon's juvenile justice community—where the use of these and other data-based strategies (a topic beyond the scope of this chapter) are helping the juvenile justice system toward the segregation of low- and high-risk juvenile offenders.

A Contingency Management System for Shaping the Practices of Organizations

Funding is a common way to influence the practices of schools and human service agencies. State and federal policies often specify practices to adopt. Sometimes organizations receive funding to implement certain practices and risk losing funding if they do not adopt them. Title IV of the Elementary and Secondary Education Act (U.S. Department of Education, 2002) provides formula-based funds for schools to implement "evidence-based" practices but gives inadequate guidance on adoption or implementation. Evidence shows that intervention fidelity is low, which compromises outcomes. These arrangements typically lack features to shape school practices effectively. Administrators often do not consult school staff when deciding what to adopt. Consequently, requirements often appear as impositions that promote resistance. When funding is available, it seldom rewards the steps needed to bring about change in staff behavior. Often the money enables teachers to devote time to develop a new practice or support training, but often funds cannot cover the time, coaching, and preparation for successful implementation of the practice. Overextended personnel result in resentment of the practice.

In theory, a contingency management system to shape school practices effectively has five key features. It is a school decision-making process with all staff discussing the proposal and the school not receiving funding unless 80% of staff agree to make the innovation one of its top three priorities (Sprague & Golly, 2004; Sugai & Horner, 1994, 2002). It includes a clear sequence of steps, each setting the stage for funding and implementation of the next. The system provides sufficient training and consultation to ensure the school's or other service agency's success at each step. Each step has sufficient funding so that no one has an increased burden. Finally, the system includes use of a database, allowing continuous monitoring for those who implement the system (Gilbert, 1987) and of its impact on staff and student/client behavior.

Acceptance and Commitment Training

Above we described how depression, burnout, and the stigmatization of students appear to obstruct school change. Recent evidence from organizational development suggests that acceptance and commitment training helps workers accept and manage depression and burnout while also making a more vital commitment to actions they value. There are book-length expositions of acceptance and commitment principles (Hayes et al., 1999) and experimental evaluations on therapeutic and organizational development versions (Bond & Bunce, 2003; Hayes et al., in press) of this approach.

The approach arises from evidence about a tendency to avoid unpleasant thoughts and feelings. Social, psychological, and clinical research indicates that avoiding such feelings and experiences is destined to fail and, in fact, makes the experience of unwanted thoughts and feelings more likely. In acceptance and commitment therapy (ACT), practitioners describe this as "When it comes to thoughts and feelings the rule is, 'If you don't want it, you've got it.' "

By design, acceptance-oriented therapy and organizational training can help people notice the ways they avoid unwanted thoughts and feelings and the ways in which doing so has not worked. It helps them develop a life approach that involves defining and committing to valued directions, while accepting (but not necessarily believing) thoughts and feelings that seem to be in the way of pursuing those directions. ACT therapists use metaphors and experiential exercises to assist people in understanding and using its principles. ACT consists of a six-step process: (1) acceptance, (2) defusion, (3) self-as-context, (4) values, (5) committed action, and (6) contact with the present moment.

Acceptance involves acknowledging thoughts and feelings. Yet acceptance is difficult and unlikely if people take their thoughts literally (e.g., most teachers cannot accept the thought of being a terrible teacher and having students hate them). Thus *defusion* helps reduce the fusion between thoughts and their subject matter. Through exercises, people increase the tendency to notice thoughts and feelings as simply what they are. Learning to notice the *self-as-context* or *observer self* facilitates taking this stance toward private experience. The self observes one's thoughts and feelings. This is changeless; whatever one experiences, the "me" experiencing it does not change. As people sense this, it becomes safe to experience even very distressing thoughts and feelings.

Often people struggle with thoughts and feelings, thinking they can progress only after overcoming negative emotional experiences. With ACT, people are helped to have negative thoughts and feelings and learn to define the *valued directions* they choose to pursue—that is, they ask themselves "What do you want your life to be about?" Upon defining that direction, they discover how to take *committed action*, as they are willing to think and feel as they progress. As the process develops, people are more apt to experience *contact with the present moment*. That is, rather than experiencing the present in terms of thoughts and feelings that color and distort the event, they can respond to what is actually happening and pursue valued directions in light of what is there to confront.

Recent research shows ACT's benefit for problems from smoking (Gifford, 2002) to schizophrenia (Bach & Hayes, 2002). More relevant to the present concern are three evaluations of an organizational development version of ACT. One involving call center workers in the United Kingdom compared ACT with a stress reduction program and a wait-list control. Relative to control, ACT improved workers' general mental health, depression, and propensity to initiate innovations. These improvements arose from increased psychological acceptance and increased ability of people to act on their values.

In a second trial, drug and alcohol abuse counselors received (1) a 1-day 6-hour ACT workshop, (2) training in multiculturalism, or (3) a control condition on education about the pharmacological effects of drugs of abuse (Hayes et al., in press). ACT had a greater effect than comparison conditions on worksite burnout. Moreover, process analyses showed that the effect in the ACT condition occurred due to significantly reduced fusion with negative thoughts about difficult clients.

A third study found that when drug abuse counselors received an ACT workshop focused on psychological barriers to new treatment approaches and acceptance of the resultant emotions, they were significantly more willing to adopt empirically supported treatment (Hayes, 2005).

These results suggest that ACT could help human services workers revitalize their commitment to work while also helping them with depression and burnout. Such a workshop would help them accept the negative thoughts and feelings that occur as they struggle with working with difficult adolescents and families. Instead, they can reconnect with the values that led them to teaching or human service work in the first place. In essence, ACT should help them become more willing to try things they previously resisted because of stress and hopelessness.

Implementation of School-Wide Positive Behavior Support

Each specific practice needs an implementation strategy. Here we describe a strategy for implementing one such practice, the Positive Behavior Support (PBS) system in schools (Sprague, Golly, Bernstein, Munkres, & March, 1999).

PBS implementation encompasses training and support of a 5- to 10-person team, including an administrator, representative faculty/staff, and parent. Administrators must take part, and the team should represent all major stakeholders in the school, including secondary students. During training and after mastery of basic material, teams meet monthly to review training content, establish a review process, and refine the school discipline plan and other school site-based activities.

School-Wide Expectations

It is critical to establish and teach school-wide behavior rules regarding student–teacher compliance, peer interaction, academic success, and study skills. Using a framework of safety, respect, and responsibility, schools actively teach year-round to establish and maintain behavior patterns with these qualities. It is valuable to post the rules publicly.

- *Recognize expected behavior and actively supervise students.* Schools should enforce, monitor, and positively reinforce adherence to the rules that specify desired behavior. This could include delivery of school-wide "tickets" stating each school rule. Weekly drawings occur. Teachers also receive rewards.
- *Define and correct problem behaviors and their consequences.* Excessive sanctions lead to more vandalism and other misbehavior (Mayer, 1995; Skiba & Peterson, 1999). Positive reinforcement is more effective than punishment and does not induce aggression or withdrawal.

Unevenly applied rules foster student misbehavior. Clear rules, rewards, business-like corrections, and sanctions signal appropriate behavior for students and respond to misbehavior predictably. Students learn expectations and consequences, develop respect, and internalize confidence in the system (Bryk & Driscoll, 1988; Gottfredson, 1987a; Gottfredson et al., 1993).

Use of Ongoing Monitoring Data for Active Decision Making

Team problem-solving efficiency improves with data-based feedback regarding implementation of SWPBS practices (see Appendix 19.1) and the impact of implementation on problem behavior as indexed by discipline referral patterns (Schoolwide Information System; Sprague, Sugai, Horner, & Walker, 1999; Sugai et al., 2000; www.swis.org/). Highly efficient systems allow teams to ask if evidence-based PBS practices are in place, and if the practices are affecting student behavior. Teams typically collect, summarize, and report quarterly the data on PBS implementation. They collect data on student behavior continuously and report to the school team weekly, the school faculty monthly, and the school district annually. Irvin, Tobin, Sprague, Sugai, and Vincent (2004) provide an evaluation documenting the value of regular access to student behavioral data for school teams.

CONCLUSION

Although research has identified practices of human service, juvenile justice, and school organizations that influence peer contagion, research on how to influence the practices of these organizations is lacking. Therefore, the present chapter has described a framework for research on how to influence the practices of schools and human service organizations. The framework is designed to pinpoint manipulable variables that influence organization practices. At the individual level, it seems important to address issues of burnout, depression, and psychological inflexibility that may be obstacles to individuals' willingness to implement the necessary changes in their practices. Closely related is the need to ensure a social climate in the organization in support of positive collegial relations, participation in decision making, and innovation. These qualities will contribute to the adoption of best practices only if the group adopts explicit goals for the implementation of those practices.

There is evidence that the practices of groups and organizations are influenced by the consequences to the group or organization of those practices. In particular, practices that undermine financial support tend to be abandoned, while those that improve financial support tend to be adopted or expanded. However, the principle of selection by consequences has not been experimentally evaluated for schools, human service agencies, or the juvenile justice system. A strategy that made sufficient funding contingent on the organization taking each of a series of steps in adopting, implementing, and maintaining the practice is a prime candidate for experimental evaluation.

ACKNOWLEDGMENTS

National Cancer Institute Grant No. CA86169 and National Institute on Drug Abuse Grant No. DA018760-01 supported the authors during their work on this chapter.

APPENDIX 19.1. Sample Needs Assessment for Planning and Evaluating School-Wide Positive Behavior Support

Effective Behavior Support (EBS) Survey Assessing and Planning Behavior Support in Schools

Name of school district _____	Date	
	State	

Person Completing the Survey:				
	Administrator	Special educator		Parent/family member
	General educator	Counselor		School psychologist
	Educational/teacher assistant	Community member		Other

1. Complete the survey independently.
2. Schedule 20–30 minutes to complete the survey.
3. Base your rating on your individual experiences in the school. If you do not work in classrooms, answer questions that are applicable to you.

To assess behavior support, first evaluate the *status* of each system feature (i.e., *in place, partially in place, not in place*) (left-hand side of survey). Next, examine each feature:

    a. "What is the *current status* of this feature (i.e., *in place, partially in place, not in place*)?"

    b. For those features rated as partially in place or not in place, "What is the *priority for improvement* for this feature (i.e., *high, medium, low*)?"

4. Return your completed survey to _____ by _____

SCHOOL-WIDE SYSTEMS

Current status			Feature	Priority for improvement		
In place	Partially in place	Not in place		High	Med	Low
			School-wide defined as involving all students, all staff, and all settings.			
			1. A small number (e.g., 3–5) of positively and clearly stated student expectations or rules defined.			
			2. Expected student behaviors taught directly.			
			3. Expected student behaviors rewarded regularly.			
			4. Problem behaviors (failure to meet expected student behaviors) defined clearly.			
			5. Consequences for problem behaviors defined clearly.			
			6. Distinctions among office- versus classroom-managed problem behaviors clear.			
			7. Options exist to allow classroom instruction to continue when problem behavior occurs.			
			8. Procedures in place to address emergency/dangerous situations.			
			9. A team exists for behavior support planning and problem solving.			
			10. School administrator is active participant on behavior support team.			
			11. Data on problem behavior patterns collected and summarized within an ongoing system.			
			12. Patterns of student problem behavior reported to teams and faculty for active decision making on a regular basis (e.g., monthly).			
			13. School has formal strategies for informing families about expected student behaviors at school.			

14. Booster training activities for students developed, modified, and conducted based on school data.					
15. School-wide behavior support team has a budget for (a) teaching students, (b) ongoing rewards, and (c) annual staff planning.					
16. All staff involved directly and/or indirectly in school-wide interventions.					
17. The school team has access to ongoing training and support from district personnel.					
18. The school required by the district to report on the social climate, discipline level, or student behavior at least annually.					

Name of School _____ Date _____

CHAPTER 20

Findings and Recommendations

A Blueprint to Minimize Deviant Peer Influence in Youth Interventions and Programs

Thomas J. Dishion, Kenneth A. Dodge,
and Jennifer E. Lansford

PEER CONTAGION EXECUTIVE SESSIONS

In the fall of 2002, a commission of leading scholars was formed to study the problem of peer contagion effects in programs and interventions for youth. The meetings were referred to as executive sessions because they consisted of a series of goal-oriented meetings focused on understanding a problem and making recommendations. The commission that prepared this report consisted of 27 members from the diverse worlds of public service (a judge, two federal program officers, a clinical psychologist), business, the media, and academia. The academic disciplines included sociology, psychology, economics, social factors engineering, epidemiology, public health, criminology, education, public policy, and political science. During a 36-month period, this group visited intervention programs, ran focus groups with practitioners and youth, reviewed program expenditures, interviewed program officials, conducted meta-analyses of the literature, convened six meetings of the Executive Sessions group, and synthesized the evidence from three streams of scientific research concerning deviant peer contagion, including (1) peer influences in the natural environment, such as the formation of gangs; (2) intervention and policy outcomes that show unintended adverse effects associated with deviant peer aggregation; and (3) intervention and policy strategies that tend to benefit children and adolescents. The group focused in particular on programs in juvenile justice, education, mental health, child welfare, and community settings.

FINDINGS

The commission's work yielded the following findings and recommendations.

• *Deviant peer contagion occurs commonly in naturally occurring peer interaction.* The behavioral science of "naturally occurring" peer interactions indicates that peer contagion effects (i.e., adverse peer influences that occur in group settings) begin in early childhood, peak during early adolescence, and continue at least through late adolescence. Developmental psychological and sociological research indicates that, in Western cultures, children begin spending more time with peers than with family members by about age 3–4, and they increase in their peer orientation at least through early adolescence. Direct observations, interviews, confidential reports, and archival record reviews have been applied to studies of preschool playgrounds, interactions and dynamics among children in public elementary schools, friendships in adolescence, formation of gangs in community settings, and assignment of roommates in college dormitories, and they all reveal significant adverse effects of association with deviant peer groups on an individual child's adjustment outcomes. Although homophily and selection effects also operate to cause deviant youth to seek each other out, the preponderance of longitudinal evidence based on studies with rigorous methodological controls suggests that, once deviant youth are aggregated, peer influences operate to exacerbate antisocial behavior among members of the deviant peer group.

Deviant peer contagion effects appear to be strongest for the following children and under the following conditions:

1. During early adolescence;
2. For youth who have experimented with deviant behavior but have not yet committed themselves to a deviant lifestyle;
3. For youth who are exposed to peers who are slightly more deviant than they are;
4. For youth who interact with deviant peers in unstructured, unsupervised settings;
5. For behaviors that are usually acquired through social processes (e.g., delinquency, substance use, violence).

The processes through which deviant peers influence youth are many, including deviancy training, modeling, labeling, enhanced exposure to opportunities for deviance, and identity formation. These processes have relatively enduring effects on problem behavior throughout childhood. Therefore, it is not surprising that peer dynamics surrounding deviance can disrupt adults' efforts to socialize youth.

- *The most common response to deviant youth is to segregate them from mainstream peers and aggregate them with each other.* When government systems in juvenile justice, education, mental health, and community programming are charged with responding to deviant behavior among youth, the majority of public dollars go to the segregation of these youth from mainstream peers and intentional aggregation of deviant youth with other deviant youth. This strategy is often the "default" strategy in education, mental health, juvenile justice, and community programming for deviant youth, especially by government agencies in the United States. Billions of dollars are spent every year to place millions of deviant children in settings with other deviant youth.

The rationales for segregation and group placement typically include (1) protection of the rest of society, (2) cost savings, and (3) optimal treatment of the deviant youth. However, except for the most dangerous of all youth, society's "protection" is short lived because these youth later return to society; unfortunately, the long-term impact of a placement is rarely weighed as strongly as its immediate effects. Cost savings through group placement and "batch processing" may also be deceptive in cases when the group placement leads to lower immediate costs but higher costs in the future. Analyses indicate that deviant youth who are not successfully socialized toward a noncriminal life cost society more than $2 million each during the course of a lifespan. Finally, the theoretical argument for group treatment of deviant youth has not been supported by empirical analyses. Optimal treatment of a deviant youth is usually individual treatment (possibly with family members) while the youth remains in the normative peer group context of education and community.

- *Treatment or placement with deviant peers reduces the potential for positive impact, and in some situations has adverse affects on youth adjustment.* It has been assumed for more than 50 years that the admitted power of deviant peer influences can be successfully harnessed to render positive change and outcomes for vulnerable and high-risk youth. Although these forces can be controlled under some circumstances, it is clear that some group-administered interventions (e.g., "Scared Straight" programs in juvenile justice, nondirective talk therapies in mental health, unsupervised community programs) have adverse effects on their recipients. Sorting out the source of these iatrogenic effects has proven difficult. Most interventions include multiple components, but most studies of outcomes compare those of a particular intervention only to those of a nontreated control group; thus it is not clear which aspect of the intervention or placement is responsible for adverse effects. As of this writing, only a handful of studies provide a methodologically strong test of whether deviant peer aggregation leads to exacerbation of problem behavior and maladjustment. Those studies that involve random assignment, long-term follow-ups, and statistical controls are particularly compelling. *On the basis of these studies, we conclude that under some circumstances the aggregation of deviant peers subverts the intended benefits of interventions and leads to less positive, sometimes even negative, outcomes for the participating youth.*

We find that youth interventions consist of multiple, distinct, active components that can operate in opposing directions. Formally, these components include the following four active ingredients, which are also depicted in Figure 20.1.

$$\text{Total intervention effect} = (T - \Gamma - I) + \Sigma\,(\mu_i * I)$$

T is the positive therapeutic effect, Γ is the group administration context effect, I is the deviant peer group effect, and μ_i are moderating factors.

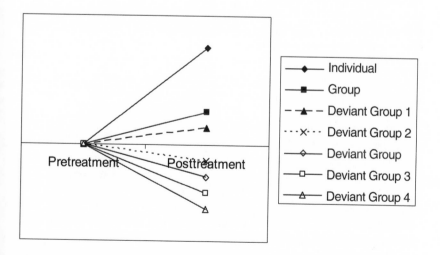

FIGURE 20.1. Prototypic evaluation of impact of interventions for deviant youth: Comparing pretreatment and posttreatment means.

• *Treatments often have positive effects.* The first component, *T*, is the intended therapeutic component, which has been shown to be positive for many interventions. The intended effect, of course, is to promote positive youth development. It is a credit to professionals who serve youth, and to the program evaluators who scrutinize their data, that most programs in mental health and juvenile justice have, on average, positive effects on the participating youth. Numerous meta-analyses, reviews of individual studies, and visits to programs in local communities confirm this average positive effect.

• *Positive treatment effects get eroded through group administration.* The maximal possible impact is partially offset, however, when those intervention programs are administered to youth in a group context. Group-based interventions are, on average, more effective than no intervention at all, but they are significantly less effective than similar interventions delivered individually. A large proportion of the intended therapeutic effect is diluted through group delivery. The dilution of the intended effect through group administration can be labeled Γ. Of course, cost and feasibility often dictate the less expensive and more politically acceptable alternative of group placement instead of individual treatment. No studies have been conducted to test whether group delivery is more or is less cost beneficial than individual delivery in the long run. Under circumstances of choice, however, the individually administered program proves superior, on average, to the group program. Such a finding may be no surprise.

• *Placement with deviant peers further erodes treatment effects.* The positive effects of intervention are often further diluted when the group placement is with other deviant or high-risk youth. Sometimes the negative impact of placement with deviant peers outweighs any therapeutic effect and leads to adverse outcomes for the youth. Placements into peer groups that are devoid of well-functioning peers and include only (or mostly) other deviant peers bring increased risk of such adverse, or iatrogenic, impact. Not only is the intended therapeutic effect further diluted in all-deviant peer group settings, a new subversive process, called *deviant peer contagion*, sometimes takes hold. The "deviant peer contagion effect" has been identified in some school-administered programs, some mental health interventions, some juvenile justice programs, and some community programs. It does not operate uniformly, but it occurs with alarming frequency.

Studies suggest that adverse effects can occur even merely by "virtual" aggregation, or public identification and labeling, of a high-risk youth as a member of a deviant group. Official processing of a youth in court may exacerbate antisocial development through perception by the youth and others that the youth is indeed a member of a deviant category. More likely, though, it is interaction among the members of the deviant peer group that promotes deviant peer contagion. A process referred to as *deviancy training*, which involves selective reinforcement among peers (laughter, attention, etc.) that increases the likelihood of problem behavior in the future, is a likely candidate. Imitation and modeling of deviant behavior is another probable mechanism. Increased problem behavior as a function of increased exposure to these opportunities by peers may be yet another mechanism, if the deviant peers have unsupervised contact in settings that allow deviant behavior. Deviancy training, modeling, and increased opportunities most likely operate on the most vulnerable youth, who may misperceive group norms or attention, identify with the most deviant youth in the group, and are otherwise personally in need of group acceptance.

• *Not all deviant peer group placements are equal.* Whatever the mechanism, the conditions that lead to deviant peer contagion are subtle. The potential for these adverse effects is well known to educators, juvenile court workers, mental health clinicians, and community programmers, but these professionals tend to believe that they are more easily controlled than rigorous evidence suggests. The situation can be likened to a maelstrom, in that intervention outcomes become less predictable when deviant peer aggregation is involved. It is commonly understood that under some conditions the weather becomes unpredictable from day to day. Similarly, outcomes associated with deviant peer aggregation seem to be, in part, unpredictable. "Unpredictability" from this perspective simply means that the variance among youth entering into deviant peer group programs increases, with some youth responding negatively, and others benefiting. This state of affairs is difficult to track because current intervention science is often narrowly focused on central tendencies (i.e., the average outcomes of youth in intervention A compared with intervention B).

In spite of the maelstrom, our analysis reveals several factors that account for some of the different outcomes that youth experience when placed in deviant peer group settings. Because the literature on deviant peer contagion is relatively new, the evidential landscape is underdeveloped. However, the literature is growing rapidly. Several factors are crucial because they often determine whether a placement ultimately results in adverse or positive impact. They also provide direction for refining future treatments and making better decisions about how to aggregate youth.

The following factors have been found to alter the effect of placement with deviant peers:

1. *Age and gender of the child.* We find evidence of a rising susceptibility to deviant peer influence during the early adolescent years, followed by a decline in susceptibility during late adolescence. Overall, young adolescents appear to be the most vulnerable age group for influence by deviant peers. Programs directed at youth of this age are at high risk for deviant peer contagion effects.

Furthermore, it is clear that problem behaviors that are of high interest to group members at a particular stage in development are the most vulnerable to influence by deviant peer contagion. There appears to be a state of readiness that influences the likelihood of peer contagion effects. For example, peer-directed aggression is salient among elementary school children, and substance use, delinquency, and sexual behavior are salient among adolescents; thus these behaviors are most susceptible to deviant peer contagion effects at these stages of development. Assembly of deviant youth during early adolescence to discuss substance use, delinquency, and sexual deviance should be avoided. Among college students, females are susceptible to disordered eating when they are exposed to it in groups, and males, especially already high-risk males, are susceptible to binge drinking when exposed to a problem-drinking roommate. Age and gender characteristics of the youth may define which behaviors are most vulnerable to the effects of deviant peer contagion for that youth.

Finally, the child's age relative to the age of the peers matters a great deal. Children are generally influenced most by peers who are slightly older than they are. Thus the child who is most susceptible to deviant peer influence is the early adolescent male who has begun delinquent or substance-using behavior but it not committed to it as a lifestyle and is placed with a group of same-ethnicity, slightly more deviant, peers who are several years older.

2. *Level of progression into deviance.* Moderately deviant youth appear to be the most at risk for negative effects associated with deviant peer aggregation. Youth derive from group interactions support for behavior trajectories that they have already initiated in their natural environment but have not yet firmly committed to enduring habit. This finding implies that the kinds of programs that are most likely to be susceptible to deviant peer contagion effects are those that target high-risk youth who are still in regular environments, including secondary prevention (i.e., selected) and early intervention programs in mental health, early diversion, and probation programs in juvenile justice, school dropout prevention programs that target high-risk youth, in-

school suspension programs, and community programs that are targeted to "at-risk" youth.

Programs that are directed toward severely deviant youth (e.g., youth with diagnosed chronic psychiatric disorders, youth sentenced to correctional facilities) are confronted with numerous challenges, ranging from cost and practical management to disorders that may be impervious to change. Many of these programs place disordered youth in groups for residential management for the safety of the community. The added risk that comes with aggregating these severely deviant youth in groups may be small in contrast with these other challenges.

Low-risk youth with social strengths and supportive family environments are apparently relatively unaffected by exposure to moderately deviant peers, at least in the small doses to which they are exposed in classrooms or short-term groups. This finding is especially encouraging because it suggests that moderately deviant youth might be able to remain in regular settings such as schools and youth groups without adversely affecting the low-risk youth. Also, it suggests that low-risk youth might be helpful in intervention group settings without being adversely affected. We note a rather modest level of confidence in this conclusion, given the paucity of rigorously collected data on system-level effects of interventions for a segment of a population. Very clearly, low-risk children represent a group worthy of additional inquiry regarding effects of various interventions and programs for others.

Yet another area worthy of further inquiry is the hypothesis that individual children might have personality characteristics that render them more susceptible to deviant peer contagion effects (or any peer influence effects) than other children would be. It is possible that specific life experiences (e.g., rejection by one's parents) might make a particular child highly vulnerable to these effects. It is also possible that personality characteristics (e.g., neurally based impulsivity) make some children more susceptible than others. Parents believe that they are intuitively aware of which of their children is likely to fall prey to "bad" peer influences. Interaction effects between child factors and environmental exposures are receiving greater attention in the scientific literature and most certainly will ultimately hold true. At the current time, however, the state of knowledge has not identified valid means of identifying which particular children will be most affected by deviant peer groups, beyond the characteristics noted above. Intuitive judgments by parents and professionals that a particular child is invulnerable to any adverse effects of placement with deviant peers are likely to be incorrect and should not guide placement.

3. *Amount of time in the group.* The effect of placement with deviant peers appears to follow a dose–response relation: the more time that

a youth spends in settings with deviant peers, the more susceptible that youth is to negative peer influences. The effects of dose accrue both within 1 day (e.g., full-day treatments probably have more adverse effects than 1-hour treatments) and across days (e.g., longer terms of treatment lead to more adverse effects than shorter term treatments). This finding is likely a result of both the deviancy training that occurs in the group and the loss of opportunities for exposure to positive socialization with prosocial peers that results from the segregation of deviant youth. Correctional institutions for juvenile offenders offer conditions that are especially conducive to deviant peer contagion; in them, delinquent youth are aggregated 24 hours a day and are cut off from associating with nondelinquent peers. Short-term holding facilities for offending youth are less likely to yield enduring contagion effects.

4. *Opportunities for interaction among members outside of the group context.* One of the mechanisms of deviant peer contagion is the opportunity that deviant peers provide for each other *outside of the peer group context* for ongoing participation in deviant behavior. Thus groups that bring together youth who establish relationships with each other that last beyond the end date of the group are more likely to inspire contagion than would groups constituted of members who will never see each other outside of the treatment or intervention setting. Corrections facilities that enroll youth according to geographic catchment areas might provide greater opportunity for home–facility contact, but they may inadvertently facilitate postcorrections opportunities for deviance.

Likewise, programs that are highly structured to prevent deviant peer contagion might risk the very problem that they attempt to prevent if they afford unstructured opportunities for the participants outside of the formal group context. Youth who are bused together to an alternative school might experience a well-managed program at the school facility but are provided unfortunate opportunities for deviance on the bus or on the street corner when the youth are dropped off. Therapy groups for conduct-disordered youth might be structured to avoid contagion effects during group sessions, but these advantages will be lost if the members are allowed to congregate before and after sessions outside the facility.

5. *Ratio of deviant to nondeviant group members and group culture.* Groups that include no more than one deviant youth appear to be immune to deviant peer contagion effects, especially if the peers establish a prosocial norm and the group leadership is skilled. At the other extreme, groups that include only deviant youth appear to be at highest risk for deviant peer contagion. One important question is whether there exists a minimal critical mass (or tipping point) of deviant group membership in

order to create deviant peer contagion. On the basis of the deviancy-training hypothesis, one would expect that the higher the risk of the individuals in the group, the more deviancy training and the stronger the iatrogenic effects. Complicating this answer is the likelihood that some group leaders (or teachers) are able to avoid contagion effects even with a relatively high ratio of deviant to nondeviant children, whereas other group leaders are able to manage only relatively benign groups.

The critical issue is likely to be the cultural norm for behavior that gets established in the group. Like cultures, groups that have been in existence for a long time have a cultural norm that is difficult to change, even when the entire cast of members has turned over to a new generation. This situation characterizes long-standing and ongoing group structures such as residential facilities, group homes, and particular schools. For newly constituted groups, the culture becomes established fairly quickly, but the opportunity for establishing a prosocial culture may be greater. The group leader's influence may be greatest during the early portion of a group.

Group culture may also be engineered to optimize the probability of establishing a prosocial norm. A sterling model is the Montessori Program method with young children. These ongoing programs often include children who stay in the same group across ages 3, 4, and 5. At the beginning of each school year, though, the previous year's 5-year-olds have "graduated" and moved on, and a new cohort of 3-year-olds is added to the group. Teachers count on the older 4- and 5-year-old children to teach the younger children established cultural norms for sharing, cooperation, and proper use of educational materials. But they don't simply hope that this norm occurs. Teachers engineer the context. The 4- and 5-year-olds attend the first sessions of the year without any 3-year-olds present, so that the prosocial cultural norms can get reestablished. Then, 3-year-olds are added to the group one at a time. After the first 3-year-old is added, the second 3-year old is added only when the norm for prosocial behavior is clear, and so on until the full cohort of 3-year-olds is complete. The outcome is maintenance of a particular cultural norm that might not be predictable merely from the pretreatment characteristics of the members.

The conclusion is clear: engineering a prosocial culture is a major task for peer group program leaders, worthy of careful planning.

6. *Group structure.* A high level of structure and organization within group interventions is likely to reduce the peer contagion phenomenon. Groups that encourage or allow free discussion of any idea, without evaluative judgment, may promote deviant peer contagion effects. Settings that allow free interaction among peers, without adults present, are more likely to promote contagion. In contrast, groups that

minimize peer interactions that include or concern deviant behavior will also minimize the contagion effect. Tight time schedules with no opportunity for deviant talk or behavior are least likely to catalyze deviant contagion.

Because behaviorist approaches to milieu therapy in school and correctional settings tend to be more highly structured than nondirective approaches, these groups are less likely than others to encourage deviant peer contagion.

7. *Level of expertise of the group leader(s).* Deviant peer contagion is a highly volatile phenomenon that can be dissipated by a truly expert group leader who knows how to divert attention, reestablish appropriate norms, and respect but control participants. Novice leaders are more vulnerable to contagion effects and should not be allowed to lead all-deviant peer groups, especially without close supervision.

8. *Cultural context of the intervention.* Finally, the cultural context of an intervention may be as important as the content for producing negative effects. For example, consider a social skills training intervention that is conducted in a university or medical setting and involves random assignment and careful attention to fidelity of intervention and removing opportunities for youth to aggregate informally around the clinic setting. Contrast this context with the same intervention offered in a community setting, close to a bus station where high-risk youth in the community "hang out" with each other. The latter intervention might lead to iatrogenic effects, whereas the former intervention obtains positive effects. The intervention offered in the community setting does not account for the incidental interactions of the youth with other high-risk youth that might contribute to the development of deviant behavior. Youth may meet after the group and smoke cigarettes or steal from the nearby shopping mall.

These differences across intervention contexts may account for some of the well-known slippage in intervention effectiveness that occurs when efficacious programs are implemented haphazardly at less cost in community settings. In this sense, the ecology of a program, intervention, or policy must be weighed carefully in the consideration of whether youth will actually benefit from the program or become vulnerable to deviant peer contagion effects.

9. *The outcome in question.* Although the outcome is not a moderator per se, we note that effects of deviant peer contagion may be stronger on some outcomes than on others. For example, depression, fears and phobias, and related emotions may be less vulnerable to deviant peer contagion than are behaviors that are acquired through exposure to others, such as delinquency and substance use. Even within the realm of externalizing behavior problems, delinquency may be more susceptible

than reactive anger. However, behaviors such as eating disorders, suicide attempts, and self-mutilation that are motivated by internalizing problems may still be vulnerable to peer contagion if high-risk youth acquire opportunity or perceive that these behaviors are more normative as a result of exposure to like-affected peers.

PEER CONTAGION AND SERVICE AND EDUCATIONAL SYSTEMS

At this juncture it is critical to discuss the issue of placing youth within group settings that aggregate deviant youth from the perspective of service delivery systems. Although the individual youth themselves may not benefit from such placements, it is plausible that youth remaining in the community (e.g., a public school) benefit from their removal. Most individual decisions regarding placement of a deviant youth have a decidedly and understandably myopic perspective. That is, parents of a deviant child want the best outcome for their child, whereas parents of non-deviant peers want their children protected from deviant youth. Elected judges are most responsive to public politics, whereas advocacy groups lobby on behalf of the interests of their constituencies. Agency directors are most attentive to cost containment and short-term outcomes. Individual parents must certainly advocate for their child, but public officials should be encouraged by the use of incentives to think more broadly at the system level.

What is needed is a more thorough and system-encompassing perspective that balances and weighs all of the stakeholders in a youth system such as the one offered by Cook and Ludwig (Chapter 4, this volume). Unfortunately, very little research has been completed at the system level, and so decision makers are left to their own values.

RECOMMENDATIONS FOR PRACTICE AND POLICY

Although the cliché "additional research is needed" certainly applies to this nascent topic, the body of knowledge is sufficient to warrant numerous recommendations for practitioners who work with youth and policymakers whose actions lead deviant youth to be segregated from mainstream peers and quarantined with each other:

• *Recommendation 1: Ineffective programs, placements, and treatments that aggregate deviant peers should be avoided whenever possible.* On the basis of available empirical evaluations and the principles described above, numerous currently popular programs, placements, and treatments (listed in Table 20.1) that aggregate deviant peers into groups should be avoided because of the high risk of adverse impact on participating youth. Not all interventions that aggregate deviant peers lead to adverse outcomes, and not all youth will suffer adverse outcomes from participation in these programs, but the risk is great enough that alternatives should be sought.

• *Recommendation 2: Effective alternatives to deviant peer group placement should be encouraged.* Examination of interventions for deviant youth that have been found to be effective and to have positive impact on participants reveals that the majority of these effective interventions do not involve aggregating high-risk children. Successful treatments that replicate in both efficacy and effectiveness trials typically mobilize adults such as parents and teachers in leadership roles that involve positive relationships with youth, behavior management, supervision, and monitoring. Some effective interventions operate at the universal level, that is, they target the entire population or community. They are group interventions, but they operate on both deviant and nondeviant members of the community. Some effective interventions are targeted toward high-risk youth (called *selective interventions*) and some are targeted toward those who already show signs of trouble, psychopathology, or maladjustment (called *indicated interventions*). The effective interventions among these operate at the individual child level, although family members and well-adjusted peers may be brought into the treatment. Most of the effective interventions focus on positive skill building rather than examination of deviant behavior, although systematic application of modest negative contingencies for disruptive behavior is an explicit part of many of these programs. Effective alternatives to deviant peer aggregation are summarized briefly below and listed in Table 20.2.

Programs that aggregate deviant youth operate in education, juvenile justice, mental health, and community programming, as do effective alternatives to deviant peer group placements. Practices that should be discouraged as well as promising alternatives are reviewed for each of these domains.

Education

Practices That Should Be Discouraged

The first group of problematic practices involves placement policies and intervention practices for deviant youth. The practice of tracking low-

TABLE 20.1. Programs and Policies That Aggregate Deviant Peers and Should Be Avoided If Possible

Education

1. Tracking of low-performing students
2. Forced grade retention for disruptive youth
3. Self-contained classrooms for unruly students in special education
4. Group counseling of homogeneously deviant youth
5. Zero tolerance policies for deviant behavior
6. Aggregation of deviant youth through in-school suspension
7. Expulsion practices
8. Alternative schools that aggregate deviant youth
9. Individuals with Disabilities Education Act (IDEA) reforms that allow disruptive special education students to be excluded from mainstream classrooms
10. School-choice policies that leave low-performing students in homogeneous low-performing schools

Juvenile justice and child welfare

1. Group incarceration
2. Military-style boot camps and wilderness challenges ("brat camp")
3. Incarceration placement with other offenders who committed the same crime
4. Custodial residential placement in training schools
5. Three strikes–mandated long prison terms
6. Scared Straight
7. Group counseling by probation officer
8. Guided group interaction
9. Positive peer culture
10. Institutional or group foster care
11. Bringing younger delinquents together in groups
12. Vocational training

Mental health

1. Any group therapy in which the ratio of deviant to nondeviant youth is high
2. Group therapies with poorly trained leaders and lack of supervision
3. Group therapies offering opportunities for unstructured time with deviant peers
4. Group homes or residential facilities
5. Discussion groups focused on eating disorders

Community programming

1. Midnight basketball
2. Unstructured settings that are unsupervised by authority figures (e.g., youth recreation centers designed as places for teens to "hang out")
3. Group programs at community and recreation centers that are restricted to deviant youth
4. After-school programs that serve only or primarily high-risk youth
5. 21st Century Community Learning Centers
6. Interventions that increase the cohesiveness of gangs
7. Gang Resistance Education and Training program
8. Comprehensive Gang Intervention program
9. Safe Futures program
10. Urban enterprise zones
11. Federal housing programs that bring together high-risk families

TABLE 20.2. Effective Programs That Represent Viable Alternatives
to Aggregating Deviant Peers

Education

1. Universal, environment-centered programs that focus on school-wide reform, including:
   a. clearly explicated expectations for student and staff behavior
   b. consistent use of proactive school discipline strategies
   c. active monitoring of "hot spots" for behavior problems
   d. improved systems to monitor student achievement and behavior.
2. Universal classroom programs to build social competence (e.g., Responding in Peaceful and Positive Ways, PATHS)
3. School-wide positive behavior support
4. Individual behavior support plan for each student
5. Improved training in behavior management practices for classroom teachers, especially:
   a. group contingencies
   b. self-management techniques
   c. differential reinforcement.
6. Incredible Years Teacher Training
7. Good Behavior Game
8. Consultation and support for classroom teachers
9. Family-based Adolescent Transitions Program
10. Matching deviant youth with well-adjusted peers (e.g., coaching, BrainPower, Peer Coping Skills Training, the Montreal Longitudinal Project)
11. Multimodal programs (e.g., LIFT, Fast Track, Seattle Social Development Project)
12. Proactive prevention programs that shape student "morals" and encourage responsible decision making

Juvenile justice and child welfare

1. Functional family therapy
2. Multisystemic therapy
3. Multidimensional treatment foster care
4. Intensive protective supervision
5. Teaching Family Home Model
6. Sending delinquent youth to programs that serve the general population of youth in their neighborhoods (e.g., Boys and Girls Clubs)
7. Community rather than custodial settings
8. Interpersonal skills training
9. Individual counseling
10. Treatment administered by mental health professionals
11. Early diversion programs
12. Victim–offender mediation
13. Teen court programs
14. Therapeutic jurisprudence
15. Community commitment orders
16. Psychiatric advance directives

Mental health

1. Individually administered treatment
2. Family-based interventions
3. Adolescent Transitions Program

(continued)

4. Linking the Interests of Families and Teachers
5. Iowa Strengthening Families Program
6. Familias Unidas
7. Mentoring programs such as Big Brothers/Big Sisters

Community programming

1. Public or private organizations that are open to all youth, regardless of risk status, and that provide structure and adult involvement (e.g., religious groups, service clubs, Scouts, Boys and Girls Clubs)
2. School-based extracurricular activities
3. Encouragement of commitments outside of gangs (e.g., to jobs, family roles, military service, mentors)
4. Early childhood interventions such as the Perry Preschool Program
5. Job Corps
6. Policing programs that target high-crime neighborhoods where high-risk youth congregate
7. Community efforts to reduce marginalization of specific groups of youth

---

performing youth into isolated classrooms serves to place these youth with each other in ways that discourage them from ever catching up to the mainstream of peers. Instead, they are at risk to influence each other in deviant ways. The policy of forced grade retention for misbehaving youth leads to school cultures that are populated by highly deviant older youth who are in a position to influence budding deviants at younger ages. Self-contained classrooms for unruly students in special education appear to exacerbate, rather than minimize, the antisocial behavior of these students. Group counseling of deviant students, especially when led by poorly trained leaders who encourage open discussion of deviance, has been shown to be ineffective and may promote deviant peer contagion. All these practices should be avoided.

Next, school disciplinary practices such as zero tolerance for deviant behavior, group in-school suspension, and placement into alternative schools are likely to lead to placements that aggregate deviant youth, thus nurturing deviant peer contagion and exacerbating the failure of these youth; thus they should be avoided. Expulsion encourages the natural aggregation of deviant youth in neighborhoods while their well-performing peers move forward in education, and it too should be terminated as a standard practice.

Finally, at the district policy level, school-choice policies that are part of the No Child Left Behind Act encourage parents to leave low-performing schools. Unfortunately, it is the well-informed parents who are most likely to take advantage of these policies, leaving the least well-informed families to remain in the lowest performing schools. These schools may well become more homogeneously low performing. Charter schools that are created for deviant students are voluntary interventions that are also likely to exacerbate deviant peer contagion. Finally, new reforms in the Individuals with Disabilities Education Act (IDEA) that allow disruptive special education students to be excluded from mainstream classrooms are likely to exacerbate deviant peer contagion. These policies should be considered as high risk to participating youth.

Promising Alternatives

Establishing universal, environment-centered programs that focus on school-wide reform should be encouraged, particularly when these efforts focus on (1) clearly explicated expectations for student and staff prosocial and negative behavior; (2) consistent utilization of proactive school discipline strategies; (3) active monitoring of "hot spots" for behavior problems; and (4) improved systems to monitor student achievement and behavior. Strategies that emphasize the behavior management practices of the entire school, without creating "pull-out" programs for deviant youth, are effective for improving the total rate of problem behavior in schools. Examples include the Good Behavior Game and School-Wide Positive Behavior Support.

System-wide training, incentives, and supports for effective behavior management practices by teachers, especially for more disruptive youth, reduce problem behavior and prevent escalations to other forms. Midcareer teaching training, teacher mentoring, and close teacher monitoring are likely to enhance effective behavior management by teachers and result in lower rates of deviant behavior. Many interpersonal conflicts can be effectively managed by peer mediation. Alternatives to school suspensions and expulsions include individually administered sanctions such as compensation to victims and individual punishments to perpetrators. These policies should be implemented, encouraged, and financially supported.

Integrating social competence enhancement into school curricula, in programs such as Responding in Peaceful and Positive Ways (RIPP) and Providing Alternative Thinking Strategies (PATHS), is likely to lower behavior problem rates. Skill development interventions within the school environment are effective for reducing disruptive behavior and preventing future problem behavior.

For selective and indicated interventions that target specific youth, numerous alternatives to aggregating deviant youth are available. Again, teacher training heads the list. Individual planning for each student can be accomplished through improved training in behavior management practices for classroom teachers, especially in the use of (1) group contingencies, (2) self-management techniques, and (3) differential reinforcement. The Incredible Years Teacher Training Program is one effective example. This training can be complemented by ongoing consultation with teachers by expert behavior managers.

Programs that match a deviant child with a single nondeviant peer for purposes of cooperative learning or skill development have yielded favorable outcomes for the deviant youth with no adverse impact on the nondeviant peer. These programs include Oden and Asher's peer coaching, Brain Power, the Peer Coping Skills Training Program, and the Montreal Longitudinal Project.

Interventions that involve individual families have proven successful, especially when these programs use behavioral principles. Often, these programs include multiple components. Examples include the Family-Based Adolescent Transitions Program, LIFT, Fast Track, and the Seattle Social Development Project.

Silver and Eddy (Chapter 14, this volume) provide a summary of the principles that guide effective programming in school contexts. These principles are repeated below:

1. Take a preventive approach that engages students and families early in elementary school and continues through middle and high school.
2. Create school-wide discipline policies that include both behavioral norms and expectations for all community members and proactive discipline approaches, including a heavy emphasis on positive reinforcement.
3. Increase use of effective and proactive classroom management techniques by (a) incorporating these skills into teacher degree programs, (b) providing in-service training in these skills, and/or (c) providing ongoing consultation services and support to teachers.
4. Use universal child-centered preventive interventions (e.g., social skills training) whenever possible.
5. When using selective prevention programs (which target at-risk or deviant youth), use strategies that minimize the risk of deviant peer contagion. Such strategies include (a) creating a highly structured program with a low teacher–student ratio and extensive training for group leaders, (b) integrating prosocial and deviant youth in mixed intervention groups or peer pairing programs, and/or (c) bringing selective interventions to the regular education classroom (e.g., behavioral modification strategies supported by consultation services).
6. Actively monitor hot spots (e.g., hallways, restrooms, playgrounds, parking lots, cafeterias) to increase school order and

decrease antisocial behavior during unstructured and unsupervised time.

7. Make parenting resources (e.g., parent training classes) accessible through schools.

8. Foster home–school collaboration by increased communication between families, teachers, administrators, and other school personnel.

9. School-based preventive efforts are most likely to be effective when they target multiple risk factors in several contexts of children's lives. Child-, parent-, classroom-, whole-school-, and community-focused components should all be considered.

Juvenile Justice and Child Welfare

Practices That Should Be Discouraged

From the perspective of the long-term welfare of the youth who has come into the juvenile justice system, incarceration with other delinquent youth, especially those who are slightly older and have committed similar crimes, is likely to exacerbate the youth's trajectory toward a life of crime. Deviancy training is a leading reason for this outcome. Similar problematic outcomes are likely if the youth is placed in a custodial residential school, training school, boot camp, or wilderness camp with other deviant youth, especially if supervision is lacking and adult leaders have not been adequately trained. Most group incarceration is bad medicine for youth. These programs should be extinguished in favor of interventions that operate at the individual level.

Evidence suggests that short-term placement such as 10-day "holding tanks" while a youth is evaluated is less likely to lead to long-term problem outcomes. Longer sentences breed bad outcomes, however. "Three strikes" law–mandated longer prison terms are worse medicine.

Of course, as noted many times in this report, the perspective of society may mandate these placements. The major finding of this report, however, is that these placements may be doing harm to the youth themselves, and the major recommendation of this report is that alternatives to these placements are available and should be expanded.

For delinquent youth who are not incarcerated, in-home treatment can have adverse or positive effects. The Scared Straight approach has been shown to be a disaster for youth and should be terminated. Adverse effects are also relatively likely if delinquent youth are placed on probation and are subjected to group counseling by poorly trained probation officers. Group-treatment programs that were once thought to be "cutting edge" have been found to have adverse effects, including guided group interaction and positive peer culture.

In child welfare cases of abuse or neglect, placement of the child vic-tim into a group home, residential facility, or group foster home has been associated with negative outcomes for the child and should be avoided if possible. The decision about placement in these cases must be weighed against the outcomes that are likely to accrue from keeping the child in an abusive home. Admittedly, these decisions are complex. When out-of-home placement is necessary, placement into a foster home headed by a parent trained in multidimensional treatment foster care is the treatment of choice.

Promising Alternatives

The good news is that randomized experiments support the implementa-tion of several alternatives to incarceration and deviant group placement for delinquent adolescents. Functional family therapy (FFT) and multi-systemic therapy (MST) have flourished under the spotlight of rigorous evaluation, including cost–benefit analyses. In general, behaviorally based family interventions to improve monitoring and supervision of youth, coupled with the appropriate application of rewards and punish-ments, should be encouraged. Strategies that address parenting practices, increase collaboration between parents and juvenile court workers, and avoid out-of-home placement should be implemented whenever possible.

When out-of-home placement is inevitable because remaining with the biological family would not be in the best interests of the child, mul-tidimensional treatment foster care (in which foster parents receive spe-cial training in parent management skills such as monitoring and clear rule setting in order to provide a therapeutic family environment) is a vi-able alternative for reducing deviant peer contagion, reducing delinquent offending, and reducing recidivism. For circumstances when residential group placement is unavoidable, programs having clear program goals, sound behavior management systems, high rates of adult supervision, and an emphasis on long-term skill development are the most likely to succeed.

Innovations are flourishing in the court system, and these reforms should be encouraged, especially with systematic evaluation of impact. Therapeutic courts are particularly likely to bring positive outcomes for delinquent youth. Innovations in supervised probation can be effec-tive if implemented regularly at the individual level. A recent case ex-ample of court-ordered probation in Los Angeles County that involved no segregation from the mainstream peer group indicated that "stu-dents are required to attend school while serving probation, and Pro-bation Department officials say allowing those teenagers to have a more typical high school experience can reduce recidivism" (Hayasaki, 2005).

Long before a child comes to the juvenile court system, individual-level prevention programs can be effective for keeping a child from initiating delinquent behavior in the first place. Early enriched preschool programs such as the High/Scope Perry Preschool Project and the Abecedarian Program have demonstrated absolutely remarkable success in long-term prevention. Prevention programs for elementary school-age high-risk youth are also proving effective in preventing antisocial behavior, especially the Montreal Longitudinal Project and Fast Track. These programs emphasize interpersonal skills training that equips a high-risk youth with a variety of skills to manage life's challenges. Nurse practitioner home visiting for high-risk new mothers has also been shown to prevent offspring crime during adolescence, a remarkable finding that demonstrates the cascading effects of early parenting.

Mental Health

Practices That Should Be Discouraged

Theoretical approaches to mental health interventions that are least likely to benefit deviant youth with externalizing problems are those that involve open, nondirective discussion with groups of deviant peers, such as guided group interaction. More critical than the theoretical orientation, though, is the group context. Residential programs for deviant youth should be avoided unless the structure is so great and the supervision is so strong that deviancy training does not occur. Any group therapy consisting solely of deviant peers or in which the ratio of deviant youth to nondeviant youth is high runs heightened risk of exacerbating deviant behavior through deviant peer contagion and should be avoided.

Additional characteristics of the context of intervention that have been shown to increase risk include numerous opportunities for unsupervised deviant peer interaction before or after group meetings, poor training of the group leaders in behavior management, and lack of use of behavioral methods to control deviant behavior during group meetings. Programs with these characteristics should be avoided.

Participants who should not be referred to deviant group interventions include, especially, early adolescent males who have begun to initiate deviant behavior but have not yet committed themselves to a deviant lifestyle.

Promising Alternatives

Mental health approaches to universal bullying prevention in communities and schools have proven effective in several European countries and are being tested in Canada. Their promise for the United States is strong, but the major barrier seems to be the unwillingness of school districts to embrace the total commitment that these programs require in this day of accountability through standardized academic testing. Perhaps such efforts would receive stronger support if gains in social competence could be tested in valid ways.

Mental health interventions that emphasize parents' behavior management skills and the child's interpersonal skills development have demonstrated the strongest effectiveness for reducing conduct problems through randomized experiments. Such interventions should replace group therapies and residential placements into all-deviant peer groups. Family-based interventions that use behavioral principles growing out of the work by Patterson should become the standard in the field. With children, the relative deficits in social-cognitive skills displayed by youth with conduct problems, coupled with strong evidence of the effectiveness of social skills training programs, suggest the wisdom of implementing social skills training programs with individual children. Programs such as social problem-solving skills training, Fast Track, and the Peer Coping Skills Program should be encouraged. When the participants in these programs are ready for practice with peers, the use of peer coaching with well-adjusted peers should be implemented.

Multimodal programs that include family involvement, skills training with youth, and school behavior management should be encouraged. Programs that include both universal and selective efforts should be encouraged, including the Adolescent Transitions Program, Linking the Interests of Families and Teachers (LIFT), the Iowa Strengthening Families Program (ISFP), and Familias Unidas.

Treatment programs directed to individual children that are family-centered have repeatedly been shown to be beneficial for reducing both emotional and behavioral problems in children and adolescents. If aggregation is necessary for treatment, then it is critical to provide substantial supervision, to be sensitive to the context of the intervention, and to continue to evaluate the potential deviant peer contagion.

Intensive parenting support that is linked to a range of mental health and substance use treatment services is a viable alternative to programs that aggregate neglected and abused children and adolescents. When out-of-home placement is necessary, then multidimensional treatment foster care with long-term adoption options is the optimal strategy for reducing deviant peer contagion.

Not all mental health interventions must be implemented by mental health professionals. Mentoring programs for deviant youth, such as Big Brothers/Big Sisters, have proven effective in randomized trials as long as the mentor stays involved with the youth for at least 1 year.

Community Programming

Practices That Should Be Discouraged

Although efforts by police and community agencies to engage street gang members in community activities were once thought to be effective, they are likely to increase gang group cohesion and thus should be avoided. Specific programs that should not be implemented include the Gang Resistance Education and Training Program (G.R.E.A.T.), the national Comprehensive Gang Intervention program, and the Safe Futures program.

Community programs that should be terminated are those well-intentioned programs that bring together deviant youth in an unstructured context without adequate adult supervision, such as Midnight Basketball and "hangouts" for youth. Community locations that inadvertently encourage deviant youth to congregate should be restructured. These locations might include malls, street corners, and convenience store parking lots, but any specific location depends on local community patterns. Any community center or recreation center group program that is restricted to high-risk youth should be scrutinized carefully and possibly be avoided.

After-school programs are currently popular, but the ones that serve exclusively or primarily deviant or high-risk youth have been found to yield adverse outcomes for their participants. These programs should be terminated or reorganized to become more highly structured and well supervised.

Sports teams at schools and community locations bring many advantages for their participants, but one disadvantage is the likelihood of increased alcohol use among adolescent participants who have already initiated alcohol use.

Although the impact of public housing, housing vouchers, and programs to move residents to different communities has not yielded uniform outcomes according to published reports, it makes sense that federal programs that bring together high-risk families against their choice should be discouraged. Finally, economic development programs such as enterprise zones have not proven effective and should be discouraged.

Promising Alternatives

The most effective community programs are those that integrate the deviant youth with the mainstream of nondeviant peers. Thus programs that combine high- and low-risk youth should be encouraged, such as 4H programs, Boys and Girls Clubs, music clubs, Scouts, and church activities. School-based extracurricular activities have been shown to have positive effects, but only if they integrate deviant youth with nondeviant peers. Sometimes these programs target inner-city or high-risk neighborhoods or groups; when they do, they should be avoided because of the risk of deviant peer contagion. One exception is participation in school and community sports programs, which have been found to have positive effects except for a tendency to increase alcohol use among participants who have already begun to try alcohol. In general, community programs have positive effects on deviant youth if they are truly integrated with nondeviant peers, if the program is highly structured, and if the participants are well supervised by trained leaders. The Job Corps Program meets these criteria and has the specific goal of training job skills and connecting youth with career opportunities. It should be encouraged.

Community strategies of collaborating with police to identify "hot spots" of illegal activity, including the spontaneous aggregation of deviant youth, have proven effective and should be encouraged. Efforts to disperse gangs, rather than increase their cohesiveness, should be encouraged. Community efforts to reduce marginalization of specific groups of families and youth are likely to reduce the possibility of the formation of gangs and peer groups that amplify deviance. In addition, providing opportunities for low resource families to "move into opportunities" are promising community strategies. It is important to note that community organization strategies must be accompanied by a long-term commitment to evaluate the impact of community change on youth problem behavior using systematic monitoring strategies.

- *Recommendation 3: When placement with deviant peers is inevitable, specific measures to minimize its impact should be implemented.* In some cases, judges, educators, and mental health officials deem it necessary to place a deviant youth with a group of deviant peers because all the available alternative placements are obviously more dangerous. Examples include the child who is being abused at home and the seriously dangerous delinquent in a community that has few individual placements available. In these communities, officials would be wise to assign their *best* leaders and *best* teachers and their *greatest* amount of resources to these placement sites in order to minimize the likelihood that they become staging grounds for the growth of deviant behavior.

Placements that aggregate deviant youth can minimize the likelihood of iatrogenic effects by adhering to specific measures. First, some youth are especially susceptible to deviant peer influences and should have the highest priority for alternative placement. These highest risk youth who should avoid deviant peer group placement are early adolescent males who have only begun to experiment with deviant behavior and are not very dangerous or committed to a deviant life style. Second, officials should be concerned with the matching among deviant youth. Younger, highly susceptible youth should not be paired with slightly older groups of deviant peers who are ready to exert their influence. Likewise, training schools and juvenile prisons should not match similar youth from the same communities in the same cottages or living units because they risk exacerbating crime development in these youth. Third, the placements should be highly structured and should provide no opportunities for deviant youth to interact freely with other deviant youth. Well-trained professionals who understand principles of behavior management should lead them.

Finally, officials should minimize the total amount of time that a youth is placed with deviant peers. Youth should be moved out of these placements as soon as an alternative can be identified or created.

• *Recommendation 4: Practitioners, programs, and policymakers should document placements and evaluate impacts of those placements.* It is well recognized that the state of evaluation for programs that aggregate youth is abysmal. Few programs document the context of a deviant youth's placement with sufficient information to determine whether the youth is placed with deviant peers, let alone devote the resources to rigorous evaluation of program impact. In order to grow knowledge that can guide public policy for the next generation of youth, all programs and placements should begin documenting the characteristics of all peers with whom a youth is placed.

Funders of programs, most of whom are government agencies but some of whom are nonprofit foundations, should demand documentation of program characteristics and peer participants, the interventions implemented to reduce deviant peer contagion, and their impact on each participant.

Finally, funders, policymakers, and citizens should demand the ethical implementation of randomized experiments that test the impact of various placements on deviant youth, their nondeviant peers, and the community at large.

LIMITATIONS OF THE SCIENCE AND RECOMMENDATIONS FOR RESEARCH

Ten years ago, there was little professional concern that peer aggregation was problematic, despite the long-standing worry of criminal justice and delinquency theorists dating back to the 19th century (Osgood &

Briddell, Chapter 8, this volume). The evidence reported in this volume brings us to a place of concern that deviant peer contagion, in some circumstances, can undermine well-intentioned efforts to improve the lives of youth. By and large, this conclusion is based on a maturing behavioral science that is integrative, uses random assignment, and reports all outcomes, regardless of whether they are positive or negative.

Despite the recent advances in intervention science, we are left with the conclusion that the existing empirical literature is woefully underdeveloped with respect to the issue of deviant peer contagion. Given that the vast majority of troubled youth are exposed to interventions and policies that aggregate them, we have very little systematic knowledge about the unique effects of peer aggregation. Schools, juvenile justice, and mental health programs rarely use random assignment and systematic observation procedures to study the risks and benefits of aggregate program delivery. Studies that do use random assignment often involve the program developers as evaluators of effectiveness. It is possible, therefore, that many studies of intervention (even those involving randomization) are biased to identify positive intervention effects and to ignore or collect no data on possible negative effects.

Detection of deviant peer contagion in the context of intervention underscores the need for data from methodologically sound research to select interventions, programs, and services and to make policy decisions that affect millions of youth. To improve our scientific database for such crucial decision making, we make the following recommendations:

1. Evaluate real-world interventions, services, and policies by the most rigorous method available. For good reason, the "gold standard" is the random assignment experiment, with the explicit goal of examining the costs and benefits of peer aggregation. It is often the case, however, that allocation of youth to existing services is a quasi-random process that can be capitalized for evaluation. For example, assignment of college roommates, prison cellmates, and training school cottage mates is often quasi-random; turning this into a random-allocation process can reveal the impact of peers on later outcomes.

2. Develop a scientific consensus on the set of variables to be measured in the context of funded intervention research, and encourage scientific reports that summarize outcomes and change processes on all measured variables. Scientific journals are beginning to require standards for reporting subject attrition, computation of effect sizes, participant characteristics, and the like. A consensus on the key variables to measure and report for intervention studies would enhance our potential for documenting a range of outcomes for any given intervention or program strategy, and, in particular, potential negative side effects. Further-

more, journal editors could ask for reports of how much interventions cost to facilitate cost–benefit analyses.

3. Report individual responses to interventions as well as central tendencies—for example, how many children improved, stayed the same, and deteriorated during the course of the intervention or program evaluation. Average effects mask variability in responses to an intervention. Some interventions, especially those that aggregate, could result in average improvement for many youth, but serious deterioration for others. This cannot be evaluated unless individual responses are summarized in scientific reports. One advantage of examining individual differences in responses would be the enhanced potential to develop interventions that may be differentially effective depending on the age, gender, ethnicity, or other characteristics of the participating youth.

4. Examine the impact of expanding the behavior management repertoire of teachers, counselors, and residential supervisors to address the process and dynamics of deviant peer contagion. It is plausible that developing adult leadership skills in the management of deviant peer contagion is a key factor in rendering interventions that aggregate more effectively for a larger proportion of youth.

5. When random assignment to real-world programs that aggregate deviant youth is not feasible or ethical, conduct observation studies in an effort to relate peer contagion to individual change. Examples of compelling observation studies conducted in the juvenile justice system suggest that youth acquire the crimes of their peers in group residential care in some circumstances (Bayer, Pintoff, & Pozen, 2003). Expanding the research framework to assess the mechanisms of deviant peer contagion and study the relation between these factors and youth outcomes is necessary for improving our potential for designing prevention and remedial strategies that actually reduce the prevalence of youth problem behavior.

6. Consider contagion effects on outcomes associated with mental health interventions for eating disorders, suicide, and other problem behaviors. In the past 10 years, there has been an increase in the number of selected prevention trials focusing on preventing the development of eating disorders among high-risk girls. It is possible that these interventions may be effective on some outcomes, yet iatrogenic for correlated problem behaviors.

7. Conduct economic evaluations that clarify the relative costs and benefits to children and adolescents in the general public with respect to interventions and policies that aggregate deviant youth. For example, what are the benefits to successful students for sending disruptive youth to alternative settings for educational services? How do children and families in the community benefit from having residential programs for delinquent youth? Such programs may run the risk of increasing the

problem behavior of deviant youth, but improve the education and socialization experiences of the majority of youth in the community.

8. Conduct research to understand how to prevent peer contagion in naturally occurring groups. For example, currently we have little understanding of how to intervene with gangs in ways that will not make the gangs more cohesive (see Klein, Chapter 13, this volume). Additional research is needed to identify strategies that will not increase the risk of deviant influence when intervening in naturally occurring groups.

REDUCING DEVIANT PEER CONTAGION

Despite the limitations of the science at this time, the chapters in this volume converge on a number of risks for adverse peer influence effects within communities and as a function of interventions and policies that target child and adolescent problem behavior. It is clear that policies that guide interventions and services that aggregate groups of high-risk youth and are not well supervised, lack structure, and provide multiple opportunities to interact are likely to amplify peer contagion and increase problem behavior and adjustment problems in youth. Examples of such strategies may include some alternative school programs that are not well funded, selected prevention programs for high-risk youth, and other well-intentioned but otherwise ill-conceived programs that bring youth together in numbers and circumstances that favor deviant peer influences.

In contrast, the empirical literature supports interventions or policies that mobilize adults to persist and skillfully manage child and adolescent behavior in the community and within the context of interventions and services. In addition, interventions and services that support adult motivation, persistence, effective behavior management practices, and positive relationships with children are likely to be effective for both prevention and treatment programs designed to benefit youth. It is generally acknowledged that behavior management and building positive relationships between parents, teachers, counselors, mentors, and children is a complex process that requires training and ongoing support. In many respects, the conceptualization of child and problem behavior driving interventions, policies, and services needs attention. Rather than a "medical model," which assumes a "cure" for youth deviance, a "preventive dentistry model" may be more appropriate. Thus the interventions that are effective for reducing deviant peer contagion and improving outcomes for youth are likely to be long-term strategies that follow youth through development in the context of the institutions within which they interact.

Overall, then, the research reviewed in this volume supports three main conclusions. First, the predominant way of dealing with deviant youth in the United States today is by grouping them together; this conclusion applies to the number of youth in some systems, such as juvenile justice when most delinquents are aggregated, and to the dollars spent in other systems, such as mental health when the most expensive treatments are residential programs that aggregate troubled youth. Second, aggregating troubled youth can reduce or degrade the positive effects of interventions and may backfire by having negative effects. Third, there are good alternatives to grouping deviant youth, but when it is necessary to aggregate such youth, there are factors to consider that might reduce the harm in grouping. Clearly, reducing total societal harm, not just harm to deviant youth, is a goal of programs that work with deviant youth.

The evidence linking deviant peer contagion to escalation in youth problem behavior underscores the need for concern and attention to how communities, educational settings, interventions, and policies can be organized to minimize this problem, and to optimize benefits to youth and families. It is clear from this comprehensive examination of the deviant peer contagion problem that simple good intentions to benefit youth are necessary but not sufficient. We have learned, once again, the value of science for studying the impact of interventions, addressing the complexity of possible outcomes, and understanding the dynamics of human behavior. With good intentions, continued research, and a comprehensive, collaborative approach, efforts to improve outcomes for youth are less likely to be inadvertently subverted, and more likely to be consistently successful and cost effective.

Finally, in the specific case, the decision to place a deviant youth in a setting with other deviant youth is a complicated one. The decision maker must contrast the likely impact of placement in the deviant peer group with the likely benefits and risks of available alternate placements. For government officials, the cost–benefit ratio for the individual deviant youth must be weighed against the costs and benefits to the rest of the community. The decision is never an easy one. This report will not make the decision easier in certain cases, but we hope that we have raised awareness of important parameters that should be considered in these cases.

References

Aaronson, D. (1997). Sibling estimates of neighborhood effects. In J. Brooks-Gunn, G. J. Duncan, & J. L. Aber (Eds.), *Neighborhood poverty Vol. 2: Policy implications in studying neighborhoods* (pp. 80–94). New York: Russell Sage Foundation.

Aaronson, D. (1998). Using sibling data to estimate the impact of neighborhoods on children's educational outcomes. *Journal of Human Resources, 33,* 915–946.

Abelson, W. D., Zigler, E., & DeBlasi, C. L. (1974). Effects of a four-year Follow Through program on economically disadvantaged children. *Journal of Educational Psychology, 66,* 756–771.

Aber, J. L., Jones, S. M., Brown, J. L., Chaudry, N., & Samples, F. (1998). Resolving conflict creatively: Evaluating the developmental effects of a school-based violence prevention program in neighborhood and classroom context. *Development and Psychopathology, 10,* 187–213.

Acker, M. M., & O'Leary, S. G. (1987). Effects of reprimands and praise on appropriate behavior in the classroom. *Journal of Abnormal Child Psychology, 15,* 549–557.

Administration for Children and Families. (2003). *The AFCARS Report: Preliminary FY 2001 estimates as of March 2003.* Retrieved September 29, 2004, from www.acf.hhs.gov/programs/cb/publications/afcars/report8.htm

Advancement Project and The Civil Rights Project. (2000). *Opportunities suspended: The devastating consequences of zero tolerance and school discipline policies.* Cambridge, MA: Harvard's Civil Rights Project.

Agnew, R., & Petersen, D. M. (1989). Leisure and delinquency. *Social Problems, 36,* 332–350.

Ahlstrom, W., & Havighurst, R. (1971). *400 Losers: Delinquent boys in high school.* San Francisco: Jossey-Bass.

Alesci, N. L., Forster, J. L., & Blaine, T. (2003). Smoking visibility, perceived acceptability, and frequency in various locations among youth and adults. *Preventive Medicine, 36,* 272–281.

Alexander, J., Barton, C., Gordon, D., Grotpeter, J., Hanson, K., Harrison, R., et al. (1998). *Blueprints for violence prevention: Vol. 3. Functional family therapy.* Boulder: University of Colorado, Institute of Behavioral Sciences.

Alexander, J. F., & Parsons, B. V. (1973). Short-term behavioral intervention with delinquent families: Impact on family process and recidivism. *Journal of Abnormal Psychology, 81,* 219–225.

Allen, J. P., Marsh, P., McFarland, C., McElhaney, K. B., Land, D. J., Jodl, K. M., et al. (2002). Attachment and autonomy as predictors of the development of social skills and delinquency during midadolescence. *Journal of Consulting and Clinical Psychology, 70,* 56–66.

Allport, F. H. (1937). The observation of societal behaviors of individuals. *Social Forces, 15,* 484–487.

Almond, R. (1974). *The healing community: Dynamics of the therapeutic milieu.* New York: Jason Aronson.

Anderson, D. (1999). The aggregate burden of crime. *Journal of Law and Economics, 42,* 611–642.

Anderson-Butcher, D., Newsome, W. S., & Ferrari, T. M. (2003). Participation in Boys and Girls Clubs and relationships to youth outcomes. *Journal of Community Psychology, 31,* 39–55.

Andrews, D. A. (1980). Some experimental investigations of the principles of differential association through deliberate manipulations of the structure of service systems. *American Sociological Review, 45,* 448–462.

Andrews, D. A., Zinger, I., Hoge, R. D., Bonta, J., Gendreau, P., & Cullen, F. T. (1990). Does correctional treatment work?: A clinically-relevant and psychologically-informed meta-analysis. *Criminology, 28,* 369–404.

Ang, R. P., & Hughes, J. N. (2002). Differential benefits of skills training with antisocial youth based on group composition: A meta-analytic investigation. *School Psychology Review, 31,* 164–185.

Angrist, J. D., Imbens, G. W., & Rubin, D. B. (1996). Identification of causal effects using instrumental variables. *Journal of the American Statistical Association, 91,* 444–472.

Aos, S., Lieb, R., Mayfield, J., Miller, M., & Pennucci, A. (2004). *Benefits and costs of prevention and early intervention programs for youth.* Olympia: Washington State Institute for Public Policy.

Aos, S., Phipps, P., Barmoski, R., & Lieb, R. (2001). *The comparative costs and benefits of programs to reduce crime.* Olympia: Washington State Institute for Public Policy. Retrieved May 2005 from www. wsipp.wa.gov/ rptfiles.costbenefit.pdf

Arnold, M. E., & Hughes, J. H. (1999). First do no harm: Adverse effects of grouping deviant youth for skills training. *Journal of School Psychology, 37,* 99–115.

Arnove, R. F., & Strout, T. (1980). Alternative schools for disruptive youth. *Educational Forum, 44,* 453–471.

Arrigo, B. A. (2004). The ethics of therapeutic jurisprudence: A critical and theoretical inquiry of law, psychology, and crime. *Psychiatry, Psychology, and Law, 11*(1). Retrieved May 2005 from infotrac.galegroup.com/itw/infomark /138/490/69077455w6/purl=rc1_EAIM_0_A121082129&dyn=4!xrn_4_ 0_A121082129?sw_aep=duke_perkins

Arum, R., & Beattie, I. (1999). High school experience and the risk of adult incarceration. *Criminology, 37,* 515–537.

Asher, S. R., & Coie, J. D. (1990). *Peer rejection in childhood.* Cambridge, UK: Cambridge University Press.

Attar, B. K., Guerra, N. G., & Tolan, P. H. (1994). Neighborhood disadvantage, stressful life events, and adjustment in urban elementary-school children. *Journal of Clinical Child Psychology, 23,* 391–400.

Avery, R. J. (2000). Perceptions and practice: Agency efforts for the hardest-to-place children. *Children and Youth Services Review, 22,* 399–420.

Bach, P., & Hayes, S. C. (2002). The use of acceptance and commitment therapy to prevent the rehospitalization of psychotic patients: A randomized controlled trial. *Journal of Consulting and Clinical Psychology, 70,* 1129–1139.

Baird, J. A., & Baldwin, D. A. (1999). Action analysis: A gateway to intentional inference. In P. Rochat (Ed.), *Early social cognition: Understanding others in the first months of life* (pp. 215–240). Mahwah, NJ: Erlbaum.

Baker, R. D., & Stevens, R. H. (1995). A random-effects model for analysis of infectious disease final-state data. *Biometrics, 51,* 956–968.

Bakeman, R., & Quera, V. (1995). *Analyzing interaction: Sequential analysis with SDIS and GSEQ.* New York: Cambridge University Press.

Baldwin, D. A. (2000). Interpersonal understanding fuels knowledge acquisition. *Current Directions in Psychological Science, 9*(2), 40–45.

Baldwin, D. A., & Moses, L. J. (1994). Early understanding of referential intent and attentional focus: Evidence from language and emotion. In C. Lewis & P. Mitchell (Eds.), *Children's early understanding of mind: Origins and development* (pp. 133–156). Hillsdale, NJ: Erlbaum.

Bandura, A. (1969). *Principles of behavior modification.* Oxford: Holt, Rinehart & Winston.

Barber, B. L., Eccles, J. S., & Stone, M. R. (2001). Whatever happened to the jock, the brain, and the princess?: Young adult pathways linked to adolescent activity involvement and social identity. *Journal of Adolescent Research, 16,* 429–455.

Barber, J. (2001). The predictors of unsuccessful transition to foster care. *Journal of Child Psychology and Psychiatry, 42,* 785–790.

Barnett, D., Manly, J. T., & Cicchetti, D. (1993). Defining child maltreatment: The interface between policy and research. In D. Cicchetti & S. L. Toth (Eds.), *Child abuse, child development, and social policy* (pp. 7–73). Norwood, NJ: Ablex.

Barrish, H. H., Saunders, M., & Wolf, M. M. (1969). Good behavior game: Effects of individual contingencies for group consequences on disruptive behavior in a classroom. *Journal of Applied Behavior Analysis, 2,* 119–124.

Barth, J., Dunlap, S., Dane, H., Lochman, J., & Wells, K. (2004). Classroom environment influences on aggression, peer relations, and academic focus. *Journal of School Psychology, 42,* 115–133.

Bartko, W. T., & Eccles, J. S. (2003). Adolescent participation in structured and unstructured activities: A person-oriented analysis. *Journal of Youth and Adolescence, 32,* 233–241.

Bartoli, P. V. (2002). Burnout and job performance among education professionals and paraprofessionals. *Dissertation Abstracts International: Section B: The Sciences and Engineering, 63*(4-B), 2049.

Battin, S. R., Hill, K. G., Abbott, R. D, Catalano, R. F., & Hawkins, J. D. (1998). The contribution of gang membership to delinquency beyond delinquent friends. *Criminology, 36,* 93–115.

Battistich, V., & Hom, A. (1997). The relationship between students' sense of their school as a community and their involvement in problem behaviors. *American Journal of Public Health, 87,* 1997–2001.

Battistich, V., Solomon, D., Kim, D., Watson, M., & Schaps, E. (1995). Schools as communities, poverty levels of student populations, and students' attitude, motives, and performance: A multilevel analysis. *American Educational Research Journal, 32,* 627–658.

Baumrind, D. (1991). The influence of parenting style on adolescent competence and substance use. *Journal of Early Adolescence, 11,* 56–95.

Bayer, P., Pintoff, R., & Pozen, D. (2003). *Building criminal capital behind bars: Social learning in juvenile corrections.* New Haven, CT: Unpublished manuscript, Yale University, Department of Economics.

Bear, G. G. (1998). School discipline in the United States: Prevention, correction, and long-term social development. *School Psychology Review, 27,* 14–32.

Bear, G. G., Webster-Stratton, C., Furlong, M. J., & Rhee, S. (2000). Preventing aggression and violence. In K. M. Minke & G. G. Bear (Eds.), *Preventing school problems, promoting school success: Strategies and programs that work* (pp. 1–69). Bethesda, MD: National Association of School Psychologists.

Beard, B. B. (1934). *Juvenile probation.* New York: American Book Company.

Becker, W. C. (1986). *Applied psychology for teachers.* Chicago: Science Research Associates.

Becker, W. C., & Gersten, R. (1982). A follow-up of Follow Through: The later effects of the direct instruction model on children in fifth and sixth grades. *American Educational Research Journal, 19,* 75–92.

Beer, J., & Beer, J. (1992). Burnout and stress, depression and self-esteem of teachers. *Psychological Reports, 71*(3, Pt. 2), 1331–1336.

Bell, R. M., Ellickson, P. L., & Harrison, E. R. (1993). Do drug prevention effects persist into high school?: How Project Alert did with ninth graders. *Preventive Medicine, 22,* 463–483.

Bennett, K., & LeCompte, M. (1990). *The way schools work.* New York: Longman.

Bentley, P. (2003). Book review of Winick and Wexler: *Judging in a therapeutic key. Criminal Law Quarterly, 48,* 267–268.

Berger, R. J., Crowley, J. E., Gold, M., Gray, J., & Arnold, M. S. (1975). *Experiment in a juvenile court: A study of a program of volunteers working with juvenile probationers.* Ann Arbor: University of Michigan, Institute for Social Research.

Berk, B. (1966). Organizational goals and inmate organization. *American Journal of Sociology, 71,* 522–534.

Berman, G. (2004). Redefining criminal courts: Problem-solving and the meaning of justice. *American Criminal Law Review, 41,* 1313.

Bernard, T. J. (1992). *The cycle of juvenile justice.* New York: Oxford University Press.

Bersoff, D. N. (2002). Concerns about law, psychology, and public policy. *Law and Human Behavior, 26,* 565–574.

Bianchi, S. (1995). The changing demographic and socioeconomic characteristics of single parent families. *Marriage and Family Review, 20,* 71–97.

Bierman, K. L. (2004). *Peer rejection: Developmental processes and intervention strategies.* New York: Guilford Press.

Bierman, K. L., Greenberg, M. T., & the Conduct Problems Prevention Research Group. (1996). Social skills training in the Fast Track program. In R. V. Peters & R. J. McMahon (Eds.), *Preventing childhood disorders, substance abuse, and delinquency* (pp. 65–86). Thousand Oaks, CA: Sage.

Biglan, A. (1995). *Changing cultural practices: A contextualist framework for intervention research.* Reno, NV: Context Press.

Biglan, A., & Hayes, S. C. (1996). Should the behavioral sciences become more pragmatic?: The case for functional contextualism in research on human behavior. *Applied and Preventive Psychology, 5,* 47–57.

Biglan, A., Mrazek, P., Carnine, D. W., & Flay, B. R. (2003). The integration of research and practice in the prevention of youth problem behaviors. *American Psychologist, 58,* 433–440.

Blumstein, A. (2002). Prisons: A policy challenge. In J. Q. Wilson & J. Petersilia (Eds.), *Crime: Public policies for crime control* (pp. 451–482). Oakland, CA: Institute for Contemporary Studies Press.

Bobashev, G. V., & Anthony, J. C. (1998). Clusters of marijuana use in the United States. *American Journal of Epidemiology, 148,* 1168–1174.

Boisjoly, J., Duncan, G. J., Kremer, M., Levy, D. M., & Eccles, J. (2003). *Peer effects in binge drinking among college students* (Working Paper). Evanston, IL: Northwestern University, Institute for Policy on Research.

Bond, F. W., & Bunce, D. (2003). The role of acceptance and job control in mental health, job satisfaction, and work performance. *Journal of Applied Psychology, 88,* 1057–1067.

Botvin, G. J. (1985). The Life Skills Training Program as a health promotion strategy: Theoretical issues and empirical findings. *Special Services in the Schools, 1,* 9–23.

Botvin, G. J. (2000). Preventing drug abuse in schools: Social and competence enhancement approaches targeting individual-level etiologic factors. *Addictive Behaviors, 25,* 887–897.

Botvin, G. J., & Botvin, E. M. (1992). Adolescent tobacco, alcohol, and drug abuse: Prevention strategies, empirical findings, and assessment issues. *Journal of Developmental and Behavioral Pediatrics, 13,* 290–301.

Bowditch, C. (1993). Getting rid of troublemakers: High school disciplinary procedures and the production of dropouts. *Social Problems, 40,* 493–507.

Bowen, G. L., Richman, J. M., Brewster, A., & Bowen, N. (1998). Sense of school coherence, perceptions of danger at school, and teacher support among youth at risk of school failure. *Child and Adolescent Social Work Journal, 15,* 273–286.

Bowlby, J. (1969). Disruption of affectional bonds and its effect on behavior. *Canada's Mental Health Supplement, 59,* 12.

Bowlby, J. (1980). *Attachment and loss*. New York: Basic Books.

Bowlby, J. (1982). Attachment and loss: Retrospect and prospect. *American Journal of Orthopsychiatry, 52,* 664–678.

Boxer, P., Guerra, N. G., Huesmann, L. R., & Morales, J. (2005). Proximal peer-level effects of a small-group selected prevention on aggression in elementary school children: An investigation of the peer contagion hypothesis. *Journal of Abnormal Child Psychology, 33,* 325–338.

Boys Clubs of America. (1991). *The effects of Boys and Girls Clubs on alcohol and other drug use and related problems in public housing projects.* New York: Author.

Bradshaw, P. (2005). Terrors and young teams: Youth gangs and delinquency in Edinburgh. In F. M. Weerman & S. H. Decker (Eds.), *European gangs and troublesome youth groups* (pp. 241–274). Walnut Creek, CA: AltaMira Press.

Braithwaite, J. (2002). Restorative justice and therapeutic jurisprudence. *Criminal Law Bulletin 38,* 244–262.

Brock, W., & Durlauf, S. N. (2001). Interactions-based models. In J. J. Heckman & E. Leamer (Eds.), *Handbook of econometrics* (Vol. 5, pp. 3297–3380). Amsterdam, The Netherlands: Elsevier Science.

Brody, G. H., & Shaffer, D. R. (1982). Contributions of parents and peers to children's moral socialization. *Developmental Review, 2,* 31–75.

Bronfenbrenner, U. (1979). *The ecology of human development: Experiments by nature and by design.* Cambridge, MA: Harvard University Press.

Bronfenbrenner, U. (1989). Ecological systems theory. In R. Vasta (Ed.), *Annals of child development: Vol. 6. Six theories of child development: Revised formulations and current issues* (pp. 187–249). London: JAI Press.

Brooks-Gunn, J., Duncan, G. J., & Aber, J. L. (Eds.). (1997a). *Neighborhood poverty: Vol. 1. Context and consequences for children.* New York: Russell Sage Foundation.

Brooks-Gunn, J., Duncan, G. J., & Aber, J. L. (Eds.). (1997b). *Neighborhood poverty: Vol. 2. Policy implications in studying neighborhoods.* New York: Russell Sage Foundation.

Brooks-Gunn, J., Duncan, G. J., Kato, P., & Sealand, N. (1993). Do neighborhoods influence child and adolescent behavior? *American Journal of Sociology, 99,* 353–395.

Brophy, J. (1996). *Teaching problem students.* New York: Guilford Press.

Brown, F. (1999, August). North Carolina's charter school law: Flexibility versus accountability. *Education and Urban Society, 31,* 465–488.

Browne, D. (2002). Coping alone: Examining the prospects of adolescent victims of child abuse placed in foster care. *Journal of Youth and Adolescence, 31,* 57–66.

Bruene-Butler, L., Hampson, J., Elias, M. J., Clabby, J. F., & Schuyler, T. (1997). The Improving Social Awareness-Social Problems Solving Project. In G. W. Albee & T. P. Gullotta (Eds.), *Primary prevention works* (pp. 239–267). Thousand Oaks, CA: Sage.

Bryk, A., & Driscoll, M. (1988). *The high school as community: Contextual influences and consequences for students and teachers.* Madison: University of Wisconsin, National Center on Effective Secondary Schools.

Bryk, A. S., & Raudenbush, S. W. (1988). Heterogeneity of variance in experimental studies: A challenge to conventional interpretations. *Psychological Bulletin, 104,* 396–404.

Buehler, R. E., Patterson, G. R., & Furniss, J. M. (1966). The reinforcement of behavior in institutional settings. *Behaviour Research and Therapy, 4,* 157–167.

Burgess, R. L., & Akers, R. L. (1966). A differential association reinforcement theory of criminal behavior. *Social Problems, 14,* 128–147.

Burton, L. M., & Jarrett, R. L. (2000). In the mix, yet on the margins: The place of families in urban neighborhood and child development research. *Journal of Marriage and the Family, 62,* 1114–1135.

Bushway, S., & Reuter, P. (2002). Labor markets and crime. In J. Q. Wilson & J. Petersilia (Eds.), *Crime: Public policies for crime control* (pp. 191–224). Oakland, CA: Institute for Contemporary Studies Press.

Butts, J. A., Buck, J., & Coggeshall, M. (2002, April 15). *The impact of teen court on young offenders* (Urban Institute, Publication No. 410457). Retrieved May 2005 from www.urban.org/UploadedPDF/410457.pdf

Byrne, J. M., Lurigio, A. J., & Petersilia, J. (1992). *Smart sentencing: The emergence of intermediate sanctions.* Newbury Park, CA: Sage.

Byrnes, D., & Yamamoto, K. (2001). Academic retention of elementary pupils: An inside look. *Education, 106,* 208–214.

Byrnes, D., Young, R. K., & Griffitt, W. (1966). The reinforcement properties of attitude statements. *Journal of Experimental Research on Personality, 1,* 266–276.

Cairns, R. B., Cairns, B., Neckerman, H., Gest, S., & Gariepy, J. (1988). Social networks and aggressive behavior: Peer support or peer rejection. *Developmental Psychology, 24,* 815–823.

Campbell, F. A., Ramey, C. T., Pungello, E., Sparling, J., & Miller-Johnson, S. (2002). Early childhood education: Young adult outcomes from the Abecedarian Project. *Applied Developmental Science, 6,* 42–57.

Caplan, N. (1968). Treatment intervention and reciprocal interaction effects. *Journal of Social Issues, 24,* 63–88.

Caprara, G. V., Dodge, K. A., Pastorelli, C., Zelli, A., Zimbardo, P., & the Conduct Problems Prevention Research Group. (2005). *Effects of marginal deviations on behavioral development and social judgment.* Unpublished manuscript, University of Rome.

Caprara, G. V., & Zimbardo, P. (1996). Aggregation and amplification of marginal deviations in the social construction of personality and maladjustment. *European Journal of Personality, 10,* 79–110.

Carlson, E. A., & Sroufe, L. A. (1995). Contribution of attachment theory to developmental psychopathology. In D. Cicchetti & D. Cohen (Eds.), *Developmental psychopathology. Vol. 1: Theory and methods* (pp. 581–617). New York: Wiley.

Carney, F., Mattick, H. W., & Callaway, J. D. (1969). *Action on the streets.* New York: Association Press.

Carnine, D. (2000). *Why education experts resist effective practices (and what it would take to make education more like medicine).* Washington, DC: Fordham Foundation.

Carson, D. (2003). Therapeutic jurisprudence and adversarial injustice: Questioning limits. *Western Criminology Review, 4.* Retrieved May 2005 from www.law.arizona.edu/depts/upr-intj/

Casey, T. (2004). When good intentions are not enough: Problem-solving courts and the impending crisis of legitimacy. *SMU Law Review, 57,* 1459–1520.

Catalano, R. F., Berglund, M. L., Ryan, J. A. M., Lonczak, H. S., & Hawkins, J. D. (2002). Positive youth development in the United States: Research findings on evaluations of positive youth development programs. *Prevention and Treatment, 5,* NP.

Catterall, J. S. (1987). An intensive group counseling dropout prevention intervention: Some cautions on isolating at-risk adolescents within high schools. *American Educational Research Journal, 24,* 521–540.

Cavell, T. A., & Hughes, J. N. (2000). Secondary prevention as context for studying change processes in aggressive children. *Journal of School Psychology, 38,* 199–235.

Center on Budget and Policy Priorities. (2003). *Introduction to the housing voucher program.* Washington, DC: Author.

Chamberlain, P. (2000). What works in treatment foster care. In M. P. Kluger & G. Alexander (Eds.), *What works in child welfare* (pp. 157–162). Washington, DC: Child Welfare League of America.

Chamberlain, P. (2003a). The Oregon Multidimensional Treatment Foster Care Model: Features, outcomes, and progress in dissemination. *Cognitive and Behavioral Practice, 10,* 303–312.

Chamberlain, P. (2003b). *Treating chronic juvenile offenders: Advances made through the Oregon Multidimensional Treatment Foster Care Model.* Washington, DC: American Psychological Association.

Chamberlain, P., & Moore, K. J. (1998). Models of community treatment for serious offenders. In J. Crane (Ed.), *Social programs that really work* (pp. 256–276). Princeton, NJ: Russell Sage Foundation.

Chamberlain, P., & Patterson, G. R. (1995). Discipline and child compliance in parenting. In M. H. Bornstein (Ed.), *Handbook of parenting* (Vol. 4, pp. 204–225). Hillsdale, NJ: Erlbaum.

Chamberlain, P., Ray, J., & Moore, K. J. (1996). Characteristics of residential care for adolescent offenders: A comparison of assumptions and practices in two models. *Journal of Child and Family Studies, 5,* 285–297.

Chamberlain, P., & Reid, J. B. (1994). Differences in risk factors and adjustment for male and female delinquents in treatment foster care. *Journal of Child and Family Studies, 3,* 23–39.

Chamberlain, P., & Reid, J. B. (1998). Comparison of two community alternatives to incarceration for chronic juvenile offenders. *Journal of Consulting and Clinical Psychology, 66,* 624–633.

Chase-Lansdale, P. L., Gordon, R. A., Brooks-Gunn, J., & Connell, J. P. (1997). Neighborhood and family influences on the intellectual and behavioral competence of preschool and early school-age children. In J. Brooks-Gunn, G. J. Duncan, & J. L. Aber (Eds.), *Neighborhood poverty: Vol. 1. Context and consequences for children* (pp. 79–118). New York: Russell Sage Foundation.

Chassin, L., Presson, C. C., Sherman, S. J., Montello, D., & McGrew, J. (1986). Changes in peer and parent influence during adolescence: Longitudinal versus cross-sectional perspectives on smoking initiation. *Developmental Psychology, 22,* 327–334.

Chen, Y. Y., Subramanian, S. V., Acevedo-Garcia, D., & Kawachi, I. (2005). Women's status and depressive symptoms: A multilevel analysis. *Social Science and Medicine, 60,* 49–60.

Chipungu, S. S. (1991). A value-based policy framework. In J. E. Everett, S. S. Chipungu, & B. R. Leashore (Eds.), *Child welfare: An Africentric perspective* (pp. 290–305). New Brunswick, NJ: Rutgers University Press.

Cho, H., Hallfors, D., & Sanchez, V. (2005). Evaluation of a high school peer group intervention for at-risk youth. *Journal of Abnormal Child Psychology, 33,* 363–374.

Christenson, S. L., Rounds, T., & Franklin, M. J. (1992). Home–school collaboration: Effects, issues, and opportunities. In S. L. Christenson & J. C. Conoley (Eds.), *Home–school collaboration: Enhancing children's academic and social competence* (pp. 19–51). Silver Spring, MD: National Association of School Psychologists.

Chubb, J. E., & Moe, T. M. (1990). *Politics, markets, and America's schools.* Washington, DC: Brookings Institution.

Cialdini, R. B. (1993). Social proof. In R. B. Cialdini (Ed.), *Influence: Science and practice* (3rd ed., pp. 94–135). New York: HarperCollins.

Cicchetti, D., Toth, S. L., & Lynch, M. (1995). Bowlby's dream comes full circle: The application of attachment to risk and psychopathology. *Advances in Clinical Child Psychology, 17,* 1–75.

Ciesielski, C., Marianos, D., Ou, C. Y., Dumbaugh, R., Witte, J., Berkelman, R., et al. (1992). Transmission of human immunodeficiency virus in a dental practice. *Annals of Internal Medicine, 116,* 798–805.

Cillessen, A. H. N., & Mayeux, L. (2004). Sociometric status and peer group behavior: Previous findings and current directions. In J. Kupersmidt & K. A. Dodge (Eds.), *Children's peer relations: From development to intervention* (pp. 3–20). Washington, DC: American Psychological Association.

Clemmer, D. (1958). *The prison community.* New York: Rinehart. (Original work published 1940)

Clotfelter, C. T., Ladd, H. F., & Vigdor, J. L. (2005). Who teaches whom?: Race and the distribution of novice teachers. *Economics of Education Review, 24,* 377–392.

Cohen, A. K. (1955). *Delinquent boys.* New York: Free Press.

Cohen, J., & Ludwig, J. (2003). Policing crime guns. In J. Ludwig & P. J. Cook (Eds.), *Evaluating gun policy* (pp. 217–250). Washington, DC: Brookings Institute Press.

Coie, J. D., & Dodge, K. A. (2006). Aggression and antisocial behavior. In W. Damon (Series Ed.) & N. Eisenberg (Vol. Ed.), *Handbook of child psychology: Vol. 3. Social, emotional, and personality development* (6th ed., pp. 779–862). New York: Wiley.

Coleman, J. S. (1966). *Equality of educational opportunity.* Washington, DC: U.S. Department of Health, Education and Welfare.

Collins, W. J., & Margo, R. A. (2000). Residential segregation and socioeconomic outcomes: When did ghettos go bad? *Economics Letters, 69,* 239–243.

Colpe, L. J. (2001). Estimates of mental and emotional problems, functional impairments, and associated disability outcomes for the U.S. child population in households. In R. W. Manderscheid & M. J. Henderson (Eds.), *Mental health, United States, 2000* (DHHS Pub. No. [SMA] 01-3537). Washington, DC: U.S. Government Printing Office.

Colvin, G., & Fernandez, E. (2000). Sustaining effective behavior support systems in an elementary school. *Journal of Positive Behavior Interventions, 2,* 251–253.

Colvin, G., Kame'enui, E. J., & Sugai, G. (1993). Reconceptualizing behavior management and school-wide discipline in general education. *Education and Treatment of Children, 16,* 361–381.

Colvin, G., Sugai, G., & Patching, B. (1993). Precorrection: An instructional approach for managing predictable problem behaviors. *Intervention in School and Clinic, 28,* 143–150.

Conduct Problems Prevention Research Group. (1992). A developmental and clinical model for the prevention of conduct problems: The FAST Track program. *Development and Psychopathology, 4,* 509–527.

Conduct Problems Prevention Research Group. (1999). Initial impact of the Fast Track Prevention Trial for conduct problems: II. Classroom effects. *Journal of Consulting and Clinical Psychology, 67,* 648–657.

Conduct Problems Prevention Research Group. (2002a). Evaluation of the first 3 years of the Fast Track Prevention Trial with children at high risk for adolescent conduct problems. *Journal of Abnormal Child Psychology, 30,* 19–35.

Conduct Problems Prevention Research Group. (2002b). The implementation of the Fast Track program: An example of a large-scale prevention science efficacy trial. *Journal of Abnormal Child Psychology, 30,* 1–17.

Conduct Problems Prevention Research Group. (2002c). Predictor variables associated with positive Fast Track outcomes at the end of third grade. *Journal of Abnormal Child Psychology, 30,* 37–52.

Cook, B. G., Landrum, T. J., Tankersley, M., & Kauffman, J. M. (2003). Bringing research to bear in practice: Effecting evidence-based instruction for students with emotional or behavioral disorders. *Education and Treatment of Children, 26,* 345–361.

Cook, P. J., & Goss, K. (1996). *A selective review of the social contagion literature.* Durham, NC: Unpublished manuscript, Duke University, Department of Public Policy Studies.

Cook, T. D., Murphy, R. F., & Hunt, H. D. (2000). Comer's School Development Program in Chicago: A theory-based evaluation. *American Educational Research Journal, 37,* 535–597.

Corrigan, M. D., & Becker, D. (2003). Moving problem-solving courts into the mainstream. *Michigan Bar Journal, 82,* 14–18.

Council of Juvenile Correctional Administrators. (2005). *Performance-based standards (PbS) for youth correction and detention facilities.* Retrieved June 23, 2005, from www.pbstandards.org/

Courtney, M. E. (1994). Factors associated with entrance into group care. In R. P. Barth, J. D. Berrick, & N. Gilbert (Eds.), *Child welfare research review* (pp. 185–204). New York: Columbia University Press.

Cover, R. (1975). *Justice accused.* New Haven, CT: Yale University Press.

Cox, S. M. (1999). An assessment of alternative education programs for at-risk delinquent youth. *Journal of Research in Crime and Delinquency, 36,* 323–336.

Crandall, C. S. (1988). Social contagion of binge eating. *Journal of Personality and Social Psychology, 55,* 588–598.

Crandall, K. A. (1995). Intraspecific phylogenetics: Support for dental transmission of human immunodeficiency virus. *Journal of Virology, 69,* 2351–2356.

Crane, J. (1991). The epidemic theory of ghettos and neighborhood effects on dropping out and teenage childbearing. *American Journal of Sociology, 96,* 1226–1259.

Crick, N. R., & Dodge, K. A. (1994). A review and reformulation of social information-processing mechanisms in children's social adjustment. *Psychological Bulletin, 115,* 74–101.

Crosnoe, R. (2002). High school curriculum track and adolescent association with delinquent friends. *Journal of Adolescent Research, 17,* 143–167.

Cunningham, C. E., Bremner, R., & Boyle, M. (1995). Large group community-based parenting programs for families of preschoolers at risk for disruptive behaviour disorders: Utilization, cost effectiveness, and outcome. *Journal of Child Psychology and Psychiatry, 36,* 1141–1159.

Currie, J., & Yelowitz, A. (2000). Are public housing projects good for kids? *Journal of Public Economics, 75,* 99–124.

Cutler, D. M., & Glaeser, E. L. (1997). Are ghettos good or bad? *Quarterly Journal of Economics, 112,* 827–872.

Cutler, D. M., Glaeser, E. L., & Vigdor, J. L. (1999). The rise and decline of the American ghetto. *Journal of Political Economy, 107,* 455–506.

Daley, D. J., & Gani, J. (1999). *Epidemic modeling: An introduction.* Cambridge, UK: Cambridge University Press.

Davidson, W. S., Redner, R., Amdur, R. L., & Mitchell, C. M. (Eds.). (1990). *Alternative treatments for troubled youth: The case of diversion from the justice system.* New York: Plenum Press.

Davis, I., Landsverk, J., & Newton, R. (1997). Duration of foster care for children reunified within the first year of care. In J. Berrick, R. Barth, & N. Gilbert (Eds.), *Child welfare research review* (Vol. 2, pp. 272–293). New York: Columbia University Press.

Dawson, P. (1998, June). A primer on student grade retention: What the research says. *NASP Communique,* pp. 26–28.

DeGarmo, D. S., Patterson, G. R., & Forgatch, M. S. (2004). How do outcomes in a specified parent training intervention maintain or wane over time? *Prevention Science, 5,* 73–89.

Dent, C. W., Sussman, S., Stacy, A. W., Craig, S., Burton, D., & Flay, B. R. (1995). Two-year behavior outcomes of Project Towards No Tobacco Use. *Journal of Consulting and Clinical Psychology, 63,* 676–677.

Derezotes, D. (1995). Evaluation of the Late Nite Basketball Project. *Child and Adolescent Social Work Journal, 12,* 33–50.

Diamond, J. (2004). *Collapse: How societies choose to fail or succeed.* New York: Viking Adult.

Dishion, T. J. (2000). Cross-setting consistency in early adolescent psychopathology:

Deviant friendships and problem behavior sequelae. *Journal of Personality*, *68*, 1109–1126.

Dishion, T. J., & Andrews, D. W. (1995). Preventing escalation in problem behaviors with high-risk young adolescents: Immediate and 1-year outcomes. *Journal of Consulting and Clinical Psychology*, *63*, 538–548.

Dishion, T. J., Andrews, D. W., & Crosby, L. (1995). Antisocial boys and their friends in early adolescence: Relationship characteristics, quality and interactional process. *Child Development*, *66*, 139–151.

Dishion, T. J., Bullock, B. M., & Granic, I. (2002). Pragmatism in modeling peer influence: Dynamics, outcomes, and change processes. *Development and Psychopathology*, *14*, 969–981.

Dishion, T. J., Capaldi, D., Spracklen, K. M., & Li, F. (1995). Peer ecology of male adolescent drug use. *Development and Psychopathology*, *7*, 803–824.

Dishion, T. J., & Dodge, K. A. (2005). Peer contagion in interventions for children and adolescents: Moving towards an understanding of the ecology and dynamics of change. *Journal of Abnormal Child Psychology*, *33(3)*, 395–400.

Dishion, T. J., Eddy, J. M., Haas, E., Li, F., & Spracklen, K. (1997). Friendships and violent behavior during adolescence. *Social Development*, *6*, 207–223.

Dishion, T. J., & Kavanaugh, K. (2000). A multilevel approach to family-centered prevention in schools: Process and outcomes. *Addictive Behaviors*, *25*, 899–911.

Dishion, T. J., & Kavanaugh, K. (2002). The Adolescent Transitions Program: A family-centered prevention strategy for schools. In J. B. Reid, G. R. Patterson, & J. Snyder (Eds.), *Antisocial behavior in children and adolescents: A developmental analysis and model for intervention* (pp. 257–272). Washington, DC: American Psychological Association.

Dishion, T. J., Kavanaugh, K., Schneiger, A., Nelson, S., & Kaufman, N. K. (2002). Preventing early adolescent substance use: A family-centered strategy for the public middle-school ecology. *Prevention Science*, *3*, 191–201.

Dishion, T. J., McCord, J., & Poulin, F. (1999). When interventions harm: Peer groups and problem behavior. *American Psychologist*, *54*, 755–764.

Dishion, T. J., Nelson, S. E., & Bullock, B. M. (2004). Premature adolescent autonomy: Parent disengagement and deviant peer process in the amplification of problem behavior. [Special issue]. *Journal of Adolescence*, *27*, 515–530.

Dishion, T. J., Nelson, S. N., Winter, C., & Bullock, B. M. (2004). Adolescent friendship as a dynamic system: Entropy and deviance in the etiology and course of male antisocial behavior. *Journal of Abnormal Child Psychology*, *32(6)*, 651–663.

Dishion, T. J., & Owen, L. D. (2002). A longitudinal analysis of friendships and substance use: Bidirectional influence from adolescence to adulthood. *Developmental Psychology*, *38*, 480–491.

Dishion, T. J., & Patterson, G. R. (in press). The development and ecology of antisocial behavior. In D. Cicchetti & D. J. Cohen (Eds.), *Developmental psychopathology: Risk, disorder, and adaptation.* New York: Wiley.

Dishion, T. J., Patterson, G. R., & Griesler, P. C. (1994). Peer adaptation in the development of antisocial behavior: A confluence model. In L. R. Huesmann

(Ed.), *Aggressive behavior: Current perspectives* (pp. 61–95). New York: Plenum Press.

Dishion, T. J., Patterson, G. R., Stoolmiller, M., & Skinner, M. L. (1991). Family, school, and behavioral antecedents to early adolescent involvement with antisocial peers. *Developmental Psychology, 27,* 172–180.

Dishion, T. J., Poulin, F., & Burraston, B. (2001). Peer group dynamics associated with iatrogenic effects in group interventions with high-risk young adolescents. *New Directions for Child and Adolescent Development, 91,* 79–92.

Dishion, T. J., Poulin, F., & Skaggs, N. M. (2000). The ecology of premature adolescent autonomy: Biological and social influences. In K. A. Kerns, S. M. Contreras, & A. M. Neal-Barnett (Eds.), *Explaining associations between family and peer relationships* (pp. 27–45). Westport, CT: Praeger.

Dishion, T. J., & Skaggs, N. M. (2000). An ecological analysis of monthly "bursts" in early adolescent substance use. *Applied Developmental Science, 4,* 89–97.

Dishion, T. J., Spracklen, K. M., & Patterson, G. R. (1996). Deviancy training in male adolescent friendships. *Behavior Therapy, 27,* 373–390.

Dishion, T. J., & Stormshak, E. (in press). *An ecological approach to child and family interventions.* Washington, DC: American Psychological Association Books.

Dodge, K. A., & Coie, J. D. (1987). Social information-processing factors in reactive and proactive aggression in children's peer groups. *Journal of Personality and Social Psychology, 53,* 1146–1158.

Dodge, K. A., & Crick, N. R. (1990). Social information-processing bases of aggressive behavior in children. *Personality and Social Psychology Bulletin, 16,* 8–22.

Dodge, K. A., Kupersmidt, J. B., & Fontaine, R. G. (2000). *Willie M: A legacy of legal, social, and policy change on behalf of children.* Durham, NC: Duke University, Center for Child and Family Policy.

Dodge, K. A., Murphy, R. R., & Buchsbaum, K. (1984). The assessment of intention-cue detection skills in children: Implications for developmental psychopathology. *Child Development, 55,* 163–173.

Dolan, L. J., Kellam, S. G., Werthamer-Larsson, L., Rebok, G. W., Mayer, L. S., Laudolff, J., et al. (1993). The short-term impact of two classroom-based preventive interventions on aggressive and shy behaviors and poor achievement. *Journal of Applied Developmental Psychology, 14,* 317–345.

Donaldson, S. I., Graham, J. W., Piccinin, A. M., & Handen, W. B. (1995). Resistance-skills training and onset of alcohol use: Evidence for beneficial and potentially harmful effects in public schools and in private Catholic schools. *Health Psychology, 14,* 291–300.

Donohue, J. J., & Siegelman, P. (1998). Allocating resources among prisons and social programs in the battle against crime. *Journal of Legal Studies, 27,* 1–43.

Dorman, J. P. (2003). Relationship between school and classroom environment and teacher burnout: A LISREL analysis. *Social Psychology of Education, 6,* 107–127.

Dornbusch, S., Glasgow, K., & Lin, I. (1996). The social structure of schooling. *Annual Review of Psychology, 47,* 401–429.

DuBois, D. L., & Neville, H. A. (1997). Youth mentoring: Investigation of relationship characteristics and perceived benefits. *Journal of Community Psychology, 25,* 227–234.

Duke University Program on Psychiatric Advance Directives. (2005). Durham, NC: Department of Psychiatry and Behavioral Sciences, Duke University Medical Center. Retrieved June 2005 from serp.mc.duke.edu/pad/index.html

Dumas, J. E., Prinz, R. J., Smith, E. P., & Laughlin, J. (1999). The Early Alliance Prevention Trial: An integrated set of interventions to promote competence and reduce risk for conduct disorder, substance abuse, and school failure. *Clinical Child and Family Psychology Review, 2,* 37–53.

Duncan, G. J., Boisjoly, J., & Harris, K. M. (2001). Sibling, peer, neighbor, and schoolmate correlations as indicators of the importance of context for adolescent development. *Demography, 38,* 437–447.

Duncan, G. J., Boisjoly, J., Kremer, M., Levy, D. M., & Eccles, J. (2005). Peer effects in drug use and sex among college students. *Journal of Abnormal Child Psychology, 33,* 375–385.

Duncan, G. J., Clark-Kauffman, E., & Snell, E. (2004). *Residential mobility interventions as treatments for the sequelae of neighborhood violence* (Mimeo). Chicago: Northwestern University.

Duncan, G. J., Connell, J. P., & Klebanov, P. K. (1997). Conceptual and methodological issues in estimating causal effects and family conditions on individual development. In J. Brooks-Gunn, G. J. Duncan, & J. L. Aber (Eds.), *Neighborhood poverty: Vol. 1. Context and consequences for children* (pp. 219–250). New York: Russell Sage Foundation.

Durlak, J. A. (1995). *School-based prevention programs for children and adolescents.* Thousand Oaks, CA: Sage.

Durlak, J. A., & Wells, A. M. (1997). Primary prevention mental health programs for children and adolescents: A meta-analytic review. *American Journal of Community Psychology, 25,* 115–152.

Eccles, J. S., & Barber, B. L. (1999). Student council, volunteering, basketball, or marching band: What kind of extracurricular involvement matters? *Journal of Adolescent Research, 10,* 10–43.

Eccles, J. S., & Goodman, J. (2002). *Community programs to promote youth development.* Washington, DC: National Academy Press.

Eddy, J. M., & Chamberlain, P. (2000). Family management and deviant peer association as mediators of the impact of treatment condition on youth antisocial behavior. *Journal of Consulting and Clinical Psychology, 68,* 857–863.

Eddy, J. M., Reid, J. B., & Fetrow, R. A. (2000). An elementary school-based prevention program targeting modifiable antecedents of youth delinquency and violence: Linking the Interests of Families and Teachers (LIFT). *Journal of Emotional and Behavioral Disorders, 8,* 165–176.

Eddy, J. M., Reid, J. B., Stoolmiller, M., & Fetrow, R. A. (2003). Outcomes during middle school for an elementary school-based preventive intervention for conduct problems: Follow-up results from a randomized trial. *Behavior Therapy, 34,* 535–552.

Eddy, J. M., Whaley, R. B., & Chamberlain, P. (2004). The prevention of violent behavior by chronic and serious male juvenile offenders: A 2-year follow-up of a randomized clinical trial. *Journal of Emotional and Behavioral Disorders, 12,* 2–8.

Ekstrom, R. B., Goertz, M. E., Pollack, J. M., & Rock, D. A. (1986). Who drops out of high school and why?: Findings from a national study. *Teacher College Record, 87,* 357–373.

Elder, C., Leaver-Dunn, D., Wang, M. Q., Nagy, S., & Green, L. (2000). Organized group activity as a protective factor against adolescent substance use. *American Journal of Health Behavior, 24,* 108–113.

Elias, M. J., Zins, J. E., Weissberg, R. P., Frey, K. S., Greenberg, M. T., Haynes, N. M., et al. (1997). *Promoting social and emotional learning: Guidelines for educators.* Alexandria, VA: Association for Supervision and Curriculum Development.

Ellen, I. G., & Turner, M. A. (1997). Does neighborhood matter?: Assessing recent evidence. *Housing Policy Debate, 8,* 833–866.

Ellickson, P., & Petersilia, J. (1983). *Implementing new ideas in criminal justice.* Santa Monica, CA: Rand.

Elliott, D. S. (1997). *Blueprints for violence prevention.* Boulder: University of Colorado, Center for the Study and Prevention of Violence.

Elliott, D. S. (2003, November). *Blueprints for violence prevention.* Presentation at the annual meeting of the American Society of Criminology, Denver, CO.

Elliott, D. S., Huizinga, D., & Menard, S. (1989). *Multiple problem youth: Delinquency, substance use, and mental health problems.* New York: Springer-Verlag.

Elliott, D. S., & Menard, S. (1996). Delinquent friends and delinquent behavior: Temporal and developmental patterns. In J. D. Hawkins (Ed.), *Delinquency and crime: Current theories* (pp. 28–67). New York: Cambridge University Press.

Elliott, D. S., & Mihalic, S. (1998). *Blueprints for violence prevention.* Boulder: University of Colorado, Institute of Behavioral Science, Center for the Study and Prevention of Violence.

Elliott, D. S., Wilson, W. J., Huizinga, D., Sampson, R. J., Elliott, A., & Rankin, B. (1996). The effects of neighborhood disadvantage on adolescent development. *Journal of Research in Crime and Delinquency, 33,* 389–426.

Embry, D. D. (2002). The Good Behavior Game: A best practice candidate as a universal behavioral vaccine. *Clinical Child and Family Psychology Review, 5,* 273–297.

Embry, D. D., Flannery, D., Vazsonyi, A., Powell, K., & Atha, H. (1996). Peace-Builders: A theoretically driven, school-based model for early violence prevention. *American Journal of Preventive Medicine, 22,* 91–100.

Empey, L. T. (1982). *American delinquency: Its meaning and construction* (rev. ed.). Homewood, IL: Dorsey Press.

Empey, L. T., & Erickson, M. L. (1972). *The Provo Experiment: Evaluating community control of delinquency.* Lexington, MA: Lexington Books.

Empey, L. T., & Lubeck, S. G. (1971). *The Silverlake Experiment: Testing delinquency theory and community intervention.* Chicago: Aldine.

Empey, L. T., & Rabow, J. (1961). The Provo Experiment in delinquency rehabilitation. *American Sociological Review, 26,* 679–695.

Emshoff, J. G., & Blakely, C. (1983). The diversion of delinquent youth: Family focused intervention. *Children and Youth Services Review, 5,* 343–356.

Engelmann, S. E., Becker, W. C., Carnine, D. W., & Gersten, R. (1988). The Direct Instruction Follow Through Model: Design and outcomes. *Education and Treatment of Children, 11,* 303–317.

Ennett, S. T., & Bauman, K. E. (1994). The contribution of influence and selection to adolescent peer group homogeneity: The case of adolescent cigarette smoking. *Journal of Personality and Social Psychology, 67(4), 653–663.*

Ennett, S. T., Ringwalt, C. L., Thorne, J., Rohrbach, L. A., Vincus, A., Simons-Rudolph, A., et al. (2003). A comparison of current practice in school-based substance use prevention programs with meta-analysis findings. *Prevention Science, 4,* 1–14.

Entwisle, D., Alexander, K. L., & Olson, L. S. (1997). *Children, schools and inequality.* Boulder, CO: Westview Press.

Esbensen, F.-A., & Huizinga, D. (1993). Gangs, drugs, and delinquency in a survey of urban youth. *Criminology, 31,* 565–587.

Espalage, D., & Swearer, S. (2003). Mini-series: Bullying prevention and intervention: Integrating research and evaluation findings: Research on school bullying and victimization: What have we learned and where do we go from here? *School Psychology Review, 32,* 365–384.

Evans, W. N., Oates, W. E., & Schwab, R. M. (1992). Measuring peer group effects: A study of teenage behavior. *Journal of Political Economy, 100,* 966–991.

Evers, W. J. G., Brouwers, A., & Tomic, W. (2002). Burnout and self-efficacy: A study on teachers' beliefs when implementing an innovative educational system in the Netherlands. *British Journal of Educational Psychology, 72,* 227–244.

Fagan, A. A., & Mihalic, S. (2003). Strategies for enhancing the adoption of school-based prevention programs: Lessons learned from the Blueprints for Violence Prevention replications of the Life Skills Training Program. *Journal of Community Psychology, 31,* 235–253.

Farrell, A. D., Meyer, A. L., Sullivan, T. N., & Kung, E. M. (2003). Evaluation of the Responding in Peaceful and Positive Ways (RIPP) seventh grade violence prevention curriculum. *Journal of Child and Family Studies, 12,* 101–120.

Farrell, W. C., Johnson, J. H., Sapp, M., Pumphrey, R. M., & Freeman, S. (1995). Redirecting the lives of urban black males: An assessment of Milwaukee's Midnight Basketball League. *Journal of Community Practice, 2,* 91–107.

Farrington, D. P., Snyder, H. N., & Finnegan, T. A. (1988). Specialization in juvenile court careers. *Criminology, 26,* 461–485.

Feder, L., Jolin, A., & Feyerherm, W. (2000). Lessons from two randomized experiments in criminal justice settings. *Crime and Delinquency, 46,* 380–400.

Fejgin, N. (1994). Participation in high school competitive sports: A subversion of school mission or contribution to academic goals? *Sociology of Sport Journal, 11,* 211–230.

Feldman, R. A. (1992). The St. Louis Experiment: Effective treatment of antisocial youths in prosocial peer groups. In J. McCord & R. E. Tremblay (Eds.), *Preventing antisocial behavior: Interventions from birth to adolescence* (pp. 233–252). New York: Guilford Press.

Feldman, R. A., Caplinger, T. E., & Wodarski, J. S. (1983). *The Saint Louis conundrum: The effective treatment of antisocial youth.* Englewood Cliffs, NJ: Prentice-Hall.

Felner, R. D., Brand, S., Adan, A. M., Mulhall, P. F., Floweres, N., Sartain, B., et al. (1993). Restructuring the ecology of the school as an approach to prevention during school transitions: Longitudinal follow-ups and extensions of the School Transitional Environment Project (STEP). *Prevention in Human Health, 10,* 103–136.

Figlio, D. N. (2005). *Testing, crime and punishment* (Working Paper No. 11194). Cambridge, MA: National Bureau of Economic Research.

Fisher, P. A., Ellis, B. H., & Chamberlain, P. (1999). Early intervention foster care: A model for preventing risk in young children who have been maltreated. *Children's Services: Social Policy, Research, and Practice, 2,* 159–182.

Fisher, P. A., Gunnar, M., Chamberlain, P., & Reid, J. (2000). Preventive intervention for maltreated preschool children: Impact on children's behavior, neuroendocrine activity, and foster parent functioning. *Journal of the American Academy of Child and Adolescent Psychiatry, 39,* 1356–1364.

Fisher, S. (1995). The amusement arcade as a social space for adolescents: An empirical study. *Journal of Adolescence, 18,* 71–86.

Fiske, D. W. (1986). Specificity of method and knowledge in social science. In D. W. Fiske & R. A. Shweder (Eds.), *Metatheory in social science: Pluralisms and subjectivities* (pp. 61–82). Chicago: University of Chicago Press.

Fiske, D. W. (1987). Construct invalidity comes from method effects. *Educational and Psychological Measurement, 47,* 285–307.

Fixsen, D. L., Phillips, E. L., & Wolf, M. M. (1978). The teaching-family model: An example of mission-oriented research. In T. A. Brigham & A. C. Catania (Eds.), *The handbook of applied behavior analysis: Social and instructional processes* (pp. 603–628). New York: Irvington Press.

Flannery, D. J., Vazsonyi, A. T., Liau, A. K., Guo, S., Powell, K. E., Atha, H., et al. (2003). Initial behavior outcomes for the Peacebuilders universal school-based violence prevention program. *Developmental Psychology, 39,* 292–308.

Fleisher, M. (1998). *Dead end kids: Gang girls and the boys they know.* Madison: University of Wisconsin Press.

Fletcher, A. C., Nickerson, P., & Wright, K. L. (2003). Structured leisure activities in middle childhood: Links to well-being. *Journal of Community Psychology, 31,* 641–659.

Fo, W. S. O., & O'Donnell, C. R. (1975). The buddy system: Effect of community intervention on delinquent offenses. *Behavior Therapy, 6,* 522–524.

Forgatch, M. S., & DeGarmo, D. S. (1999). Parenting through change: An effective prevention program for single mothers. *Journal of Consulting and Clinical Psychology, 67,* 711–724.

French, J. R. P., Jr., & Raven, B. (1960). The bases of social power. In D. Cartwright & A. Zander (Eds.), *Group dynamics* (pp. 607–623). New York: Harper & Row.

Friedman, M., & Friedman, R. (1980). *Free to choose: A personal statement.* New York: Harcourt Brace Jovanovich.

Frith, U., & Frith, C. (2001). The biological basis of social interaction. *Current Directions in Psychological Science, 10*, 151–155.

Fuhrer, M. J., & Baer, P. E. (1965). Differential classical conditioning: Verbalization of stimulus contingencies. *Science, 150*, 1479–1481.

Galster, G. C., Quercia, R. G., & Cortes, A. (2000). Identifying neighborhood thresholds: An empirical exploration. *Housing Policy Debate, 11*, 701–732.

Garbarino, J., Kostelny, K., & Grady, J. (1993). Children in dangerous environments: Child maltreatment in the context of community violence. In D. Cicchetti & S. L. Toth (Eds.), *Child abuse, child development, and social policy* (pp. 167–189). Norwood, NJ: Ablex.

Garces, E., Thomas, D., & Currie, J. (2002). Longer-term effects of Head Start. *American Economic Review, 92*, 999–1012.

Garland, A. F., Ellis-MacLeod, E., Landsverk, J. A., Ganger, W., & Johnson, I. (1998). Minority populations in the child welfare system: The visibility hypothesis reexamined. *American Journal of Orthopsychiatry, 68*, 142–146.

Garnier, H., & Stein, J. (2002). An 18-year model of family and peer effects on adolescent drug use and juvenile delinquency. *Journal of Youth and Adolescence, 31*, 45–56.

Gatti, U., Tremblay, R. E., Vitaro, F., & McDuff, P. (2003). *Youth gangs, delinquency, and drug use: Results from the Montreal Longitudinal Experimental Study.* Unpublished manuscript, University of Montreal.

Gaviria, A. (2000). Increasing returns and the evolution of violent crime: The case of Colombia. *Journal of Development Economics, 61*, 1–25.

Gendreau, P., & Andrews, D. A. (1994). *The Correctional Program Assessment Inventory* (5th ed.). Saint John, New Brunswick, Canada: University of New Brunswick.

Gendreau, P., Goggin, C., & Smith, P. (1999). The forgotten issue in effective correctional treatment: Program implementation. *International Journal of Offender Therapy and Comparative Criminology, 43*, 180–187.

Gephart, M. A. (1997). Neighborhoods and communities as contexts for development. In J. Brooks-Gunn, G. J. Duncan, & J. L. Aber (Eds.), *Neighborhood poverty: Vol. 1. Context and consequences for children* (pp. 1–43). New York: Russell Sage Foundation.

Giffin, G., & Jenuwine, M. J. (2002). Using therapeutic jurisprudence to bridge the juvenile justice and mental health systems. *University of Cincinnati Law Review, 71*, 65–87.

Gifford, E. (2002). *Acceptance and commitment therapy versus nicotine replacement therapy as methods of smoking cessation.* Reno: University of Nevada.

Gilbert, J., Grimm, R., & Parnham, J. (2001). Applying therapeutic principles to a family-focused juvenile justice model (delinquency). *Alabama Law Review, 52*, 1153–1212.

Gilbert, R. O. (1987). *Statistical methods for environmental pollution monitoring.* New York: Van Nostrand Reinhold.

Ginther, D., Haveman, R., & Wolfe, B. (2000). Neighborhood attributes as determinants of children's outcomes: How robust are the relationships? *Journal of Human Resources, 35*, 603–642.

Gladwell, M. (2000). *The tipping point: How little things can make a big difference.* Boston: Little, Brown.

Glaeser, E. L., Sacerdote, B., & Scheinkman, J. A. (1996). Crime and social interactions. *Quarterly Journal of Economics, 111,* 507–548.

Glaeser, E. L., Sacerdote, B., & Scheinkman, J. A. (2003). The social multiplier. *Journal of the European Economic Association, 1,* 345–353.

Glasgow, R. E., Vogt, T. M., & Boles, S. M. (1999). Evaluating the public health impact of health promotion interventions: The RE-AIM framework. *American Journal of Public Health, 89,* 1322–1327.

Glenn, S. S. (1986). Metacontingencies in Walden Two. *Behavior Analysis and Social Action, 5,* 2–12.

Glenn, S. S. (1988). Contingencies and metacontingencies: Toward a synthesis of behavior analysis and cultural materialism. *Behavior Analyst, 11,* 161–179.

Glenn, S. S. (2004). Individual behavior, culture, and social change. *Behavior Analyst, 27,* 133–151.

Goering, J., & Feins, J. D. (2003). *Choosing a better life?: Evaluating the Moving to Opportunity social experiment.* Washington, DC: Urban Institute Press.

Goffman, E. (1961). *Asylums: Essays on the social situation of mental patients and other inmates.* Chicago: Aldine.

Gold, M., & Osgood, D. W. (1992). *Personality and peer influence in juvenile corrections.* Westport, CT: Greenwood Press.

Goldberg, L., Elliot, D. L., Clarke, G. N., MacKinnon, D. P., Moe, E., Zoref, L., et al. (1996). Effects of a multi-dimensional anabolic steroid prevention intervention: The A.T.L.A.S. (Adolescents Training and Learning to Avoid Steroids) program. *Journal of the American Medical Association, 276,* 1555–1562.

Goodnight, J. A., Bates, J. E., Newman, J. P., Dodge, K. A., & Petit, G. S. (in press). The interactive influence of friend deviance, disinhibition tendencies, and gender on the emergence of externalizing behavior during early and middle adolescence. *Journal of Abnormal Psychology.*

Gordon, R. A., Savage, C., Lahey, B. B., Goodman, S. H., Jensen, P. S., Rubio-Stipec, M., et al. (2003). Family and neighborhood income: Additive and multiplicative associations with youths' well-being. *Social Science Research, 32,* 191–219.

Gormley, W. T., & Gayer, T. (2005, December 29). Promoting school readiness in Oklahoma: An evaluation of Tulsa's pre-K program. *Journal of Human Resources, 40*(3). Retrieved from www.ssc.wisc.edu/jhr/toc2005.html

Gottfredson, D. C. (1987a). An evaluation of an organization development approach to reducing school disorder. *Evaluation Review, 11,* 739–763.

Gottfredson, D. C. (1987b). Examining the potential for delinquency prevention through alternative education. *Today's Delinquent, 6,* 87–100.

Gottfredson, D. C. (1987c). Peer group interventions to reduce the risk of delinquent behavior: A selective review and new evaluation. *Criminology, 25,* 671–714.

Gottfredson, D. C., Gerstenblith, S. A., Soule, D. A., Womer, S. C., & Lu, S. (2004). Do after school programs reduce delinquency? *Prevention Science, 5,* 253–266.

Gottfredson, D. C., Gottfredson, G. D., & Hybl, K. G. (1993). Managing adolescent behavior: A multiyear, multischool study. *American Educational Research Journal, 30*, 179–215.

Gottfredson, D. C., & Wilson, D. B. (2003). Characteristics of effective school-based substance abuse prevention. *Prevention Science, 4*, 27–38.

Gottfredson, G. D., & Gottfredson, D. C. (2001). What schools do to prevent problem behavior and promote safe environments. *Journal of Educational and Psychological Consultation, 12*, 313–344.

Gottfredson, G. D., Gottfredson, D. C., Czeh, E. R., Cantor, D., Crosse, S. B., & Hantman, I. (2000). *Summary: National Study of Delinquency Prevention in Schools.* Ellicott City, MD: Gottfredson Associates, Inc.

Gramlich, E., Laren, D., & Sealand, N. (1992). Moving into and out of poor urban areas. *Journal of Policy Analysis and Management, 11*, 273–287.

Granic, I., & Dishion, T. J. (2002, May). *Measuring deviant talk between adolescents as an attractor: Predictions to antisocial outcomes.* Invited talk, first annual workshop, Linking Dynamic Systems and Reinforcement Mechanisms: Complementarities, Disparities and Data, Port Townsend, WA.

Greenberg, M. T., Domitrovich, C., & Bumbarger, B. (1999). *Preventing mental disorders in school-aged children: A review of the effectiveness of prevention programs.* Report submitted to the Center for Mental Health Services (SAM HSA), Prevention Research Center, Pennsylvania State University. Retrieved from www.psu. edu/dept/prevention/

Greenberg, M. T., Domitrovich, C., & Bumbarger, B. (2001, March). The prevention of mental disorders in school-aged children: Current state of the field. *Prevention and Treatment, 4*, Article 1. Retrieved April 24, 2001, from journals.apa.org/prevention/volume4/pre0040001a.html

Greenberg, M. T., Kusche, C. A., Cook, E. T., & Quamma, J. P. (1995). Promoting emotional competence in school-aged children: The effects of the PATHS curriculum [Special issue]. *Development and Psychopathology, 7*, 117–136.

Greenberg, M. T., Speltz, M. L., Deklyen, M., & Endriga, M. C. (1991). Attachment security in preschoolers with and without externalizing behavior problems: A replication. *Development and Psychopathology, 3*, 413–430.

Greenwood, M., & Yule, G. U. (1920). An inquiry into the nature of the frequency distributions representative of multiple happenings with particular reference to the occurrence of multiple attacks of disease or of repeated accidents. *Journal of the Royal Statistical Society, 83*, 255–279.

Greenwood, P. W., Model, K. E., Rydell, C. P., & Chiesa, J. (1996). *Diverting children from a life of crime: Measuring costs and benefits.* Santa Monica, CA: RAND.

Griffin, K. W., Botvin, G. J., Nichols, T. R., & Doyle, M. M. (2003). Effectiveness of a universal drug abuse prevention approach for youth at high risk for substance use initiation. *Preventive Medicine, 36*, 1–7.

Grogger, J. (2002). The effects of civil gang injunctions on reported violent crime: Evidence from Los Angeles County. *Journal of Law and Economics, 45*, 69–90.

Grossman, D. C., Neckerman, H. J., Koepsell, T. D., Liu, P. Y., Asher, K. N., Beland, K., et al. (1997). Effectiveness of a violence prevention curriculum among children in elementary school: A randomized controlled trial. *Journal of the American Medical Association, 277,* 1605–1611.

Grossman, J. B., & Tierney, J. P. (1998). Does mentoring work?: An impact study of the Big Brothers Big Sisters program. *Evaluation Review, 22,* 403–426.

Hahn, A., Leavitt, T., & Aaron, P. (1994). *Evaluation of the Quantum Opportunities Program (QOP): Did the program work?* Waltham, MA: Brandeis University, Center for Human Resources.

Halberstam, D. (1986). *The reckoning.* New York: Morrow.

Hallinger, P., & Heck, R. H. (1998). Exploring the principal's contribution to school effectiveness: 1980–1995. *School Effectiveness and School Improvement, 9,* 157–191.

Halpern-Felsher, B. L., Connell, J. P., Spencer, M. B., Aber, J. L., Duncan, G. J., Clifford, E., et al. (1997). Neighborhood and family factors predicting educational risk and attainment in African American and white children and adolescents. In J. Brooks-Gunn, G. J. Duncan, & J. L. Aber (Eds.), *Neighborhood poverty: Vol. 1. Context and consequences for children* (pp. 146–173). New York: Russell Sage Foundation.

Hamm, J. V. (2000). Do birds of a feather flock together?: The variable bases for African American, Asian American, and European American adolescents' selection of similar friends. *Developmental Psychology, 36,* 209–219.

Hampton, R. L. (1991). Child abuse in the African American community. In J. E. Everett, S. S. Chipungu, & B. R. Leashore (Eds.), *Child welfare: An Africentric perspective* (pp. 220–246). New Brunswick, NJ: Rutgers University Press.

Hanish, L. D., Martin, C. L., Fabes, R. A., Leonard, S., & Herzog, M. (2005). Exposure to externalizing peers in early childhood: Homophily and peer contagion processes. *Journal of Abnormal Child Psychology, 33,* 267–281.

Harding, D. J. (2003). Counterfactual models of neighborhood effects: The effect of neighborhood poverty on dropping out and teenage pregnancy. *American Journal of Sociology, 109,* 676–719.

Harrell, A., Cavanagh, S., & Sridharan, S. (1998). *Impact of the Children At Risk Program: Comprehensive final report II.* Washington, DC: Urban Institute.

Harrington, N. G., Giles, S. M., Hoyle, R. H., Feeney, G. J., & Yungbluth, S. C. (2001). Evaluation of the All Stars character education and problem behavior prevention program: Effects on mediator and outcome variables for middle school students. *Health Education and Behavior, 28,* 533–546.

Harris, M. (1979). *Cultural materialism: The struggle for a science of culture.* New York: Simon & Schuster.

Harris, M. (1981). *Why nothing works: The anthropology of daily life.* New York: Simon & Schuster.

Harris, M. J. (1994). Self-fulfilling prophesies in the clinical context: Review and implications for clinical practice. *Applied and Preventative Psychology, 3,* 145–158.

Hartmann, D. (2001). Notes on Midnight Basketball and the cultural politics of recreation, race, and at-risk urban youth. *Journal of Sport and Social Issues, 25,* 339–371.

Hastings, R. P., & Bham, M. S. (2003). The relationship between student behaviour patterns and teacher burnout. *School Psychology International*, 24, 115–127.

Hausman, J. (1978). Specification tests in econometrics. *Econometrica*, 46, 1251–1271.

Hawkins, J. D., Catalano, R. F., Kosterman, R., Abbott, R., & Hill, K. G. (1999). Preventing adolescent health-risk behaviors by strengthening protection during childhood. *Archives of Pediatric and Adolescent Medicine*, 153, 226–234.

Hawkins, J. D., Catalano, R. F., Morrison, D. M., O'Donnell, J., Abbott, R. D., & Day, L. E. (1992a). Risk and protective factors for alcohol and other drug problems in adolescence and early adulthood: Implications for substance abuse prevention. *Psychological Bulletin*, 112, 64–105.

Hawkins, J. D., Catalano, R. F., Morrison, D. M., O'Donnell, J., Abbott, R. D., & Day, L. E. (1992b). The Seattle Social Development Project: Effects of the first four years on protective factors and problem behaviors. In J. McCord & R. E. Tremblay (Eds.), *Preventing antisocial behavior: Interventions from birth through adolescence* (pp. 139–161). New York: Guilford Press.

Hawkins, J. D., Farrington, D. P., & Catalano, R. F. (1998). Reducing violence through the schools. In D. S. Elliot, B. A. Hamburg, & K. R. Williams (Eds.), *Violence in American schools* (pp. 188–216). Cambridge, UK: Cambridge University Press.

Hawkins, J. D., Von Cleve, E., & Catalano, R. F. (1991). Reducing early childhood aggression: Results of a primary prevention program. *Journal of the American Academy of Child and Adolescent Psychiatry*, 30, 208–217.

Hawthorne, G. (2001). Drug education: Myth and reality. *Drug and Alcohol Review*, 20, 111–119.

Hayasaki, E. (2005, May 30). Standing between the lockup and a diploma. *Los Angeles Times*. Available at http://www.prisontalk.com/forums/showthread.php?t=127964

Hayes, S. C. (1989). Nonhumans have not yet shown stimulus equivalents. *Journal of the Experimental Analysis of Behavior*, 51, 385–392.

Hayes, S. C. (2004). Measuring experiential avoidance: A preliminary test of a working model. *Psychological Record*, 54, 553–578.

Hayes, S. C. (2005, July 18–22). *Creating a psychology more adequate to the challenge of the human condition: State of the ACT evidence.* Paper presented at the ACT Summer Institute II, LaSalle University, Philadelphia.

Hayes, S. C., Barnes-Holmes, D., & Roche, D. (Eds.). (2001). *Relational frame theory: A post-Skinnerian account of human language and cognition.* New York: Kluwer.

Hayes, S. C., Bissett, R. T., Roget, N., Padilla, M., Kohlenberg, B. S., Fisher, G., et al. (in press). The impact of acceptance and commitment training and multicultural training on the stigmatizing attitudes and professional burnout of substance abuse counselors. *Prevention Science*.

Hayes, S. C., & Hayes, L. J. (1989). The verbal action of the listener as a basis for rule-governance. In S. C. Hayes (Ed.), *Rule-governed behavior: Cognition, contingencies, and instructional control* (pp. 153–190). New York: Plenum Press.

Hayes, S. C., Hayes, L. J., & Reese, H. W. (1988). Finding the philosophical core: A review of Stephen C. Pepper's *World hypotheses. Journal of the Experimental Analysis of Behavior, 50,* 97–111.

Hayes, S. C., Hayes, L. J., Reese, H. W., & Sarbin, T. R. (1993). *Varieties of scientific contextualism.* Reno, NV: Context Press.

Hayes, S. C., Strosahl, K. D., & Wilson, K. G. (1999). *Acceptance and commitment therapy: An experiential approach to behavior change.* New York: Guilford Press.

Haynie, D. L., & Osgood, D. W. (2005). Reconsidering peers and delinquency: How do peers matter? *Social Forces, 84,* 1107–1128.

Hedges, L. V. (1981). Distribution theory for Glass's estimator of effect size and related estimators. *Journal of Educational Statistics, 6,* 107–128.

Hedges, L. V., & Olkin, I. (1985). *Statistical methods for meta-analysis.* New York: Academic Press.

Henggeler, S. W., Melton, G. B., Brondino, M. J., Scherer, D. G., & Hanley, J. H. (1997). Multisystemic therapy with violent and chronic juvenile offenders and their families: The role of treatment fidelity in successful dissemination. *Journal of Consulting and Clinical Psychology, 65,* 821–833.

Henggeler, S. W., Mihalic, S. F., Rone, L., Thomas, C., & Timmons-Mitchell, J. (1998). *Blueprints for violence prevention: Vol. 6. Multisystemic therapy.* Boulder: University of Colorado.

Henggeler, S. W., Pickrel, S. G., & Brondino, M. J. (1999). Multisystemic treatment of substance-abusing and dependent delinquents: Outcomes, treatment fidelity, and transportability. *Mental Health Services Research, 1,* 171–184.

Herrnstein, R. J. (1970). The law of effect. *Journal of the Experimental Analysis of Behavior, 13,* 243–266.

Hindelang, M. J., Hirschi, T., & Weis, J. G. (1979). Correlates of delinquency: The illusion of discrepancy between self-report and official measures. *American Sociological Review, 44,* 995–1014.

Hirsch, E. (1998, June). A new chapter for charters. *State Legislatures,* pp. 20–24.

Hirschfeld, R. M. A., Montgomery, S. A., Keller, M. B., Kasper, S., Schatzberg, A. F., Moeller, H. J., et al. (2000). Social functioning in depression: A review. *Journal of Clinical Psychiatry, 61,* 268–275.

Hirschi, T. (1969). *Causes of delinquency.* Berkeley: University of California Press.

Hochschild, J. (2003). Social class in public schools. *Journal of Social Issues, 59,* 821–840.

Hoglund, W. L., & Leadbeater, B. J. (2004). The effects of family, school, and classroom ecologies on changes in children's social competence and emotional and behavioral problems in first grade. *Developmental Psychology, 40,* 533–544.

Holmes, C. T. (1989). Grade level retention effects: A meta-analysis of research studies. In L. A. Shepard & M. L. Smith (Eds.), *Flunking grades: Research and policies on retention* (pp. 16–33). Philadelphia: Falmer Press.

Hops, H. (1978). CLASS: A standardized in-class program for acting-out children: II. Field test evaluations. *Journal of Educational Psychology, 70,* 636–644.

Horowitz, R. (1983). *Honor and the American dream.* New Brunswick, NJ: Rutgers University Press.

Howell, W. G., & Peterson, P. E. (2002). *The education gap: Vouchers and urban schools.* Washington, DC: Brookings Institution Press.

Howell, W. G., Wolf, P. J., Campbell, D. E., & Peterson, P. E. (2002). School vouchers and academic performance: Results from three randomized field trials. *Journal of Policy Analysis and Management, 21,* 191–218.

Hsieh, C.-T., & Urquiola, M. (2002). *When schools compete, how do they compete?: An assessment of Chile's nationwide school voucher program* (Working Paper). New York: Columbia University, Department of Economics.

Hudley, C., Britsch, B., Wakefield, W. D., Smith, T., Demorat, M., & Cho, S. (1998). An attributional retraining program to reduce aggression in elementary school students. *Psychology in the Schools, 35,* 271–282.

Hudley, C., & Graham, S. (1993). An attributional intervention to reduce peer-directed aggression among African-American boys. *Child Development, 64,* 124–138.

Hughes, R. E. (2001). Deciding to leave but staying: Teacher burnout, precursors, and turnover. *International Journal of Human Resource Management, 12,* 288–298.

Huizinga, D., & Elliot, D. S. (1986). Reassessing the reliability and validity of self-report delinquency measures. *Journal of Quantitative Criminology, 2,* 293–327.

Hundleby, J. D. (1987). Adolescent drug use in a behavioral matrix: A confirmation and comparison of the sexes. *Addictive Behaviors, 12,* 103–112.

Ialongo, N. S., Poduska, J., Werthamer, L., & Kellam, S. G. (2001). The distal impact of two first-grade preventive interventions on conduct problems and disorder in early adolescence. *Journal of Emotional and Behavioral Disorders, 9,* 146–190.

Ialongo, N. S., Werthamer, L., Kellam, S. G., Brown, C. H., Wang, S., & Lin, Y. (1999). Proximal impact of two first-grade preventive interventions on the early risk behaviors for later substance abuse, depression, and antisocial behavior. *American Journal of Community Psychology, 27,* 599–641.

Illinois Juvenile Court Act, 1899 Illinois Laws, 132 et seq. (1899).

Imbens, G. (2003). *Nonparametric estimation of average treatment effects under exogeneity: A review* (Technical Working Paper No. 294). Cambridge, MA: National Bureau of Economic Research.

Imbens, G. W., & Angrist, J. D. (1994). Identification and estimation of local average treatment effects. *Econometrica, 62,* 467–475.

Ingersoll, R. M. (1996). Teachers' decision-making power and school conflict. *Sociological Quarterly, 69,* 159–176.

Ingersoll, R. M. (2001). Teacher turnover and teacher shortages: An organizational analysis. *American Educational Research Journal, 38,* 499–534.

In Re Gault, 387 U.S. 1 (1967).

Irvin, L. K., Tobin, T. J., Sprague, J. R., Sugai, G., & Vincent, C. G. (2004). Validity of office discipline referral measures as indices of school-wide behavioral status and effects of school-wide behavioral interventions. *Journal of Positive Behavior Interventions, 6,* 131–147.

Jacob, B. A. (2004). Public housing, housing vouchers, and student achievement: Evidence from public housing demolitions in Chicago. *American Economic Review, 94,* 233–258.

Jacobsen, N. S., & Truax, P. (1991). Clinical significance: A statistical approach to defining meaningful change in psychotherapy research. *Journal of Consulting and Clinical Psychology, 59*, 12–19.

James-Burdumy, S., Dynarski, M., Moore, M., Deke, J., Mansfield, W., & Pistorino, C. (2005). *When schools stay open late: The national evaluation of the 21st Century Community Learning Centers Program: Final report.* Washington, DC: U.S. Department of Education, Institute of Education Sciences, National Center for Education Evaluation and Regional Assistance. Retrieved from http://www.ed.gov/ies/ncee

Jargowsky, P. A. (1997). *Poverty and place: Ghettos, barrios, and the American city.* New York: Russell Sage Foundation.

Jargowsky, P. A. (2003). *Stunning progress, hidden problems: The dramatic decline of concentrated poverty in the 1990s.* Washington, DC: Brookings Institution, Center on Urban and Metropolitan Policy.

Jencks, C., & Mayer, S. E. (1990). The social consequences of growing up in a poor neighborhood. In L. E. Lynn Jr. & M. G. H. McGeary (Eds.), *Inner-city poverty in the United States* (pp. 111–186). Washington, DC: National Academy Press.

Jensen, G. F., & Rojek, D. G. (1998). *Delinquency and youth crime.* Prospect Heights, IL: Waveland Press.

Jimerson, S. R. (2001). Meta-analysis of grade retention research: Implications for practice in the 21st century. *School Psychology Review, 30*, 420–437.

Jimerson, S. R., Anderson, G., & Whipple, A. (2002). Winning the battle and losing the war: Examining the relation between grade retention and dropping out of high school. *Psychology in the Schools, 39*, 441–457.

Jimerson, S. R., & Kaufman, A. M. (2003). Reading, writing, and retention: A primer on grade retention research. *The Reading Teacher, 56*, 622–635.

Johnson, D. W., & Johnson, R. T. (1996). Conflict resolution and peer mediation programs in elementary and secondary schools: A review of research. *Review of Educational Research, 66*, 459–506.

Johnson, L. M., Simons, L., & Conger, R. D. (2004). Criminal justice system involvement and continuity of youth crime: A longitudinal analysis. *Youth and Society, 36*, 3–29.

Johnson, M., Ladd, H. F., & Ludwig, J. (2002). The benefits and costs of residential mobility programs. *Housing Studies, 17*, 125–138.

Johnson, S. L., & Jacob, T. (1997). Marital interactions of depressed men and women. *Journal of Consulting and Clinical Psychology, 65*, 15–23.

Jones, M. B., & Jones, D. R. (2000). The contagious nature of antisocial behavior. *Criminology, 38*, 25–46.

Jonson-Reid, M. (1998). Youth violence and exposure to violence in childhood: An ecological review. *Aggression and Violent Behavior, 30*, 159–179.

Jonson-Reid, M. (2002a) After a child abuse report: Early adolescents and the child welfare system. *Journal of Early Adolescence, 22*, 24–48.

Jonson-Reid, M. (2002b). Exploring the relationship between child welfare intervention and juvenile corrections involvement. *American Journal of Orthopsychiatry, 72*, 559–576.

Jonson-Reid, M., & Barth, R. (2000a). From maltreatment to juvenile incarceration: Uncovering the role of child welfare services. *Child Abuse and Neglect*, 24, 505–520.

Jonson-Reid, M., & Barth, R. (2000b). From placement to prison: The path to adolescent incarceration from child welfare supervised foster or group care. *Children and Youth Services Review*, 22, 493–516.

Jurado, D., Gurpegui, M., Moreno, O., & de Dios, L. J. (1998). School setting and teaching experience as risk factors for depressive symptoms in teachers. *European Psychiatry*, 13, 78–82.

Jussim, L., & Osgood, D. W. (1989). Influence and similarity among friends: An integrative model applied to incarcerated adolescents. *Social Psychology Quarterly*, 52, 98–112.

Juvonen, J., & Graham, S. (2001). *Peer harassment in school: The plight of the vulnerable and victimized*. New York: Guilford Press.

Kain, J. F. (1968). Housing segregation, Negro employment, and metropolitan decentralization. *Quarterly Journal of Economics*, 82, 175–197.

Kam, C. M., Greenberg, M. T., & Walls, C. T. (2003). Examining the role of implementation quality in school-based prevention using the PATHS curriculum. *Prevention Science*, 4, 55–63.

Kane, T. J. (2004). *The impact of after-school programs: Interpreting the results of four recent evaluations* (Working Paper). New York: William T. Grant Foundation.

Kanfer, F. H., & Grimm, L. G. (1978). Freedom of choice and behavioral change. *Journal of Consulting and Clinical Psychology*, 2, 193–207.

Kang, C. (2005). *Classroom peer effects and academic achievement: Quasi-randomization evidence from South Korea*. Singapore: National University of Singapore. Retrieved July 23, 2005, from nt2.fas.nus.edu.sg/ecs/res/seminars/seminar-papers/14042005.pdf

Kaplan, H. B. (1975). Increase in self-rejection as an antecedent of deviant responses. *Journal of Youth and Adolescence*, 4, 281–292.

Kaplan, H. B. (1976). Self-attitudes and deviant responses. *Social Forces*, 54, 788–801.

Kaplan, H. B., & Liu, X. (1994). A longitudinal analysis of mediating variables in the drug use-dropping out relationship. *Criminology*, 32, 415–439.

Kaplan, R. M. (1984). The connection between clinical health promotion and health status: A critical overview. *American Psychologist*, 39, 755–765.

Kapp, S. A., McDonald, T. P., & Diamond, K. L. (2001). The path to adoption for children of color. *Child Abuse and Neglect*, 25, 215–229.

Karoly, L. A., Greenwood, P. W., Everingham, S. S., Houbé, J., Kilburn, M. R., Rydell, C. P., et al. (1998). *Investing in our children: What we know and don't know about the costs and benefits of early childhood interventions*. Santa Monica, CA: RAND.

Katz, L. F., Kling, J. R., & Liebman, J. B. (2001). Moving to Opportunity in Boston: Early results of a randomized mobility experiment. *Quarterly Journal of Economics*, 116, 607–654.

Kauffman, J. (2005). *Characteristics of emotional and behavioral disorders of children and youth*. Columbus, OH: Prentice-Hall.

Kazdin, A. E., & Weisz, J. R. (Eds.). (2003). *Evidence-based psychotherapies for children and adolescents*. New York: Guilford Press.

Keels, M., Duncan, G. J., & Rosenbaum, J. E. (2004). *The long-term effects of the*

Gautreaux Residential-Mobility Program (Working Paper). Evanston, IL: Northwestern University, Institute for Policy Research.

Keenan, K., Loeber, R., Zhang, Q., Stouthamer-Loeber, M., & Van Kammen, W. (1995). The influence of deviant peers on the development of boys' disruptive and delinquent behavior: A temporal analysis. *Development and Psychopathology, 7,* 715–726.

Kellam, S. G., Ling, X., Merisca, R., Brown, C. H., & Ialongo, N. (1998). The effect of the level of aggression in the first grade classroom on the course and malleability of aggressive behavior into middle school. *Development and Psychopathology, 10,* 165–185.

Kellam, S. G., Rebok, G. W., Ialongo, N., & Mayer, L. S. (1994). The course and malleability of aggressive behavior from early first grade into middle school: Results of a developmental epidemiologically-based prevention trial. *Journal of Child Psychology and Psychiatry, 35,* 259–281.

Kelly, J. G. (1988). *A guide to conducting prevention research in the community: First steps.* Binghamton, NY: Haworth Press.

Kennedy, D. M., Braga, A. A., Piehl, A. M., & Waring, E. J. (2001). *Reducing gun violence: The Boston Gun Project's Operation Cease Fire.* Washington, DC: National Institute of Justice.

Kernan, E., & Lansford, J. E. (2004). Providing for the best interests of the child?: The Adoption and Safe Families Act of 1997. *Journal of Applied Developmental Psychology, 25,* 523–539.

Khan, J. E. (2001). Adolescents in foster care: A descriptive study of self-concept and behavioral indicators of psychosocial adjustment. *Dissertation Abstracts International: Section B: The Sciences and Engineering, 61*(9-B), 4989.

Kingery, P. (2000). *Zero tolerance: The alternative is education.* Washington, DC: Hamilton Fish Institute.

Klebanov, P. K., Brooks-Gunn, J., Chase-Lansdale, P. L., & Gordon, R. A. (1997). Are neighborhood effects on young children mediated by features of the home environment? In J. Brooks-Gunn, G. J. Duncan, & J. L. Aber (Eds.), *Neighborhood poverty: Vol. 1. Context and consequences for children* (pp. 199–145). New York: Russell Sage Foundation.

Klein, M. W. (1971). *Street gangs and street workers.* Englewood Cliffs, NJ: Prentice-Hall.

Klein, M. W. (1995). *The American street gang: Its nature, prevalence, and control.* New York: Oxford University Press.

Klein, M. W. (1997). *Guiding Los Angeles's response to street gangs: An SC 2 Project Failure.* Los Angeles: University of Southern California, Social Science Research Institute.

Klein, M. W. (2004). *Gang cop: The words and ways of Officer Paco Domingo.* Walnut Creek, CA: Altamira Press.

Klein, M. W. (2005). The value of comparisons in street gang research. *Journal of Contemporary Criminal Justice, 21,* 135–152.

Klein, M. W., Kerner, H.-J., Maxson, C. L., & Weitekamp, E. G. M. (Eds.). (2001). *The Eurogang paradox: Street gangs and youth groups in the U.S. and Europe.* Dordrecht, The Netherlands: Kluwer Academic Press.

Klein, M. W., & Maxson, C. L. (in press). *Street gang patterns and policies*. New York: Oxford University Press.

Kleiner, B., Porch, R., & Farris, E. (2002). *Public alternative schools and programs for students at risk of education failure: 2000–01* (NCES Pub. No. 2002-004). Washington, DC: U.S. Department of Education, National Center for Education Statistics.

Kling, J. R., & Liebman, J. B. (2004a). *Experimental analysis of neighborhood effects on youth* (Working Paper No. 483). Princeton, NJ: Princeton University, Department of Economics.

Kling, J. R., & Liebman, J.B. (2004b). *Experimental analysis of neighborhood effects on youth* (Working Paper No. RWP04-034). Cambridge, MA: Harvard University, Kennedy School of Government.

Kling, J. R., Liebman, J. B., Katz, L. F., & Sanbonmatsu, L. (2004). *Moving to opportunity and tranquility: Neighborhood effects on adult economic self-sufficiency and health from a randomized housing voucher experiment* (Working Paper No. 481). Princeton, NJ: Princeton University, Department of Economics.

Kling, J., Ludwig, J., & Katz, L. (2004). *Youth criminal behavior in the Moving to Opportunity experiment* (Working Paper No. 482). Princeton, NJ: Princeton University, Department of Economics.

Kling, J. R., Ludwig, J., & Katz, L. F. (2005). Neighborhood effects on crime for male and female youth: Evidence from a randomized housing voucher experiment. *Quarterly Journal of Economics, 120*, 87–130.

Knoff, H. M., & Batsche, G. M. (1995). Project Achieve: Analyzing a school reform process for at-risk and underachieving students. *School Psychology Review, 24*, 579–603.

Kramer, L., Laumann, G., & Brunson, L. (2000). Implementation and diffusion of the Rainbows Program in rural communities: Implications for school-based prevention programs. *Journal of Education and Psychological Consultation, 11*, 37–64.

Krueger, A. (1999). Experimental estimates of educational production functions. *Quarterly Journal of Economics, 114*, 497–532.

Kubitscheck, W., & Hallinan, M. (1998). Tracking and students' friendships. *Social Psychology Quarterly, 61*, 1–15.

Kumpfer, K. L., Molgaard, V., & Spoth, R. (1996). The Strengthening Families Program for the prevention of delinquency and drug use. In R. D. Peters & R. J. McMahon (Eds.), *Preventing childhood disorders, substance abuse, and delinquency* (pp. 241–267). Thousand Oaks, CA: Sage.

Kunz, J., Page, M. E., & Solon, G. (2003). Are point-in-time measures of neighborhood characteristics useful proxies for children's long-run neighborhood environment? *Economics Letter, 79*, 231–237.

Ladd, G. W. (1990). Having friends, keeping friends, making friends, and being liked by peers in the classroom: Predictors of children's early school adjustment? *Child Development, 61*, 1081–1100.

Ladd, H. F. (1994). Spatially targeted economic development strategies: Do they work? *Cityscape: A Journal of Policy Development and Research, 1*, 193–218.

Larson, J. (1994). Violence prevention in the schools: A review of selected programs and procedures. *School Psychology Review*, 23, 151–164.

Larson, J. (1998). Managing student aggression in high schools: Implications for practice. *Psychology in the Schools*, 35, 283–295.

Larson, R. (1994). Youth organizations, hobbies, and sports as developmental contexts. In R. K. Silberiesen & E. Todt (Eds.), *Adolescence in context* (pp. 46–65). New York: Springer-Verlag.

Latessa, E. J. (2004). The challenge of change: Correctional programs and evidence-based practices. *Criminology and Public Policy*, 3, 547–559.

Latessa, E. J., Listwan, S. J., & Hubbard, D. J. (2005). *Correctional interventions: Changing offender behavior.* Los Angeles: Roxbury.

Lavallee, K. L., Bierman, K. L., Nix, R. L., & the Conduct Problems Prevention Research Group. (2005). The impact of first-grade "friendship group" experiences on child social outcomes in the Fast Track program. *Journal of Abnormal Child Psychology*, 33, 307–324.

Leathers, S. (2002). Foster children's behavioral disturbance and detachment from caregivers and community institutions. *Children and Youth Services Review*, 24, 239–268.

Le Blanc, M., Vallieres, E., & McDuff, P. (1992). Adolescent's school experience and self-reported offending: An empirical elaboration of an interactional and developmental school social control theory. *International Journal of Adolescence and Youth*, 3, 197–247.

Lederman, C. (1999). The juvenile court: Putting research to work for prevention. *Juvenile Justice*, 6, 22–31.

Lemertt, E. M. (1951). *Social pathology.* New York: McGraw-Hill.

Lemertt, E. M. (1972). *Human deviance, social problems and social control* (2nd ed.). Englewood Cliffs, NJ: Prentice-Hall.

Leve, L. D., & Chamberlain, P. (2004). Female juvenile offenders: Defining an early-onset pathway for delinquency. *Journal of Child and Family Studies*, 13, 439–452.

Leve, L. D., & Chamberlain, P. (2005). Association with delinquent peers: Intervention effects for youth in the juvenile justice system. *Journal of Abnormal Child Psychology*, 33, 339–347.

Levitt, S. D. (1996). The effect of prison population size on crime rates: Evidence from prison overcrowding litigation. *Quarterly Journal of Economics*, 111, 319–352.

Levitt, S. D. (1997). Using electoral cycles in police hiring to estimate the effect of police on crime. *American Economic Review*, 87, 270–290.

Levitt, S. D. (2002). Using electoral cycles in police hiring to estimate the effect of police on crime: A reply. *American Economic Review*, 92, 1244–1250.

Levitt, S. D. (2004). Understanding why crime fell in the 1990s: Four factors that explain the decline and six that do not. *Journal of Economic Perspectives*, 18, 163–190.

Lewin, K. (1936). *Principles of topological psychology* (F. Heider & G. M. Heider, Trans.). New York: McGraw-Hill.

Lewis, R. V. (1983). Scared Straight—California style. *Criminal Justice and Behavior*, 10, 284–289.

Lewis, T. J., Sugai, G., & Colvin, G. (1998). Reducing problem behavior through a school-wide system of effective behavioral support: Investigation of a school-wide social skills training program and contextual interventions. *School Psychology Review, 27*, 446–459.

Liebman, J., Katz, L. F., & Kling, J. R. (2004). *Beyond treatment effects: Estimating the relationship between neighborhood poverty and individual outcomes in the MTO experiment* (Working Paper No. 493). Princeton, NJ: Princeton University, Industrial Relations Section.

Lipsey, M. W. (1992). Juvenile delinquency treatment: A meta-analytic inquiry into the variability of effects. In T. D. Cook, H. Cooper, D. S. Condray, H. Hartman, L. V. Hodges, R. J. Light, et al. (Eds.), *Meta-analysis for explanation: A casebook* (pp. 83–127). New York: Russell Sage Foundation.

Lipsey, M. W. (1995). What do we learn from 400 research studies on the effectiveness of treatment with juvenile delinquents? In J. McGuire (Ed.), *What works?: Reducing reoffending* (pp. 63–78). New York: Wiley.

Lipsey, M. W., & Derzon, J. H. (1998). Predictors of violent or serious delinquency in adolescence and early adulthood: A synthesis of longitudinal research. In R. Loeber & D. P. Farrington (Eds.), *Serious and violent juvenile offenders: Risk factors and successful interventions* (pp. 86–105). Thousand Oaks, CA: Sage.

Lipsey, M. W., & Wilson, D. B. (1998). Effective intervention for serious juvenile offenders: A synthesis of research. In R. Loeber & D. P. Farrington (Eds.), *Serious and violent juvenile offenders: Risk factors and successful interventions* (pp. 313–345). Thousand Oaks, CA: Sage.

Lipsey, M. W., Wilson, D. B., & Cothern, L. (2000). *Effective intervention for serious juvenile offenders*. Washington DC: U.S. Department of Justice, Office of Juvenile Justice and Delinquency Prevention.

Little, J. W. (1982). Norms of collegiality and experimentation: Workplace conditions of school success. *American Educational Research Journal, 19*, 325–340.

Lochman, J. E., & Van den Steenhoven, A. (2002). Family-based approaches to substance abuse prevention. *Journal of Primary Prevention, 23*, 49–114.

Loeber, R., Farrington, D. P., Stouthamer-Loeber, M., Moffitt, T. E., & Caspi, A. (1998). The development of male offending: Key findings from the first decade of the Pittsburgh Youth Study. *Studies on Crime and Crime Prevention, 7*, 141–171.

Loeber, R., Wei, E., Stouthamer-Loeber, M., Huizanga, D., & Thornberry, T. P. (1999). Behavioral antecedents to serious and violent offending: Joint analyses from the Denver Youth Survey, Pittsburgh Youth Study and the Rochester Youth Development Study. *Studies on Crime and Crime Prevention, 8*, 245–263.

Lohrmann-O'Rourke, S., Knoster, T., Sabatine, K., Smith, D., Horvath, B., & Llewellyn, G. (2000). School-wide application of PBS in the Bangor area school district. *Journal of Positive Behavior Interventions, 2*, 238–240.

Lopez Turley, R. N. (2003). When do neighborhoods matter?: The role of race and neighborhood peers. *Social Science Research, 32*, 61–79.

Loughran, E. J., Godfrey, K., Holyoke, S., Conroy, D., & Dugan, B. (2004). *Juvenile corrections: A national perspective 2004*. Braintree, MA: Council of Juvenile Correctional Administrators.

Ludwig, J., Duncan, G., & Hirschfield, P. (2001). Urban poverty and juvenile crime: Evidence from a randomized housing experiment. *Quarterly Journal of Economics, 116,* 655–680.

Ludwig, J., Ladd, H. F., & Duncan, G. J. (2001). Urban poverty and educational outcomes. In W. Gale & J. R. Pack (Eds.), *Brookings–Wharton papers on urban affairs* (pp. 147–201). Washington, DC: Brookings Institution.

Ludwig, J., & Miller, D. L. (2005). *Does Head Start have long term effects?: Evidence from a regression discontinuity design* (Working Paper). Washington, DC: Georgetown University, Georgetown Public Policy Institute.

Lutzker, J. R., Touchette, P. E., & Campbell, R. V. (1988). Parental positive reinforcement might make a difference: A rejoinder to Forehand. *Child and Family Behavior Therapy, 10,* 2–33.

Lynam, D. R., Milich, R., Zimmerman, R., Novak, S. P., Logan, T. K., Martin, C., et al. (1999). Project DARE: No effects at 10-year follow-up. *Journal of Consulting and Clinical Psychology, 67,* 590–593.

Lyons-Ruth, K. (1996). Attachment relationships among children with aggressive behavior problems: The role of disorganized early attachment patterns. *Journal of Consulting and Clinical Psychology, 64,* 64–73.

Maccoby, E. A., & Martin, J. A. (1983). Socialization in the context of the family: Parent–child interaction. In P. H. Mussen (Ed.), *Handbook of child psychology* (4th ed., Vol. 4., pp. 1–101). New York: Wiley.

MacKenzie, D. (1997). Criminal justice and crime prevention. In L. W. Sherman, D. Gottfredson, D. MacKenzie, J. Eck, P. Reuter, & S. Bushway (Eds.), *Preventing crime: What works, what doesn't, what's promising* (pp. 9-1–9-76). Washington, DC: U.S. Department of Justice, Office of Justice Programs.

MacKenzie, D. L. (2002). Reducing the criminal activities of known offenders and delinquents. In L. W. Sherman, D. P. Farrington, B. C. Welsh, & D. L. MacKenzie (Eds.), *Evidence-based crime prevention* (pp. 330–404). London: Routledge.

MacKinnon, D. P., Johnson, C. A., Pentz, M. A., Dwyer, J. H., Hansen, W. B., Flay, B. R., et al. (1991). Mediating mechanisms in a school-based drug prevention program: First-year effects of the Midwestern Prevention Project. *Health Psychology, 10,* 164–172.

Madden, J. F. (1996). Changes in the distribution of poverty across and within U.S. metropolitan areas, 1979–89. *Urban Studies, 33,* 1581–1600.

Madsen, C. H., Becker, W. C., & Thomas, D. R. (1968). Rules, praise, and ignoring: Elements of elementary classroom control. *Journal of Applied Behavior Analysis, 1,* 139–150.

Mager, W., Milich, R., Harris, M. J., & Howard, A. (2005). Intervention groups for adolescents with conduct problems: Is aggregation harmful or helpful? *Journal of Abnormal Child Psychology, 33,* 349–362.

Magnusson, D., Stattin, H., & Allen, J. L. (1985). Biological maturation and social development: A longitudinal study of some adjustment processes from mid-adolescence to adulthood. *Journal of Youth and Adolescence, 14*(4), 267–283.

Mahoney, J. L. (2000). School extracurricular activity participation as a moderator in the development of antisocial patterns. *Child Development, 71,* 502–516.

Mahoney, J. L., & Cairns, R. B. (1997). Do extracurricular activities protect against early school dropout? *Developmental Psychology, 33,* 241–253.

Mahoney, J. L., Lord, H., & Carryl, E. (2005). An ecological analysis of after-school program participation and the development of academic performance and motivational attributes for disadvantaged children. *Child Development*, 76, 811–825.

Mahoney, J. L., Schweder, A. E., & Stattin, H. (2002). Structured after-school activities as a moderator of depressed mood for adolescents with detached relations to their parents. *Journal of Community Psychology*, 30, 69–86.

Mahoney, J. L., & Stattin, H. (2000). Leisure activities and adolescent antisocial behavior: The role of structure and social context. *Journal of Adolescence*, 23, 113–127.

Mahoney, J. L., Stattin, H., & Lord, H. (2004). Participation in unstructured youth recreation centers and the development of antisocial behavior: Selection processes and the moderating role of deviant peers. *International Journal of Behavioral Development*, 28, 553–560.

Mahoney, J. L., Stattin, H., & Magnusson, D. (2001). Youth recreation centre participation and criminal offending: A 20-year longitudinal study of Swedish boys. *International Journal of Behavioral Development*, 25, 509–520.

Malle, B. F. (1999). How people explain behavior: A new theoretical framework. *Personality and Social Psychology Review*, 3, 23–48.

Malle, B. F., & Knobe, J. C. (1997). Which behaviors do people explain?: A basic actor–observer asymmetry. *Journal of Personality and Social Psychology*, 72, 288–304.

Mann, T., Nolen-Hoeksema, S., Burgard, D., Wright, A., & Hanson, K. (1997). Are two interventions worse than none?: Joint primary and secondary prevention of eating disorders in college females. *Health Psychology*, 16, 215–225.

Manski, C. F. (1993). Identification of endogenous social effects: The reflection problem. *Review of Economic Studies*, 60, 531–542.

Martinez, C. R., & Forgatch, M. S. (2001). Preventing problems with boys' noncompliance: Effects of a parent training intervention for divorcing mothers. *Journal of Consulting and Clinical Psychology*, 69, 416–428.

Martinez, C. R. Jr., & Forgatch, M. S. (2002). Adjusting to change: Linking family structure transitions with parenting and boys' adjustment. *Journal of Family Psychology*, 16, 107–117.

Martinson, R. (1974). What works?: Questions and answers about prison reform. *The Public Interest*, 35, 22–54.

Maslach, C. (1999). Progress in understanding teacher burnout. In A. M. Huberman & R. Vandenberghe (Eds.), *Understanding and preventing teacher burnout: A sourcebook of international research and practice* (pp. 211–222). New York: Cambridge University Press.

Maslach, C., & Jackson, S. E. (1984). Burnout in organizational settings. *Applied Social Psychology Annual*, 5, 133–153.

Mayer, G. O. (1995). Preventing antisocial behavior in the schools. *Journal of Applied Behavior Analysis*, 28, 467–478.

Mayer, G. R., Butterworth, T. W., Nafpaktitis, M., & Sulzer-Azaroff, B. (1983). Preventing school vandalism and improving discipline: A three-year study. *Journal of Applied Behavior Analysis*, 16, 355–369.

Mayer, G. R., Sulzer, B., & Cody, J. J. (1968). The use of punishment in modifying student behavior. *Journal of Special Education, 2,* 323–328.

Mayeux, L., Bellmore, A. D., & Kaplan, A. M. (2002, April). *Stability and correlates of perceived popularity in adolescence.* Paper presented at the biennial meeting of the Society for Research in Adolescence, New Orleans, LA.

Mays, G. L., & Winfree, L. T. Jr. (2000). *Juvenile justice.* Boston: McGraw-Hill.

McClendon, M. J. (1995). *Multiple regression and causal analysis.* Itasca, IL: Peacock.

McCord, J. (1978). A thirty-year follow-up of treatment effects. *American Psychologist, 33,* 284–289.

McCord, J. (1992). The Cambridge–Somerville Study: A pioneering longitudinal-experimental study of delinquency prevention. In J. McCord & R. E. Tremblay (Eds.), *Preventing antisocial behavior: Interventions from birth through adolescence* (pp. 196–206). New York: Guilford Press.

McCord, J. (1997). He did it because he wanted to. . . . In D. W. Osgood (Ed.), *Motivation and delinquency: Nebraska Symposium on Motivation* (Vol. 44, pp. 1–43). Lincoln: University of Nebraska Press.

McCord, J. (1999). Understanding childhood and subsequent crime. *Aggressive Behavior, 25,* 241–253.

McCord, J. (2003). Cures that harm: Unanticipated outcomes of crime prevention programs. *Annals of the American Academy of Political and Social Science, 587,* 16–30.

McCord, J., Widom, C. S., & Crowell, N. (Eds.). (2001). *Juvenile crime, juvenile justice.* Washington, DC: National Academy Press.

McCorkle, L. W. (1953). The present status of group therapy in United States correctional institutions. *International Journal of Group Psychotherapy, 3,* 79–87.

McCulloch, A., & Joshi, H. E. (2001). Neighbourhood and family influences on the cognitive ability of children in the British National Child Development Study. *Social Science and Medicine, 53,* 579–591.

McDowell, J. J. (1988). Matching theory in natural human environments. *Behavior Analyst, 11,* 95–109.

McEvoy, A., & Welker, R. (2000). Antisocial behavior, academic failure, and school climate: A critical review. *Journal of Emotional and Behavioral Disorders, 8,* 130–140.

McRoy, R. G., Oglesby, Z., & Grape, H. (1997). Achieving same-race adoptive placements for African American children: Culturally sensitive practice approaches. *Child Welfare, 76,* 85–104.

Mendel, R. A. (2001). *Less hype, more help: Reducing juvenile crime, what works—and what doesn't.* Washington, DC: American Youth Policy Forum.

Mendenhall, R., Duncan, G. J., & DeLuca, S. (2004). *Neighborhood resources and economic mobility: Results from the Gautreaux Program.* Evanston, IL: Unpublished manuscript, Northwestern University, Institute for Policy Research.

Metropolitan Area Child Study Research Group & Gorman-Smith, D. (2003). Effects of teacher training and consultation on teacher behavior towards students at high risk for aggression. *Behavior Therapy, 34,* 437–452.

Metzler, C. W., Biglan, A., Rusby, J. C., & Sprague, J. R. (2001). Evaluation of a comprehensive behavior management program to provide school-wide positive behavior support. *Education and Treatment of Children, 24,* 448–479.

Metzler, C. W., Eddy, J. M., Taylor, T., & Lichtenstein, D. (2005). *Identifying best practices in prevention through the aggregation of research based lists.* Unpublished manuscript, Department of Psychology, University of Oregon.

Midnight basketball. (n.d.). Retrieved May 5, 2004, from www.lockjaw.net/project/mbasketball

Midnight basketball: How to give young people a chance. (n.d.). Retrieved May 5, 2004 from www.housingresearch.org/hrf/HRF_REFLIB.Nsf320d38 b6b455f6fb8525699a005e0617/8e6ba5fc3ea 317148525699a 005e503e? OpenDocument

Mihalic, S., & Aultman-Bettridge, T. (2002). A guide to effective school-based prevention programs. In W. L. Tulk (Ed.), *Policing and school crime* (pp. 202–229). Englewood Cliffs, NJ: Prentice-Hall.

Mihalic, S. F., & Irwin, K. (2003). Blueprints for violence prevention: From research to real world settings—Factors influencing the successful replication of model programs. *Youth Violence and Juvenile Justice, 1,* 307–329.

Miller, J. (2001). *One of the guys: Girls, gangs, and gender.* New York: Oxford University Press.

Miller, W. B. (1973). Race, sex, and gangs: The molls. *Society, 11,* 32–35.

Minuchin, S., & Fishman, C. H. (1981). *Family therapy techniques.* Cambridge, MA: Harvard University Press.

Mitchell, J., Dodder, R. A., & Norris, T. D. (1990). Neutralization and delinquency: A comparison by sex and ethnicity. *Adolescence, 25,* 487–497.

Moberg, D. P., & Piper, D. L. (1998). The healthy for life project: Sexual risk behavior outcomes. *AIDS Education and Prevention, 10,* 128–148.

Moffitt, R. A. (2001). Policy interventions, low-level equilibria, and social interactions. In S. Durlauf & P. Young (Eds.), *Social dynamics* (pp. 45–82). Cambridge, MA: MIT Press.

Monahan, J. (2003). Violence risk assessment . In A. Goldstein (Ed.), *Handbook of psychology: Forensic psychology* (Vol. 11, pp. 527–540). New York: Wiley.

Monahan, J., Swartz, M., & Bonnie, R. (2003). Mandated community treatment for mental disorders. *Health Affairs, 22,* 28–38.

Moore, J. W. (1991). *Going down to the barrio: Homeboys and homegirls in change.* Philadelphia: Temple University Press.

Moore, J. W., & Vigil, J. D. (1989). Chicano gangs: Group norms and individual factors related to adult criminality. *Aztlan, 18,* 27–44.

Moore, K. J., Osgood, D. W., Larzelere, R. E., & Chamberlain, P. (1994). Use of pooled time series in the study of naturally occurring clinical events and problem behavior in a foster care setting. *Journal of Consulting and Clinical Psychology, 62,* 718–728.

Morrison, G. M., & D'Incau, B. (1997). The web of zero tolerance: Characteristics of students who are recommended for expulsion from school. *Education and Treatment of Children, 20,* 316–335.

Moss, B. G. (1996). *Perceptions of church leaders regarding the role of the church in combating juvenile delinquency in San Antonio, Texas: Implications for church and community-based programs.* Unpublished doctoral dissertation, St. Mary's University, San Antonio, TX.

Mrazek, P. G., & Haggerty, R. J. (Eds.). (1994). *Reducing risks for mental disor-*

ders: Frontiers for preventive intervention research. Washington, DC: National Academy Press.

Muthén, B. O., & Curran, P. J. (1997). General longitudinal modeling of individual differences in experimental designs: A latent variable framework for analysis and power estimation. *Psychological Methods, 2,* 371–402.

Muthén, B. O., & Muthén, L. K. (2000). Integrating person-centered and variable-centered analysis: Growth mixture modeling with latent trajectory classes. *Alcoholism: Clinical and Experimental Research, 24,* 882–891.

Nafpaktitis, M., Mayer, G. R., & Butterworth, T. W. (1985). Natural rates of teacher approval and disapproval and their relation to student behavior in intermediate school classrooms. *Journal of Educational Psychology, 77,* 362–367.

Nagin, D. (2001). Measuring the economic benefits of developmental prevention programs. In M. Tonry (Ed.), *Crime and justice: A review of research* (Vol. 28, pp. 247–384). Chicago: University of Chicago Press.

National Center for Educational Statistics. (2001). *Public alternative schools and programs for students at risk of educational failure: 2000–01.* Washington, DC: U.S. Department of Education, Office of Educational Research and Improvement.

National Collaboration for Youth. (1990). *Making the grade: A report card on American youth.* Washington, DC: Author.

National Council on Disability. (2003). *Addressing the needs of youth with disabilities in the juvenile justice system: The status of evidence-based research.* Washington, DC: Author.

National Institutes of Health. (2004, October). *Preventing violence and related health-risking social behaviors in adolescents* (State-of-the-Science Conference Statement). Washington, DC: Author. Retrieved May 2005 from consensus.nih.gov

National Institute of Mental Health. (2004). *Preventing child and adolescent mental disorders: Research roundtable on economic burden and cost effectiveness.* Retrieved from www.nimh.nih.gov/scientificmeetings/economicroundtable.cfm

National Research Council. (2002). *Minority students in special and gifted education.* Washington, DC: National Academy Press.

National Youth Gang Center. (1998). *1998 National Youth Gang Survey: Summary.* Washington, DC: U.S. Department of Justice, Office of Juvenile Justice and Delinquency Prevention.

Nelson, F. H., Rosenberg, B., & Van Meter, N. (2004). *Charter school achievement on the 2003 National Assessment of Educational Progress.* Washington, DC: American Federation of Teachers.

Nelson, J. R., Crabtree, M., Marchard-Martella, N., & Martella, R. (1998). Teaching good behavior in the whole school. *Teaching Exceptional Children, 30,* 4–9.

Newcomb, T. M. (1943). *Personality and social change: Attitude formation in a student community.* New York: Dryden.

Newmann, F. M., Rutter, R. A., & Smith, M. S. (1989). Organizational factors that affect school sense of efficacy, community, and expectations. *Sociology of Education, 62,* 221–238.

Nickerson, D. W. (2005). Scalable protocols offer efficient design for field experiments. *Political Analysis, 13*, 233–252.

Nolan, J. L. (2003). Redefining criminal courts: Problem-solving and the meaning of justice. *American Criminal Law Review, 40*, 1541–1566.

Nugent, W., Umbreit, M., Winimaki, L., & Paddock, J. (2001). Participation in victim–offender mediation and reoffense. *Research on Social Work Practice, 11*, 5–23.

O'Donnell, J., Hawkins, J. D., Catalano, R. F., Abbott, R. D., & Day, L. E. (1995). Preventing school failure, drug use, and delinquency among low-income children: Long-term intervention in elementary schools. *American Journal of Orthopsychiatry, 65*, 87–100.

Office of Juvenile Justice and Delinquency Prevention. (1994). *The mandates: Fact sheet, March 1994* (No. FS9407). Washington, DC: U.S. Department of Justice.

Office of Juvenile Justice and Delinquency Prevention. (1995). *Guide for implementing a comprehensive strategy for serious, violent, and chronic juvenile offenders.* Washington, DC: U.S. Department of Justice.

Office of Juvenile Justice and Delinquency Prevention. (2003). *OJJDP statistical briefing book.* Retrieved from ojjdp.ncjrs.org/ojstatbb/court/qa06301.asp?qaDate=20030811

Office of Management and Budget. (2004). What constitutes evidence of program effectiveness (Memo). Retrieved from www.whitehouse.gov/omb/part/2004_program_eval.pdf

Olds, D. L. (2002). Prenatal and infancy home visiting by nurses: From randomized trials to community replication. *Prevention Science, 3*, 153–172.

Olsen, E. A. (2003). Housing programs for low-income households. In R. A. Moffitt (Ed.), *Means-tested transfer programs in the United States* (pp. 365–442). Chicago: University of Chicago Press.

Olweus, D. (1992). Bullying among schoolchildren: Intervention and prevention. In R. D. Peters, R. J. McMahon, & V. L. Quinsey (Eds.), *Aggression and violence throughout the life span* (pp. 100–125). Newbury Park, CA: Sage.

Olweus, D. (1993). *Bullying at school: What we know and what we can do.* Oxford, UK: Blackwell.

Olweus, D. (1997). Bully victim problems in school: Knowledge base and an effective intervention program. *Irish Journal of Psychology, 17*, 170–190.

O'Neil, R., Horner, R., Albin, R., Sprague, J., Storey, K., & Newton, J. S. (1997). *Functional assessment and program development for problem behavior: A practical handbook* (2nd ed.). New York: Brooks/Cole.

Orange County Probation Department. (2005). *The 8% solution.* Retrieved May 2005 from www.ocgov.com/Probation/solution/index.asp and www.ncjrs.org/pdffiles1/ojjdp/fs200139.pdf

Oreopoulos, P. (2003). The long-run consequences of living in a poor neighborhood. *Quarterly Journal of Economics, 118*, 1533–1575.

Orr, L., Feins, J. D., Jacob, R., Beecroft, E., Sanbonmatsu, L., Katz, L. F., et al. (2003). *Moving to Opportunity interim impact evaluation.* Washington, DC: U.S. Department of Housing and Urban Development, Office of Policy Development and Research. Retrieved from www.wws.princeton.edu/~kling/ mto/MTO_OMB.pdf

Osgood, D. W., Wilson, J. K., O'Malley, P. M., Bachman, J. G., & Johnston, L. D. (1996). Routine activities and individual deviant behavior. *American Sociological Review, 61,* 635–655.

Oxford, M. L., Harachi, T. W., Catalano, R. F., & Abbott, R. D. (2001). Preadolescent predictors of substance initiation: A test of both the direct and mediated effect of family social control factors on deviant peer associations and substance initiation. *American Journal of Drug and Alcohol Abuse, 27,* 599–616.

Page, M. E., & Solon, G. (2003). Correlations between brothers and neighboring boys in their adult earnings. *Journal of Labor Economics, 21,* 831–855.

Palinkas, L. A., Atkins, C. J., Miller, C., & Ferreira, D. (1996). Social skills training for drug prevention in high-risk female adolescents. *Preventive Medicine, 25,* 692–701.

Pantin, H., Coatsworth, J. D., Feaster, D. J., Newman, F. L., Birones, E., Prado, G., et al. (2003). Familias Unidas: The efficacy of an intervention to promote parental investment in Hispanic immigrant families. *Prevention Science, 4,* 189–201.

Patrick, J. (1973). *A Glasgow gang observed.* London: Methuen.

Patrick, S., Marsh, R., Bundy, W., Mimura, S., & Perkins, T. (2004). Control group study of juvenile diversion programs. *Social Science Journal, 41,* 129–135.

Patterson, G. R. (1973). Changes in status of family members as controlling stimuli: A basis for describing treatment process. In L. A. Hamerlynck, L. C. Handy, & E. J. Mash (Eds.), *Behavior change: Methodology, concepts, and practices* (pp. 169–191). Champaign, IL: Research Press.

Patterson, G. R. (1982). *Coercive family process.* Eugene, OR: Castalia.

Patterson, G. R. (1993). Orderly change in a stable world: The antisocial trait as a chimera. *Journal of Consulting and Clincial Psychology, 61,* 911–919.

Patterson, G. R., & Cobb, J. A. (1973). Stimulus control for classes of noxious behaviors. In J. F. Knutson (Ed.), *The control of aggression: Implications from basic research* (pp. 144–199). Chicago: Aldine.

Patterson, G. R., Dishion, T. J., & Yoerger, K. (2000). Adolescent growth in new forms of problem behavior: Macro- and micropeer dynamics. *Prevention Science, 1,* 3–13.

Patterson, G. R., Reid, J. B., & Dishion, T. J. (1992). *Antisocial boys.* Eugene, OR: Castalia Press.

Pearson, K. (1912). On the appearance of multiple cases of disease in the same house. *Biometrika, 8,* 404–412.

Peeples, F., & Loeber, R. (1994). Do individual factors and neighborhood context explain ethnic differences in juvenile delinquency? *Journal of Quantitative Criminology, 10,* 141–157.

Pentz, M. A., Dwyer, J. H., Flay, B. R., Hansen, W. B., & Johnson, C. A. (1989). A multi-community trial for primary prevention of adolescent drug abuse: Effects on drug use prevalence. *Journal of the American Medical Association, 261,* 3259–3266.

Pentz, M. A., Trebow, E. A., Hansen, W. B., MacKinnon, D. P., Dwyer, J. H., Johnson, C. A., et al. (1990). Effects of program implementation on adolescent drug use behavior: The Midwestern Prevention Project (MPP). *Evaluation Review, 14,* 264–289.

Perry, C. L., Williams, C. L., Komro, K. A., Veblen-Mortenson, S., Stigler, M. H., Munson, K. A., et al. (2002). Project Northland: Long-term outcomes of community action to reduce adolescent alcohol use. *Health Education Research, 17,* 117–132.

Perry, C. L., Williams, C. L., Veblen-Mortenson, S., Toomey, T. L., Komro, K. A., Anstine, P. S., et al. (1996). Project Northland: Outcomes of a community-wide alcohol use prevention program during early adolescence. *American Journal of Public Health, 86,* 956–965.

Persson, A., Kerr, M., & Stattin, H. (2002, September). *Explaining why a leisure context is bad for some girls and not for others.* Paper presented at the Individual Development and Adaptation Conference, Stockholm, Sweden.

Petronis, K. R., & Anthony, J. C. (2003). A different kind of contextual effect: Geographical clustering of cocaine incidence in the USA. *Journal of Epidemiology and Community Health, 57,* 893–900.

Petrosino, A., Turpin-Petrosino, C., & Finckenauer, J. O. (2000). Well-meaning programs can have harmful effects! Lessons from experiments of programs such as Scared Straight. *Crime and Delinquency, 46,* 354–379.

Petrucci, C. J., & Hartley, C. C. (2004). Practicing culturally competent therapeutic jurisprudence: A collaboration between social work and law. *Washington University Journal of Law and Policy, 14,* 133–181.

Pettit, G. S., Bates, J. E., Dodge, K. A., & Meece, D. W. (1999). The impact of after-school peer contact on early adolescent externalizing problems is moderated by parental monitoring, neighborhood safety, and prior adjustment. *Child Development, 70,* 768–778.

Pfiffner, L. J., & O'Leary, S. G. (1987). The efficacy of all-positive management as a function of the prior use of negative consequences. *Journal of Applied Behavior Analysis, 20,* 265–271.

Pfiffner, L. J., Rosen, L. A., & O'Leary, S. G. (1985). The efficacy of an all-positive approach to classroom management. *Journal of Applied Behavior Analysis, 18,* 257–261.

Phillips, E. L., Phillips, E.A., Fixsen, D. L., & Wolf, M. M. (1974). *The teaching-family handbook* (2nd ed.). Lawrence, KS: University Printing Service.

Phillips, E. L., Wolf, M. M., Fixsen, D. L., & Bailey, J. S. (1975). The achievement place model: A community-based, family style behavior modification program for predelinquents. In J. L. Khanna (Ed.), *New treatment approaches to juvenile delinquency.* Springfield, IL: Charles C. Thomas.

Phillips, M. (1997). What makes schools effective?: A comparison of the relationships of communitarian climate and academic climate to mathematics achievement and attendance during middle school. *American Educational Research Journal, 34,* 633–662.

Pianta, R. C., Steinberg, M. S., & Rollins, K. B. (1995). The first two years of school: Teacher–child relationships and deflections in children's classroom adjustment. *Development and Psychopathology, 7,* 295–312.

Pinderhughes, E. E., Nix, R., Foster, E. M., Jones, D., & the Conduct Problems Prevention Research Group. (2001). Parenting in context: Impact of neighborhood poverty, residential stability, public services, social networks, and danger on parental behaviors. *Journal of Marriage and Family, 63,* 941–53.

Pinnock, D. (1997). *Gangs, rituals and rites of passage.* Capetown, South Africa: African Sun Press.

Platek, S. M., Mohamed, F. B., & Gallup, G. G. Jr. (2005). Contagious yawning and the brain. *Brain Research Cognitive Brain Research, 23,* 448–452.

Platt, A. M. (1977). *The child savers: The invention of delinquency* (2nd ed.). Chicago: University of Chicago Press.

Plotnick, R. D., & Hoffman, S. D. (1999). The effect of neighborhood characteristics on young adult outcomes: Alternative estimates. *Social Science Quarterly, 80,* 1–18.

Polivy, J., & Federoff, I. (1997). Group psychotherapy. In D. M. Garner & P. E. Garfinkel (Eds.), *Handbook of treatment for eating disorders* (2nd ed., pp. 462–475). New York: Guilford Press.

Ponting, C. (1991). *A green history of the world.* New York: Penguin Books.

Pope, A. W., Bierman, K. L., & Mumma, G. H. (1989). Relations between hyperactive and aggressive behavior and peer relations at three elementary grade levels. *Journal of Abnormal Child Psychology, 17,* 253–267.

Popkin, S. J., Harris, L. E., & Cunningham, M. K. (2001). *Families in transition: A qualitative analysis of the MTO experience.* Washington, DC: Urban Institute.

Posner, M. I., & Rothbart, M. K. (2000). Developing mechanisms of self-regulation. *Development and Psychopathology, 12,* 427–441.

Poulin, F., & Boivin, M. (2000). Proactive and reactive aggression: Evidence of a two-factor model. *Psychological Assessment, 12,* 115–122.

Poulin, F., & Dishion, T. J. (2002). *Methodological issues in the use of sociometric assessment with middle school youth.* Unpublished manuscript.

Poulin, F., Dishion, T. J., & Burraston, B. (2001). 3-year iatrogenic effects associated with aggregating high-risk adolescents in cognitive-behavioral preventive interventions. *Applied Developmental Science, 5,* 214–224.

Powers, E., & Witmer, H. (1951). *An experiment in the prevention of delinquency: The Cambridge–Somerville youth study.* New York: Columbia University Press.

Prinstein, M. J., & Wang, S. S. (2005). False consensus and adolescent peer contagion: Examining discrepancies between perceptions and actual reported levels of friends' deviant and health risk behaviors. *Journal of Abnormal Child Psychology, 33*(3), 293–306.

Prinz, R. J., Blechman, E. A., & Dumas, J. E. (1994). An evaluation of peer coping-skills training for childhood aggression. *Journal of Clinical Child Psychology, 23,* 193–203.

Provine, R. R., Tate, B. C., & Geldmacher, L. L. (1987). Yawning: No effect of 3–5% CO_2, 100% O_2, and exercise. *Behavioural and Neural Biology, 48,* 382–393.

Public Schools of North Carolina. (2003). *Alternative learning programs evaluation: 2001–2002.* Durham: North Carolina State Board of Education/Department of Public Instruction.

Puzzanchera, C., Stahl, A. L., Finnegan, T. A., Tierney, N., & Snyder, H. N. (2003).

Juvenile court statistics 1999 (NCJ 201241). Pittsburgh, PA: National Center for Juvenile Justice.

Quinn, J. (1999). Where need meets opportunity: Youth development programs for early teens. *The Future of Children, 9,* 96–116.

Rabiner, D. L., & Coie, J. D. (1989). The effect of expectancy inductions on rejected children's acceptance by unfamiliar peers. *Developmental Psychology, 25,* 450–457.

Radloff, L. S. (1977). The CES-D Scale: A self-report scale for research in the general population. *Applied Psychological Measurement, 1,* 385–401.

Raywid, M. A. (1981). The first decade of public school alternatives. *Phi Delta Kappan, 62,* 551–54.

Raywid, M. A. (1994). Alternative schools: The state of the art. *Educational Leadership, 52,* 26–34.

Reid, J. B., Eddy, J. M., Fetrow, R. A., & Stoolmiller, M. (1999). Description and immediate impacts of a preventive intervention for conduct problems. *American Journal of Community Psychology, 27,* 483–517.

Reid, J. B., Patterson, G. R., & Snyder, J. J. (2002). *Antisocial behavior in children and adolescents: A developmental analysis and the Oregon Model for intervention.* Washington, DC: American Psychological Association.

Reid, M. J., Webster-Stratton, C., & Hammond, M. (2003). Follow-up of children who received the Incredible Years intervention for oppositional defiant disorder: Maintenance and prediction of 2-year outcome. *Behavior Therapy, 34,* 471–491.

Reinke, W. M., & Herman, K. C. (2002). Creating school environments that deter antisocial behaviors in youth. *Psychology in the Schools, 39,* 549–559.

Rescorla, R. A. (1987). A Pavlovian analysis of goal-directed behavior. *American Psychologist, 42,* 119–129.

Reynolds, A. J., Temple, J. A., Robertson, D. L., & Mann, E. A. (2001). Long-term effects of an early childhood intervention on educational achievement and juvenile arrest: A 15-year follow-up of low-income children in public school. *Journal of the American Medical Association, 285,* 2339–2346.

Rhodes, P. H., Halloran, M. E., & Longini, I. M. Jr. (1996). Counting process models for infectious disease data: Distinguishing exposure to infection from susceptibility. *Journal of Royal Statistical Society, Series B: Methodological, 58,* 751–762.

Ringwalt, C. L., Ennett, S., Johnson, R., Rohrbach, L. A., Simons-Rudolph, A., Vincus, A., et al. (2003). Factors associated with fidelity to substance use prevention curriculum guides in the nation's middle schools. *Health Education and Behavior, 30,* 375–391.

Ringwalt, C. L., Greene, J. M., Ennett, S. T., Iachan, R., Clayton, R. R., & Leukefeld, C. G. (1994). *Past and future directions of the D.A.R.E. program: An evaluation review.* Retrieved from www.ncjrs.org/txtfiles/darerev.txt

Rodick, J. D., Henggeler, S. W., & Hanson, C. L. (1986). An evaluation of the Family Adaptability and Cohesion Evaluation Scales and the circumplex model. *Journal of Abnormal Child Psychology, 14,* 77–87.

Rodkin, P. C., Farmer, T. W., Pearl, R., & Van Acker, R. (2000). Heterogeneity of popular boys: Antisocial and prosocial configurations. *Developmental Psychology, 36,* 14–34.

Roffman, J. G., Pagano, M. E., & Hirsch, B. J. (2001). Youth functioning and the experiences of inner-city after-school programs among age, gender, and race groups. *Journal of Child and Family Studies, 10,* 85–100.

Rose, A., Lockerd, E., & Swenson, L. (2001, April). *Prosocial behavior, overt aggression, and relational aggression among sociometrically popular and perceived popular children.* Paper presented at the biennial meeting of the Society for Research in Child Development, Minneapolis, MN.

Rosenholtz, S. J. (1985). Effective schools: Interpreting the evidence. *American Journal of Education, 93,* 352–388.

Rosenthal, R. (1994). Interpersonal expectancy effects: A 30-year perspective. *Current Directions in Psychological Science, 3,* 176–179.

Rosenthal, R. (2003). Covert communication in laboratories, classrooms and the truly real world. *Current Directions in Psychological Science, 12,* 151–159.

Roth, J. L., & Brooks-Gunn, J. (2003). Youth development programs: Risk, prevention, and policy. *Journal of Adolescent Health, 32,* 170–182.

Roth, J., Brooks-Gunn, J., Murray, L., & Foster, W. (1998). Promoting healthy adolescents: Synthesis of youth development program evaluations. *Journal of Research on Adolescence, 8,* 423–459.

Rothbart, M. K., & Bates, J. E. (1998). Temperament. In W. Damon & N. Eisenberg (Eds.), *Handbook of child psychology: Vol. 3. Social, emotional, and personality development* (4th ed., pp. 105–176). Hoboken, NJ: Wiley.

Rothbart, M. K., Ellis, L. K., Rueda, M. R., & Posner, M. I. (2003). Developing mechanisms of temperamental effortful control. *Journal of Personality, 71*(6), 1113–1143.

Rouse, C. E. (1998). Private school vouchers and student achievement: An evaluation of the Milwaukee Parental Choice Program. *Quarterly Journal of Economics, 113,* 553–602.

Rowan, B., Chiang, F. S., & Miller, R. J. (1997). Using research on employees' performance to study the effects of teachers on students' achievement. *Sociology of Education, 70,* 256–284.

Rubinowitz, L. S., & Rosenbaum, J. E. (2001). *Crossing the class and color lines: From public housing to white suburbia.* Chicago: University of Chicago Press.

Rusby, J. C., Forrester, K. K., Biglan, A., & Metzler, C. W. (2005). Relationships between peer harassment and adolescent problem behaviors. *Journal of Early Adolescence, 25,* 453–477.

Ryan, J. P., & Testa, M. F. (2005). Child maltreatment and juvenile delinquency: Investigating the role of placement and placement instability. *Children and Youth Services Review, 27,* 227–249.

Sacerdote, B. (2001). Peer effects with random assignment: Results for Dartmouth roommates. *Quarterly Journal of Economics, 116,* 681–703.

Sah, R. (1991). Social osmosis and patterns of crime. *Journal of Political Economy, 99,* 1272–1295.

Sameroff, A. J. (1981). Development and the dialectic: The need for a systems approach. In W. A. Collins (Ed.), *Minnesota Symposium on Child Psychology* (pp. 83–103). Hillsdale, NJ: Erlbaum.

Samples, F., & Aber, L. (1998). Evaluations of school-based violence prevention programs. In D. S. Elliot, B. A. Hamburg, & K. R. Williams (Eds.), *Violence in American schools* (pp. 217–252). Cambridge, UK: Cambridge University Press.

Sampson, R. J., Morenoff, J. D., & Earls, F. (1999). Beyond social capital: Spatial dynamics of collective efficacy for children. *American Sociological Review*, *64*, 633–660.

Sampson, R. J., Raudenbush, S. W., & Earls, F. (1997). Neighborhoods and violent crime: A multilevel study of collective efficacy. *Science*, *277*, 918–924.

Sanbonmatsu, L., Kling, J. R., Duncan, G. L., & Brooks-Gunn, J. (2004). *Neighborhoods and academic achievement: Results from the Moving to Opportunity experiment* (Working Paper No. 492). Princeton, NJ: Princeton University, Industrial Relations Section.

Sawka, K. D., McCurdy, B. L., & Mannella, M. C. (2002). Strengthening emotional support services: An empirically based model for training teachers of students with behavior disorders. *Journal of Emotional and Behavioral Disorders*, *10*, 223–232.

Schafer, W. E., & Armer, J. M. (1968). Athletes are not inferior students. *Transaction*, *6*, 21–26.

Schlegel, A., & Barry, H. (1991). *Adolescence: An anthropological enquiry.* New York: Free Press.

Schlossman, S. L. (1977). *Love and the American delinquent: The theory and practice of progressive juvenile justice, 1825–1920.* Chicago: University of Chicago Press.

Schochet, P. Z., Burghardt, J., & Glazerman, S. (2000). *National Job Corps Study: The short-term impacts of Job Corps on participants' employment and related outcomes.* Princeton, NJ: Mathematica Policy Research.

Schonfeld, I. S. (1992). School conditions induce teacher depression. *Teaching and Teacher Education*, *8*, 151–158.

Schur, E. M. (1973). *Radical non-intervention: Rethinking the delinquency problem.* Englewood Cliffs, NJ: Prentice-Hall.

Schurmann, M., Hesse, M. D., Stephan, K. E., Saarela, M., Zilles, K., Hari, R., et al. (2005). Yearning to yawn: The neural basis of contagious yawning. *Neuroimage*, *24*, 1260–1264.

Schweinhart, L. J., Montie, J., Xiang, Z., Barnett, W. S., Belfield, C. R., & Nores, M. (2005). *Lifetime effects: The High/Scope Perry Preschool Study through age 40.* Ypsilanti, MI: High/Scope Press.

Segal, Z. V., Teasdale, J. D., & Williams, J. M. G. (2004). Mindfulness-based cognitive therapy: Theoretical rationale and empirical status. In S. C. Hayes, V. M. Follette, & M. M. Linehan (Eds.), *Mindfulness and acceptance: Expanding the cognitive-behavioral tradition* (pp. 270–289). New York: Guilford Press.

Sexton, T. L., & Alexander, J. F. (2002). Family-based empirically supported interventions. *Counseling Psychologist*, *30*, 238–261.

Shadish, W., & Meyers, D. (2002). Campbell collaboration research design policy brief. Retrieved from www.missouri.edu/~c2method/ResDesPolicyBrief.htm

Shaw, C., & McKay, H. 1972. *Juvenile delinquency and urban areas.* Chicago: University of Chicago Press.

Shelton, T. L., Barkley, R. A., Crosswait, C., Moorehouse, M., Fletcher, K., Barrett, S., et al. (2000). Multimethod psychoeducational intervention for preschool children with disruptive behavior: Two-year post-treatment follow-up. *Journal of Abnormal Child Psychology, 28*, 253–266.

Shepard, R. (1999). The juvenile court at 100 years. *Juvenile Justice, 6*, 3–21.

Shepherd, J. P., & Farrington, D. P. (1995). Preventing crime and violence: Preschool education, early family support, and situational prevention can be effective. *British Medical Journal, 310*, 271–272.

Sherman, L. W. (2002). Fair and effective policing. In J. Q Wilson & J. Petersillia (Eds.), *Crime: Public policies for crime control* (pp. 383–412). Oakland, CA: ICS Press.

Sherman, L. W., Gottfredson, D., MacKenzie, D., Eck, J., Reuter, P., & Bushway, S. (1997). *Preventing crime: What works, what doesn't, what's promising.* Washington, DC: U.S. Department of Justice, Office of Justice Programs.

Sherman, L. W., & Strang, H. (2004). Verdicts or inventions?: Interpreting results from randomized controlled experiments in criminology. *American Behavioral Scientist, 47*, 575–607.

Sherman, L. W., & Weisburd, D. (1995). General deterrent effects of police patrol in crime "hot spots": A randomized, controlled trial. *Justice Quarterly, 12*, 625–648.

Short, J. F., Jr., & Strodtbeck, F. L. (1965). *Group process and gang delinquency.* Chicago: University of Chicago Press.

Shure, M. B. (1997). Interpersonal problem cognitive problem solving: Primary prevention of early high-risk behaviors in the preschool and primary years. In G. W. Albee & T. P. Gullotta (Eds.), *Primary prevention works* (pp. 167–188). Thousand Oaks, CA: Sage.

Shure, M. B. (2001a). *I can problem solve: An interpersonal cognitive problem solving program: Preschool.* Champaign, IL: Research Press.

Shure, M. B. (2001b). *I can problem solve: An interpersonal cognitive problem solving program: Kindergarten and primary grades.* Champaign, IL: Research Press.

Shure, M. B., & Spivack, G. (1982). Interpersonal problem-solving in young children: A cognitive approach to prevention. *American Journal of Community Psychology, 10*, 341–356.

Silliker, S. A., & Quirk, J. T. (1997). The effect of extracurricular activity participation on the academic performance of male and female high school students. *School Counselor, 44*, 288–293.

Silver, R. B., Measelle, J., Essex, M., & Armstrong, J. M. (2005). Trajectories of externalizing behavior problems in the classroom: Contributions of child characteristics, family characteristics, and the teacher–child relationship during the school transition. *Journal of School Psychology, 43*, 39–60.

Skiba, R. J. (2000). *Zero tolerance, zero evidence: An analysis of school disciplinary practice* (Policy Research Report). Bloomington: Indiana University, Education Policy Center.

Skiba, R. J., & Peterson, R. L. (1999). The dark side of zero tolerance: Can punishment lead to safe schools? *Phi Delta Kappan, 80*, 372–376, 381–382.

Skiba, R. J., & Peterson, R. L. (2000). School discipline at a crossroads: From zero tolerance to early response. *Exceptional Children, 66,* 335–347.

Slaikeu, K. A. (1973). Evaluation on group treatment of juvenile and group offenders in correctional institutions: A review of the literature. *Journal of Research in Crime and Delinquency, 10,* 87–100.

Slobogin, C. (1995). Therapeutic jurisprudence: Five dilemmas to ponder. *Psychology, Public Policy, and Law, 1,* 193–219.

Smith, D., & Paternoster, R. (1990). Formal processing and future delinquency. *Law and Society Review, 24,* 1109–1132.

Smith, E. P., Boutte, G. S., Zigler, E., & Finn-Stevenson, M. (2004). Opportunities for schools to promote resilience in children and youth. In K. I. Maton, C. J. Schellenbach, B. J. Leadbetter, & A. L. Solarz (Eds.), *Investing in children, youth, families, and communities: Strengths-based research and policy* (pp. 213–231). Washington, DC: American Psychological Association.

Smith, E. P., Gorman-Smith, D. G., Quinn, W., Horne, A., Rabiner, D., Miller-Johnson, S., et al. (2004). Community-based multiple family groups to prevent and reduce violent and aggressive behavior: The GREAT Families Program. *American Journal of Preventive Medicine, 26,* 39–47.

Snow, D. L., Tebes, J. K., Arther, M. W., & Tapasak, R. C. (1992). Two-year follow-up of a social-cognitive intervention to prevent substance use. *Journal of Drug Education, 22,* 101–114.

Snyder, H. N. (1997). *Juvenile arrests 1996.* Washington, DC: U.S. Department of Justice, Office of Justice Programs, Office of Juvenile Justice and Delinquency Prevention.

Snyder, H. N., Sickmund, M., & Poe-Yamagata, E. (2000). *Juvenile transfers to criminal court in the 1990's: Lessons learned from four studies.* Washington, DC: U.S. Department of Justice, Office of Justice Programs, Office of Juvenile Justice and Delinquency Prevention.

Snyder, J., Schrepferman, L., Oeser, J., Patterson, G., Stoolmiller, M., Johnson, K., et al. (2005). Deviancy training and association with deviant peers in young children: Occurrence and contribution to early-onset conduct problems. *Development and Psychopathology, 17*(2), 397–413.

Snyder, J. J., & Huntley, D. (1990). Troubled families and troubled youth: The development of antisocial behavior and depression in children. In P. E. Leone (Ed.), *Understanding troubled and troubling youth* (pp. 194–225). Newbury Park, CA: Sage.

Solomon, J., George, C., & DeJong, A. (1995). Children classified as controlling at age six: Evidence for disorganized representational strategies and aggression at home and at school. *Development and Psychopathology, 7,* 447–463.

Solon, G., Page, M. E., & Duncan, G. L. (2000). Correlations between neighboring children in their subsequent educational attainment. *Review of Economics and Statistics, 83,* 383–392.

Sontheimer, H., & Goodstein, L. (1993). Evaluation of juvenile intensive aftercare. *Justice Quarterly, 10,* 197–227.

Spencer, M. B., Cole, S. P., Jones, S. M., & Swanson, D. P. (1997). Neighborhood and family influences on young urban adolescents' behavior problems: A multisample, multisite analysis. In J. Brooks-Gunn, G. J. Duncan, & J. L. Aber (Eds.), *Neighborhood poverty: Vol. 1. Context and consequences for children* (pp. 200–218). New York: Russell Sage Foundation.

Spielberger, C. D. (1965). Theoretical and epistemological issues and verbal conditioning. In S. Rosenberger (Ed.), *Directions in psycholinguistics* (pp. 111–200). New York: Macmillan.

Spitzer, S., Cupp, R., & Parke, R. D. (1995). School entrance age, social acceptance, and self-perception in kindergarten and 1st grade. *Early Childhood Research Quarterly, 10,* 433–450.

Spoth, R. L., Kavanaugh, K. A., & Dishion, T. J. (2002). Family-centered preventive intervention science: Towards benefits to larger populations of children, youth, and families. *Prevention Science, 3,* 145–152.

Spoth, R. L., & Redmond, C. (2002). Project Family prevention trials based in community-university partnerships: Toward scaled-up preventive interventions. *Prevention Science, 3,* 203–221.

Spoth, R., Redmond, C., Shin, C., & Azevedo, K. (2004). Brief family intervention effects on adolescent substance initiation: School-level growth curve analysis 6 years following baseline. *Journal of Consulting and Clinical Psychology, 72,* 535–542.

Sprague, J. R., & Golly, A. (2004). *Best behavior: Building positive behavior supports in schools.* Longmont, CO: Sopris West Educational Services.

Sprague, J., Golly, A., Bernstein, L., Munkres, A. M., & March, R. M. (1999). *Effective school and classroom discipline: A training manual.* Eugene: University of Oregon, Institute on Violence and Destructive Behavior.

Sprague, J. R., Sugai, G., Horner, R. H., & Walker, H. M. (1999). Using office discipline referral data to evaluate school-wide discipline and violence prevention interventions. *Oregon School Study Council Bulletin, 42*(2). Eugene: University of Oregon, College of Education.

Sprague, J. R., Sugai, G., & Walker, H. M. (1998a). *Antisocial behavior in schools.* Eugene: University of Oregon, College of Education.

Sprague, J., Sugai, G., & Walker, H. M. (1998b). Antisocial behavior in schools. In S. Watson & F. M. Gresham (Eds.), *Child behavior therapy: Ecological considerations in assessment, treatment, and evaluation* (pp. 451–474). New York: Plenum Press.

Sprick, R., Sprick, M., & Garrison, M. (1992). *Foundations: Developing positive school discipline policies.* Longmont, CO: Sopris West Educational Services.

St. Pierre, T. L., Mark, M. M., Kaltreider, D. L., & Campbell, B. (2001). Boys and Girls Clubs and school collaborations: A longitudinal study of a multi-component substance abuse prevention program for high-risk elementary school children. *Journal of Community Psychology, 29,* 87–106.

Stage, S. A., & Quiroz, D. R. (1997). A meta-analysis of interventions to decrease disruptive.classroom behavior in public education settings. *School Psychology Review, 26,* 333–368.

Steele, C. M., Spencer, S. J., & Aronson, J. (2002). Contending with group image: The psychology of stereotype threat and social identity threat. In M. P. Zanna (Ed.), *Advances in experimental social psychology* (Vol. 34). San Diego, CA: Academic Press.

Sternberg, K. J. (1993). Child maltreatment: Implications for policy from cross-cultural research. In D. Cicchetti & S. L. Toth (Eds.), *Child abuse, child development, and social policy* (pp. 191–211). Norwood, NJ: Ablex.

Stewart, W. F., Ricci, J. A., Chee, E., Hahn, S. R., & Morganstein, D. (2003). Cost of lost productive work time among U.S. workers with depression. *Journal of the American Medical Association, 289,* 3135–3144.

Stoolmiller, M. (1992). *Wandering and deviant peer involvement as predictors of later police arrest.* Manuscript in preparation.

Stoolmiller, M., Eddy, J. M., & Reid, J. B. (2000). Detecting and describing preventive intervention effects in a universal school-based randomized trial targeting delinquent and violent behavior. *Journal of Consulting and Clinical Psychology, 68,* 296–306.

Stormshak, E. A., Bierman, K. L., Bruschi, C., Dodge, K. A., Coie, J. D., & the Conduct Problems Prevention Research Group. (1999). The relation between behavior problems and peer preference in different classroom contexts. *Child Development, 70,* 169–182.

Stormshak, E. A., & Dishion, T. J. (2002). An ecological approach to child and family clinical and counseling psychology. *Clinical Child and Family Psychology Review, 51,* 197–215.

Straus, M. A., Gelles, R. J., & Steinmetz, S. (1980). *Behind closed doors: Violence in the American family.* New York: Doubleday.

Street, D., Vinter, R., & Perrow, C. (1966). *Organization for treatment.* New York: Free Press.

Substance Abuse and Mental Health Services Administration. (n.d.). *Youth violence: A report of the surgeon general.* Retrieved May 6, 2004, from www.mentalhealth.samhsa.gov/youthviolence/surgeongeneral/SG_Site/chapter5/sec5.asp

Sugai, G., & Horner, R. (1994). Including students with severe behavior problems in general education settings: Assumptions, challenges, and solutions. In J. Marr, G. Sugai, & B. Tindal (Eds.), *The Oregon Conference monograph* (Vol. 6, pp. 102–120). Eugene: University of Oregon, College of Education.

Sugai, G., & Horner, R. (2002). The evolution of discipline practices: School-wide positive behavior supports. *Child and Family Behavior Therapy, 24,* 23–50.

Sugai, G., Horner, R., & Gresham, F. (2002). Behaviorally effective school environments. In M. Shinn, H. Walker, & G. Stoner (Eds.), *Interventions for academic and behavior problems: Vol. 2. Prevention and remedial approaches* (pp. 315–350). Bethesda, MD: National Association of School Psychologists.

Sugai, G., Sprague, J. R., Horner, R. H., & Walker, H. M. (2000). Preventing school violence: The use of office discipline referrals to assess and monitor school-wide discipline interventions. *Journal of Emotional and Behavioral Disorders, 8,* 94–101.

Swanson, J. W., Tepper, M. C., Backlar, P., & Swartz, M. S. (2000). Psychiatric advanced directives: An alternative to coercive treatment? *Psychiatry, 63,* 160–172.

Swartz, M. S., Swanson, J. W., Hiday, V. A., Wagner, H. R., Burns, B. J., & Borum, R. (2001). A randomized controlled trial of outpatient commitment in North Carolina. *Psychiatric Services, 52,* 325–329.

Sykes, G. (1958). *Society of captives*. Princeton, NJ: Princeton University Press.

Szapocznik, J., & Kurtines, W. M. (1989). *Breakthroughs in family therapy with drug-abusing and problem youth*. New York: Springer.

Taibleson, M. H. (1974). Distinguishing between contagion, heterogeneity, and randomness in stochastic models. *American Sociological Review, 39,* 877–880.

Tajfel, H., & Turner, J. C. (2004). The social identity theory of intergroup behavior. In J. T. Jost & J. Sidanius (Eds.), *Political psychology: Key readings* (pp. 276–293). New York: Psychology Press.

Tannenbaum, F. (1938). *Crime and the community*. New York: Columbia University Press.

Task Force on Youth Development and Community Programs. (1992). *A matter of time: Risk and opportunity in the nonschool hours*. New York: Carneig Corporation, Carnegie Council on Adolescent Development.

Tatara, T. (1991). Overview of child abuse and neglect. In J. E. Everett, S. S. Chipungu, & B. R. Leashore (Eds.), *Child welfare: An Africentric perspective* (pp. 187–219). New Brunswick, NJ: Rutgers University Press.

Taylor-Greene, S., Brown, D., Nelson, L., Longton, J., Gassman, T., Cohen, J., et al. (1997). School-wide behavioral support: Starting the year off right. *Journal of Behavioral Education, 7,* 99–112.

Taylor-Greene, S. J., & Kartub, D. T. (2000). Durable implementation of school-wide behavior support. *Journal of Positive Behavior Interventions, 2,* 333–335.

Thornberry, T. P., & Krohn, M. D. (1997). Peers, drug use, and delinquency. In D. Stoff, J. Breiling, & J. Maser (Eds.), *Handbook of antisocial behavior* (pp. 218–233). New York: Wiley.

Thornberry, T. P., Krohn, M. D., Lizotte, A. J., & Chard-Wierschem, D. (1993). The role of juvenile gangs in facilitating delinquent behavior. *Journal of Research in Crime and Delinquency, 30,* 55–87.

Thornberry, T. P., Krohn, M. D., Lizotte, A. J., Smith, C., & Tobin, K. (2003). *Gangs and delinquency in developmental perspective*. Cambridge, UK: Cambridge University Press.

Thornton, T. N., Craft, C. A., Dahlberg, L. L., Lynch, B. S., & Baer, K. (2000). *Best practices of youth violence prevention: A sourcebook for community action*. Atlanta, GA: Centers for Disease Control and Prevention, National Center for Injury Prevention and Control.

Tiebout, C. M. (1956). A pure theory of local expenditures. *Journal of Political Economy, 64,* 416–424.

Tierney, J. P., & Grossman, J. B. (1995). *Making a difference: An impact study of Big Brothers Big Sisters*. Philadelphia: Public/Private Ventures.

Tobin, T., & Sprague, J. (2002). Alternative educational programs: Accommodating tertiary level, at-risk students. In M. Shinn, H. Walker, & G. Stoner (Eds.), *Interventions for academic and behavior problems: Vol. 2. Preventive and remedial approaches* (pp. 961–992). Bethesda, MD: National Association of School Psychologists.

Tobin, T., Sugai, G., & Colvin, G. (1996). Patterns in middle school discipline records. *Journal of Emotional and Behavioral Disorders, 4,* 82–94.

Tobler, N. S., & Stratton, H. H. (1997). Effectiveness of school-based drug prevention programs: A meta-analysis of the research. *Journal of Primary Prevention, 18*, 71–128.

Tremblay, R. E., Masse, L. C., Vitaro, F., & Dobkin, P. L. (1995). The impact of friends' deviant behavior on early onset delinquency: Longitudinal data from 6 to 13 years of age. *Development and Psychopathology, 7*, 649–667.

Trojanowicz, R., & Bucqueroux, B. (1994). *Community policing: How to get started.* Cincinnati, OH: Anderson.

Tucker, D. M., & Luu, P. (in press). Adaptive binding. In H. Zimmer, A. Mecklinger, & U. Lindenberger (Eds.), *Binding in human memory: A neurocognitive approach.* Oxford: Oxford University Press.

U.S. Department of Education. (1990). *National Education Longitudinal Study of 1988: A profile of the American eighth grader.* Washington, DC: Author.

U.S. Department of Education. (2000). *21st Century Community Learning Centers: Providing quality afterschool learning opportunities for America's families.* Washington, DC: Author.

U.S. Department of Education. (2002). *No Child Left Behind Act of 2001.* Washington, DC: U.S. Department of Education, Office of Elementary and Secondary Education.

U.S. Department of Education, Office of the Under Secretary. (2003). *When schools stay open late: The national evaluation of the 21st-Century Community Learning Centers Program, first year findings.* Washington, DC: Author.

U.S. Department of Education. (2004). *10 facts about K–12 education funding.* Washington, DC: National Center for Education Statistics.

U.S. Department of Health and Human Services. (2001). *Youth violence: A report of the surgeon general.* Rockville, MD: Author.

U.S. Department of Housing and Urban Development. (2000). *Section 8 tenant-based housing assistance: A look back after 30 years.* Washington, DC: Author.

U.S. Department of Justice. (1994). *Conditions of confinement: Juvenile detention and corrections facilities* (Report No. NCJ 145793). Washington, DC: U.S. Department of Justice, Office of Juvenile Justice and Delinquency Prevention.

Umbreit, M. (1993). Juvenile offenders meet their victims: The impact of mediation in New Mexico. *Family and Conciliation Courts Review, 31*, 90–100.

Umbreit, M. (1994). Crime victims confront their offenders: The impact of a Minneapolis mediation program. *Research on Social Work Practice, 4*, 436–447.

Umbreit, M., Coates, R., & Vos, B. (2001). The impact of victim–offender mediation: Two decades of research. *Federal Probation, 65*, 29–35.

Valdez, A. (2000). *Gangs: A guide to understanding street gangs* (3rd ed.). San Clemente, CA: Law Tech.

Vigdor, J. L. (2002a). Does gentrification harm the poor? In W. G. Gale & J. R. Pack (Eds.), *Brookings–Wharton papers on urban affairs* (pp. 133–173). Washington, DC: Brookings Institution Press.

Vigdor, J. L. (2002b). Locations, outcomes, and selective migration. *Review of Economics and Statistics, 84*, 751–755.

Vigil, J. D. (1988). *Barrio gangs: Street life and identity in Southern California.* Austin: University of Texas Press.

Vintner, R. D. (Ed.). (1967). *Readings in group work practice*. Ann Arbor, MI: Campus.

Vitaro, F., Brendgen, M., Pagani, L., Tremblay, R. E., & McDuff, P. (1999). Disruptive behavior, peer association, and conduct disorder: Testing the developmental links through early intervention. *Development and Psychopathology*, *11*, 287–304.

Vitaro, F., Brendgen, M., & Tremblay, R. E. (1999). Prevention of school dropout through the reduction of disruptive behaviors and school failure in elementary school. *Journal of School Psychology*, *37*, 205–226.

Vitaro, F., Brendgen, M., & Trembley, R. E. (2000). Influence of deviant friends on delinquency: Searching for moderator variables. *Journal of Abnormal Child Psychology*, *28*, 313–325.

Vitaro, F., Tremblay, R. E., Kerr, M., Pagani, L., & Bukowski, W. M. (1997). Disruptiveness, friends' characteristics, and delinquency in early adolescence: A test of two competing models of development. *Child Development*, *68*, 676–689.

Vorrath, H. H., & Brendtro, L. K. (1985). *Positive peer culture* (3rd ed.). New York: Aldine.

Wagner, M. (1991). *Drop-outs with disabilities: What do we know? What can we do?: A report from the National Longitudinal Transition Study of Special Education Students*. Menlo Park, CA: SRI International.

Wagner, M. (1995). Outcomes for youths with serious emotional disturbance in secondary school and early adulthood. *The Future of Children*, *5*, 90–112.

Wagner, M., Blackorby, J., & Hebbeler, K. (1993). *Beyond the report card: The multiple dimensions of secondary school performance of students with disabilities*. Menlo Park, CA: SRI International.

Wagner, M., Marder, C., Blackorby, J., Cameto, R., Newman, L., Levine, P., et al. (2003). *The achievements of youth with disabilities during secondary school: National Longitudinal Transition Study 2*. Menlo Park, CA: SRI International.

Waldron, H. B., & Kaminer, Y. (2004). On the learning curve: The emerging evidence supporting cognitive-behavioral therapies for adolescent substance abuse. *Addiction*, *99*(12), 93–105.

Waldron, H. B., Slesnick, N., Brody, J. L., Turner, C. W., & Peterson, T. R. (2001). Treatment outcomes for adolescent substance abuse at 4 and 7 month assessments. *Journal of Consulting and Clinical Psychology*, *69*, 802–813.

Walker, H. M., Colvin, G., & Ramsey, E. (1995). *Antisocial behavior in school: Strategies and best practices*. Pacific Grove, CA: Brooks/Cole.

Walker, H. M., Kavanaugh, K., Stiller, B., Golly, A., Severson, H. H., & Feil, E. G. (1998). First Step to Success: An early intervention approach for preventing school antisocial behavior. *Journal of Emotional and Behavioral Disorders*, *6*, 66–80.

Walker, H. M., Stieber, S., & Bullis, M. (1997). Longitudinal correlates of arrest status among at-risk males. *Journal of Child and Family Studies*, *6*, 289–309.

Walker, H. M., Stiller, B., Severson, H. H., Golly, A., & Feil, E. G. (1998). First Step to Success: Intervening at the point of school entry to prevent antisocial behavior patterns. *Psychology in the Schools*, *35*, 259–269.

Wallace, J. M., & Bachman, J. G. (1991). Explaining racial/ethnic differences in adolescent drug use: The impact of background and lifestyle. *Social Problems, 38,* 333–357.

Warr, M. (1993). Age, peers, and delinquency. *Criminology, 31,* 17–40.

Warr, M. (1996). Organization and instigation in delinquent groups. *Criminology, 34,* 11–37.

Warren, K., Schoppelrey, S., Moberg, D., & McDonald, M. (2005). A model of contagion through competition in the aggressive behaviors of elementary school students. *Journal of Abnormal Child Psychology, 33,* 283–292.

Wasserman, S., & Galaskiewicz, J. (Eds.). (1994). *Advances in social network analysis: Research in the social and behavioral sciences.* Thousand Oaks, CA: Sage.

Webster-Stratton, C. (2001). The Incredible Years: Parents, teachers, and children training series. In S. I. Pfeiffer & L. A. Reddy (Eds.), *Innovative mental health interventions for children: Programs that work* (pp. 31–45). Binghamton, NY: Hawthorn Press.

Webster-Stratton, C., & Hammond, M. (1997). Treating children with early-onset conduct problems: A comparison of child and parent training interventions. *Journal of Counseling and Clinical Psychology, 65,* 93–109.

Webster-Stratton, C., Reid, M. J., & Hammond, M. (2001). Social skills and problem-solving training for children with early-onset conduct problems: Who benefits? *Journal of Child Psychology and Psychiatry, 42,* 943–952.

Webster-Stratton, C., Reid, M. J., & Hammond, M. (2004). Treating children with early-onset conduct problems: Intervention outcomes for parent, child, and teacher training. *Journal of Clinical Child and Adolescent Psychology, 33,* 105–124.

Webster-Stratton, C., & Taylor, T. (2001). Nipping early risk factors in the bud: Preventing substance abuse, delinquency, and violence in adolescence through interventions targeted at young children (0–8 years). *Prevention Science, 3,* 165–192.

Weerman, F. M., & Decker, S. H. (2005). *European gangs and troublesome youth groups.* Walnut Creek, CA: AltaMira Press.

Wegner, D. M. (1992). You can't always think what you want: Problems in the suppression of unwanted thoughts. In M. P. Zanna (Ed.), *Advances in experimental social psychology* (Vol. 25, pp. 193–225). San Diego, CA: Academic Press.

Weisburd, D., Lum, C. M., & Petrosino, A. (2001). Does research design affect study outcomes in criminal justice? *Annals of the American Academy of Political and Social Science, 578,* 50–70.

Weiss, B., Caron, A., Ball, S., Tapp, J., Johnson, M., & Weisz, J. R. (2005). Iatrogenic effects of group treatment for antisocial youths. *Journal of Consulting and Clinical Psychology, 73,* 1036–1044.

Weisz, J. R. (2004). *Psychotherapy for children and adolescents: Evidence-based treatments and case examples.* Cambridge, UK: Cambridge University Press.

Weisz, J. R., & Jensen, A. L. (2001). Child and adolescent psychotherapy in research and practice contexts: Review of the evidence and suggestions for improving the field. *European Journal of Child and Adolescent Psychiatry, 10,* 12–18.

Weisz, J. R., Weiss, B., Alicke, M. D., & Klotz, M. L. (1987). Effectiveness of psychotherapy with children and adolescents: A meta-analysis for clinicians. *Journal of Consulting and Clinical Psychology, 55,* 542–549.

Weisz, J. R., Weiss, B., Han, S. S., Granger, D. A., & Morton, T. (1995). Effects of psychotherapy with children and adolescents: A meta-analysis of treatment outcome studies. *Psychological Bulletin, 117,* 450–468.

Wells, K. B., & Guo, S. (1999). Reunification and reentry of foster care. *Children and Youth Services Review, 21,* 273–294.

Wells, K. B., & Sherbourne, C. D. (1999). Functioning and utility for current health of patients with depression or chronic medical conditions in managed, primary care practices. *Archives of General Psychiatry, 56,* 897–904.

Welsh, W. N., Stokes, R., & Greene, J. R. (2000). A macro-level model of school disorder. *Journal of Research in Crime and Delinquency, 37,* 243–283.

Werch, C. E., & Owen, D. M. (2002). Iatrogenic effects of alcohol and drug prevention programs. *Journal of Studies on Alcohol, 63,* 581–590.

Wexler, D. (1992). Putting mental health into mental health law: Therapeutic jurisprudence. *Law and Human Behavior, 16,* 27–38.

Wexler, D. (2005). *Therapeutic jurisprudence: An overview.* Retrieved May 2005 from www.law.arizona.edu/depts/upr-intj/ (Originally published in 2000 as Therapeutic jurisprudence: An overview, *Thomas M. Cooley Law Review, 17,* 125–134).

Whitaker, H. J., Farrington, C. P., Spiessens, B., & Musonda, P. (in press). Tutorial in biostatistics: The self-controlled case series method. *Statistics in Medicine.*

Whitlock, M. (2004). *Family-based risk and protective mechanisms for youth at-risk of gang joining.* Los Angeles: Unpublished doctoral dissertation, University of Southern California, Department of Sociology.

Wilhelmus, M. (1998). Mediation in kinship care: Another step in the provision of culturally relevant child welfare services. *Social Work, 43,* 117–126.

Wills, T. A., & Dishion, T. J. (2003). Temperament and adolescent substance use: A transactional analysis of emerging self-control. In P. Frick & W. Silverman (Eds.), Temperament and childhood psychopathology [Special issue]. *Journal of Clinical Child and Adolescent Psychology, 33,* 69–81.

Wills, T. A., McNamara, G., Vaccaro, D., & Hirky, A. E. (1996). Escalated substance use: A longitudinal grouping analysis from early to middle adolescence. *Journal of Abnormal Child Psychology, 105,* 166–180.

Wilson, D. B., Gottfredson, D. C., & Najaka, S. S. (2001). School-based prevention of problem behaviors: A meta-analysis. *Journal of Quantitative Criminology, 17,* 247–272.

Wilson, J. Q., & Hernstein, R. (1985). *Crime and human nature.* New York: Simon & Schuster.

Wilson, M. N., & Saft, E. W. (1993). Child maltreatment in the African American community. In D. Cicchetti & S. L. Toth (Eds.), *Child abuse, child development, and social policy* (pp. 213–247). Norwood, NJ: Ablex.

Wilson, W. J. (1987). *The truly disadvantaged: The inner city, the underclass, and publis policy.* Chicago: University of Chicago Press.

Wolfe, B., & Scrivner, S. (2003). Providing universal preschool for four-year-olds.

In I. V. Sawhill (Ed.), *One percent for the kids* (pp. 113–135). Washington, DC: Brookings Institution Press.

Woods, L. N. (2004). *Cultural risk and protective factors of delinquency in African American adolescents*. Unpublished doctoral dissertation, University of Virginia, Department of Psychology.

Wu, L. T., & Anthony, J. C. (2000). The use of the case-crossover design in studying illicit drug use. *Substance Use and Misuse, 25*(6–8), 1035–1050.

Yasumoto, J. Y., Uekawa, K., & Bidwell, C. E. (2001). The collegial focus and high school students' achievement. *Sociology of Education, 74*, 181–209.

Youth violence: A report of the Surgeon General. (n.d.). Retrieved May 6, 2004, from www.mentalhealth.samhsa.gov/youthviolence/surgeongeneral/SG_Site/chapter5/sec5.asp

Zaff, J. F., Moore, K. A., Papillo, A. R., & Williams, S. (2003). Implications of extracurricular activity participation during adolescence on positive outcomes. *Journal of Adolescent Research, 18*, 599–630.

Zimmerman, M. A., & Maton, K. I. (1992). Life-style and substance use among male African-American urban adolescents: A cluster analytic approach. *American Journal of Community Psychology, 20*, 121–138.

Index

Page numbers followed by an *f* indicate figure, *n* indicate note, and *t* indicate table